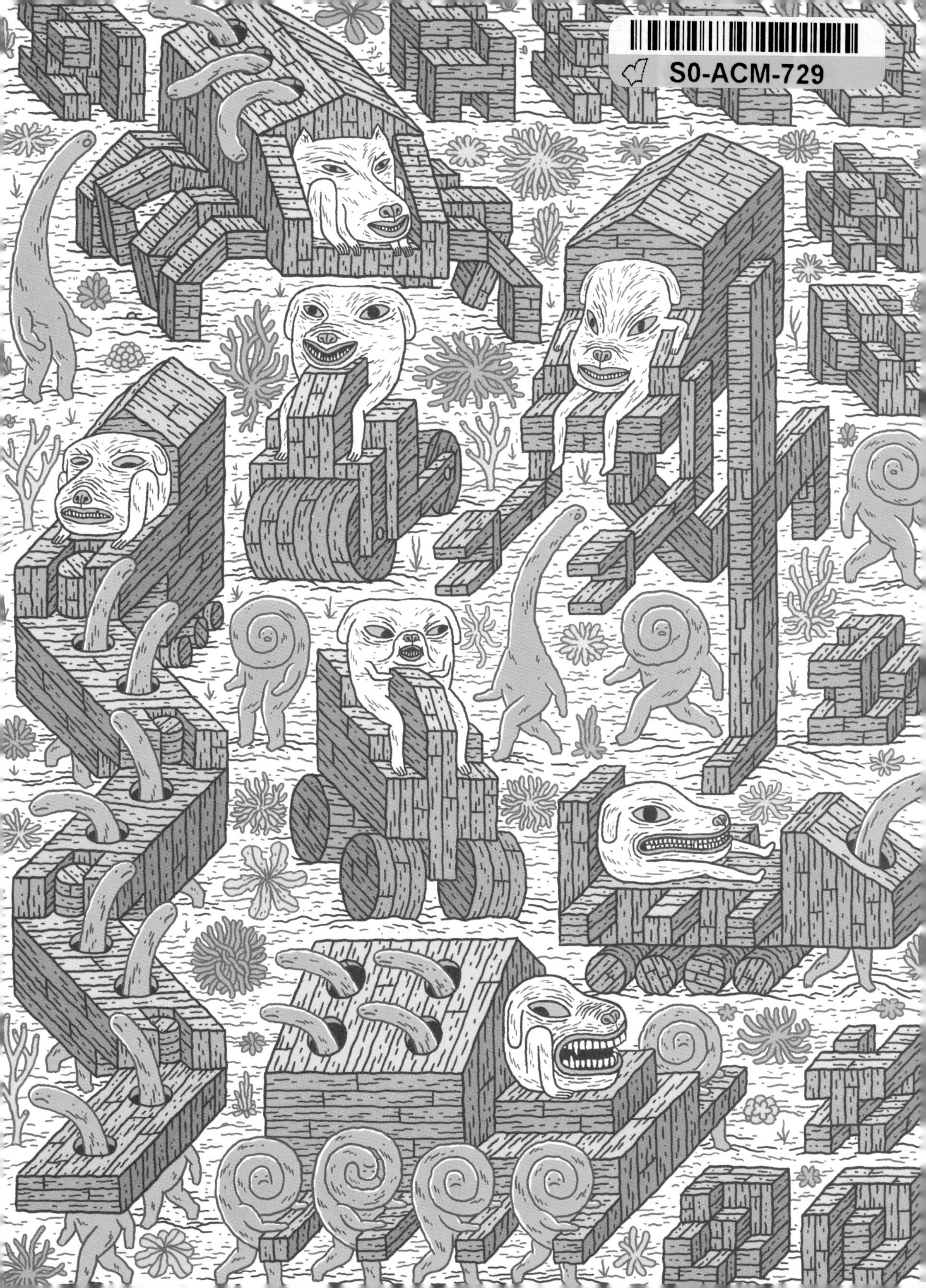

THE BEST AMERICAN

Comics 2012

Guest Editors of
the Best American Comics

2006 HARVEY PEKAR
2007 CHRIS WARE
2008 LYNDA BARRY
2009 CHARLES BURNS
2010 NEIL GAIMAN
2011 ALISON BECHDEL
2012 FRANÇOISE MOULY

THE BEST AMERICAN

Comics

2012

EDITED *and with an*
INTRODUCTION *by* Françoise Mouly

JESSICA ABEL & MATT MADDEN,
series editors

HOUGHTON MIFFLIN HARCOURT
BOSTON ▪ NEW YORK   2012

www.hmhbooks.com

Library of Congress Cataloging-in-Publication Data is available.

ISBN 978-0-547-69112-1

Book design: Robert Overholtzer   Cover design: Françoise Mouly
Cover illustration: Gary Panter   Endpaper art: Jesse Jacobs

PRINTED IN THE UNITED STATES OF AMERICA

DOC 10 9 8 7 6 5 4 3 2 1

Permissions credits are located on page 364.

Contents

Comics for Kids

Foreword

JESSICA: I CAN STILL REMEMBER my first editing job. I sat on the carpeted floor of my student apartment, pasting photocopies of comics onto blue-line grid paper, creating (that is, drawing) a table of contents by hand, numbering pages . . . at four in the morning. I had taken on the editorship of our school comics anthology with no help, and no idea what I was doing. And this was way pre-InDesign. It was all done totally analog. I drove the layouts to the printer myself and, a week later, picked up two thousand comics. A proud day. By my third issue, I knew not to leave the pasting up to the last night, but I decided to add a spot color so found myself at that same early-morning crisis hour making overlays on ads I'd sold (and drawn) myself. Then I retired.

But not for long. Editing is an addictive business. Most cartoonists have their first brush with editorial work when they design and publish their first minicomics. Soon, many are helming self-published anthologies and even starting small publishing houses. Take a look at Kickstarter.com if you don't believe us. Making a comic, soup to nuts, and then causing it to take on printed form — a book, like every other book — is just a little bit of magic.

Matt: Making minicomics was my introduction to the editing and design work that is an integral part of the cartoonist's job. My first few minicomics were collections of some short comics. In making the zines as much as making the comics themselves, I was learning by doing, with little to guide me but trial and error and a shelf full of examples to copy and learn from. From the beginning, I figured out that you couldn't just drop off some drawings at the local copy shop and come back later to pick up your minicomic. No, you had to come up with a sequence of comics that flowed well; you needed cover art and title page, a letters or "plugs" page; and you needed to pick a size and make sure all the artwork fit the format — these are editing and design decisions. Pretty quickly I understood that these choices had creative consequences as well. Even the color and weight of paper you chose affected the reading experience (as well as your budget). Before I knew it, I was designing a story so that it would have a fold-out surprise ending.

So what is an "editor"? From what we've said so far, you may think that we have quite a different idea of the job than you do. But that's not necessarily the case. An editor may be many things. First of all, an editor may actually assess a work at some draft stage and offer criticism and advice. When people hear the word "editor," this is often the kind of work they picture. An editor may also compile, curate, and coordinate, as we and the guest editors do on this series, and then hand off production tasks to other professionals.

Finally, an editor may also be something like what we think of as a publisher, whether he or she personally handles design, production, and printing (as is often the case at small, independent publishers), or at a larger publishing house, he or she oversees the production of a book from purchasing the rights to shepherding it through the editorial, production, and launch processes until it's in your, the readers', hands.

Let's return to the primary definition of an editor: someone who guides the creative development of a work. When you're talking about prose, the way an editor might do this is pretty straightforward. You turn in a draft, and then your editor marks it up and you have a conversation about what he or she thinks. You make whatever changes you need to, and voilà. Editing comics is more complicated. Putting aside the fact that many editors at traditional publishing houses are not well-versed in the visual language of comics, there's the more basic problem of figuring out at what point an editor can get involved. If you have your editor read a script, you won't get feedback on the way you are telling your story visually. If you wait until you have penciled pages (or, God forbid, inks), you will have done such a lot of work, and locked your pages into such a complex structure, that making more than the most minimal changes is really not very feasible. You can't just remove a panel from a page of comics the way you can cut a sentence or paragraph from a novel—the page will collapse like a house of cards. The best time to get feedback is when you've done a complete set of thumbnails, that is, the sketch stage of comics, where you've roughed out the visual storytelling but haven't done so much on it that you can't stand to change anything. However, that's easier said than done. There aren't that many cartoonists out there who are in the habit of making full thumbnails of a work that are also legible to another set of eyes. So it's tricky.

When we teach, editing is one of the skills we try to build in our students: we train them to make and discuss thumbnails at a pretty high level and then to do the additional work of revising them before moving to pencils. We get a few students who take to this process and incorporate it seamlessly into their work. But for most, it's pretty difficult. The drawing in a thumbnail isn't complex or demanding, but the intellectual work of it is the hardest part of comics, and redrawing panels and pages can be draining and, at first, discouraging. The best students learn to internalize this process by the time they graduate, and they need to, since it's a rare case where quality editorial input is available at the right moment for a young, unpublished cartoonist. Many of them miss the regular editing that their peers and teachers provide.

But editing for content is just one part of cartooning. Any good cartoonist will tell you that a huge part of making comics successfully (in the artistic sense of success) is planning for publication from the moment you put pencil to paper. Comics are an art form that really comes to life only in reproduction (whether in print or electronic form), and cartoonists are constantly thinking about that. So it's natural that most of us take the plunge and self-publish at some point.

Again, our students provide good examples of what happens next. Every year, we see fifteen to thirty-five students through the process of self-publishing for the first time. The questions are always the same: How do you get the pages to appear in the right order in the finished book? What order should I put my stories in? Should I use page numbers? (Yes! Please! We editors plead with you: Use page numbers!) Do I need a table of contents? Title pages? What should I call it? How can I design a cover that indicates what's inside and also attracts notice? How should I physically bind the book? How about cover decoration?

We wrote about a lot of these issues recently in our new comics textbook, *Mastering Comics*. We spent a long time discussing how to present these decisions, and how much detail to get into. It's just so easy to go down the rabbit hole and try to convey each possible iteration of each possible decision. It's so very interesting when you're doing it, and when it's your own work, you can feel the difference between one choice and another.

Students learn reading order, laying stories out on the correct side (starting on the right page, usually), how to consider spreads, how to plan for and trim bleeds. Abstract story ideas now take up physical real estate, and the pages make interesting new relationships with one another. Facing, turning, visible, invisible. It's not until the whole thing is done—and you can see how one story leads into another, how your bleeds worked here but failed there, how your center spread rocks—that you really feel that having a book in your hands you made from the ground up is like nothing else. And then you're hooked.

We decided to write our foreword on the subject of editing and production because of our spectacular guest editor this year, Françoise Mouly. We were really pleased when she accepted the job, because for years she has been such an important advocate, designer, and editor of comics. And while she is widely known from her days coediting and publishing *RAW* magazine with her husband, Art Spiegelman, and her current position as art director at *The New Yorker*, we are thrilled to give her an opportunity to put her own singular vision of the state of our art form on this year's volume. And she has done that, to be sure!

Françoise is an editor's editor. Regular readers of this series will notice a few changes in the overall look this time around. From the moment she began her work, the eventual look and feel of the book you hold in your hands was her foremost concern. She chose stories carefully and with an eye to their inherent quality, but also to how they would work with the stories that surround them. She decided that each comic should have a title page, asking the artists to fill out short interviews and provide self-portraits and cover art. A particular passion of Françoise's in recent years has been comics for children. (If you're a parent or teacher, you really should look into her TOON Books series—our children recommend them highly!) And to showcase this underrepresented field of our medium, she designated a separate kids' section at the back of the book. She was thinking about the wonderful cover by Gary Panter before we had even handed her all of our selections.

Working with Françoise is like getting swept up in an editorial tornado. Her passion and vision mark this volume as the work of a master.

The Best American Comics 2012 represents a selection of the outstanding comics published in North America between September 1, 2010, and August 31, 2011. As series editors, we search out and review comics in as many formats and publications as we can find, from hand-produced minicomics to individual pamphlet issues to graphic novels and collections to webcomics. Our goal is to put as much interesting and worthwhile material in front of our guest editors as they can stand to read through. This includes works that we consider excellent by reasonable objective standards, but it also certainly includes comics we have a particular fondness for, as well as left-field choices that may not be our cup of tea but that we feel may turn out to be someone else's "best"—and in particular the guest editor's.

Guest editors will sometimes seek out material on their own, as well. The guest editor makes the final selections from this large and varied pool of titles. Idiosyncrasy is encouraged. One of the things we love most about this series is the way it changes from year to year. Each volume is indisputably the best of that year—as seen through one particular pair of eyes. And that vision of the guest editor is the most valuable and intriguing aspect of the ongoing series. This is now our fifth outing, and each time a new guest editor turns in his or her choices, we are surprised and pleased anew.

Our final choices are wonderful, but please don't fail to take a look at our list of Notable Comics in the back of this volume. You'll find so much more there that you're likely to enjoy. Don't forget that we also have this list posted online, with some helpful links so that you may be able to track down even the most obscure minicomics in the list.

As we discussed above, the mountains of good comics always threaten to bury us, so we depend on your advice and submissions. Here are the submission guidelines: Comics eligible for consideration must have been published in the eligibility period either on paper or electronically, in English, by a North American author, or one who makes his or her home here. As this 2012 volume hits the shelves, we will have already passed the deadline for the 2013 volume and will be on to collecting for the 2014 volume, whose eligibility window is September 1, 2012, to August 31, 2013. A note about webcomics (and comics on the Web): We do our best to find what's out there, and we rely on friends, blogs, and "best of" lists to track down important work, but we are aware that webcomics deserve better coverage. Therefore we'd like to especially encourage you Web cartoonists and publishers to send us submissions either on paper or digitally. Printed submissions can be sent to the address below. Digital submissions can be made in the form of a PDF of the comics published in the eligibility window, with each comic labeled with the exact date it was published online. Better yet, you might make a subselection of what you consider your best strips from the year or send a self-contained continuity, as long as it appeared in the eligibility period. You can mail a CD of the PDF to us or e-mail a download link to bestamericancomics@hmhpub.com.

All comics should be labeled with their release date and contact information and mailed to us at the following address:

Jessica Abel and Matt Madden
Series Editors
The Best American Comics
Houghton Mifflin Harcourt Publishing Company
215 Park Avenue South
New York, NY 10003

Further information is available on the Best American Comics website: bestamericancomics.com.

We'd like to thank all the people who helped us with this volume, starting with the excellent team at Houghton Mifflin Harcourt: our editor Johnathan Wilber; our production team, Christopher Moisan, Beth Burleigh Fuller, and David Futato; as well as Tom Bouman and Christina Mamangakis. We would not have been able to pull this thing together without Mina Kaneko from Françoise's office. Thanks also to our great studio assistants Hilary Allison, Li-Or Zaltzman, Wyeth Yates, and Eric Arroyo; and of course to all the artists and publishers from all over who sent in submissions.

JESSICA ABEL and MATT MADDEN

Introduction

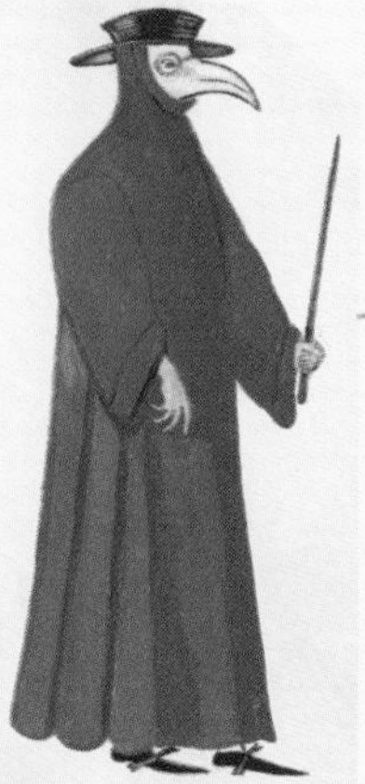

Découpage*

Selecting the Best American Comics 2012

by Françoise Mouly

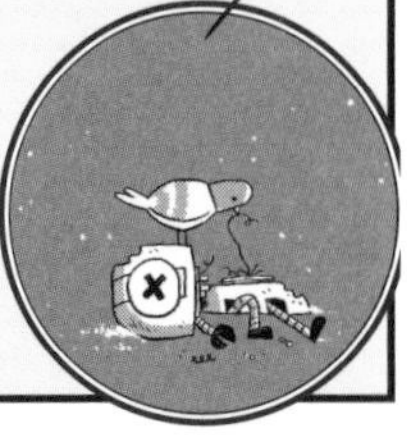

with apologies to Maira Kalman, John Martz, Roz Chast, Jillian Tamaki, Laura Park, Trade Loeffler, Ben Katchor, Dan Clowes, Pascal Girard, Lilli Carré, Art Spiegelman, Ted Stearn, Kevin Huizenga, Jason Lutes, Lynda Barry, Michael DeForge, Joseph Lambert, Gabrielle Bell, Marc Bell, Seth, Josh Neufeld & Brooke Gladstone, Tin Can Forest, Jeffrey Brown, and the many others who couldn't work in the final mix, but who all belong in an anthology such as this.

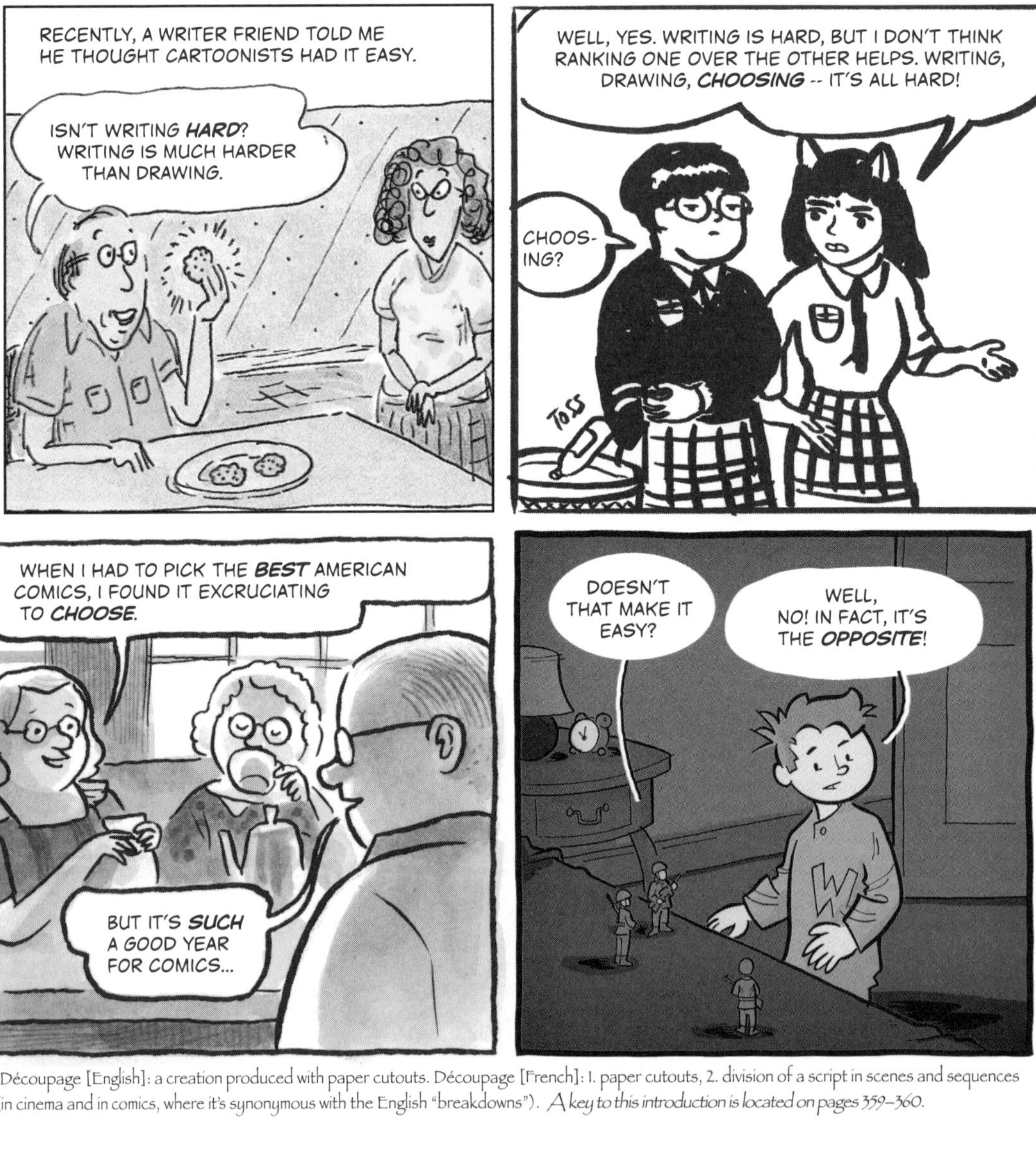
RECENTLY, A WRITER FRIEND TOLD ME HE THOUGHT CARTOONISTS HAD IT EASY.
ISN'T WRITING HARD? WRITING IS MUCH HARDER THAN DRAWING.
WELL, YES. WRITING IS HARD, BUT I DON'T THINK RANKING ONE OVER THE OTHER HELPS. WRITING, DRAWING, CHOOSING -- IT'S ALL HARD!
CHOOS-ING?
TOSS
WHEN I HAD TO PICK THE BEST AMERICAN COMICS, I FOUND IT EXCRUCIATING TO CHOOSE.
BUT IT'S SUCH A GOOD YEAR FOR COMICS...
DOESN'T THAT MAKE IT EASY?
WELL, NO! IN FACT, IT'S THE OPPOSITE!

*Découpage [English]: a creation produced with paper cutouts. Découpage [French]: 1. paper cutouts, 2. division of a script in scenes and sequences (in cinema and in comics, where it's synonymous with the English "breakdowns"). *A key to this introduction is located on pages 359–360.*

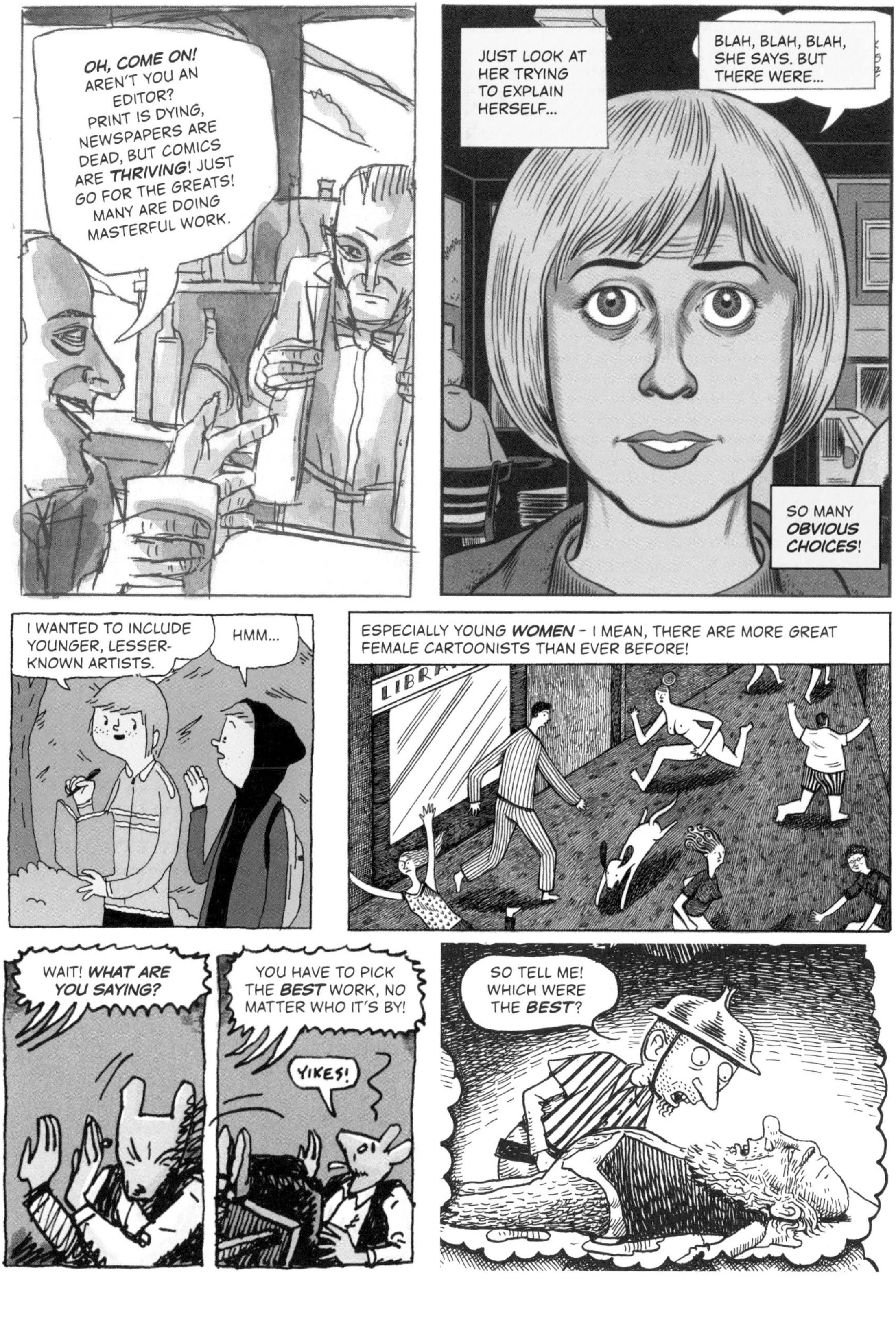
OH, COME ON! AREN'T YOU AN EDITOR? PRINT IS DYING, NEWSPAPERS ARE DEAD, BUT COMICS ARE THRIVING! JUST GO FOR THE GREATS! MANY ARE DOING MASTERFUL WORK.
JUST LOOK AT HER TRYING TO EXPLAIN HERSELF...
BLAH, BLAH, BLAH, SHE SAYS. BUT THERE WERE...
SO MANY OBVIOUS CHOICES!
I WANTED TO INCLUDE YOUNGER, LESSER-KNOWN ARTISTS.
HMM...
ESPECIALLY YOUNG WOMEN – I MEAN, THERE ARE MORE GREAT FEMALE CARTOONISTS THAN EVER BEFORE!
WAIT! WHAT ARE YOU SAYING?
YOU HAVE TO PICK THE BEST WORK, NO MATTER WHO IT'S BY!
YIKES!
SO TELL ME! WHICH WERE THE BEST?

WAIT! LET ME EXPLAIN. WHEN I STARTED *RAW* MAGAZINE, IN THE 80'S...

THERE WERE MOSTLY SUPERHEROES, A FEW CHILDREN'S COMICS...

AND THE DIRTY, INTENTIONALLY LOWBROW, UNDERGROUND *COMIX.*

AND NOW...

YES?

...COMICS CAN TACKLE *ANY* TOPIC.

I SEE A FEW STRONG TENDENCIES: ONE IS *AUTOBIOGRAPHY,* WHICH TAKES ADVANTAGE OF THE FACT THAT COMICS ARE A HANDWRITTEN MEDIUM.

WHATCHA DOIN'?

NOTHIN'.

THEN WHY YA DOIN' IT?

WATCH TV WITH ME.

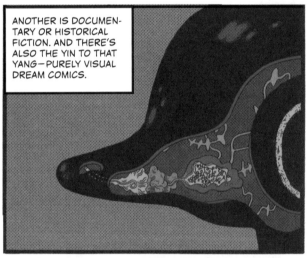

ANOTHER IS DOCUMENTARY OR HISTORICAL FICTION. AND THERE'S ALSO THE YIN TO THAT YANG—PURELY VISUAL DREAM COMICS.

ANOTHER EXCITING TREND IS THE GREAT NEW *KIDS* COMICS.

HA! YOU SAID THERE USED TO BE SOME. DID THEY DISAPPEAR?...

...AND AREN'T *ALL* COMICS FOR KIDS ANYWAY?

NO! MOST COMICS ARE *NOT* FOR KIDS!

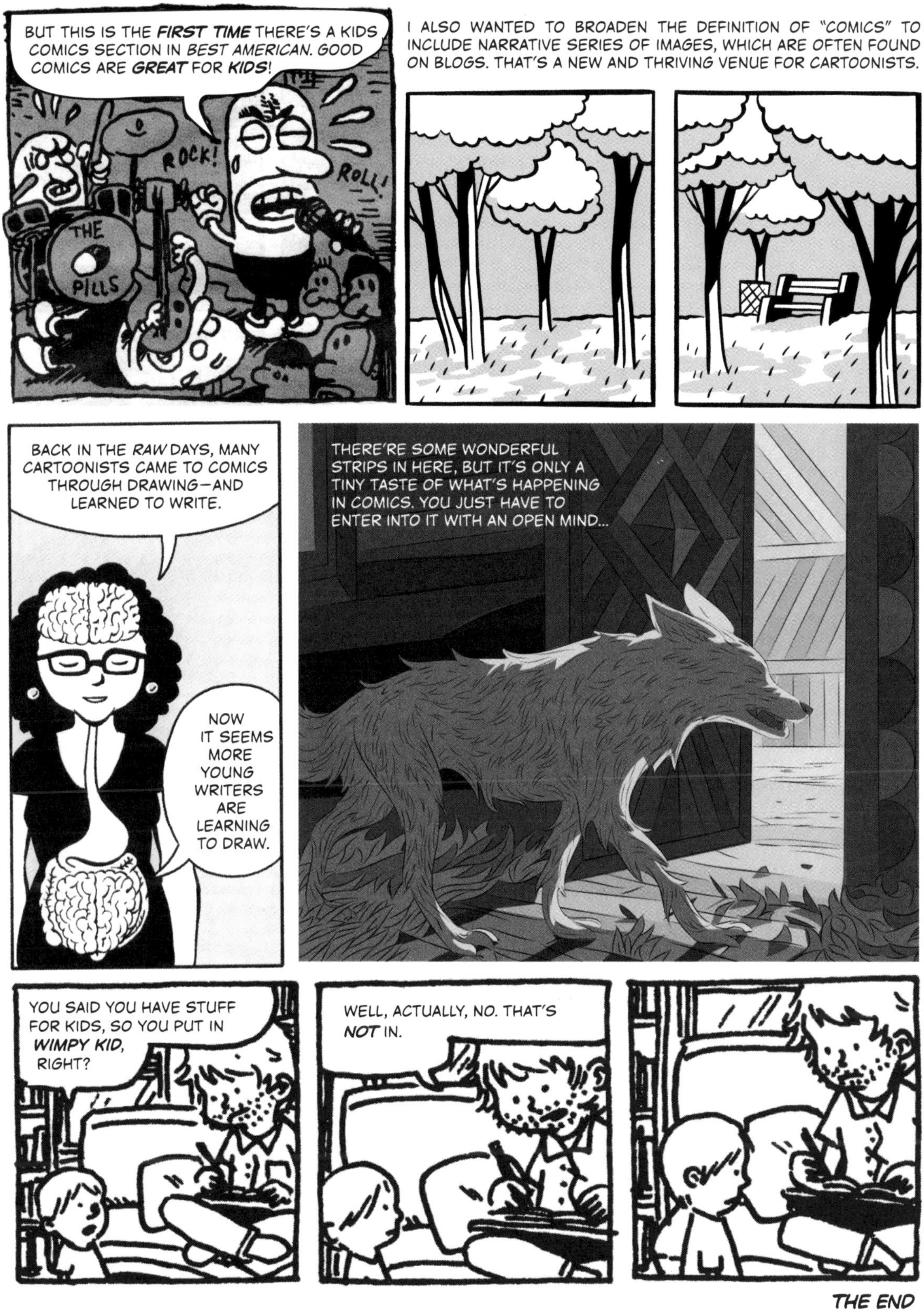
BUT THIS IS THE FIRST TIME THERE'S A KIDS COMICS SECTION IN BEST AMERICAN. GOOD COMICS ARE GREAT FOR KIDS!
ROCK!
ROLL!
THE PILLS
I ALSO WANTED TO BROADEN THE DEFINITION OF "COMICS" TO INCLUDE NARRATIVE SERIES OF IMAGES, WHICH ARE OFTEN FOUND ON BLOGS. THAT'S A NEW AND THRIVING VENUE FOR CARTOONISTS.
BACK IN THE RAW DAYS, MANY CARTOONISTS CAME TO COMICS THROUGH DRAWING—AND LEARNED TO WRITE.
NOW IT SEEMS MORE YOUNG WRITERS ARE LEARNING TO DRAW.
THERE'RE SOME WONDERFUL STRIPS IN HERE, BUT IT'S ONLY A TINY TASTE OF WHAT'S HAPPENING IN COMICS. YOU JUST HAVE TO ENTER INTO IT WITH AN OPEN MIND...
YOU SAID YOU HAVE STUFF FOR KIDS, SO YOU PUT IN WIMPY KID, RIGHT?
WELL, ACTUALLY, NO. THAT'S NOT IN.
THE END

THE BEST AMERICAN

Comics 2012

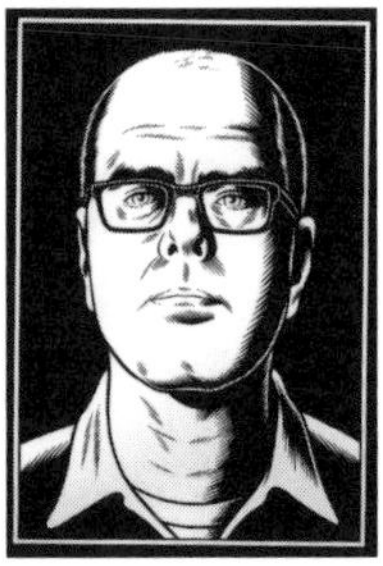

CHARLES BURNS

X'ed Out *(Excerpt)*

FOR ME, DRAWING COMICS IS

Getting it down on paper.

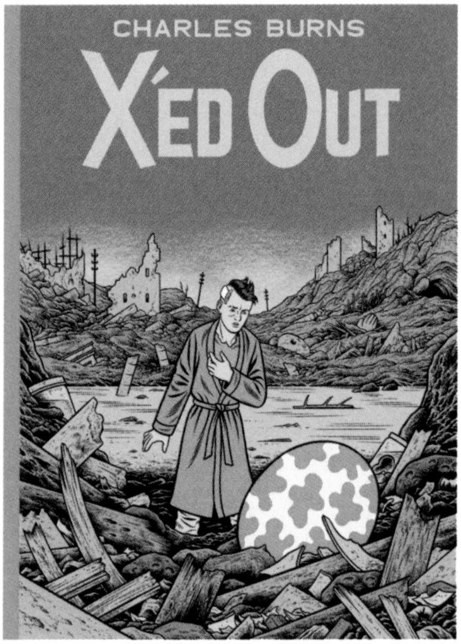
CHARLES BURNS
X'ED OUT

THE SELECTION

Doug (our protagonist) is hiding out in his dead father's basement office, ingesting large doses of opiates. With a bandaged head, it's clear he's recently suffered through a traumatic incident — but what exactly?

WHAT I'M KNOWN FOR

Black Hole, Big Baby, Skin Deep.

WHERE I LIVE

Philadelphia, Pennsylvania.

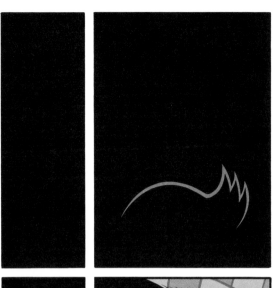

THIS IS
THE ONLY
PART I'LL
REMEMBER.

THE PART
WHERE
I WAKE
UP AND
DON'T
KNOW
WHERE
I AM.

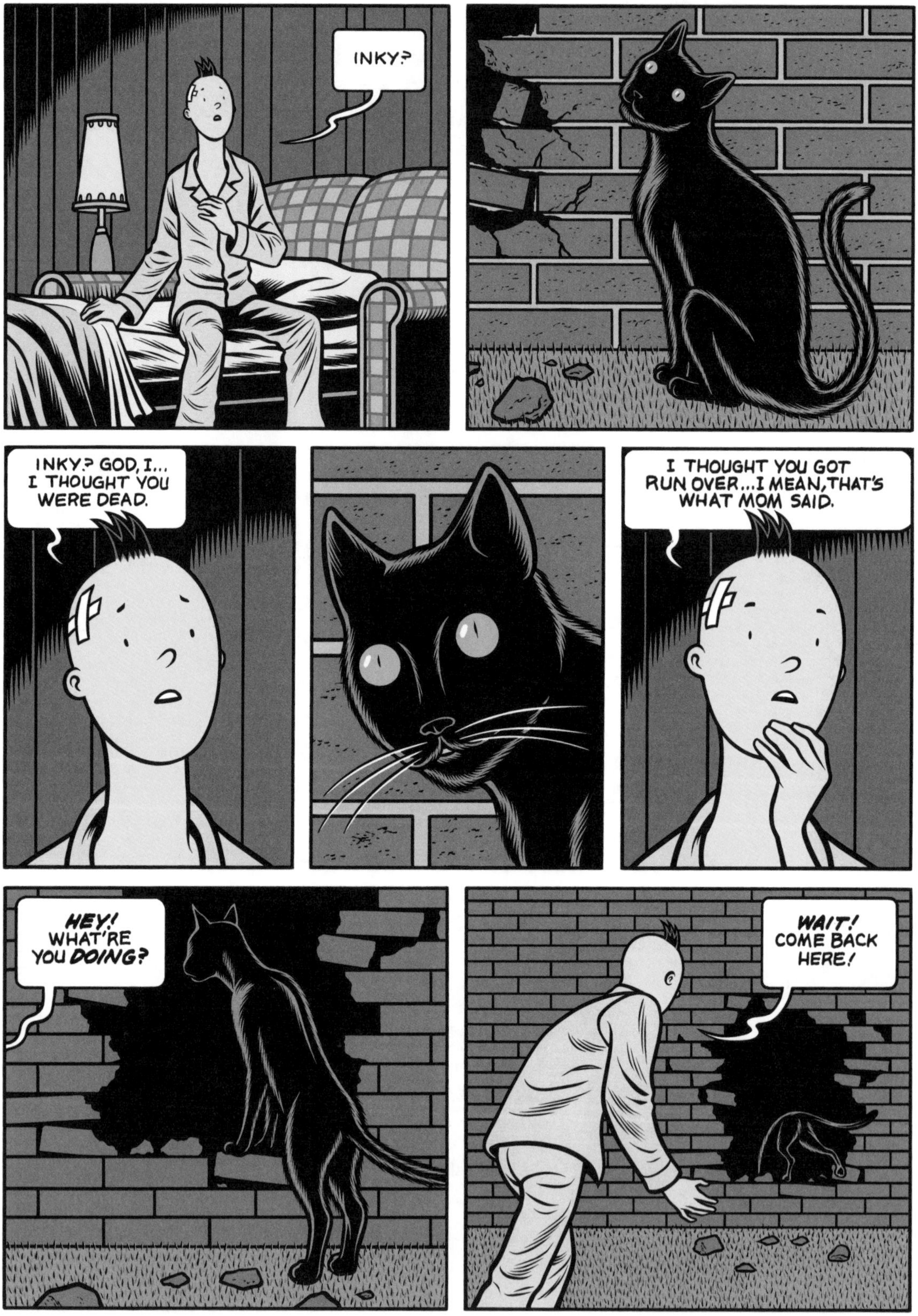
INKY?
INKY? GOD, I... I THOUGHT YOU WERE DEAD.
I THOUGHT YOU GOT RUN OVER...I MEAN, THAT'S WHAT MOM SAID.
HEY! WHAT'RE YOU DOING?
WAIT! COME BACK HERE!

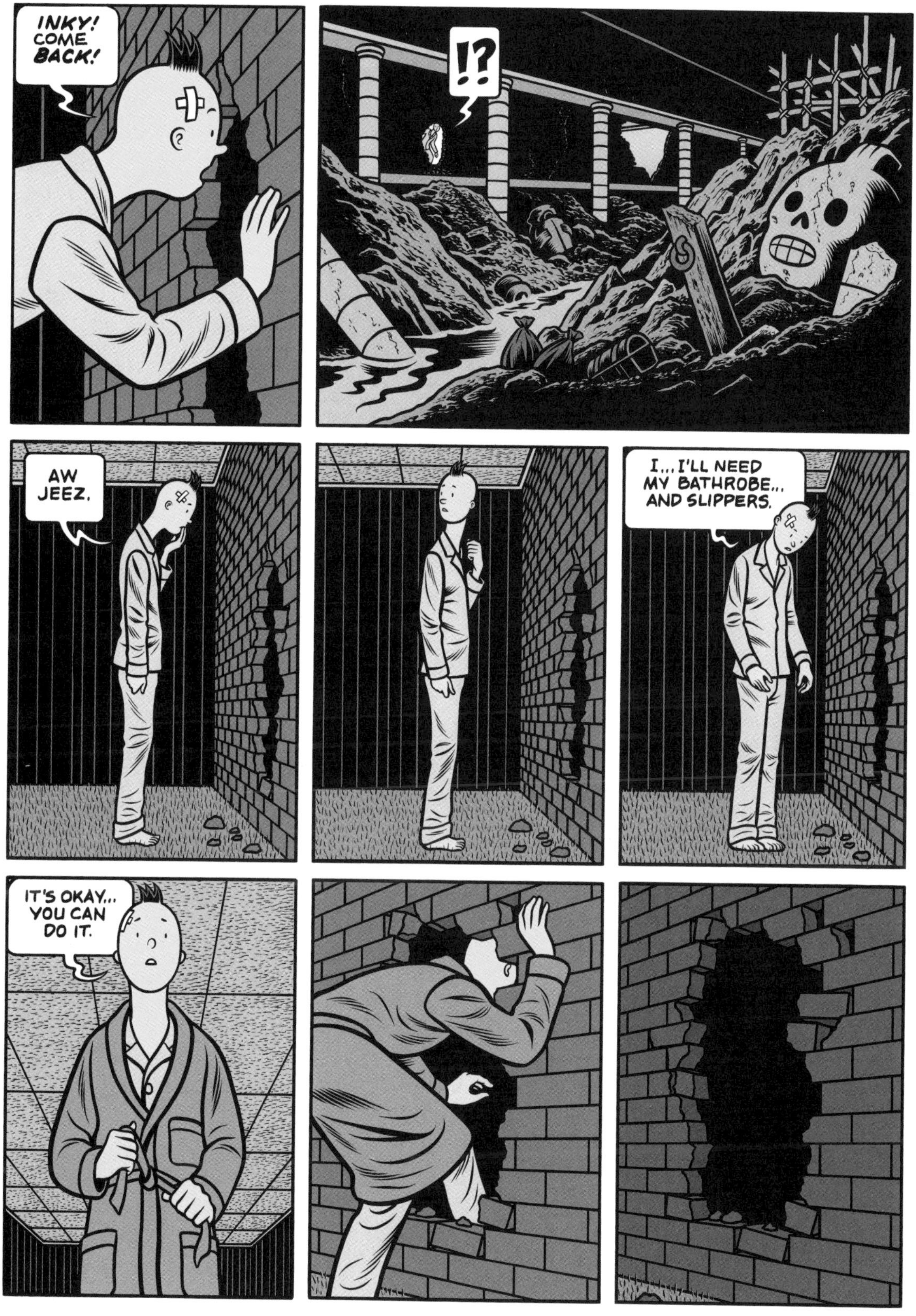

INKY! COME BACK!
!?
AW JEEZ.
I... I'LL NEED MY BATHROBE... AND SLIPPERS.
IT'S OKAY... YOU CAN DO IT.

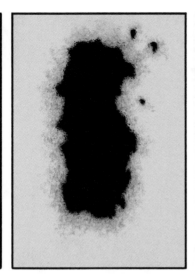

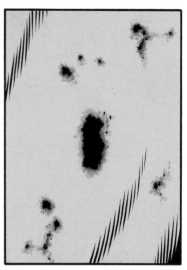

STALE
CIGARETTE
SMOKE...

ICE CUBES
CLINKING
IN A GLASS.

THE FLICKER
OF A DISTANT
TELEVISION...

SOME NEWS
SHOW ABOUT
THE FLOODS...

NUMM?
NUH?

NUMM?
UMMM?

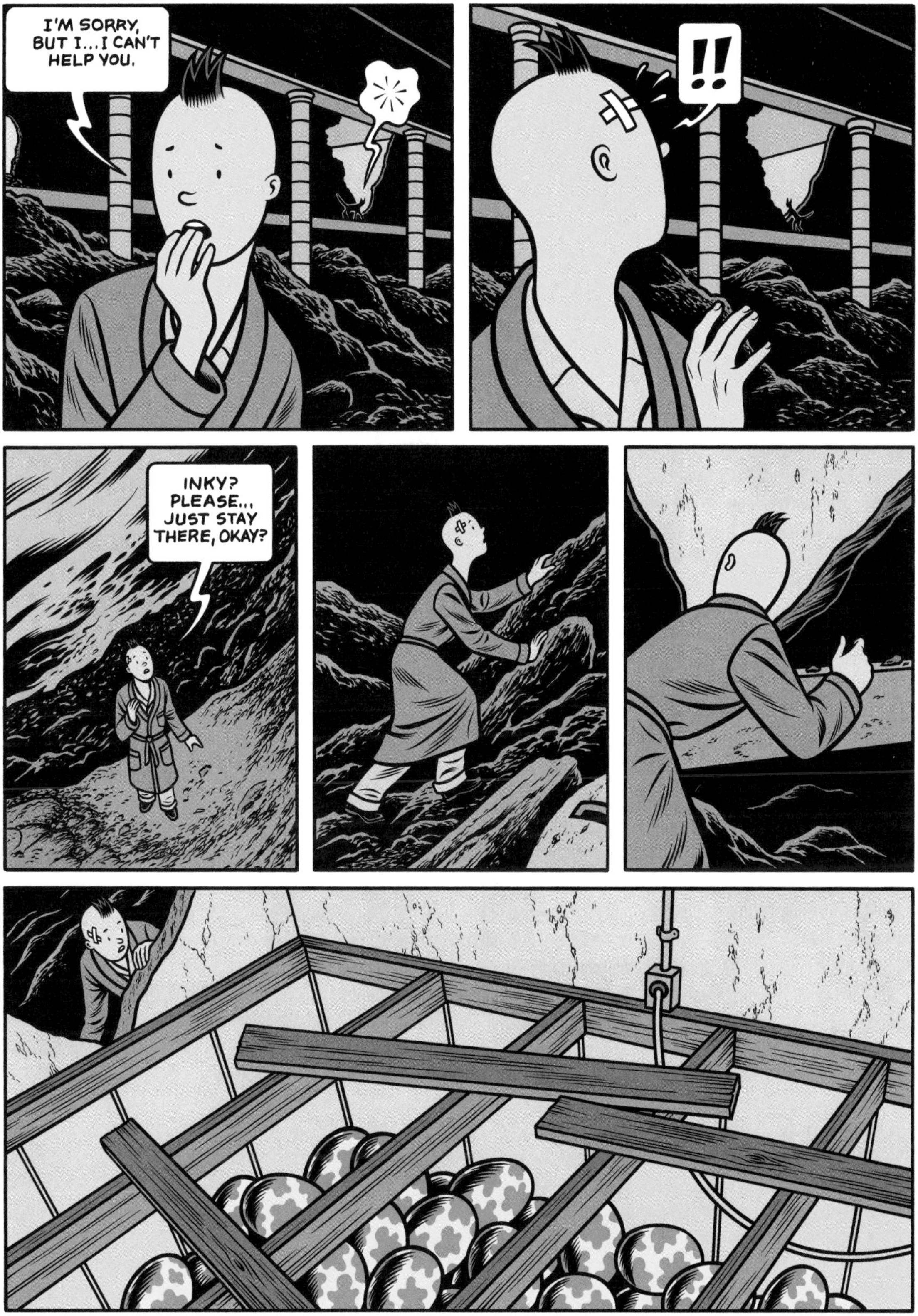
I'M SORRY, BUT I... I CAN'T HELP YOU.
!!
INKY? PLEASE... JUST STAY THERE, OKAY?

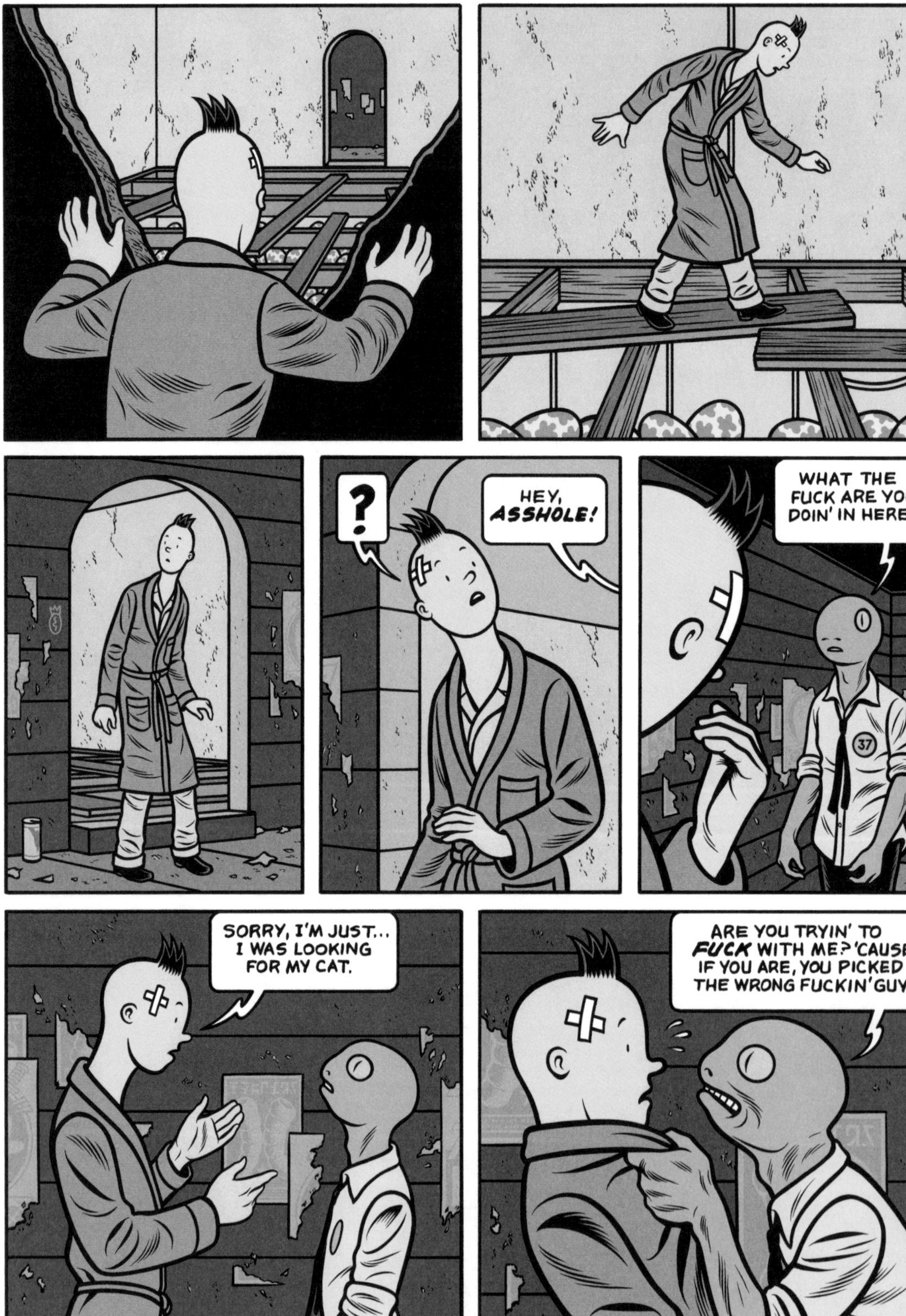

?
HEY, ASSHOLE!
WHAT THE FUCK ARE YOU DOIN' IN HERE?
SORRY, I'M JUST... I WAS LOOKING FOR MY CAT.
ARE YOU TRYIN' TO FUCK WITH ME? 'CAUSE IF YOU ARE, YOU PICKED THE WRONG FUCKIN' GUY!

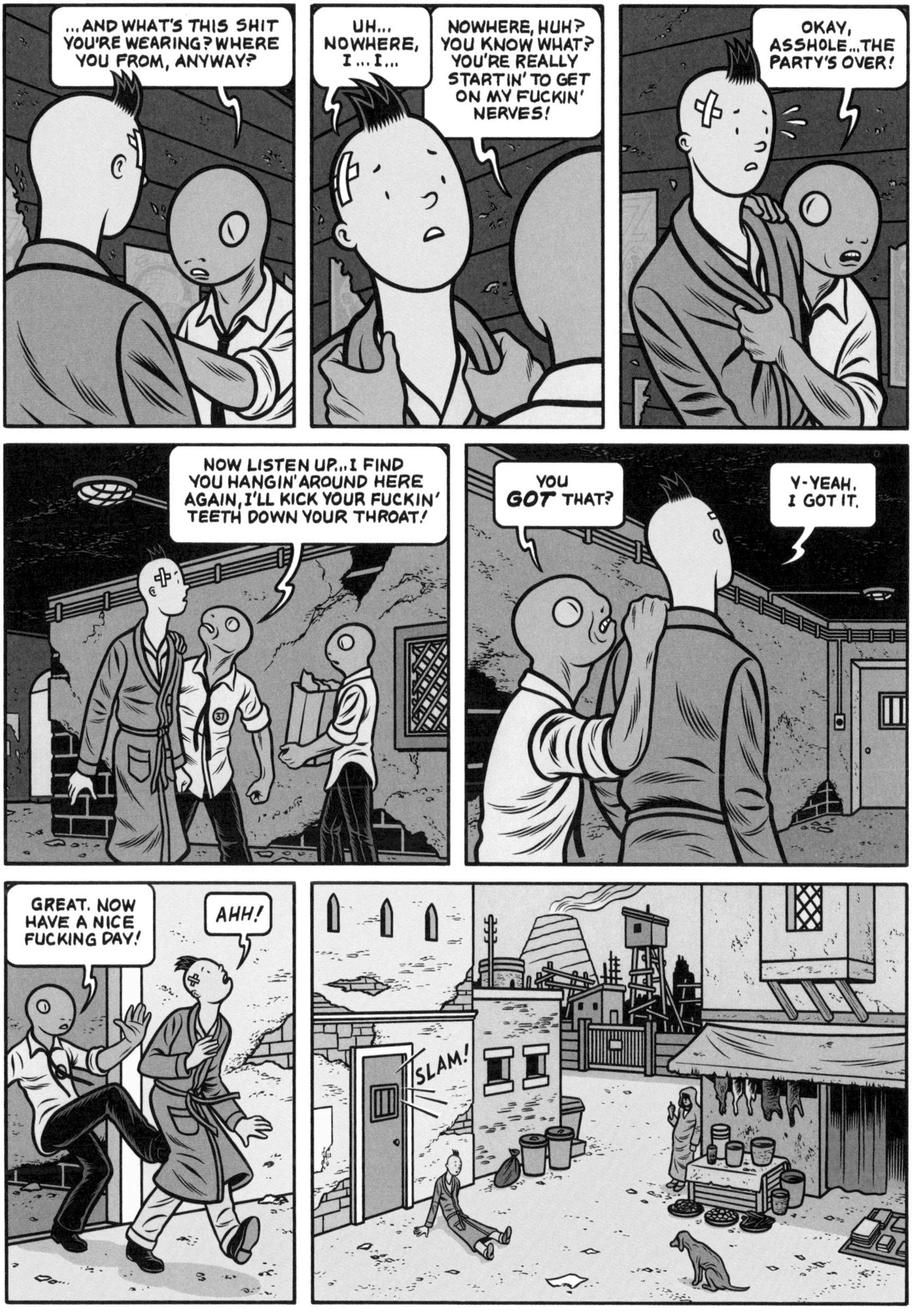
...AND WHAT'S THIS SHIT YOU'RE WEARING? WHERE YOU FROM, ANYWAY?
UH... NOWHERE, I... I...
NOWHERE, HUH? YOU KNOW WHAT? YOU'RE REALLY STARTIN' TO GET ON MY FUCKIN' NERVES!
OKAY, ASSHOLE... THE PARTY'S OVER!
NOW LISTEN UP... I FIND YOU HANGIN' AROUND HERE AGAIN, I'LL KICK YOUR FUCKIN' TEETH DOWN YOUR THROAT!
YOU GOT THAT?
Y-YEAH, I GOT IT.
GREAT. NOW HAVE A NICE FUCKING DAY!
AHH!
SLAM!

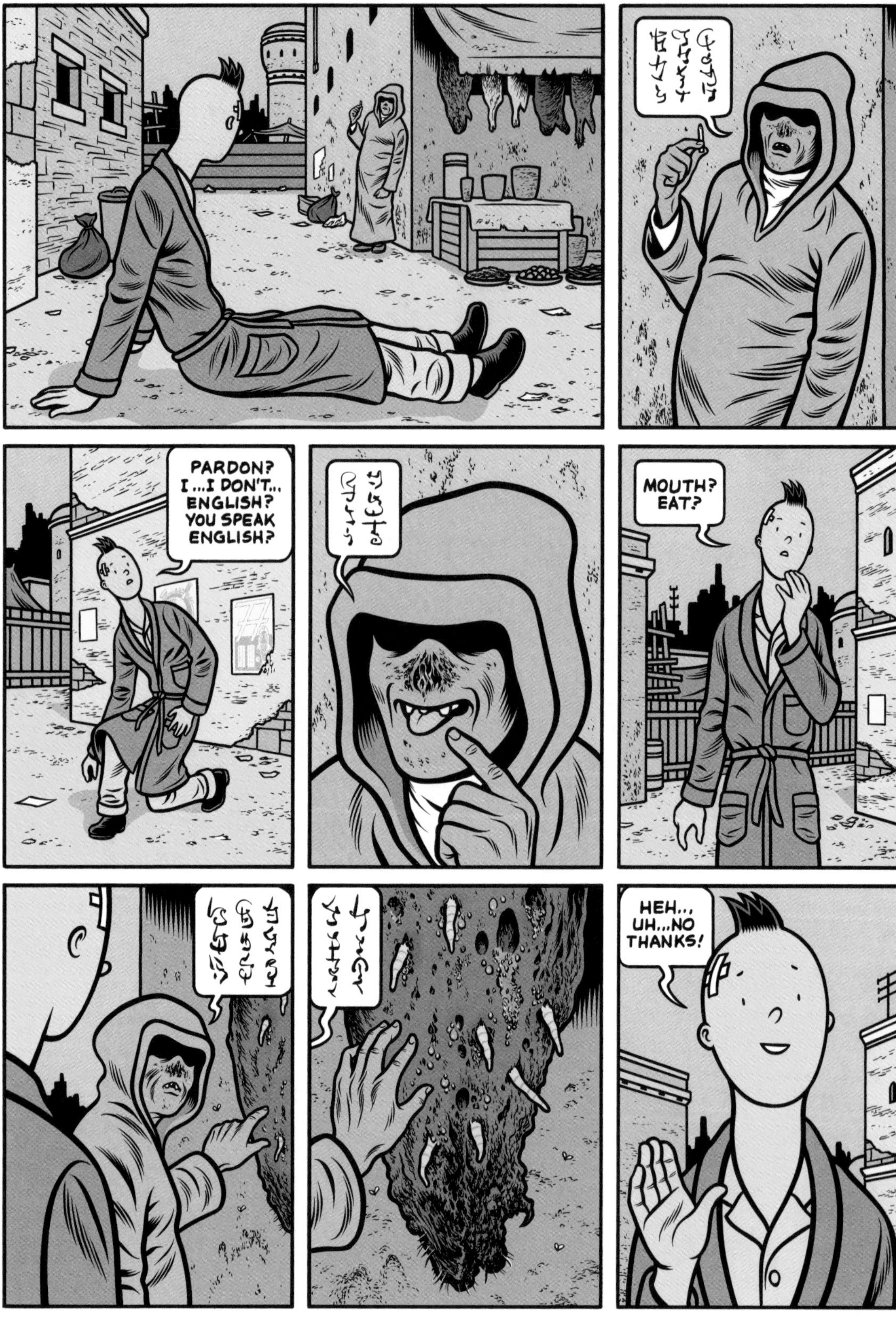
PARDON? I...I DON'T... ENGLISH? YOU SPEAK ENGLISH?
MOUTH? EAT?
HEH.., UH...NO THANKS!

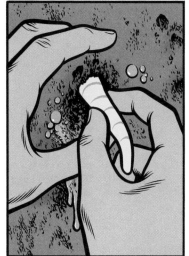

HEY... HEY, MISTER!

YOU DON'T WANNA EAT THAT JUNK... IT'LL MAKE YOU SICK.

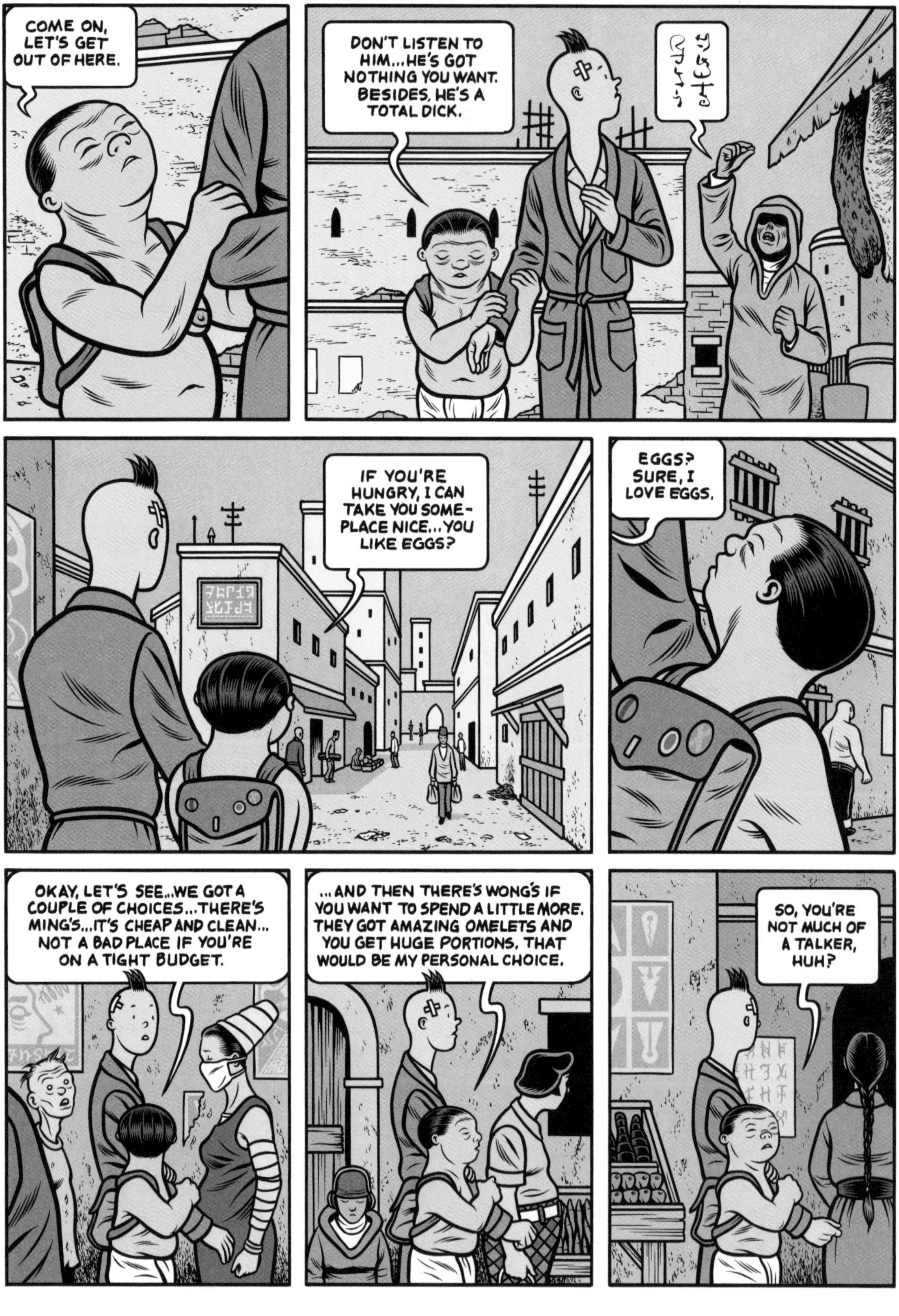
COME ON, LET'S GET OUT OF HERE.
DON'T LISTEN TO HIM...HE'S GOT NOTHING YOU WANT. BESIDES, HE'S A TOTAL DICK.
IF YOU'RE HUNGRY, I CAN TAKE YOU SOME-PLACE NICE... YOU LIKE EGGS?
EGGS? SURE, I LOVE EGGS.
OKAY, LET'S SEE...WE GOT A COUPLE OF CHOICES...THERE'S MING'S...IT'S CHEAP AND CLEAN... NOT A BAD PLACE IF YOU'RE ON A TIGHT BUDGET.
...AND THEN THERE'S WONG'S IF YOU WANT TO SPEND A LITTLE MORE. THEY GOT AMAZING OMELETS AND YOU GET HUGE PORTIONS. THAT WOULD BE MY PERSONAL CHOICE.
SO, YOU'RE NOT MUCH OF A TALKER, HUH?

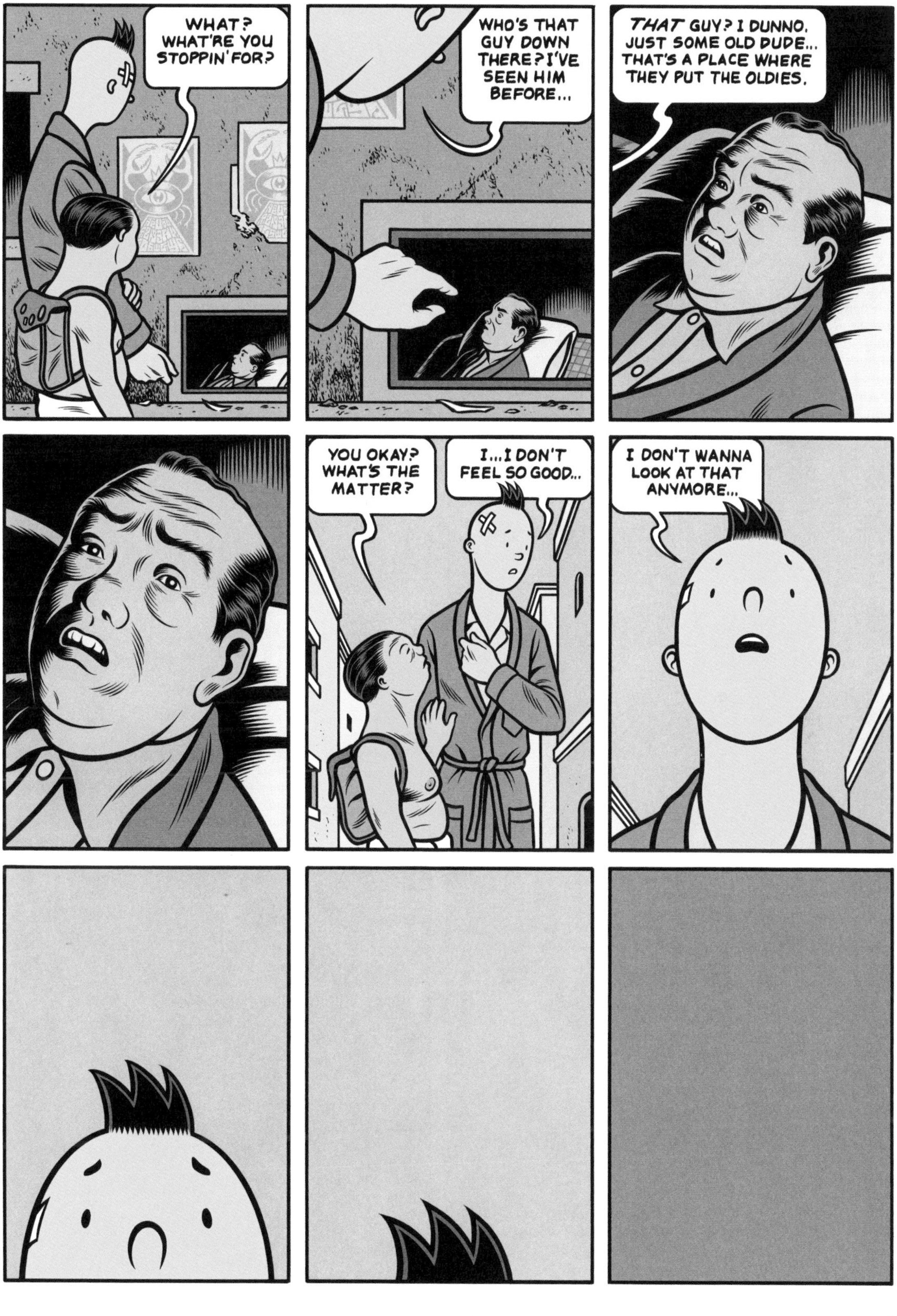
WHAT? WHAT'RE YOU STOPPIN' FOR?
WHO'S THAT GUY DOWN THERE? I'VE SEEN HIM BEFORE...
THAT GUY? I DUNNO. JUST SOME OLD DUDE... THAT'S A PLACE WHERE THEY PUT THE OLDIES.
YOU OKAY? WHAT'S THE MATTER?
I...I DON'T FEEL SO GOOD...
I DON'T WANNA LOOK AT THAT ANYMORE...

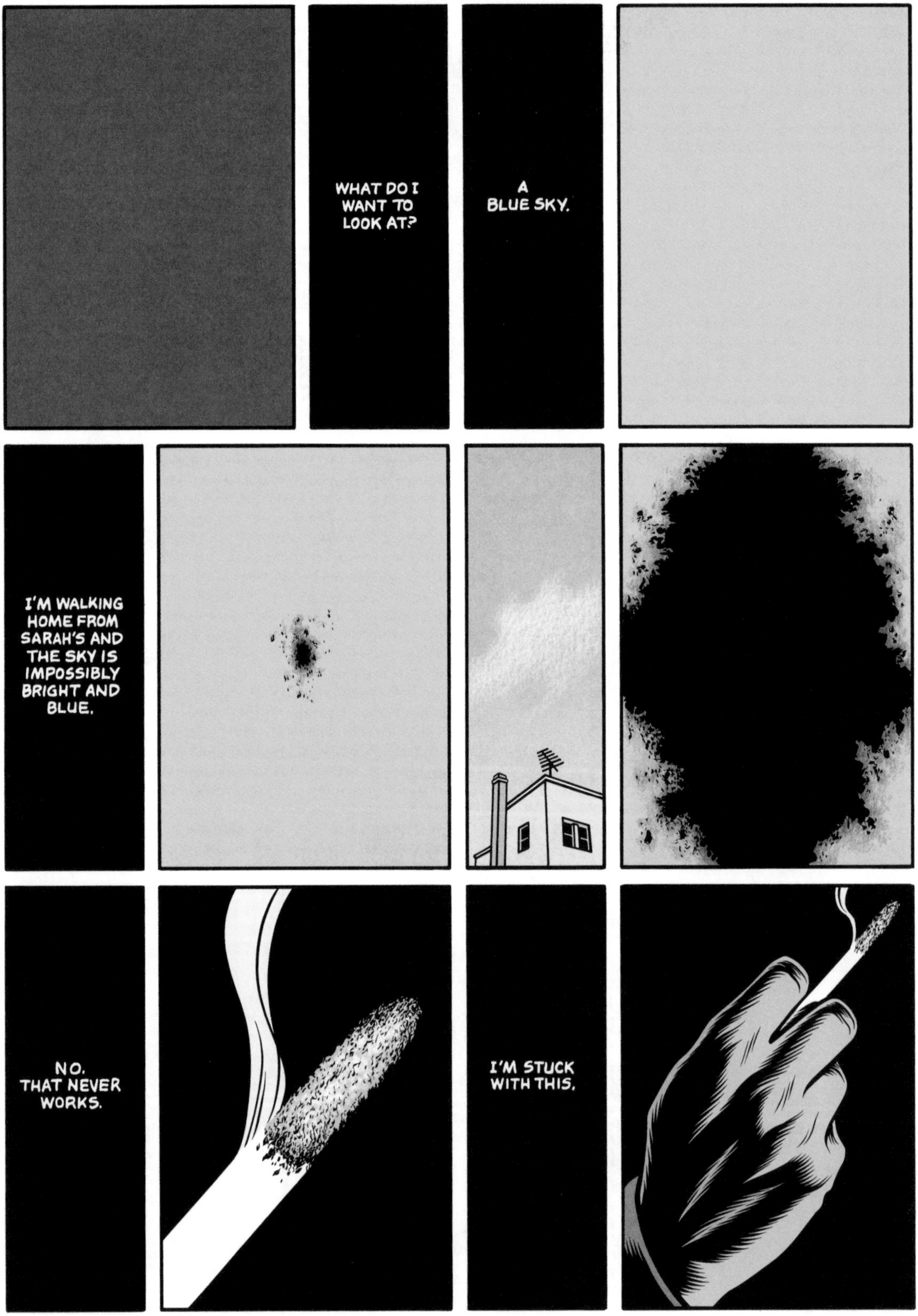
WHAT DO I
WANT TO
LOOK AT?
A
BLUE SKY.
I'M WALKING
HOME FROM
SARAH'S AND
THE SKY IS
IMPOSSIBLY
BRIGHT AND
BLUE.
NO.
THAT NEVER
WORKS.
I'M STUCK
WITH THIS.

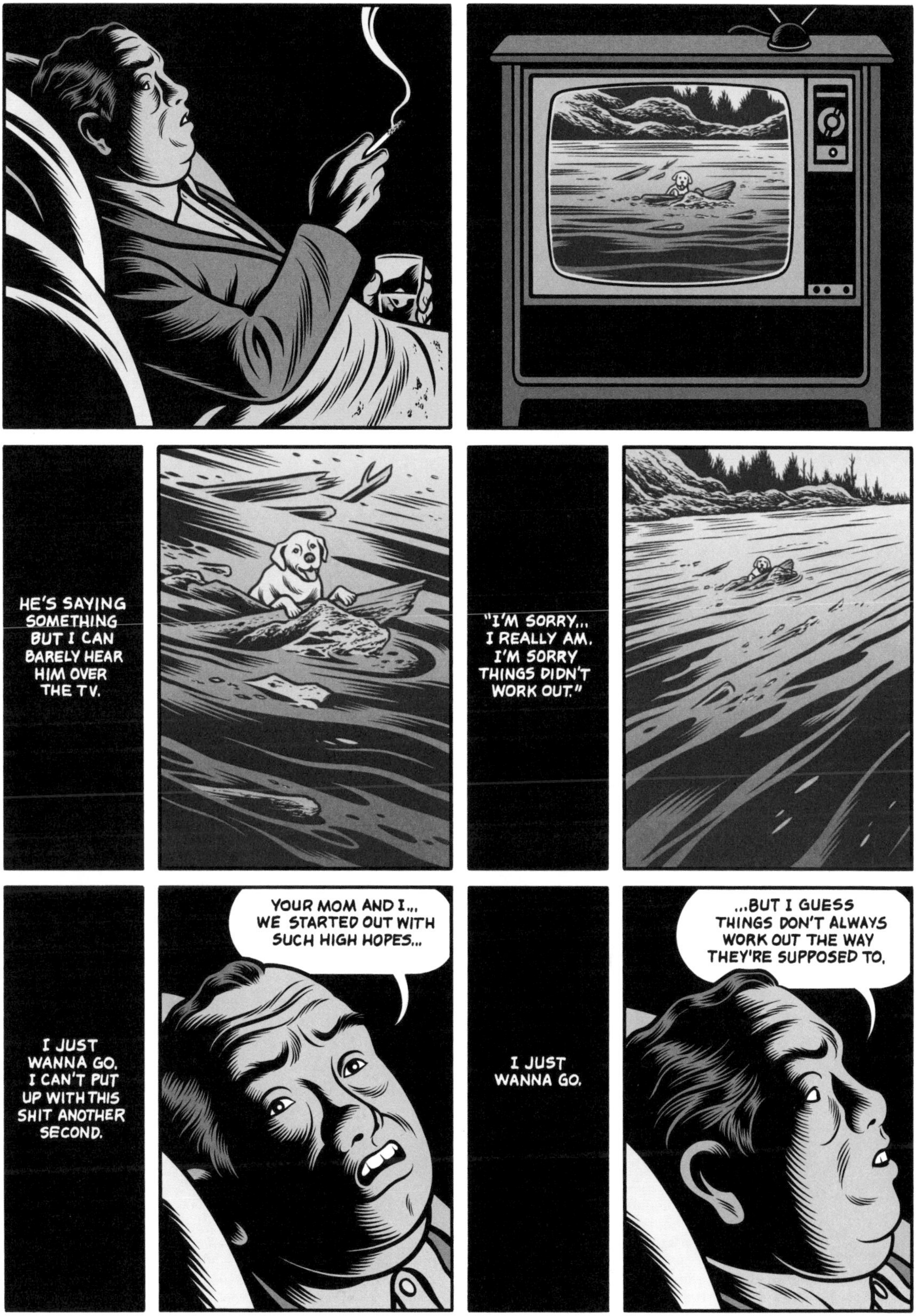
HE'S SAYING SOMETHING BUT I CAN BARELY HEAR HIM OVER THE TV.
"I'M SORRY... I REALLY AM. I'M SORRY THINGS DIDN'T WORK OUT."
I JUST WANNA GO. I CAN'T PUT UP WITH THIS SHIT ANOTHER SECOND.
YOUR MOM AND I... WE STARTED OUT WITH SUCH HIGH HOPES...
I JUST WANNA GO.
...BUT I GUESS THINGS DON'T ALWAYS WORK OUT THE WAY THEY'RE SUPPOSED TO.

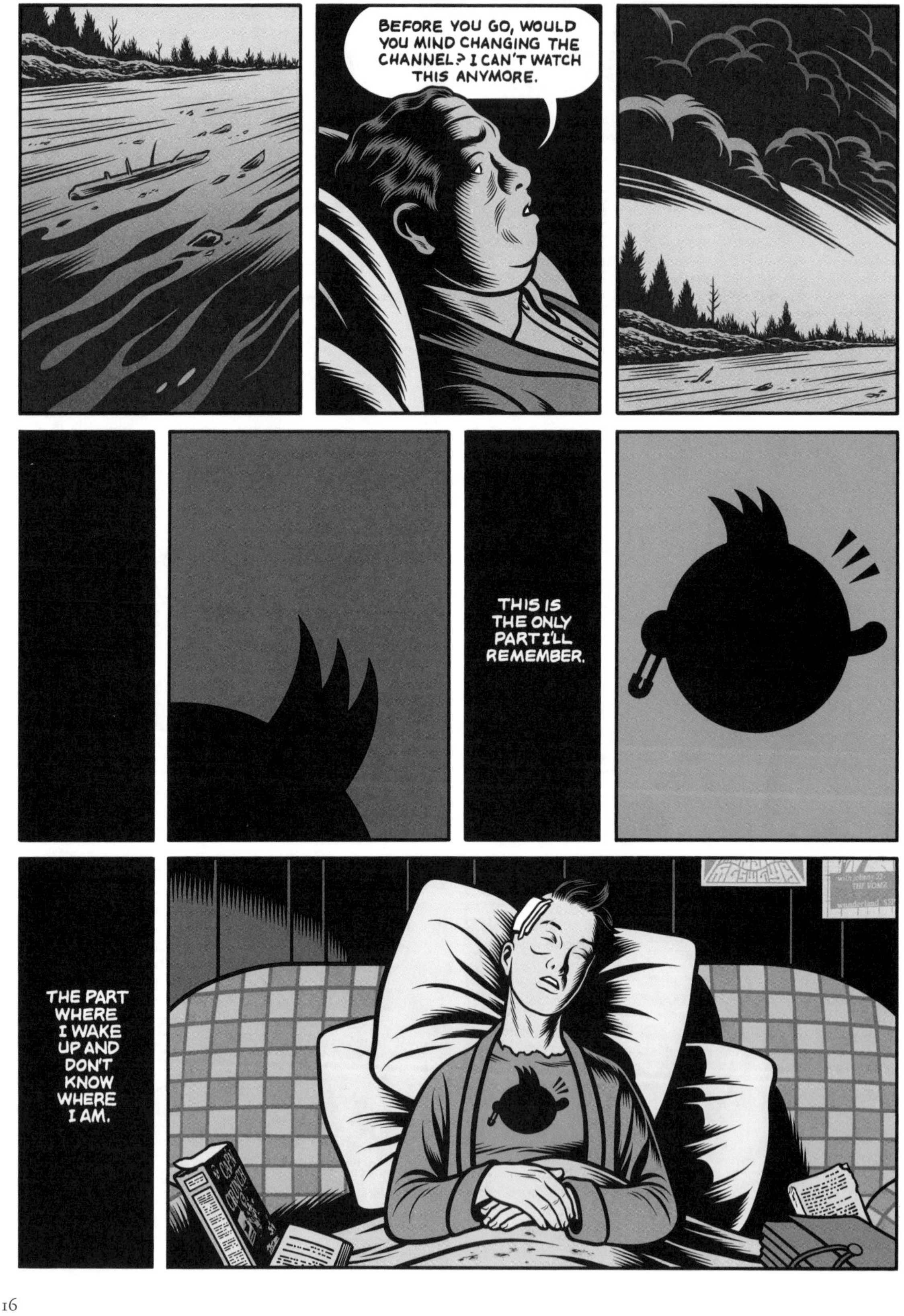
BEFORE YOU GO, WOULD YOU MIND CHANGING THE CHANNEL? I CAN'T WATCH THIS ANYMORE.
THIS IS THE ONLY PART I'LL REMEMBER.
THE PART WHERE I WAKE UP AND DON'T KNOW WHERE I AM.

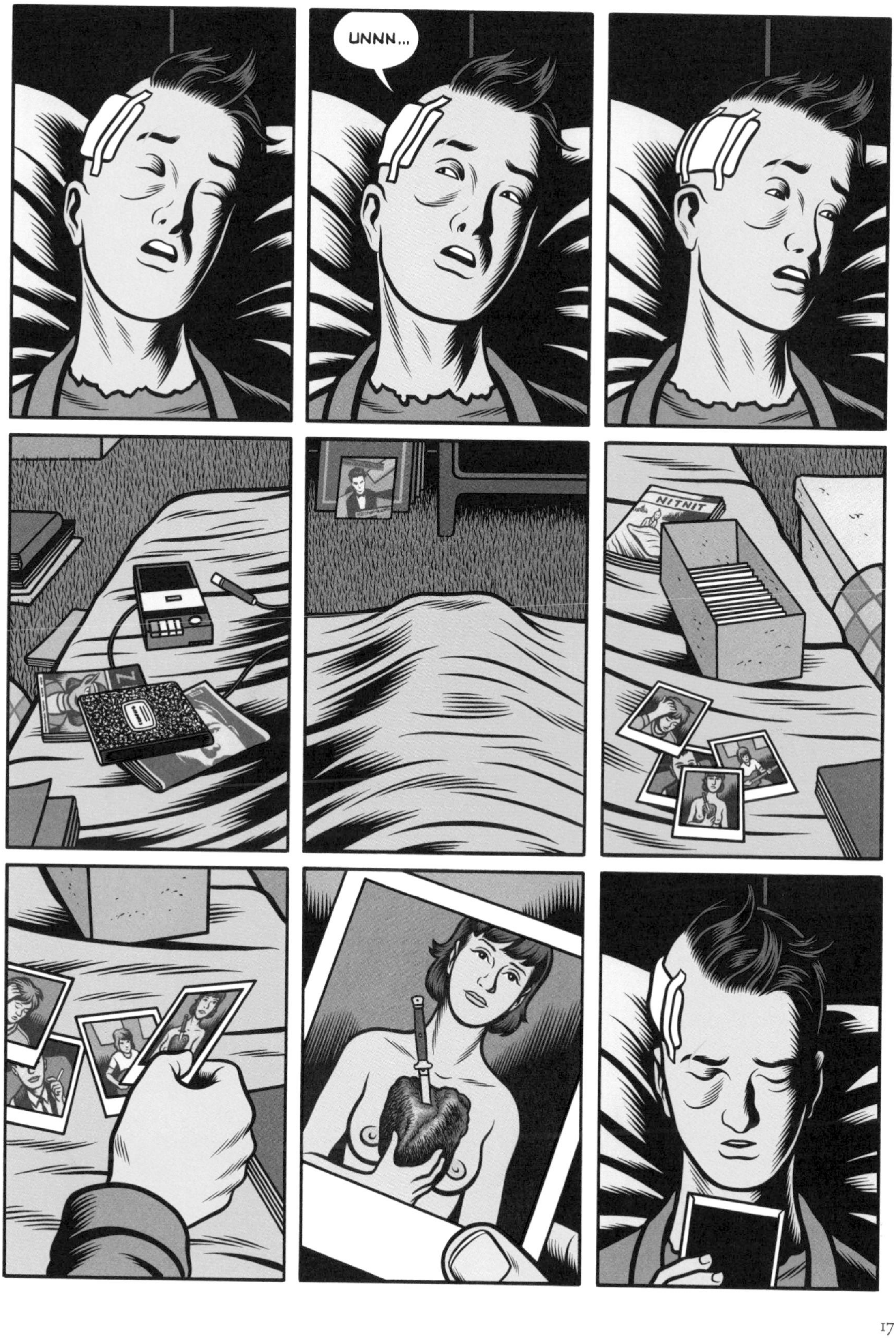
UNNN...
NITNIT

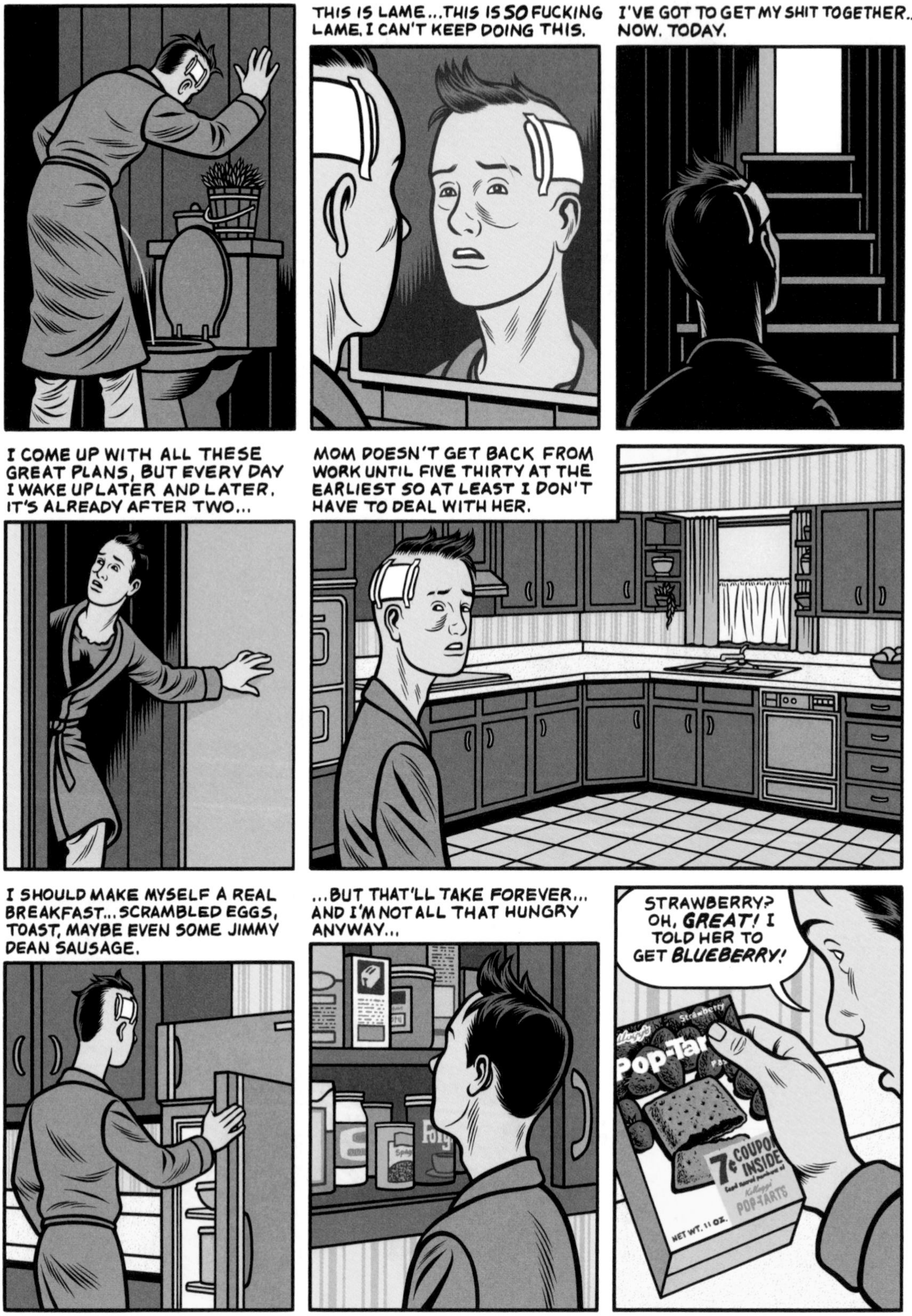
THIS IS LAME...THIS IS SO FUCKING LAME. I CAN'T KEEP DOING THIS.
I'VE GOT TO GET MY SHIT TOGETHER... NOW. TODAY.
I COME UP WITH ALL THESE GREAT PLANS, BUT EVERY DAY I WAKE UP LATER AND LATER. IT'S ALREADY AFTER TWO...
MOM DOESN'T GET BACK FROM WORK UNTIL FIVE THIRTY AT THE EARLIEST SO AT LEAST I DON'T HAVE TO DEAL WITH HER.
I SHOULD MAKE MYSELF A REAL BREAKFAST... SCRAMBLED EGGS, TOAST, MAYBE EVEN SOME JIMMY DEAN SAUSAGE.
...BUT THAT'LL TAKE FOREVER... AND I'M NOT ALL THAT HUNGRY ANYWAY...
STRAWBERRY? OH, GREAT! I TOLD HER TO GET BLUEBERRY!
Strawberry
Pop-Tar
7¢ COUPON INSIDE
Kellogg's POP-TARTS
NET WT. 11 OZ.

MMM...SMELLS SO GOOD. BUT I SHOULD WAIT A FEW SECONDS TO LET THEM COOL DOWN.

KA-CHNK!

I DON'T WANT TO BURN MY TONGUE LIKE LAST TIME, I'VE GOTTA LEARN TO BE PATIENT.

...I'VE GOTTA

BZZZZZ!

AHHH! AW, SHIT!

COME ON, IT'S OKAY! IT'S ONLY THE DOORBELL! IT'S...IT'S THE MAILMAN OR...WHO THE FUCK KNOWS? BUT I DON'T HAVE TO ANSWER IT.

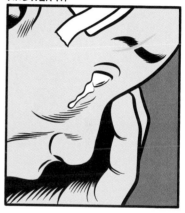

IF ANYONE ASKS, I CAN JUST SAY I WAS DOWNSTAIRS, SICK IN BED AND COULDN'T GET UP TO ANSWER THE DOOR...

...AND IT'S TRUE. I FEEL AWFUL, I FEEL LIKE SHIT.

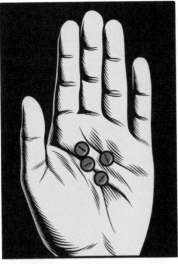

THIS
ISN'T GOING
TO LAST
FOREVER.

IT CAN'T,

I'VE COUNTED
OUT ALL OF
MY PILLS
AND IT'S ONLY
A MATTER
OF TIME...

IT'S GOING TO COME TO AN END
NO MATTER WHAT...'CAUSE THERE'S
ALWAYS A LAST *EVERYTHING*, RIGHT?

...YOUR LAST PILL, YOUR LAST
CIGARETTE, YOUR LAST SIP OF
WATER...

...YOUR LAST GOOD KISS.

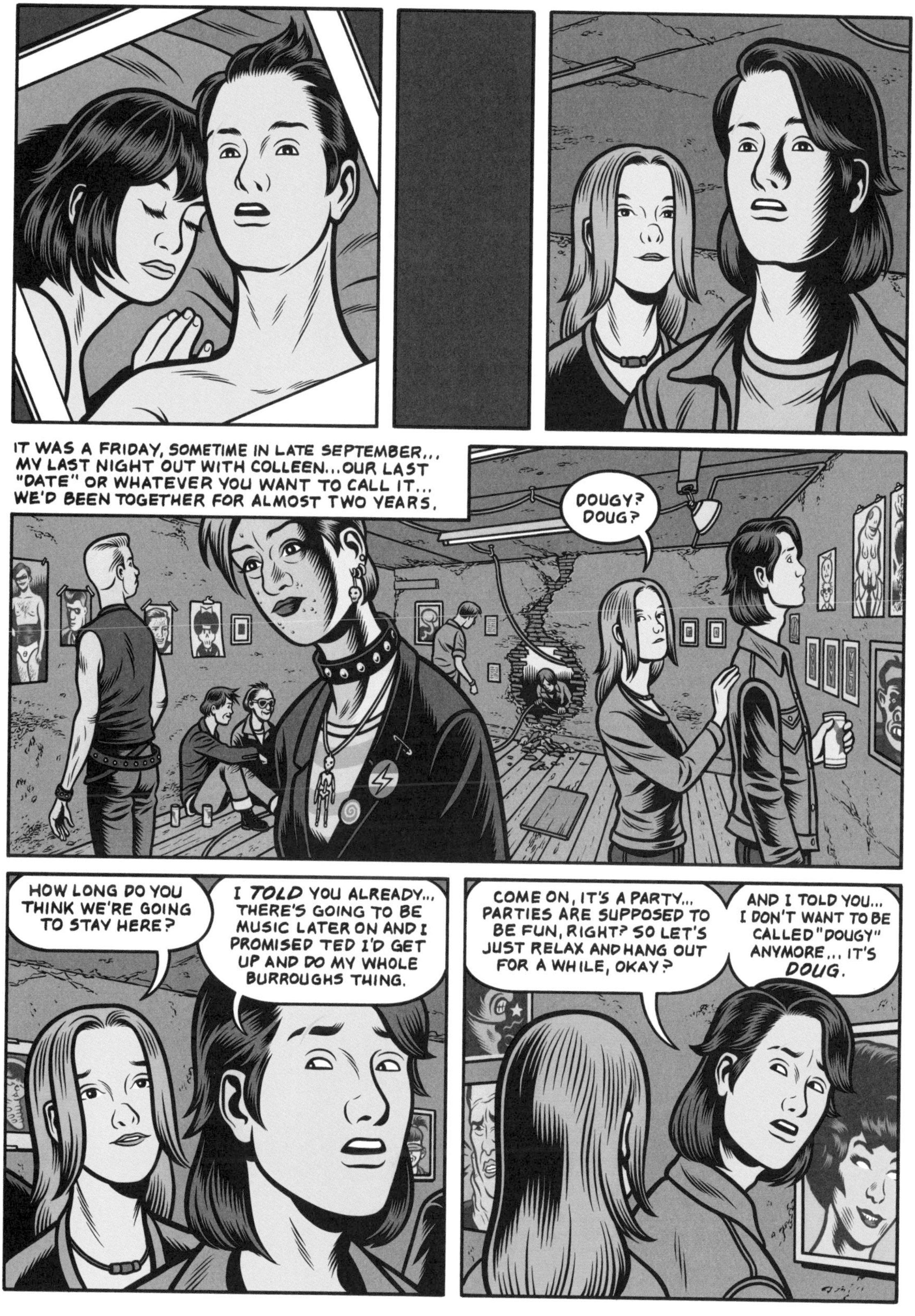

IT WAS A FRIDAY, SOMETIME IN LATE SEPTEMBER... MY LAST NIGHT OUT WITH COLLEEN...OUR LAST "DATE" OR WHATEVER YOU WANT TO CALL IT... WE'D BEEN TOGETHER FOR ALMOST TWO YEARS.
DOUGY? DOUG?
HOW LONG DO YOU THINK WE'RE GOING TO STAY HERE?
I *TOLD* YOU ALREADY... THERE'S GOING TO BE MUSIC LATER ON AND I PROMISED TED I'D GET UP AND DO MY WHOLE BURROUGHS THING.
COME ON, IT'S A PARTY... PARTIES ARE SUPPOSED TO BE FUN, RIGHT? SO LET'S JUST RELAX AND HANG OUT FOR A WHILE, OKAY?
AND I TOLD YOU... I DON'T WANT TO BE CALLED "DOUGY" ANYMORE... IT'S *DOUG*.

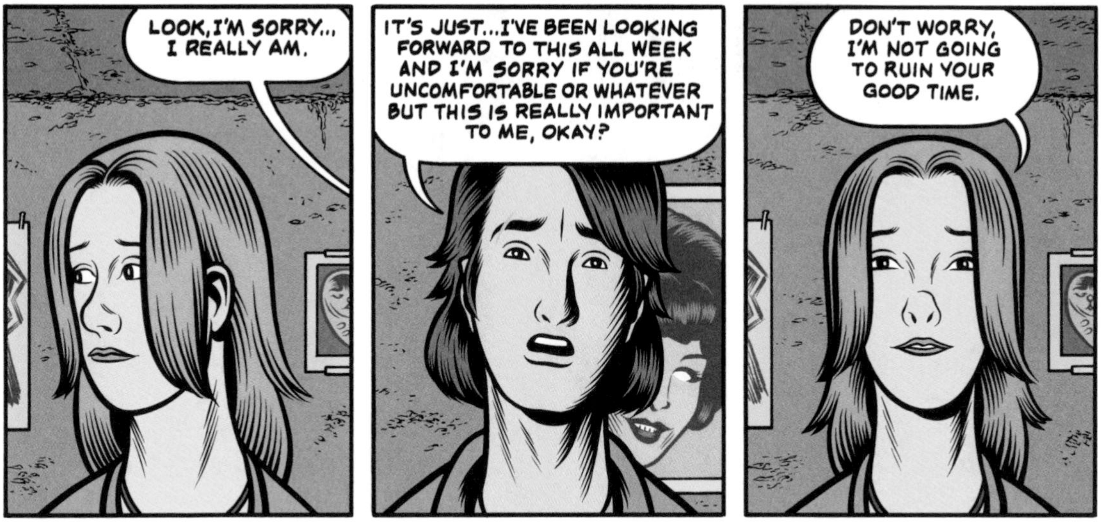
LOOK, I'M SORRY... I REALLY AM.
IT'S JUST...I'VE BEEN LOOKING FORWARD TO THIS ALL WEEK AND I'M SORRY IF YOU'RE UNCOMFORTABLE OR WHATEVER BUT THIS IS REALLY IMPORTANT TO ME, OKAY?
DON'T WORRY, I'M NOT GOING TO RUIN YOUR GOOD TIME.

AFTER A WHILE, COLLEEN RAN INTO SOME FRIENDS FROM SCHOOL SO I WAS ABLE TO SLIP OFF ON MY OWN.

THE PLACE WAS HUGE...IT WAS AN OLD OFFICE BUILDING THAT TED AND A BUNCH OF OTHER GUYS RENTED FOR NEXT TO NOTHING.

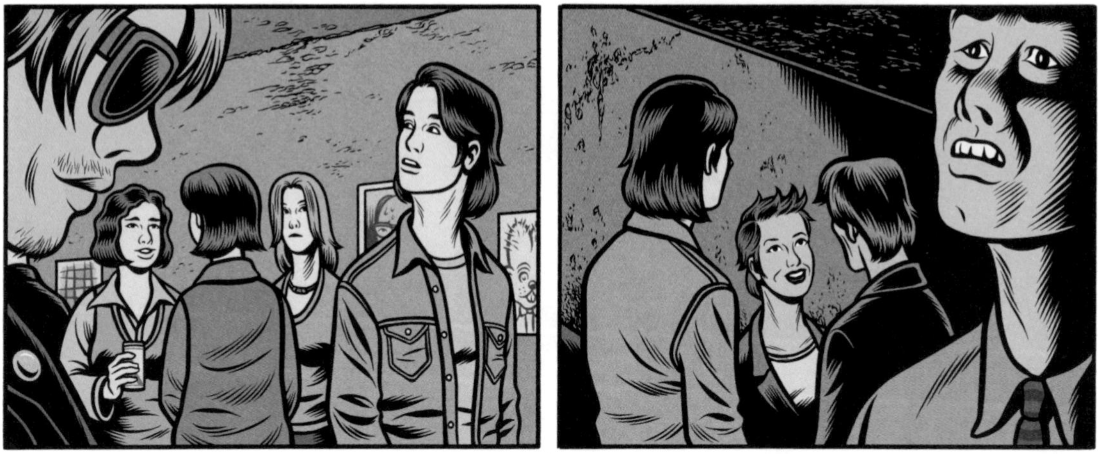

AT SOME POINT THEY STARTED BUSTING THROUGH THE WALLS TO THE ABANDONED WAREHOUSE NEXT DOOR.

I'D HEARD ALL KINDS OF STORIES ABOUT THE SHOWS AND PARTIES THEY PUT ON BUT IT WAS MY FIRST TIME OVER THERE.

I HAD NO IDEA WHAT I WAS GETTING MYSELF INTO.

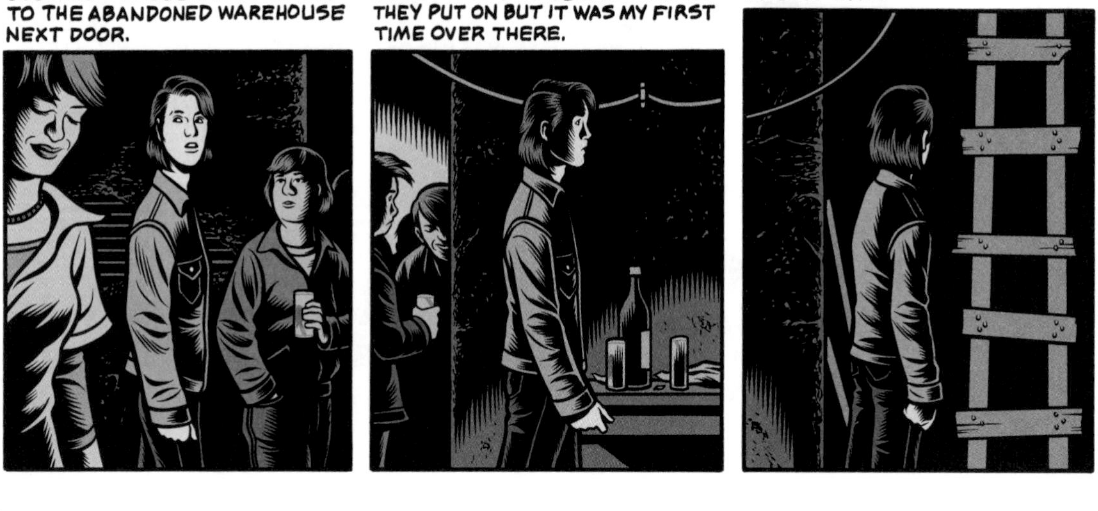

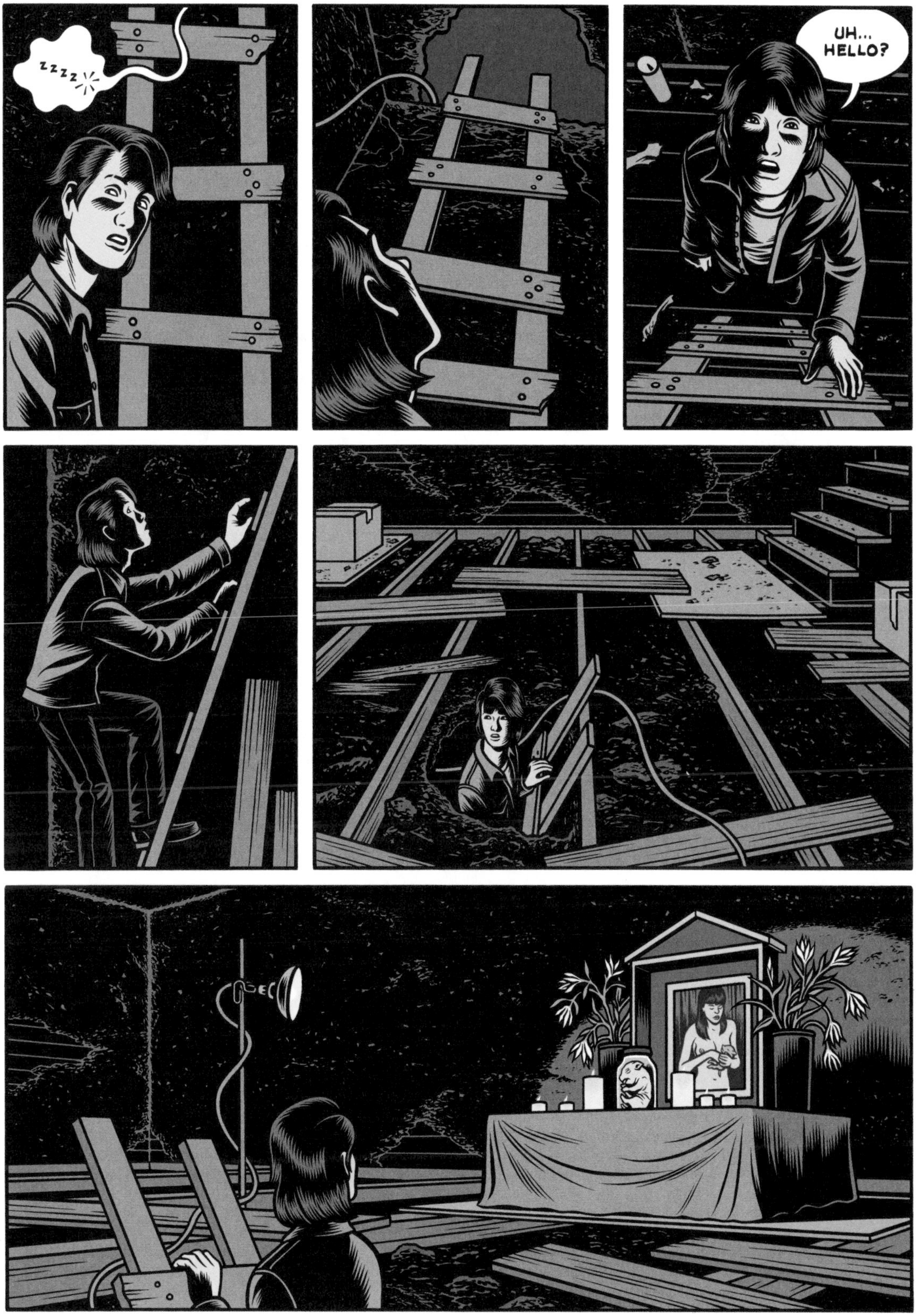
ZZZZ
UH... HELLO?

SCOTT CHANTLER

The Battle of Buron

from *Two Generals*

TWO GENERALS
SCOTT CHANTLER

FOR ME, DRAWING COMICS IS

The single most effective way to express yourself if you're someone who's able to use words and pictures interchangeably. I sometimes balk at how time-consuming and isolating it can be, but anytime I stop, I'm usually sketching and tinkering with story ideas again within a week.

THE CONTEXT

Having gone overseas together in 1943, young lieutenants Law (my grandfather) and Jack have survived rigorous training, mortal fear, and the landing at Juno Beach on D-day. Now the job of punching through German defenses at Buron (the most well-fortified obstacle between them and the Canadian objective, the French city of Caen) has fallen to their regiment.

PUBLICATIONS MY WORK HAS APPEARED IN

The *New York Daily News*, the *National Post*, the *Toronto Star*, *Maclean's*, *Quill and Quire*.

AWARDS

Winner of the 2011 Joe Shuster Award for Best Comic for Kids (for *Tower of Treasure*). Nominated for the Eisner, Harvey, Russ Manning, and Doug Wright awards, as well as the Ontario Library Association's White Pine Award for Non-Fiction and Canada Reads 2012 (both for *Two Generals*).

WHAT I'M KNOWN FOR

Northwest Passage (2007) from Oni Press, and the kids' fantasy series Three Thieves (the first two books of which, *Tower of Treasure* and *The Sign of the Black Rock*, are in stores).

WHERE I LIVE

Waterloo, Ontario.

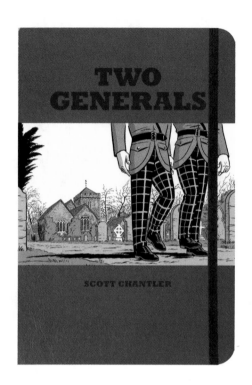

ON JULY 7TH, FIVE HUNDRED ALLIED PLANES TOOK PART IN THE BOMBING OF CAEN.

THE HLI WAR DIARY CALLS IT "A GRAND SHOW."

THAT NIGHT, THE REGIMENT FINALLY MOVED ON FROM WHERE THEY'D DUG IN A MONTH BEFORE.

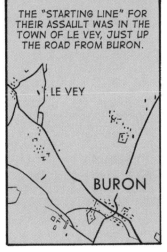

THE "STARTING LINE" FOR THEIR ASSAULT WAS IN THE TOWN OF LE VEY, JUST UP THE ROAD FROM BURON.

LE VEY

BURON

AFTER A SLEEPLESS NIGHT, THEY FORMED UP AT 7:30 AM.

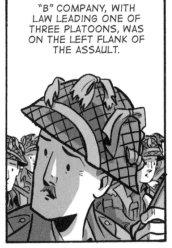

"B" COMPANY, WITH LAW LEADING ONE OF THREE PLATOONS, WAS ON THE LEFT FLANK OF THE ASSAULT.

"A" COMPANY, WITH JACK LEADING HIS PLATOON, WAS IN BEHIND.

ONCE THE OTHER COMPANIES HAD TAKEN BURON, THEY WERE TO PUSH THROUGH TO THE HIGH GROUND SOUTH OF TOWN.

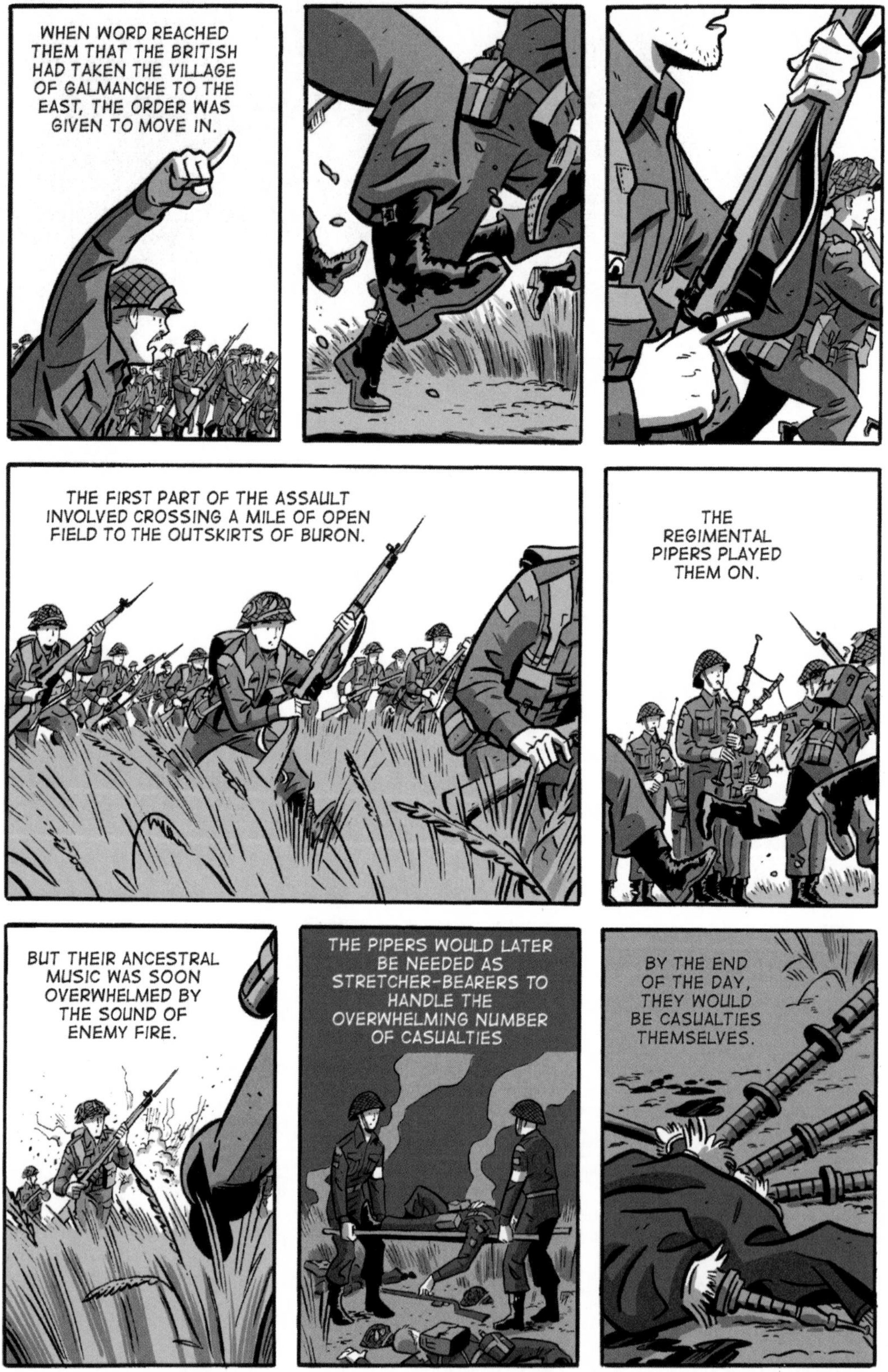
WHEN WORD REACHED THEM THAT THE BRITISH HAD TAKEN THE VILLAGE OF GALMANCHE TO THE EAST, THE ORDER WAS GIVEN TO MOVE IN.
THE FIRST PART OF THE ASSAULT INVOLVED CROSSING A MILE OF OPEN FIELD TO THE OUTSKIRTS OF BURON.
THE REGIMENTAL PIPERS PLAYED THEM ON.
BUT THEIR ANCESTRAL MUSIC WAS SOON OVERWHELMED BY THE SOUND OF ENEMY FIRE.
THE PIPERS WOULD LATER BE NEEDED AS STRETCHER-BEARERS TO HANDLE THE OVERWHELMING NUMBER OF CASUALTIES.
BY THE END OF THE DAY, THEY WOULD BE CASUALTIES THEMSELVES.

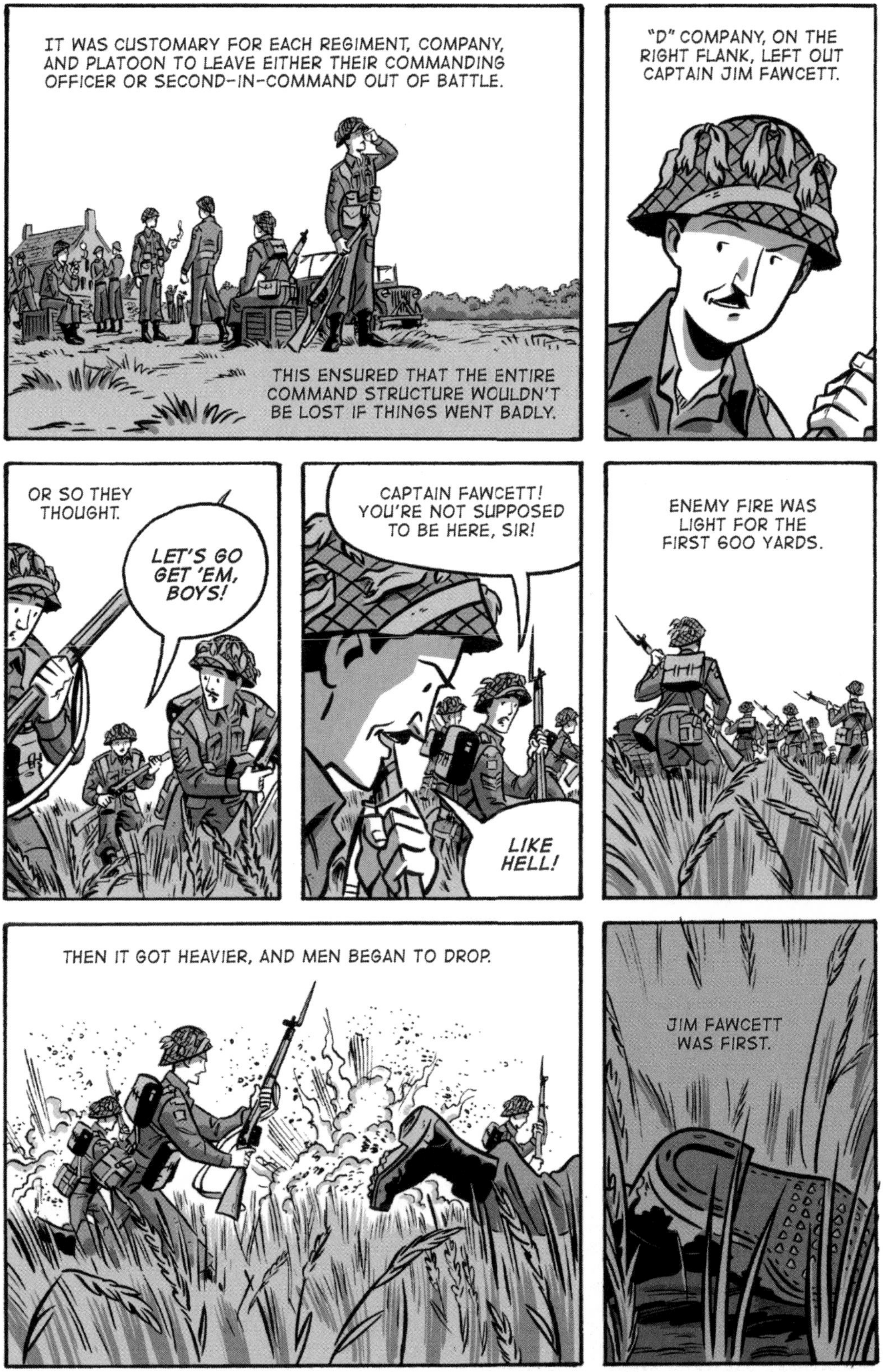
IT WAS CUSTOMARY FOR EACH REGIMENT, COMPANY, AND PLATOON TO LEAVE EITHER THEIR COMMANDING OFFICER OR SECOND-IN-COMMAND OUT OF BATTLE.
THIS ENSURED THAT THE ENTIRE COMMAND STRUCTURE WOULDN'T BE LOST IF THINGS WENT BADLY.
"D" COMPANY, ON THE RIGHT FLANK, LEFT OUT CAPTAIN JIM FAWCETT.
OR SO THEY THOUGHT.
LET'S GO GET 'EM, BOYS!
CAPTAIN FAWCETT! YOU'RE NOT SUPPOSED TO BE HERE, SIR!
LIKE HELL!
ENEMY FIRE WAS LIGHT FOR THE FIRST 600 YARDS.
THEN IT GOT HEAVIER, AND MEN BEGAN TO DROP.
JIM FAWCETT WAS FIRST.

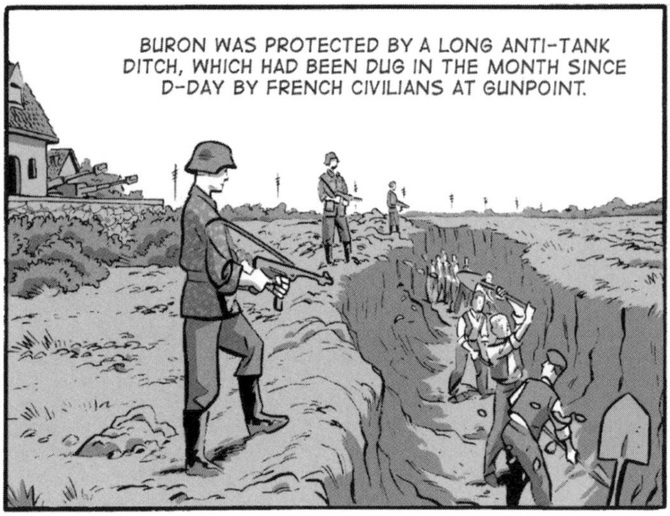
BURON WAS PROTECTED BY A LONG ANTI-TANK DITCH, WHICH HAD BEEN DUG IN THE MONTH SINCE D-DAY BY FRENCH CIVILIANS AT GUNPOINT.

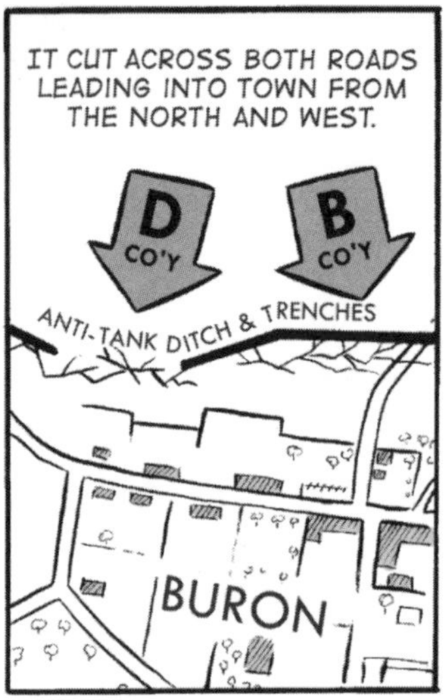
IT CUT ACROSS BOTH ROADS LEADING INTO TOWN FROM THE NORTH AND WEST.
D CO'Y
B CO'Y
ANTI-TANK DITCH & TRENCHES
BURON

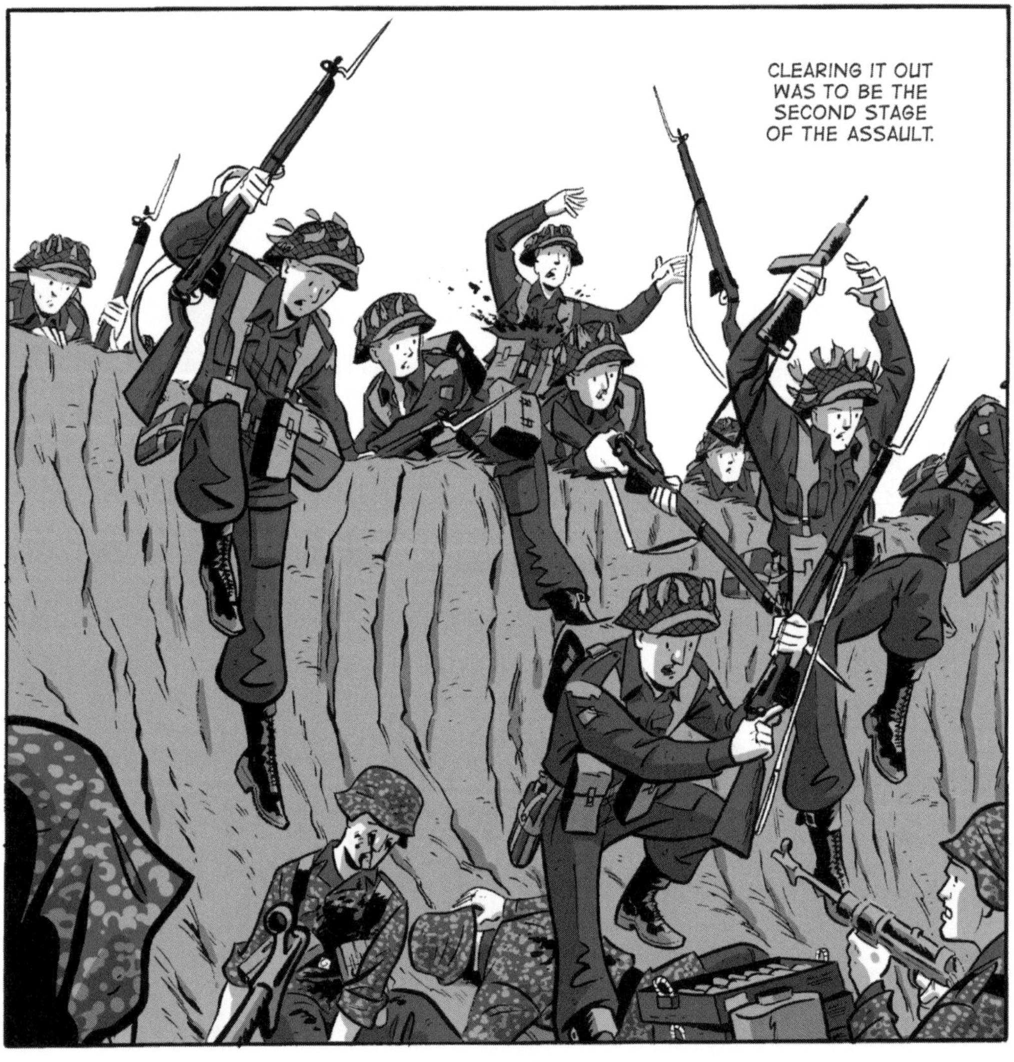
CLEARING IT OUT WAS TO BE THE SECOND STAGE OF THE ASSAULT.

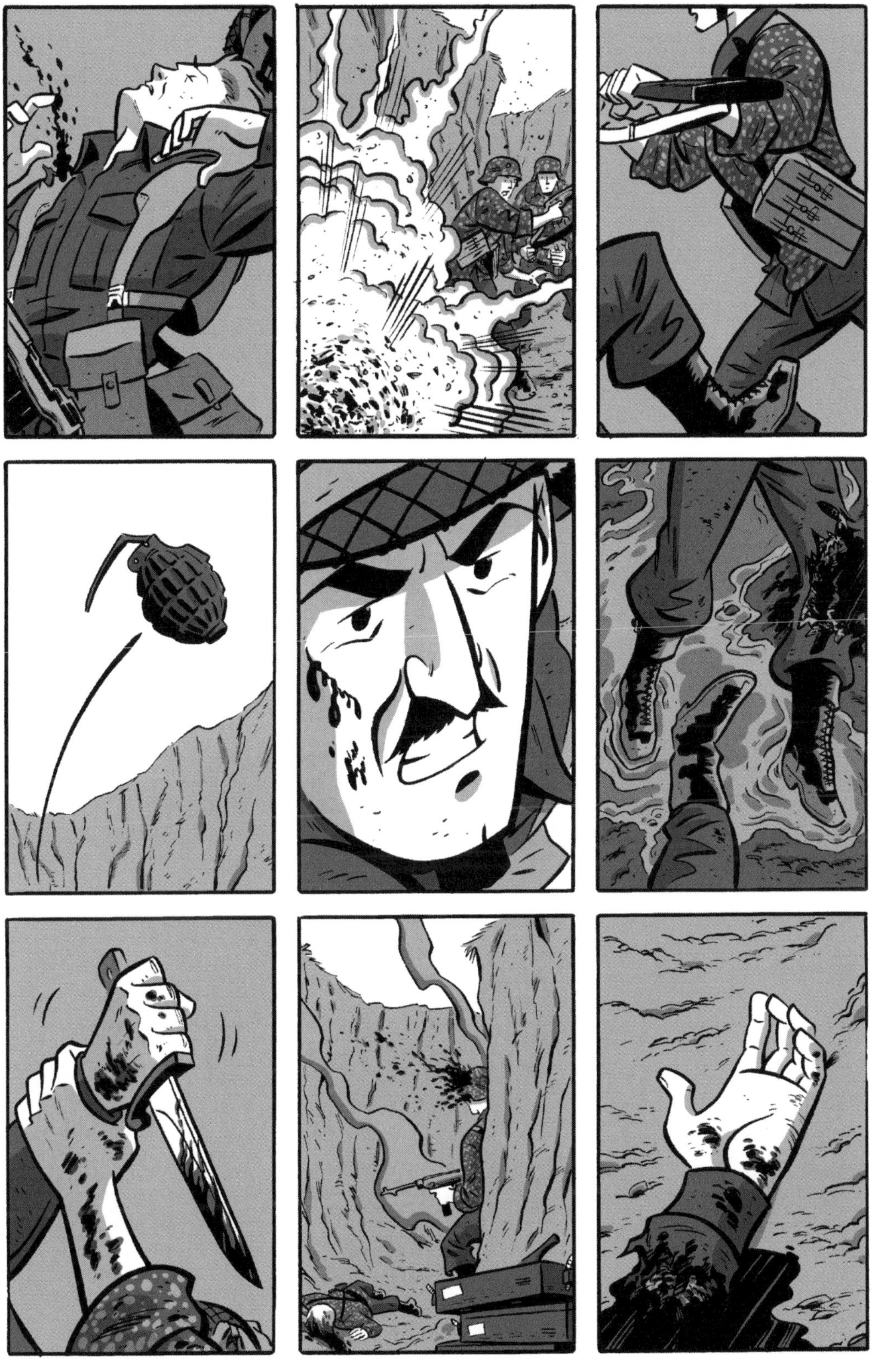

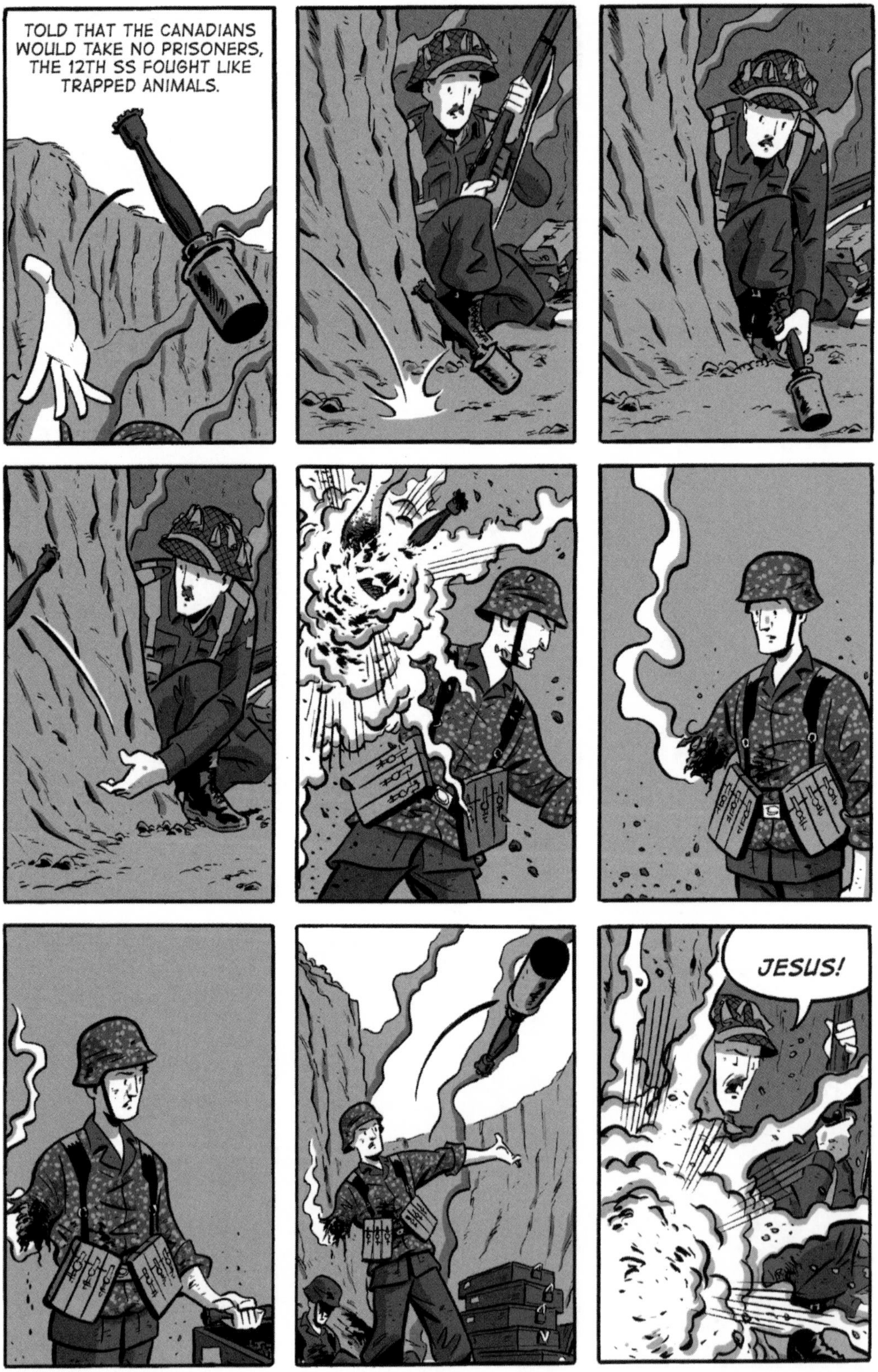
TOLD THAT THE CANADIANS WOULD TAKE NO PRISONERS, THE 12TH SS FOUGHT LIKE TRAPPED ANIMALS.
JESUS!

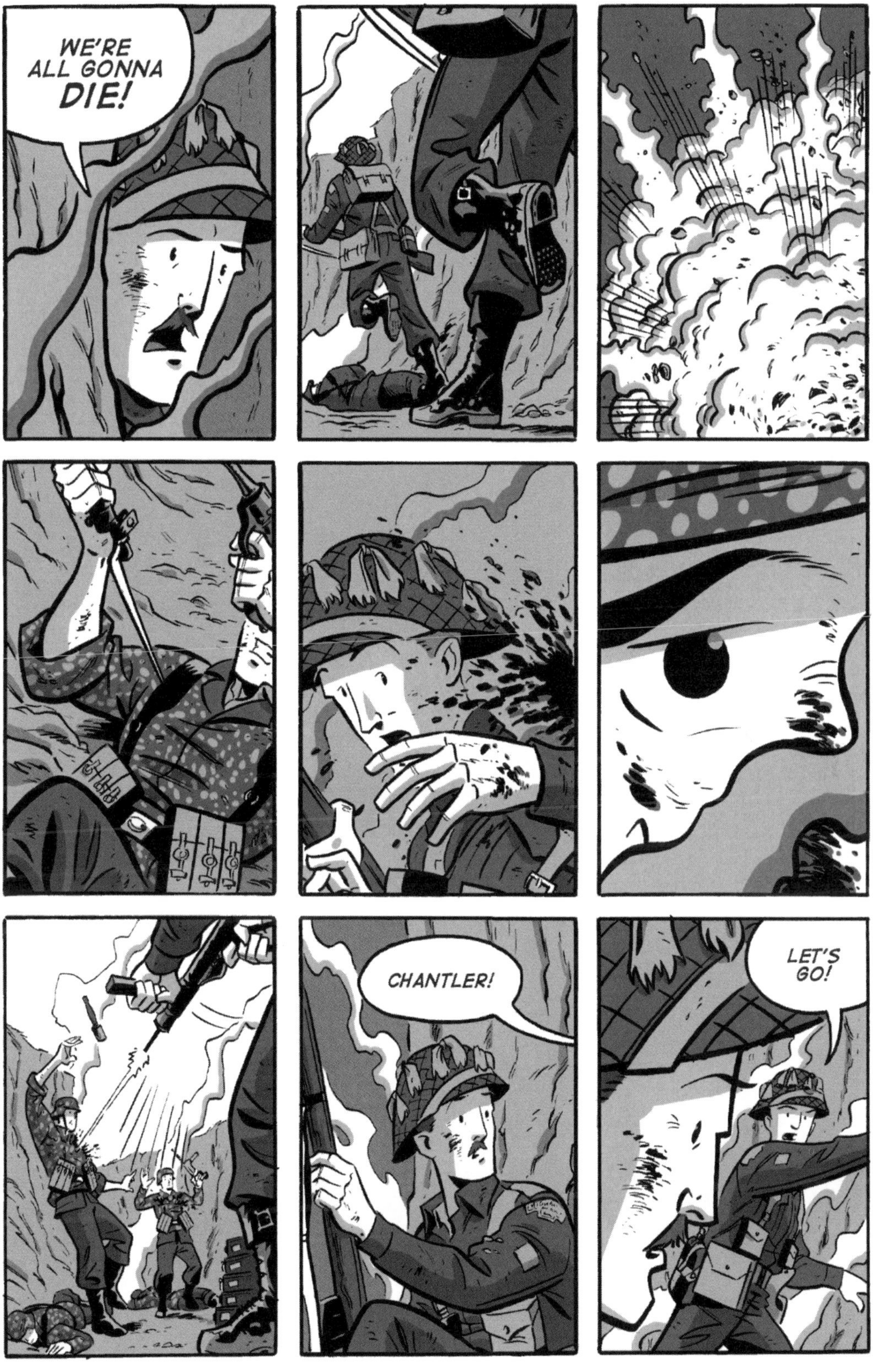

WE'RE ALL GONNA DIE!
CHANTLER!
LET'S GO!

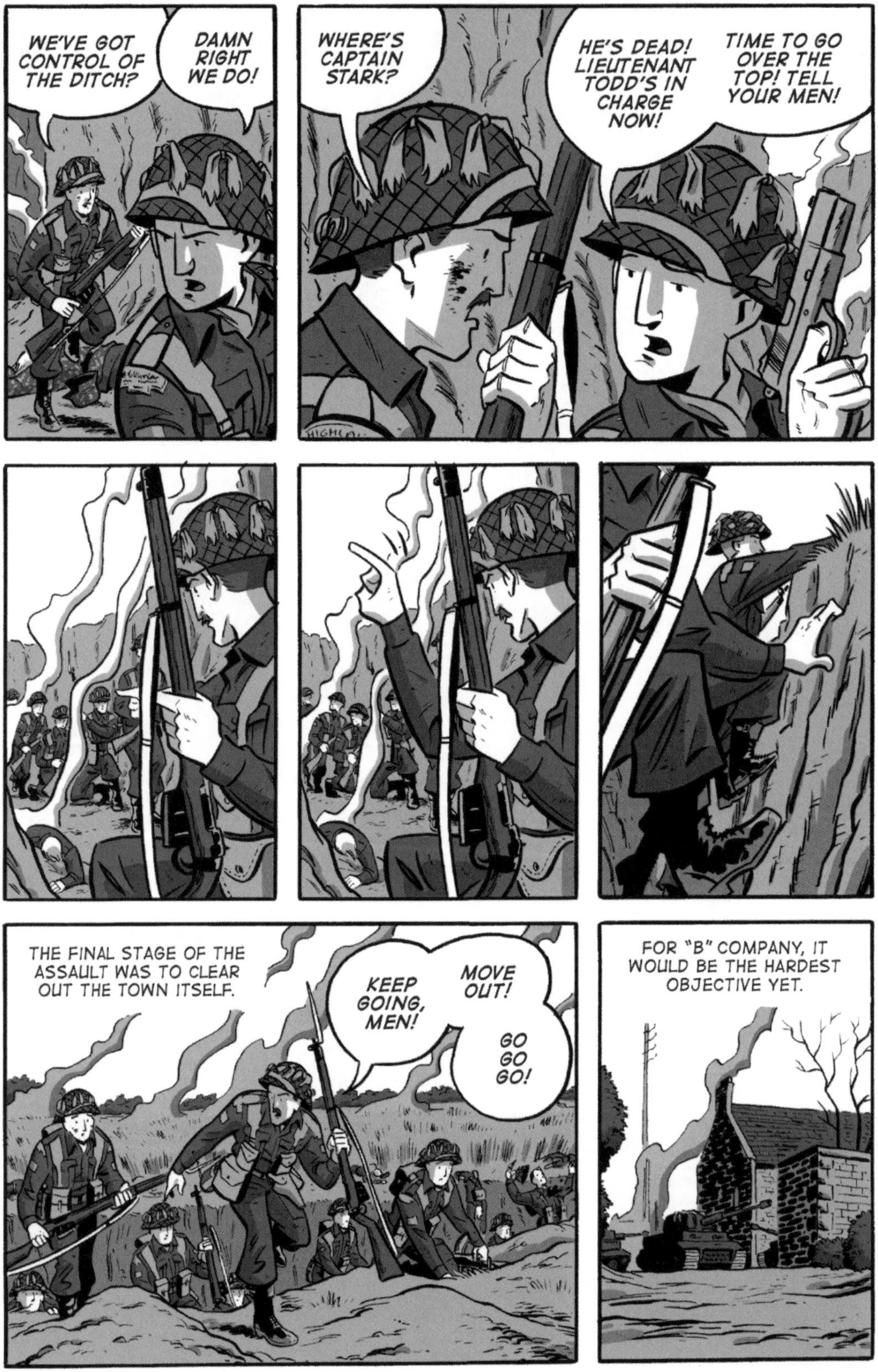
WE'VE GOT CONTROL OF THE DITCH?
DAMN RIGHT WE DO!
WHERE'S CAPTAIN STARK?
HE'S DEAD! LIEUTENANT TODD'S IN CHARGE NOW!
TIME TO GO OVER THE TOP! TELL YOUR MEN!
THE FINAL STAGE OF THE ASSAULT WAS TO CLEAR OUT THE TOWN ITSELF.
KEEP GOING, MEN!
MOVE OUT!
GO GO GO!
FOR "B" COMPANY, IT WOULD BE THE HARDEST OBJECTIVE YET.

THEY WERE PINNED DOWN BY MORTAR AND MACHINE GUN FIRE FROM THE TOWN.

WHERE THE HELL ARE THE **TANKS?!**

RADIO THE COMMAND GROUP AND TELL THEM WE NEED THE TANKS OVER HERE **NOW!**

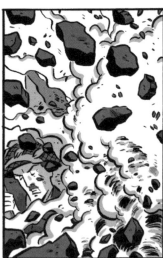

GOD DAMMIT! I—

SO MANY SIGNALLERS HAD BECOME CASUALTIES THAT IT WAS IMPOSSIBLE TO GET INFORMATION ABOUT WHAT WAS GOING ON ELSEWHERE IN THE BATTLE.

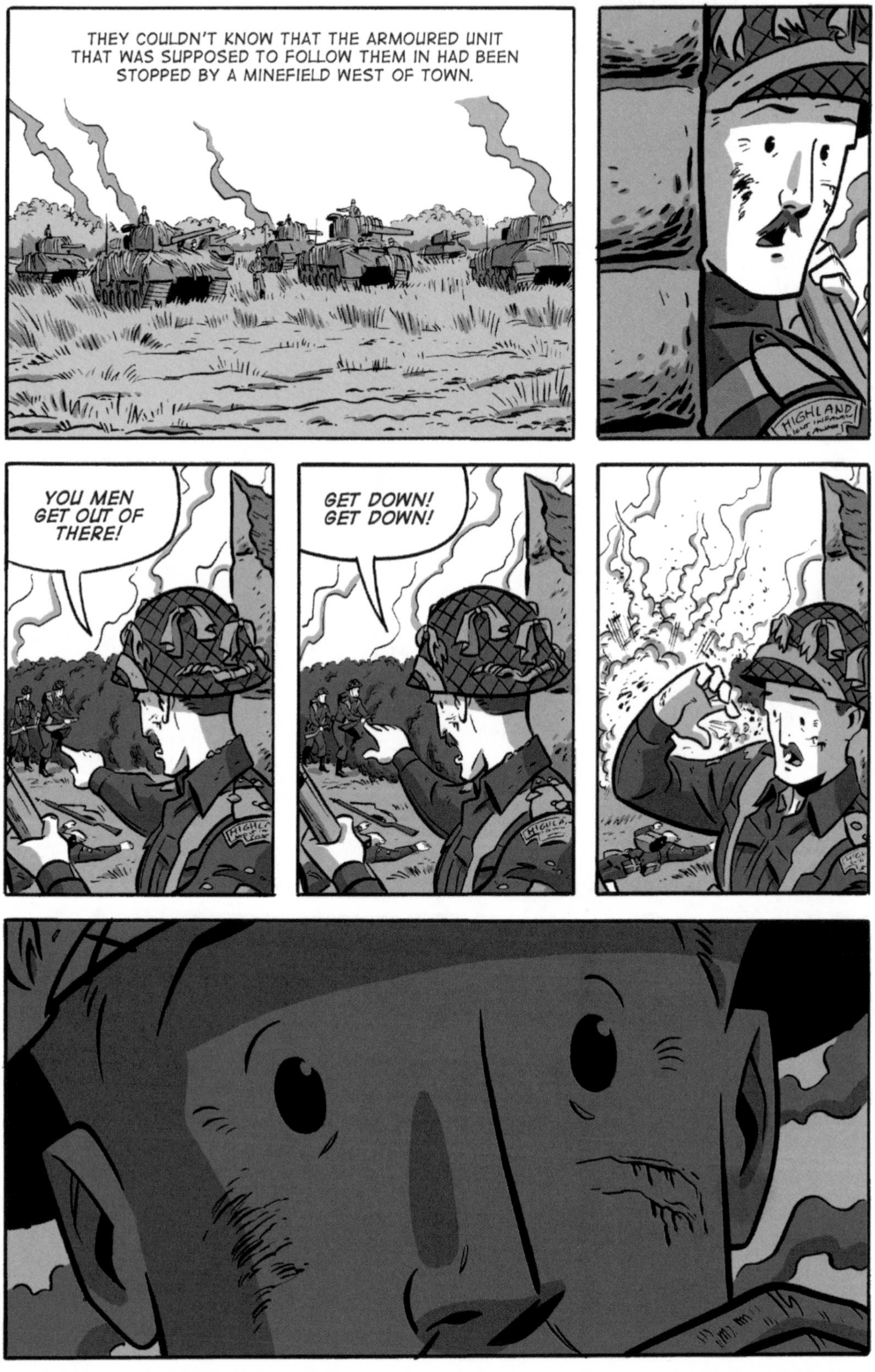
THEY COULDN'T KNOW THAT THE ARMOURED UNIT THAT WAS SUPPOSED TO FOLLOW THEM IN HAD BEEN STOPPED BY A MINEFIELD WEST OF TOWN.
HIGHLAND
YOU MEN GET OUT OF THERE!
GET DOWN! GET DOWN!

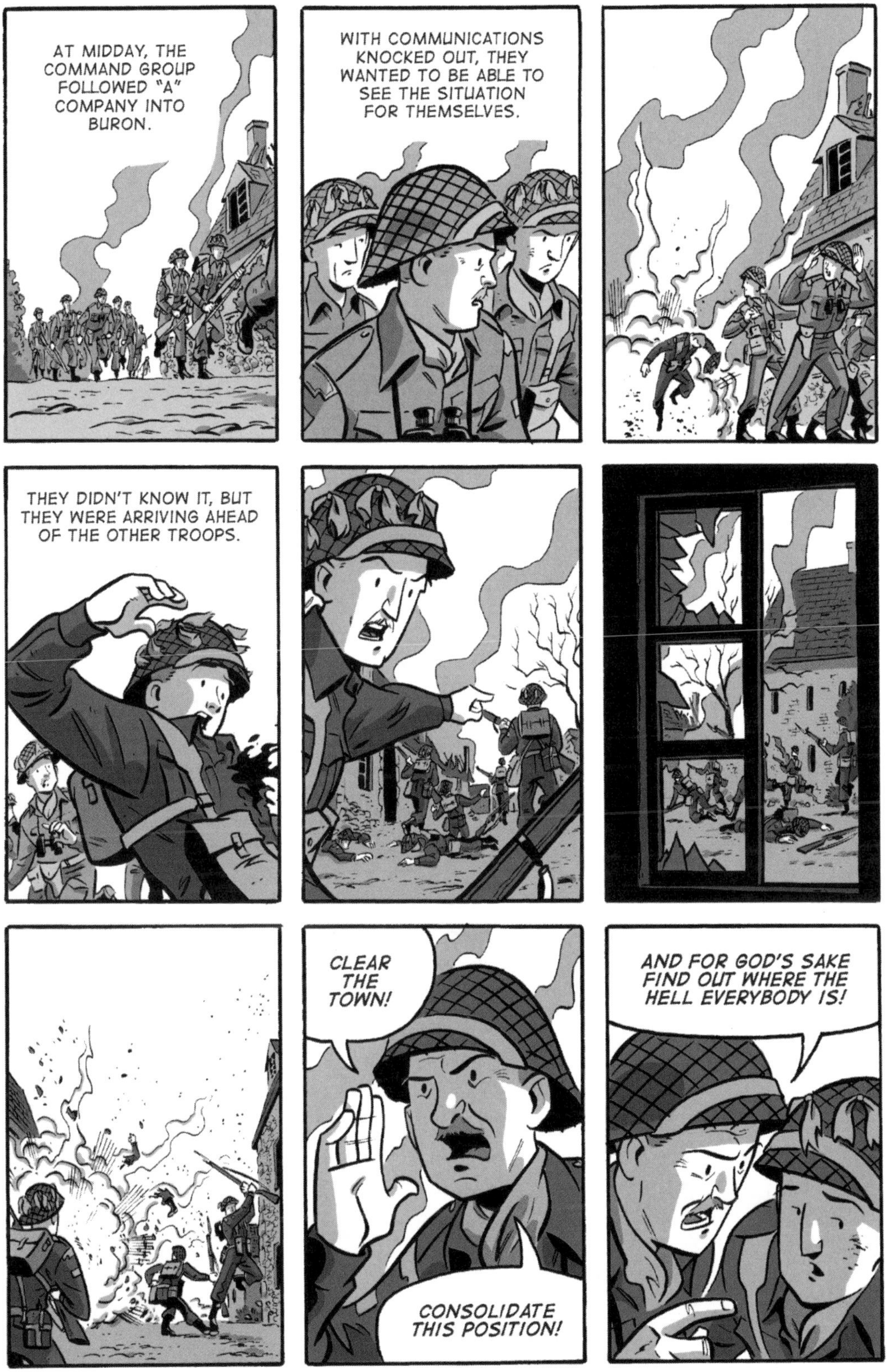
AT MIDDAY, THE COMMAND GROUP FOLLOWED "A" COMPANY INTO BURON.
WITH COMMUNICATIONS KNOCKED OUT, THEY WANTED TO BE ABLE TO SEE THE SITUATION FOR THEMSELVES.
THEY DIDN'T KNOW IT, BUT THEY WERE ARRIVING AHEAD OF THE OTHER TROOPS.
CLEAR THE TOWN!
CONSOLIDATE THIS POSITION!
AND FOR GOD'S SAKE FIND OUT WHERE THE HELL EVERYBODY IS!

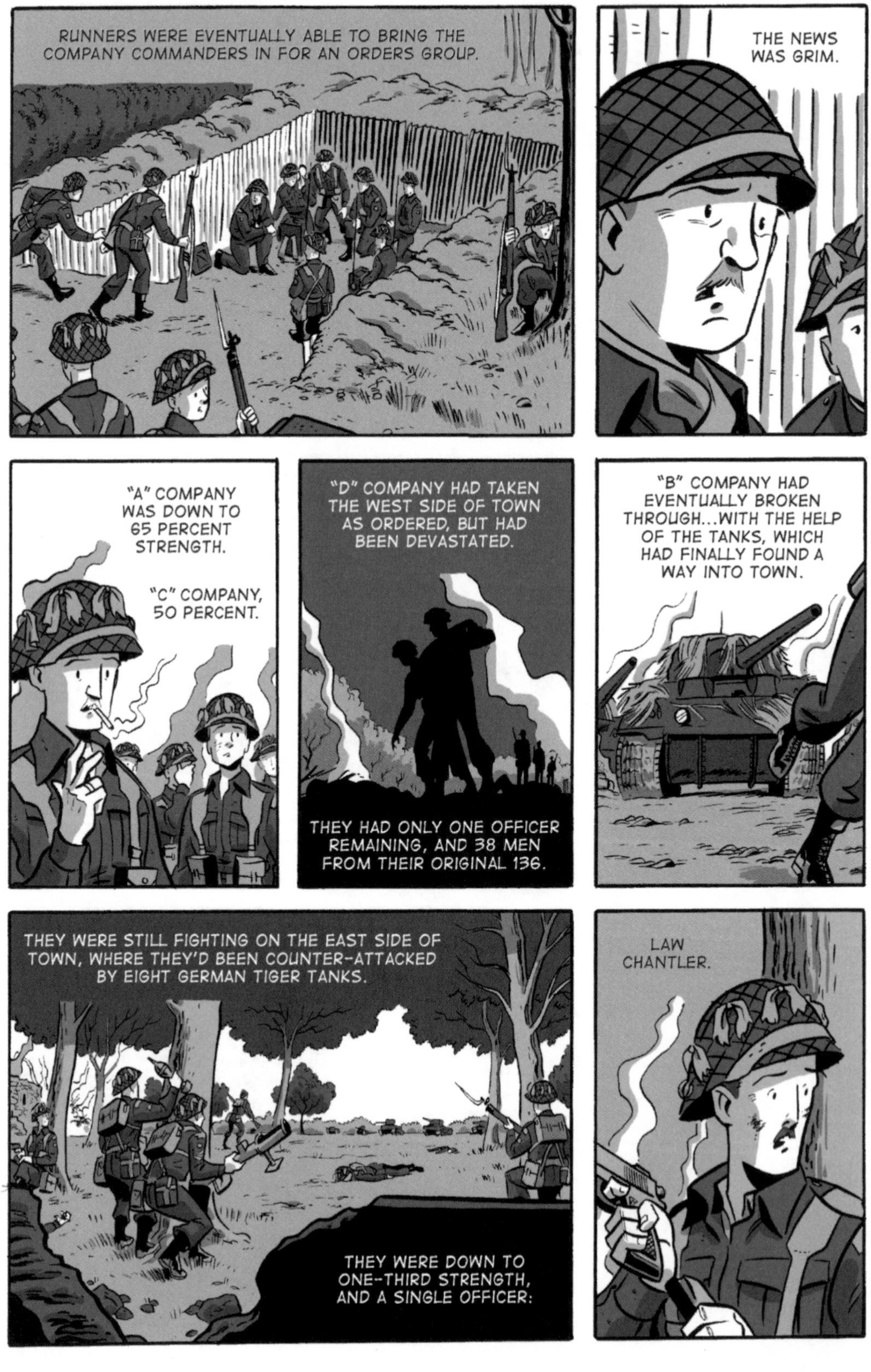
RUNNERS WERE EVENTUALLY ABLE TO BRING THE COMPANY COMMANDERS IN FOR AN ORDERS GROUP.
THE NEWS WAS GRIM.
"A" COMPANY WAS DOWN TO 65 PERCENT STRENGTH.
"C" COMPANY, 50 PERCENT.
"D" COMPANY HAD TAKEN THE WEST SIDE OF TOWN AS ORDERED, BUT HAD BEEN DEVASTATED.
THEY HAD ONLY ONE OFFICER REMAINING, AND 38 MEN FROM THEIR ORIGINAL 136.
"B" COMPANY HAD EVENTUALLY BROKEN THROUGH...WITH THE HELP OF THE TANKS, WHICH HAD FINALLY FOUND A WAY INTO TOWN.
THEY WERE STILL FIGHTING ON THE EAST SIDE OF TOWN, WHERE THEY'D BEEN COUNTER-ATTACKED BY EIGHT GERMAN TIGER TANKS.
THEY WERE DOWN TO ONE-THIRD STRENGTH, AND A SINGLE OFFICER:
LAW CHANTLER.

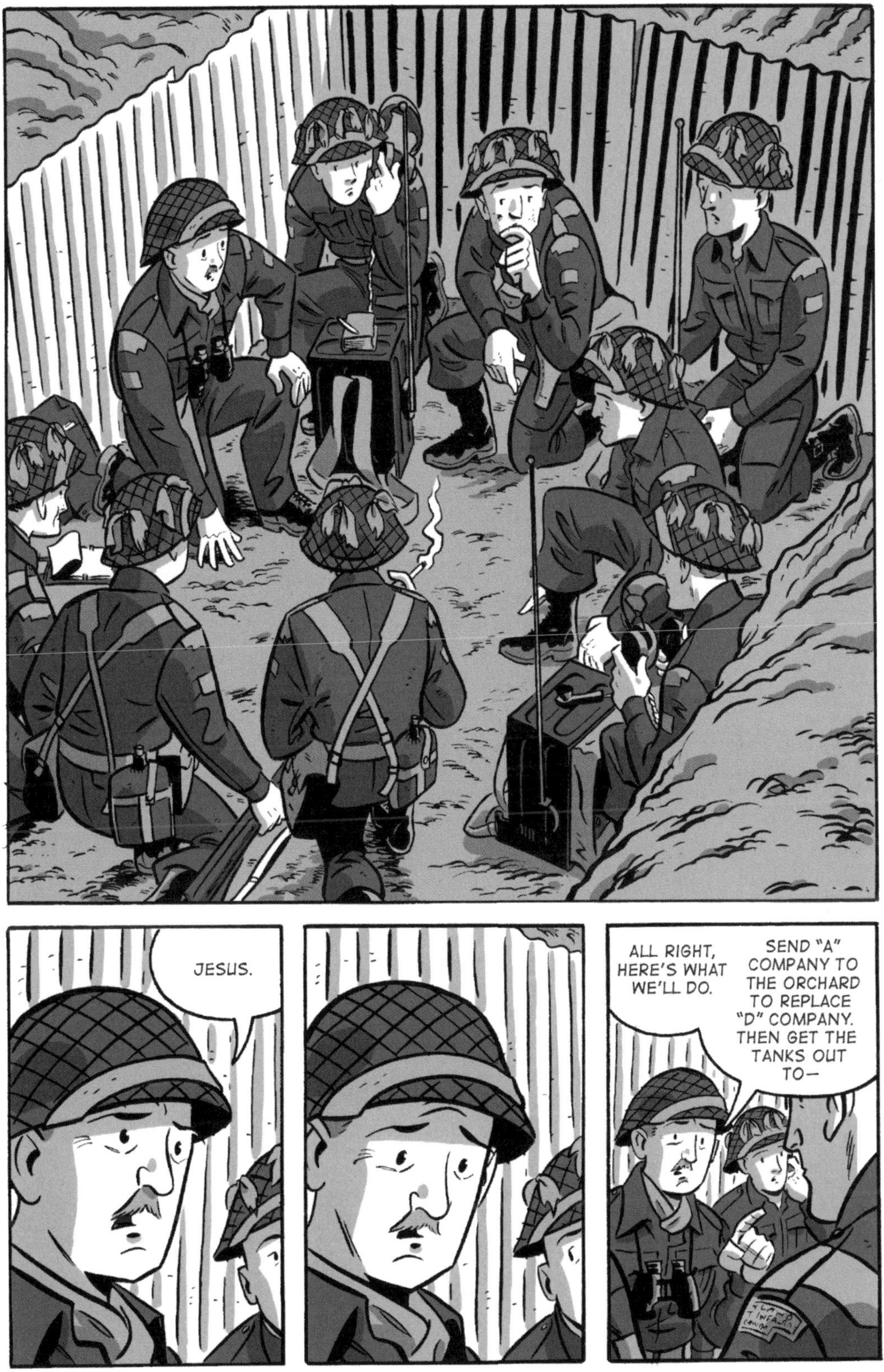
JESUS.
ALL RIGHT, HERE'S WHAT WE'LL DO.
SEND "A" COMPANY TO THE ORCHARD TO REPLACE "D" COMPANY. THEN GET THE TANKS OUT TO—

THAT'S WHEN
THE COMMAND
GROUP WAS HIT.

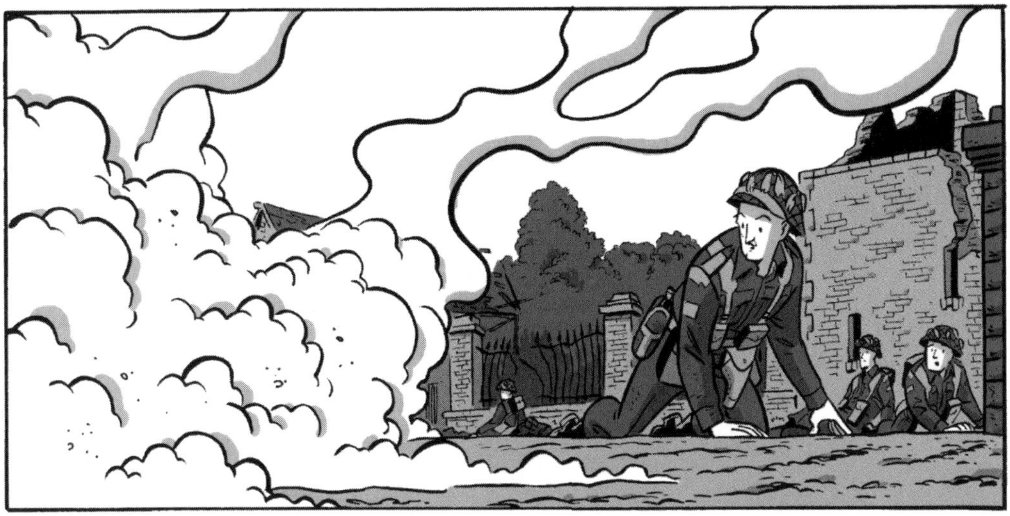

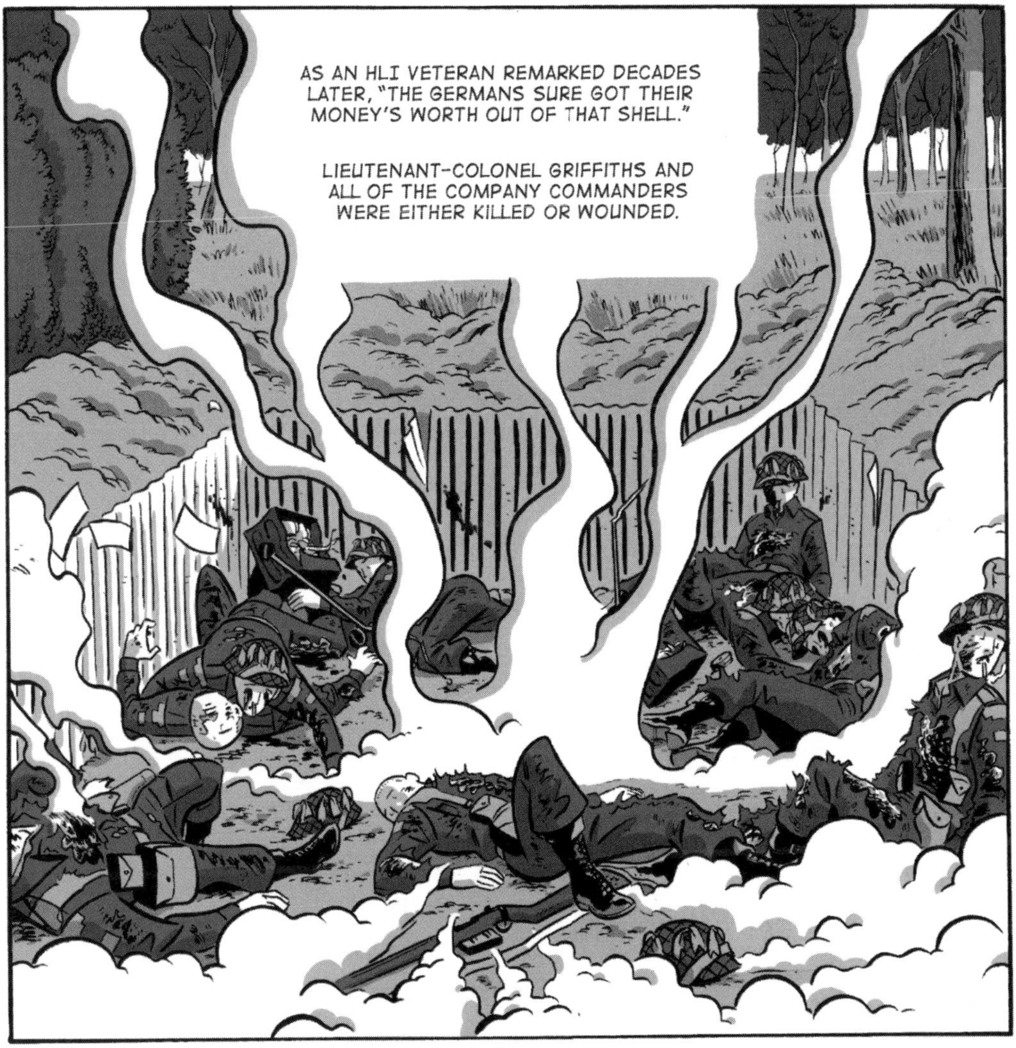
AS AN HLI VETERAN REMARKED DECADES LATER, "THE GERMANS SURE GOT THEIR MONEY'S WORTH OUT OF THAT SHELL."
LIEUTENANT-COLONEL GRIFFITHS AND ALL OF THE COMPANY COMMANDERS WERE EITHER KILLED OR WOUNDED.

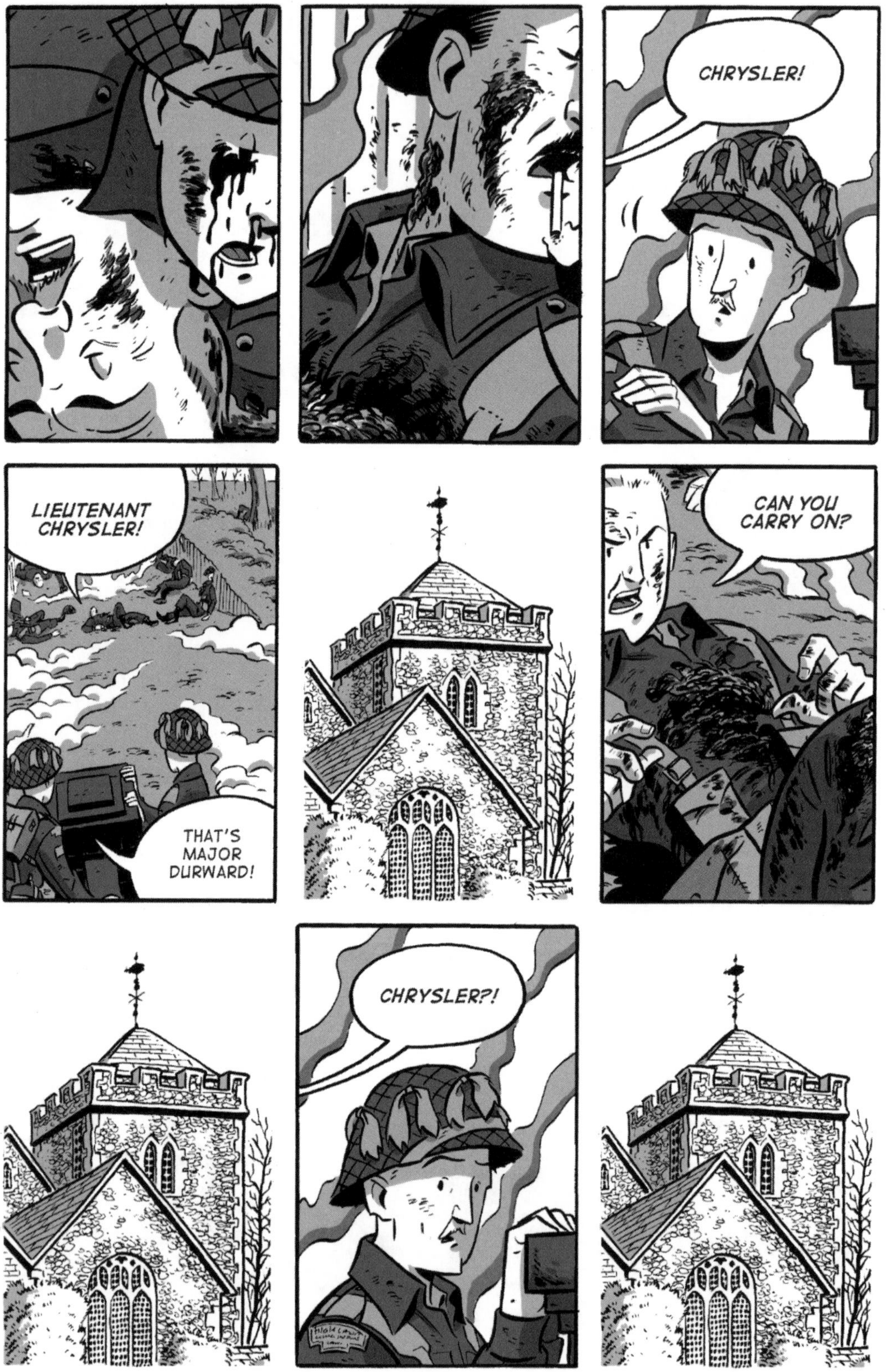
CHRYSLER!
LIEUTENANT CHRYSLER!
THAT'S MAJOR DURWARD!
CAN YOU CARRY ON?
CHRYSLER?!

ADRIAN TOMINE

Scenes from an Impending Marriage *(Excerpt)*

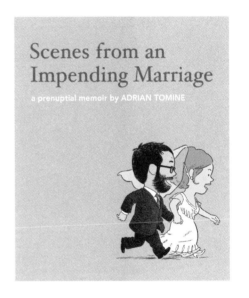

Scenes from an
Impending Marriage

a prenuptial memoir by ADRIAN TOMINE

FOR ME, DRAWING COMICS IS

Slightly less daunting and frustrating than not drawing comics.

THE SELECTION

This was originally a limited-edition, hand-assembled booklet that was given out as a "wedding favor" when I got married. After the wedding, I kept adding pages in my sketchbook, and it turned into the published book.

A PUBLICATION MY WORK HAS APPEARED IN

The New Yorker.

WHAT I'M KNOWN FOR

Optic Nerve (comic book) and *Shortcomings* (graphic novel).

WHERE I LIVE

Brooklyn, New York.

Hundred Dollar Necktie

*"...And you're <u>sure</u> I can't just wear the one
I bought for your grandma's funeral?"*

Registering

UGH...THIS ENTIRE STORE IS FILLED WITH HAPPY, YOUNG COUPLES "REGISTERING" FOR THEIR WEDDING!

IMAGINE HOW ANNOYING THIS WOULD BE IF YOU WERE SOME LONELY, SINGLE PERSON WHO JUST NEEDED A NEW BATH MAT!

WHAT A BIZARRE RITUAL! IT'S BASICALLY MAKING A LIST OF EXPENSIVE STUFF YOU EXPECT PEOPLE TO BUY FOR YOU!

AND WHAT'S WITH THESE BAR-CODE SCANNERS? IT LOOKS LIKE EVERYONE'S CASUALLY AIMING A GUN AT WICKER TISSUE BOX HOLDERS OR WHATEVER!

IT'S EMBLEMATIC OF OUR WHOLE CULTURE: "I WANT LOTS OF STUFF, AND I WANT TO SHOOT A GUN!"

AND YOU KNOW... NO ONE SEEMS EMBARRASSED OR—

ENOUGH!

JUST MAKE UP YOUR MIND: DO YOU LIKE THE "GRAND HOTEL" FLATWARE OR THE "CHARLEMAGNE"?

Florist

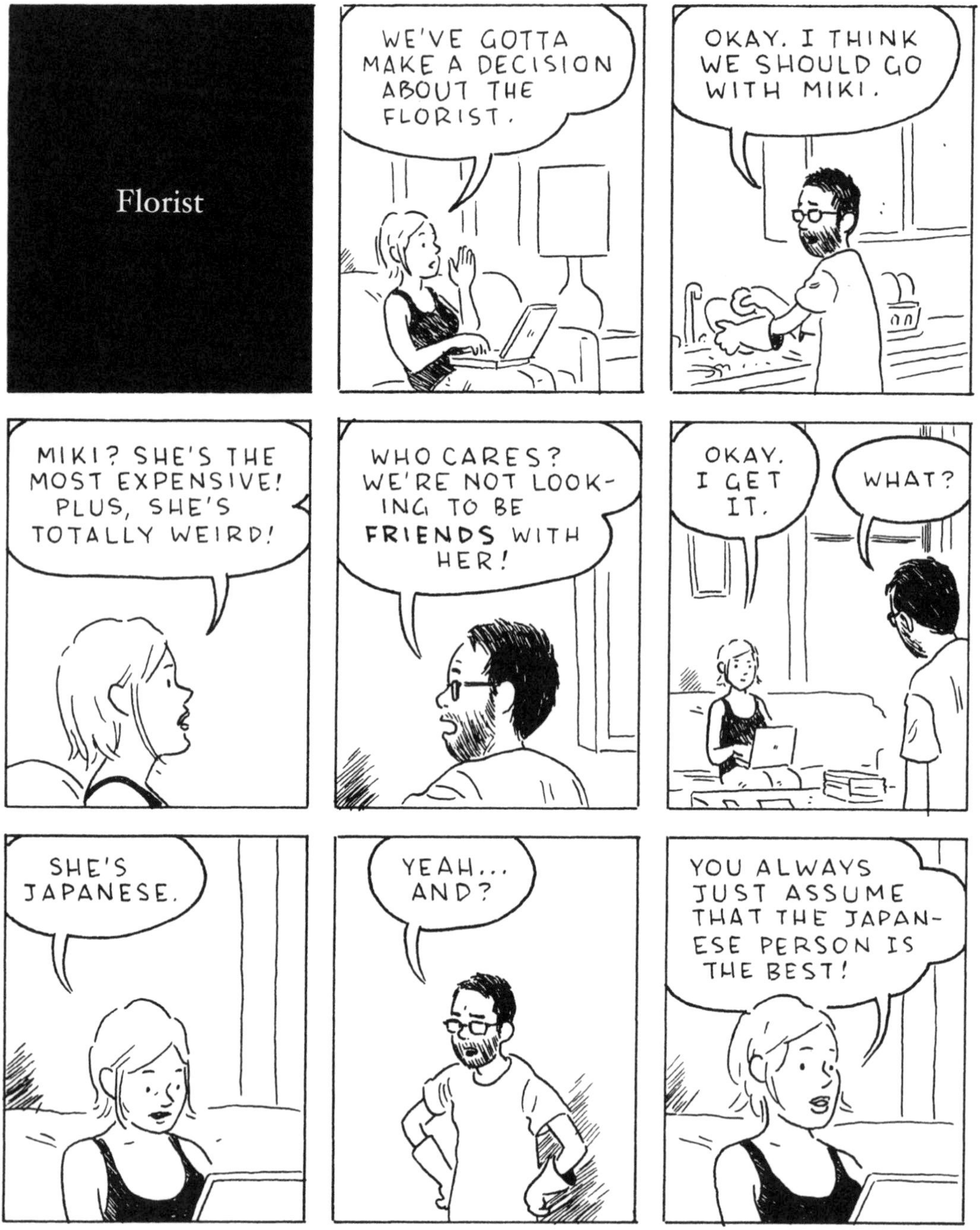

WE'VE GOTTA MAKE A DECISION ABOUT THE FLORIST.
OKAY. I THINK WE SHOULD GO WITH MIKI.
MIKI? SHE'S THE MOST EXPENSIVE! PLUS, SHE'S TOTALLY WEIRD!
WHO CARES? WE'RE NOT LOOK-ING TO BE **FRIENDS** WITH HER!
OKAY. I GET IT.
WHAT?
SHE'S JAPANESE.
YEAH... AND?
YOU ALWAYS JUST ASSUME THAT THE JAPAN-ESE PERSON IS THE BEST!

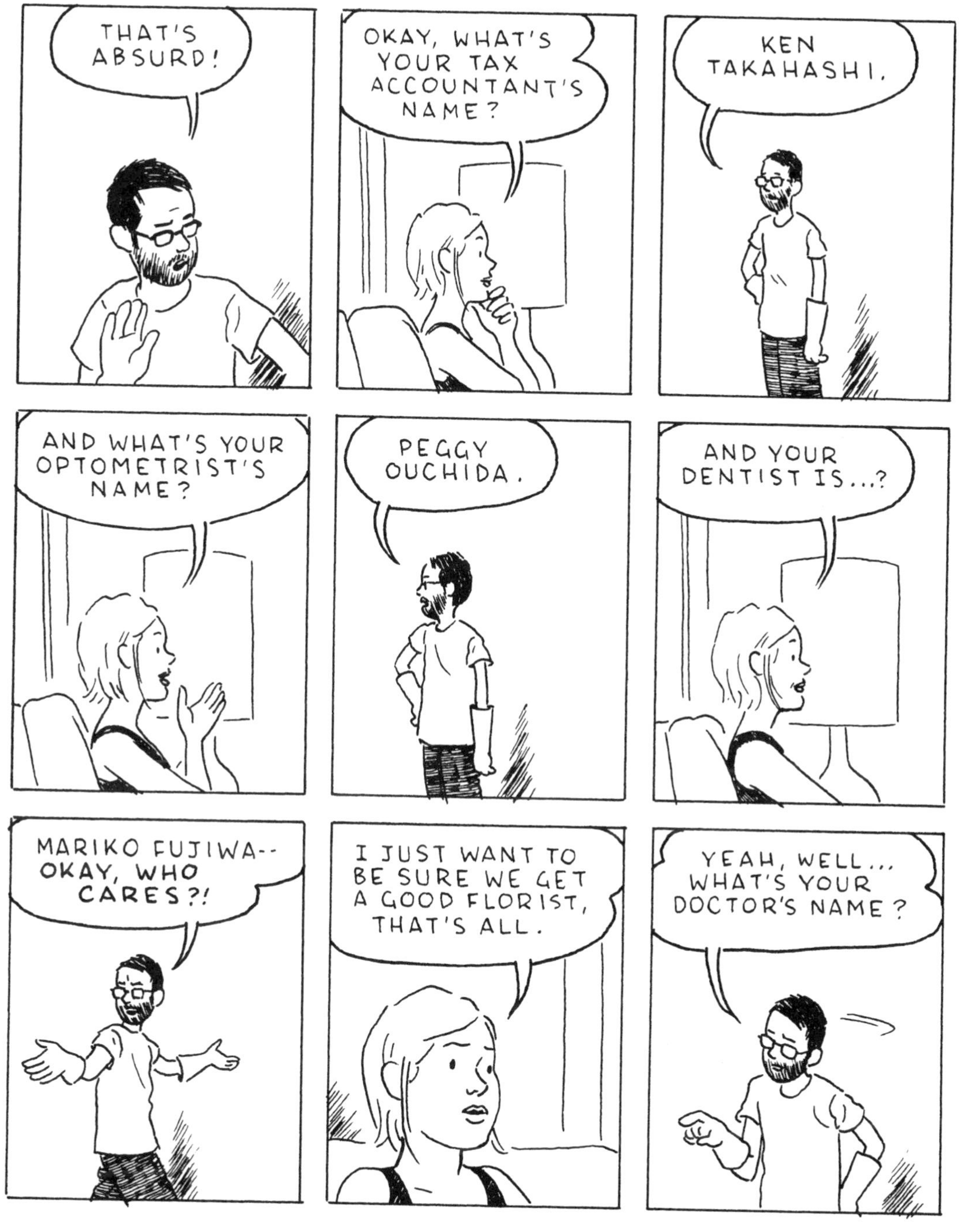
THAT'S ABSURD!
OKAY, WHAT'S YOUR TAX ACCOUNTANT'S NAME?
KEN TAKAHASHI.
AND WHAT'S YOUR OPTOMETRIST'S NAME?
PEGGY OUCHIDA.
AND YOUR DENTIST IS...?
MARIKO FUJIWA-- OKAY, WHO CARES?!
I JUST WANT TO BE SURE WE GET A GOOD FLORIST, THAT'S ALL.
YEAH, WELL... WHAT'S YOUR DOCTOR'S NAME?

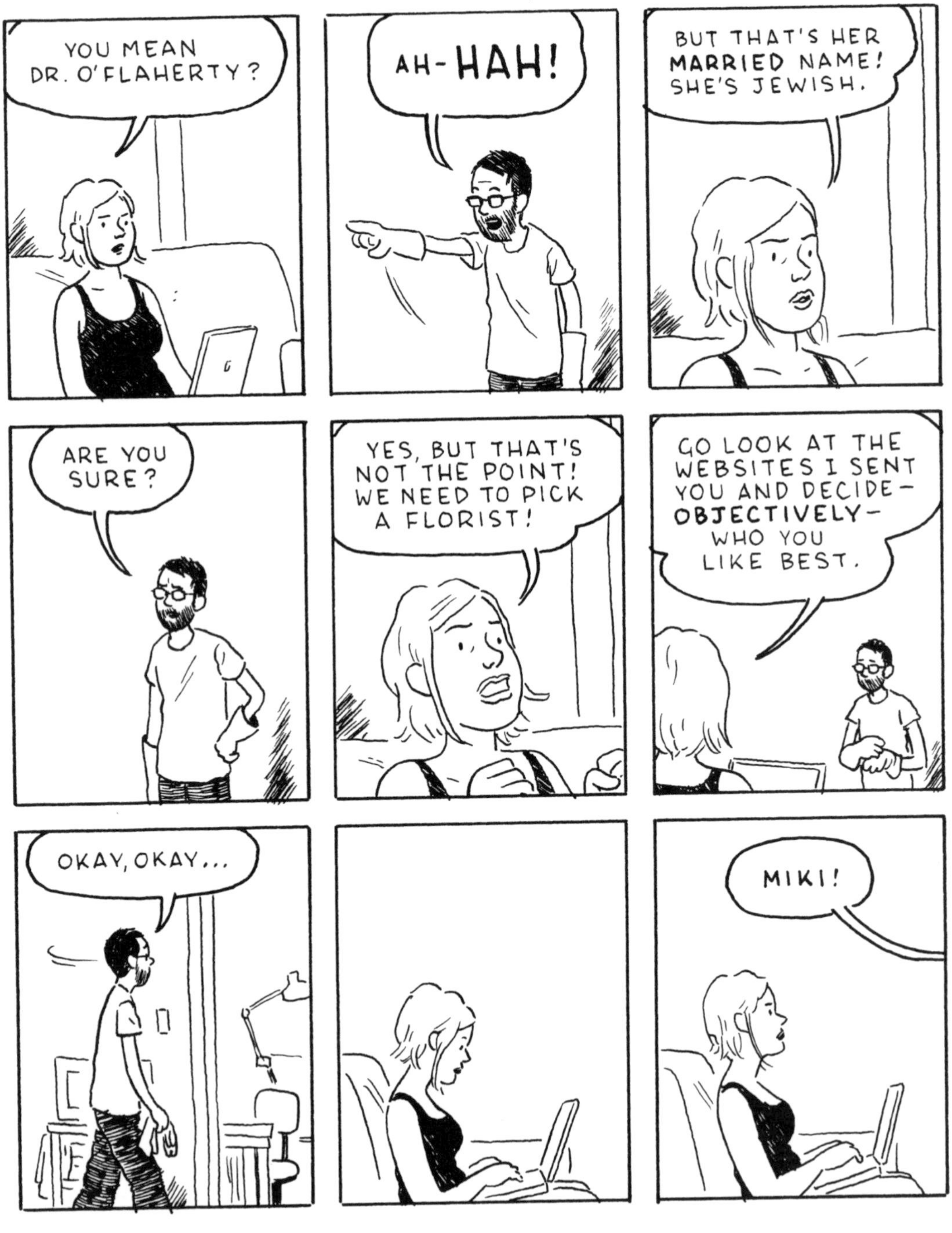
YOU MEAN DR. O'FLAHERTY?
AH-HAH!
BUT THAT'S HER MARRIED NAME! SHE'S JEWISH.
ARE YOU SURE?
YES, BUT THAT'S NOT THE POINT! WE NEED TO PICK A FLORIST!
GO LOOK AT THE WEBSITES I SENT YOU AND DECIDE—OBJECTIVELY—WHO YOU LIKE BEST.
OKAY, OKAY...
MIKI!

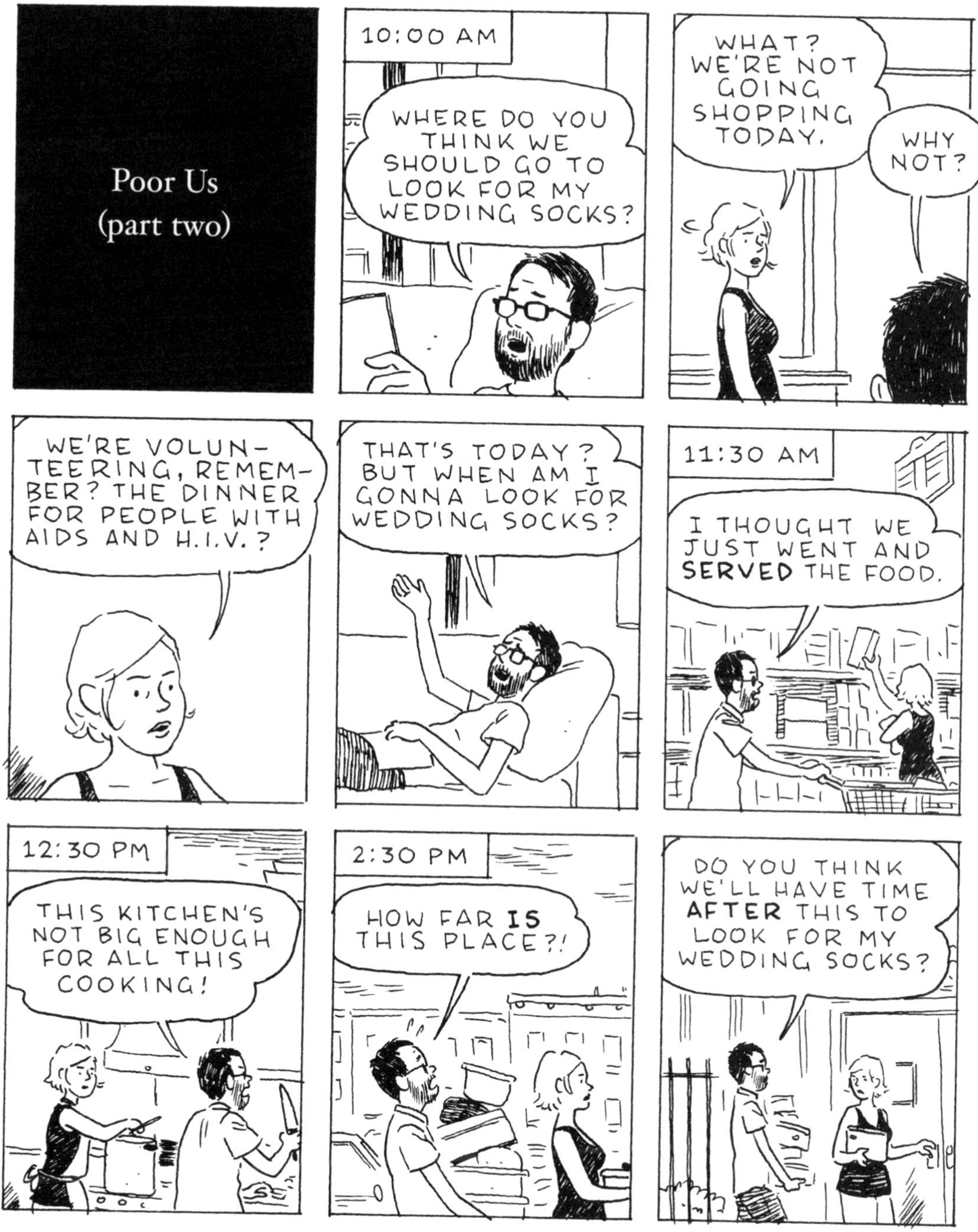
Poor Us (part two)
10:00 AM
WHERE DO YOU THINK WE SHOULD GO TO LOOK FOR MY WEDDING SOCKS?
WHAT? WE'RE NOT GOING SHOPPING TODAY.
WHY NOT?
WE'RE VOLUN-TEERING, REMEM-BER? THE DINNER FOR PEOPLE WITH AIDS AND H.I.V.?
THAT'S TODAY? BUT WHEN AM I GONNA LOOK FOR WEDDING SOCKS?
11:30 AM
I THOUGHT WE JUST WENT AND SERVED THE FOOD.
12:30 PM
THIS KITCHEN'S NOT BIG ENOUGH FOR ALL THIS COOKING!
2:30 PM
HOW FAR IS THIS PLACE?!
DO YOU THINK WE'LL HAVE TIME AFTER THIS TO LOOK FOR MY WEDDING SOCKS?

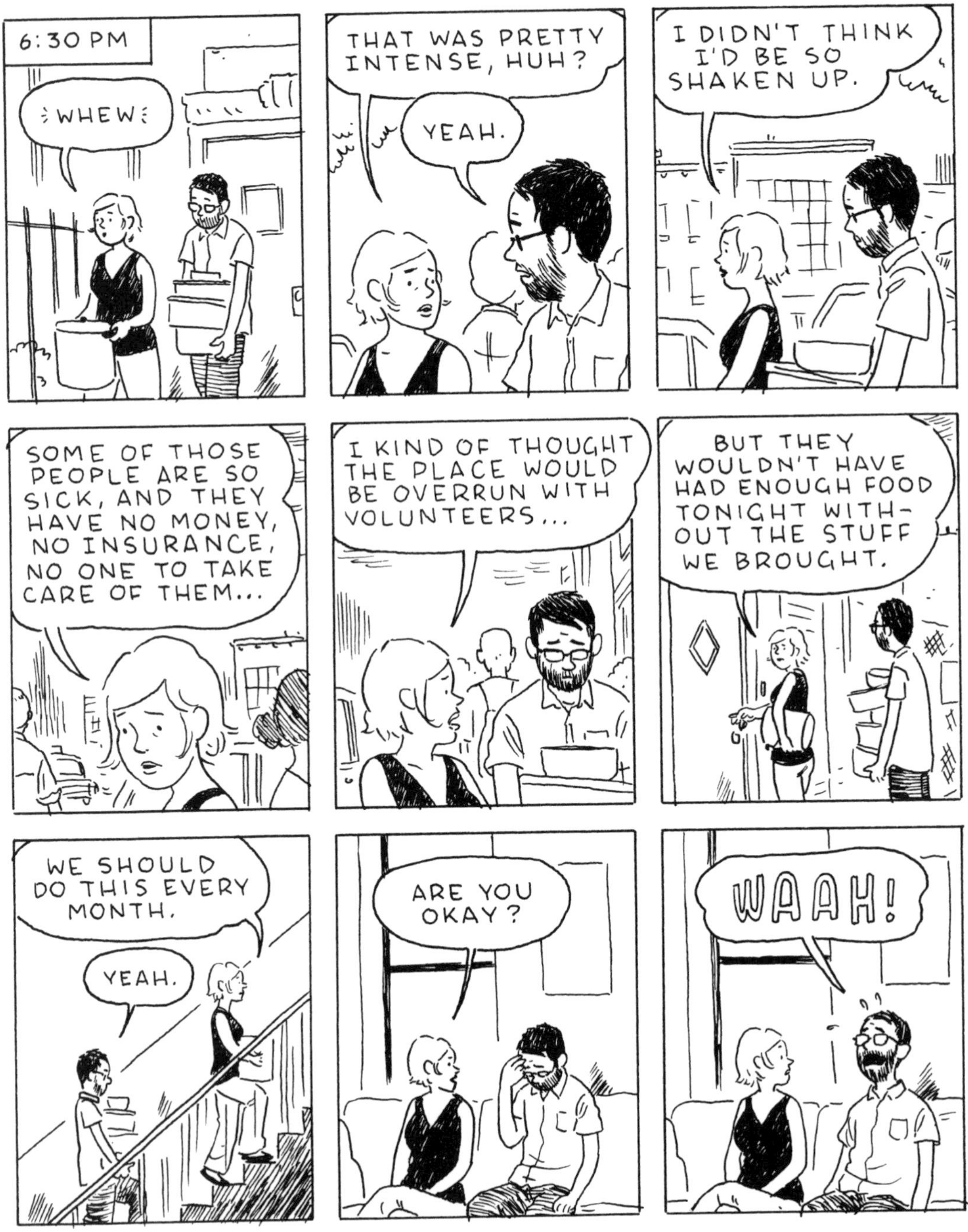
6:30 PM
WHEW
THAT WAS PRETTY INTENSE, HUH?
YEAH.
I DIDN'T THINK I'D BE SO SHAKEN UP.
SOME OF THOSE PEOPLE ARE SO SICK, AND THEY HAVE NO MONEY, NO INSURANCE, NO ONE TO TAKE CARE OF THEM...
I KIND OF THOUGHT THE PLACE WOULD BE OVERRUN WITH VOLUNTEERS...
BUT THEY WOULDN'T HAVE HAD ENOUGH FOOD TONIGHT WITHOUT THE STUFF WE BROUGHT.
WE SHOULD DO THIS EVERY MONTH.
YEAH.
ARE YOU OKAY?
WAAH!

Eyebrow Tweezing

"This nonsense stops the minute we're—OW! $#@&!!!"*

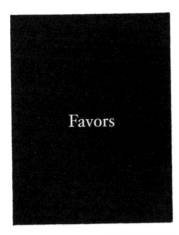

Favors

WHAT ARE YOU UP TO?

I'M LOOKING ONLINE FOR WEDDING FAVORS.

I GUESS I DON'T GET THE POINT OF THOSE THINGS.

IT'S JUST A LITTLE MEMENTO FOR PEOPLE TO TAKE HOME. IT'S NICE.

OKAY, OKAY... WHAT ARE SOME OF OUR OPTIONS?

WELL, THIS COMPANY MAKES CUSTOM CHOCOLATE BARS. WE CAN HAVE OUR NAMES PRINTED ON THEM.

BUT HOW IS THAT A "MEMENTO" IF IT'S JUST GONNA GET EATEN?

OKAY, SMARTY-PANTS. MAYBE YOU'D PREFER TO DRAW SOMETHING?

LIKE, MAYBE A SPECIAL CARD, OR... **OOH!** HOW ABOUT A LITTLE COMIC BOOK?

YOU MUST BE JOKING.

IT WOULD BE SO **CUTE!** YOU COULD DO A BUNCH OF SHORT STRIPS ABOUT US GETTING READY FOR THE WEDDING!

I DON'T HAVE TIME FOR SOMETHING LIKE THAT! LET'S JUST GET THE CHOCOLATE, AND—

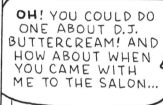

OH! YOU COULD DO ONE ABOUT D.J. BUTTERCREAM! AND HOW ABOUT WHEN YOU CAME WITH ME TO THE SALON...

LOOK...EVERYONE LIKES CHOCOLATE! ESPECIALLY WHEN IT'S CUSTOMIZED! IT'S PERFECT!

IF YOU REALLY, REALLY, REALLY LOVED ME, YOU'D DO THIS.

⸪SIGH⸪

LET ME THINK ABOUT IT.

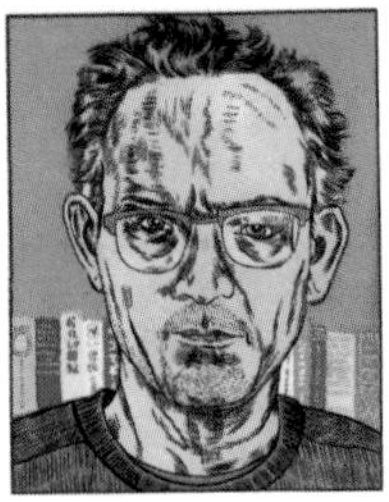

GARY PANTER

Jimbo

(see also cover)

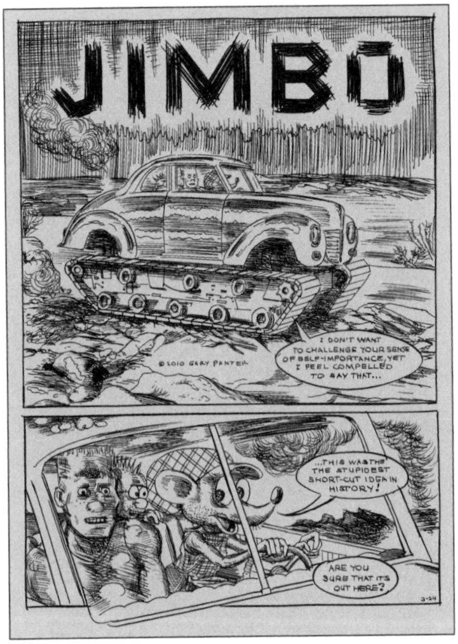

JIMBO
©2010 GARY PANTER
I DON'T WANT TO CHALLENGE YOUR SENSE OF SELF-IMPORTANCE, YET I FEEL COMPELLED TO SAY THAT...
...THIS WAS THE THE STUPIDEST SHORT-CUT IDEA IN HISTORY!
ARE YOU SURE THAT IT'S OUT HERE?
3-24

FOR ME, DRAWING COMICS IS

Calming. Dreaming while awake. A place to draw.

THE SELECTION

Two primal adversaries meet by an elevated highway.

PUBLICATIONS MY WORK HAS APPEARED IN

RAW, *Time*, *Rolling Stone*, *McSweeney's*.

AWARDS

Winner of a 2000 Chrysler Design Award and three Emmy Awards.

WHAT I'M KNOWN FOR

Jimbo in Purgatory and *Dal Tokyo*.

WHERE I LIVE

Brooklyn, New York.

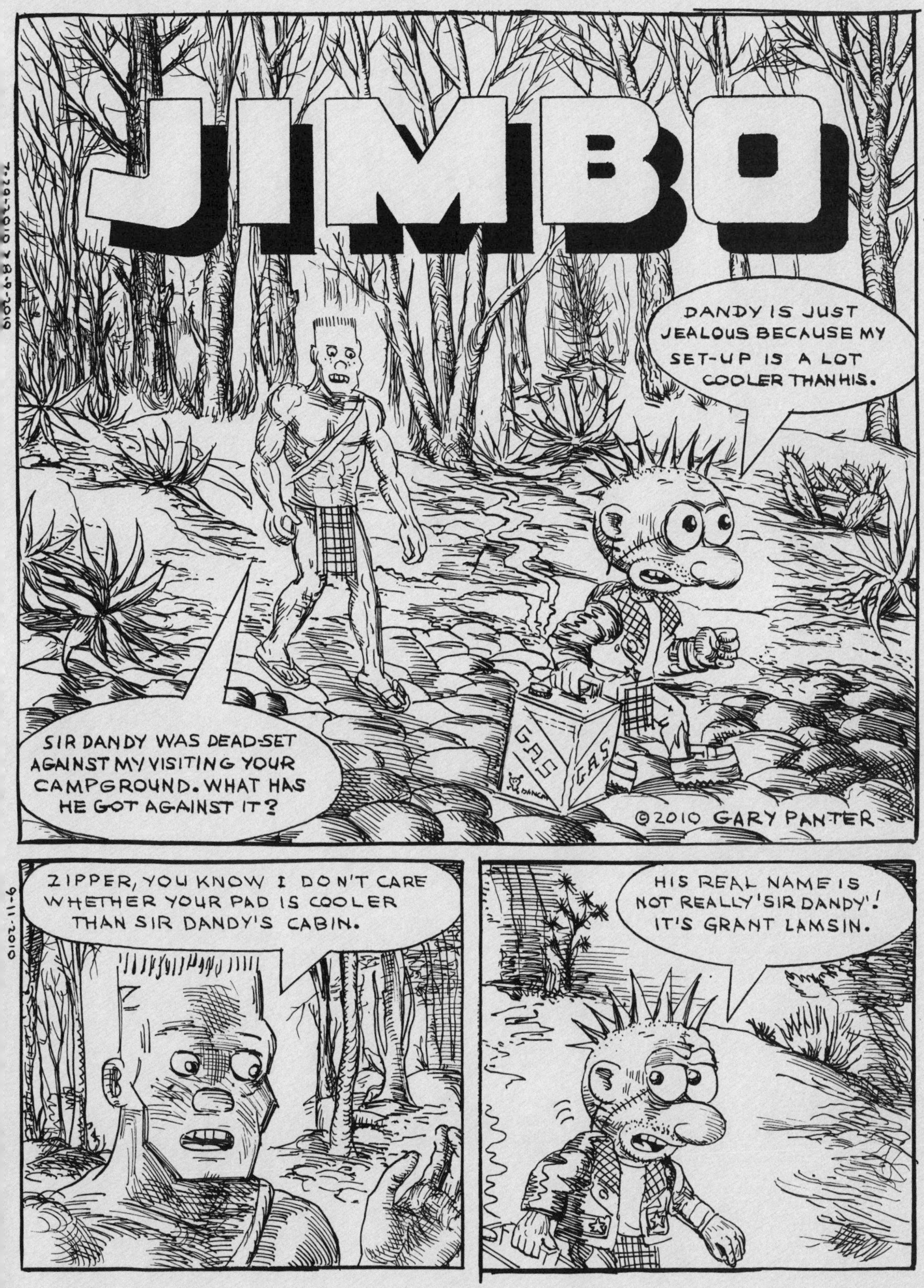

JIMBO
7-29-2010 / 8-9-2010
SIR DANDY WAS DEAD-SET AGAINST MY VISITING YOUR CAMPGROUND. WHAT HAS HE GOT AGAINST IT?
DANDY IS JUST JEALOUS BECAUSE MY SET-UP IS A LOT COOLER THAN HIS.
GAS
©2010 GARY PANTER
9-11-2010
ZIPPER, YOU KNOW I DON'T CARE WHETHER YOUR PAD IS COOLER THAN SIR DANDY'S CABIN.
HIS REAL NAME IS NOT REALLY 'SIR DANDY'! IT'S GRANT LAMSIN.

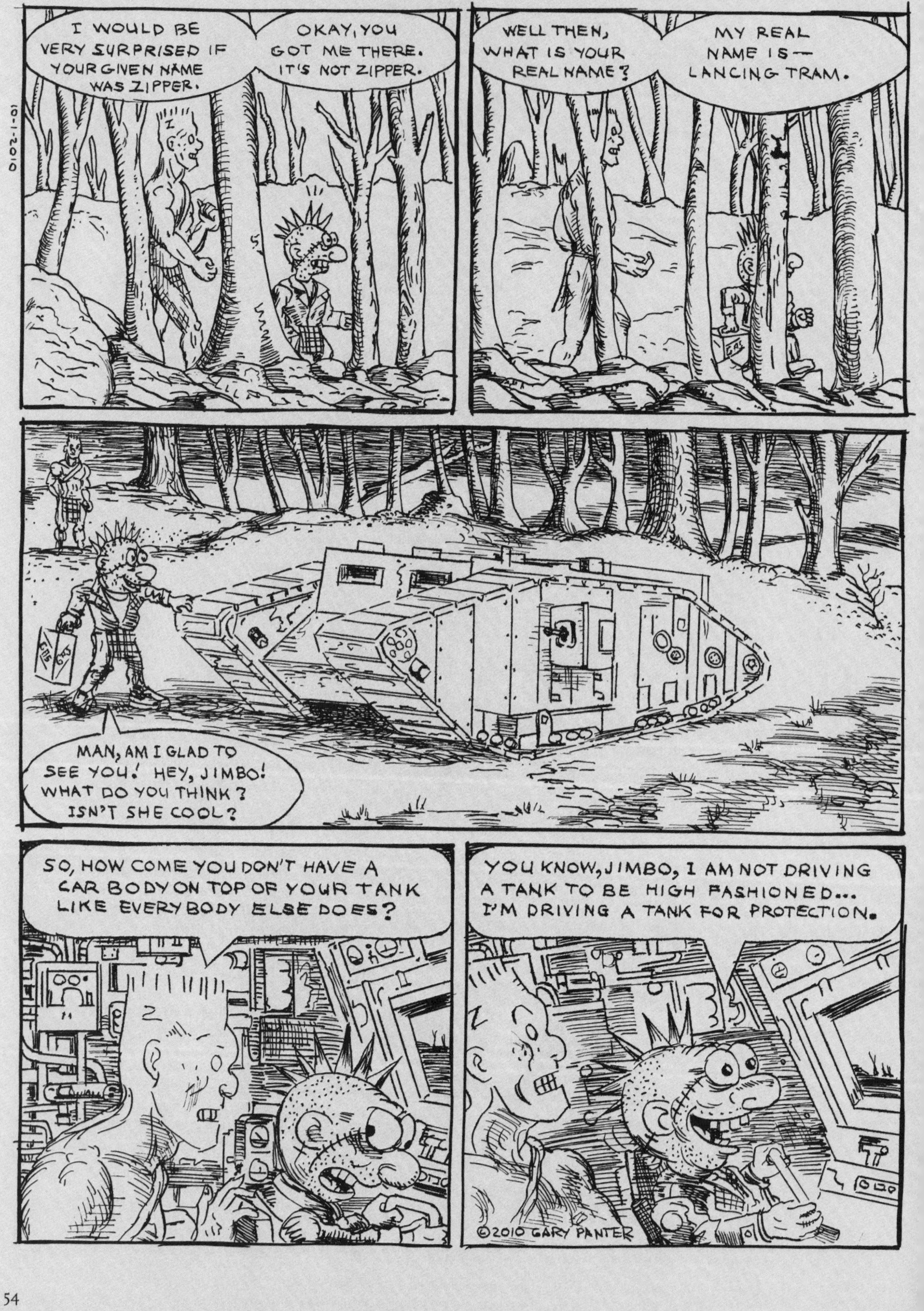
10-1-2010
I WOULD BE VERY SURPRISED IF YOUR GIVEN NAME WAS ZIPPER.
OKAY, YOU GOT ME THERE. IT'S NOT ZIPPER.
WELL THEN, WHAT IS YOUR REAL NAME?
MY REAL NAME IS— LANCING TRAM.
MAN, AM I GLAD TO SEE YOU! HEY, JIMBO! WHAT DO YOU THINK? ISN'T SHE COOL?
SO, HOW COME YOU DON'T HAVE A CAR BODY ON TOP OF YOUR TANK LIKE EVERYBODY ELSE DOES?
YOU KNOW, JIMBO, I AM NOT DRIVING A TANK TO BE HIGH FASHIONED... I'M DRIVING A TANK FOR PROTECTION.
©2010 GARY PANTER

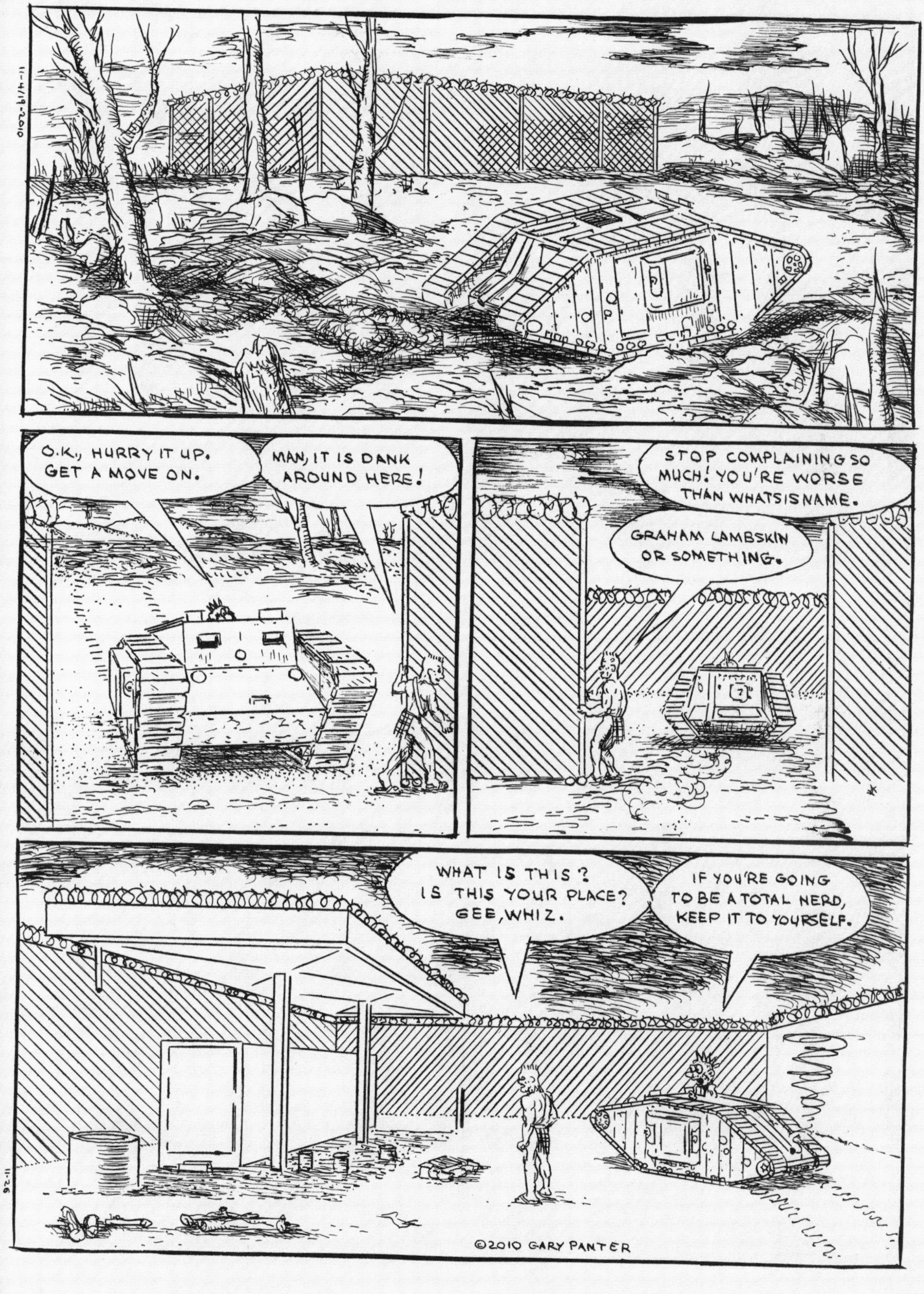

O.K., HURRY IT UP. GET A MOVE ON.
MAN, IT IS DANK AROUND HERE!
STOP COMPLAINING SO MUCH! YOU'RE WORSE THAN WHATSISNAME.
GRAHAM LAMBSKIN OR SOMETHING.
WHAT IS THIS? IS THIS YOUR PLACE? GEE, WHIZ.
IF YOU'RE GOING TO BE A TOTAL NERD, KEEP IT TO YOURSELF.
©2010 GARY PANTER

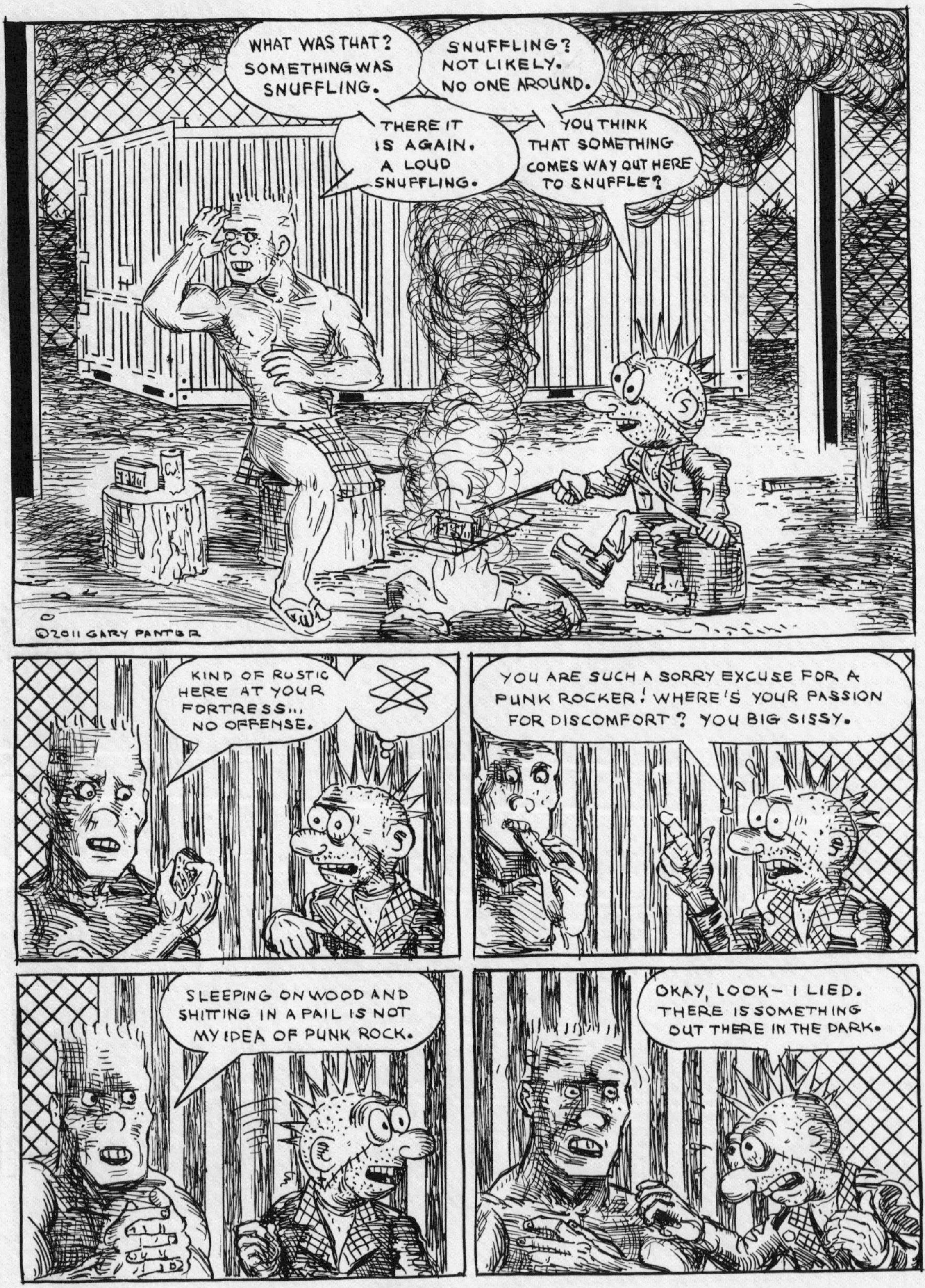
WHAT WAS THAT? SOMETHING WAS SNUFFLING.
SNUFFLING? NOT LIKELY. NO ONE AROUND.
THERE IT IS AGAIN. A LOUD SNUFFLING.
YOU THINK THAT SOMETHING COMES WAY OUT HERE TO SNUFFLE?
©2011 GARY PANTER
KIND OF RUSTIC HERE AT YOUR FORTRESS... NO OFFENSE.
YOU ARE SUCH A SORRY EXCUSE FOR A PUNK ROCKER! WHERE'S YOUR PASSION FOR DISCOMFORT? YOU BIG SISSY.
SLEEPING ON WOOD AND SHITTING IN A PAIL IS NOT MY IDEA OF PUNK ROCK.
OKAY, LOOK— I LIED. THERE IS SOMETHING OUT THERE IN THE DARK.

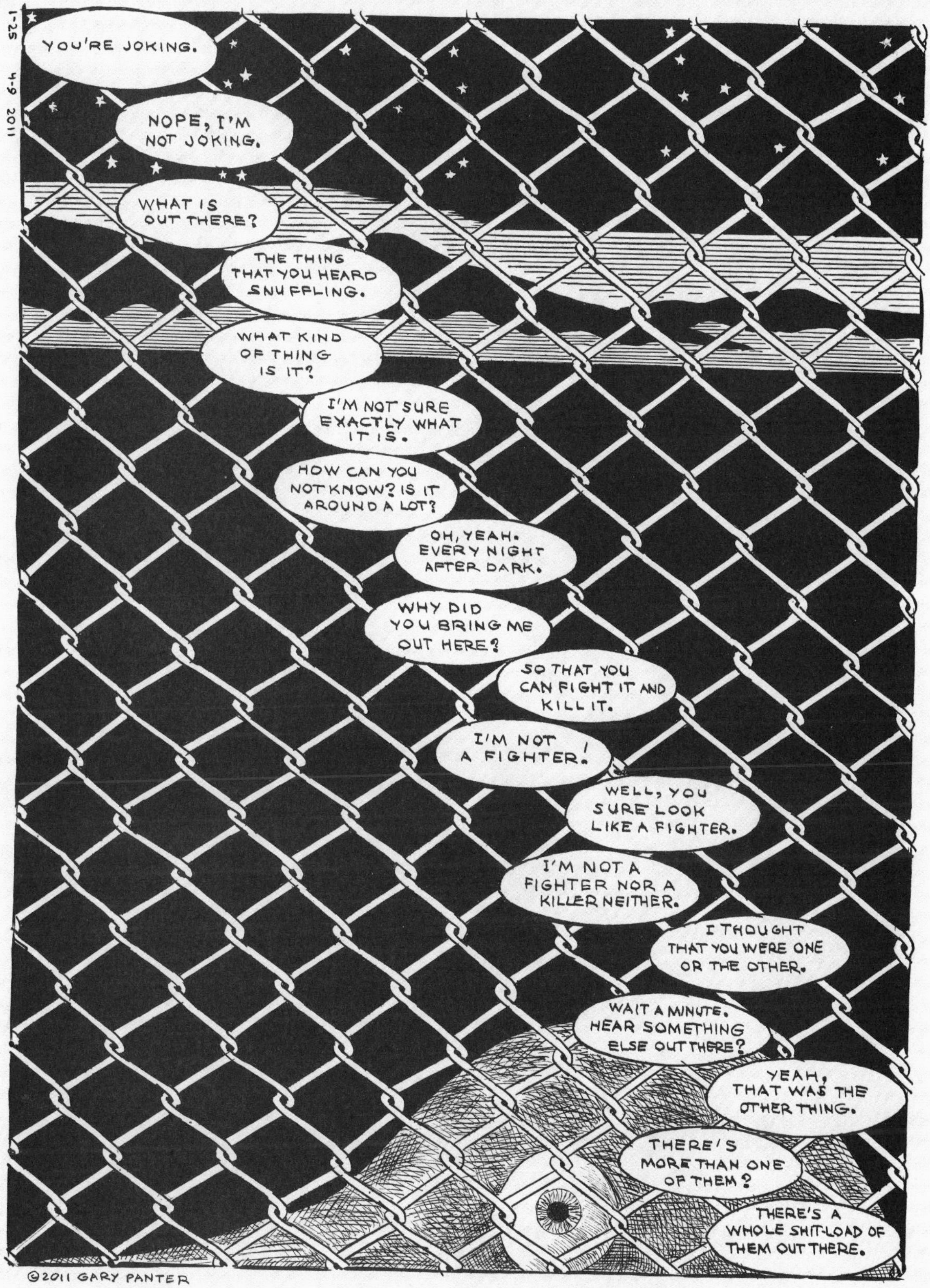
YOU'RE JOKING.
NOPE, I'M NOT JOKING.
WHAT IS OUT THERE?
THE THING THAT YOU HEARD SNUFFLING.
WHAT KIND OF THING IS IT?
I'M NOT SURE EXACTLY WHAT IT IS.
HOW CAN YOU NOT KNOW? IS IT AROUND A LOT?
OH, YEAH. EVERY NIGHT AFTER DARK.
WHY DID YOU BRING ME OUT HERE?
SO THAT YOU CAN FIGHT IT AND KILL IT.
I'M NOT A FIGHTER!
WELL, YOU SURE LOOK LIKE A FIGHTER.
I'M NOT A FIGHTER NOR A KILLER NEITHER.
I THOUGHT THAT YOU WERE ONE OR THE OTHER.
WAIT A MINUTE. HEAR SOMETHING ELSE OUT THERE?
YEAH, THAT WAS THE OTHER THING.
THERE'S MORE THAN ONE OF THEM?
THERE'S A WHOLE SHIT-LOAD OF THEM OUT THERE.

5-26

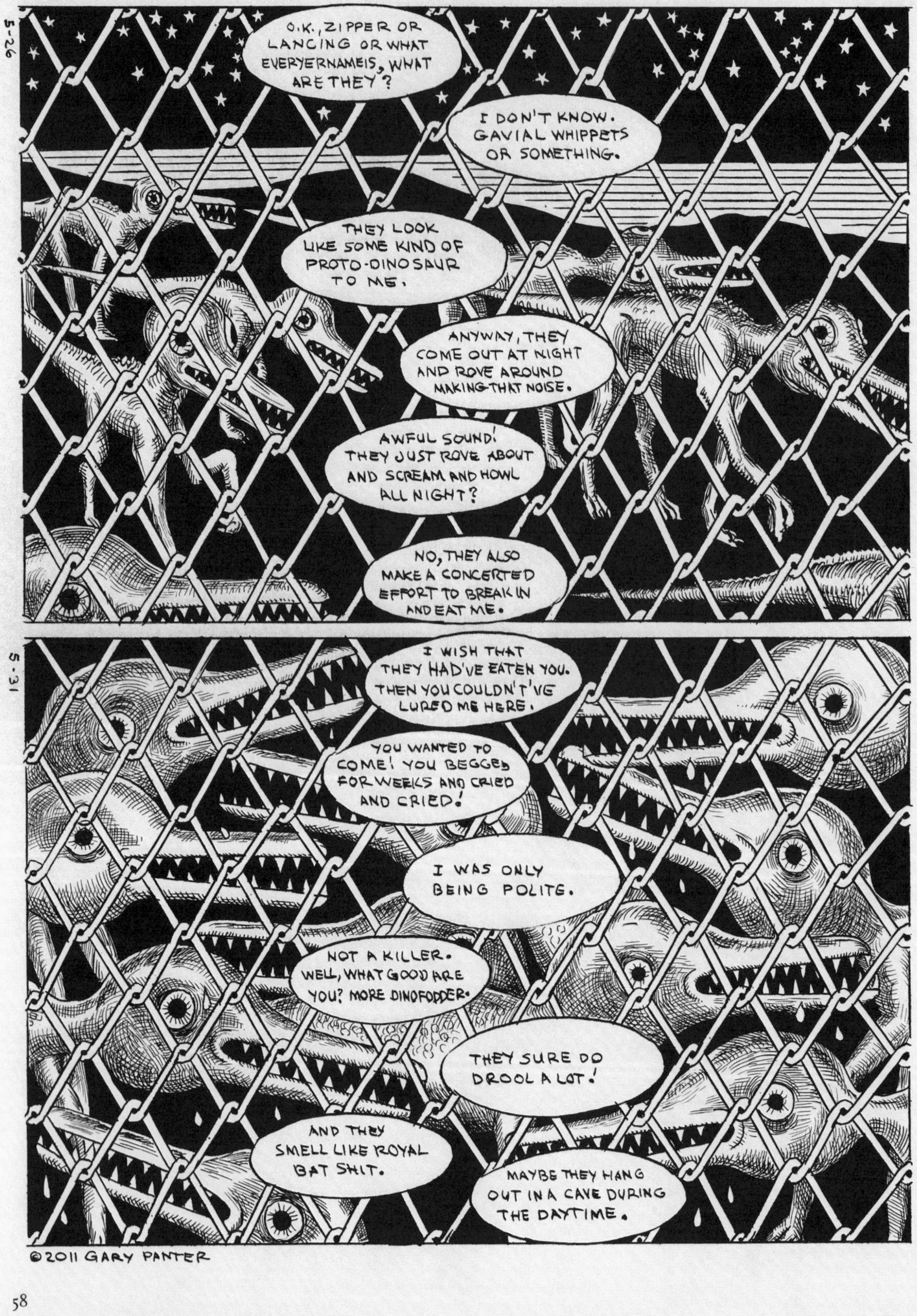
O.K., ZIPPER OR LANCING OR WHAT EVERYERNAMEIS, WHAT ARE THEY?
I DON'T KNOW. GAVIAL WHIPPETS OR SOMETHING.
THEY LOOK LIKE SOME KIND OF PROTO-DINOSAUR TO ME.
ANYWAY, THEY COME OUT AT NIGHT AND ROVE AROUND MAKING THAT NOISE.
AWFUL SOUND! THEY JUST ROVE ABOUT AND SCREAM AND HOWL ALL NIGHT?
NO, THEY ALSO MAKE A CONCERTED EFFORT TO BREAK IN AND EAT ME.
I WISH THAT THEY HAD'VE EATEN YOU. THEN YOU COULDN'T'VE LURED ME HERE.
YOU WANTED TO COME! YOU BEGGED FOR WEEKS AND CRIED AND CRIED!
I WAS ONLY BEING POLITE.
NOT A KILLER. WELL, WHAT GOOD ARE YOU? MORE DINOFODDER.
THEY SURE DO DROOL A LOT!
AND THEY SMELL LIKE ROYAL BAT SHIT.
MAYBE THEY HANG OUT IN A CAVE DURING THE DAYTIME.

5-31

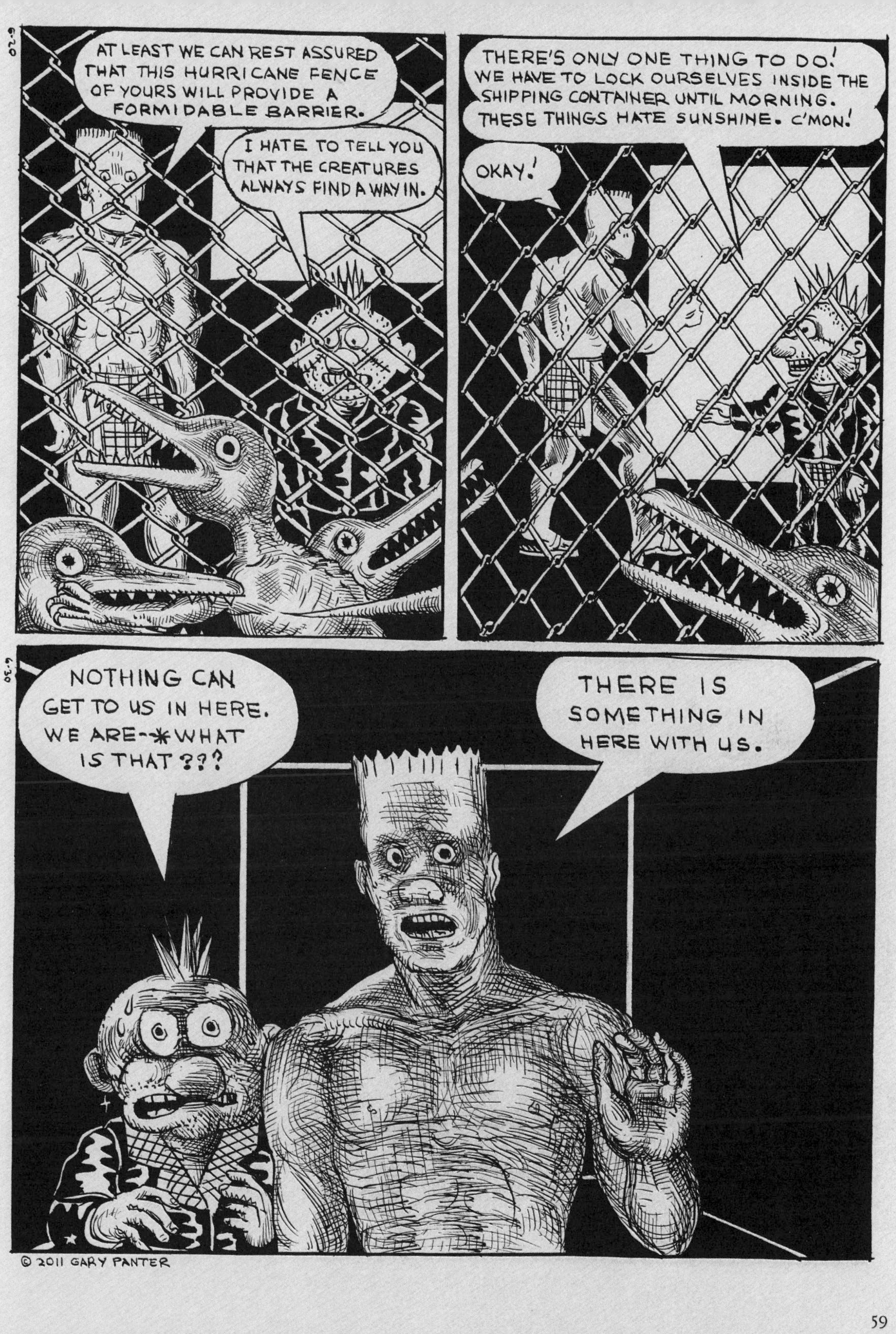
AT LEAST WE CAN REST ASSURED THAT THIS HURRICANE FENCE OF YOURS WILL PROVIDE A FORMIDABLE BARRIER.
I HATE TO TELL YOU THAT THE CREATURES ALWAYS FIND A WAY IN.
THERE'S ONLY ONE THING TO DO! WE HAVE TO LOCK OURSELVES INSIDE THE SHIPPING CONTAINER UNTIL MORNING. THESE THINGS HATE SUNSHINE. C'MON!
OKAY!
NOTHING CAN GET TO US IN HERE. WE ARE--*WHAT IS THAT???
THERE IS SOMETHING IN HERE WITH US.

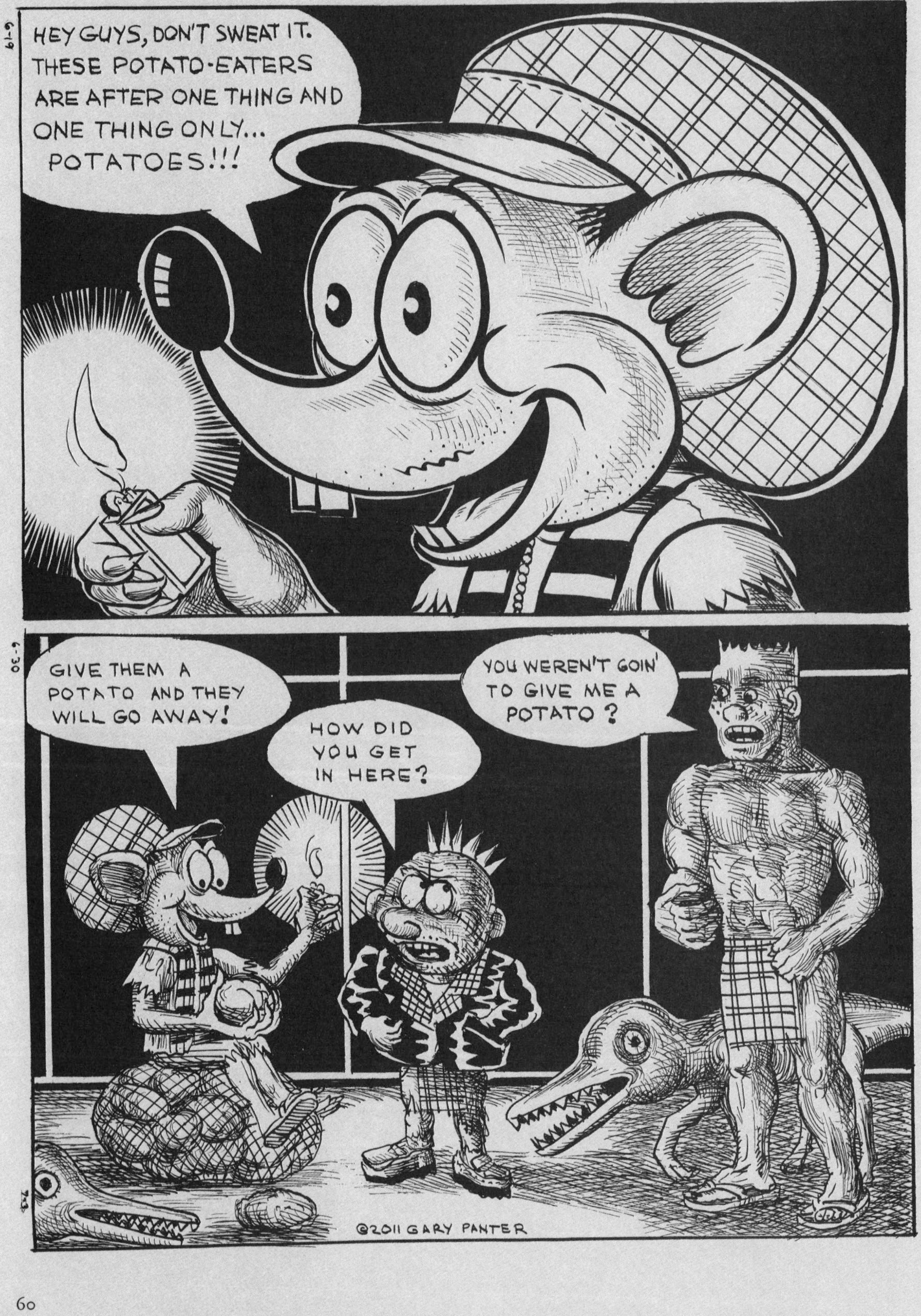
HEY GUYS, DON'T SWEAT IT. THESE POTATO-EATERS ARE AFTER ONE THING AND ONE THING ONLY... POTATOES!!!
GIVE THEM A POTATO AND THEY WILL GO AWAY!
HOW DID YOU GET IN HERE?
YOU WEREN'T GOIN' TO GIVE ME A POTATO?
©2011 GARY PANTER

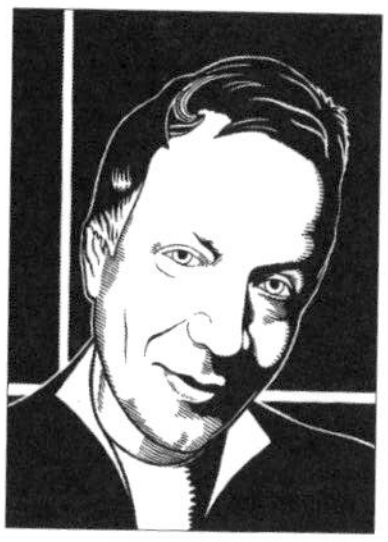

MICHAEL KUPPERMAN

Are Comics Moronic Dribble? / Skull Groin / Diner Food / House of Shouts

from *Up All Night* in the *Washington City Paper*

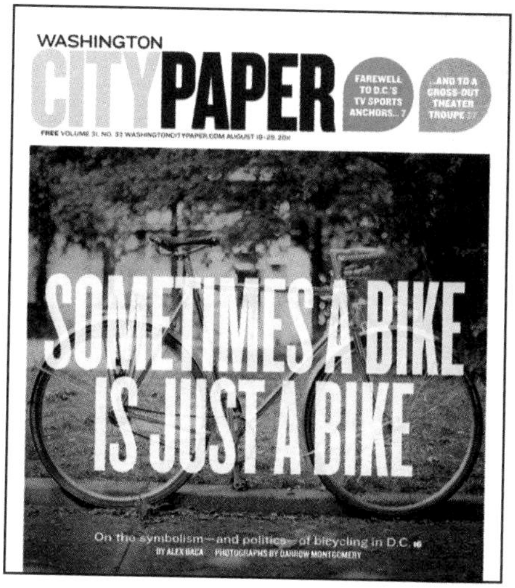
WASHINGTON
CITY PAPER
FAREWELL TO D.C.'S TV SPORTS ANCHORS... 7
SOMETIMES A BIKE IS JUST A BIKE
On the symbolism—and politics—of bicycling in D.C.

FOR ME, DRAWING COMICS IS

A beautiful nightmare, a horrible dream.

THE SELECTION

Just some nonsense designed to amuse. These strips are meant to be like laughter candy.

PUBLICATIONS MY WORK HAS APPEARED IN

The New Yorker, McSweeney's, Heavy Metal, Nickelodeon.

WHAT I'M KNOWN FOR

Snake'N'Bacon's Cartoon Cabaret, Tales Designed to Thrizzle, Mark Twain's Autobiography 1910–2010; also *TV Funhouse* and *Saturday Night Live.*

WHERE I LIVE

Crown Heights, Brooklyn, New York.

SELECTIONS

ARE COMICS MORONIC DRIBBLE?
COMICS ARE NOTHING BUT MORONIC DRIBBLE!
NO, THEY'RE NOT
SELL GRIT
YUK
COMICS ARE PROFOUND! IN FACT, *YOU AND I ARE IN A COMIC STRIP RIGHT NOW!*
WHAT?
HOLY SHIT, YOU'RE RIGHT!

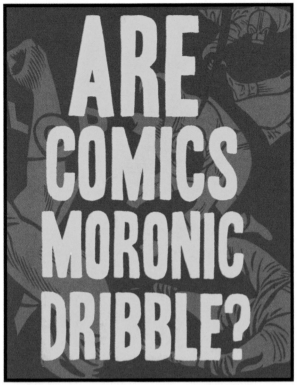

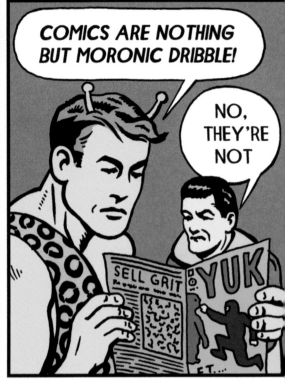

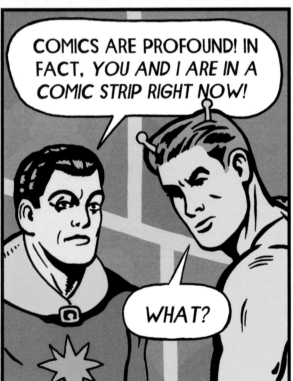

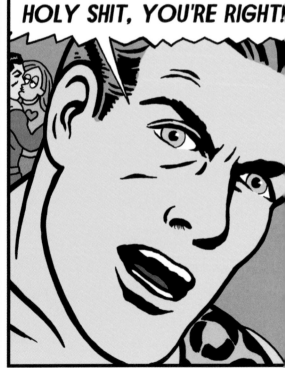

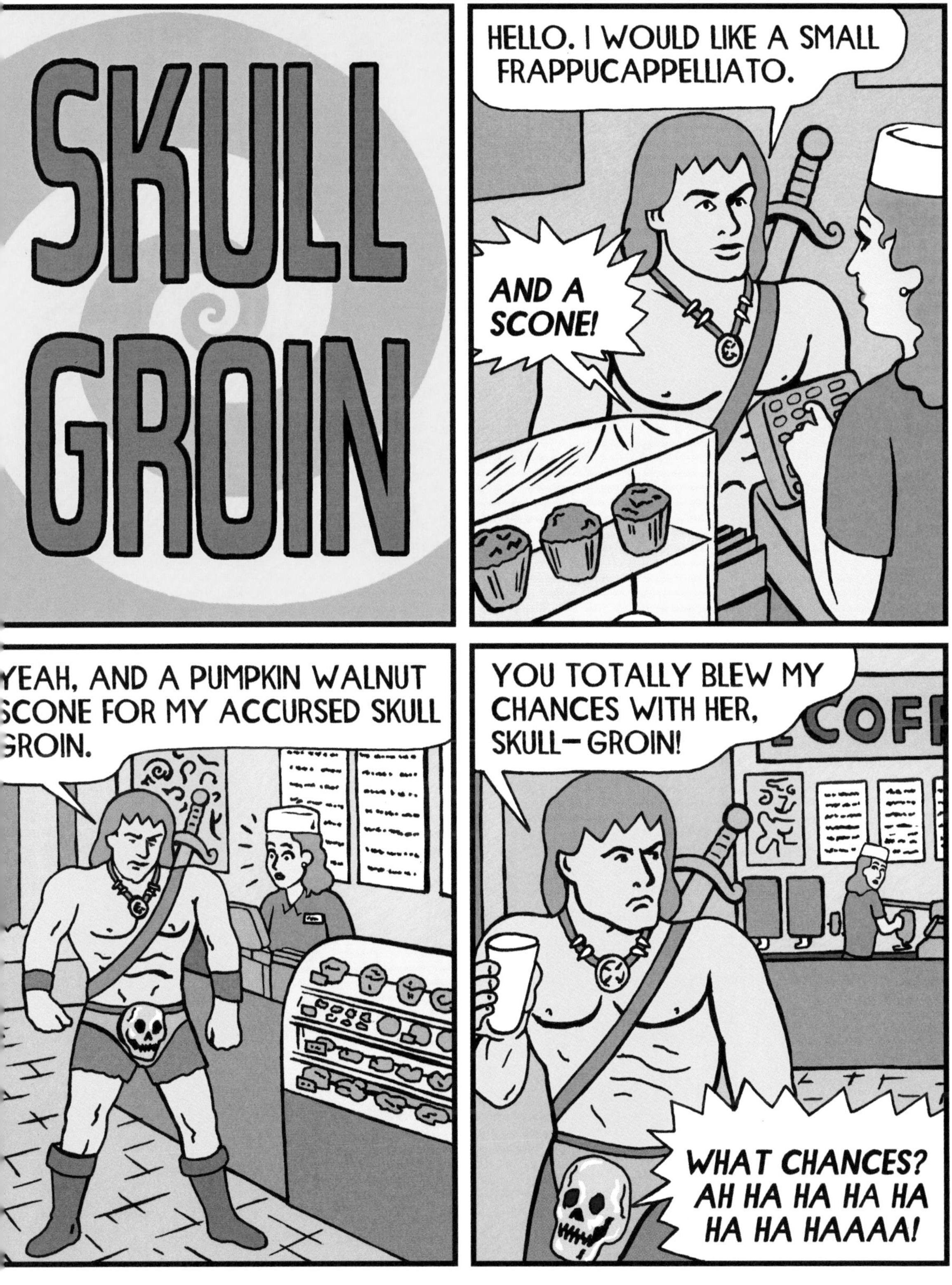
SKULL GROIN
HELLO. I WOULD LIKE A SMALL FRAPPUCAPPELLIATO.
AND A SCONE!
YEAH, AND A PUMPKIN WALNUT SCONE FOR MY ACCURSED SKULL GROIN.
YOU TOTALLY BLEW MY CHANCES WITH HER, SKULL-GROIN!
WHAT CHANCES? AH HA HA HA HA HA HA HAAAA!

NORA KRUG

Kamikaze

from *A Public Space*

FOR ME, DRAWING COMICS IS

Like acting: I try to put myself into the mind of a character and use illustration to communicate their thoughts and emotions.

KAMIKAZE
神風
by Nora Krug

THE SELECTION

Kamikaze is one in a series of biographical narratives about ordinary individuals impacted by extraordinary political circumstances. The subject of this particular story is Ena Takehiko, a Japanese WWII kamikaze pilot who survived his mission because of unexpected engine failure midair, and who today lives as a peace activist and retired soybean exporter in Japan.

PUBLICATIONS MY WORK HAS APPEARED IN

The *New York Times*, the *Guardian*, *Le Monde Diplomatique*, *Print* magazine's "20 Under 30," and in anthologies published by Simon and Schuster and Chronicle Books. I also illustrated the children's book *My Cold Went on Vacation.*

WHERE I LIVE

Brooklyn, New York.

AWARDS

Awards from the New York Art Director's Club and American Illustration, and two gold medals from the Society of Illustrators. My animations were selected for showing at the Sundance Film Festival, Ars Electronica, and ZKM (Center for Art and Media, Karlsruhe); and my illustrations have been exhibited at the *New York Times*, the Society of Illustrators, and Illustrative, among others.

WHAT I'M KNOWN FOR

Red Riding Hood Redux is a wordless comic album for grownups, retelling the original fairy tale in five books, each one representing the viewpoint of each character in the original tale.

KAMIKAZE 神 風

by Nora Krug

December 1943, 20-year-old Ena akehiko was drafted into the Japanese imperial navy.

In 1944, the political situation in Japan drastically worsened

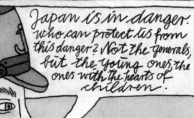

Japan is in danger. who can protect us from this danger? Not the generals, but the young ones, the ones with the hearts of children.

and admiral Ohnishi proposed a "special attack unit" made up of kamikaze pilots.

A young, very talented pilot named Seki was asked if he wanted to lead the first ever kamikaze attack and die a hero.

I accept your offer. Please assign me to the post.

Seki had recently gotten married.

You are already gods. And just like gods you don't have any desire... you will sleep for a long time...

He didn't want to commit suicide.

Right before his sortie, he handed one of the officers a lock of his hair

which was delivered to his mother right after his death.

From then on, young soldiers were asked if they would volunteer to be part of the "special attack units." Most of them were 17-26 years old.

Volunteers were asked to write down their names on a piece of paper. Everyone else was supposed to leave the sheet blank.

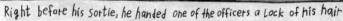

Almost all of the pilots volunteered. No one wanted to stay alive while seeing their friends die.

If a soldier refused, he was listed anyway.

Many weeks passed

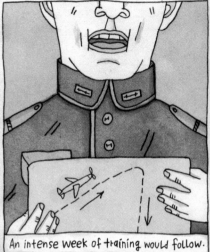

松村 堀
西屋

...til the day and time of the ...diers' sorties were scheduled.

An intense week of training would follow.

The night before the sortie was spent cele-brating, drinking sake, eating dried fish,

...probably never see ...face again. Mother, ...show your face a little ...er. I don't want to leave ...u a souvenir because I kn... ...that you would cry over it ...twenty-years from now. When I depart, I will fly over our house. This is my last farewell. Saburo Mogi

...writing farewell letters.

武運
長久

Village girls made dolls and waist-bands, stained with their own blood

and gave them to the pilots as gifts before takeoff.

...lots had a ritual last cup of sake and bowed ...stward, in the direction of the imperial palace.

The girls decorated the planes' cockpits with cherry branches.

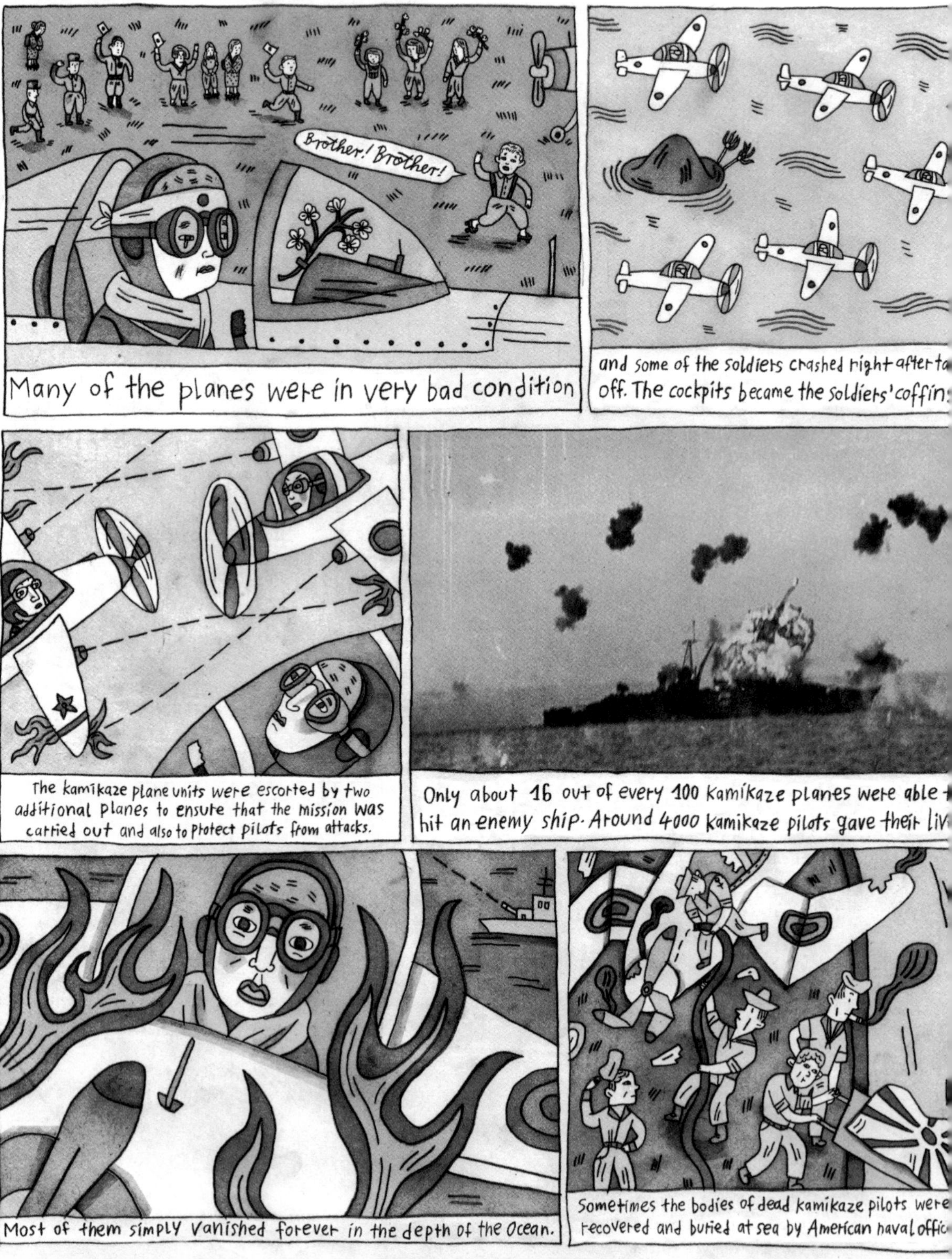
Brother! Brother!
Many of the planes were in very bad condition
and some of the soldiers crashed right after ta
off. The cockpits became the soldiers' coffin
The kamikaze plane units were escorted by two additional planes to ensure that the mission was carried out and also to protect pilots from attacks.
Only about 16 out of every 100 kamikaze planes were able t
hit an enemy ship. Around 4000 kamikaze pilots gave their liv
Most of them simply vanished forever in the depth of the ocean.
Sometimes the bodies of dead kamikaze pilots were
recovered and buried at sea by American naval offic

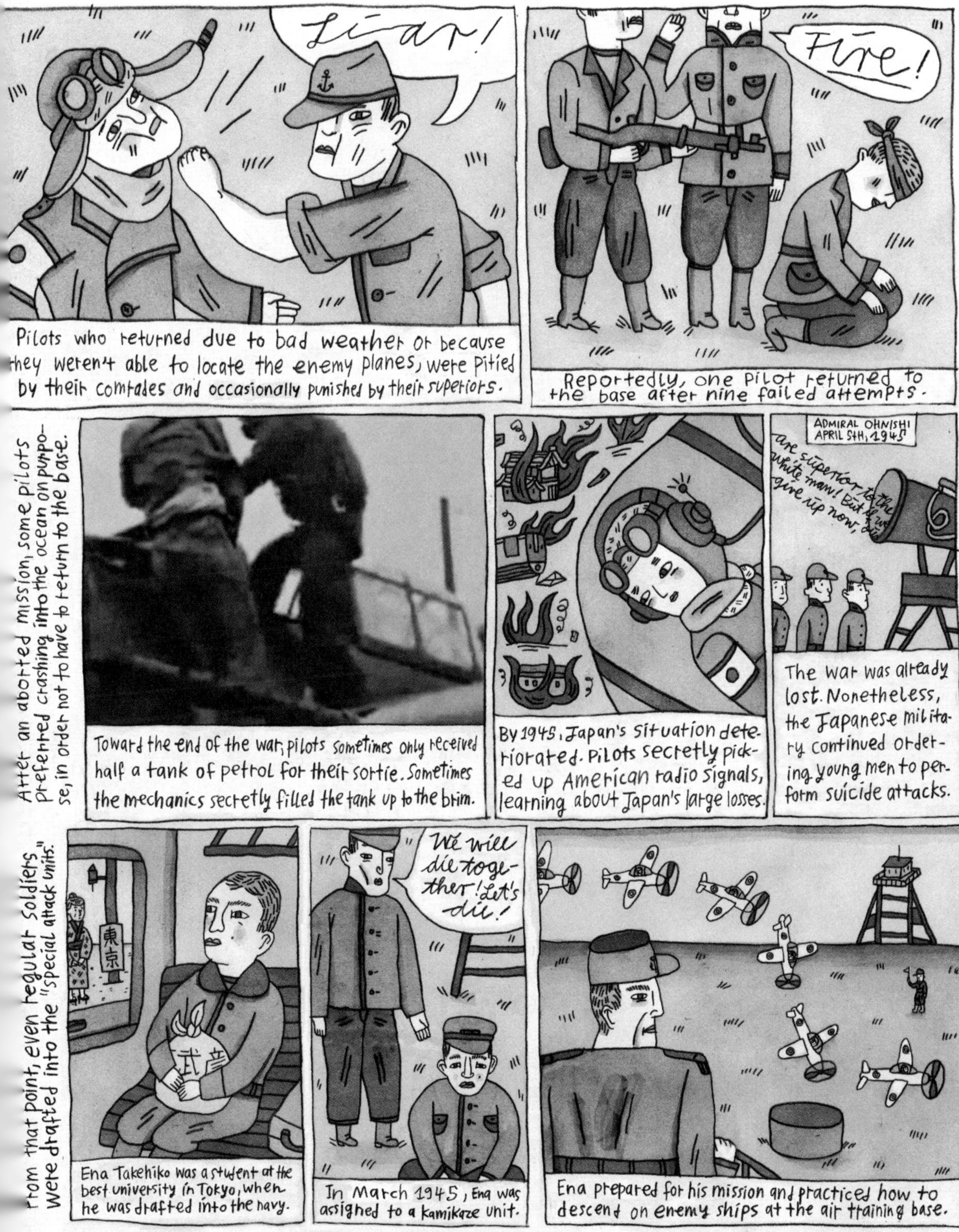
Liar!
Pilots who returned due to bad weather or because they weren't able to locate the enemy planes, were pitied by their comrades and occasionally punished by their superiors.
Fire!
Reportedly, one pilot returned to the base after nine failed attempts.
After an aborted mission, some pilots preferred crashing into the ocean on purpose, in order not to have to return to the base.
Toward the end of the war, pilots sometimes only received half a tank of petrol for their sortie. Sometimes the mechanics secretly filled the tank up to the brim.
By 1945, Japan's situation deteriorated. Pilots secretly picked up American radio signals, learning about Japan's large losses.
ADMIRAL OHNISHI APRIL 5TH, 1945
are superior to the white man! But if we give up now,
The war was already lost. Nonetheless, the Japanese military continued ordering young men to perform suicide attacks.
From that point, even regular soldiers were drafted into the "special attack units."
東京
Ena Takehiko was a student at the best university in Tokyo, when he was drafted into the navy.
We will die together! Let's die!
In March 1945, Ena was assigned to a kamikaze unit.
Ena prepared for his mission and practiced how to descend on enemy ships at the air training base.

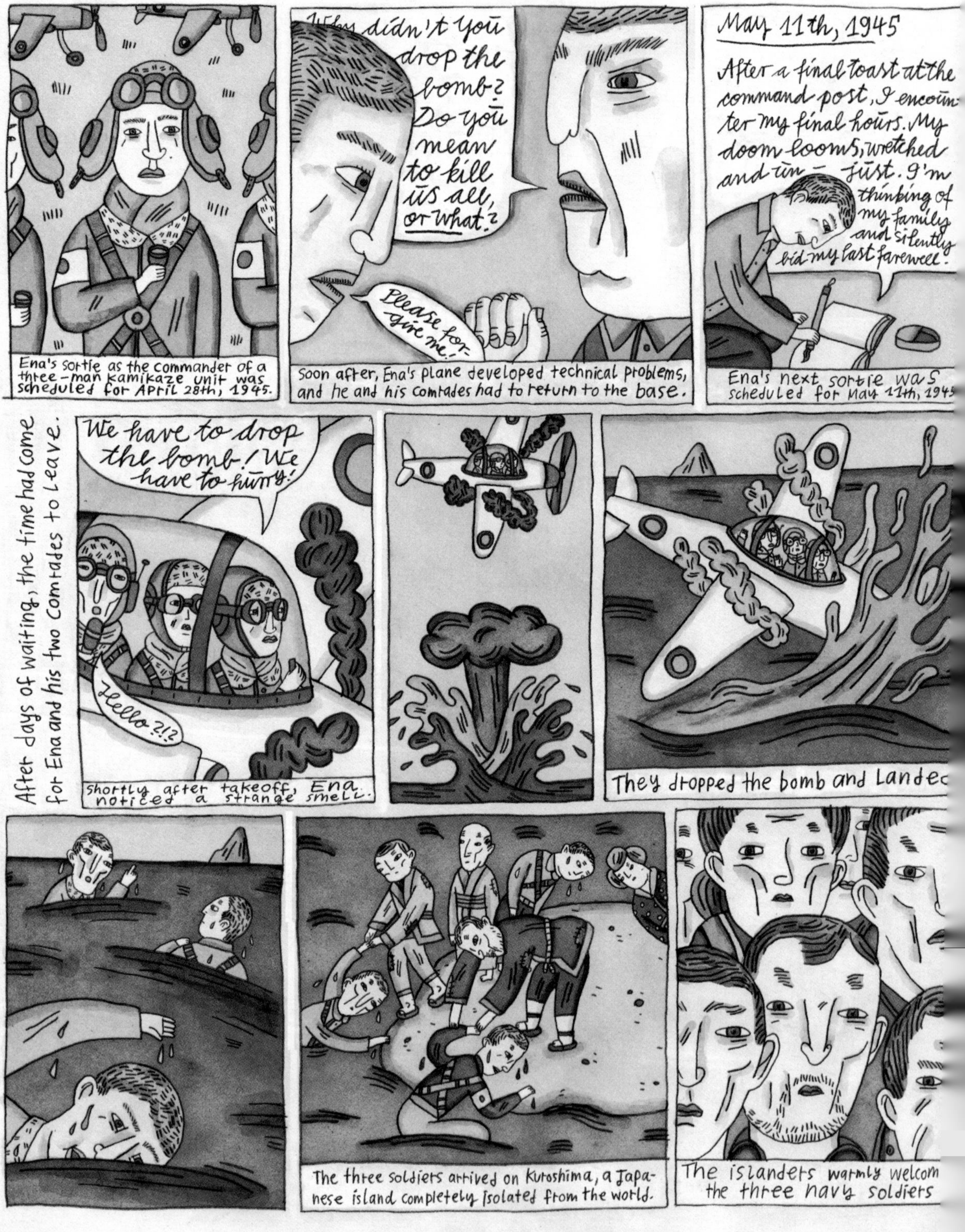

Ena's sortie as the commander of a three-man kamikaze unit was scheduled for April 28th, 1945.
Why didn't you drop the bomb? Do you mean to kill us all, or what?
Please forgive me.
Soon after, Ena's plane developed technical problems, and he and his comrades had to return to the base.
May 11th, 1945
After a final toast at the command post, I encounter my final hours. My doom looms, wretched and unjust. I'm thinking of my family and silently bid my last farewell.
Ena's next sortie was scheduled for May 11th, 1945
After days of waiting, the time had come for Ena and his two comrades to leave.
We have to drop the bomb! We have to hurry!
Hello?!?
Shortly after takeoff, Ena noticed a strange smell.
They dropped the bomb and landed
The three soldiers arrived on Kuroshima, a Japanese island completely isolated from the world.
The islanders warmly welcom the three navy soldiers

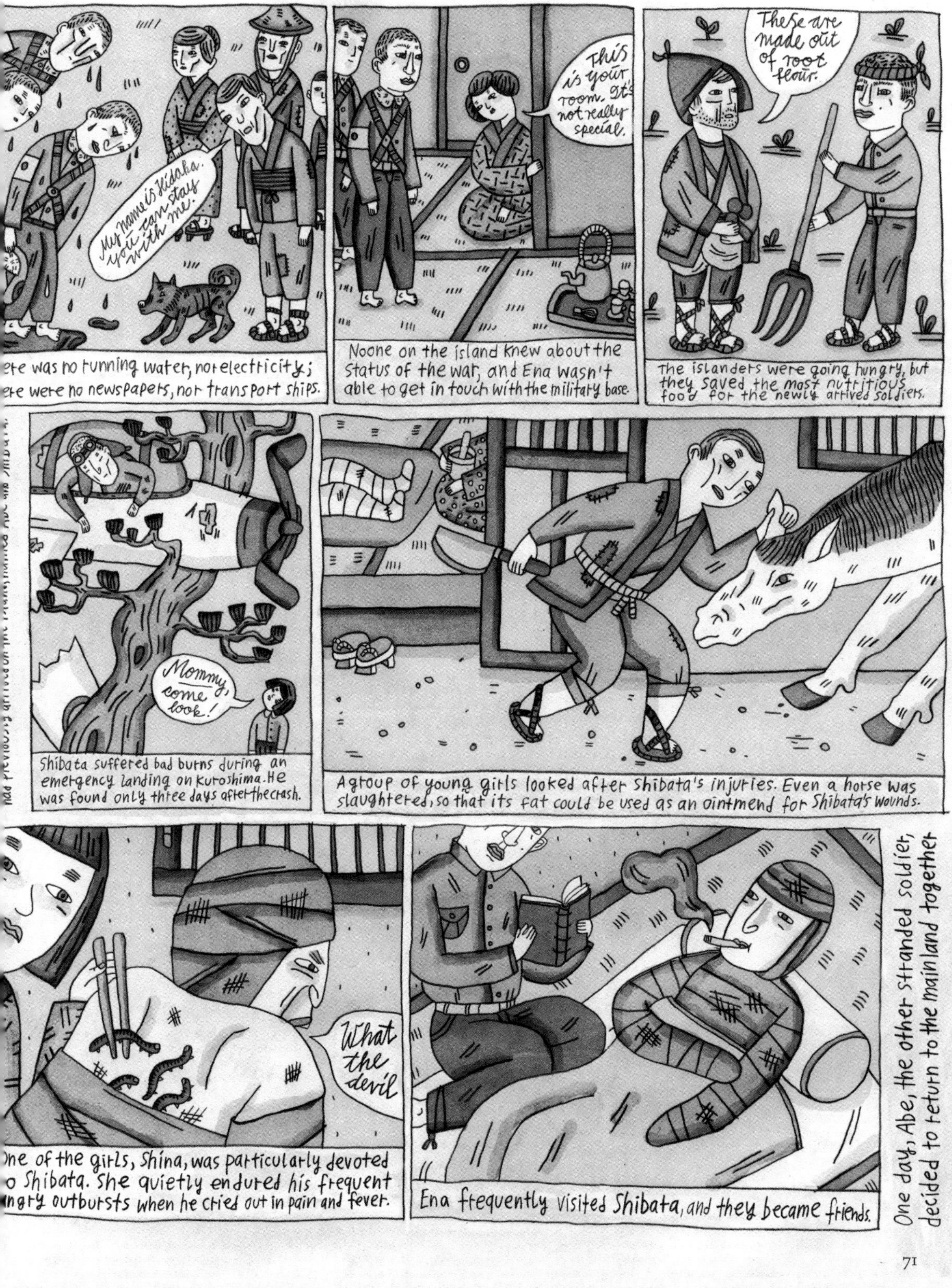

My name is Hidaka. You can stay with me.
ere was no running water, nor electricity;
ere were no newspapers, nor transport ships.
This is your room. It's not really special.
Noone on the island knew about the status of the war, and Ena wasn't able to get in touch with the military base.
These are made out of root flour.
The islanders were going hungry, but they saved the most nutritious food for the newly arrived soldiers.
Mommy, come look!
Shibata suffered bad burns during an emergency landing on Kuroshima. He was found only three days after the crash.
A group of young girls looked after Shibata's injuries. Even a horse was slaughtered, so that its fat could be used as an ointmend for Shibata's wounds.
What the devil
One of the girls, Shina, was particularly devoted o Shibata. She quietly endured his frequent ngry outbursts when he cried out in pain and fever.
Ena frequently visited Shibata, and they became friends.
One day, Abe, the other stranded soldier, decided to return to the mainland together

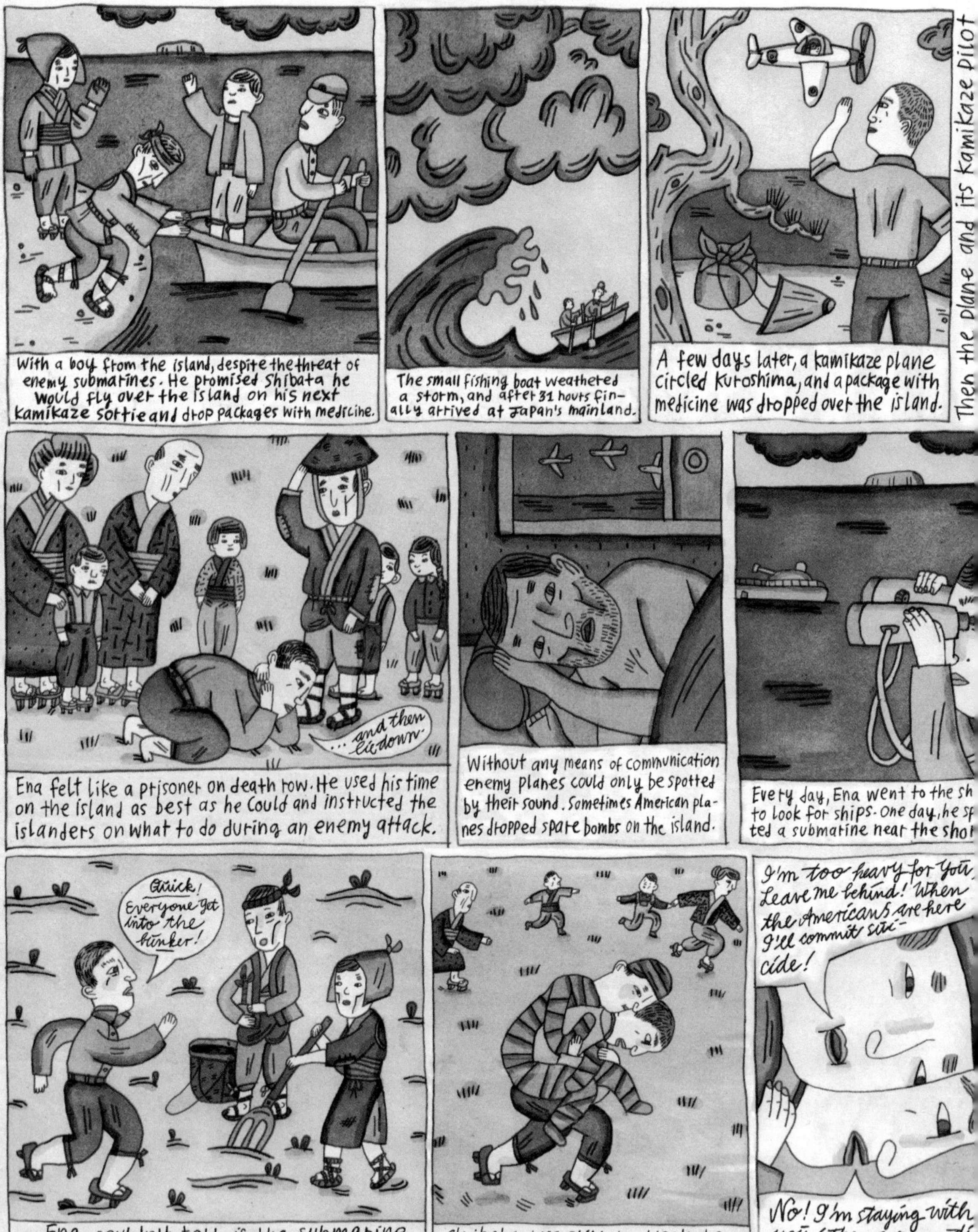

With a boy from the island, despite the threat of enemy submarines. He promised Shibata he would fly over the island on his next kamikaze sortie and drop packages with medicine.
The small fishing boat weathered a storm, and after 31 hours finally arrived at Japan's mainland.
A few days later, a kamikaze plane circled Kuroshima, and a package with medicine was dropped over the island.
Then the plane and its kamikaze pilot
... and then lie down.
Ena felt like a prisoner on death row. He used his time on the island as best as he could and instructed the islanders on what to do during an enemy attack.
Without any means of communication enemy planes could only be spotted by their sound. Sometimes American planes dropped spare bombs on the island.
Every day, Ena went to the sh
to look for ships. One day, he sp
ted a submarine near the sho
Quick! Everyone get into the bunker!
Ena couldn't tell if the submarine was Japanese or American.
Shibata was still too weak to walk and Ena came to his aid.
I'm too heavy for you. Leave me behind! When the Americans are here I'll commit suicide!
No! I'm staying with you! Then we can di together right here

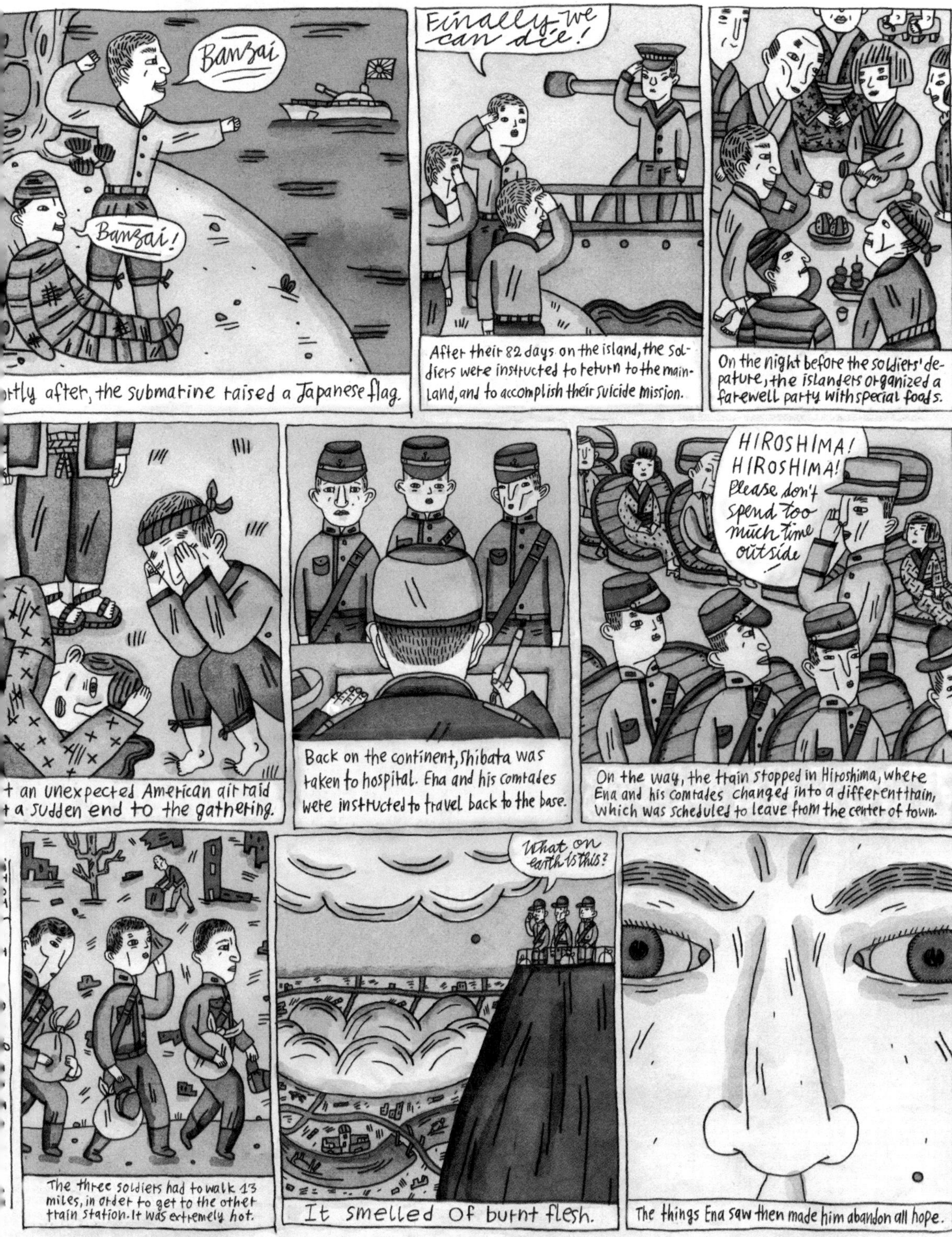
Banzai
Banzai!
rtly after, the submarine raised a Japanese flag.
Finally we can die!
After their 82 days on the island, the soldiers were instructed to return to the mainland, and to accomplish their suicide mission.
On the night before the soldiers' depature, the islanders organized a farewell party with special foods.
t an unexpected American air raid
t a sudden end to the gathering.
Back on the continent, Shibata was taken to hospital. Ena and his comrades were instructed to travel back to the base.
HIROSHIMA! HIROSHIMA!
Please don't spend too much time outside!
On the way, the train stopped in Hiroshima, where Ena and his comrades changed into a different train, which was scheduled to leave from the center of town.
The three soldiers had to walk 13 miles, in order to get to the other train station. It was extremely hot.
What on earth is this?
It smelled of burnt flesh.
The things Ena saw then made him abandon all hope.

He saw a man who was alive, but whose intestines hung down from his belly.

He saw someone whose face was swollen to a degree that it was impossible to make out the person's eyes, nose and mouth.

Ena felt as though his soul was cleanse

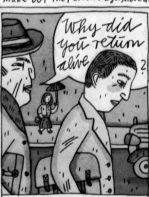

He swore to never again be involved in any form of war.

Why did you return alive?

On August 15th, the emperor broadcast his capitulation. Ena was no longer a soldier, but, as a surviving kamikaze pilot, despised by some.

Club soda makes you feel less hungry

Ena went back to university in Tokyo. Onl half of his former college friends had survived

Ena and Shibata met frequently in Tokyo.

I'm already engaged.
A few years after the war, Ena returned to Kuroshima. Shibata asked him to find Shina, the girl who had looked after him, and to ask her if she would marry Shibata.

In 2004, Ena erected a Buddhist statue o Kuroshima, and he decided that he woulc commemorate his friends who had died kamikaze pilots every year on the islan

Ena Takehiko is in his late 80s and lives as a retired soy-bean exporter in Japa
Sources: Wings of Defeat (Dir. Risa Morimoto), Kamikaze in Color (Dir. Ron Marans), Kamikaze Diaries (Auth. Emiko Ohnuki-Tierney TOKKOU NO MACHI: CHIRAN (AUTH. SANAE SATO). THANK YOU to: Ena Takehiko, Ai Tatebayashi, William Gordon (Wesley Universit

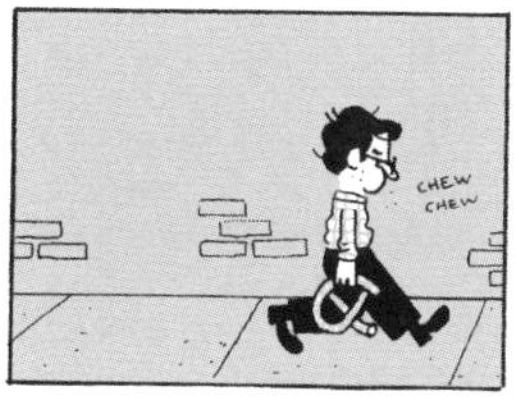
CHEW
CHEW

JONATHAN BENNETT

Skyline / Hot Stuff / Hibern-8 / Prophets / Dead Soles / Haggling

from *The Believer*

FOR ME, DRAWING COMICS IS

A challenge. I don't really have any ideas for stories or fiction, so the strips are simple, semiautobiographical sketches. I struggle to come up with an idea each month for my brief *Believer* strip. I just try to write the strip quickly. To put down on paper something that resembles a genuine wandering of my mind, to amuse myself, I guess. To document something that seems like it might be worth preserving in my own way.

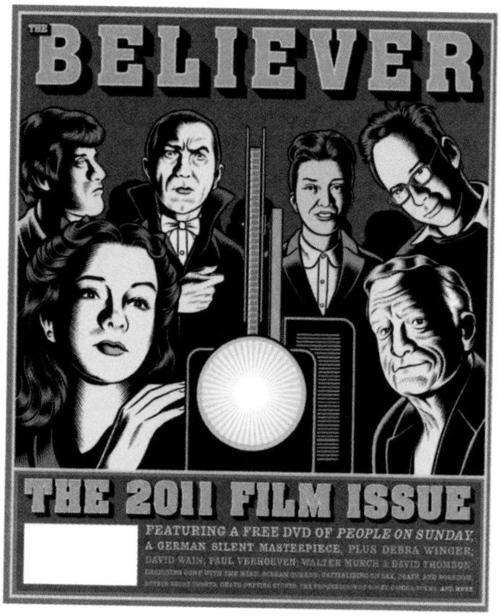
THE BELIEVER
THE 2011 FILM ISSUE
FEATURING A FREE DVD OF PEOPLE ON SUNDAY,
A GERMAN SILENT MASTERPIECE, PLUS DEBRA WINGER;
DAVID WAIN; PAUL VERHOEVEN; WALTER MURCH & DAVID THOMSON

THE SELECTION

I created these strips for the monthly comics section in *The Believer*, edited by Alvin Buenaventura.

PUBLICATIONS MY WORK HAS APPEARED IN

MOME, The Believer, Kramer's Ergot, Spin.

WHAT I'M KNOWN FOR

Most of my time is taken up as a book designer. I designed a few comics-related monographs for Abrams (*The Art of Harvey Kurtzman, The Art of Daniel Clowes*), some special publications from the Library of America (Lynd Ward, Edgar Rice Burroughs), and helped Françoise Mouly package the TOON Books line of comics for kids.

WHERE I LIVE

Brooklyn Heights, New York.

SELECTIONS

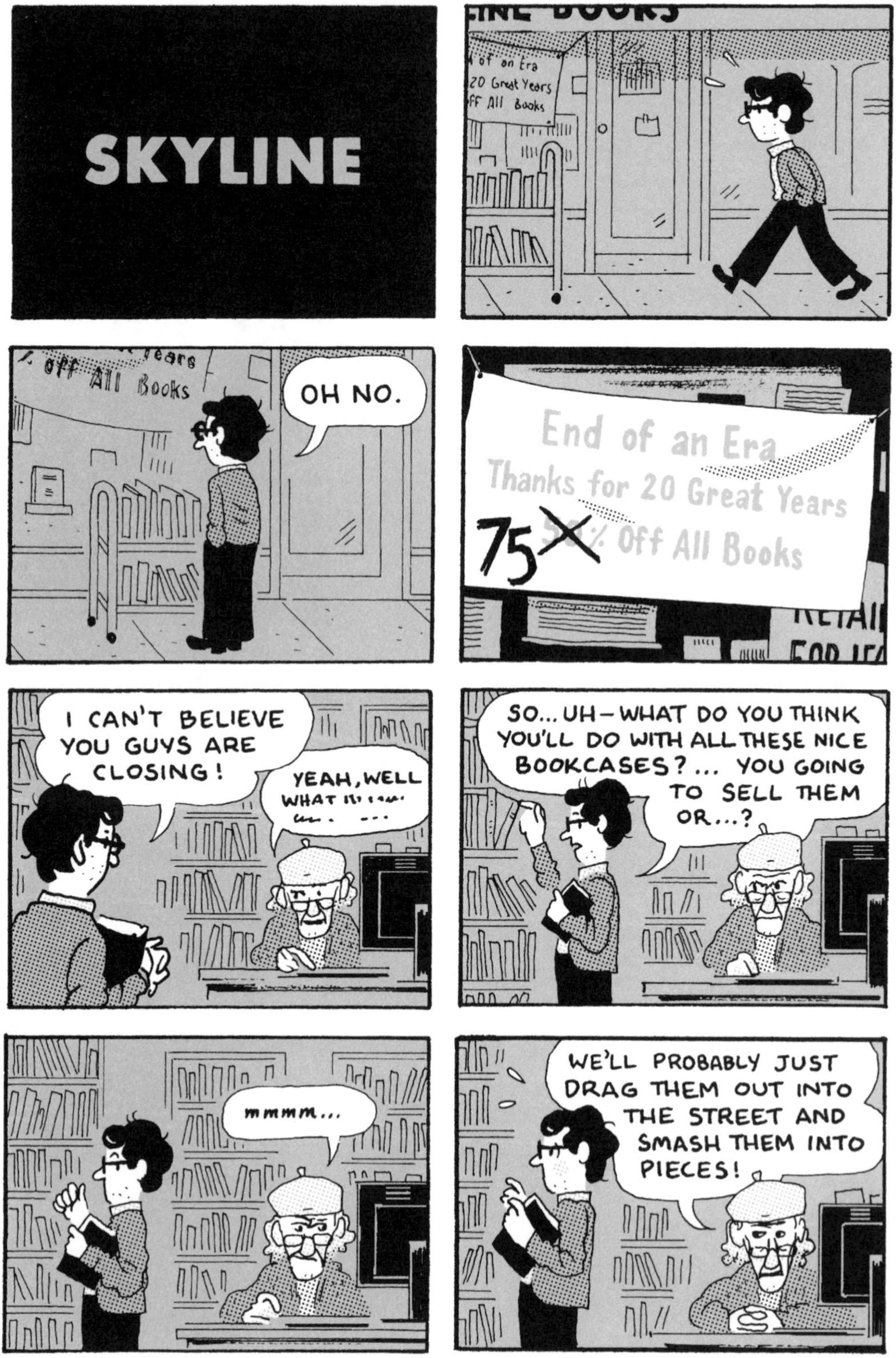
SKYLINE
OH NO.
End of an Era
Thanks for 20 Great Years
75 Off All Books
I CAN'T BELIEVE YOU GUYS ARE CLOSING!
YEAH, WELL
SO... UH—WHAT DO YOU THINK YOU'LL DO WITH ALL THESE NICE BOOKCASES? ... YOU GOING TO SELL THEM OR...?
mmmm...
WE'LL PROBABLY JUST DRAG THEM OUT INTO THE STREET AND SMASH THEM INTO PIECES!

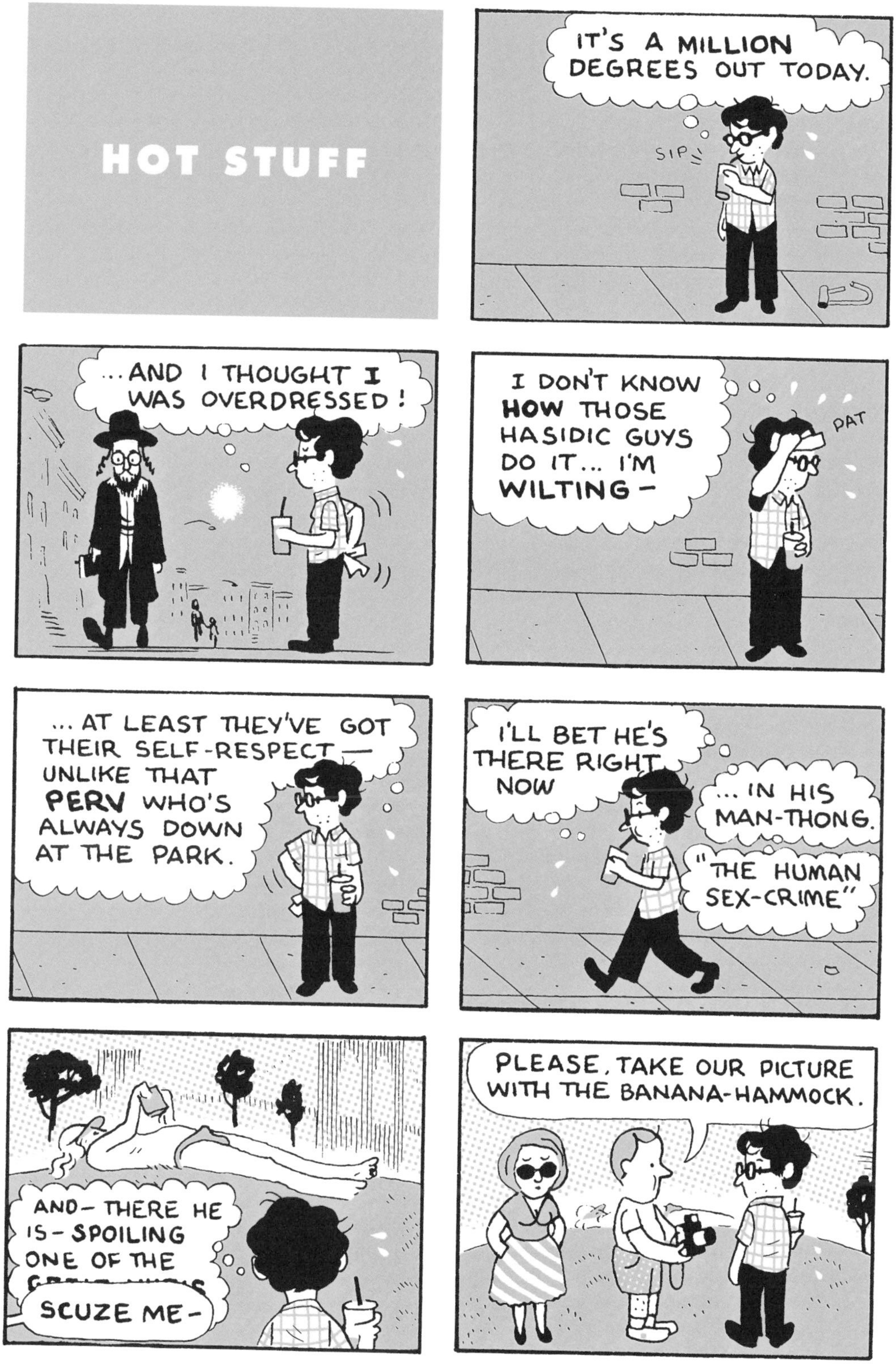
HOT STUFF
IT'S A MILLION DEGREES OUT TODAY.
SIP
...AND I THOUGHT I WAS OVERDRESSED!
I DON'T KNOW HOW THOSE HASIDIC GUYS DO IT... I'M WILTING –
PAT
...AT LEAST THEY'VE GOT THEIR SELF-RESPECT — UNLIKE THAT PERV WHO'S ALWAYS DOWN AT THE PARK.
I'LL BET HE'S THERE RIGHT NOW
...IN HIS MAN-THONG.
"THE HUMAN SEX-CRIME"
AND – THERE HE IS – SPOILING ONE OF THE
SCUZE ME –
PLEASE, TAKE OUR PICTURE WITH THE BANANA-HAMMOCK.

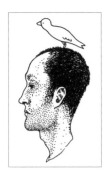

ANDERS NILSEN

The Pilot Learns to Fly

from *Big Questions*

big questions
anders nilsen

FOR ME, DRAWING COMICS IS

I still can't believe people pay me to do this.

THE SELECTION

This piece is an excerpt from *Big Questions*, an epic existential fable about some little birds who think a bomb is an egg and a crashed airplane might be a giant bird. There are a couple of human characters as well, including an idiot boy exploring the world on his own for the first time, and the pilot of the plane.

THE CONTEXT

The Pilot here has just had a dramatic confrontation with the Idiot and some of the birds, and, in the mêlée, been bitten on the ankle by a snake. He'd already been having trouble keeping his dreams and real life apart. They now get hopelessly tangled.

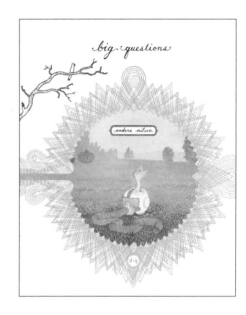

PUBLICATIONS MY WORK HAS APPEARED IN

The *Chicago Reader*, *Interview Magazine*, *Punk Planet*, *The Best American Comics*, *The Best American Non-Required Reading*, Yale's *Anthology of Graphic Fiction*, *The Believer*, *Kramer's Ergot*.

AWARDS

Ignatz Award 2005, Outstanding Story: *Dogs and Water*; Ignatz Award 2007, Outstanding Graphic Novel: *Don't Go Where I Can't Follow*.

WHAT I'M KNOWN FOR

Dogs and Water (Drawn & Quarterly), *Don't Go Where I Can't Follow* (Drawn & Quarterly), *Monologues for the Coming Plague* (Fantagraphics).

WHERE I LIVE

Minneapolis, Minnesota.

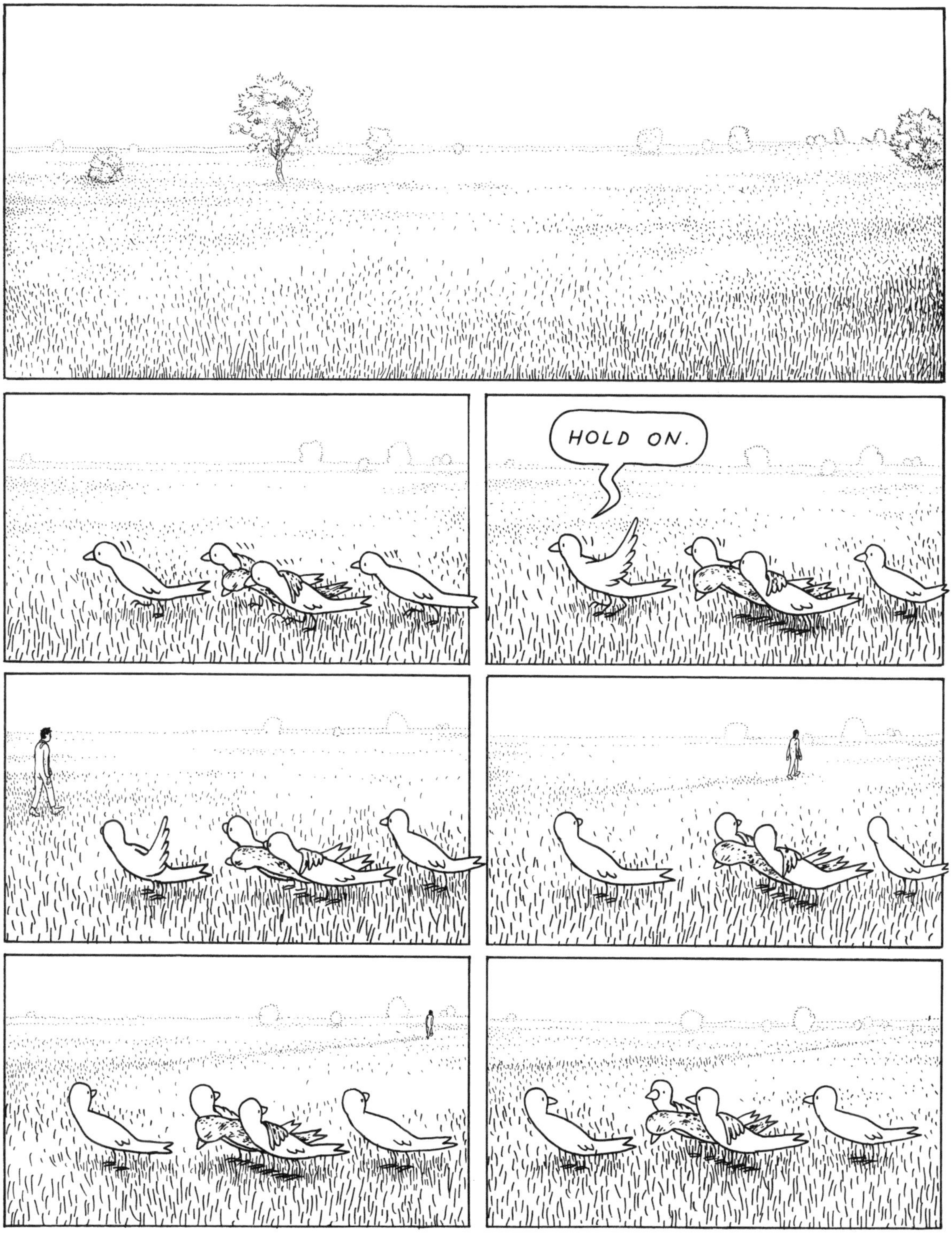
HOLD ON.

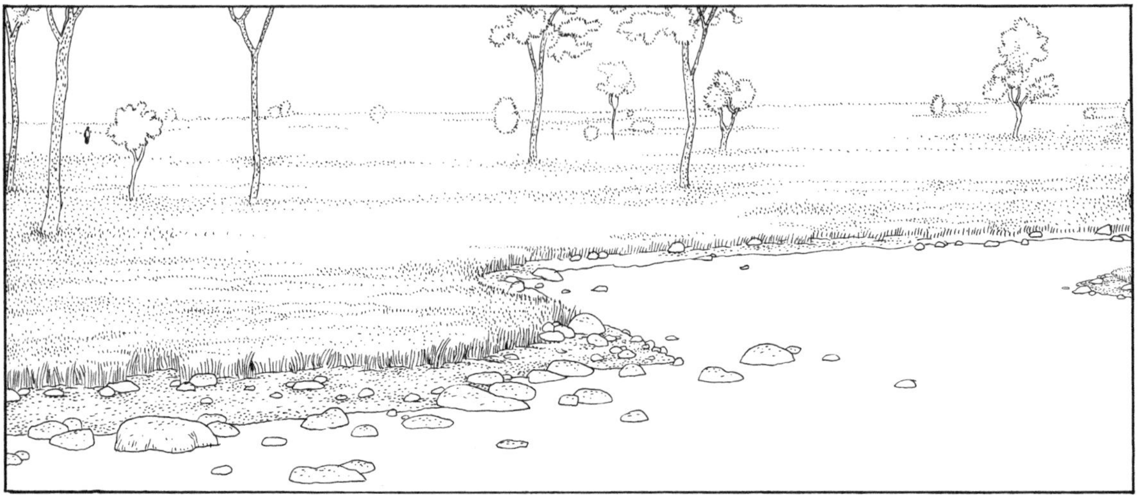

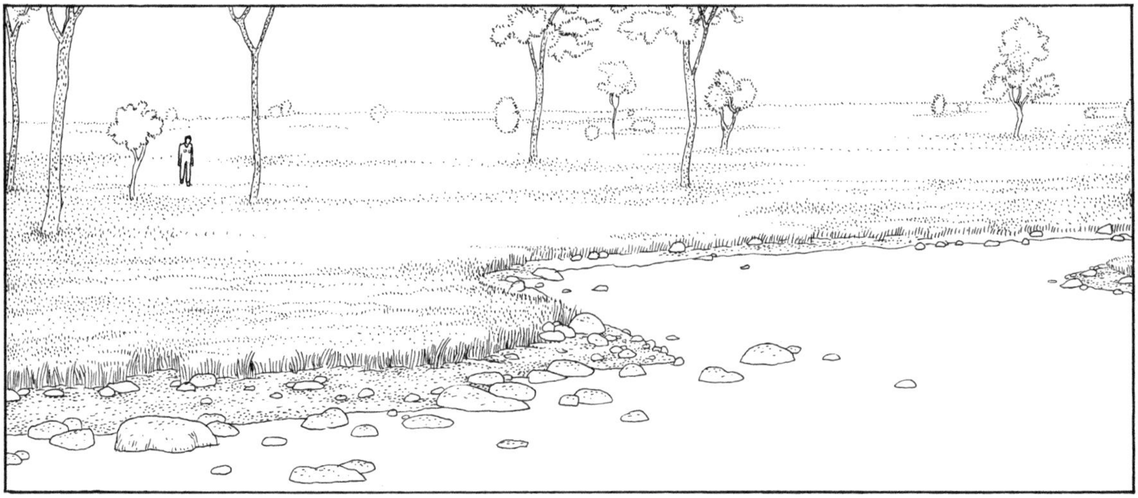

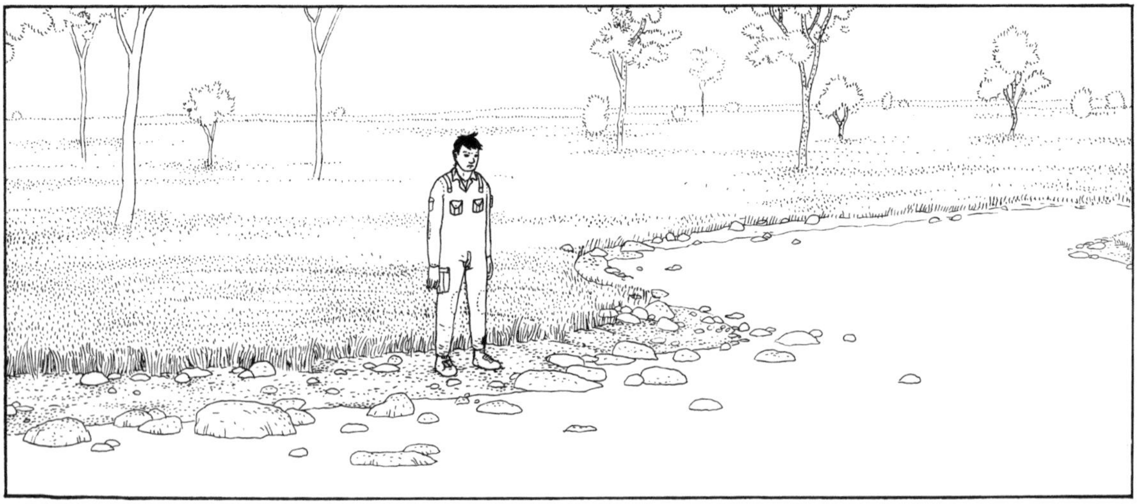

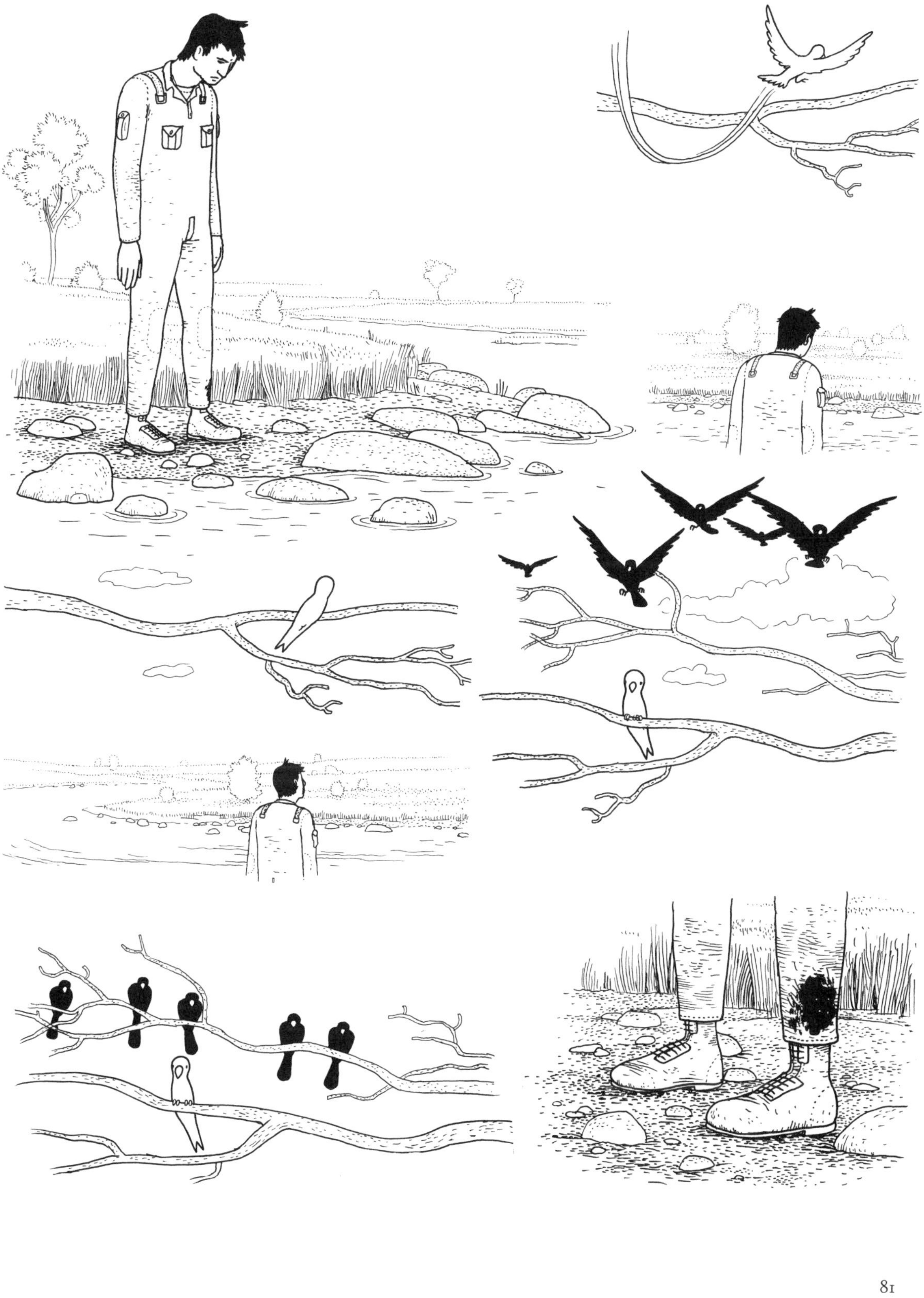

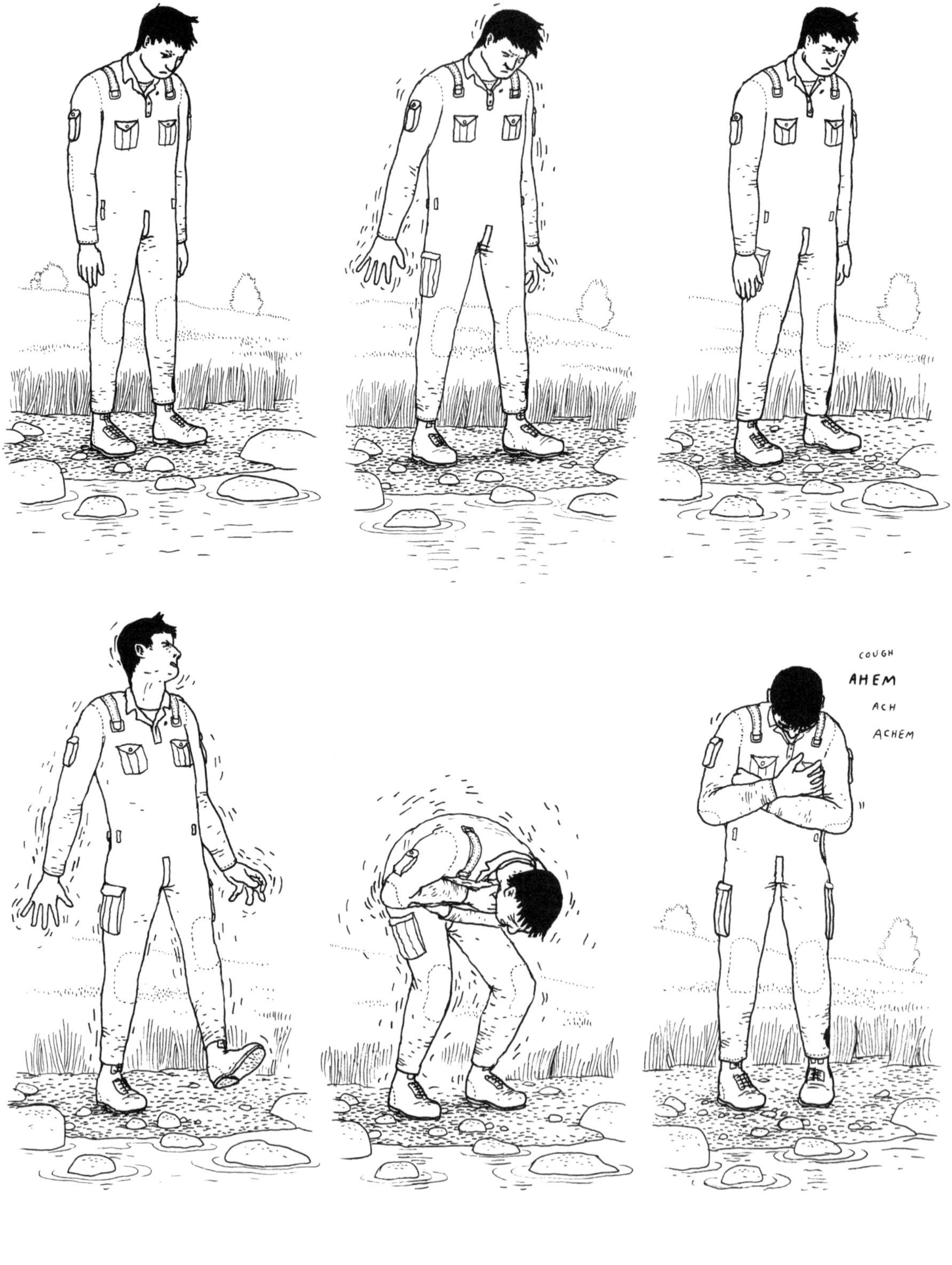
COUGH
AHEM
ACH
ACHEM

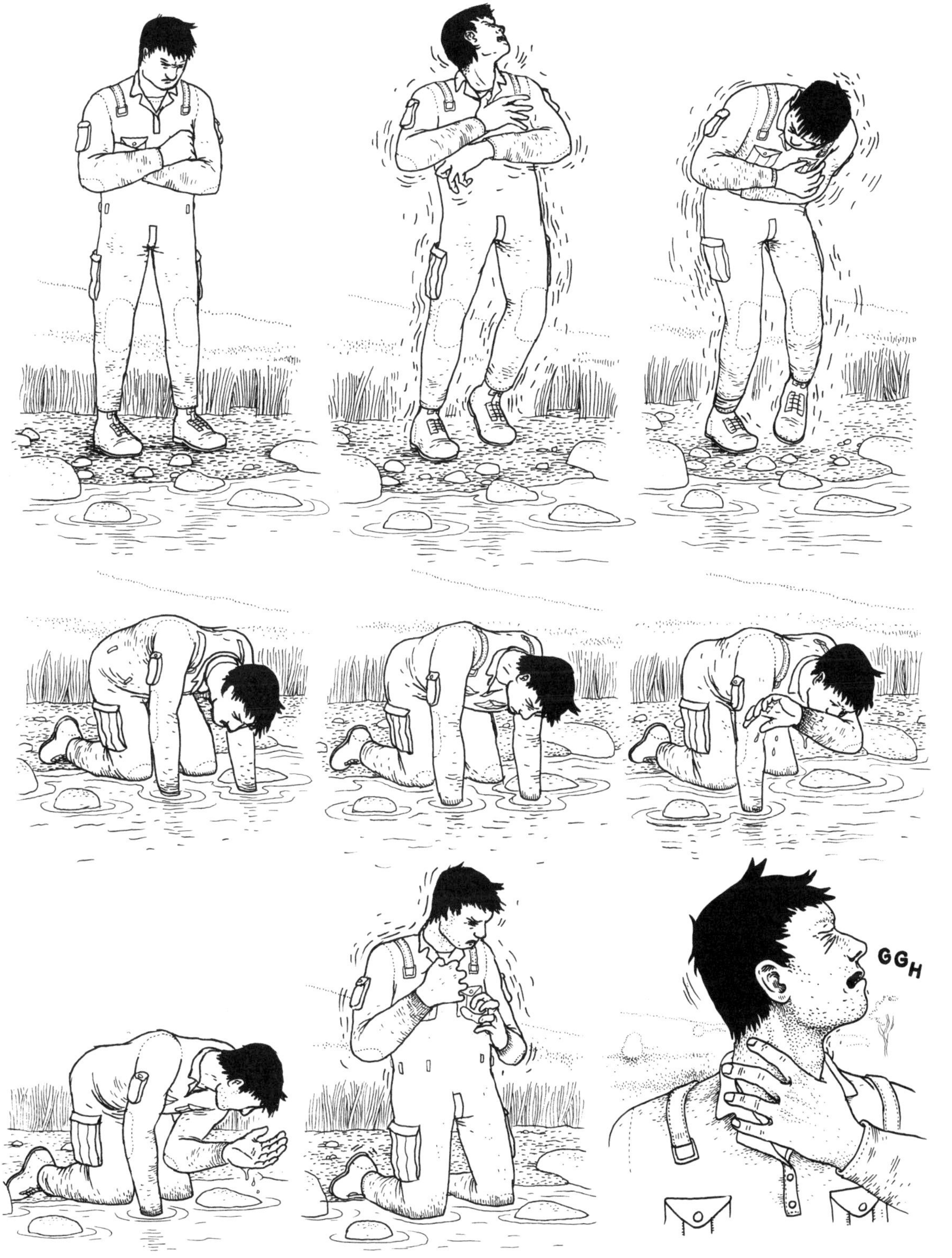
GGH

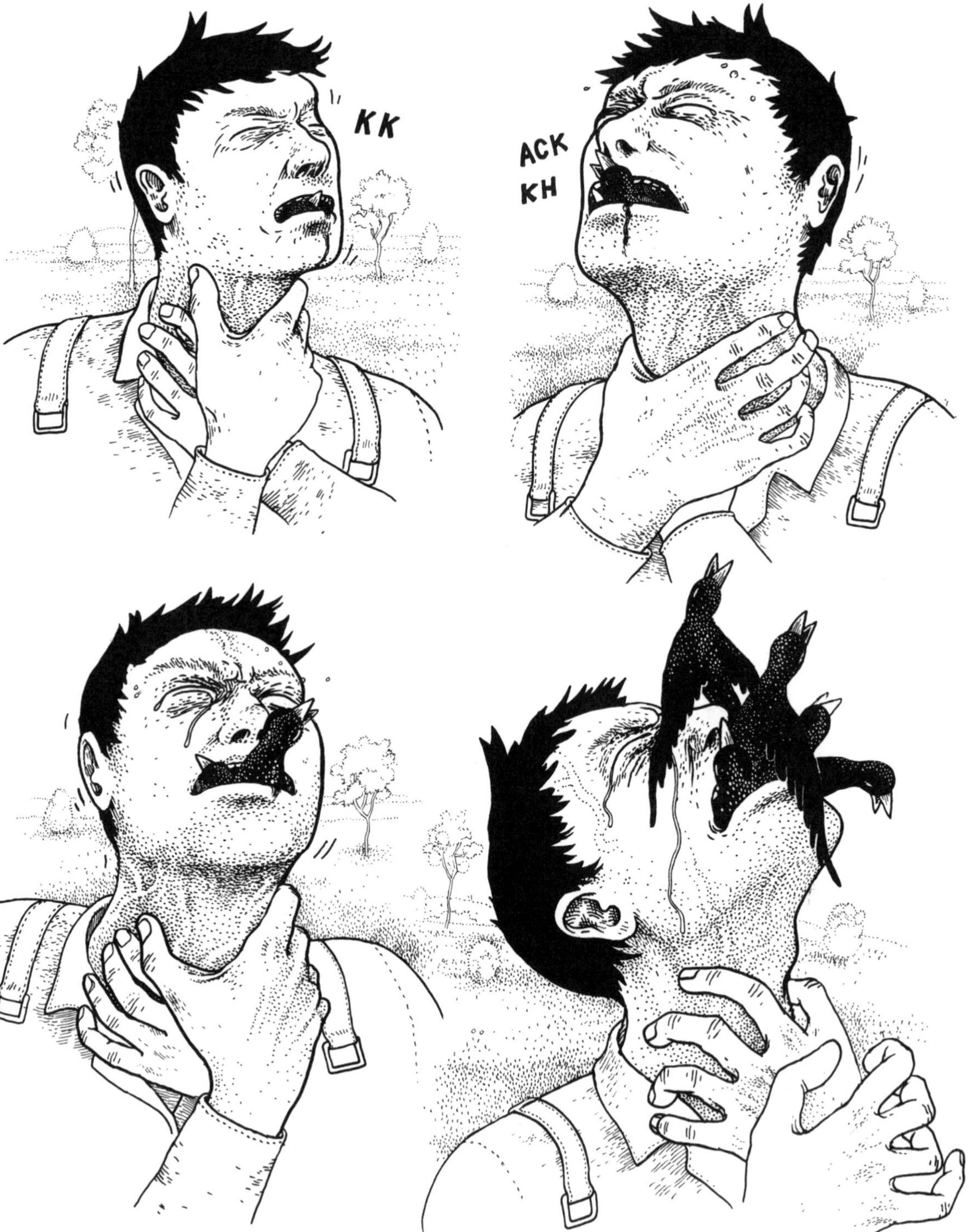
KK
ACK
KH

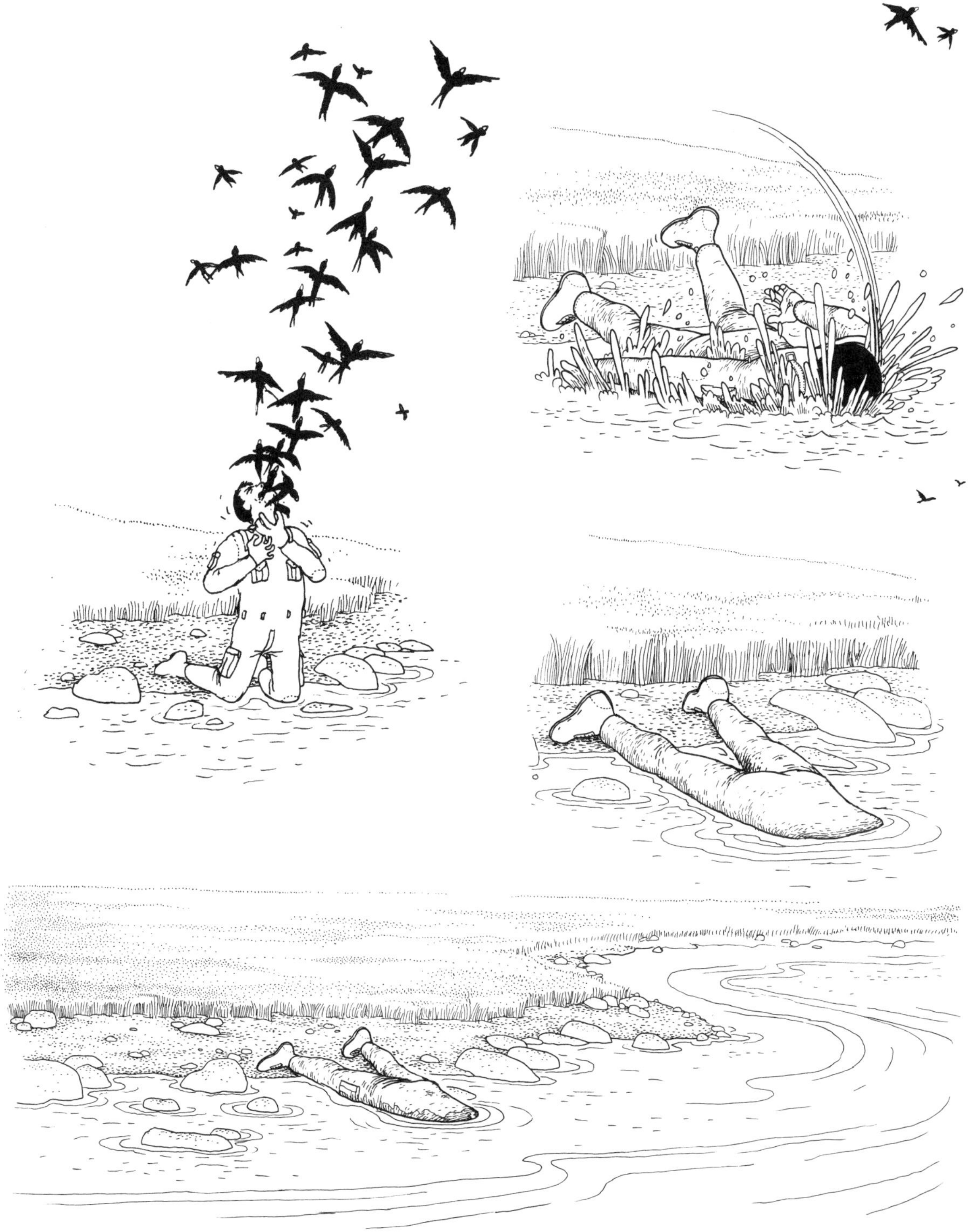

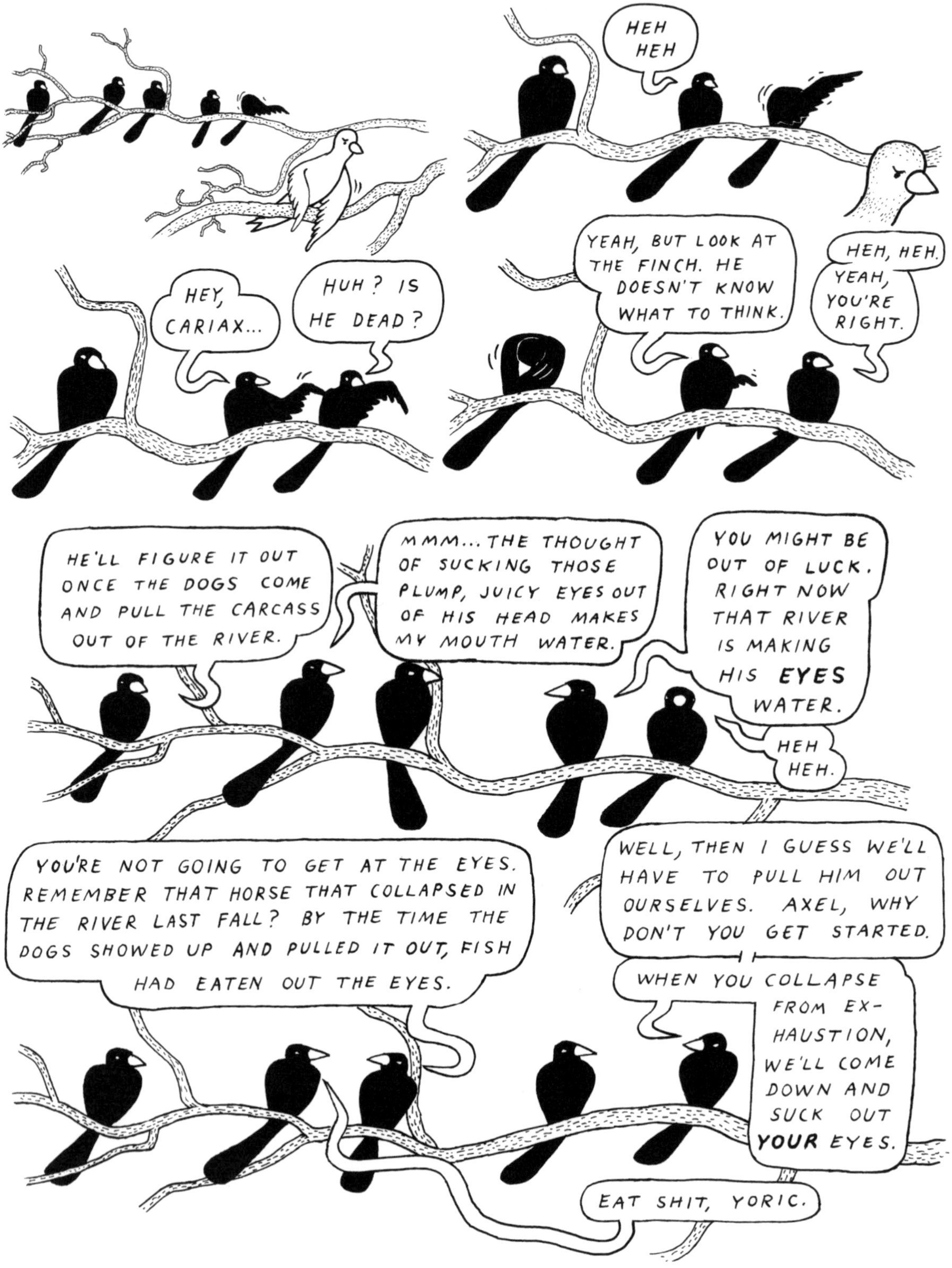
HEH HEH
HEY, CARIAX...
HUH? IS HE DEAD?
YEAH, BUT LOOK AT THE FINCH. HE DOESN'T KNOW WHAT TO THINK.
HEH, HEH. YEAH, YOU'RE RIGHT.
HE'LL FIGURE IT OUT ONCE THE DOGS COME AND PULL THE CARCASS OUT OF THE RIVER.
MMM... THE THOUGHT OF SUCKING THOSE PLUMP, JUICY EYES OUT OF HIS HEAD MAKES MY MOUTH WATER.
YOU MIGHT BE OUT OF LUCK. RIGHT NOW THAT RIVER IS MAKING HIS **EYES** WATER.
HEH HEH.
YOU'RE NOT GOING TO GET AT THE EYES. REMEMBER THAT HORSE THAT COLLAPSED IN THE RIVER LAST FALL? BY THE TIME THE DOGS SHOWED UP AND PULLED IT OUT, FISH HAD EATEN OUT THE EYES.
WELL, THEN I GUESS WE'LL HAVE TO PULL HIM OUT OURSELVES. AXEL, WHY DON'T YOU GET STARTED.
WHEN YOU COLLAPSE FROM EX-HAUSTION, WE'LL COME DOWN AND SUCK OUT **YOUR** EYES.
EAT SHIT, YORIC.

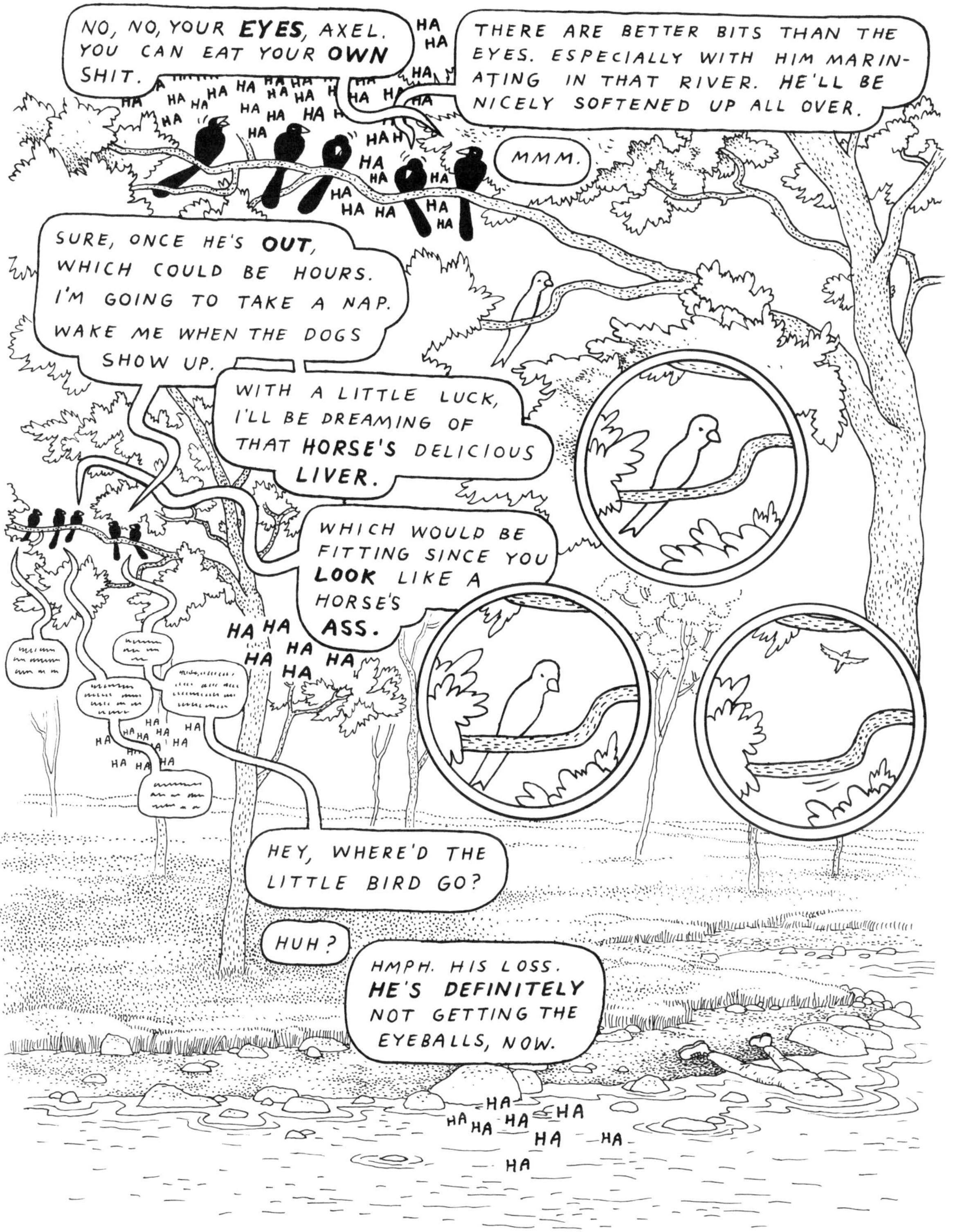
NO, NO, YOUR EYES, AXEL. YOU CAN EAT YOUR OWN SHIT.
HA HA HA HA HA HA HA HA HA HA HA
THERE ARE BETTER BITS THAN THE EYES. ESPECIALLY WITH HIM MARINATING IN THAT RIVER. HE'LL BE NICELY SOFTENED UP ALL OVER.
MMM.
SURE, ONCE HE'S OUT, WHICH COULD BE HOURS. I'M GOING TO TAKE A NAP. WAKE ME WHEN THE DOGS SHOW UP.
WITH A LITTLE LUCK, I'LL BE DREAMING OF THAT HORSE'S DELICIOUS LIVER.
WHICH WOULD BE FITTING SINCE YOU LOOK LIKE A HORSE'S ASS.
HA HA HA HA HA HA HA
HA HA HA HA HA HA HA HA HA HA
HEY, WHERE'D THE LITTLE BIRD GO?
HUH?
HMPH. HIS LOSS. HE'S DEFINITELY NOT GETTING THE EYEBALLS, NOW.
HA HA HA HA HA HA HA HA

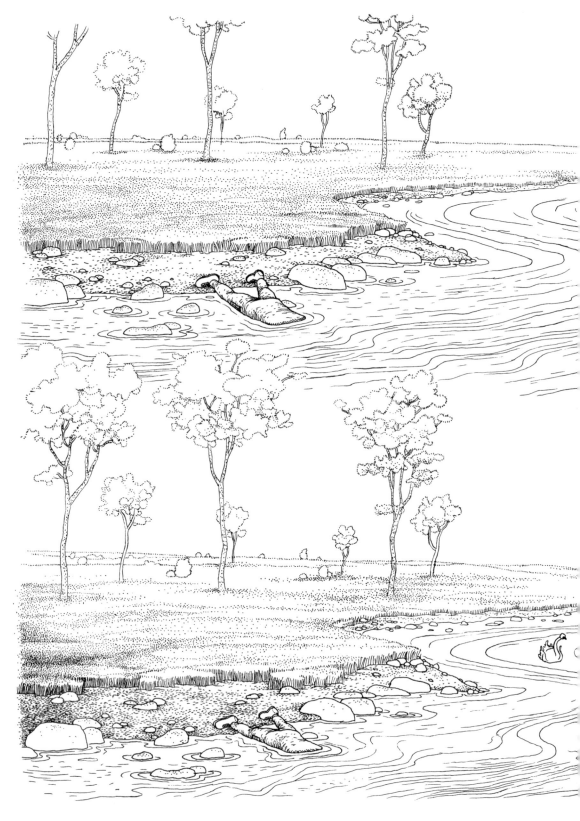

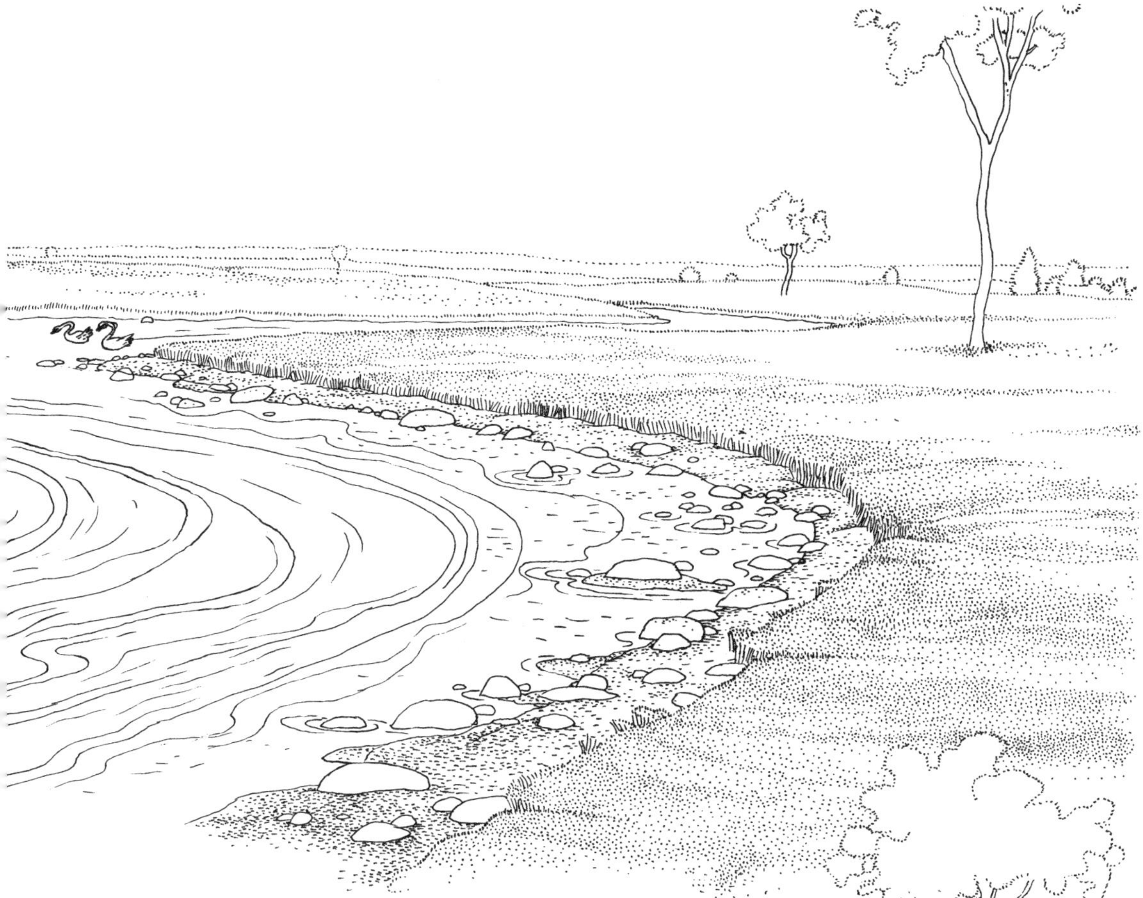

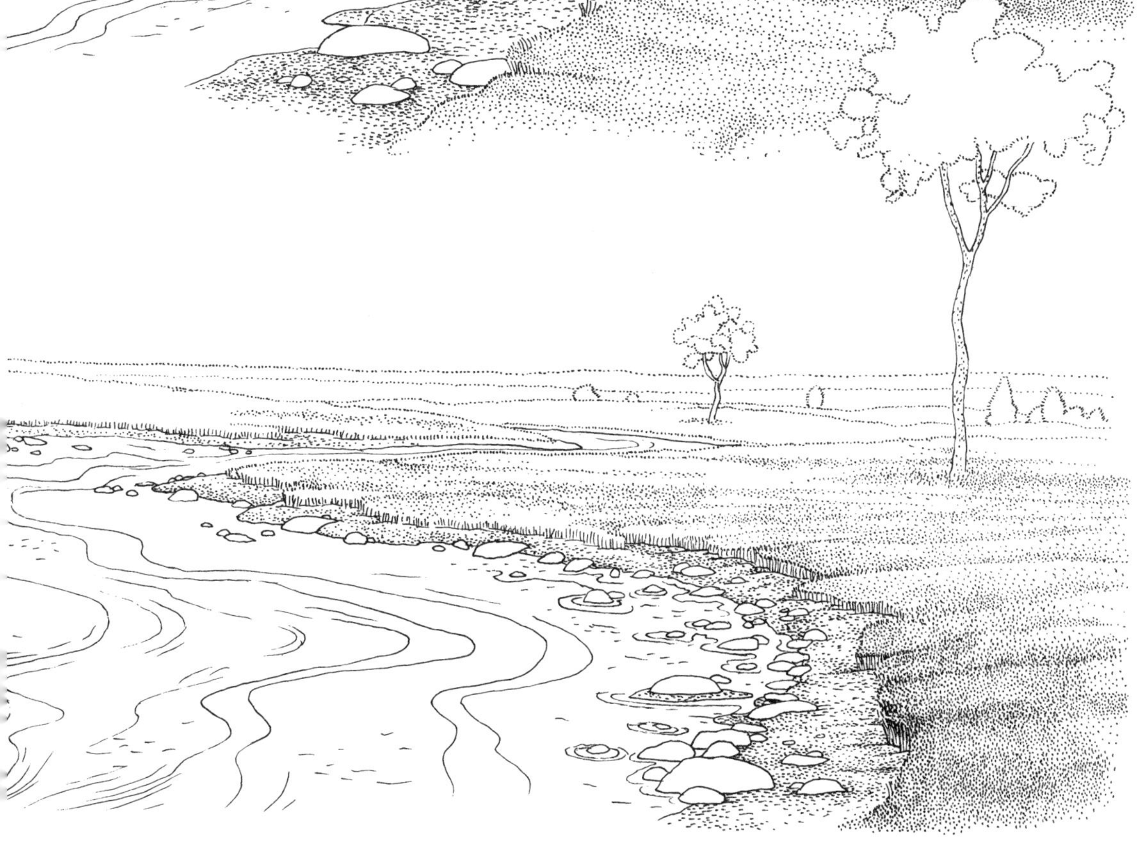

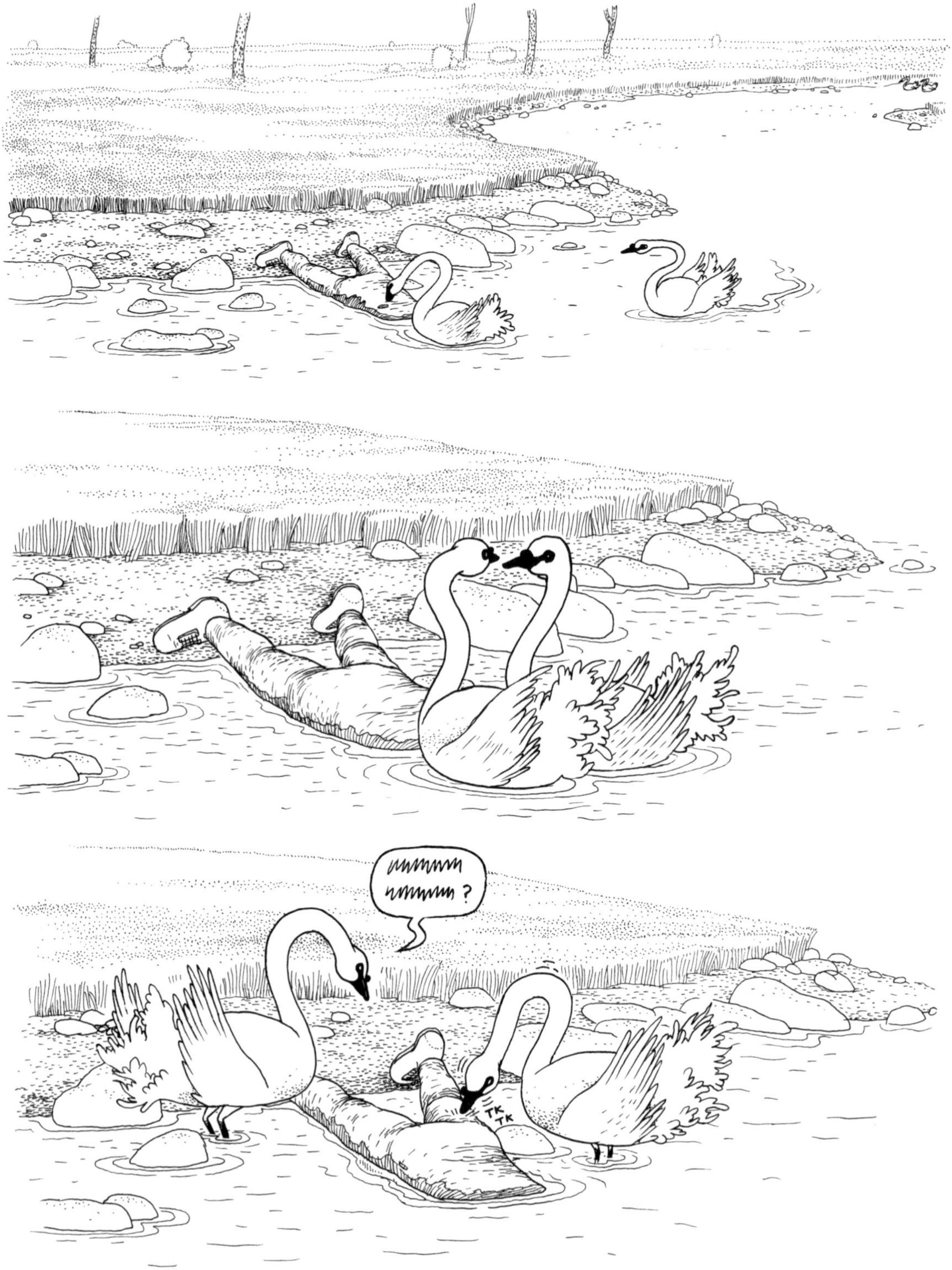
?
TK TK

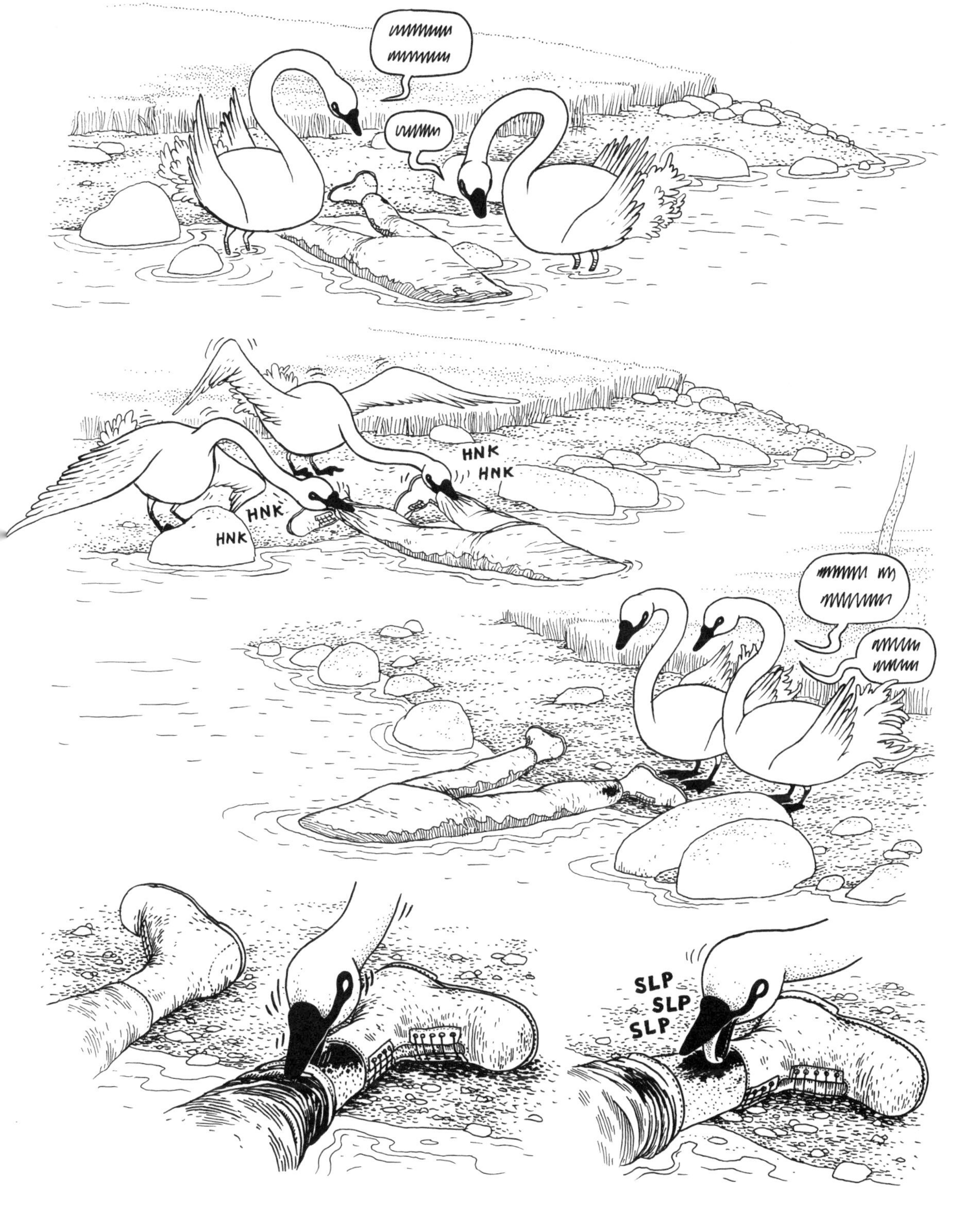
HNK
HNK
HNK
HNK
SLP
SLP
SLP

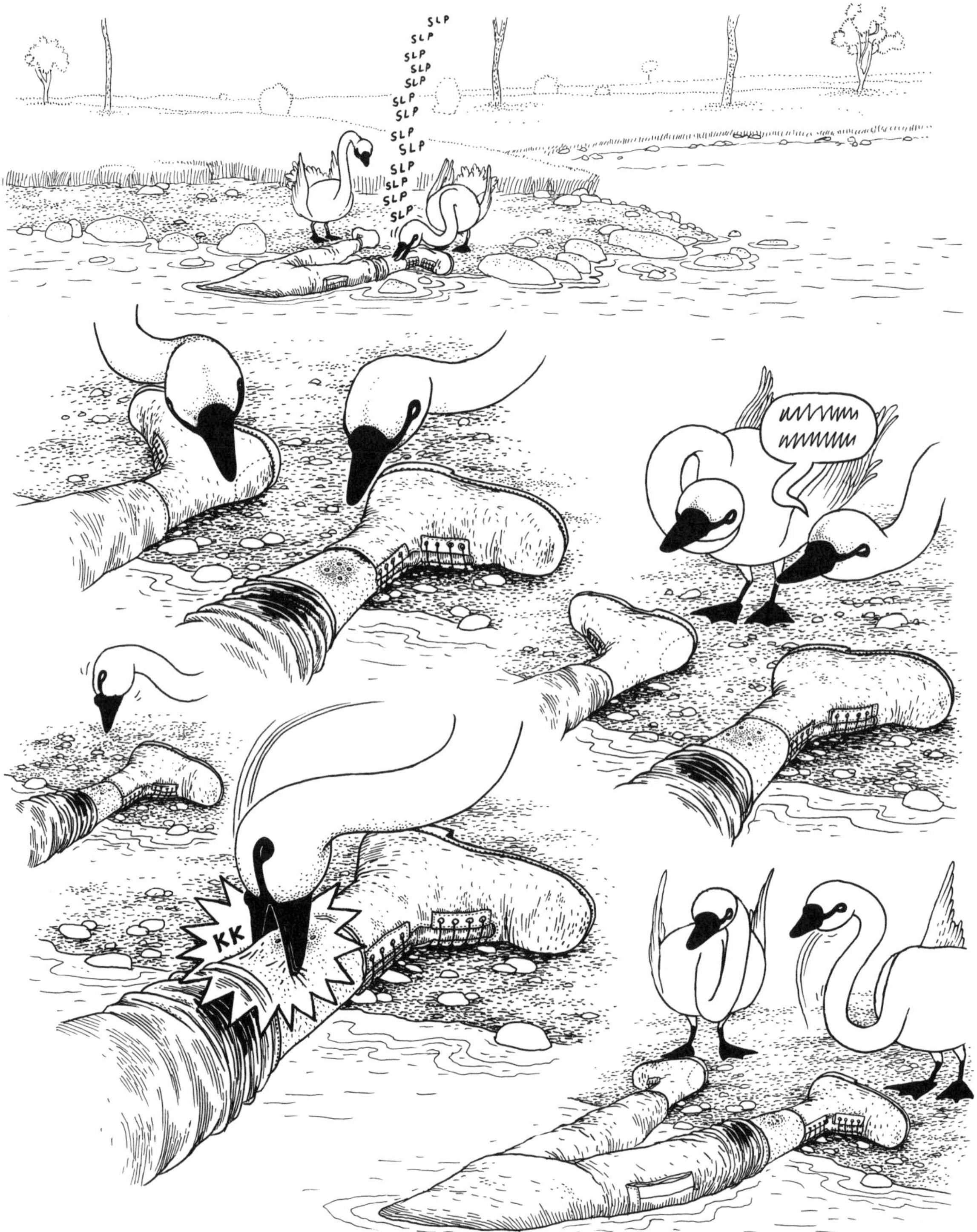
SLP SLP SLP SLP SLP SLP SLP SLP SLP SLP SLP SLP SLP
KK

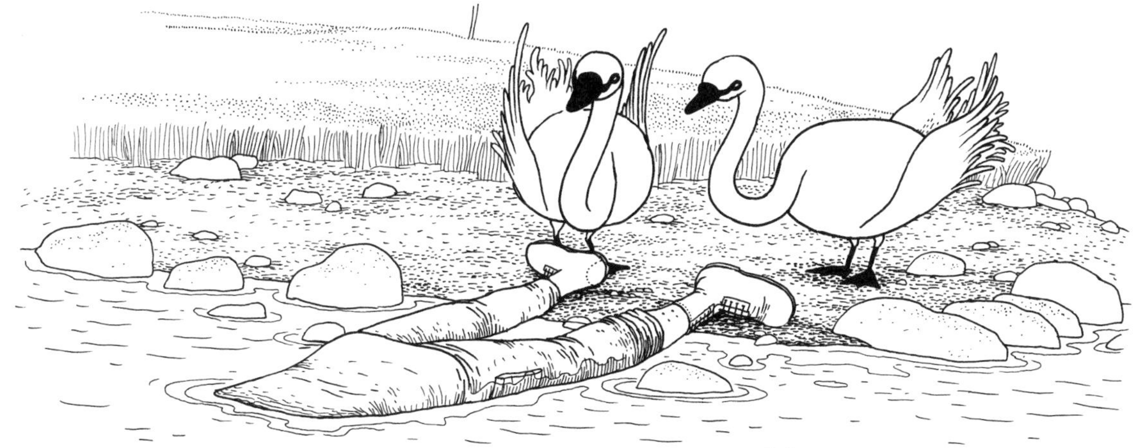

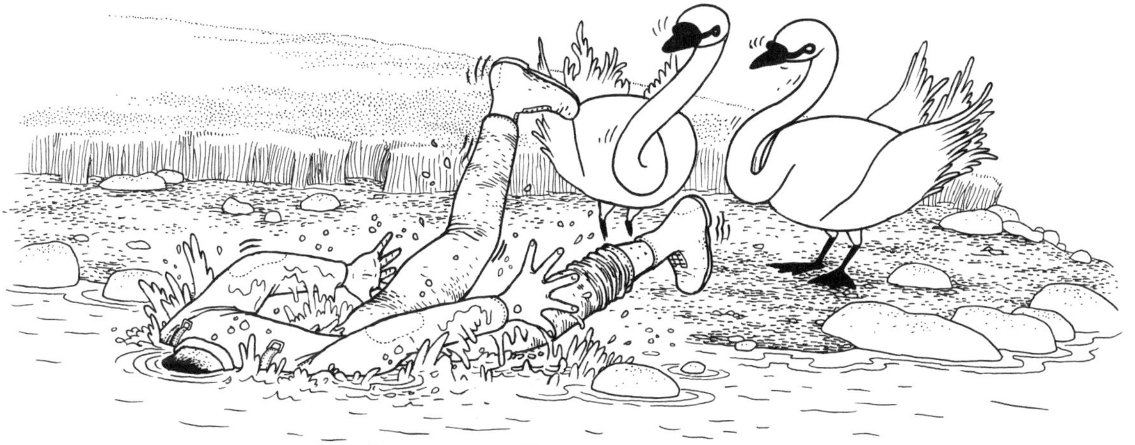

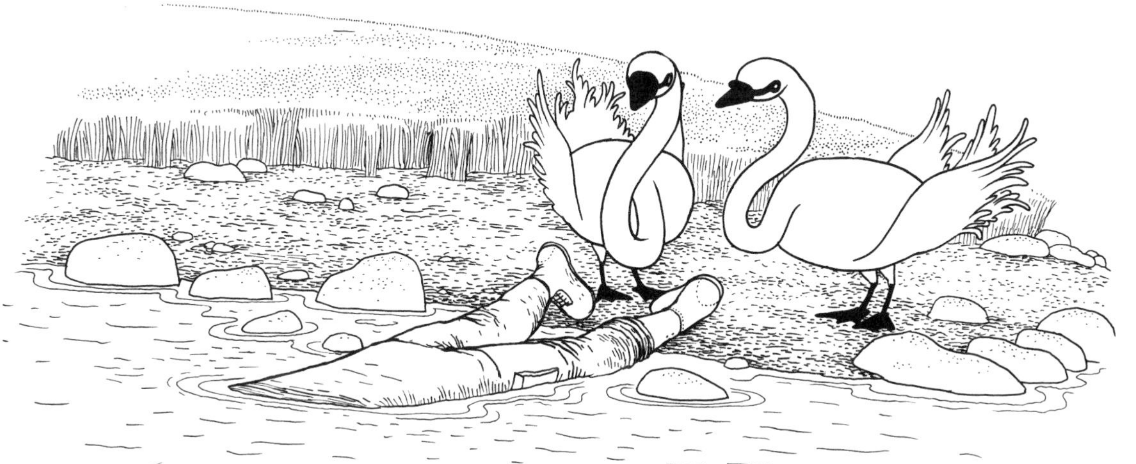

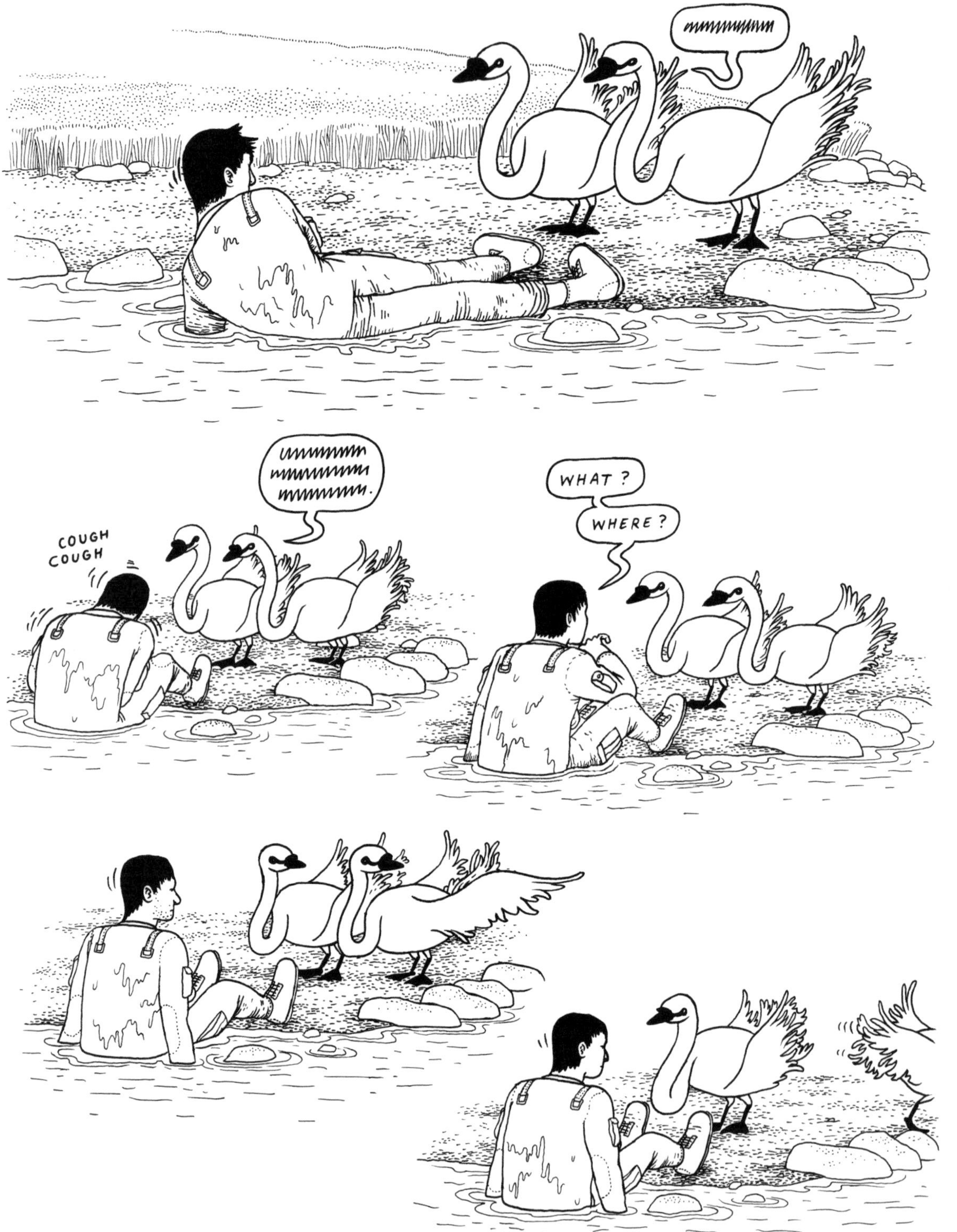
COUGH COUGH
WHAT ?
WHERE ?

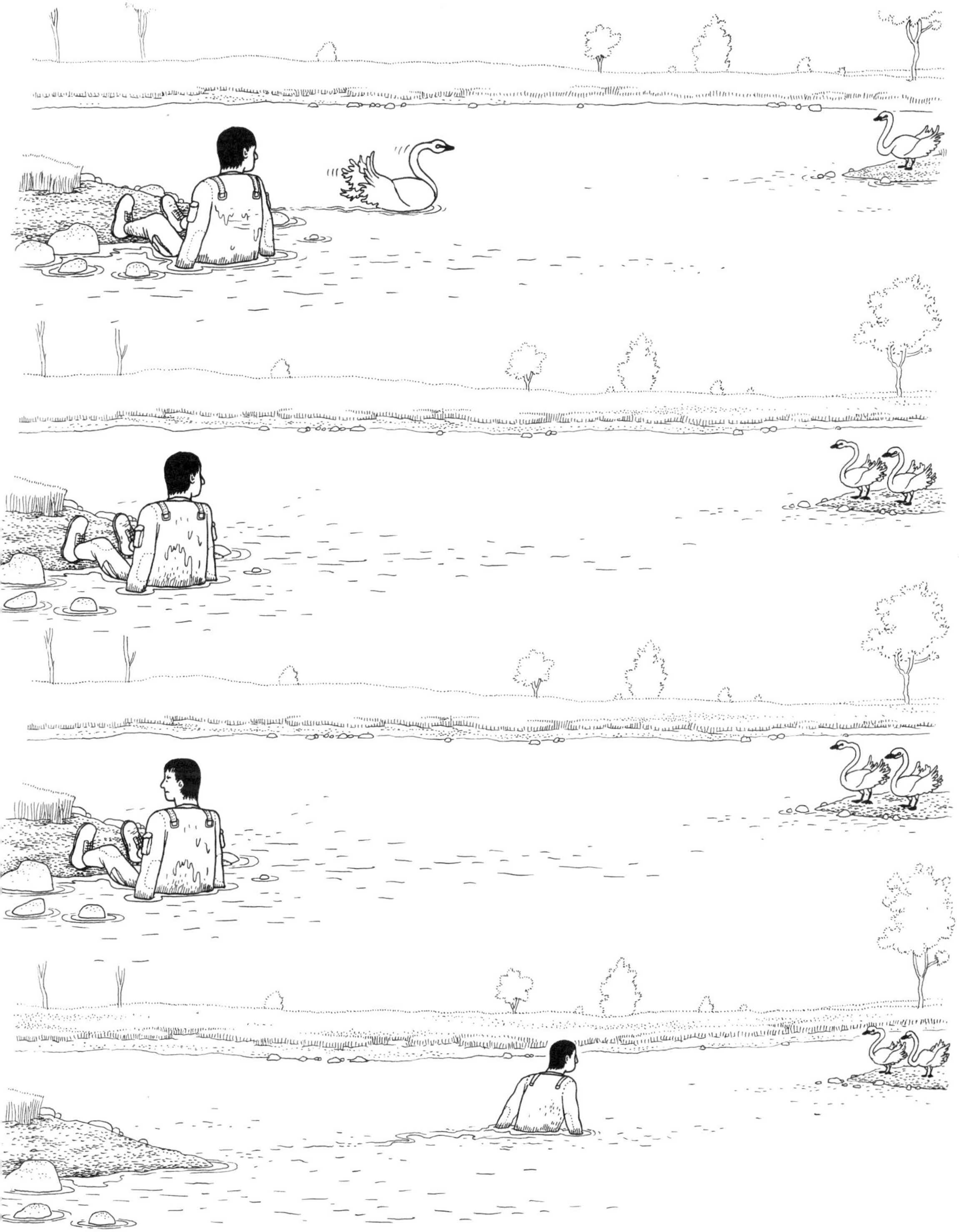

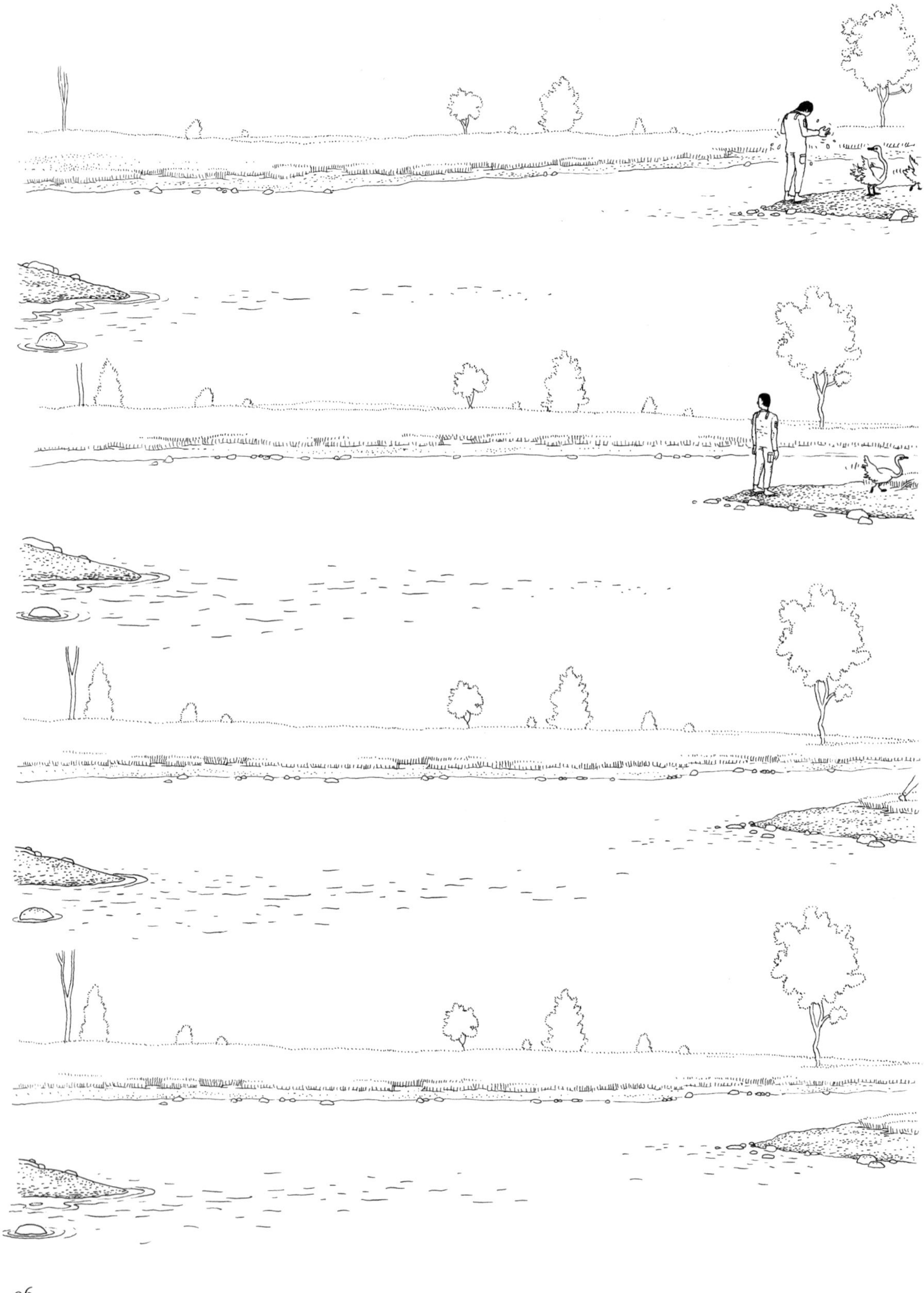

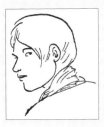

SARAH GLIDDEN

The Golan Heights

from *How to Understand Israel in 60 Days or Less*

FOR ME, DRAWING COMICS IS

A way to share stories that people might have difficulty relating to otherwise.

THE SELECTION

As a group of young Jewish-American tour participants is being told about the capture of the Golan Heights by Israel during the Six Day War in 1967, I try to imagine the human stories behind the history.

PUBLICATIONS MY WORK HAS APPEARED IN

The *Jewish Quarterly, Ha'aretz, Cartoon Movement* (www.cartoonmovement.com).

AWARDS

2008 Ignatz Award for Promising New Talent, 2008 Masie Kukoc Award for Comics Inspiration.

WHERE I LIVE

Brooklyn, New York.

HOW TO UNDERSTAND
ISRAEL
IN 60 DAYS OR LESS
SARAH GLIDDEN
VERTIGO

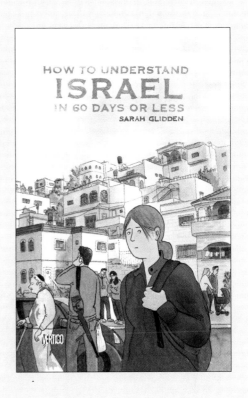

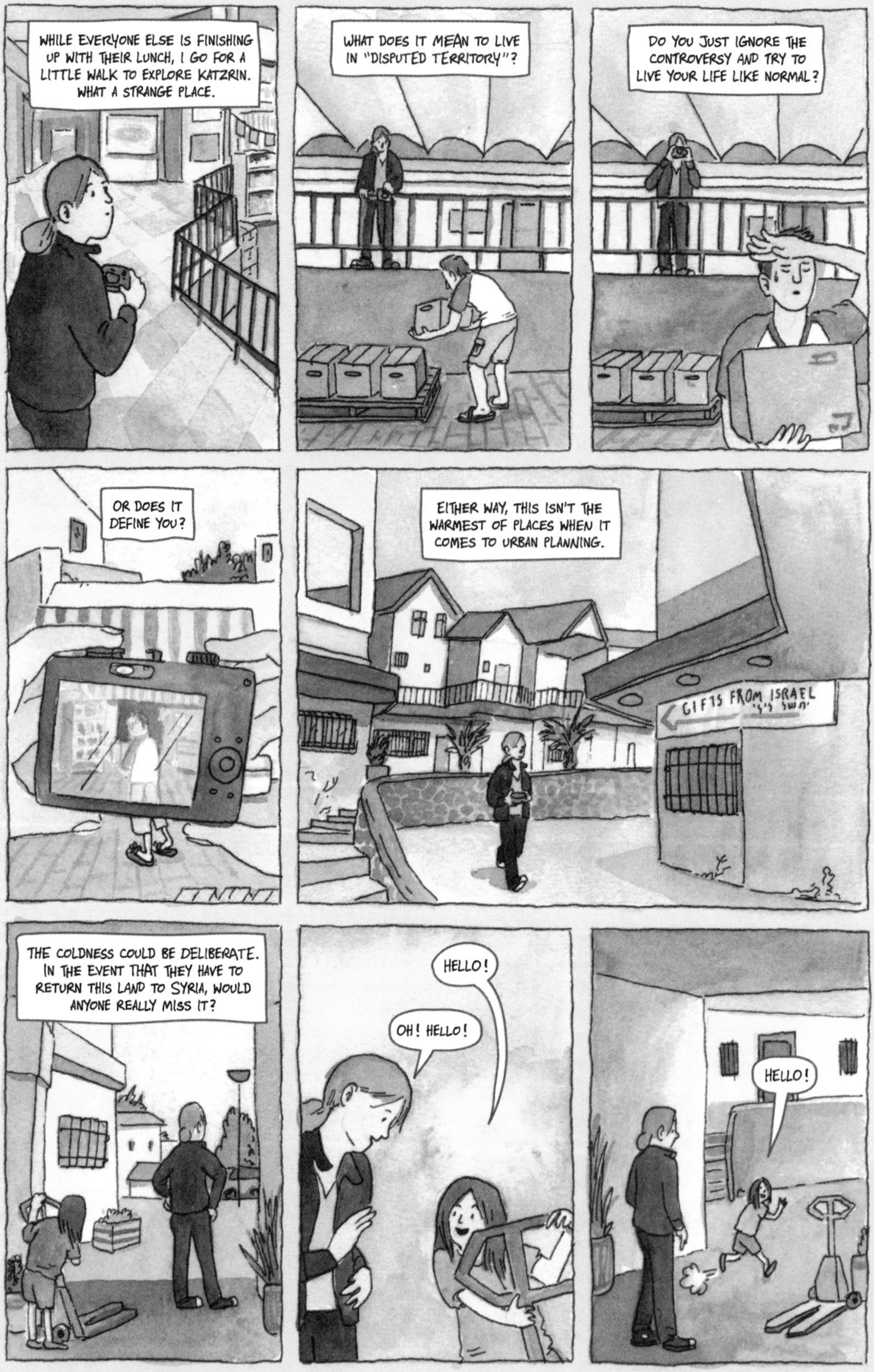
WHILE EVERYONE ELSE IS FINISHING UP WITH THEIR LUNCH, I GO FOR A LITTLE WALK TO EXPLORE KATZRIN. WHAT A STRANGE PLACE.
WHAT DOES IT MEAN TO LIVE IN "DISPUTED TERRITORY"?
DO YOU JUST IGNORE THE CONTROVERSY AND TRY TO LIVE YOUR LIFE LIKE NORMAL?
OR DOES IT DEFINE YOU?
EITHER WAY, THIS ISN'T THE WARMEST OF PLACES WHEN IT COMES TO URBAN PLANNING.
GIFTS FROM ISRAEL
THE COLDNESS COULD BE DELIBERATE. IN THE EVENT THAT THEY HAVE TO RETURN THIS LAND TO SYRIA, WOULD ANYONE REALLY MISS IT?
HELLO!
OH! HELLO!
HELLO!

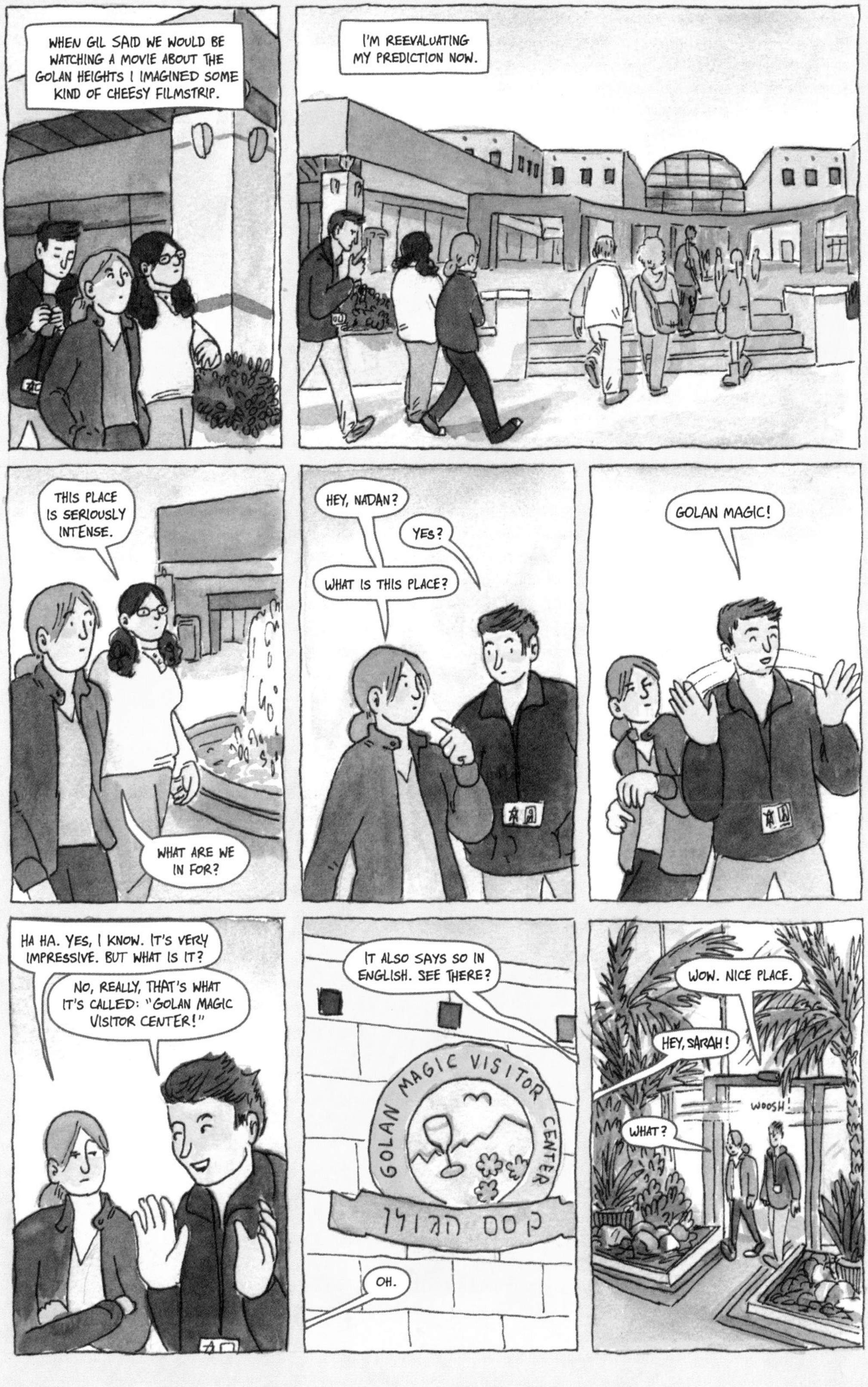
WHEN GIL SAID WE WOULD BE WATCHING A MOVIE ABOUT THE GOLAN HEIGHTS I IMAGINED SOME KIND OF CHEESY FILMSTRIP.
I'M REEVALUATING MY PREDICTION NOW.
THIS PLACE IS SERIOUSLY INTENSE.
WHAT ARE WE IN FOR?
HEY, NADAN?
YES?
WHAT IS THIS PLACE?
GOLAN MAGIC!
HA HA. YES, I KNOW. IT'S VERY IMPRESSIVE. BUT WHAT IS IT?
NO, REALLY, THAT'S WHAT IT'S CALLED: "GOLAN MAGIC VISITOR CENTER!"
IT ALSO SAYS SO IN ENGLISH. SEE THERE?
GOLAN MAGIC VISITOR CENTER
קסם הגולן
OH.
WOW. NICE PLACE.
HEY, SARAH!
WOOSH!
WHAT?

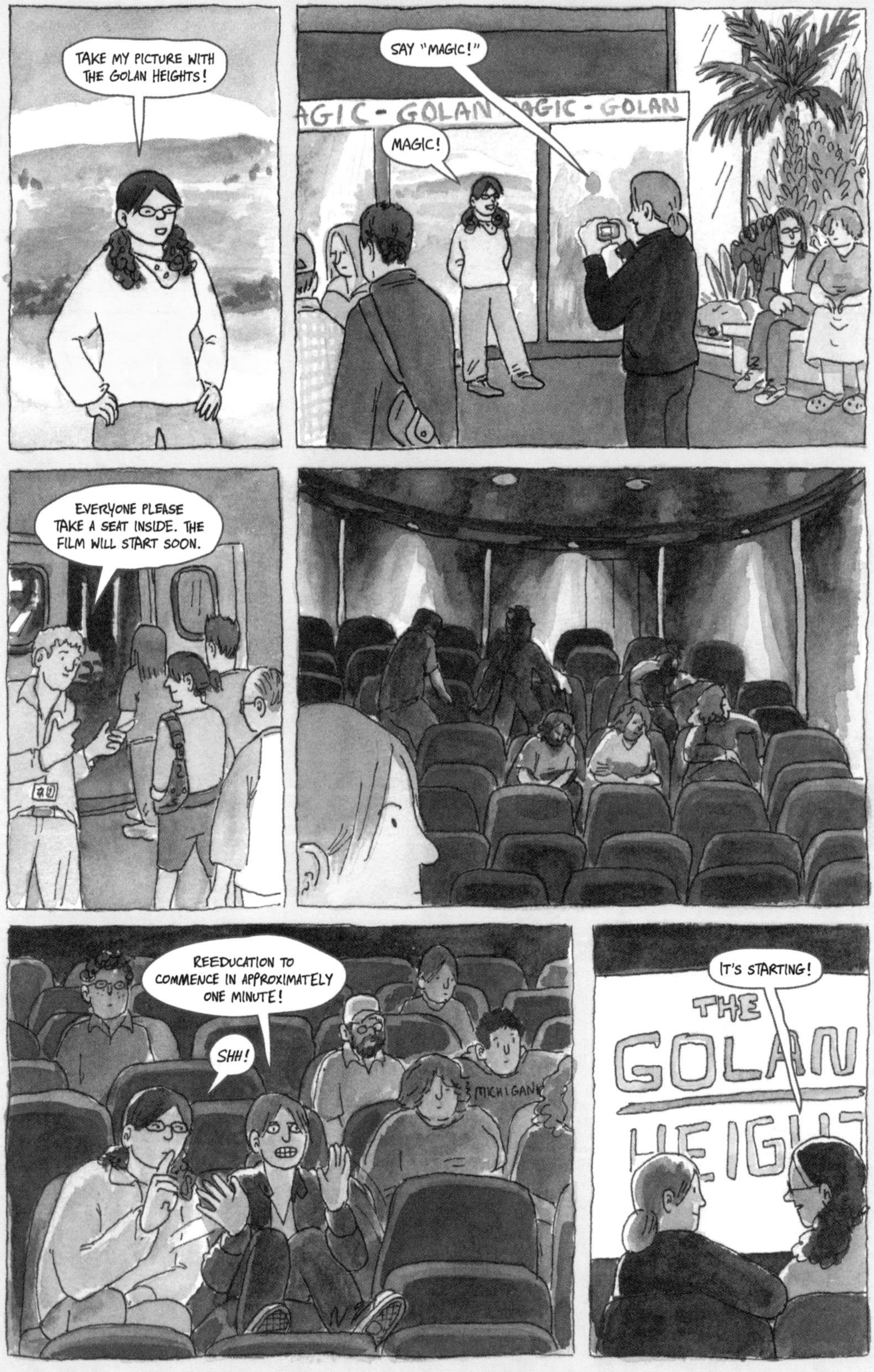
TAKE MY PICTURE WITH THE GOLAN HEIGHTS!
SAY "MAGIC!"
MAGIC - GOLAN MAGIC - GOLAN
MAGIC!
EVERYONE PLEASE TAKE A SEAT INSIDE. THE FILM WILL START SOON.
REEDUCATION TO COMMENCE IN APPROXIMATELY ONE MINUTE!
SHH!
MICHIGAN
IT'S STARTING!
THE GOLAN HEIGHT

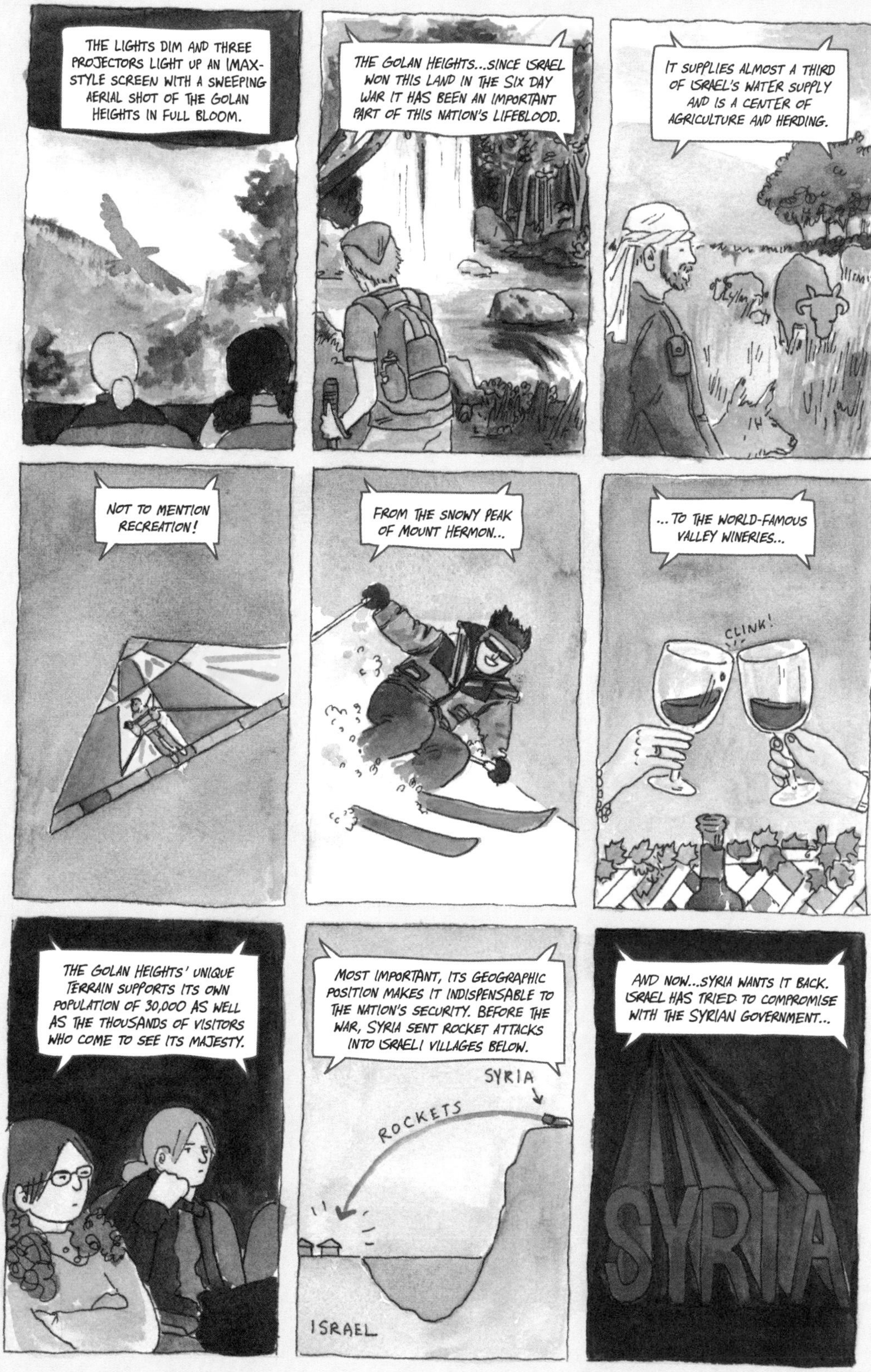
THE LIGHTS DIM AND THREE PROJECTORS LIGHT UP AN IMAX-STYLE SCREEN WITH A SWEEPING AERIAL SHOT OF THE GOLAN HEIGHTS IN FULL BLOOM.
THE GOLAN HEIGHTS...SINCE ISRAEL WON THIS LAND IN THE SIX DAY WAR IT HAS BEEN AN IMPORTANT PART OF THIS NATION'S LIFEBLOOD.
IT SUPPLIES ALMOST A THIRD OF ISRAEL'S WATER SUPPLY AND IS A CENTER OF AGRICULTURE AND HERDING.
NOT TO MENTION RECREATION!
FROM THE SNOWY PEAK OF MOUNT HERMON...
...TO THE WORLD-FAMOUS VALLEY WINERIES...
CLINK!
THE GOLAN HEIGHTS' UNIQUE TERRAIN SUPPORTS ITS OWN POPULATION OF 30,000 AS WELL AS THE THOUSANDS OF VISITORS WHO COME TO SEE ITS MAJESTY.
MOST IMPORTANT, ITS GEOGRAPHIC POSITION MAKES IT INDISPENSABLE TO THE NATION'S SECURITY. BEFORE THE WAR, SYRIA SENT ROCKET ATTACKS INTO ISRAELI VILLAGES BELOW.
SYRIA
ROCKETS
ISRAEL
AND NOW...SYRIA WANTS IT BACK. ISRAEL HAS TRIED TO COMPROMISE WITH THE SYRIAN GOVERNMENT...
SYRIA

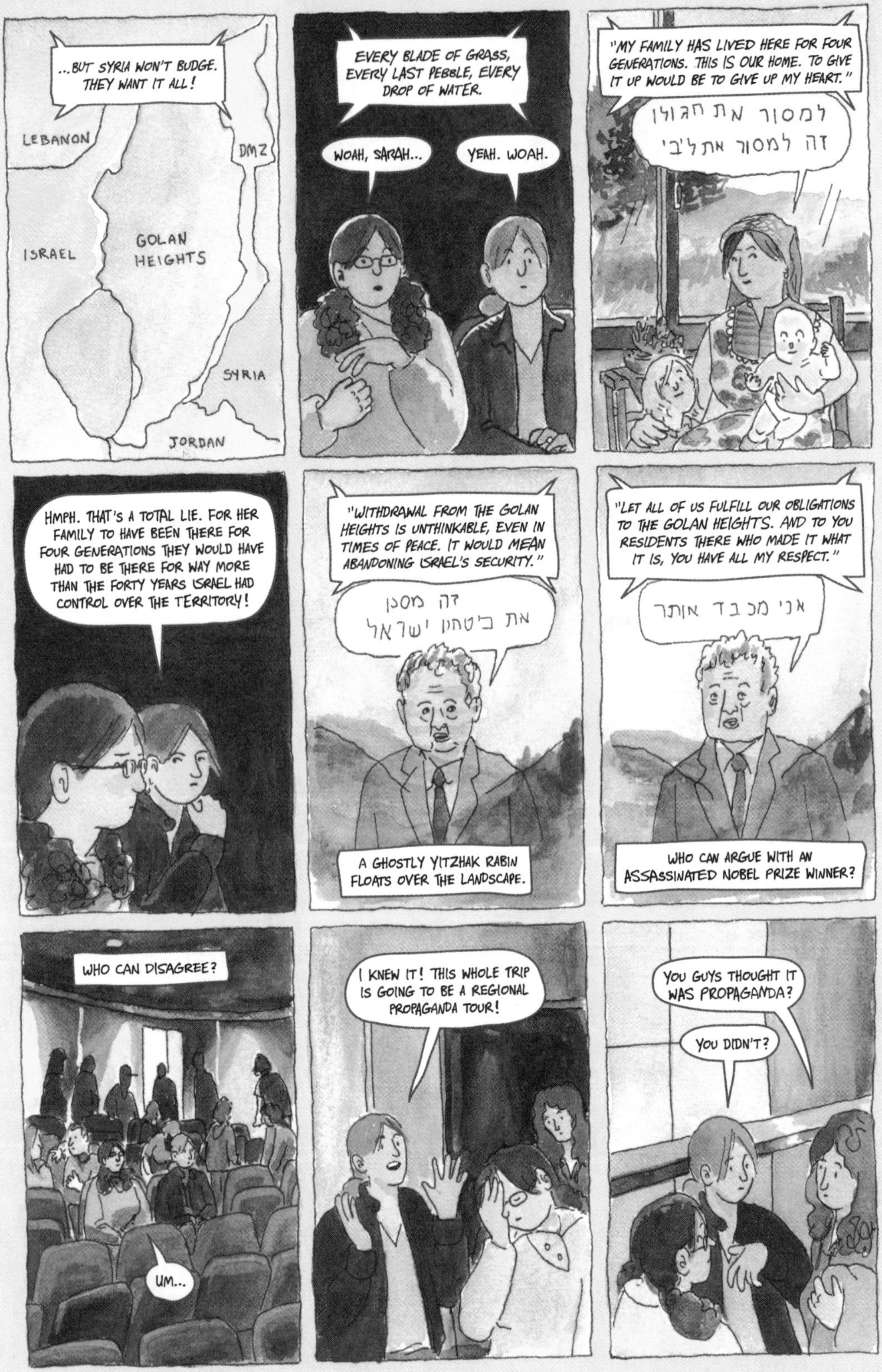
...BUT SYRIA WON'T BUDGE. THEY WANT IT ALL!
LEBANON
DMZ
ISRAEL
GOLAN HEIGHTS
SYRIA
JORDAN
EVERY BLADE OF GRASS, EVERY LAST PEBBLE, EVERY DROP OF WATER.
WOAH, SARAH...
YEAH. WOAH.
"MY FAMILY HAS LIVED HERE FOR FOUR GENERATIONS. THIS IS OUR HOME. TO GIVE IT UP WOULD BE TO GIVE UP MY HEART."
למסור את הגולן
זה למסור את לבי
HMPH. THAT'S A TOTAL LIE. FOR HER FAMILY TO HAVE BEEN THERE FOR FOUR GENERATIONS THEY WOULD HAVE HAD TO BE THERE FOR WAY MORE THAN THE FORTY YEARS ISRAEL HAD CONTROL OVER THE TERRITORY!
"WITHDRAWAL FROM THE GOLAN HEIGHTS IS UNTHINKABLE, EVEN IN TIMES OF PEACE. IT WOULD MEAN ABANDONING ISRAEL'S SECURITY."
זה מסכן
את ביטחון ישראל
A GHOSTLY YITZHAK RABIN FLOATS OVER THE LANDSCAPE.
"LET ALL OF US FULFILL OUR OBLIGATIONS TO THE GOLAN HEIGHTS. AND TO YOU RESIDENTS THERE WHO MADE IT WHAT IT IS, YOU HAVE ALL MY RESPECT."
אני מכבד אותך
WHO CAN ARGUE WITH AN ASSASSINATED NOBEL PRIZE WINNER?
WHO CAN DISAGREE?
UM...
I KNEW IT! THIS WHOLE TRIP IS GOING TO BE A REGIONAL PROPAGANDA TOUR!
YOU GUYS THOUGHT IT WAS PROPAGANDA?
YOU DIDN'T?

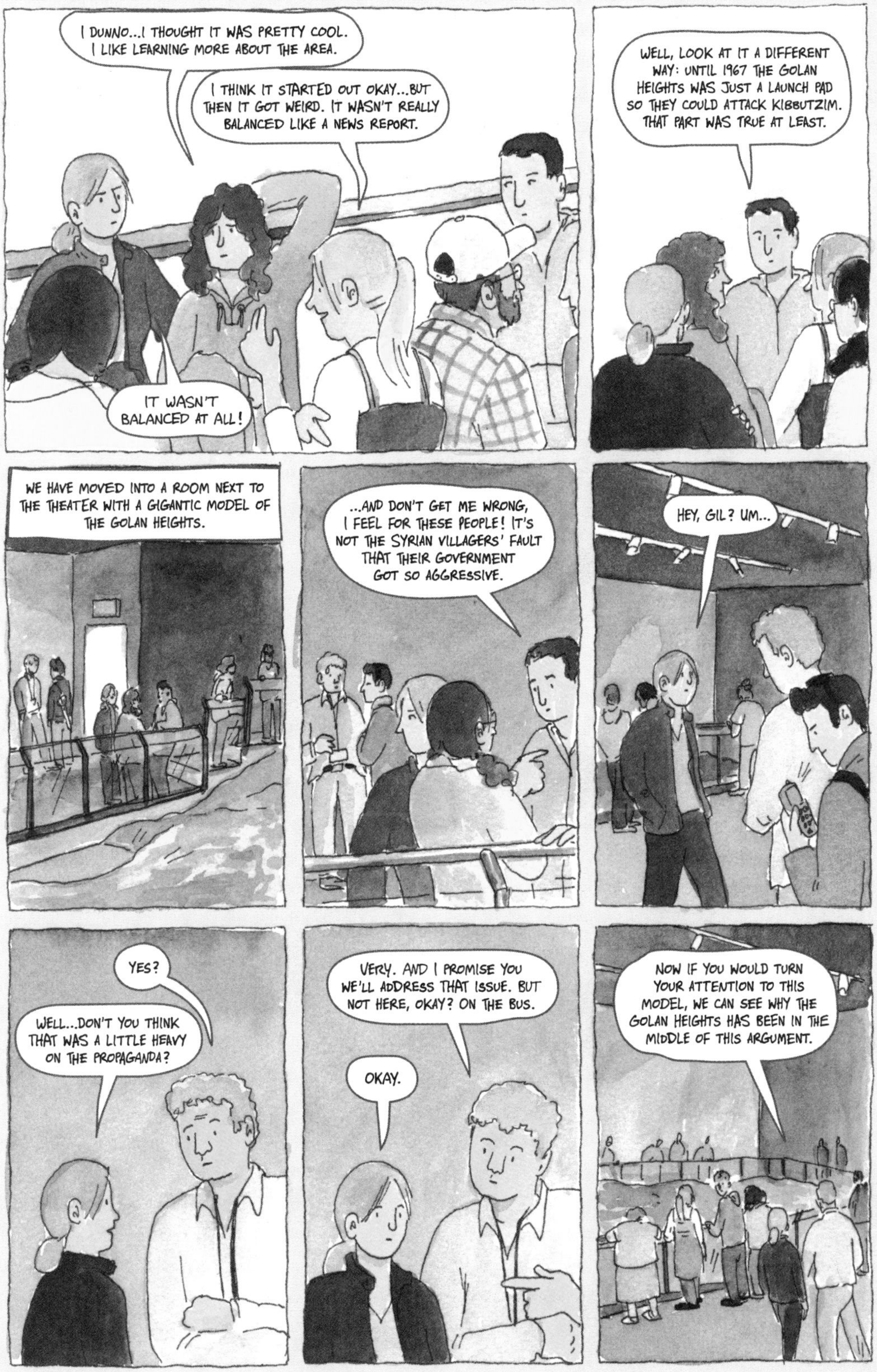
I DUNNO...I THOUGHT IT WAS PRETTY COOL. I LIKE LEARNING MORE ABOUT THE AREA.
I THINK IT STARTED OUT OKAY...BUT THEN IT GOT WEIRD. IT WASN'T REALLY BALANCED LIKE A NEWS REPORT.
IT WASN'T BALANCED AT ALL!
WELL, LOOK AT IT A DIFFERENT WAY: UNTIL 1967 THE GOLAN HEIGHTS WAS JUST A LAUNCH PAD SO THEY COULD ATTACK KIBBUTZIM. THAT PART WAS TRUE AT LEAST.
WE HAVE MOVED INTO A ROOM NEXT TO THE THEATER WITH A GIGANTIC MODEL OF THE GOLAN HEIGHTS.
...AND DON'T GET ME WRONG, I FEEL FOR THESE PEOPLE! IT'S NOT THE SYRIAN VILLAGERS' FAULT THAT THEIR GOVERNMENT GOT SO AGGRESSIVE.
HEY, GIL? UM...
YES?
WELL...DON'T YOU THINK THAT WAS A LITTLE HEAVY ON THE PROPAGANDA?
VERY. AND I PROMISE YOU WE'LL ADDRESS THAT ISSUE. BUT NOT HERE, OKAY? ON THE BUS.
OKAY.
NOW IF YOU WOULD TURN YOUR ATTENTION TO THIS MODEL, WE CAN SEE WHY THE GOLAN HEIGHTS HAS BEEN IN THE MIDDLE OF THIS ARGUMENT.

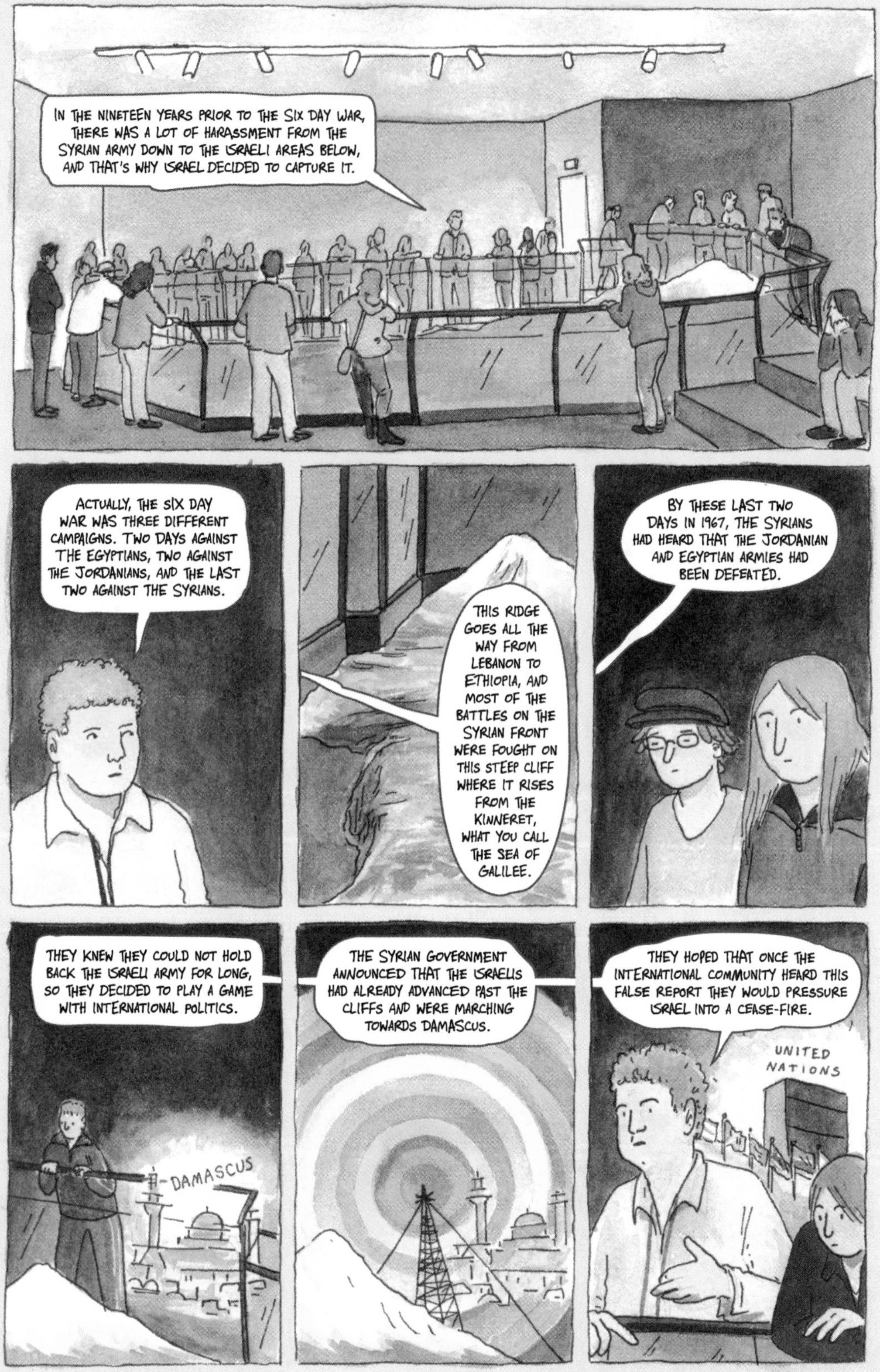
IN THE NINETEEN YEARS PRIOR TO THE SIX DAY WAR, THERE WAS A LOT OF HARASSMENT FROM THE SYRIAN ARMY DOWN TO THE ISRAELI AREAS BELOW, AND THAT'S WHY ISRAEL DECIDED TO CAPTURE IT.
ACTUALLY, THE SIX DAY WAR WAS THREE DIFFERENT CAMPAIGNS. TWO DAYS AGAINST THE EGYPTIANS, TWO AGAINST THE JORDANIANS, AND THE LAST TWO AGAINST THE SYRIANS.
THIS RIDGE GOES ALL THE WAY FROM LEBANON TO ETHIOPIA, AND MOST OF THE BATTLES ON THE SYRIAN FRONT WERE FOUGHT ON THIS STEEP CLIFF WHERE IT RISES FROM THE KINNERET, WHAT YOU CALL THE SEA OF GALILEE.
BY THESE LAST TWO DAYS IN 1967, THE SYRIANS HAD HEARD THAT THE JORDANIAN AND EGYPTIAN ARMIES HAD BEEN DEFEATED.
THEY KNEW THEY COULD NOT HOLD BACK THE ISRAELI ARMY FOR LONG, SO THEY DECIDED TO PLAY A GAME WITH INTERNATIONAL POLITICS.
DAMASCUS
THE SYRIAN GOVERNMENT ANNOUNCED THAT THE ISRAELIS HAD ALREADY ADVANCED PAST THE CLIFFS AND WERE MARCHING TOWARDS DAMASCUS.
THEY HOPED THAT ONCE THE INTERNATIONAL COMMUNITY HEARD THIS FALSE REPORT THEY WOULD PRESSURE ISRAEL INTO A CEASE-FIRE.
UNITED NATIONS

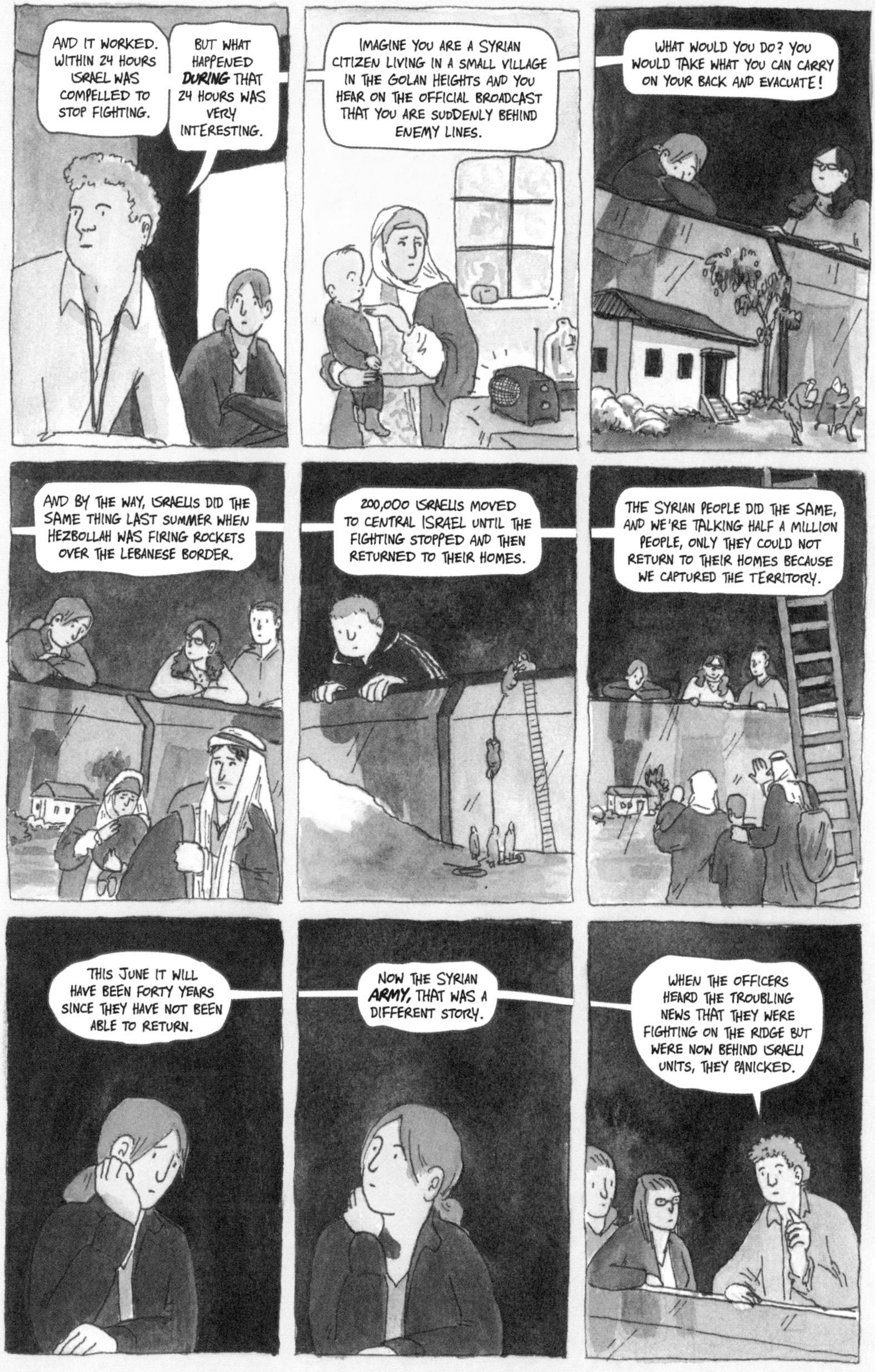
AND IT WORKED. WITHIN 24 HOURS ISRAEL WAS COMPELLED TO STOP FIGHTING.
BUT WHAT HAPPENED DURING THAT 24 HOURS WAS VERY INTERESTING.
IMAGINE YOU ARE A SYRIAN CITIZEN LIVING IN A SMALL VILLAGE IN THE GOLAN HEIGHTS AND YOU HEAR ON THE OFFICIAL BROADCAST THAT YOU ARE SUDDENLY BEHIND ENEMY LINES.
WHAT WOULD YOU DO? YOU WOULD TAKE WHAT YOU CAN CARRY ON YOUR BACK AND EVACUATE!
AND BY THE WAY, ISRAELIS DID THE SAME THING LAST SUMMER WHEN HEZBOLLAH WAS FIRING ROCKETS OVER THE LEBANESE BORDER.
200,000 ISRAELIS MOVED TO CENTRAL ISRAEL UNTIL THE FIGHTING STOPPED AND THEN RETURNED TO THEIR HOMES.
THE SYRIAN PEOPLE DID THE SAME, AND WE'RE TALKING HALF A MILLION PEOPLE, ONLY THEY COULD NOT RETURN TO THEIR HOMES BECAUSE WE CAPTURED THE TERRITORY.
THIS JUNE IT WILL HAVE BEEN FORTY YEARS SINCE THEY HAVE NOT BEEN ABLE TO RETURN.
NOW THE SYRIAN ARMY, THAT WAS A DIFFERENT STORY.
WHEN THE OFFICERS HEARD THE TROUBLING NEWS THAT THEY WERE FIGHTING ON THE RIDGE BUT WERE NOW BEHIND ISRAELI UNITS, THEY PANICKED.

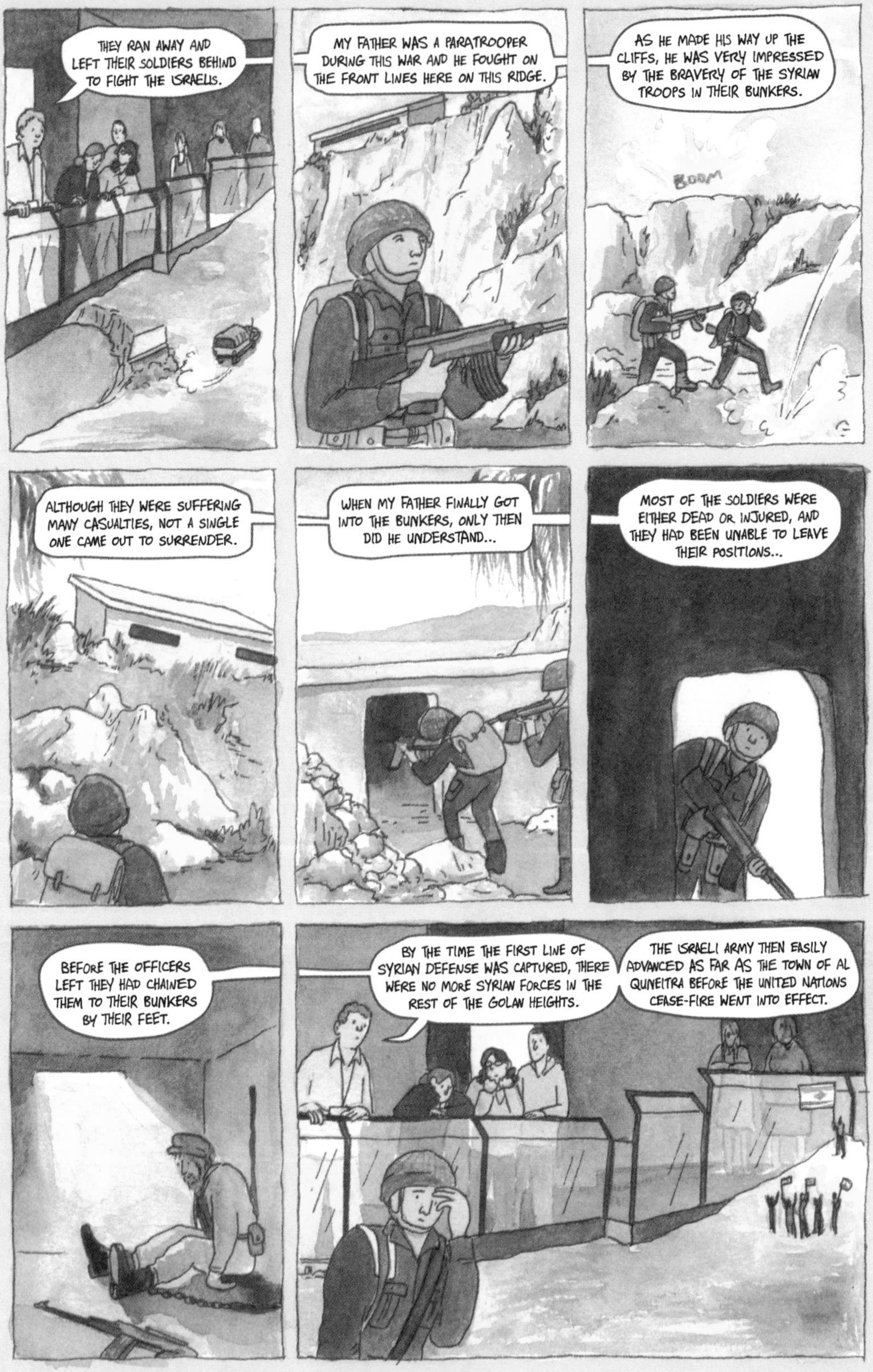
THEY RAN AWAY AND LEFT THEIR SOLDIERS BEHIND TO FIGHT THE ISRAELIS.
MY FATHER WAS A PARATROOPER DURING THIS WAR AND HE FOUGHT ON THE FRONT LINES HERE ON THIS RIDGE.
AS HE MADE HIS WAY UP THE CLIFFS, HE WAS VERY IMPRESSED BY THE BRAVERY OF THE SYRIAN TROOPS IN THEIR BUNKERS.
BOOM
ALTHOUGH THEY WERE SUFFERING MANY CASUALTIES, NOT A SINGLE ONE CAME OUT TO SURRENDER.
WHEN MY FATHER FINALLY GOT INTO THE BUNKERS, ONLY THEN DID HE UNDERSTAND...
MOST OF THE SOLDIERS WERE EITHER DEAD OR INJURED, AND THEY HAD BEEN UNABLE TO LEAVE THEIR POSITIONS...
BEFORE THE OFFICERS LEFT THEY HAD CHAINED THEM TO THEIR BUNKERS BY THEIR FEET.
BY THE TIME THE FIRST LINE OF SYRIAN DEFENSE WAS CAPTURED, THERE WERE NO MORE SYRIAN FORCES IN THE REST OF THE GOLAN HEIGHTS.
THE ISRAELI ARMY THEN EASILY ADVANCED AS FAR AS THE TOWN OF AL QUNEITRA BEFORE THE UNITED NATIONS CEASE-FIRE WENT INTO EFFECT.

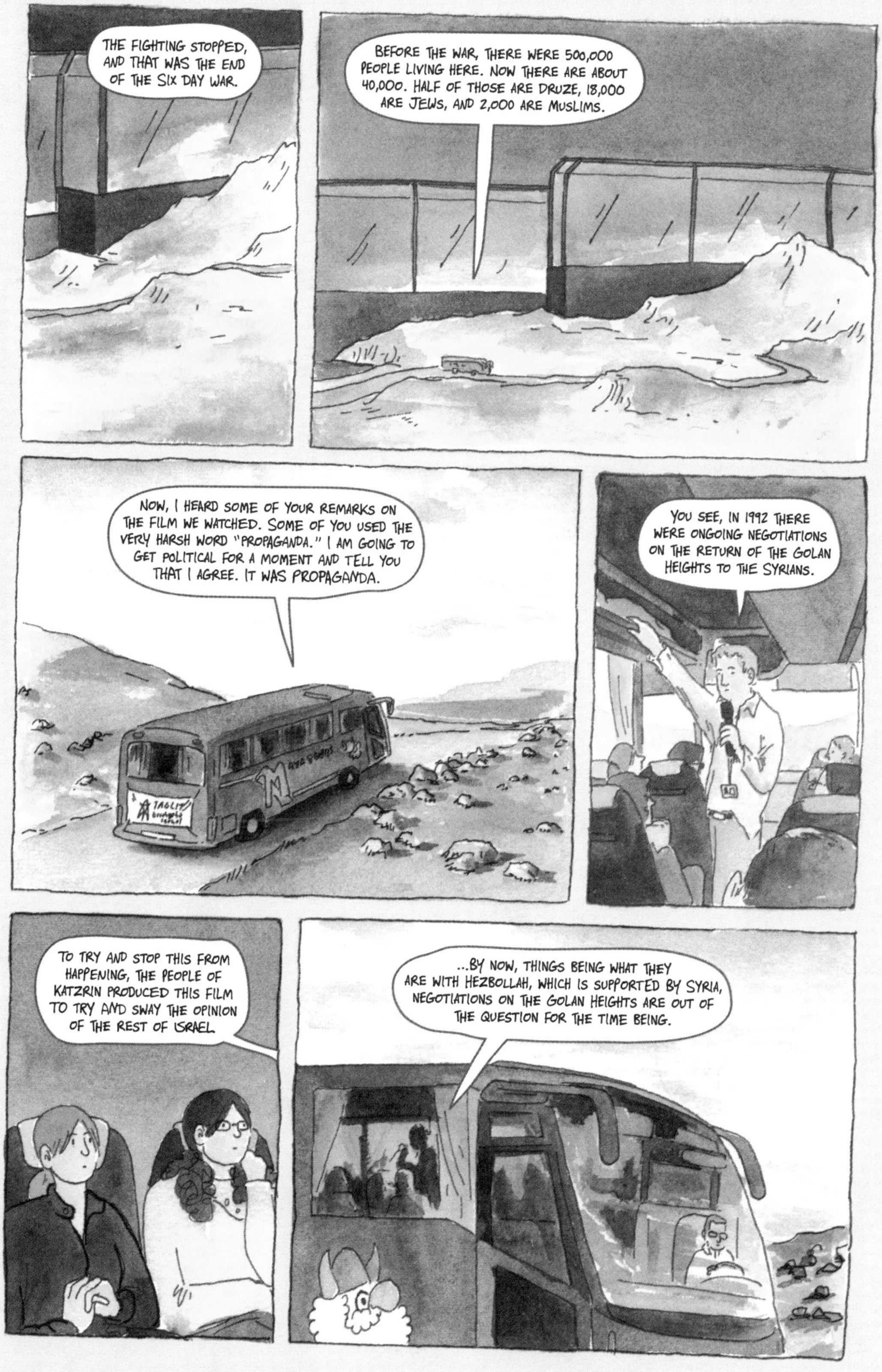
THE FIGHTING STOPPED, AND THAT WAS THE END OF THE SIX DAY WAR.
BEFORE THE WAR, THERE WERE 500,000 PEOPLE LIVING HERE. NOW THERE ARE ABOUT 40,000. HALF OF THOSE ARE DRUZE, 18,000 ARE JEWS, AND 2,000 ARE MUSLIMS.
NOW, I HEARD SOME OF YOUR REMARKS ON THE FILM WE WATCHED. SOME OF YOU USED THE VERY HARSH WORD "PROPAGANDA." I AM GOING TO GET POLITICAL FOR A MOMENT AND TELL YOU THAT I AGREE. IT WAS PROPAGANDA.
YOU SEE, IN 1992 THERE WERE ONGOING NEGOTIATIONS ON THE RETURN OF THE GOLAN HEIGHTS TO THE SYRIANS.
TO TRY AND STOP THIS FROM HAPPENING, THE PEOPLE OF KATZRIN PRODUCED THIS FILM TO TRY AND SWAY THE OPINION OF THE REST OF ISRAEL.
...BY NOW, THINGS BEING WHAT THEY ARE WITH HEZBOLLAH, WHICH IS SUPPORTED BY SYRIA, NEGOTIATIONS ON THE GOLAN HEIGHTS ARE OUT OF THE QUESTION FOR THE TIME BEING.

SAMMY HARKHAM

Blood of the Virgin (Excerpt)

from *Crickets*

FOR ME, DRAWING COMICS IS
Fun and terrifying!

THE SELECTION
Blood of the Virgin takes place in Los Angeles in 1971. A young father and husband named Seymour gets a chance to jump rank as an editor at a tiny film company where he works to writing and producing a screenplay he wrote.

THE CONTEXT
Earlier in the story, Seymour has sold his script, *Blood of the Virgin*, to the film company he works for as an editor. Despite his requests, they won't let him direct it but have agreed to let him be one of the producers. Production is slated to start in a couple weeks.

AWARDS
2008 Ignatz Award for Best Anthology for *Kramer's Ergot* 8.

WHAT I'M KNOWN FOR
Editor of *Kramer's Ergot*, and of Bart Simpson's "Treehouse of Horror #15."

WHERE I LIVE
Los Angeles, California.

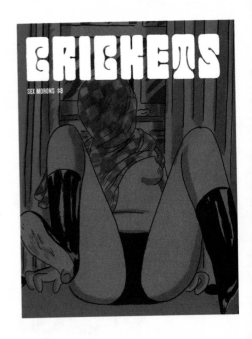

DON'T YOU WANT TO EAT? AREN'T YOU HUNGRY?

IS JUNIOR STILL AWAKE?

HE'S ASLEEP. YOU KNOW HE'S ASLEEP. YOU'RE AN HOUR LATE.

I SAID I WAS SORRY.

HERE.

EAT.

CHEW

THIS IS COLD.

I'M NOT EATING THIS.

WHAT THE FUCK HAVE YOU DONE TODAY? I WORKED. DINNER IS NOT MY JOB.

YOU'RE A MORON.

"YOU SHOULDN'T SMOKE IN THE HOUSE!"

GO FUCK YOURSELF.

BYE!

WHERE'D YOU PUT THE REMOTE?

GO IN THE STINKY COUNTRY HA HA

WHAT'S THAT?

THE NEW ISSUE!

FANTACINE

FALL '71

HORROR OF FRAN...

THEY RAN MY REVIEW!

FLIP

THEY CHANGED EVERY WORD!

109

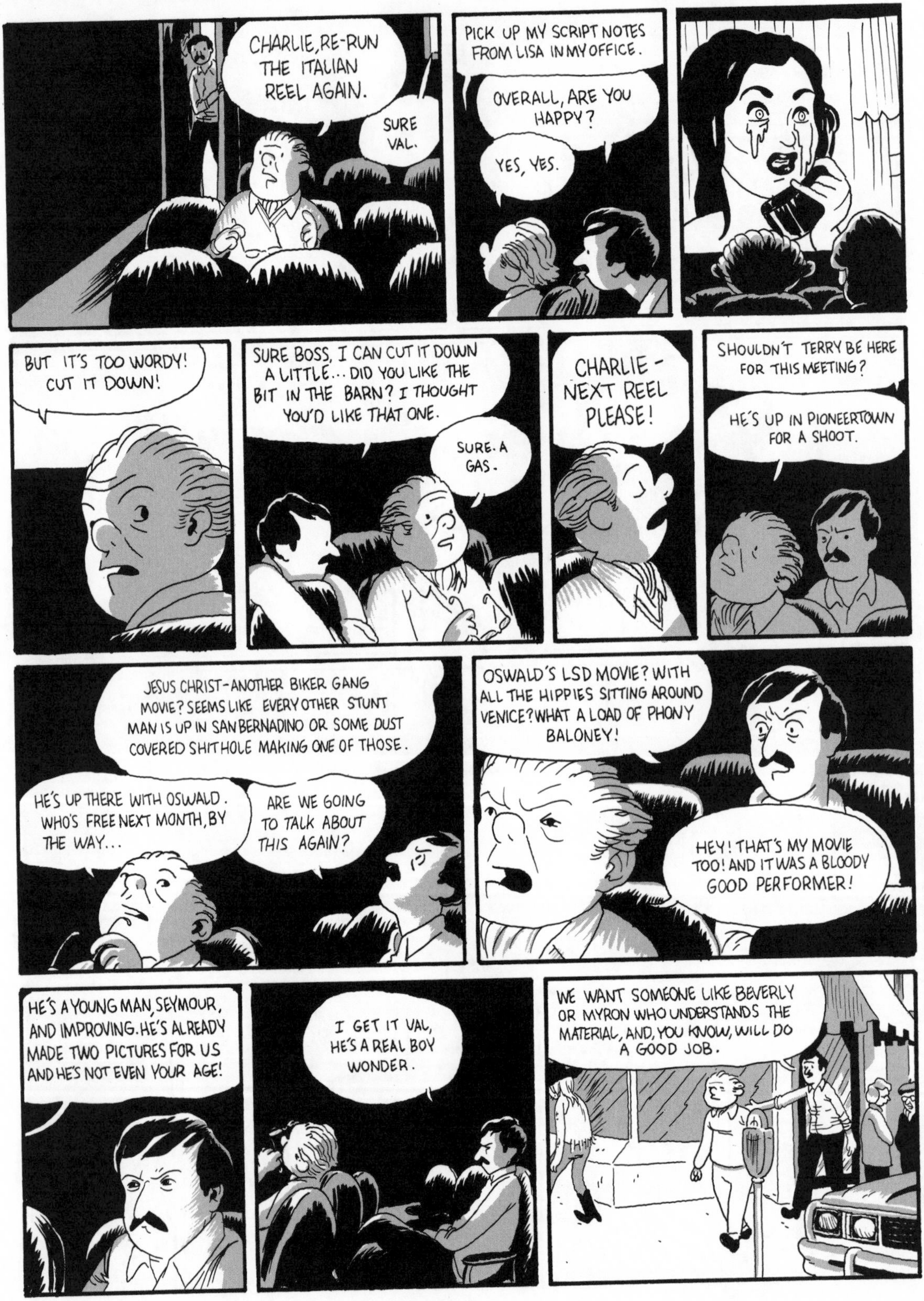

CHARLIE, RE-RUN THE ITALIAN REEL AGAIN.
SURE VAL.
PICK UP MY SCRIPT NOTES FROM LISA IN MY OFFICE.
OVERALL, ARE YOU HAPPY?
YES, YES.
BUT IT'S TOO WORDY! CUT IT DOWN!
SURE BOSS, I CAN CUT IT DOWN A LITTLE... DID YOU LIKE THE BIT IN THE BARN? I THOUGHT YOU'D LIKE THAT ONE.
SURE. A GAS.
CHARLIE - NEXT REEL PLEASE!
SHOULDN'T TERRY BE HERE FOR THIS MEETING?
HE'S UP IN PIONEERTOWN FOR A SHOOT.
JESUS CHRIST-ANOTHER BIKER GANG MOVIE? SEEMS LIKE EVERY OTHER STUNT MAN IS UP IN SAN BERNADINO OR SOME DUST COVERED SHITHOLE MAKING ONE OF THOSE.
HE'S UP THERE WITH OSWALD. WHO'S FREE NEXT MONTH, BY THE WAY...
ARE WE GOING TO TALK ABOUT THIS AGAIN?
OSWALD'S LSD MOVIE? WITH ALL THE HIPPIES SITTING AROUND VENICE? WHAT A LOAD OF PHONY BALONEY!
HEY! THAT'S MY MOVIE TOO! AND IT WAS A BLOODY GOOD PERFORMER!
HE'S A YOUNG MAN, SEYMOUR, AND IMPROVING. HE'S ALREADY MADE TWO PICTURES FOR US AND HE'S NOT EVEN YOUR AGE!
I GET IT VAL, HE'S A REAL BOY WONDER.
WE WANT SOMEONE LIKE BEVERLY OR MYRON WHO UNDERSTANDS THE MATERIAL, AND, YOU KNOW, WILL DO A GOOD JOB.

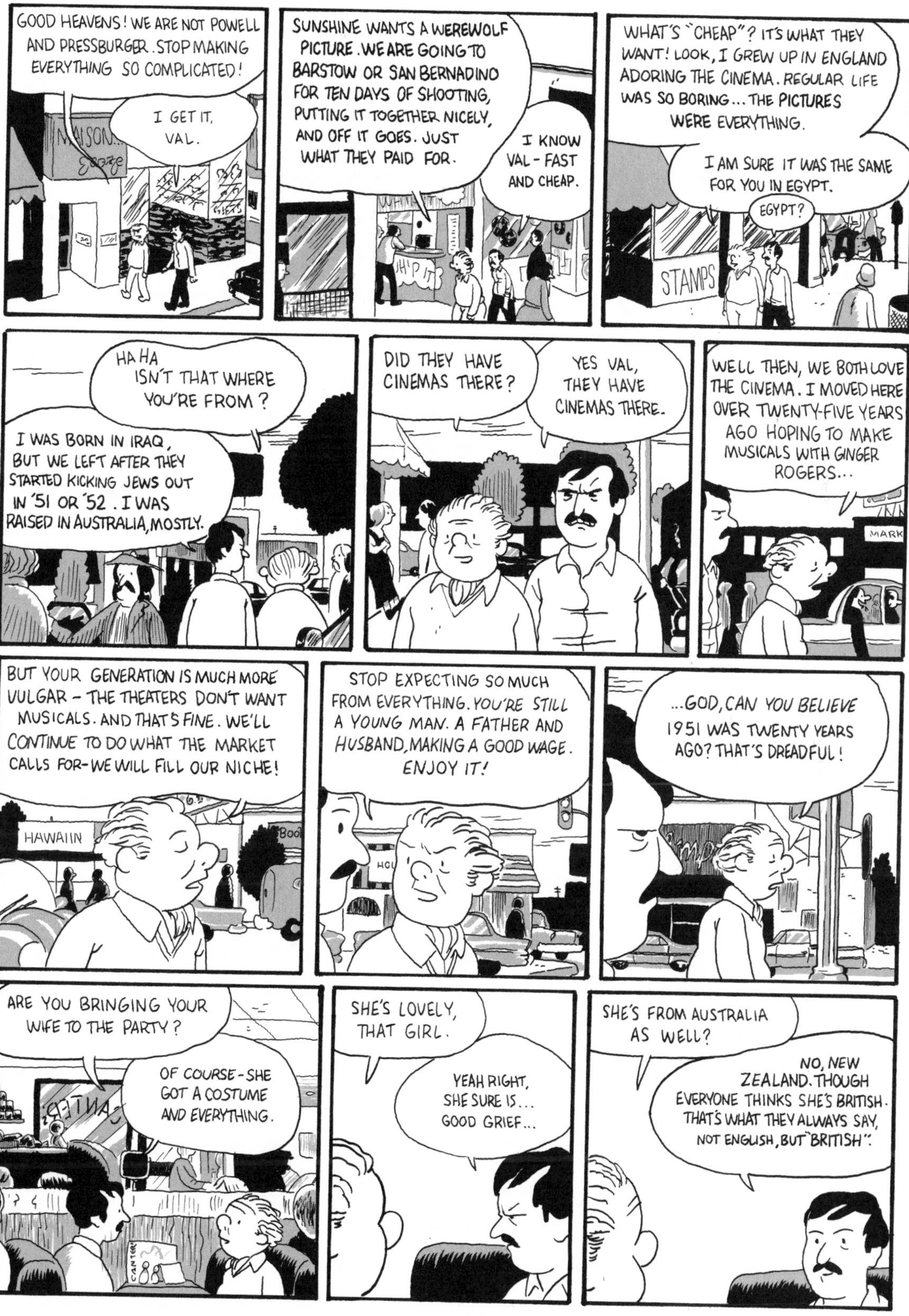
GOOD HEAVENS! WE ARE NOT POWELL AND PRESSBURGER. STOP MAKING EVERYTHING SO COMPLICATED!
I GET IT, VAL.
SUNSHINE WANTS A WEREWOLF PICTURE. WE ARE GOING TO BARSTOW OR SAN BERNADINO FOR TEN DAYS OF SHOOTING, PUTTING IT TOGETHER NICELY, AND OFF IT GOES. JUST WHAT THEY PAID FOR.
I KNOW VAL - FAST AND CHEAP.
WHAT'S "CHEAP"? IT'S WHAT THEY WANT! LOOK, I GREW UP IN ENGLAND ADORING THE CINEMA. REGULAR LIFE WAS SO BORING... THE PICTURES WERE EVERYTHING.
I AM SURE IT WAS THE SAME FOR YOU IN EGYPT.
EGYPT?
STAMPS
HA HA ISN'T THAT WHERE YOU'RE FROM?
I WAS BORN IN IRAQ, BUT WE LEFT AFTER THEY STARTED KICKING JEWS OUT IN '51 OR '52. I WAS RAISED IN AUSTRALIA, MOSTLY.
DID THEY HAVE CINEMAS THERE?
YES VAL, THEY HAVE CINEMAS THERE.
WELL THEN, WE BOTH LOVE THE CINEMA. I MOVED HERE OVER TWENTY-FIVE YEARS AGO HOPING TO MAKE MUSICALS WITH GINGER ROGERS...
BUT YOUR GENERATION IS MUCH MORE VULGAR - THE THEATERS DON'T WANT MUSICALS. AND THAT'S FINE. WE'LL CONTINUE TO DO WHAT THE MARKET CALLS FOR - WE WILL FILL OUR NICHE!
HAWAIIN
STOP EXPECTING SO MUCH FROM EVERYTHING. YOU'RE STILL A YOUNG MAN. A FATHER AND HUSBAND, MAKING A GOOD WAGE. ENJOY IT!
...GOD, CAN YOU BELIEVE 1951 WAS TWENTY YEARS AGO? THAT'S DREADFUL!
ARE YOU BRINGING YOUR WIFE TO THE PARTY?
OF COURSE - SHE GOT A COSTUME AND EVERYTHING.
SHE'S LOVELY, THAT GIRL.
YEAH RIGHT, SHE SURE IS... GOOD GRIEF...
SHE'S FROM AUSTRALIA AS WELL?
NO, NEW ZEALAND. THOUGH EVERYONE THINKS SHE'S BRITISH. THAT'S WHAT THEY ALWAYS SAY, NOT ENGLISH, BUT "BRITISH".

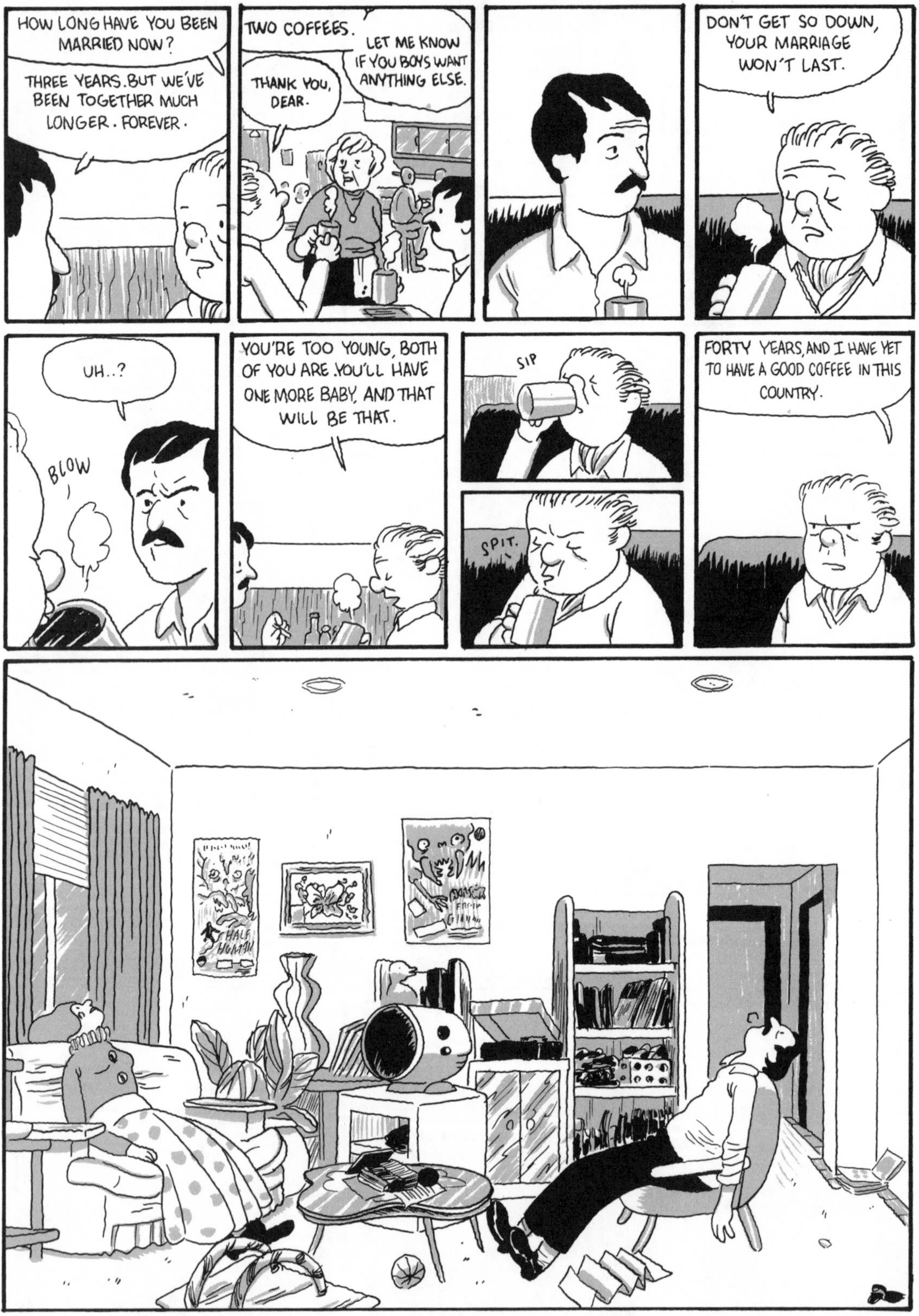
HOW LONG HAVE YOU BEEN MARRIED NOW?
THREE YEARS. BUT WE'VE BEEN TOGETHER MUCH LONGER. FOREVER.
TWO COFFEES.
LET ME KNOW IF YOU BOYS WANT ANYTHING ELSE.
THANK YOU, DEAR.
DON'T GET SO DOWN, YOUR MARRIAGE WON'T LAST.
UH..?
BLOW
YOU'RE TOO YOUNG, BOTH OF YOU ARE. YOU'LL HAVE ONE MORE BABY, AND THAT WILL BE THAT.
SIP
SPIT.
FORTY YEARS, AND I HAVE YET TO HAVE A GOOD COFFEE IN THIS COUNTRY.

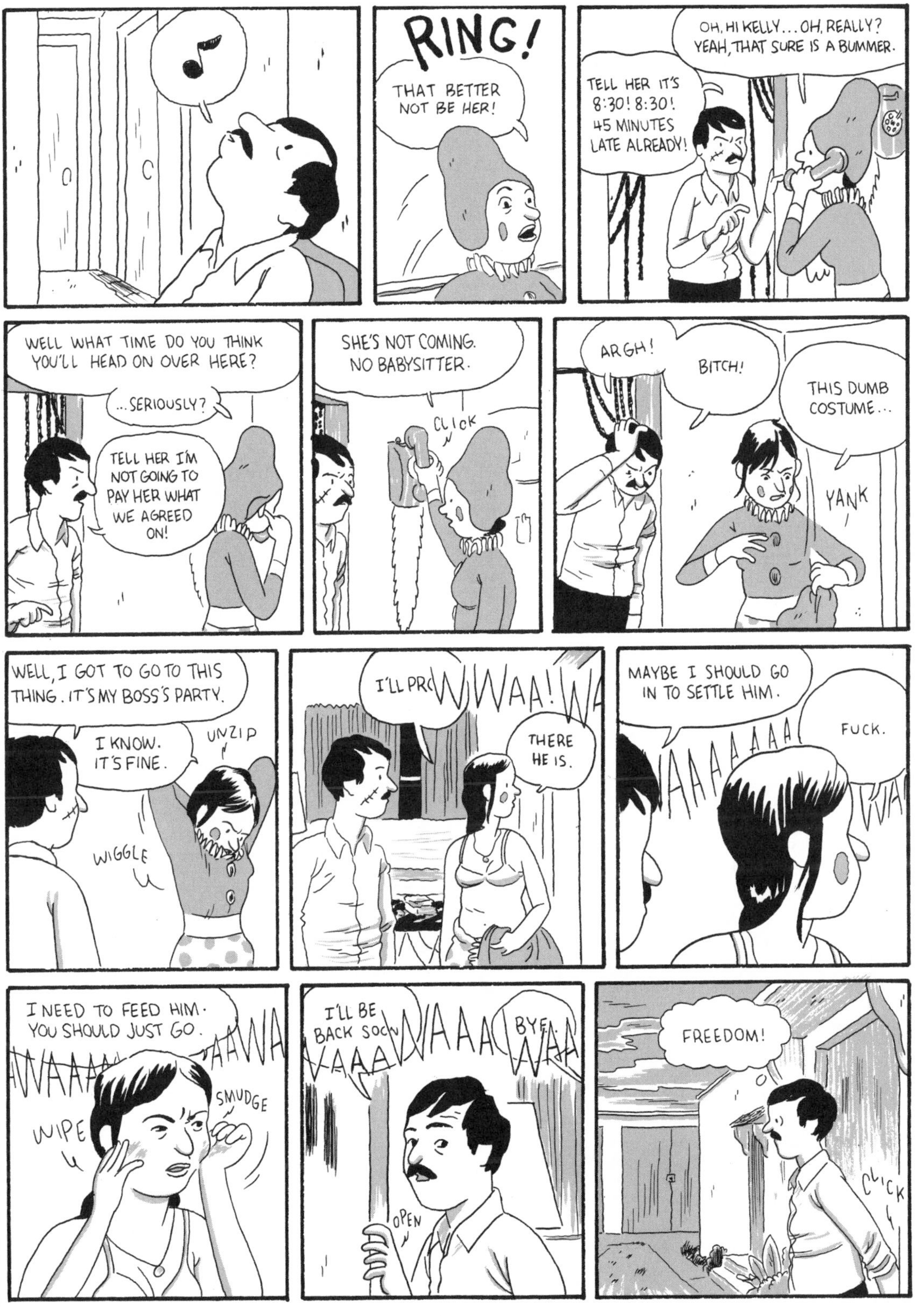
RING!
THAT BETTER NOT BE HER!
OH, HI KELLY... OH, REALLY? YEAH, THAT SURE IS A BUMMER.
TELL HER IT'S 8:30! 8:30! 45 MINUTES LATE ALREADY!
WELL WHAT TIME DO YOU THINK YOU'LL HEAD ON OVER HERE?
...SERIOUSLY?
TELL HER I'M NOT GOING TO PAY HER WHAT WE AGREED ON!
SHE'S NOT COMING. NO BABYSITTER.
CLICK
ARGH!
BITCH!
THIS DUMB COSTUME...
YANK
WELL, I GOT TO GO TO THIS THING. IT'S MY BOSS'S PARTY.
I KNOW. IT'S FINE.
UNZIP
WIGGLE
I'LL PR
WWAA! WA
THERE HE IS.
MAYBE I SHOULD GO IN TO SETTLE HIM.
AAAAAAA
FUCK.
WA
I NEED TO FEED HIM. YOU SHOULD JUST GO.
WAAAAA
AAWA
WIPE
SMUDGE
I'LL BE BACK SOO
WAAA
VAAA
BYE.
WAA
OPEN
FREEDOM!
CLICK

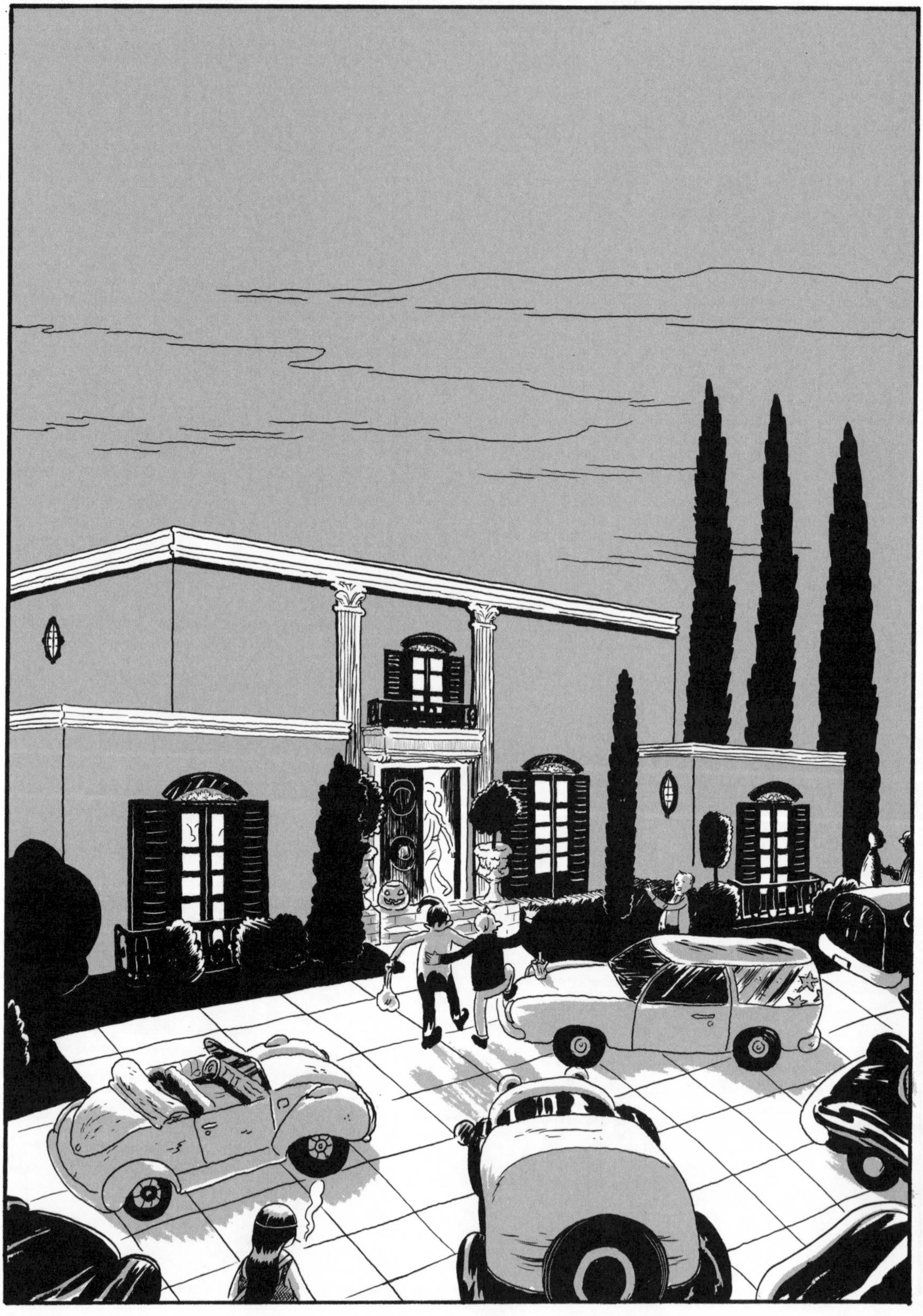

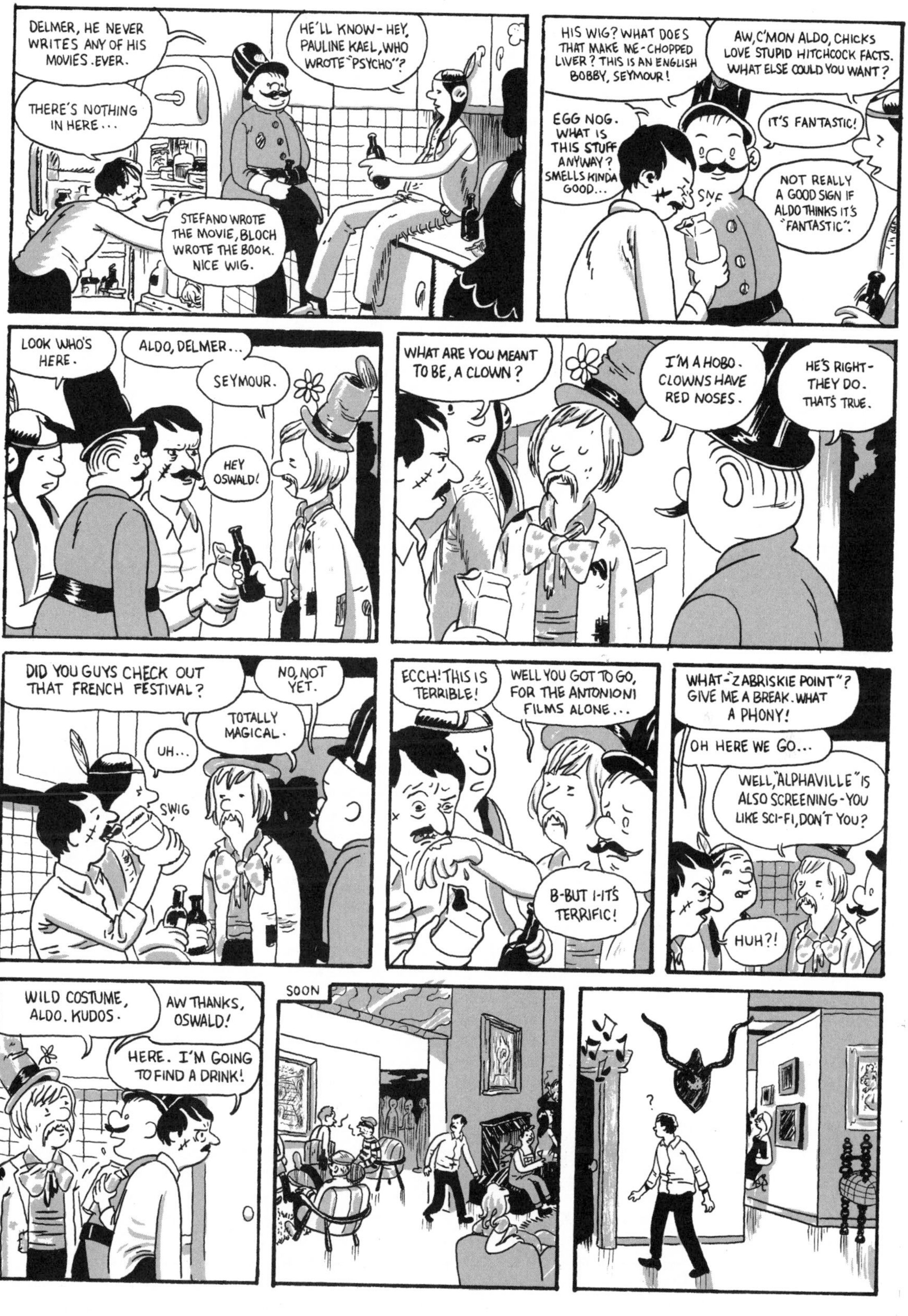

DELMER, HE NEVER WRITES ANY OF HIS MOVIES. EVER.
HE'LL KNOW- HEY, PAULINE KAEL, WHO WROTE "PSYCHO"?
THERE'S NOTHING IN HERE...
STEFANO WROTE THE MOVIE, BLOCH WROTE THE BOOK. NICE WIG.
HIS WIG? WHAT DOES THAT MAKE ME- CHOPPED LIVER? THIS IS AN ENGLISH BOBBY, SEYMOUR!
AW, C'MON ALDO, CHICKS LOVE STUPID HITCHCOCK FACTS. WHAT ELSE COULD YOU WANT?
EGG NOG. WHAT IS THIS STUFF ANYWAY? SMELLS KINDA GOOD...
SNF
IT'S FANTASTIC!
NOT REALLY A GOOD SIGN IF ALDO THINKS IT'S "FANTASTIC".
LOOK WHO'S HERE.
ALDO, DELMER...
SEYMOUR.
HEY OSWALD!
WHAT ARE YOU MEANT TO BE, A CLOWN?
I'M A HOBO. CLOWNS HAVE RED NOSES.
HE'S RIGHT- THEY DO. THAT'S TRUE.
DID YOU GUYS CHECK OUT THAT FRENCH FESTIVAL?
NO, NOT YET.
TOTALLY MAGICAL.
UH...
SWIG
ECCH! THIS IS TERRIBLE!
WELL YOU GOT TO GO, FOR THE ANTONIONI FILMS ALONE...
B-BUT I-IT'S TERRIFIC!
WHAT- "ZABRISKIE POINT"? GIVE ME A BREAK. WHAT A PHONY!
OH HERE WE GO...
WELL, "ALPHAVILLE" IS ALSO SCREENING- YOU LIKE SCI-FI, DON'T YOU?
HUH?!
WILD COSTUME, ALDO. KUDOS.
AW THANKS, OSWALD!
HERE. I'M GOING TO FIND A DRINK!
SOON
?

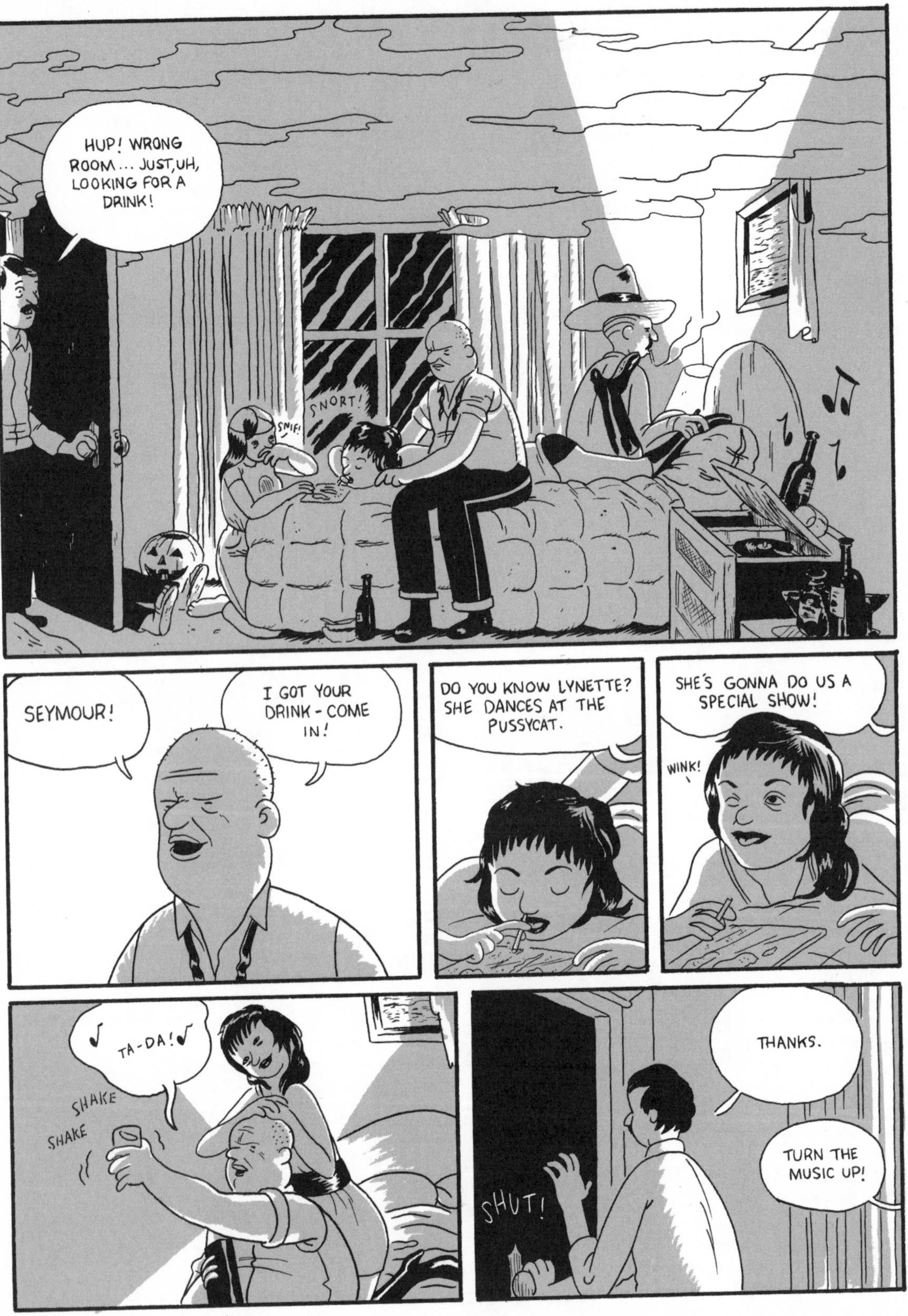
HUP! WRONG ROOM... JUST, UH, LOOKING FOR A DRINK!
SNIF!
SNORT!
SEYMOUR!
I GOT YOUR DRINK - COME IN!
DO YOU KNOW LYNETTE? SHE DANCES AT THE PUSSYCAT.
SHE'S GONNA DO US A SPECIAL SHOW!
WINK!
TA-DA!
SHAKE
SHAKE
THANKS.
TURN THE MUSIC UP!
SHUT!

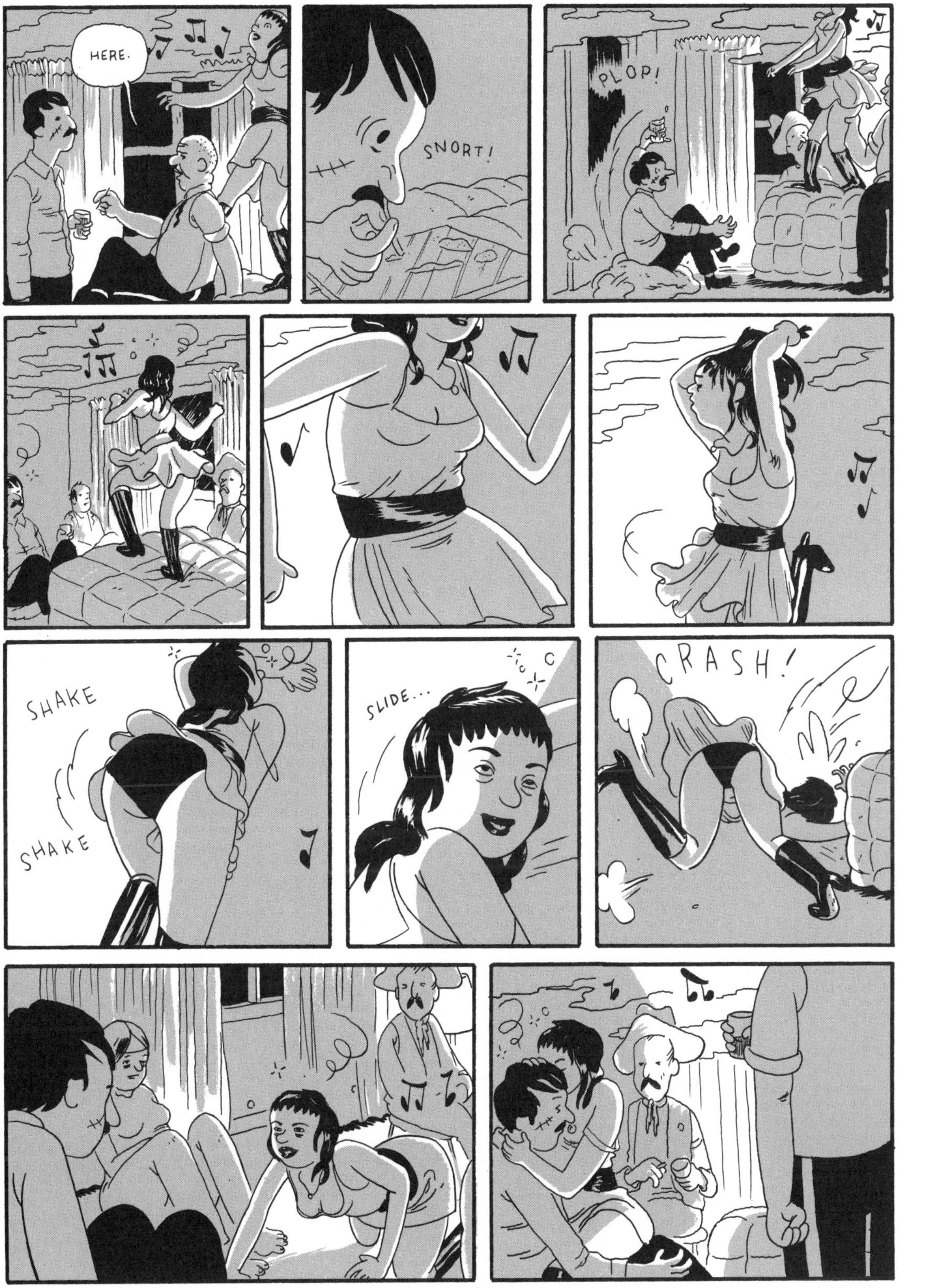
HERE.
SNORT!
PLOP!
SHAKE
SHAKE
SLIDE...
CRASH!

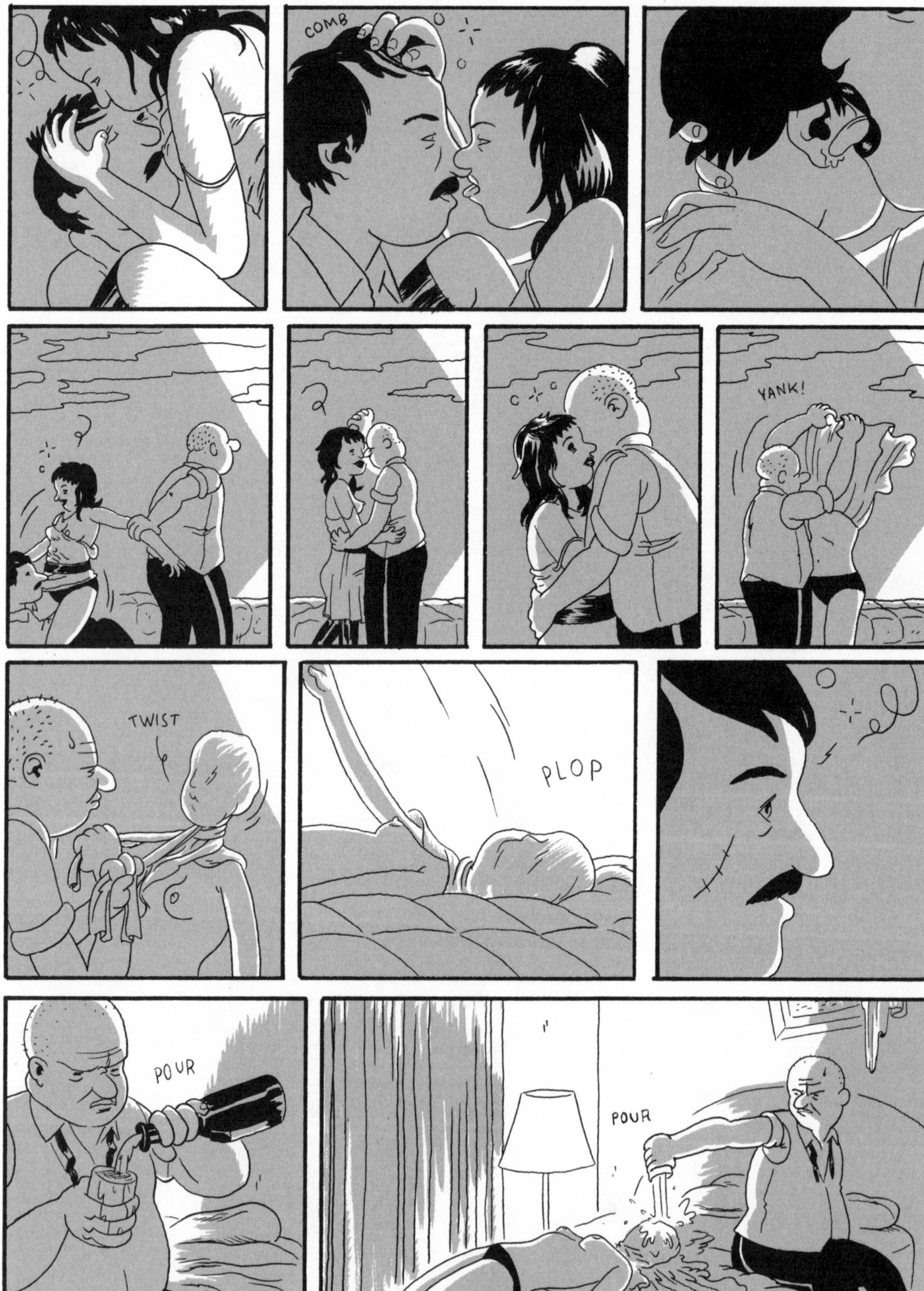
COMB
YANK!
TWIST
PLOP
POUR
POUR

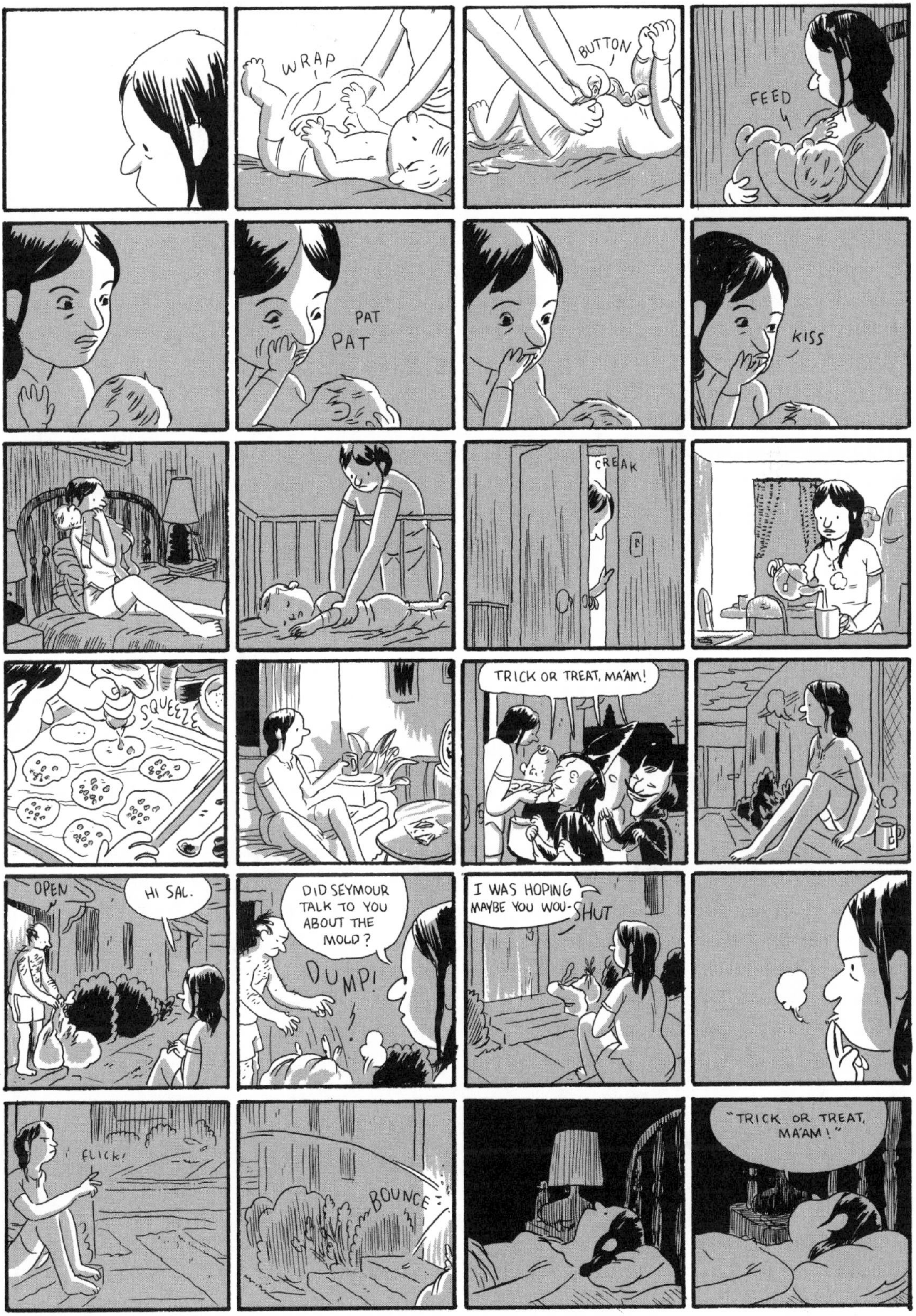

WRAP
BUTTON
FEED
PAT
PAT
KISS
CREAK
SQUEEZE
TRICK OR TREAT, MA'AM!
OPEN
HI SAL.
DID SEYMOUR TALK TO YOU ABOUT THE MOLD?
DUMP!
I WAS HOPING MAYBE YOU WOU-
SHUT
FLICK!
BOUNCE
"TRICK OR TREAT, MA'AM!"

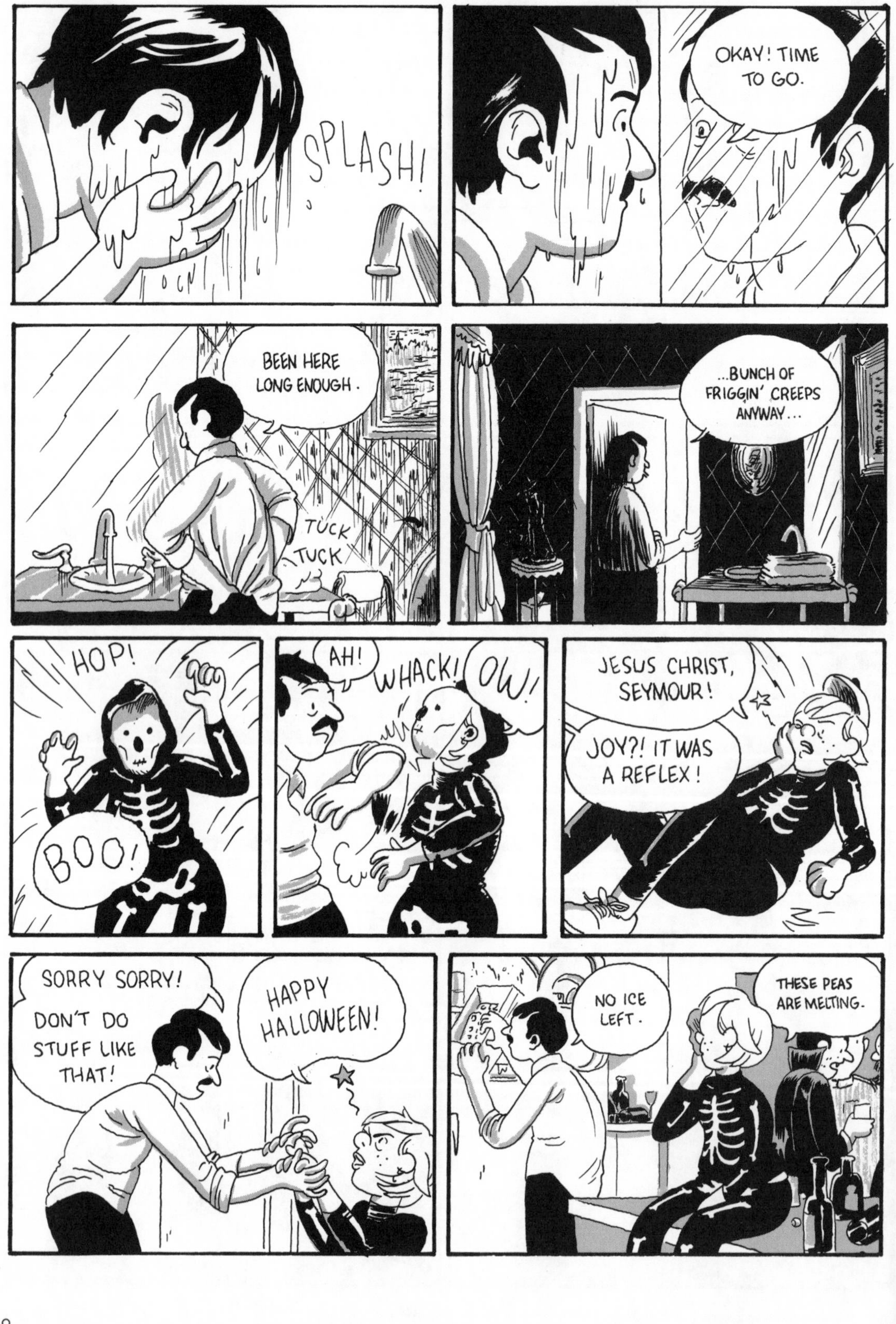
SPLASH!
OKAY! TIME TO GO.
BEEN HERE LONG ENOUGH.
TUCK
TUCK
...BUNCH OF FRIGGIN' CREEPS ANYWAY...
HOP!
BOO!
AH!
WHACK!
OW!
JESUS CHRIST, SEYMOUR!
JOY?! IT WAS A REFLEX!
SORRY SORRY!
DON'T DO STUFF LIKE THAT!
HAPPY HALLOWEEN!
NO ICE LEFT.
THESE PEAS ARE MELTING.

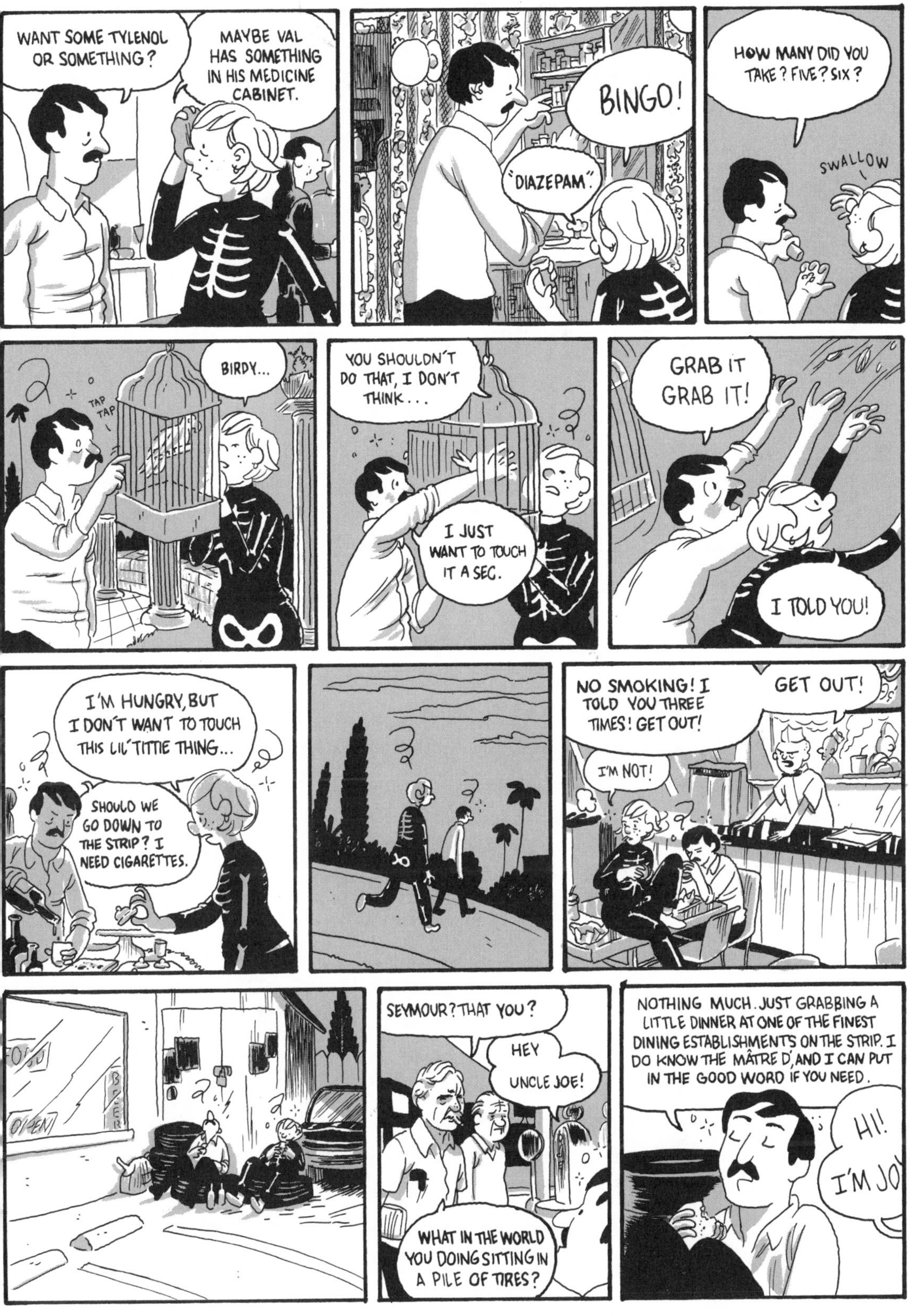
WANT SOME TYLENOL OR SOMETHING?
MAYBE VAL HAS SOMETHING IN HIS MEDICINE CABINET.
BINGO!
"DIAZEPAM."
HOW MANY DID YOU TAKE? FIVE? SIX?
SWALLOW
TAP TAP
BIRDY...
YOU SHOULDN'T DO THAT, I DON'T THINK...
I JUST WANT TO TOUCH IT A SEC.
GRAB IT GRAB IT!
I TOLD YOU!
I'M HUNGRY, BUT I DON'T WANT TO TOUCH THIS LIL' TITTIE THING...
SHOULD WE GO DOWN TO THE STRIP? I NEED CIGARETTES.
NO SMOKING! I TOLD YOU THREE TIMES! GET OUT!
GET OUT!
I'M NOT!
OPEN
SEYMOUR? THAT YOU?
HEY
UNCLE JOE!
WHAT IN THE WORLD YOU DOING SITTING IN A PILE OF TIRES?
NOTHING MUCH. JUST GRABBING A LITTLE DINNER AT ONE OF THE FINEST DINING ESTABLISHMENTS ON THE STRIP. I DO KNOW THE MÂTRE D', AND I CAN PUT IN THE GOOD WORD IF YOU NEED.
HI!
I'M JO

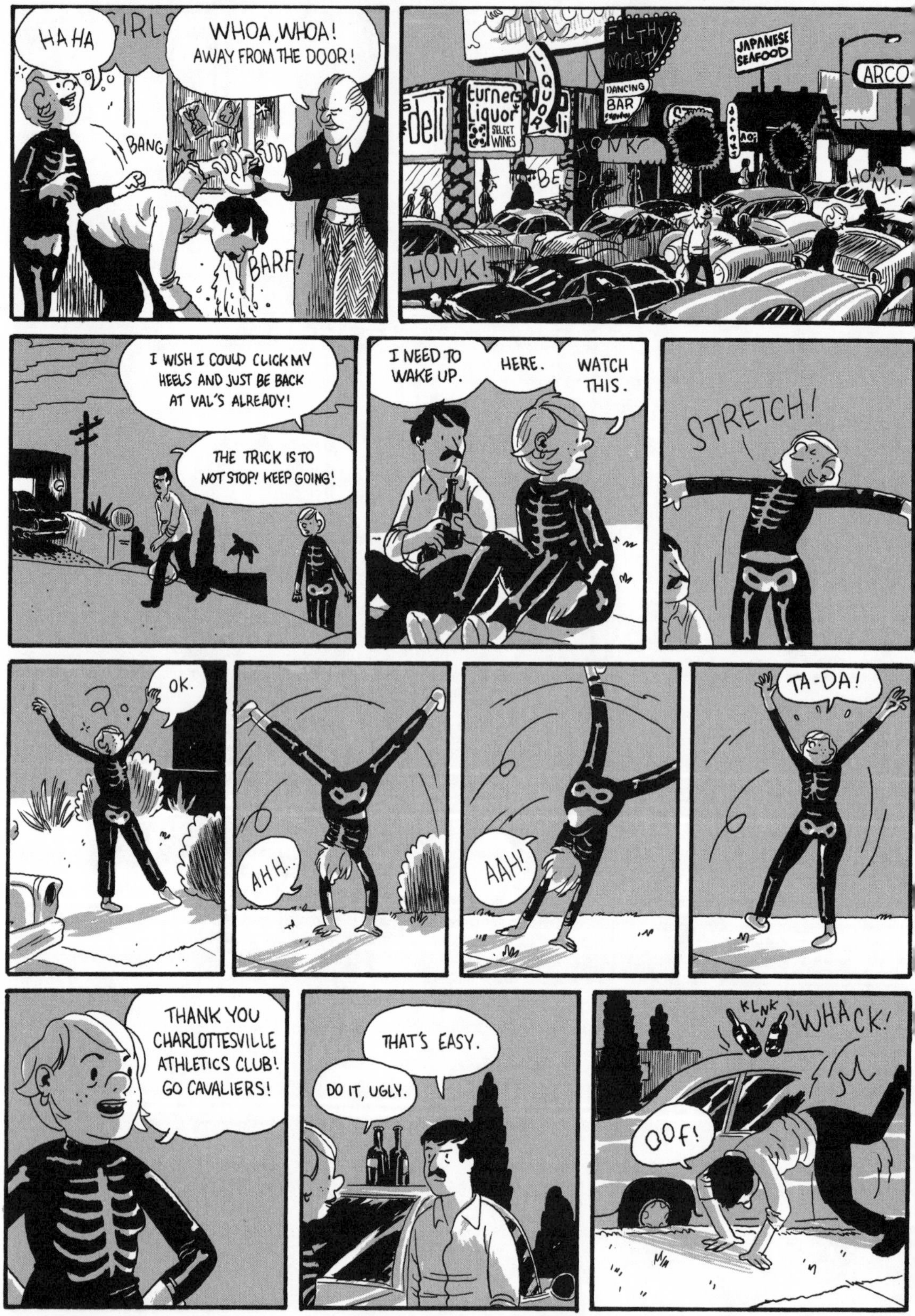
HA HA
GIRLS
WHOA, WHOA! AWAY FROM THE DOOR!
BANG!
BARF!
FILTHY McNasty
LIQUOR
JAPANESE SEAFOOD
ARCO
deli
turners Liquor SELECT WINES
DANCING BAR
HONK
BEEP!
HONK!
HONK!
I WISH I COULD CLICK MY HEELS AND JUST BE BACK AT VAL'S ALREADY!
THE TRICK IS TO NOT STOP! KEEP GOING!
I NEED TO WAKE UP.
HERE.
WATCH THIS.
STRETCH!
OK.
AHH...
AAH!
TA-DA!
THANK YOU CHARLOTTESVILLE ATHLETICS CLUB! GO CAVALIERS!
THAT'S EASY.
DO IT, UGLY.
KLNK
WHACK!
OOF!

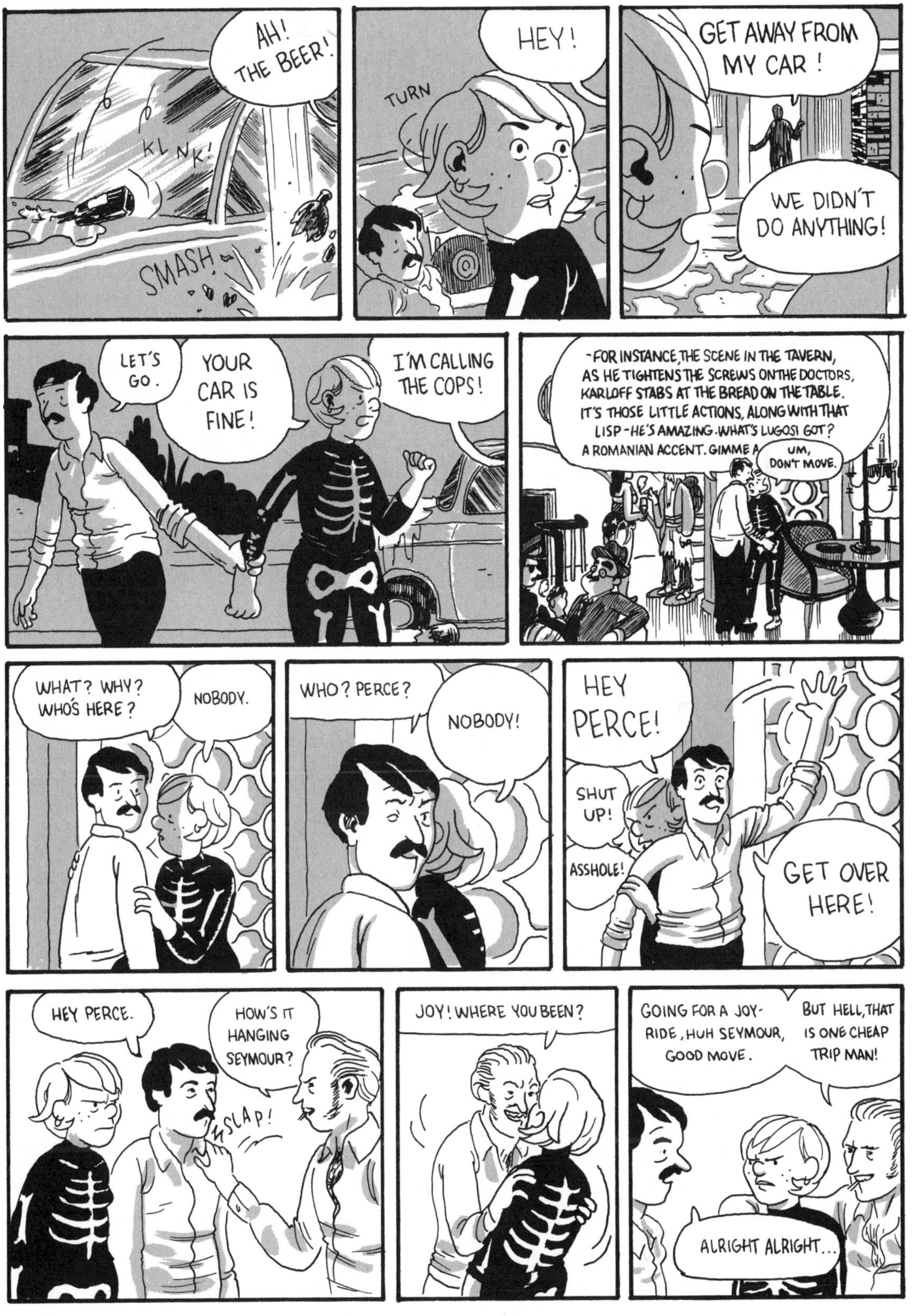
AH! THE BEER!
KLNK!
SMASH!
TURN
HEY!
GET AWAY FROM MY CAR!
WE DIDN'T DO ANYTHING!
LET'S GO.
YOUR CAR IS FINE!
I'M CALLING THE COPS!
-FOR INSTANCE, THE SCENE IN THE TAVERN, AS HE TIGHTENS THE SCREWS ON THE DOCTORS, KARLOFF STABS AT THE BREAD ON THE TABLE. IT'S THOSE LITTLE ACTIONS, ALONG WITH THAT LISP - HE'S AMAZING. WHAT'S LUGOSI GOT? A ROMANIAN ACCENT. GIMME A
UM, DON'T MOVE.
WHAT? WHY? WHO'S HERE?
NOBODY.
WHO? PERCE?
NOBODY!
HEY PERCE!
SHUT UP!
ASSHOLE!
GET OVER HERE!
HEY PERCE.
HOW'S IT HANGING SEYMOUR?
SLAP!
JOY! WHERE YOU BEEN?
GOING FOR A JOY-RIDE, HUH SEYMOUR, GOOD MOVE.
BUT HELL, THAT IS ONE CHEAP TRIP MAN!
ALRIGHT ALRIGHT...

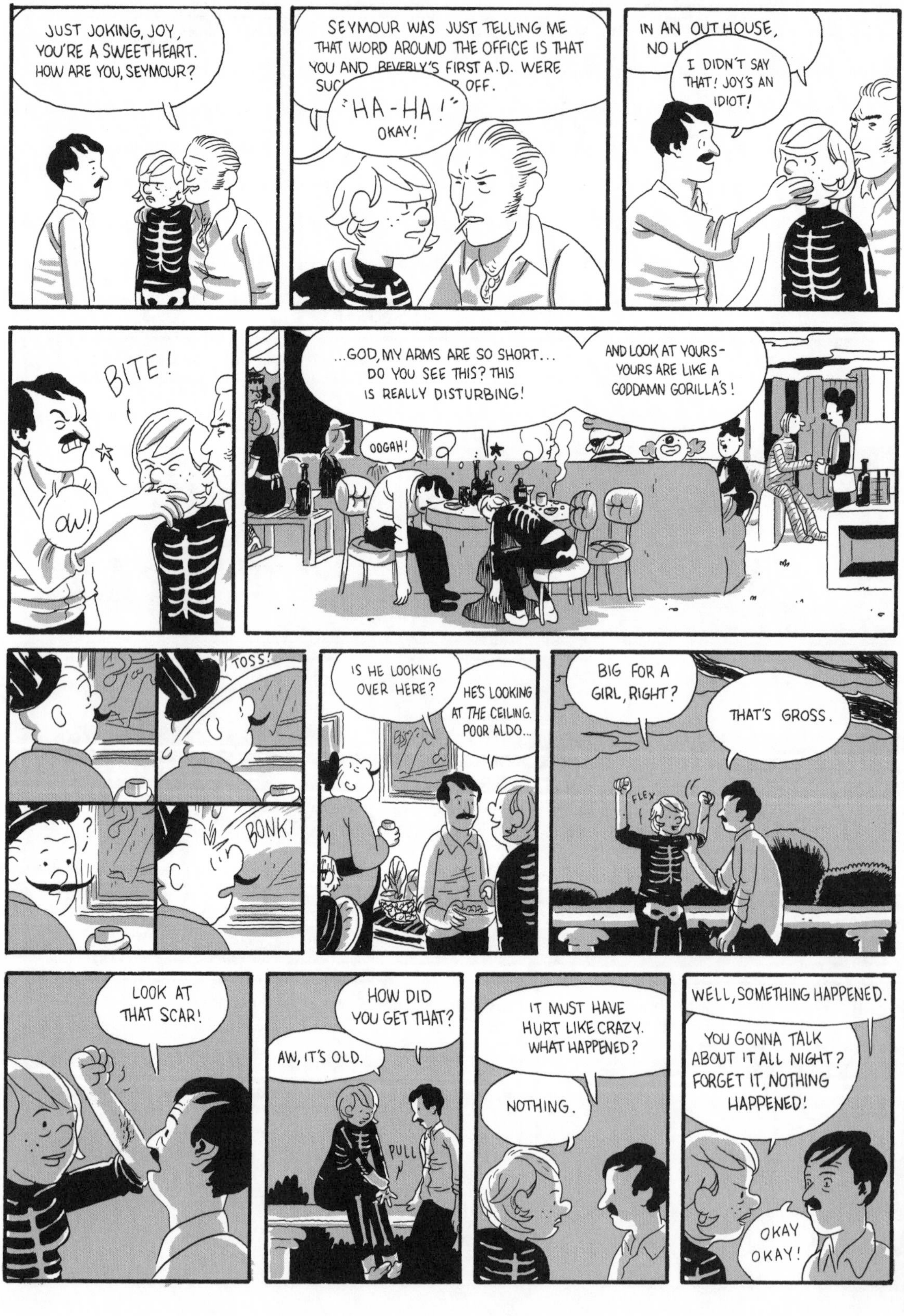
JUST JOKING, JOY, YOU'RE A SWEETHEART. HOW ARE YOU, SEYMOUR?
SEYMOUR WAS JUST TELLING ME THAT WORD AROUND THE OFFICE IS THAT YOU AND BEVERLY'S FIRST A.D. WERE
OFF.
HA-HA! OKAY!
IN AN OUTHOUSE, NO
I DIDN'T SAY THAT! JOY'S AN IDIOT!
BITE!
OW!
...GOD, MY ARMS ARE SO SHORT... DO YOU SEE THIS? THIS IS REALLY DISTURBING!
AND LOOK AT YOURS-YOURS ARE LIKE A GODDAMN GORILLA'S!
OOGAH!
TOSS!
?
BONK!
IS HE LOOKING OVER HERE?
HE'S LOOKING AT THE CEILING. POOR ALDO...
BIG FOR A GIRL, RIGHT?
THAT'S GROSS.
FLEX
LOOK AT THAT SCAR!
HOW DID YOU GET THAT?
AW, IT'S OLD.
PULL
IT MUST HAVE HURT LIKE CRAZY. WHAT HAPPENED?
NOTHING.
WELL, SOMETHING HAPPENED.
YOU GONNA TALK ABOUT IT ALL NIGHT? FORGET IT, NOTHING HAPPENED!
OKAY OKAY!

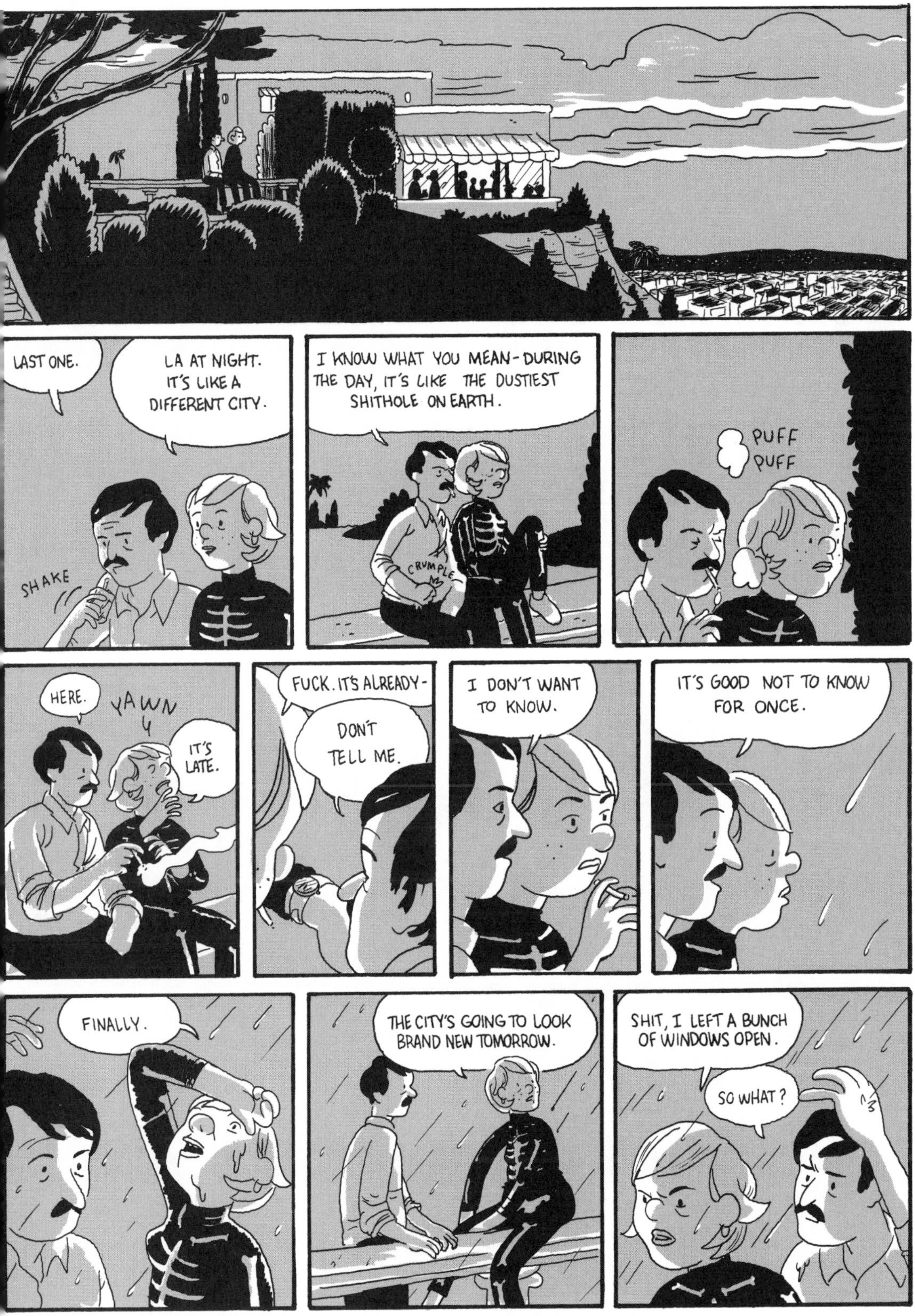
LAST ONE.
LA AT NIGHT. IT'S LIKE A DIFFERENT CITY.
SHAKE
I KNOW WHAT YOU MEAN- DURING THE DAY, IT'S LIKE THE DUSTIEST SHITHOLE ON EARTH.
CRUMPLE
PUFF PUFF
HERE.
YAWN
IT'S LATE.
FUCK. IT'S ALREADY-
DON'T TELL ME.
I DON'T WANT TO KNOW.
IT'S GOOD NOT TO KNOW FOR ONCE.
FINALLY.
THE CITY'S GOING TO LOOK BRAND NEW TOMORROW.
SHIT, I LEFT A BUNCH OF WINDOWS OPEN.
SO WHAT?

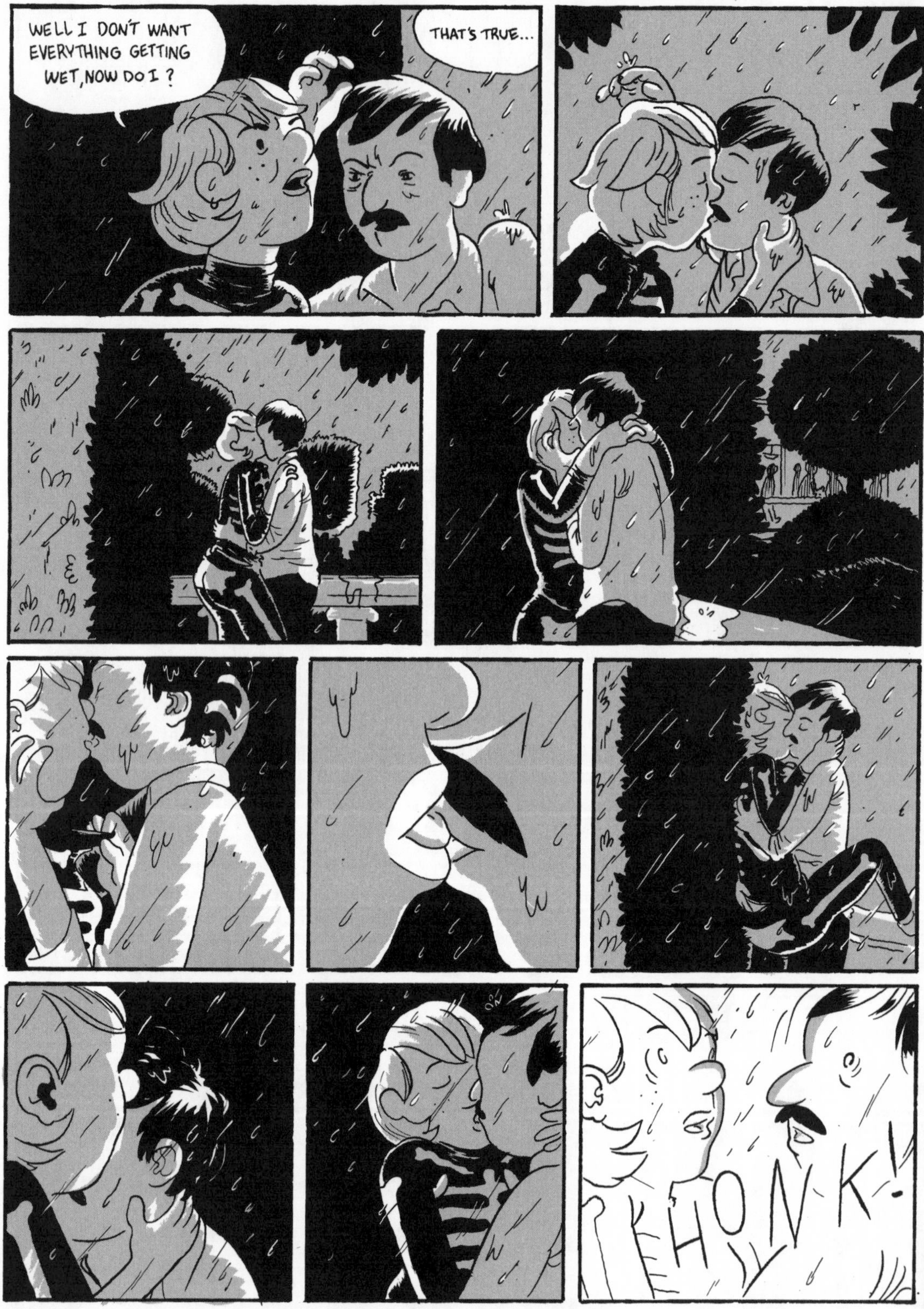
WELL I DON'T WANT EVERYTHING GETTING WET, NOW DO I ?
THAT'S TRUE...
HONK!

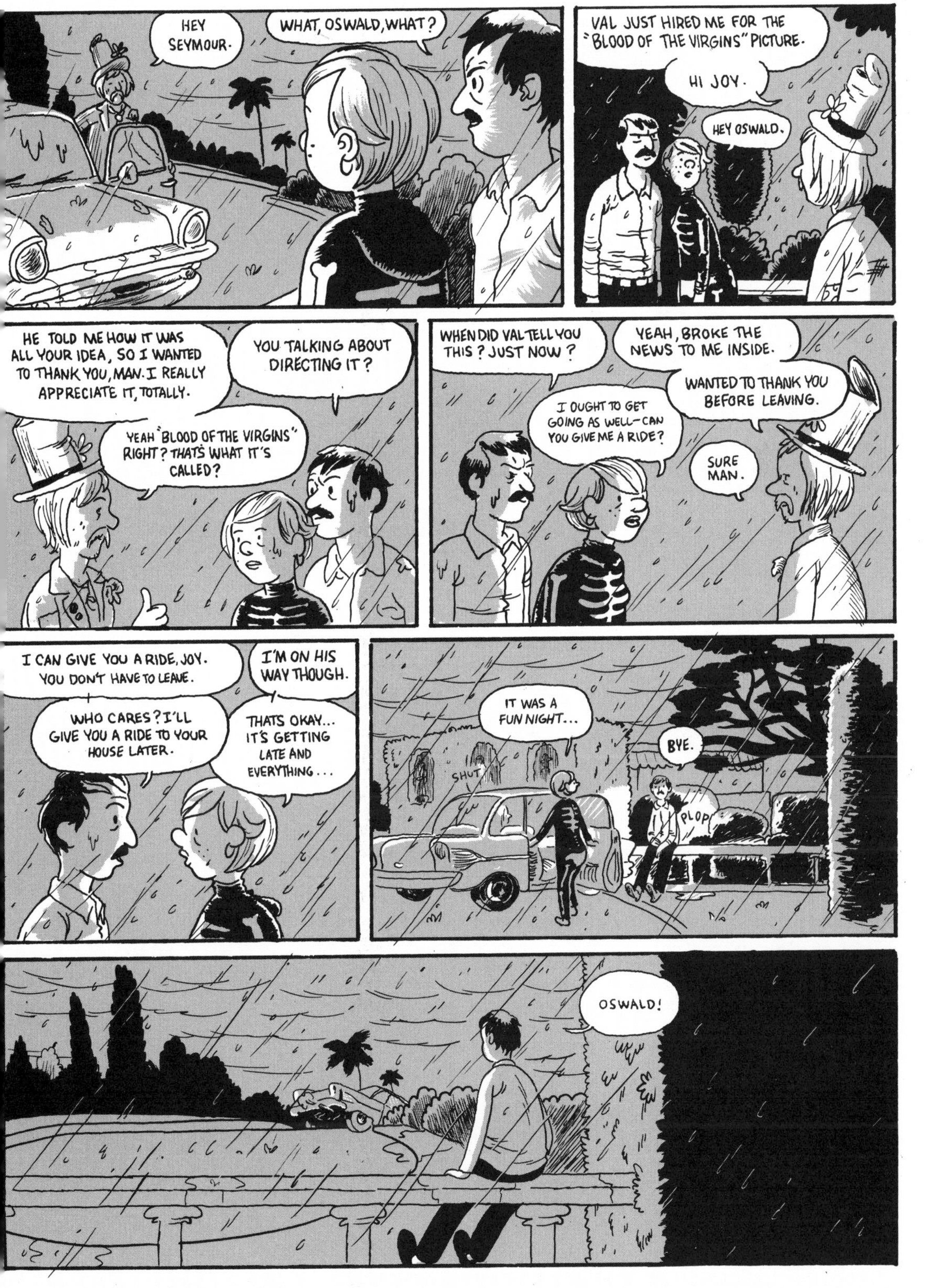
HEY SEYMOUR.
WHAT, OSWALD, WHAT?
VAL JUST HIRED ME FOR THE "BLOOD OF THE VIRGINS" PICTURE.
HI JOY.
HEY OSWALD.
HE TOLD ME HOW IT WAS ALL YOUR IDEA, SO I WANTED TO THANK YOU, MAN. I REALLY APPRECIATE IT, TOTALLY.
YOU TALKING ABOUT DIRECTING IT?
YEAH "BLOOD OF THE VIRGINS" RIGHT? THAT'S WHAT IT'S CALLED?
WHEN DID VAL TELL YOU THIS? JUST NOW?
YEAH, BROKE THE NEWS TO ME INSIDE.
WANTED TO THANK YOU BEFORE LEAVING.
I OUGHT TO GET GOING AS WELL—CAN YOU GIVE ME A RIDE?
SURE MAN.
I CAN GIVE YOU A RIDE, JOY. YOU DON'T HAVE TO LEAVE.
I'M ON HIS WAY THOUGH.
WHO CARES? I'LL GIVE YOU A RIDE TO YOUR HOUSE LATER.
THATS OKAY... IT'S GETTING LATE AND EVERYTHING...
IT WAS A FUN NIGHT...
BYE.
SHUT
PLOP
OSWALD!

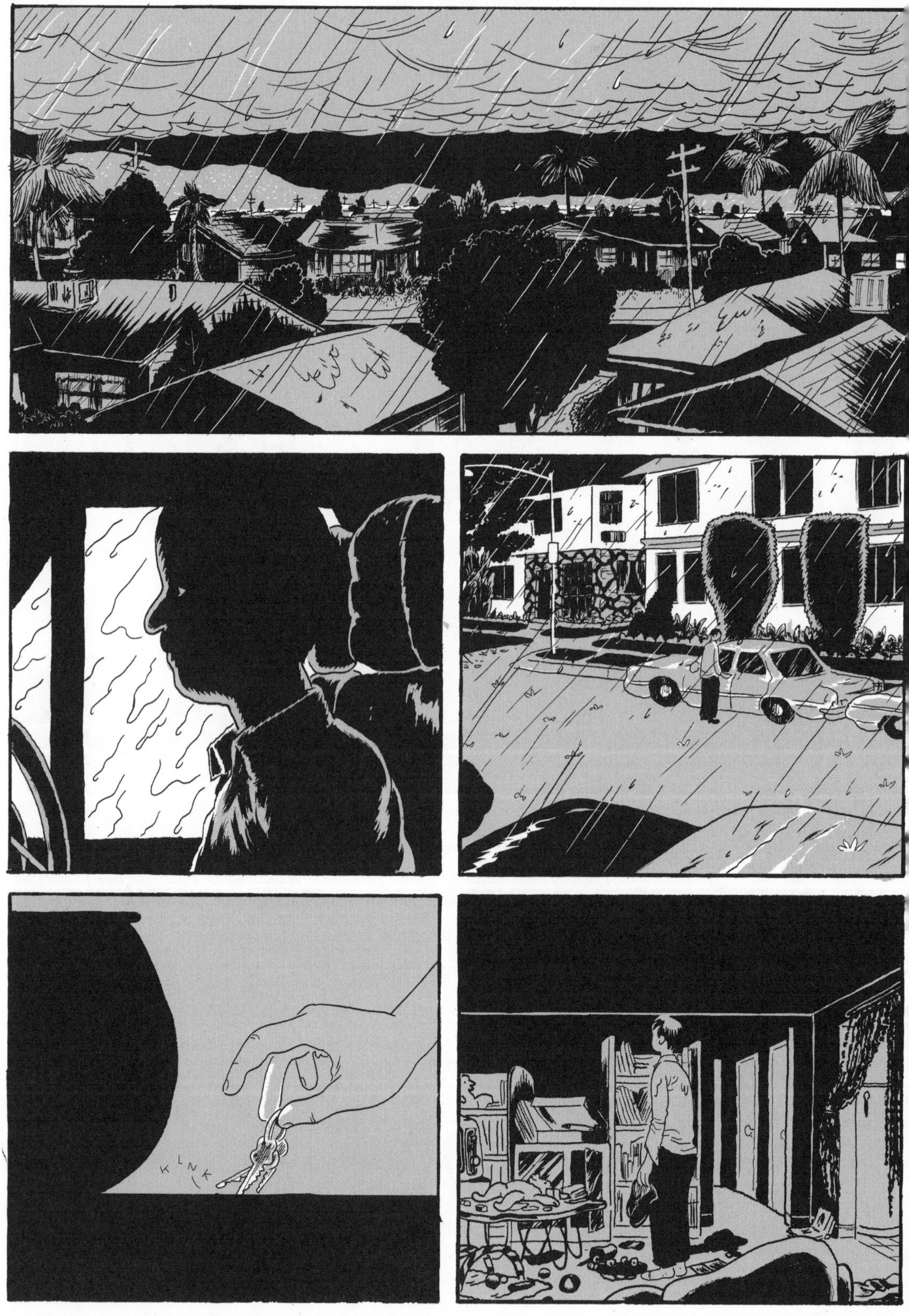
KLNK

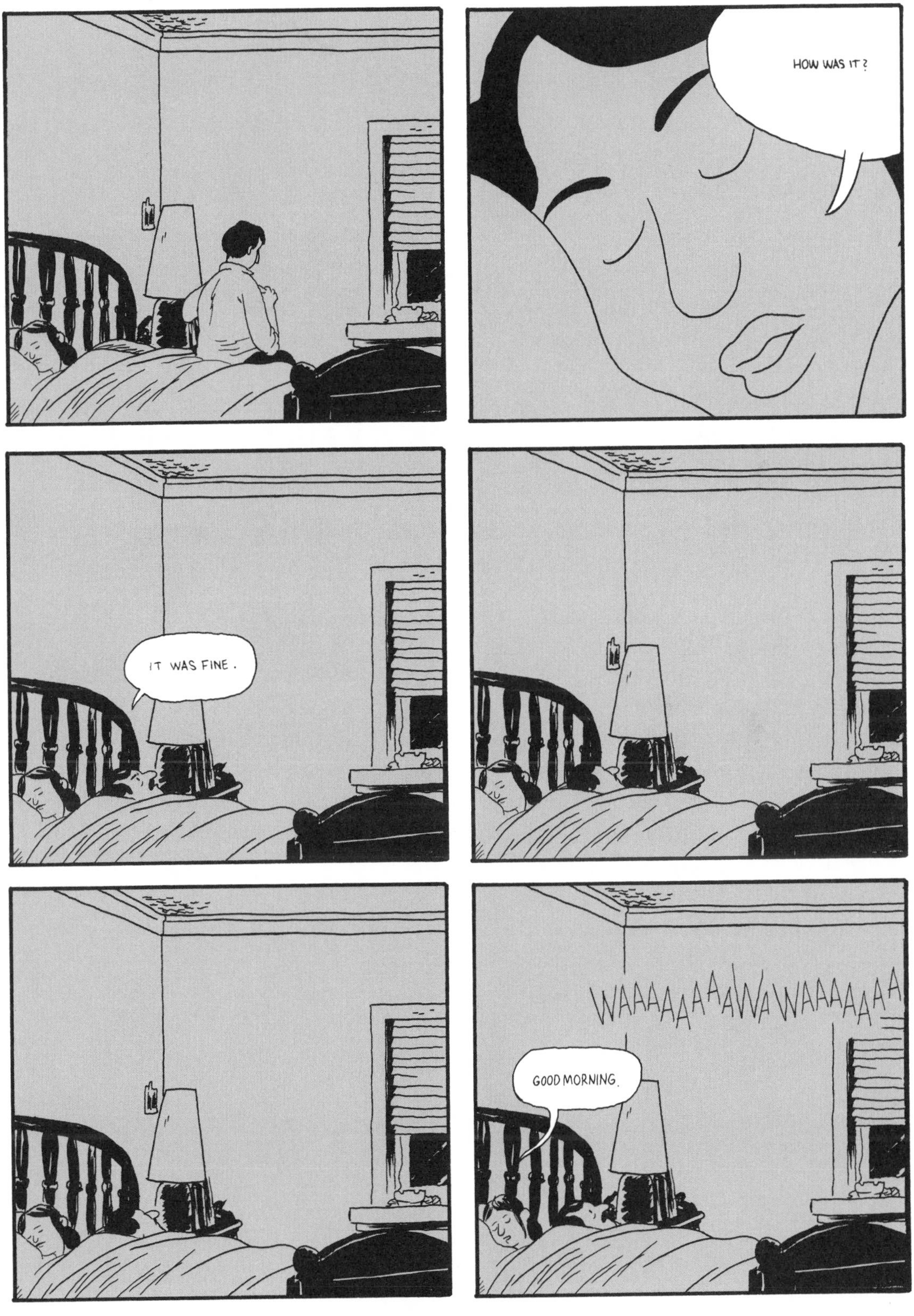
HOW WAS IT?
IT WAS FINE.
WAAAAAAAAWAWAAAAAAA
GOOD MORNING.

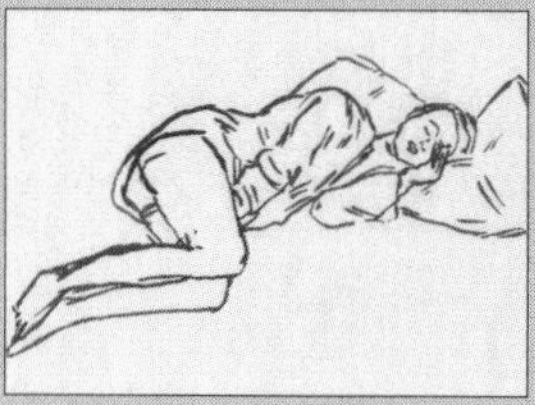

LEANNE SHAPTON

A Month Of...

from the *New York Times*

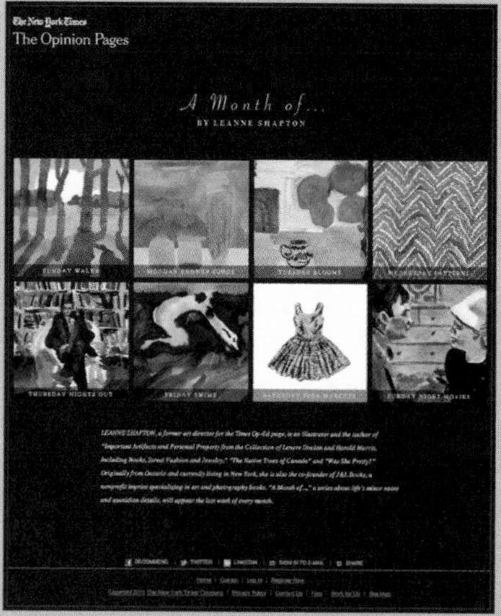
The New York Times
The Opinion Pages
A Month of...
BY LEANNE SHAPTON

FOR ME, DRAWING COMICS IS

Something I admire, but not what I do, as I find it impossible to draw the same face twice. In this case, it's an extension of my series work and writing projects.

THE SELECTION

This is a piece of an eight-month series of 243 paintings that focused on the banalities and quotidian details of daily life. The interactive series appeared at the end of each month on the *New York Times* Opinionator website.

PUBLICATIONS MY WORK HAS APPEARED IN

The *New York Times*, the *Wall Street Journal*, *Time*, *Newsweek*, *The New Yorker*, *New York Magazine*, *Harper's Magazine*, the *Paris Review*, *The Believer*, the *National Post*, *Elle*, *Glamour*.

WHAT I'M KNOWN FOR

Cofounder and publisher, J&L Books.
Was She Pretty, FSG/Sarah Crichton Books, 2006.
Important Artifacts, FSG/Sarah Crichton Books, 2009.
Native Trees of Canada, Drawn & Quarterly, 2010.
Swimming Studies, Blue Rider Press, 2012.

WHERE I LIVE

New York City, New York.

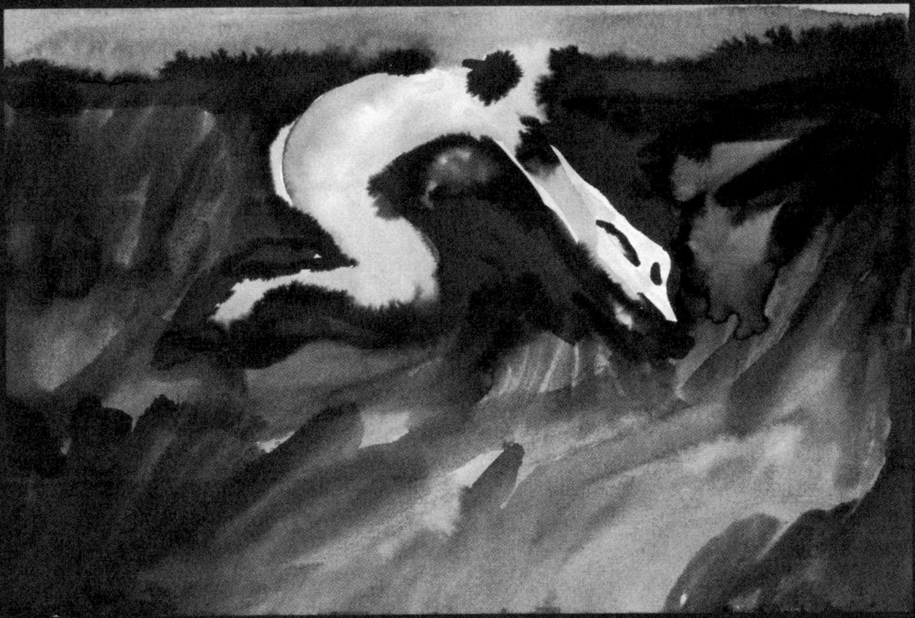

To get to the natural pool we clamber down and over the steep rocks. The water in the pool is clear, calmer and warmer than the water in the surrounding sea. We swim here at least twice a day, trying to understand each other, circling each other and pointing things out to each other underwater: a fish, a shell, a sharp rock. Aug. 5, 2005, Deià, Mallorca, Spain.

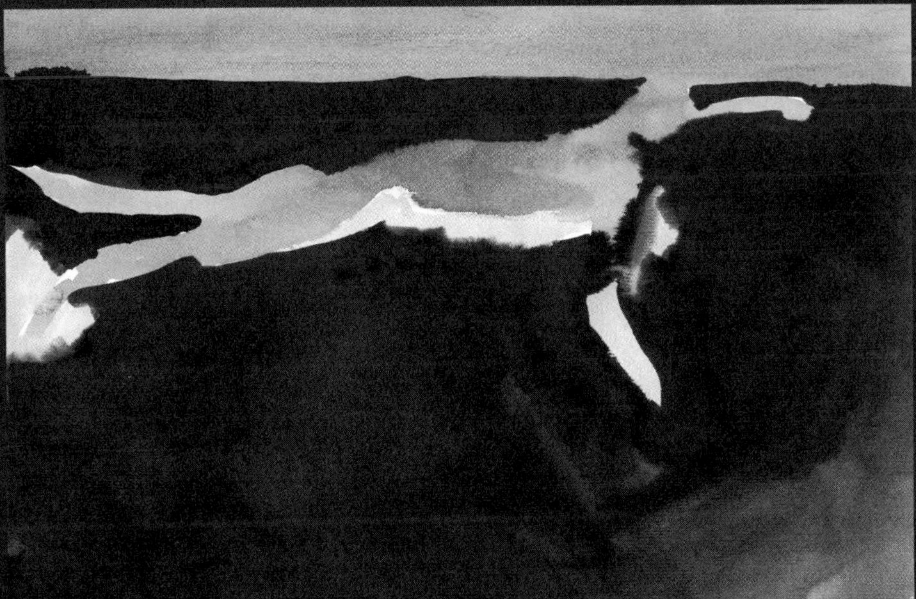

A 30-minute swim. Heading up the lane I glance at the clock as I breathe to my right. Heading down I breathe to my left. I am already tired 10 minutes in and dread the next 20. October 1, 2004, McBurney YMCA, New York City.

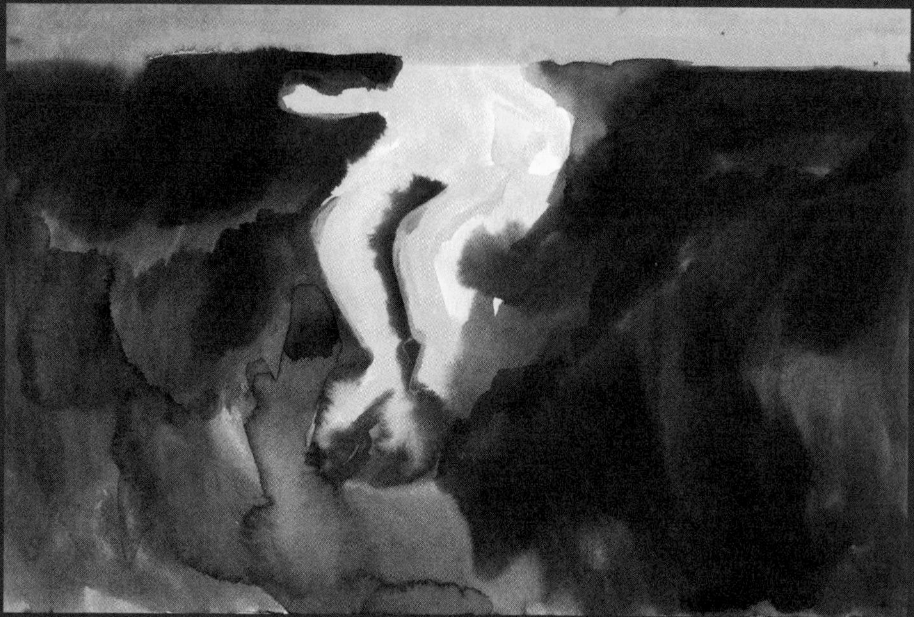

After three hours of tennis, the Lake Manitouwabing water is cold. I swim around the dock, then tread water and look down at my legs disappearing into the green dark. I think of the Charles Sprawson title, "Haunts of the Black Masseur." September 1, 2006, The Inn at Manitou, McKeller, Ontario.

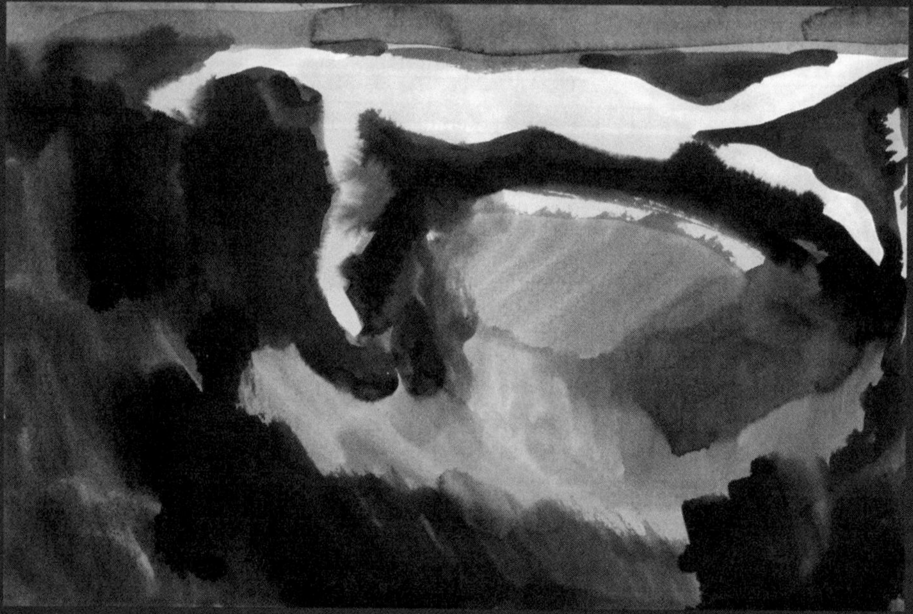

I haven't packed sneakers or flip-flops, so I wear my rubber boots under my robe and leave them standing on the tiles at the side while I do laps in the unusually warm water. It looks, as I breathe and glimpse them, as though someone is watching me swim. February 4, 2011, Windsor Arms Hotel, Toronto.

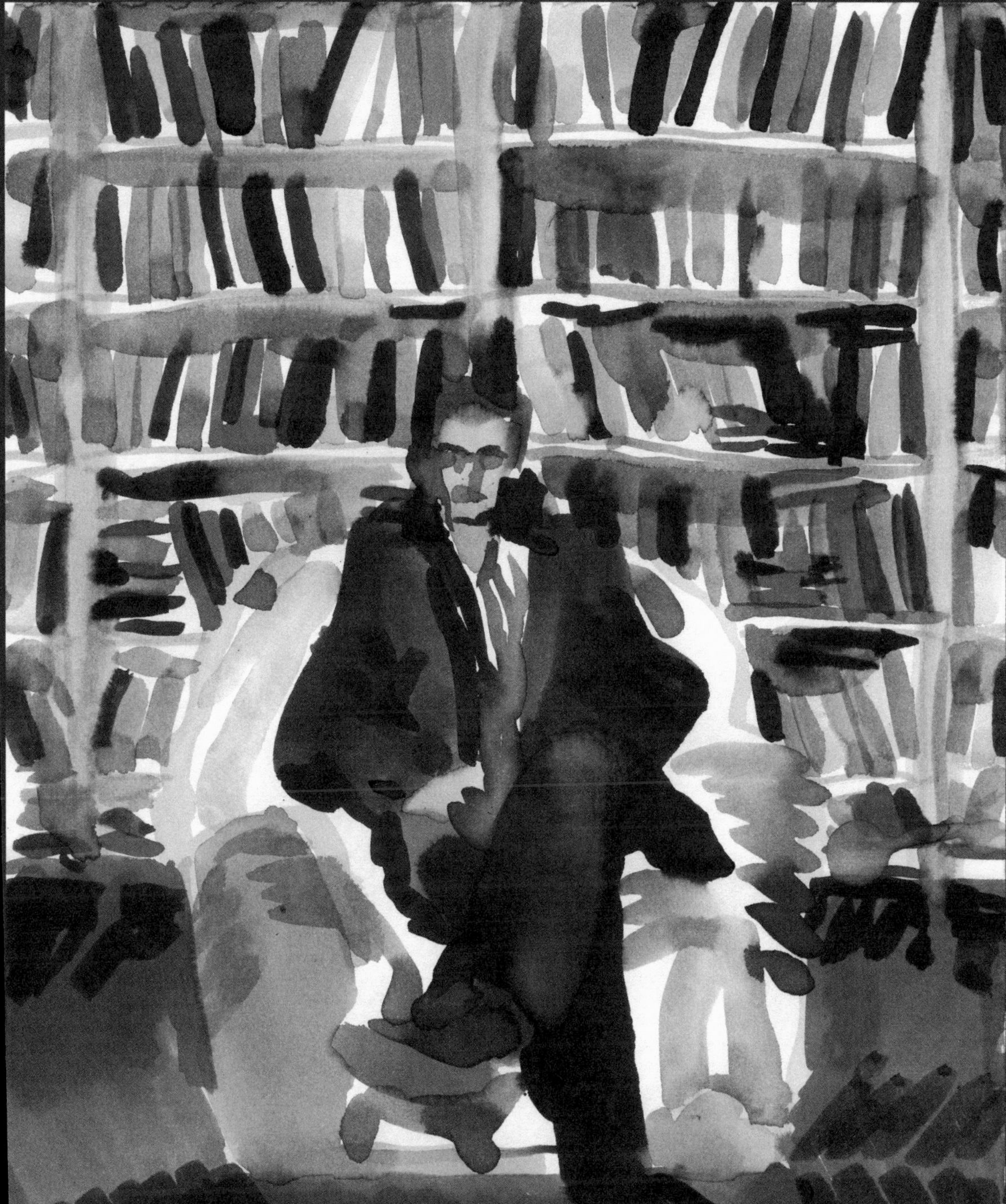

Gianluigi sitting in a chair covered with a sheet to keep off dog hair. We had gone to look at the view of the city from his balcony before dinner at Ristorante Consorzio. Nov. 4, 2010, Turin, Italy.

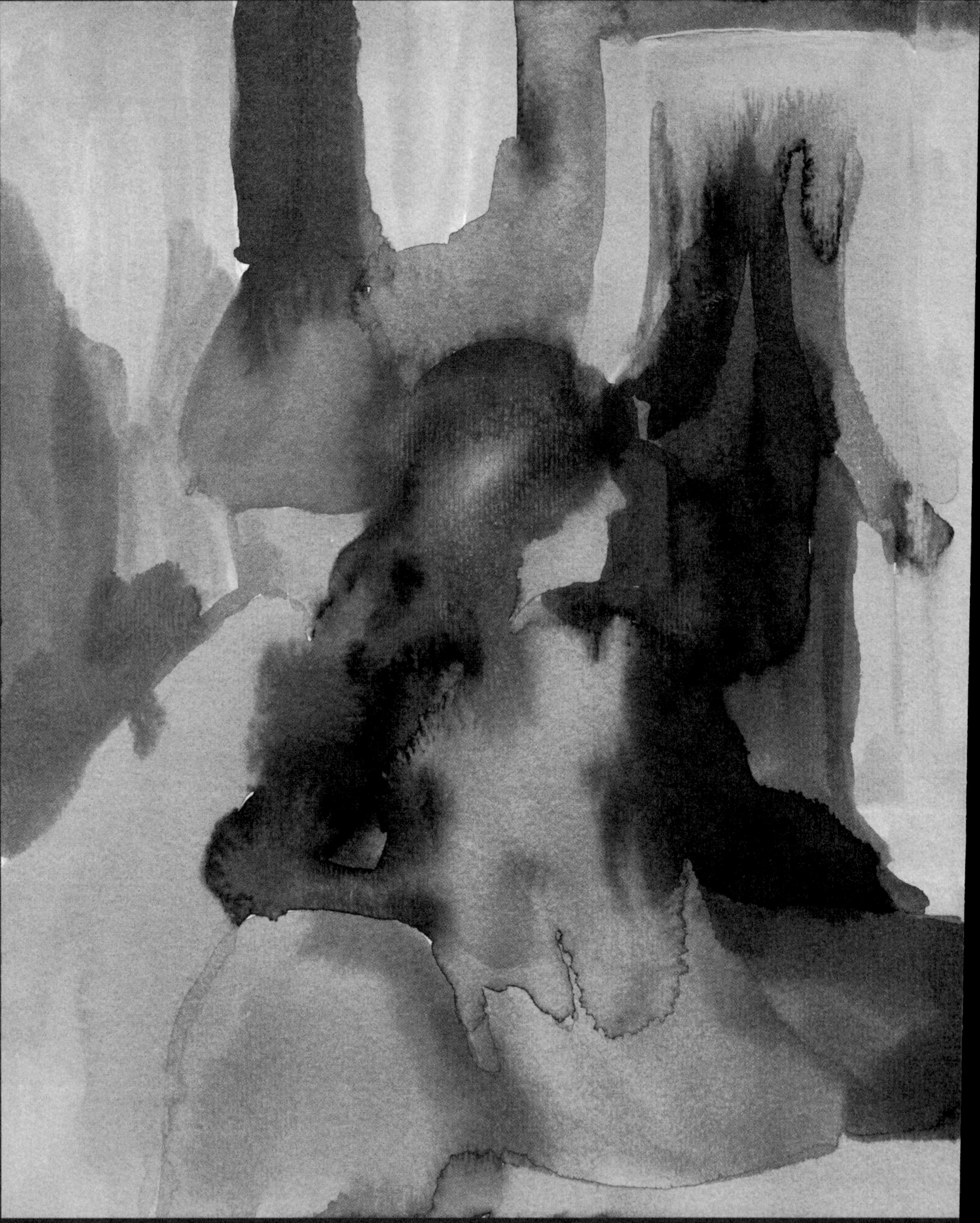

Agnes on the sofa at Deirdre's birthday party, watching Michael take Craig's author photo. May 5, 2011, New York City.

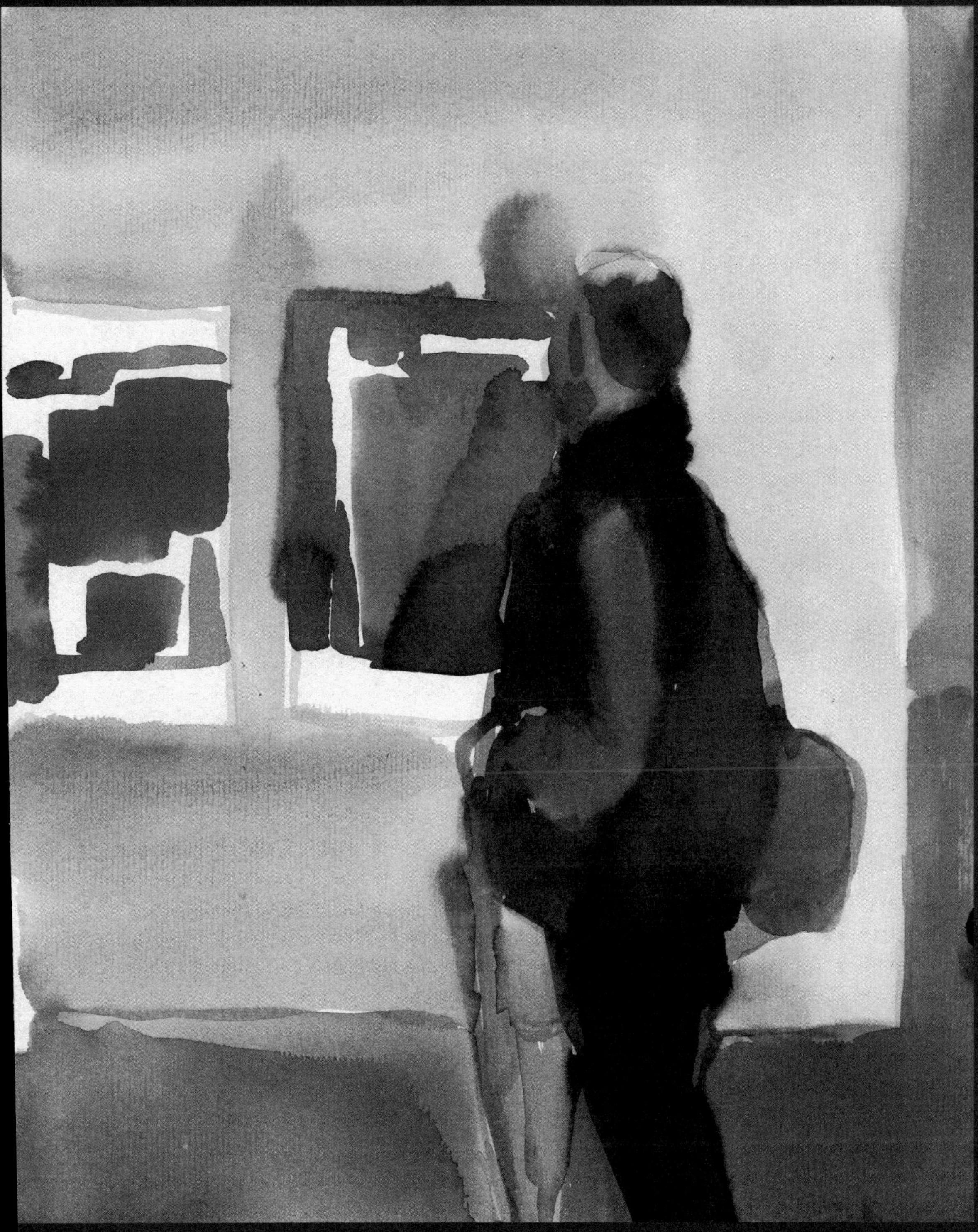

Michael looking at two of Andrew Kuo's paintings at Taxter and Spengemann gallery, before heading to a reading in SoHo. March 31, 2011, New York City.

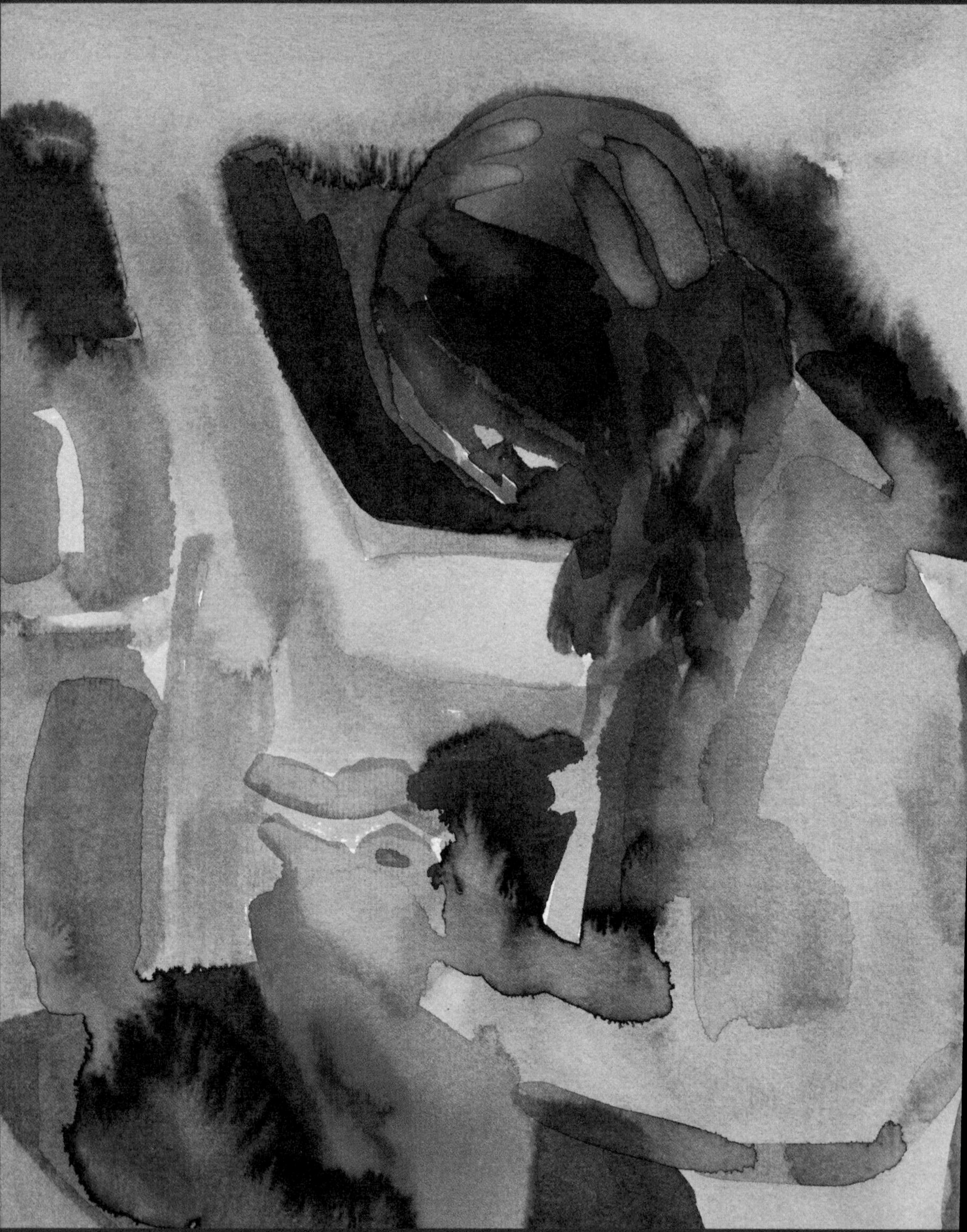

Vivian texting from the backseat of a van on the way to dinner, holding a box of champagne in her lap. Jan. 6, 2011, Ocho Rios, Jamaica.

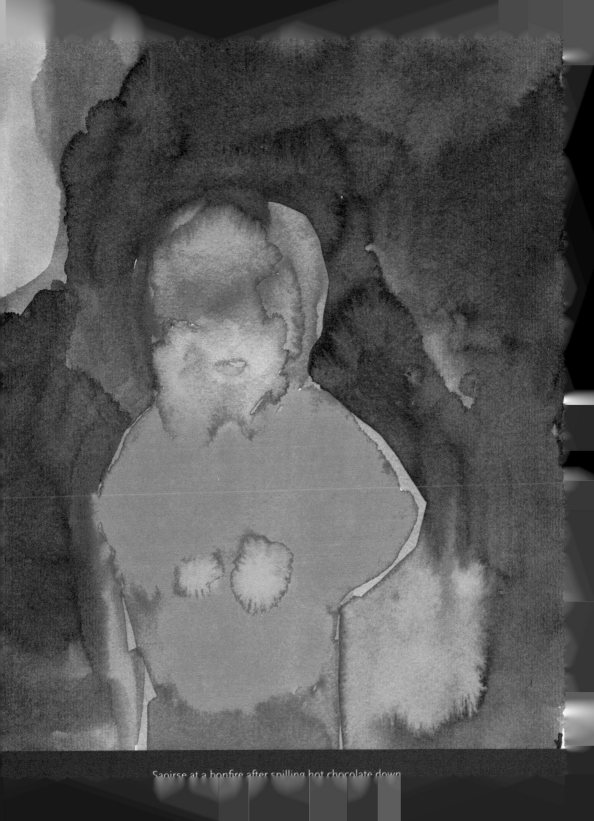
Saoirse at a bonfire after spilling hot chocolate down

JOYCE FARMER

Special Exits *(Excerpt)*

FOR ME, DRAWING COMICS IS

A way of communication that can be both fun and informative for the reader. It's a lot of work, it's fun to do, and it's rewarding when other people enjoy the finished product.

THE SELECTION

Laura, daughter of Lars and Rachel, tries to help her aging parents whether they want help or not. Her parents are trying hard to maintain their independence.

THE CONTEXT

Laura's parents live in South Los Angeles, isolated from their friends and family. Their health is failing and their home is crowded with over fifty years of accumulated possessions.

AWARDS

Reuben Award from the National Cartoonists Society for 2011; Inkpot Award from the Comic Con; nominated for a 2011 Eisner.

WHAT I'M KNOWN FOR

Tits & Clits Comix, seven issues 1972 to 1987; *Wimmen's Comix*; various other underground publications from 1972 to 1987.

WHERE I LIVE

Laguna Beach, California.

SPECIAL
A Graphic Memoir
JOYCE FARMER
"One of the best long-narrative comics I've ever read, right up there with Maus...
I actually found myself moved to tears." — R. CRUMB
EXITS

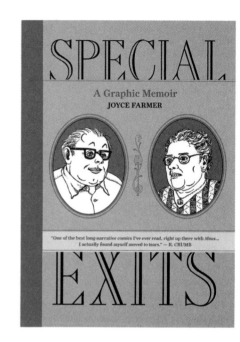

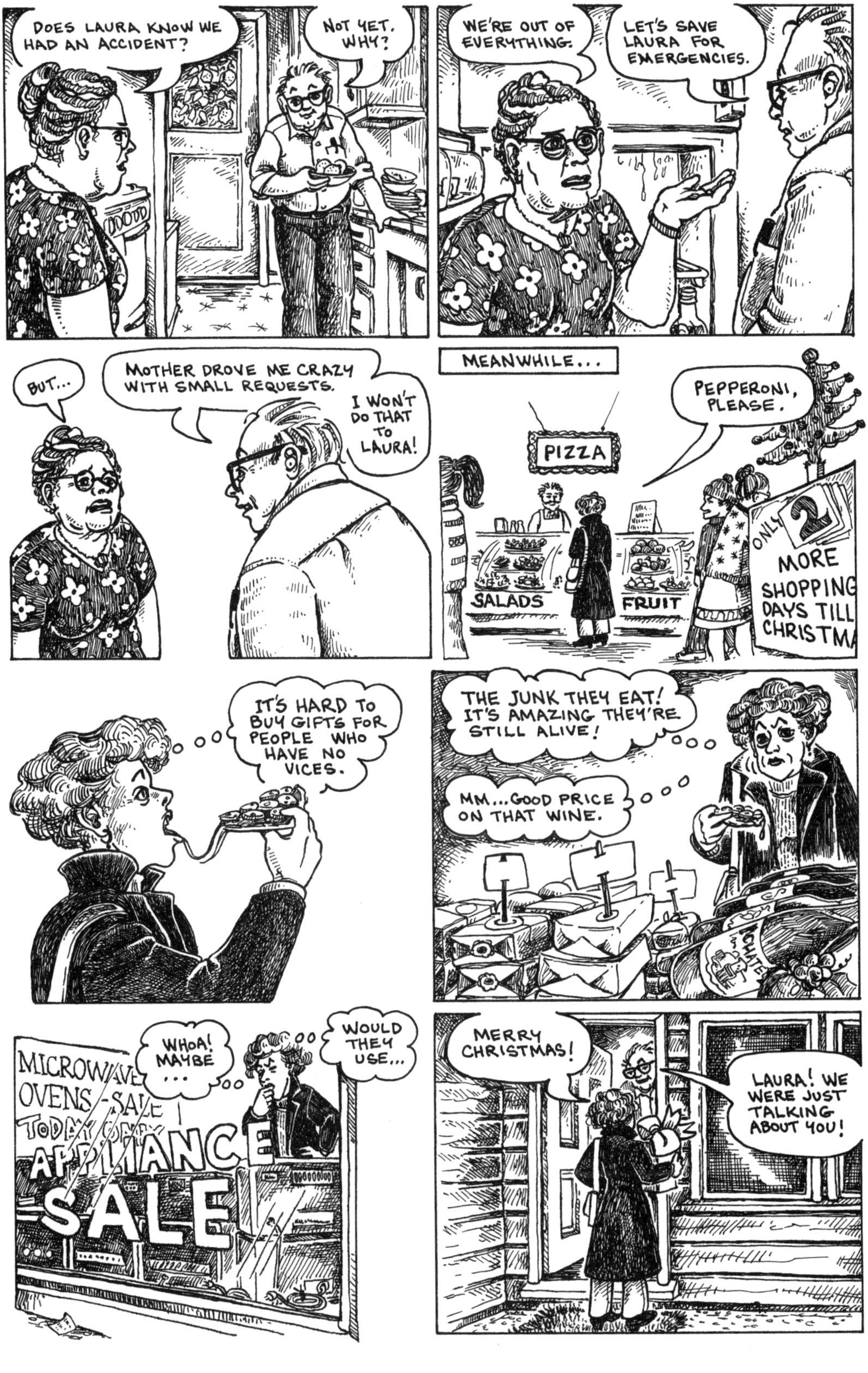
DOES LAURA KNOW WE HAD AN ACCIDENT?
NOT YET. WHY?
WE'RE OUT OF EVERYTHING.
LET'S SAVE LAURA FOR EMERGENCIES.
BUT...
MOTHER DROVE ME CRAZY WITH SMALL REQUESTS.
I WON'T DO THAT TO LAURA!
MEANWHILE...
PIZZA
PEPPERONI, PLEASE.
SALADS
FRUIT
ONLY 2 MORE SHOPPING DAYS TILL CHRISTMA
IT'S HARD TO BUY GIFTS FOR PEOPLE WHO HAVE NO VICES.
THE JUNK THEY EAT! IT'S AMAZING THEY'RE STILL ALIVE!
MM... GOOD PRICE ON THAT WINE.
MICROWAVE OVENS SALE TODAY ONLY
APPLIANCE SALE
WHOA! MAYBE...
WOULD THEY USE...
MERRY CHRISTMAS!
LAURA! WE WERE JUST TALKING ABOUT YOU!

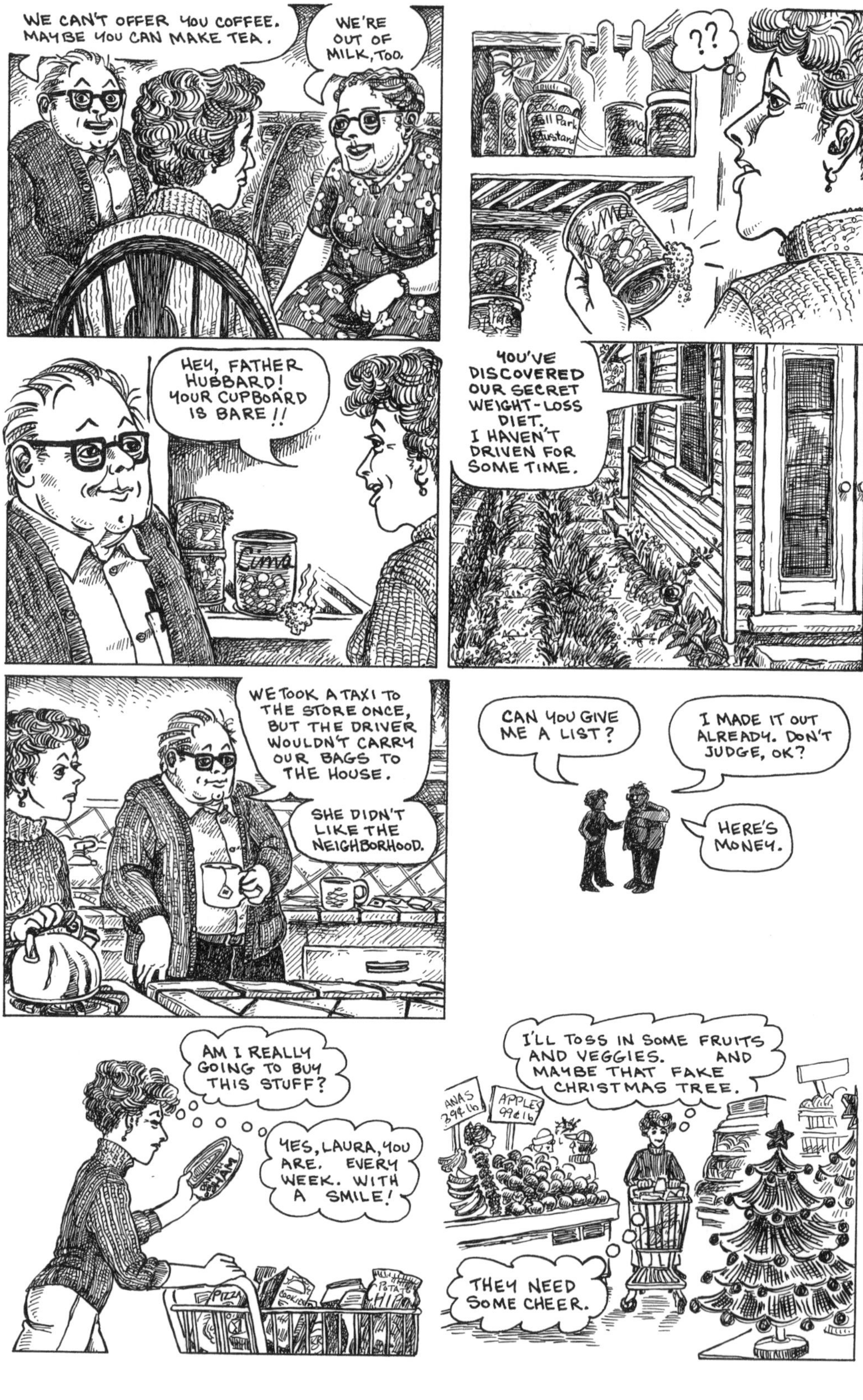
WE CAN'T OFFER YOU COFFEE. MAYBE YOU CAN MAKE TEA.
WE'RE OUT OF MILK, TOO.
??
Ball Park Mustard
HEY, FATHER HUBBARD! YOUR CUPBOARD IS BARE!!
Lima
YOU'VE DISCOVERED OUR SECRET WEIGHT-LOSS DIET. I HAVEN'T DRIVEN FOR SOME TIME.
WE TOOK A TAXI TO THE STORE ONCE, BUT THE DRIVER WOULDN'T CARRY OUR BAGS TO THE HOUSE.
SHE DIDN'T LIKE THE NEIGHBORHOOD.
CAN YOU GIVE ME A LIST?
I MADE IT OUT ALREADY. DON'T JUDGE, OK?
HERE'S MONEY.
AM I REALLY GOING TO BUY THIS STUFF?
YES, LAURA, YOU ARE. EVERY WEEK. WITH A SMILE!
PIZZA
I'LL TOSS IN SOME FRUITS AND VEGGIES. AND MAYBE THAT FAKE CHRISTMAS TREE.
APPLES 99¢ lb
THEY NEED SOME CHEER.

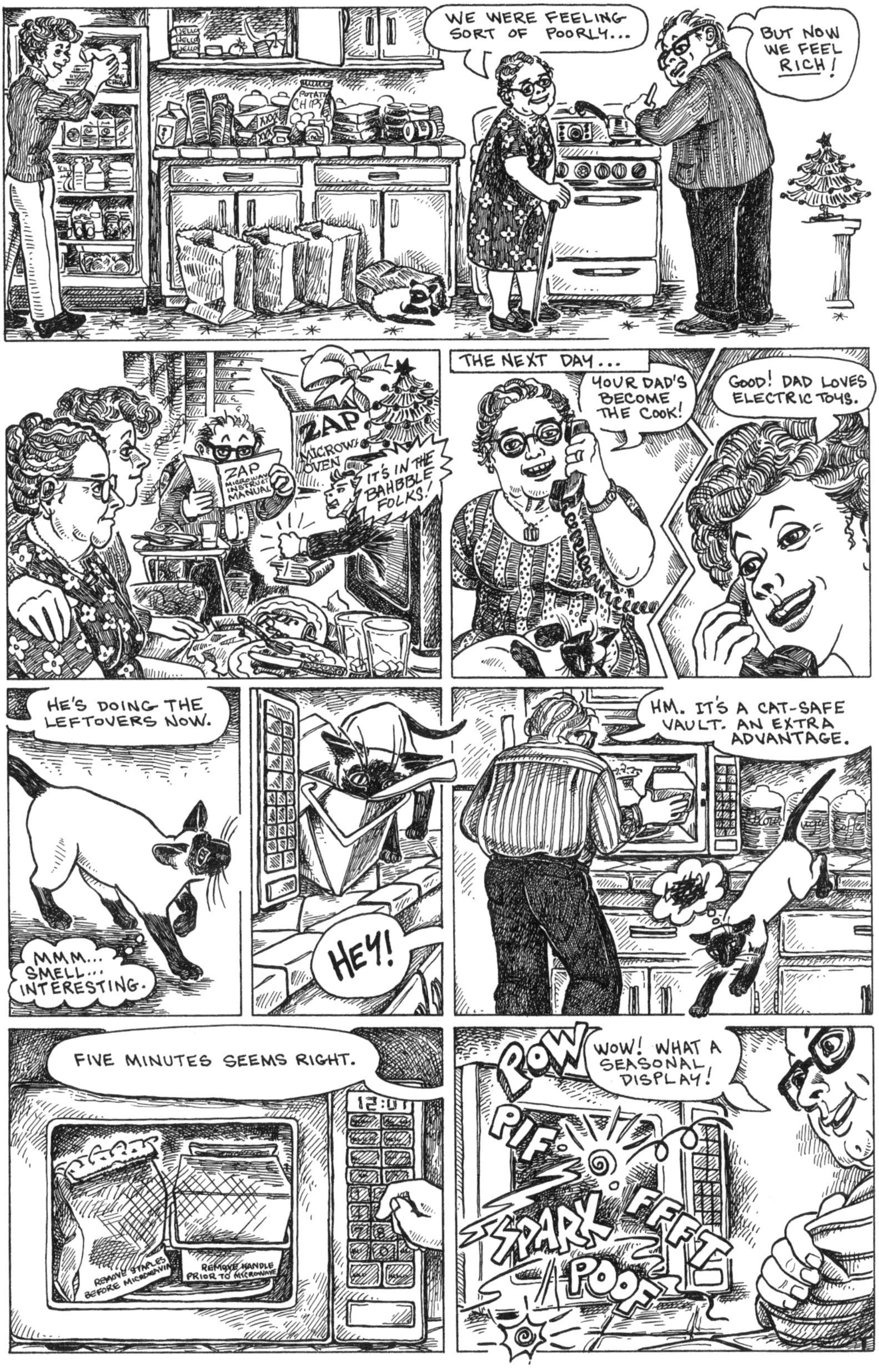

WE WERE FEELING SORT OF POORLY...
BUT NOW WE FEEL RICH!
JELLO
POTATO CHIPS
ZAP MICROWAVE OVEN
ZAP MICROWAVE INSTRUCT MANUAL
IT'S IN THE BAHBBLE FOLKS!
THE NEXT DAY...
YOUR DAD'S BECOME THE COOK!
GOOD! DAD LOVES ELECTRIC TOYS.
HE'S DOING THE LEFTOVERS NOW.
MMM... SMELL... INTERESTING.
HEY!
HM. IT'S A CAT-SAFE VAULT. AN EXTRA ADVANTAGE.
FIVE MINUTES SEEMS RIGHT.
12:01
REMOVE STAPLES BEFORE MICROWAVING
REMOVE HANDLE PRIOR TO MICROWAVE
POW
WOW! WHAT A SEASONAL DISPLAY!
PIF
SPARK
FFFT
POOF

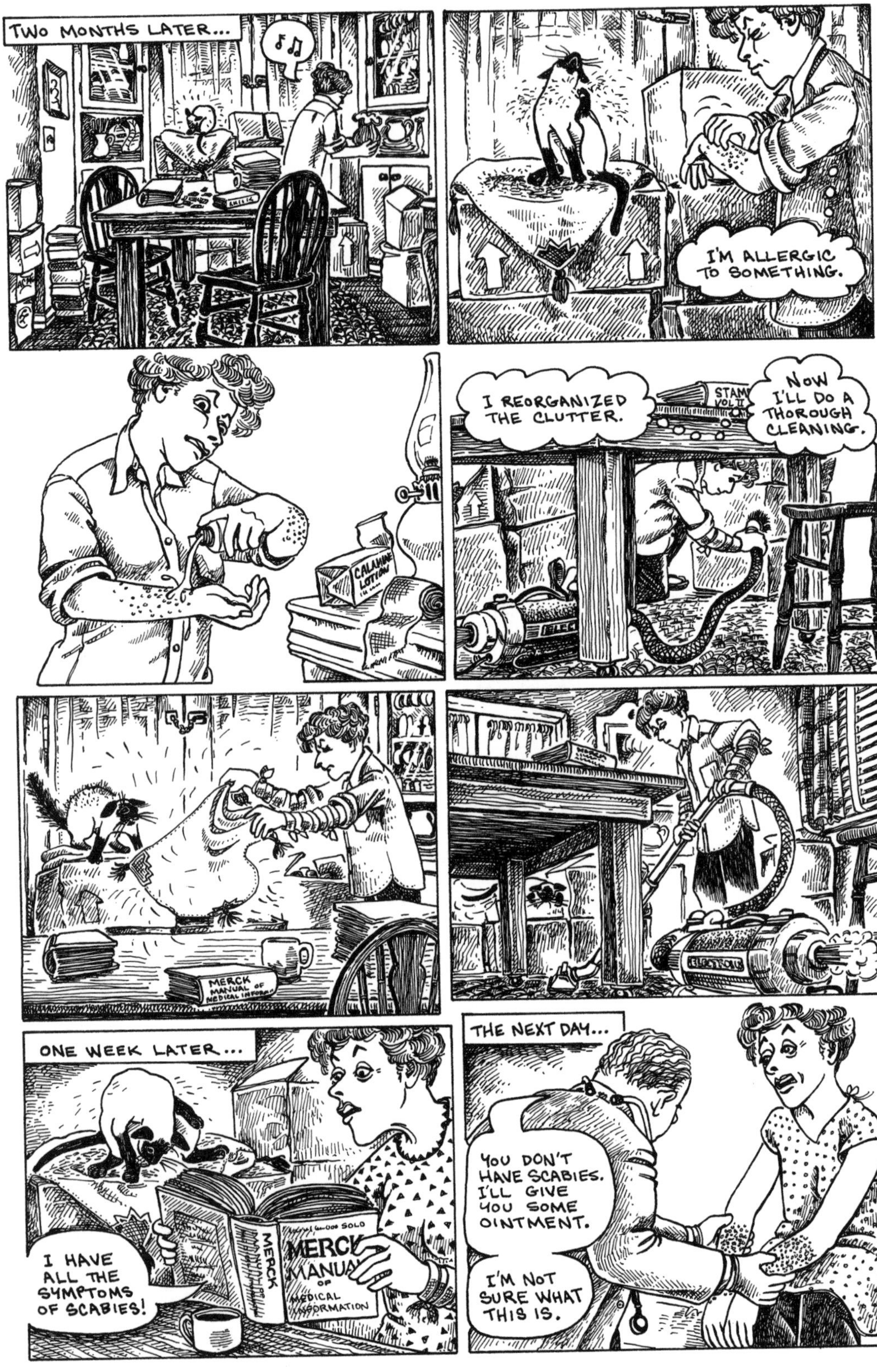

TWO MONTHS LATER...
I'M ALLERGIC TO SOMETHING.
CALAMINE LOTION
I REORGANIZED THE CLUTTER.
NOW I'LL DO A THOROUGH CLEANING.
MERCK MANUAL OF MEDICAL INFORM
ELECTROLUX
ONE WEEK LATER...
I HAVE ALL THE SYMPTOMS OF SCABIES!
MERCK MANUAL OF MEDICAL INFORMATION
THE NEXT DAY...
YOU DON'T HAVE SCABIES. I'LL GIVE YOU SOME OINTMENT.
I'M NOT SURE WHAT THIS IS.

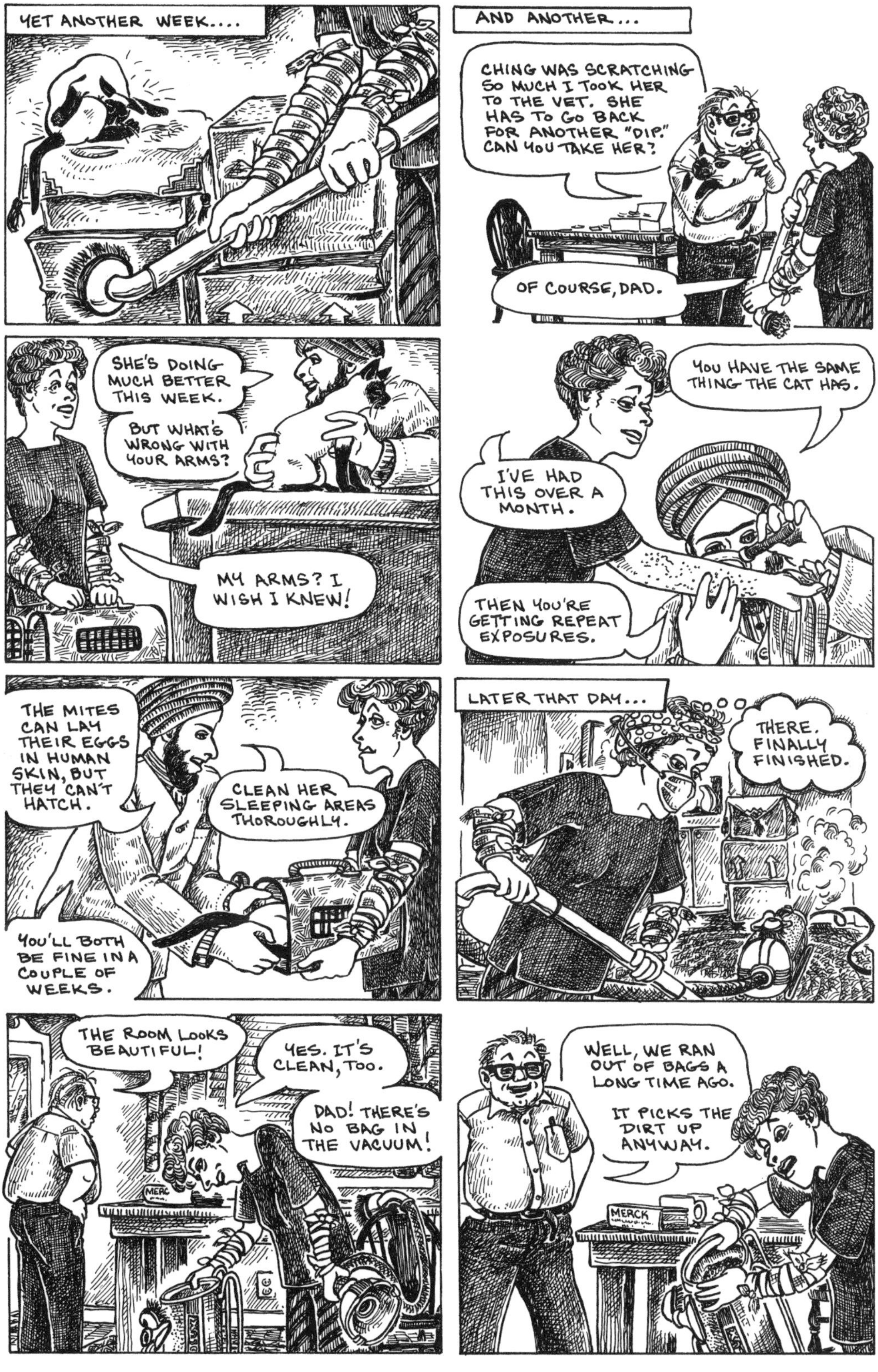

YET ANOTHER WEEK....
AND ANOTHER...
CHING WAS SCRATCHING SO MUCH I TOOK HER TO THE VET. SHE HAS TO GO BACK FOR ANOTHER "DIP." CAN YOU TAKE HER?
OF COURSE, DAD.
SHE'S DOING MUCH BETTER THIS WEEK.
BUT WHAT'S WRONG WITH YOUR ARMS?
MY ARMS? I WISH I KNEW!
YOU HAVE THE SAME THING THE CAT HAS.
I'VE HAD THIS OVER A MONTH.
THEN YOU'RE GETTING REPEAT EXPOSURES.
THE MITES CAN LAY THEIR EGGS IN HUMAN SKIN, BUT THEY CAN'T HATCH.
CLEAN HER SLEEPING AREAS THOROUGHLY.
YOU'LL BOTH BE FINE IN A COUPLE OF WEEKS.
LATER THAT DAY...
THERE. FINALLY FINISHED.
THE ROOM LOOKS BEAUTIFUL!
YES. IT'S CLEAN, TOO.
DAD! THERE'S NO BAG IN THE VACUUM!
WELL, WE RAN OUT OF BAGS A LONG TIME AGO.
IT PICKS THE DIRT UP ANYWAY.
MERCK

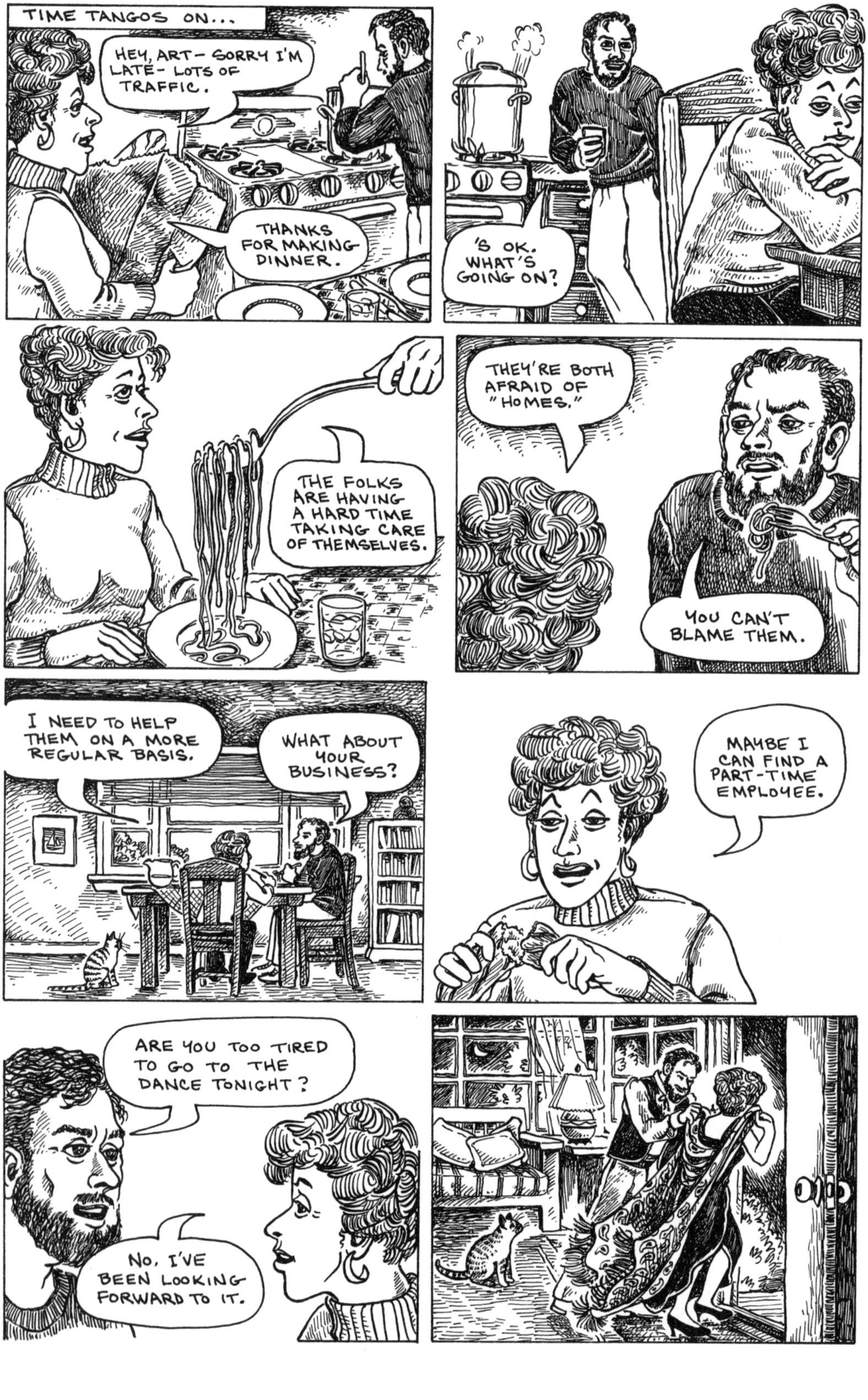
TIME TANGOS ON...
HEY, ART- SORRY I'M LATE- LOTS OF TRAFFIC.
THANKS FOR MAKING DINNER.
'S OK. WHAT'S GOING ON?
THE FOLKS ARE HAVING A HARD TIME TAKING CARE OF THEMSELVES.
THEY'RE BOTH AFRAID OF "HOMES."
YOU CAN'T BLAME THEM.
I NEED TO HELP THEM ON A MORE REGULAR BASIS.
WHAT ABOUT YOUR BUSINESS?
MAYBE I CAN FIND A PART-TIME EMPLOYEE.
ARE YOU TOO TIRED TO GO TO THE DANCE TONIGHT?
NO, I'VE BEEN LOOKING FORWARD TO IT.

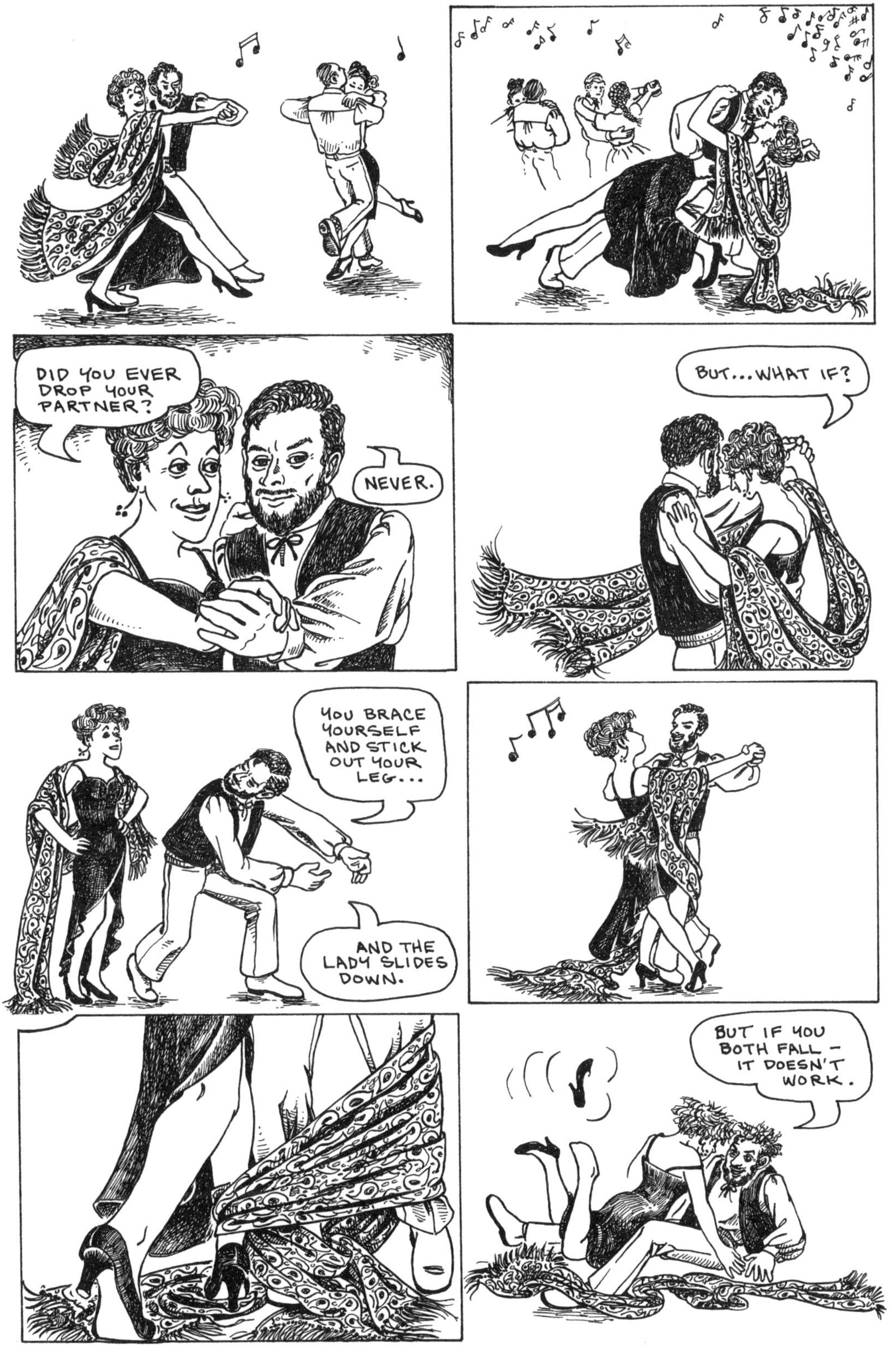
DID YOU EVER DROP YOUR PARTNER?
NEVER.
BUT...WHAT IF?
YOU BRACE YOURSELF AND STICK OUT YOUR LEG...
AND THE LADY SLIDES DOWN.
BUT IF YOU BOTH FALL - IT DOESN'T WORK.

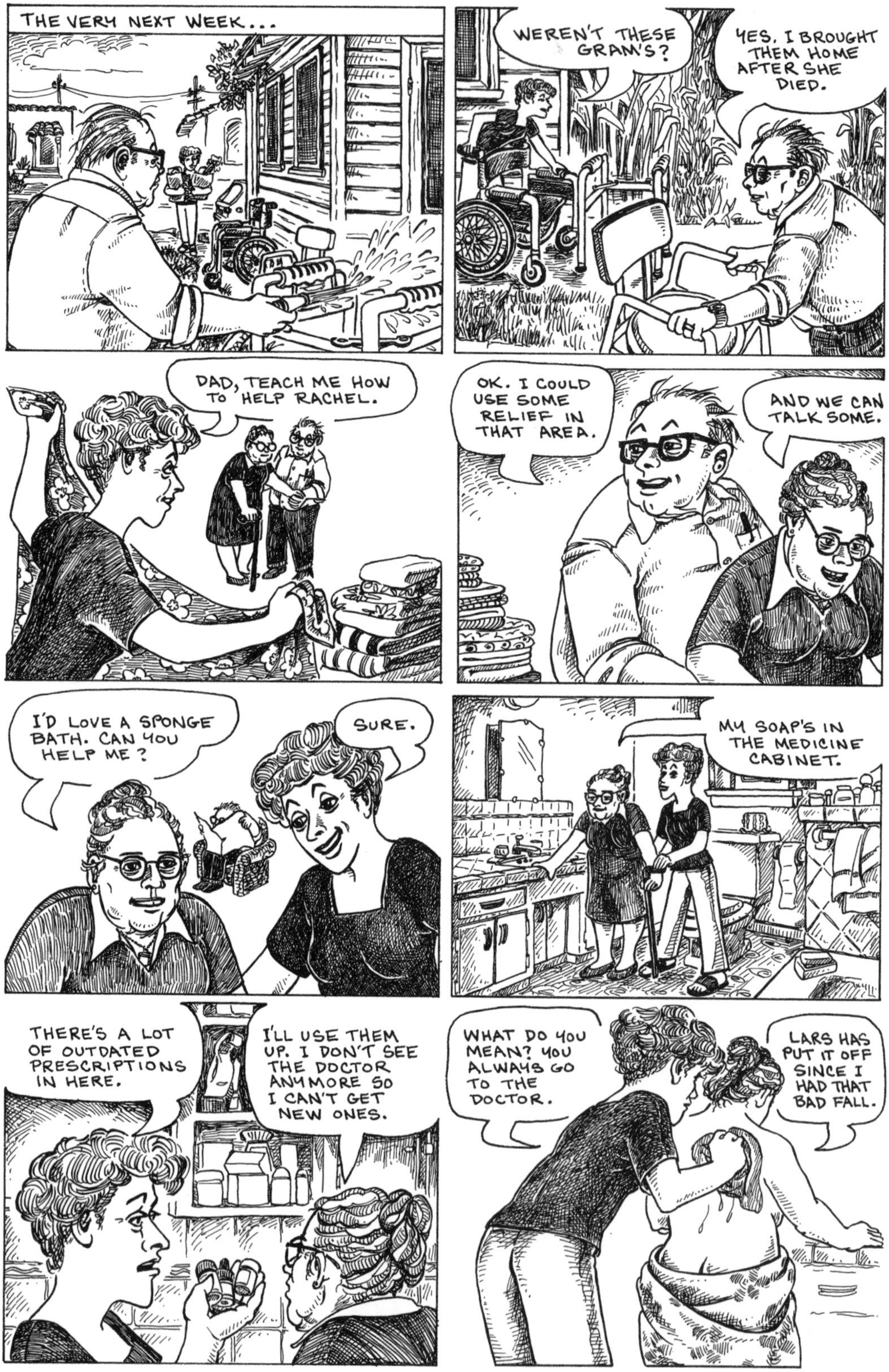
THE VERY NEXT WEEK...
WEREN'T THESE GRAM'S?
YES. I BROUGHT THEM HOME AFTER SHE DIED.
DAD, TEACH ME HOW TO HELP RACHEL.
OK. I COULD USE SOME RELIEF IN THAT AREA.
AND WE CAN TALK SOME.
I'D LOVE A SPONGE BATH. CAN YOU HELP ME?
SURE.
MY SOAP'S IN THE MEDICINE CABINET.
THERE'S A LOT OF OUTDATED PRESCRIPTIONS IN HERE.
I'LL USE THEM UP. I DON'T SEE THE DOCTOR ANYMORE SO I CAN'T GET NEW ONES.
WHAT DO YOU MEAN? YOU ALWAYS GO TO THE DOCTOR.
LARS HAS PUT IT OFF SINCE I HAD THAT BAD FALL.

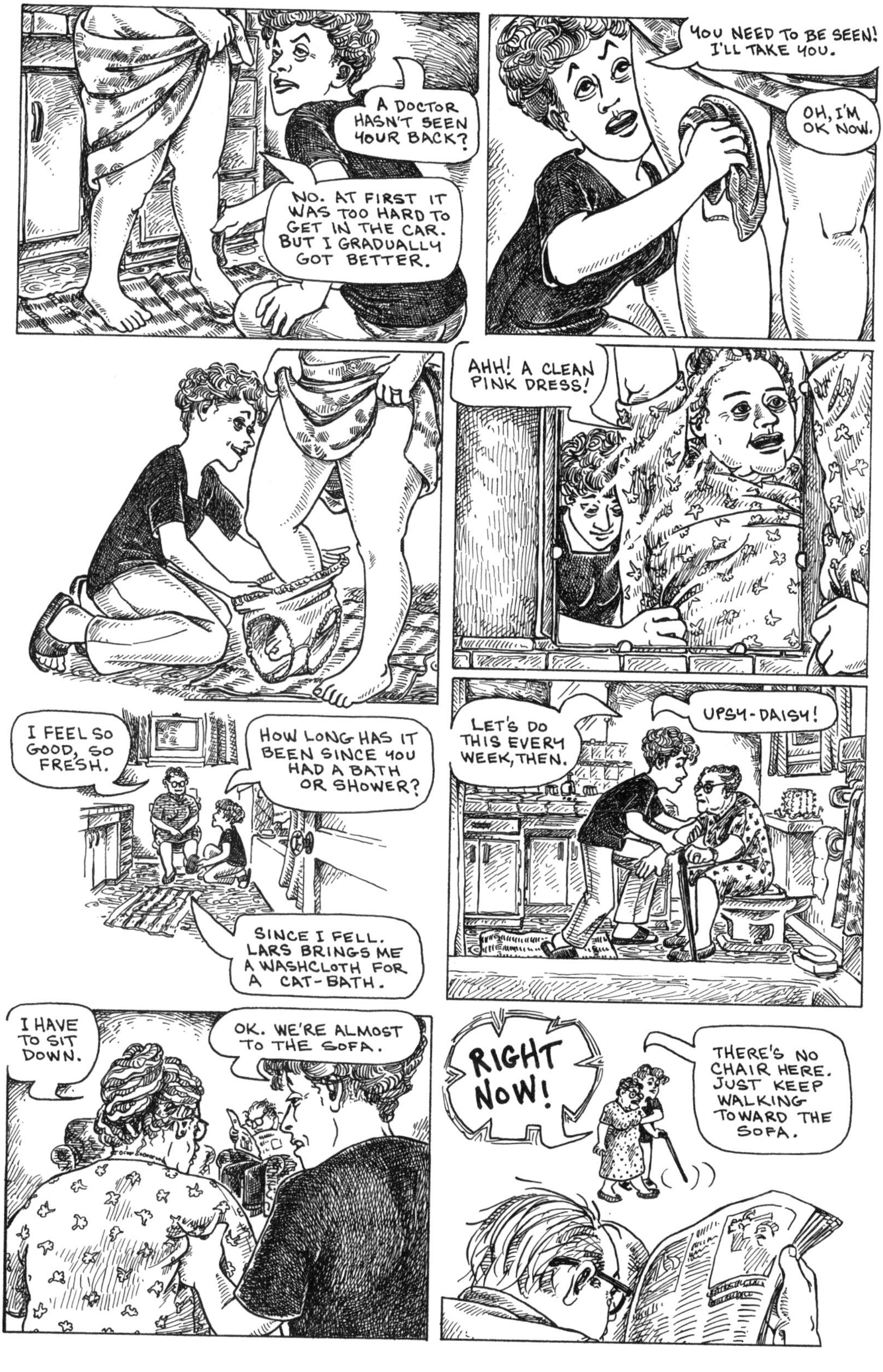
A DOCTOR HASN'T SEEN YOUR BACK?
NO. AT FIRST IT WAS TOO HARD TO GET IN THE CAR. BUT I GRADUALLY GOT BETTER.
YOU NEED TO BE SEEN! I'LL TAKE YOU.
OH, I'M OK NOW.
AHH! A CLEAN PINK DRESS!
I FEEL SO GOOD, SO FRESH.
HOW LONG HAS IT BEEN SINCE YOU HAD A BATH OR SHOWER?
SINCE I FELL. LARS BRINGS ME A WASHCLOTH FOR A CAT-BATH.
LET'S DO THIS EVERY WEEK, THEN.
UPSY-DAISY!
I HAVE TO SIT DOWN.
OK. WE'RE ALMOST TO THE SOFA.
RIGHT NOW!
THERE'S NO CHAIR HERE. JUST KEEP WALKING TOWARD THE SOFA.

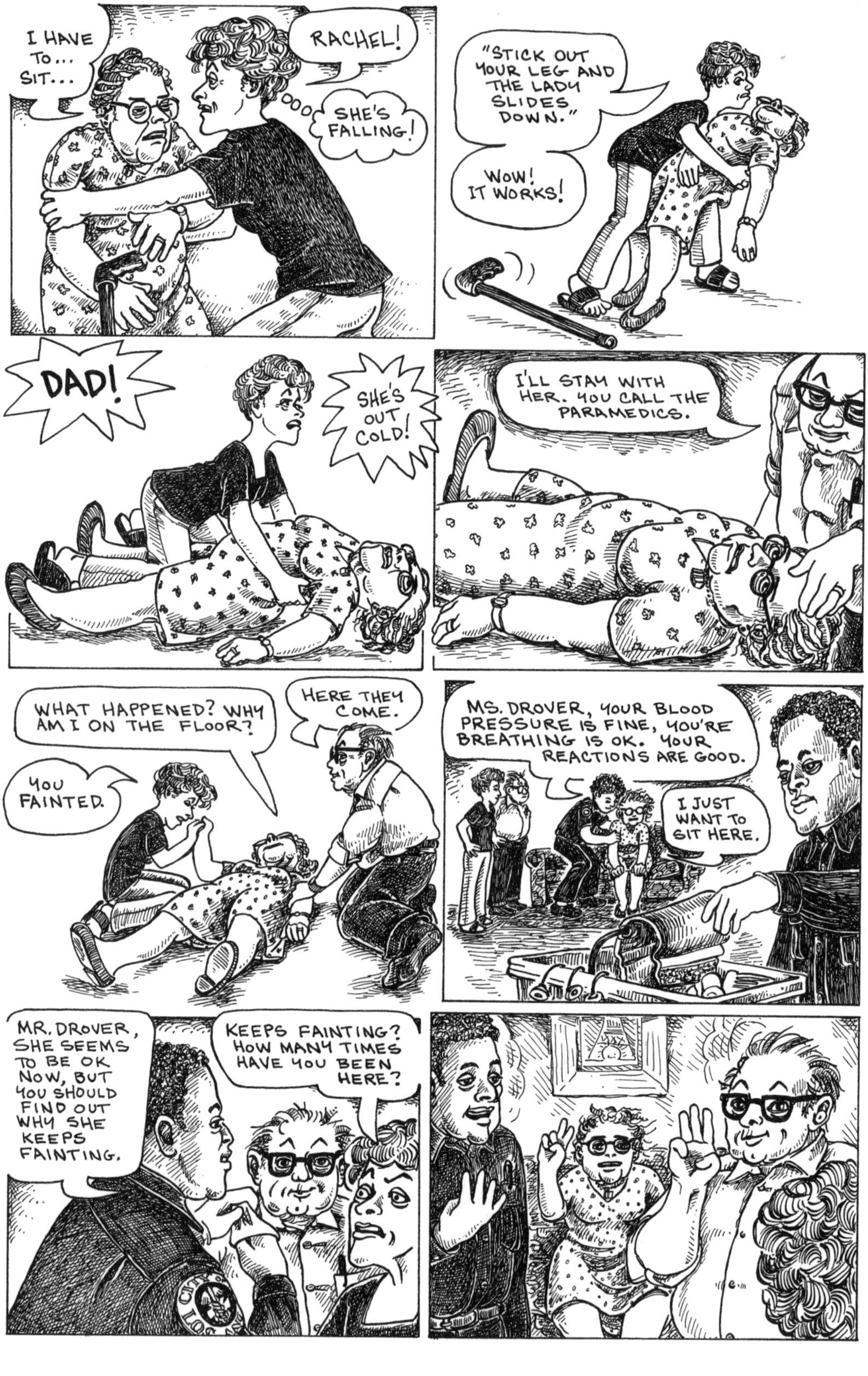
I HAVE TO... SIT...
RACHEL!
SHE'S FALLING!
"STICK OUT YOUR LEG AND THE LADY SLIDES DOWN."
WOW! IT WORKS!
DAD!
SHE'S OUT COLD!
I'LL STAY WITH HER. YOU CALL THE PARAMEDICS.
WHAT HAPPENED? WHY AM I ON THE FLOOR?
HERE THEY COME.
YOU FAINTED.
MS. DROVER, YOUR BLOOD PRESSURE IS FINE, YOU'RE BREATHING IS OK. YOUR REACTIONS ARE GOOD.
I JUST WANT TO SIT HERE.
MR. DROVER, SHE SEEMS TO BE OK NOW, BUT YOU SHOULD FIND OUT WHY SHE KEEPS FAINTING.
KEEPS FAINTING? HOW MANY TIMES HAVE YOU BEEN HERE?

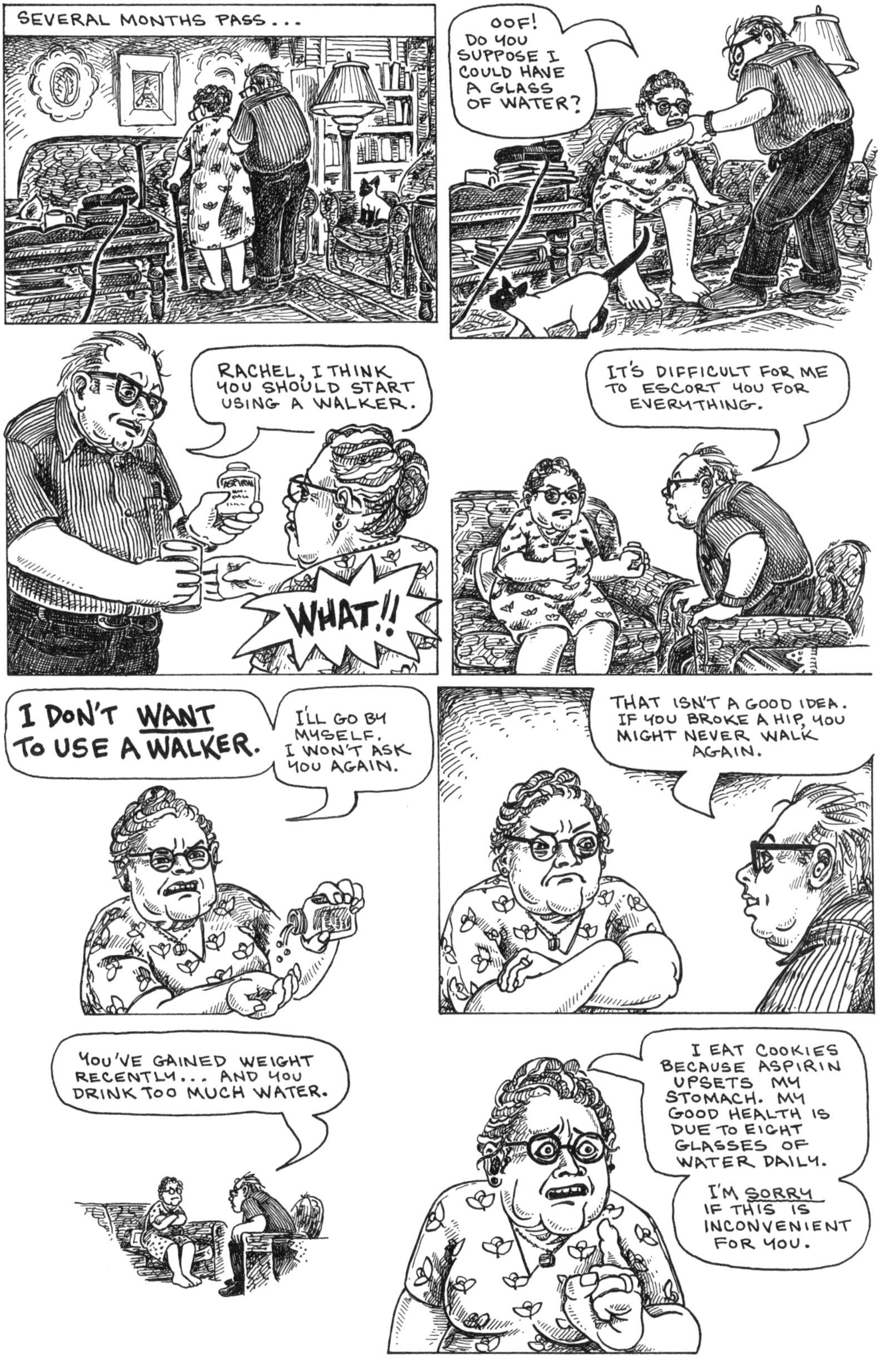
SEVERAL MONTHS PASS...
OOF! DO YOU SUPPOSE I COULD HAVE A GLASS OF WATER?
RACHEL, I THINK YOU SHOULD START USING A WALKER.
WHAT!!
IT'S DIFFICULT FOR ME TO ESCORT YOU FOR EVERYTHING.
I DON'T WANT TO USE A WALKER.
I'LL GO BY MYSELF. I WON'T ASK YOU AGAIN.
THAT ISN'T A GOOD IDEA. IF YOU BROKE A HIP, YOU MIGHT NEVER WALK AGAIN.
YOU'VE GAINED WEIGHT RECENTLY... AND YOU DRINK TOO MUCH WATER.
I EAT COOKIES BECAUSE ASPIRIN UPSETS MY STOMACH. MY GOOD HEALTH IS DUE TO EIGHT GLASSES OF WATER DAILY.
I'M SORRY IF THIS IS INCONVENIENT FOR YOU.

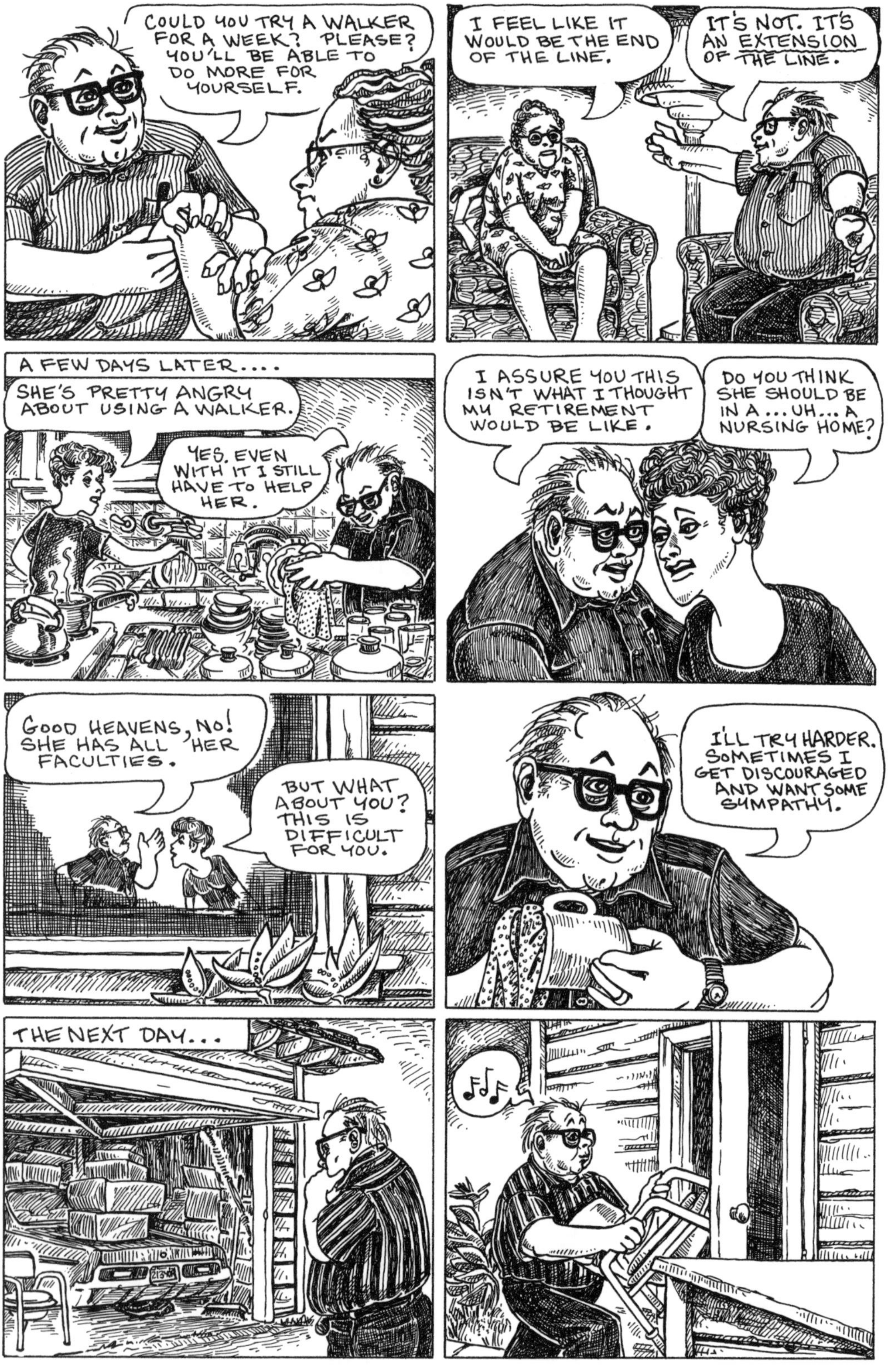
COULD YOU TRY A WALKER FOR A WEEK? PLEASE? YOU'LL BE ABLE TO DO MORE FOR YOURSELF.
I FEEL LIKE IT WOULD BE THE END OF THE LINE.
IT'S NOT. IT'S AN EXTENSION OF THE LINE.
A FEW DAYS LATER....
SHE'S PRETTY ANGRY ABOUT USING A WALKER.
YES. EVEN WITH IT I STILL HAVE TO HELP HER.
I ASSURE YOU THIS ISN'T WHAT I THOUGHT MY RETIREMENT WOULD BE LIKE.
DO YOU THINK SHE SHOULD BE IN A...UH...A NURSING HOME?
GOOD HEAVENS, NO! SHE HAS ALL HER FACULTIES.
BUT WHAT ABOUT YOU? THIS IS DIFFICULT FOR YOU.
I'LL TRY HARDER. SOMETIMES I GET DISCOURAGED AND WANT SOME SYMPATHY.
THE NEXT DAY...

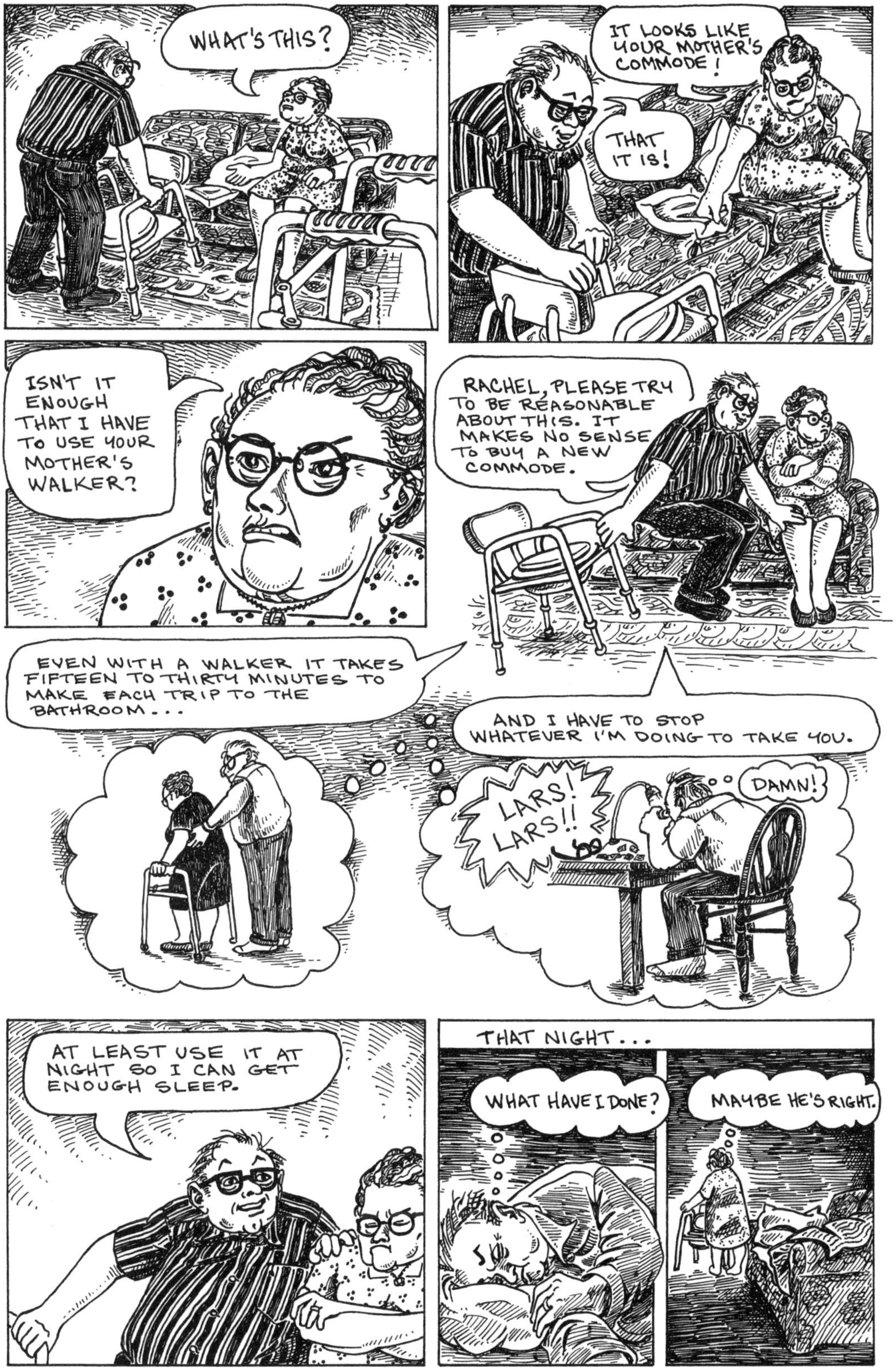
WHAT'S THIS?
IT LOOKS LIKE YOUR MOTHER'S COMMODE!
THAT IT IS!
ISN'T IT ENOUGH THAT I HAVE TO USE YOUR MOTHER'S WALKER?
RACHEL, PLEASE TRY TO BE REASONABLE ABOUT THIS. IT MAKES NO SENSE TO BUY A NEW COMMODE.
EVEN WITH A WALKER IT TAKES FIFTEEN TO THIRTY MINUTES TO MAKE EACH TRIP TO THE BATHROOM...
AND I HAVE TO STOP WHATEVER I'M DOING TO TAKE YOU.
LARS! LARS!!
DAMN!
AT LEAST USE IT AT NIGHT SO I CAN GET ENOUGH SLEEP.
THAT NIGHT...
WHAT HAVE I DONE?
MAYBE HE'S RIGHT.

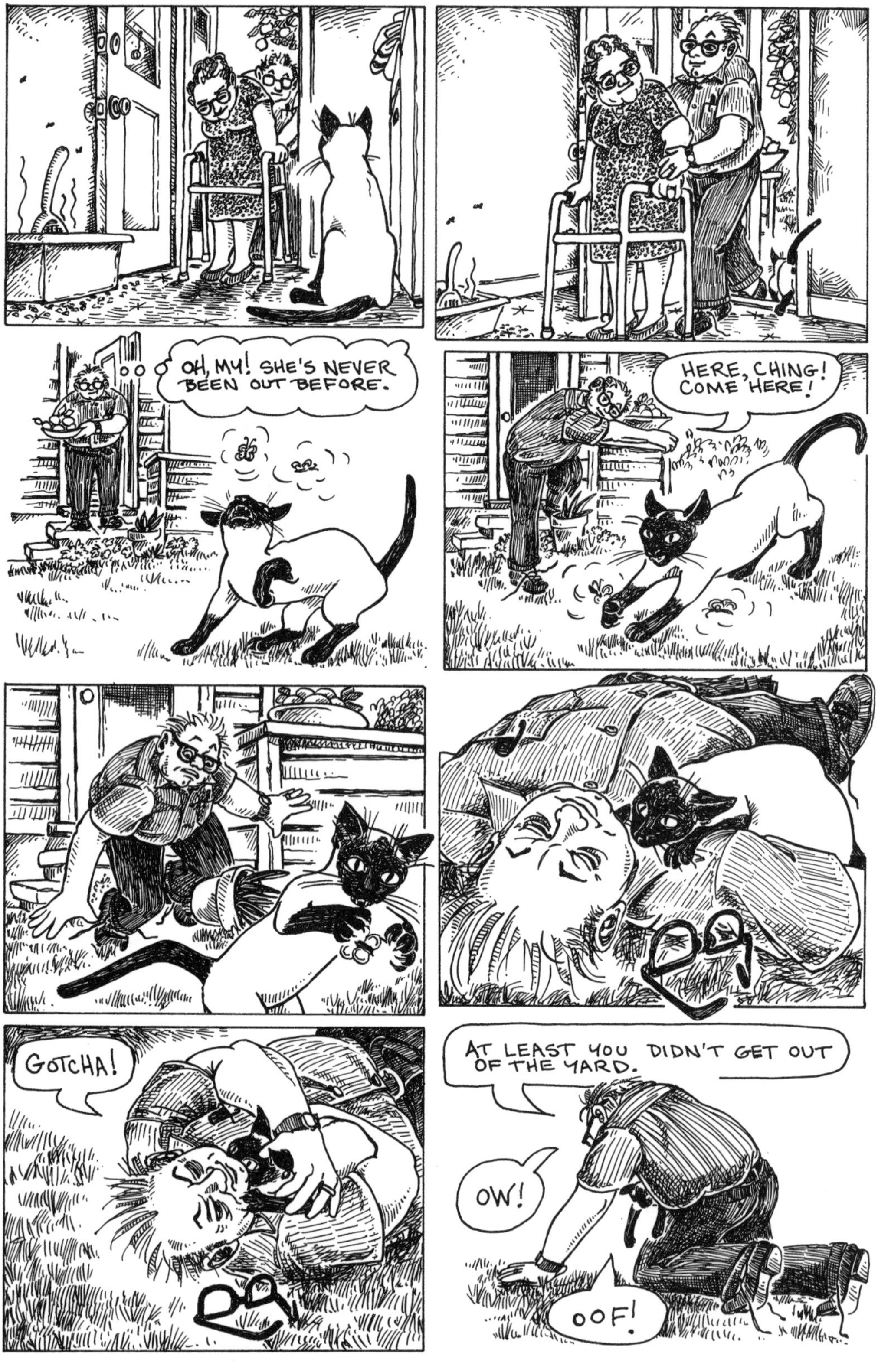
OH, MY! SHE'S NEVER BEEN OUT BEFORE.
HERE, CHING! COME HERE!
GOTCHA!
AT LEAST YOU DIDN'T GET OUT OF THE YARD.
OW!
OOF!

JIM WOODRING

Frank Among the Gut-Worshippers

from *Congress of the Animals*

Jim Woodring
Congress Of The Animals
Fantagraphics Books

FOR ME, DRAWING COMICS IS

One way among many of getting my ideas across.

THE SELECTION

The generic anthropomorph Frank finds himself detained by a tribe of viscera-obsessed man-things. Following a communications impasse, Frank's hosts use a cosmonucleus as an anesthetic to examine his works, which they find deficient in every way.

THE CONTEXT

Congress of the Animals is the story of how Frank profited from venturing beyond the boundaries of his homeland, the Unifactor. His path to glory is strewn with demoralizing obstacles, including the grotesque events portrayed in this sequence.

PUBLICATIONS MY WORK HAS APPEARED IN

The *New York Times, Print, World Art, Abitare, Weirdo, The Comics Journal,* the *Kenyon Review, Wired, Publishers Weekly.*

AWARDS

2006 United States Artists Fellowship; 2008 Artist Trust Fellowship.

WHAT I'M KNOWN FOR

JIM magazine, 1980 to 1992; *Seeing Things,* a drawing collection, 2007; Nibbus Maximus, a seven-foot functioning dip pen, 2010.

WHERE I LIVE

Seattle, Washington.

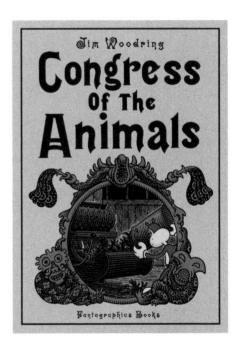

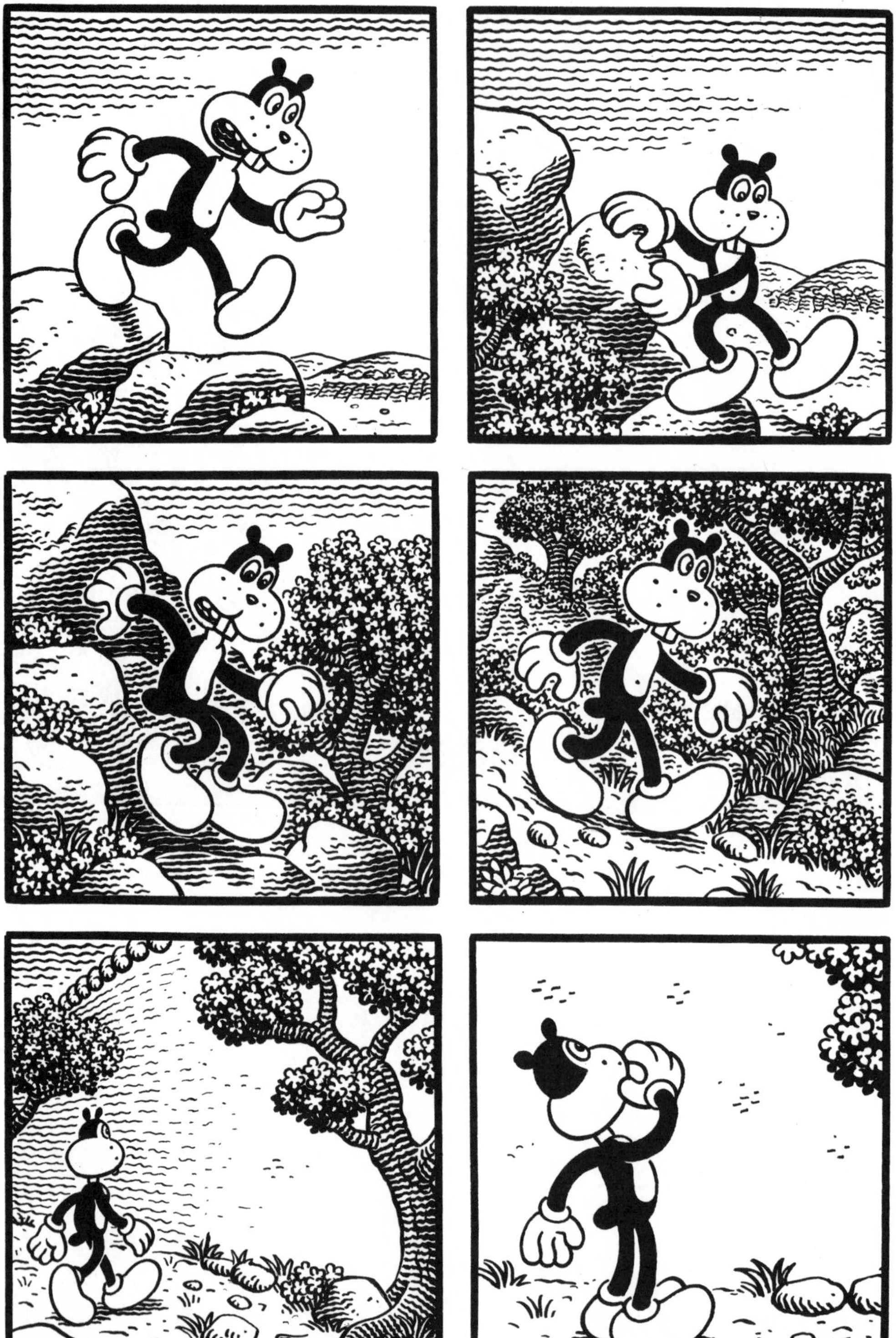

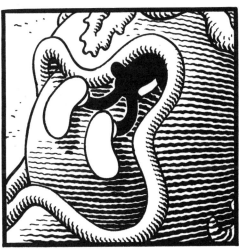

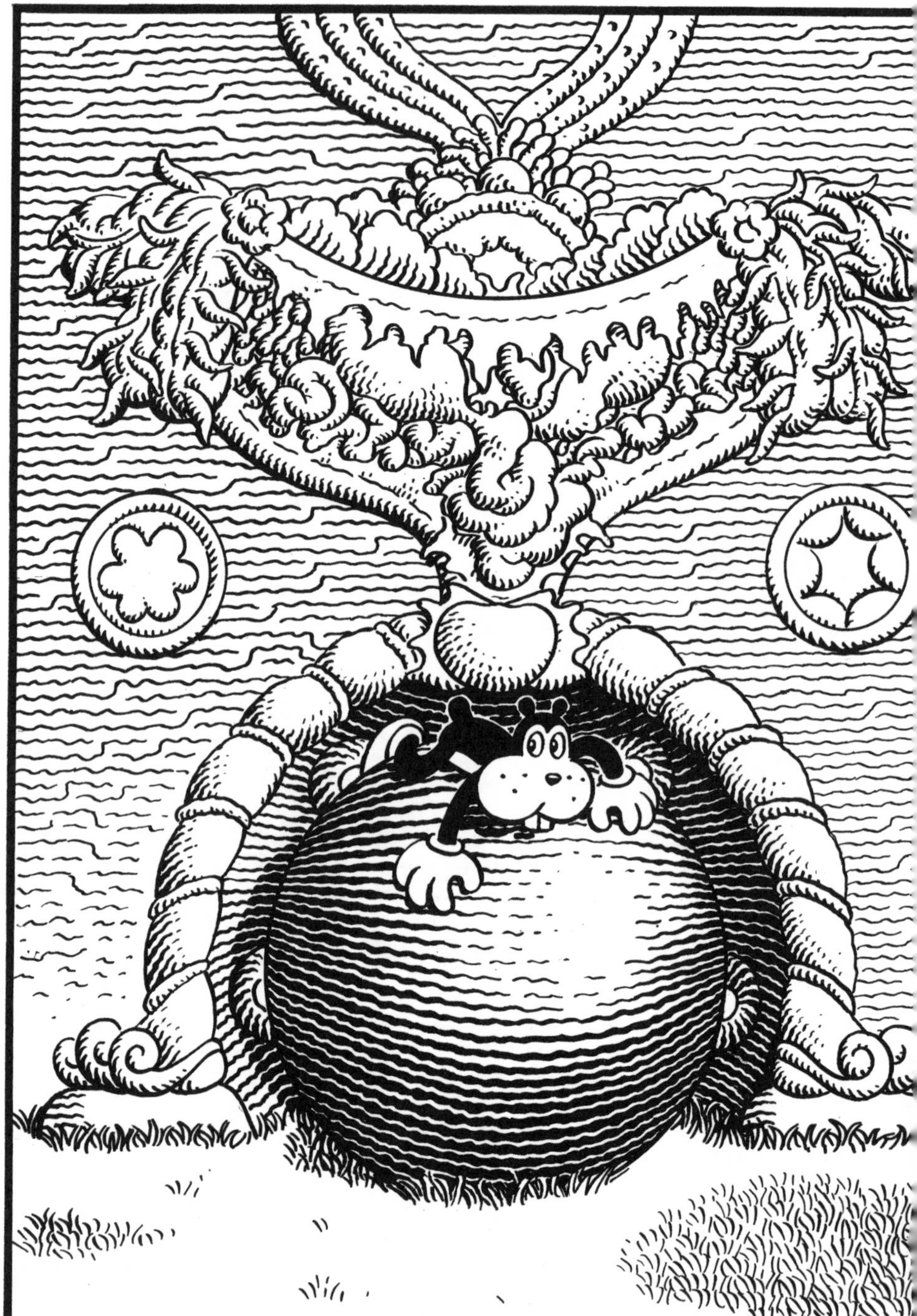

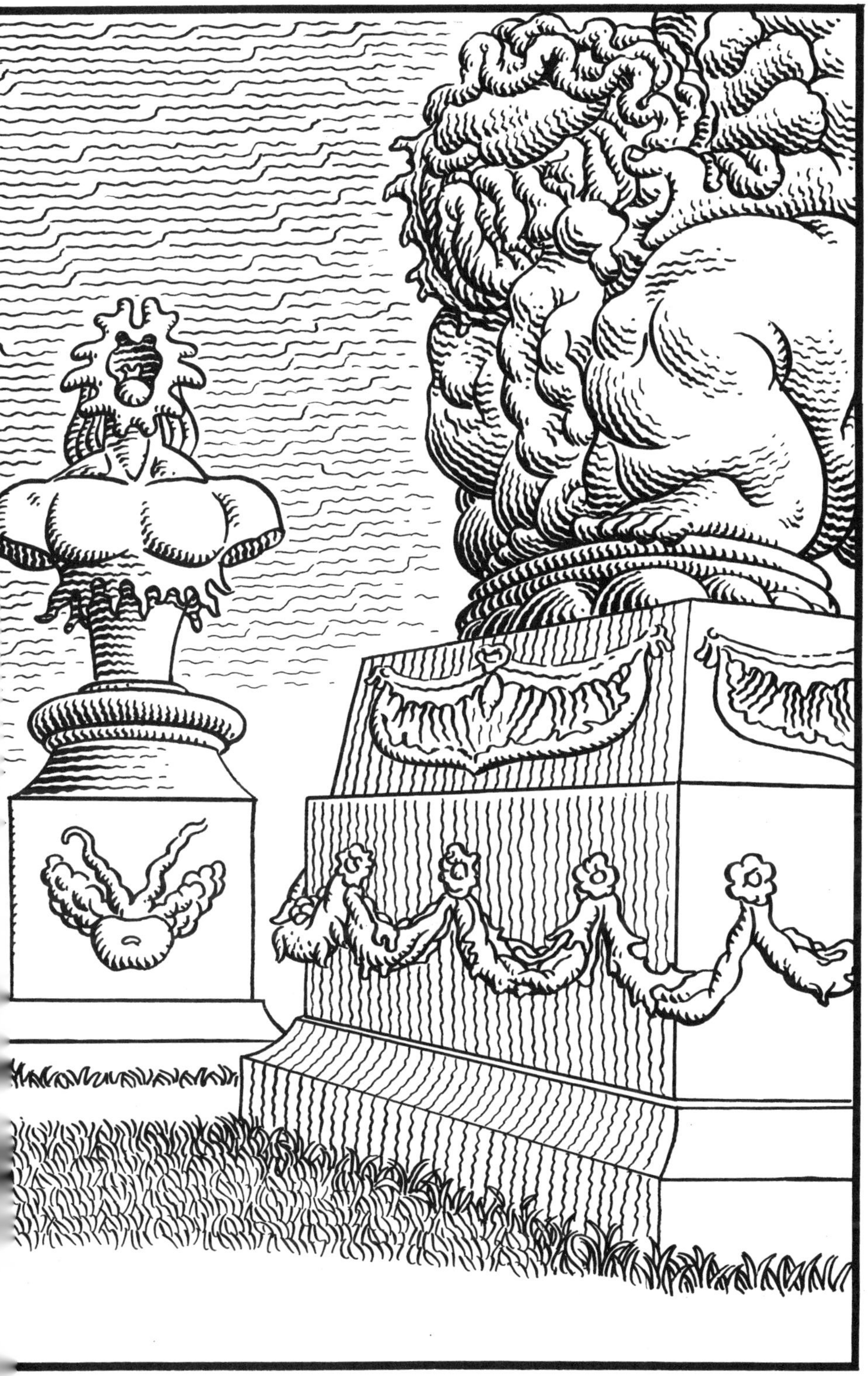

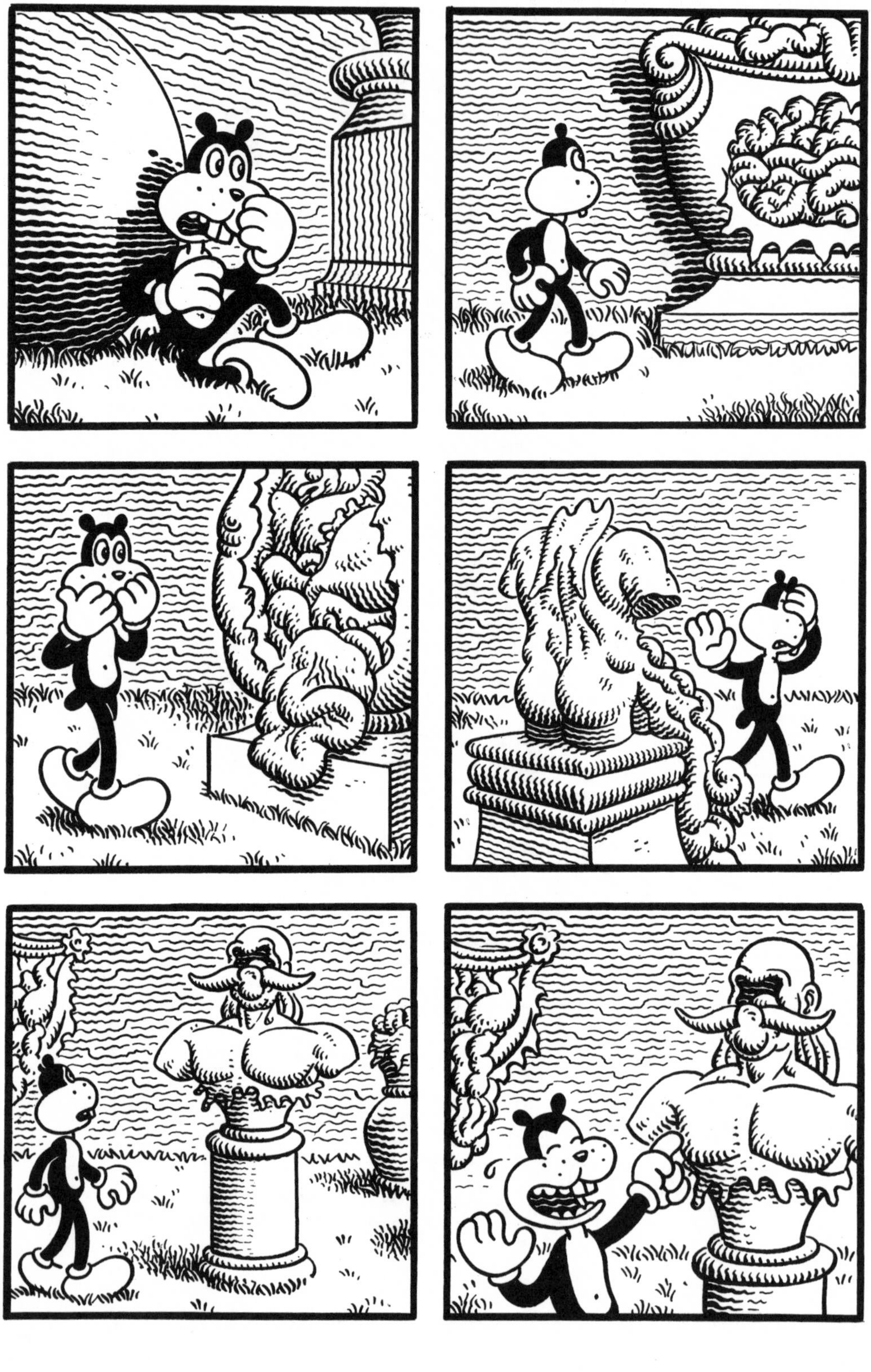

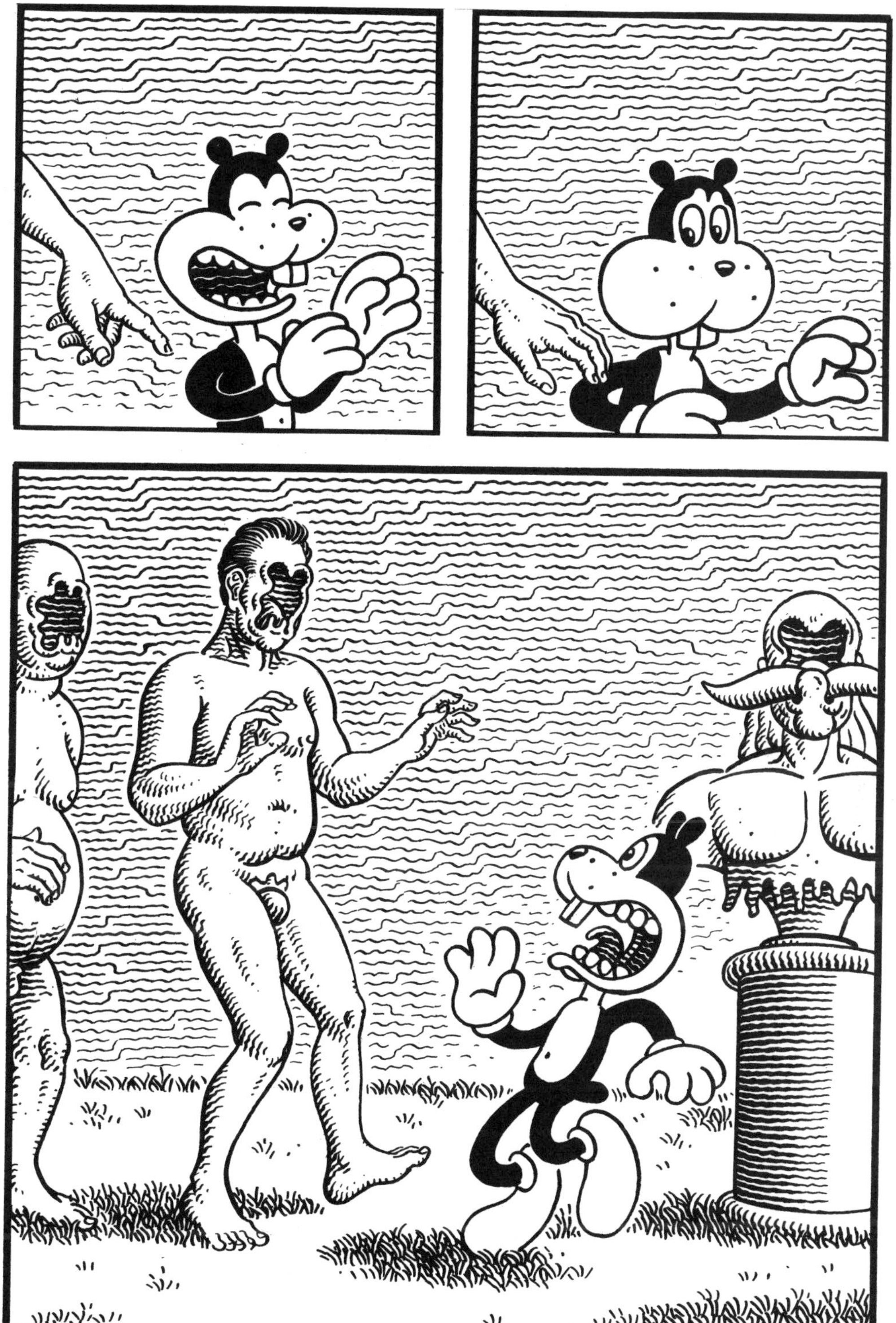

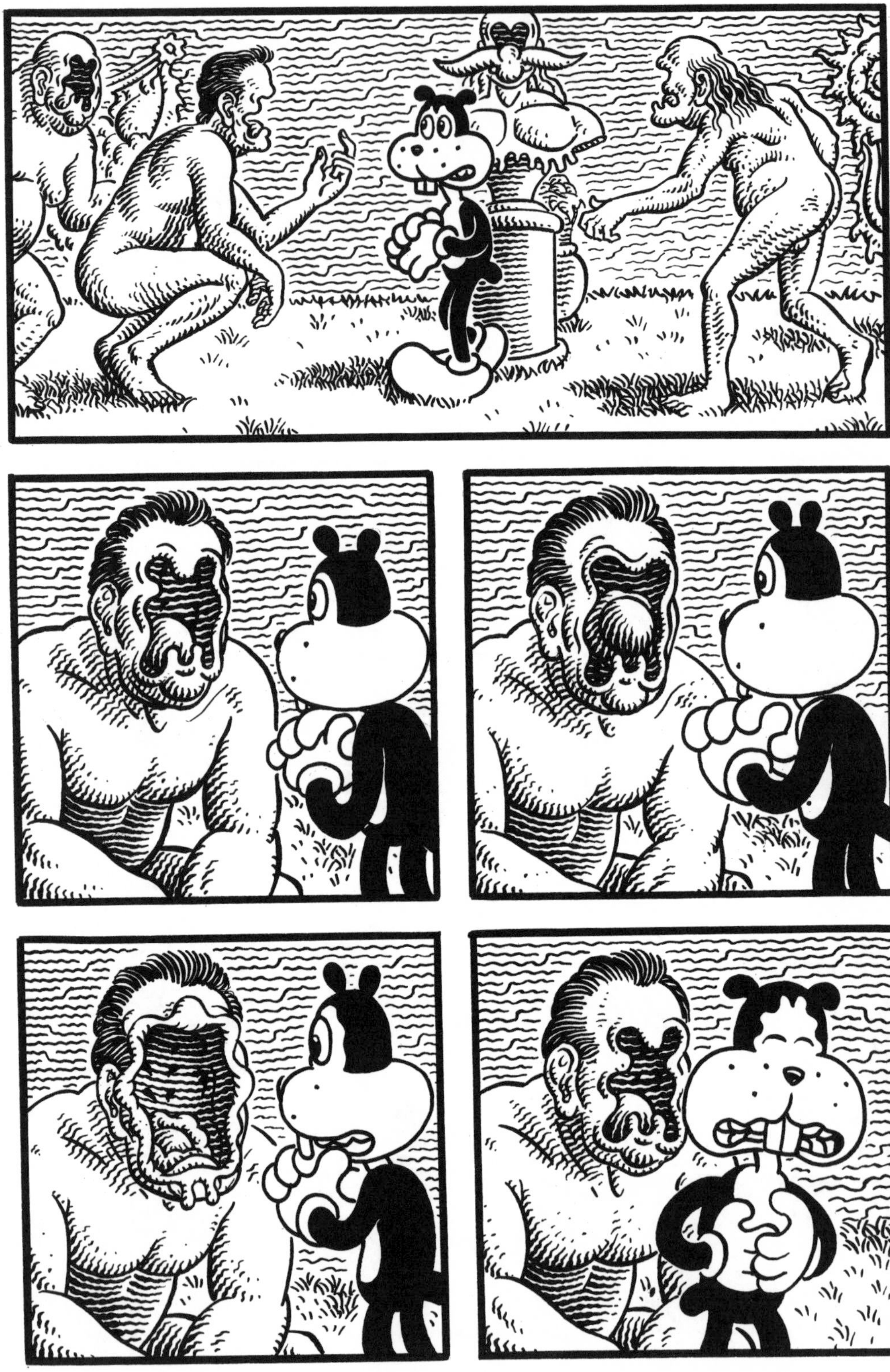

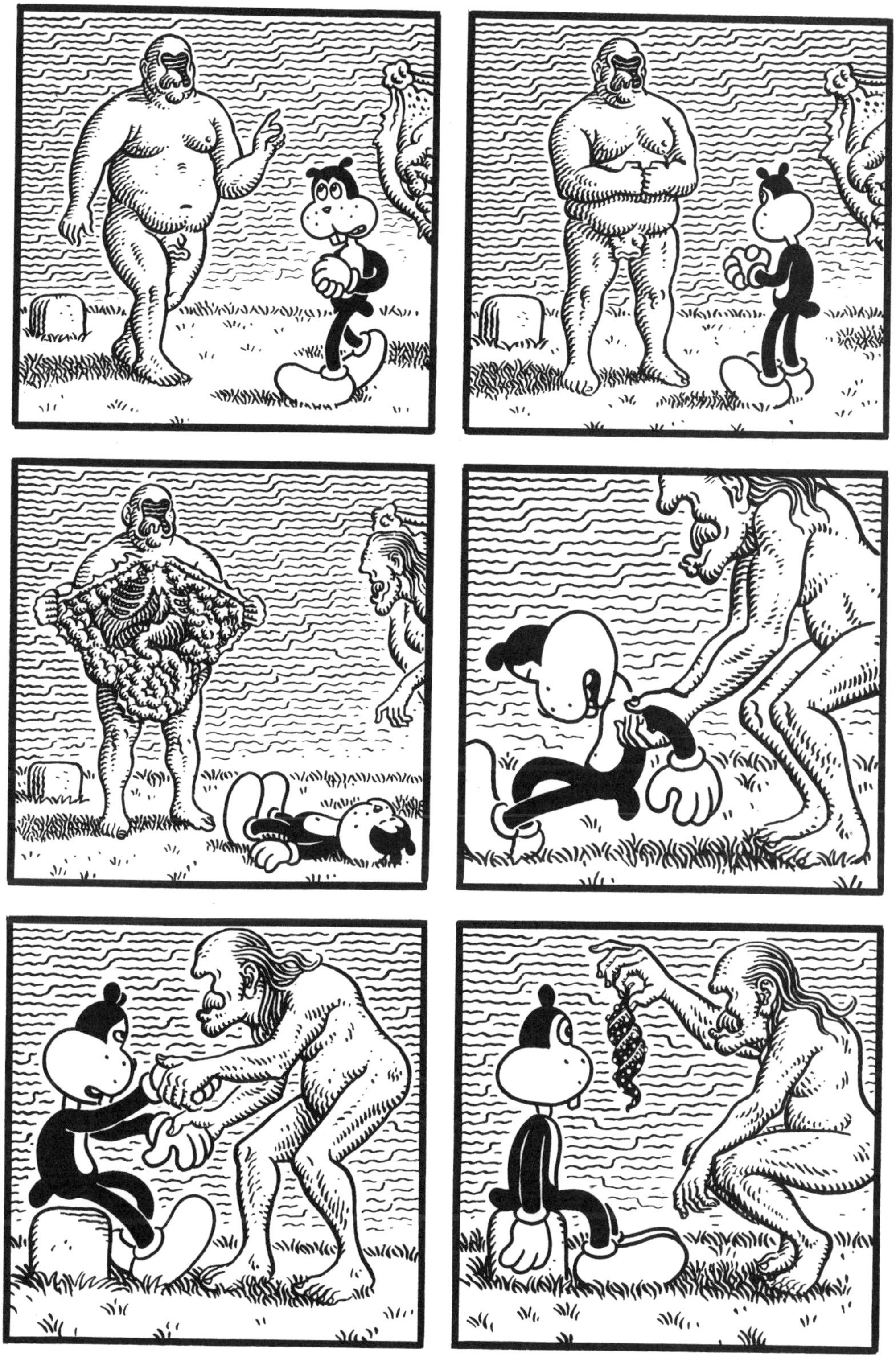

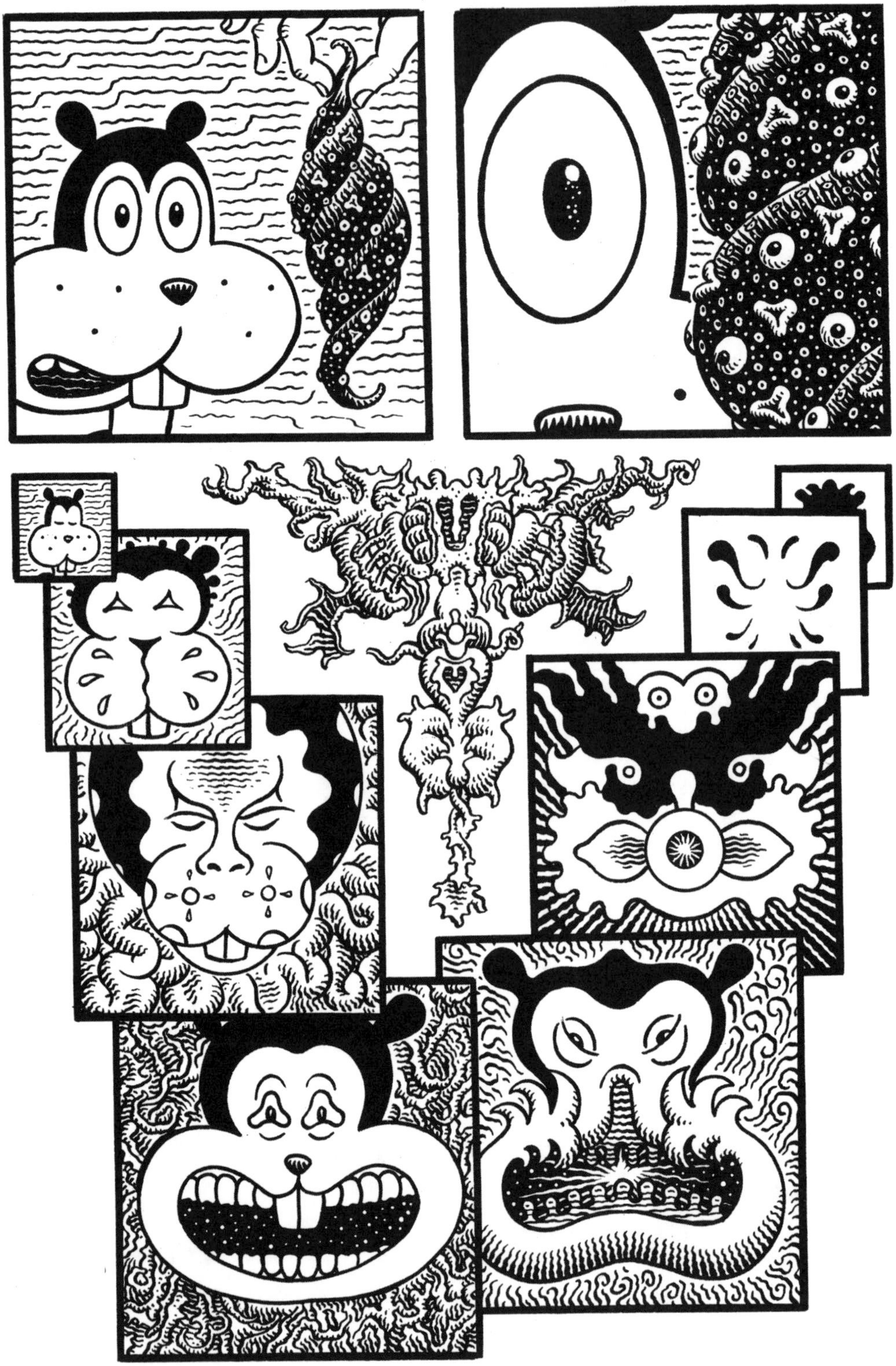

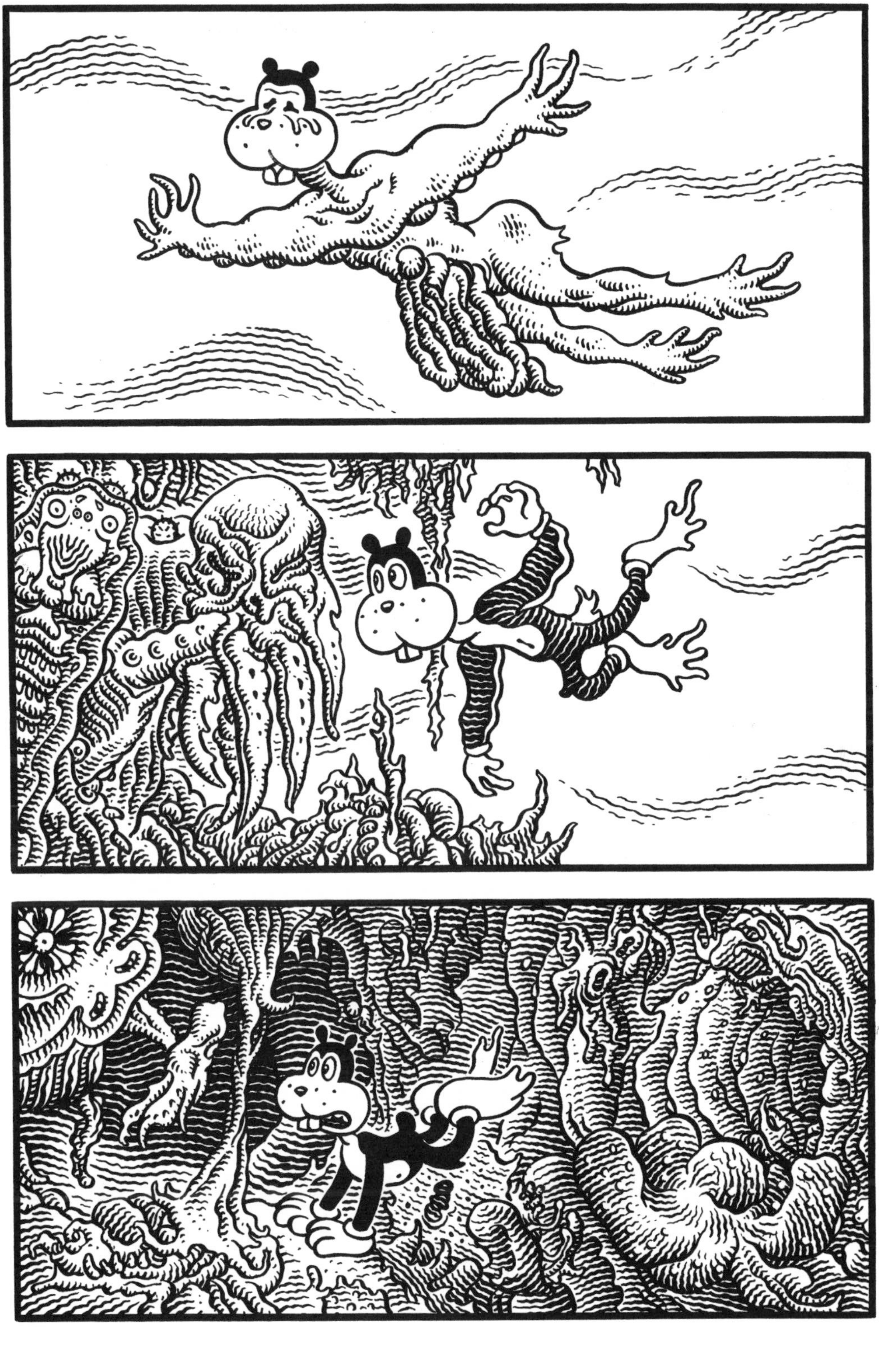

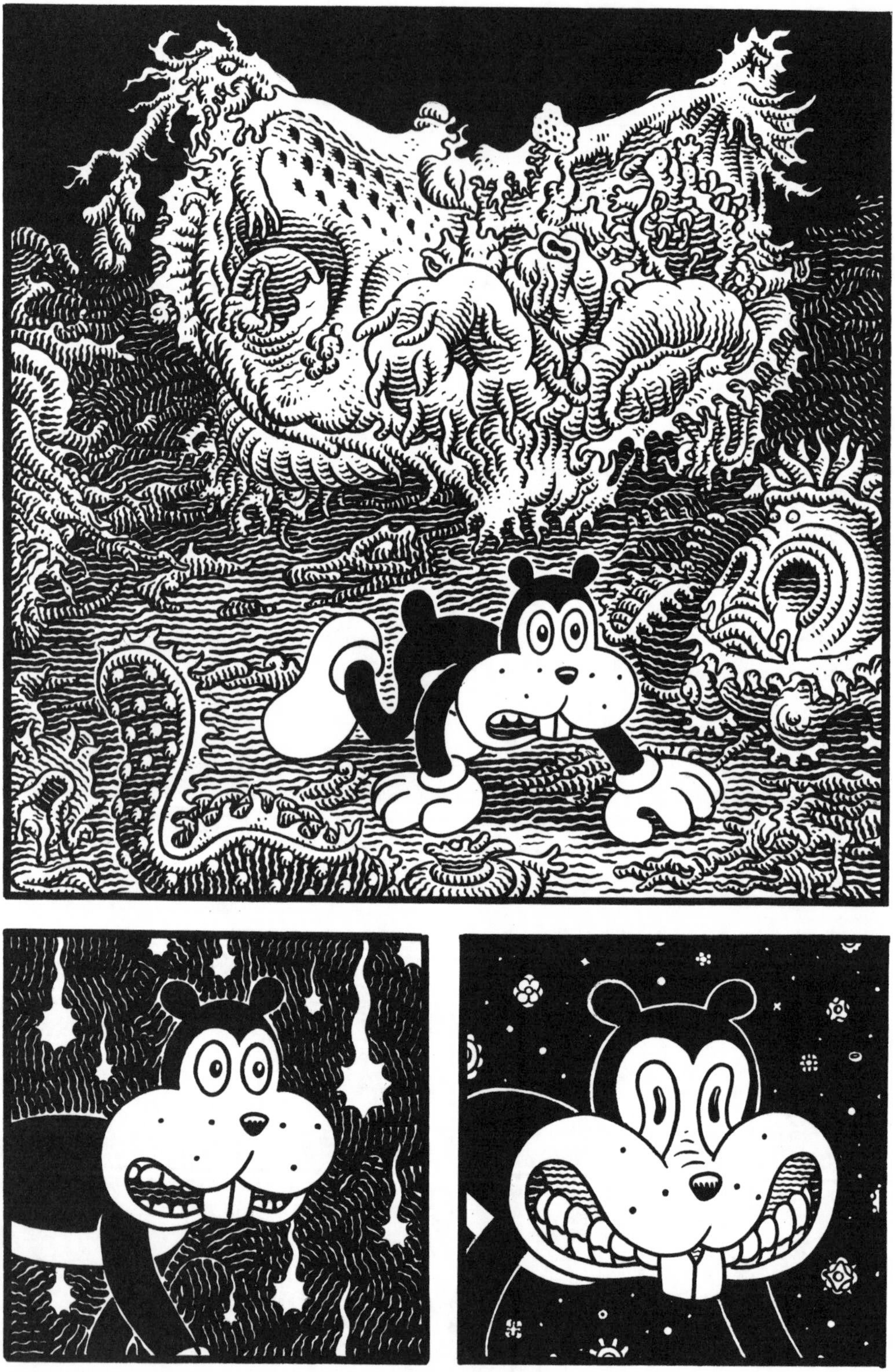

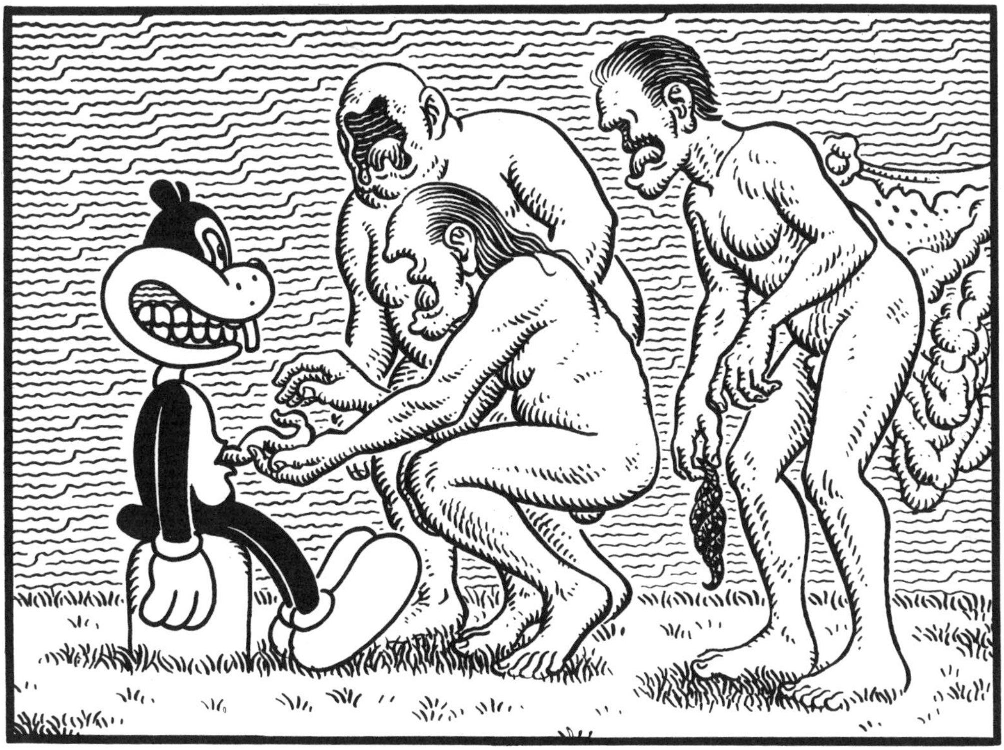

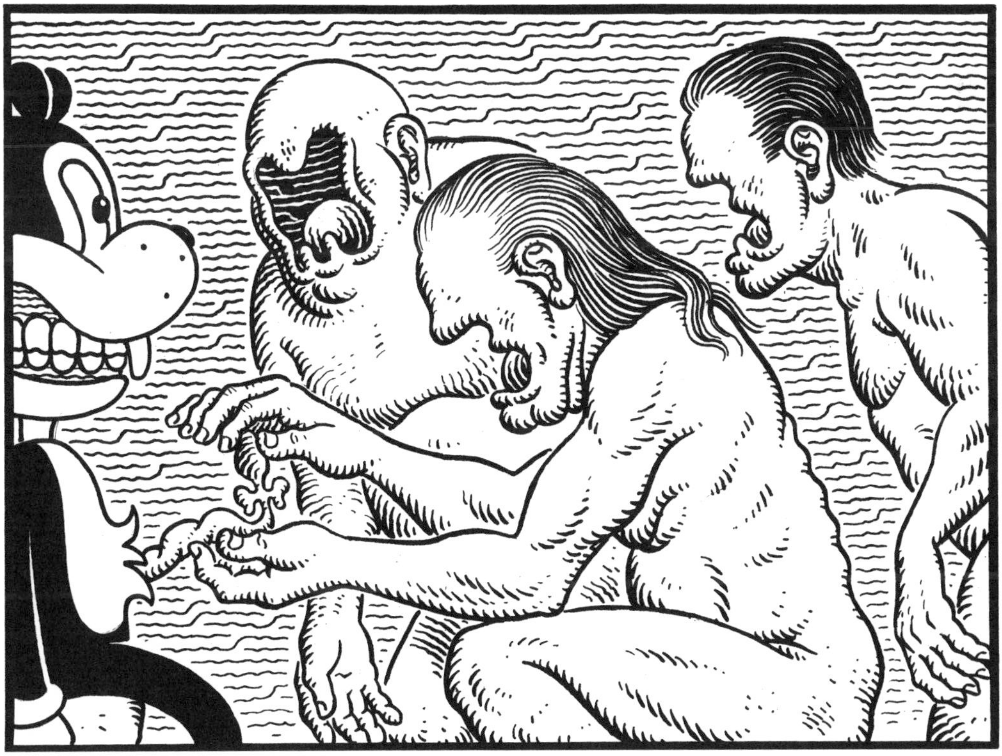

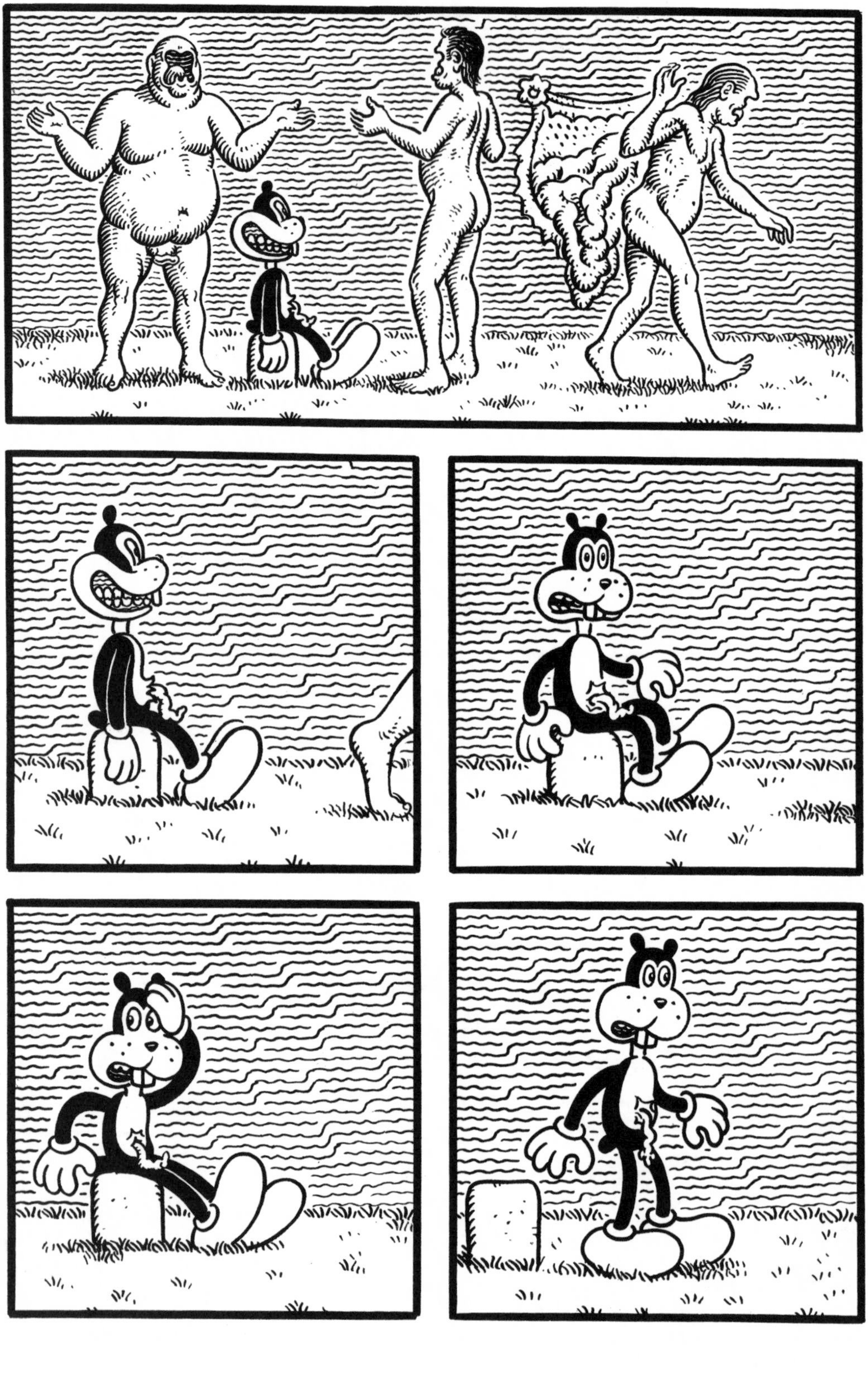

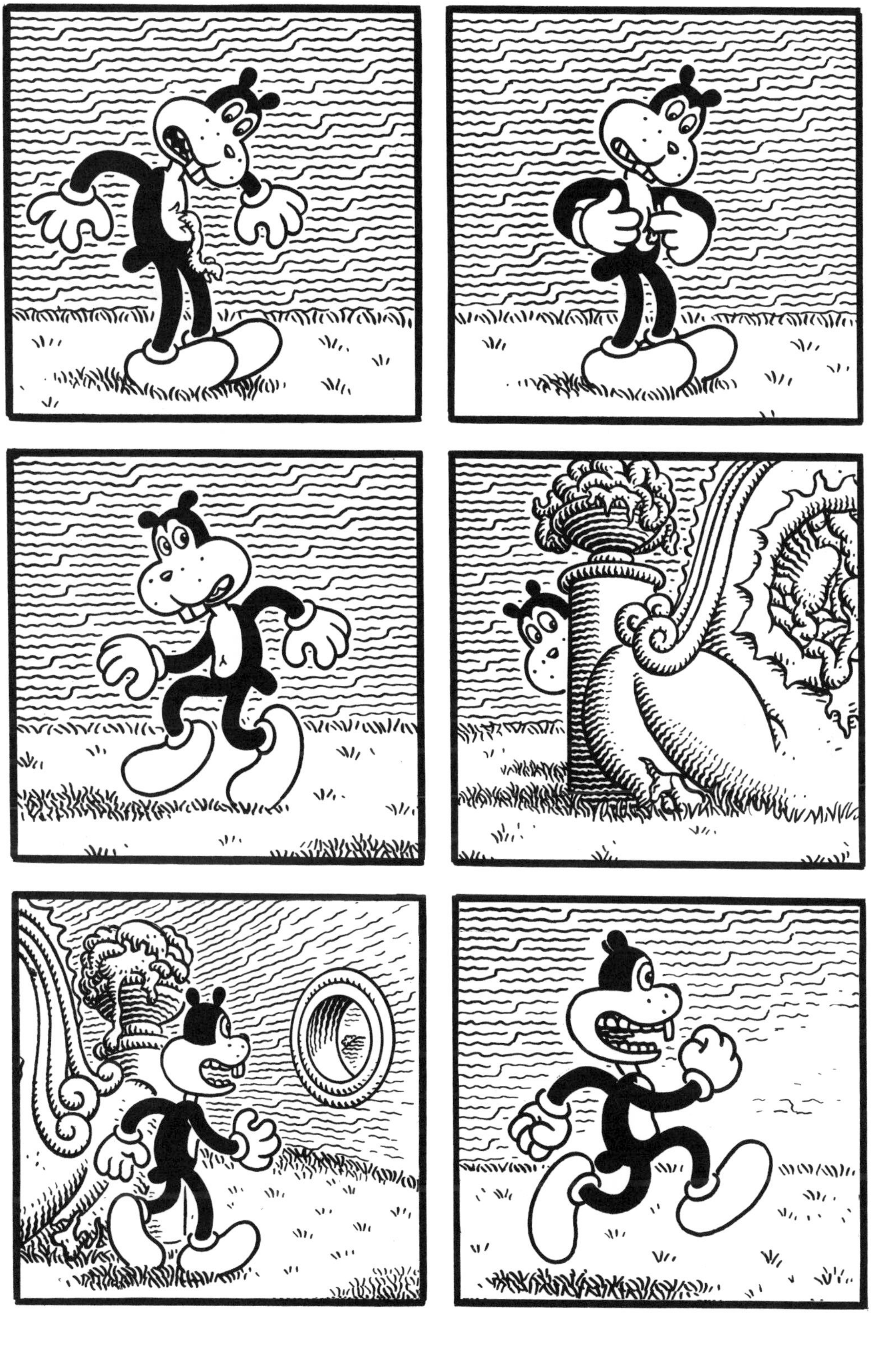

CHESTER BROWN

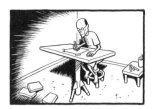

Angelina

from *Paying for It*

PAYING FOR IT
a comic-strip memoir about being a john
CHESTER BROWN
introduction by
ROBERT CRUMB

FOR ME, DRAWING COMICS IS

I don't have an answer for this — sorry. Anything I come up with just seems silly and reductive.

THE SELECTION

The narrative mostly focuses on what happened when I paid for sex from 1999 to 2010.

THE CONTEXT

Chapter 1 explained why I began to consider seeing sex workers, and Chapter 2 recounted my experiences in a particular brothel with the first prostitute I had sex with. In the chapter you're reading, I visit a second brothel.

WHAT I'M KNOWN FOR

The major projects I'd be known for would be my comic book series, *Yummy Fur,* and my graphic novels, *Ed the Happy Clown, The Playboy, I Never Liked You,* and *Louis Riel.*

WHERE I LIVE

Toronto, Ontario.

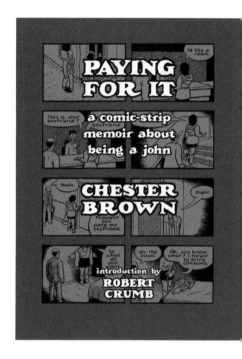

CHAPTER 3

ANGELINA

MAY 13th 1999:
Here's an ad for a girl named Tina -- "19, thin, busty, very pretty".
I'm calling about Tina. How much does she charge?
Bell
80 dollars for a half-hour.
Wow! That's a lot less than 120.
And where are you located?

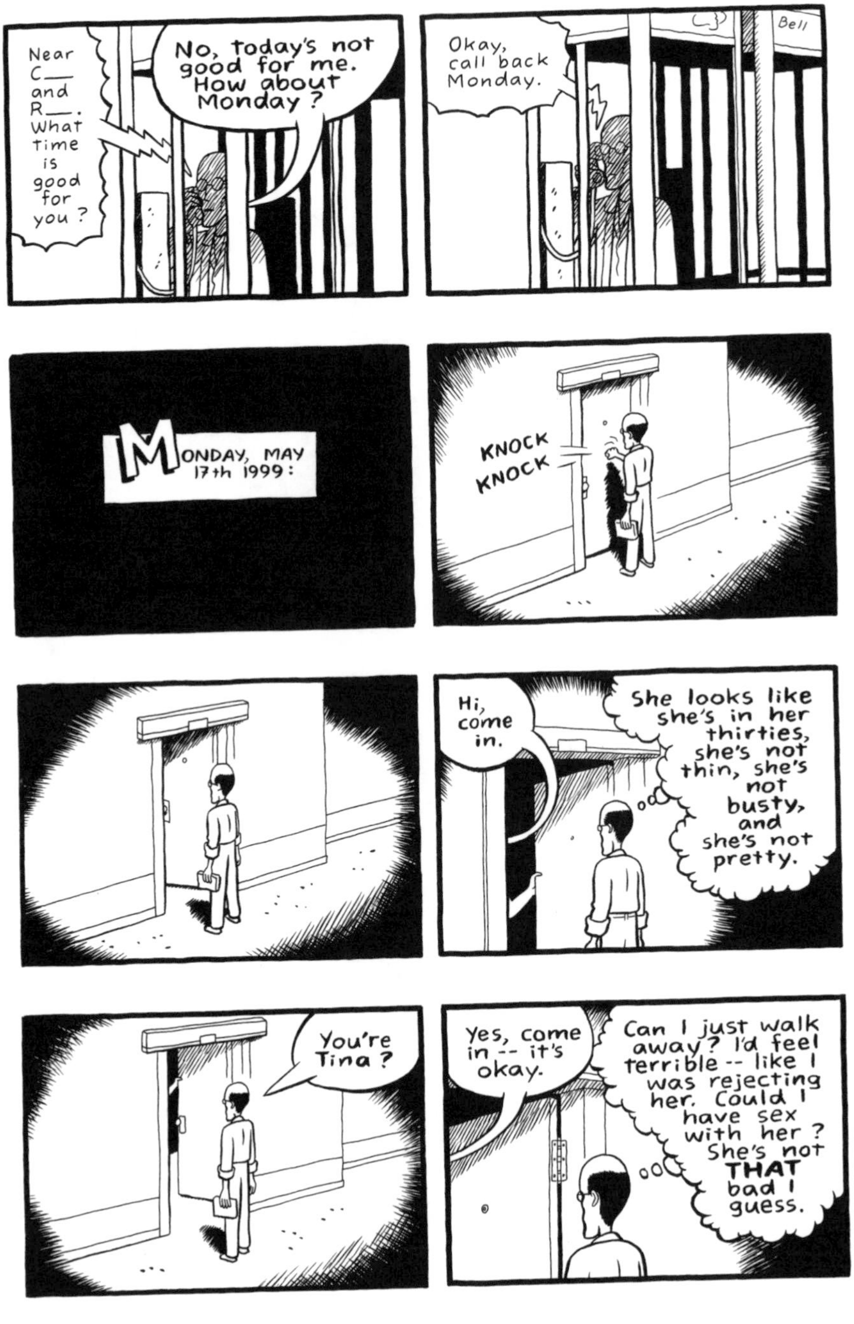
Near C__ and R__. What time is good for you?
No, today's not good for me. How about Monday?
Bell
Okay, call back Monday.
MONDAY, MAY 17th 1999:
KNOCK KNOCK
Hi, come in.
She looks like she's in her thirties, she's not thin, she's not busty, and she's not pretty.
You're Tina?
Yes, come in -- it's okay.
Can I just walk away? I'd feel terrible -- like I was rejecting her. Could I have sex with her? She's not THAT bad I guess.

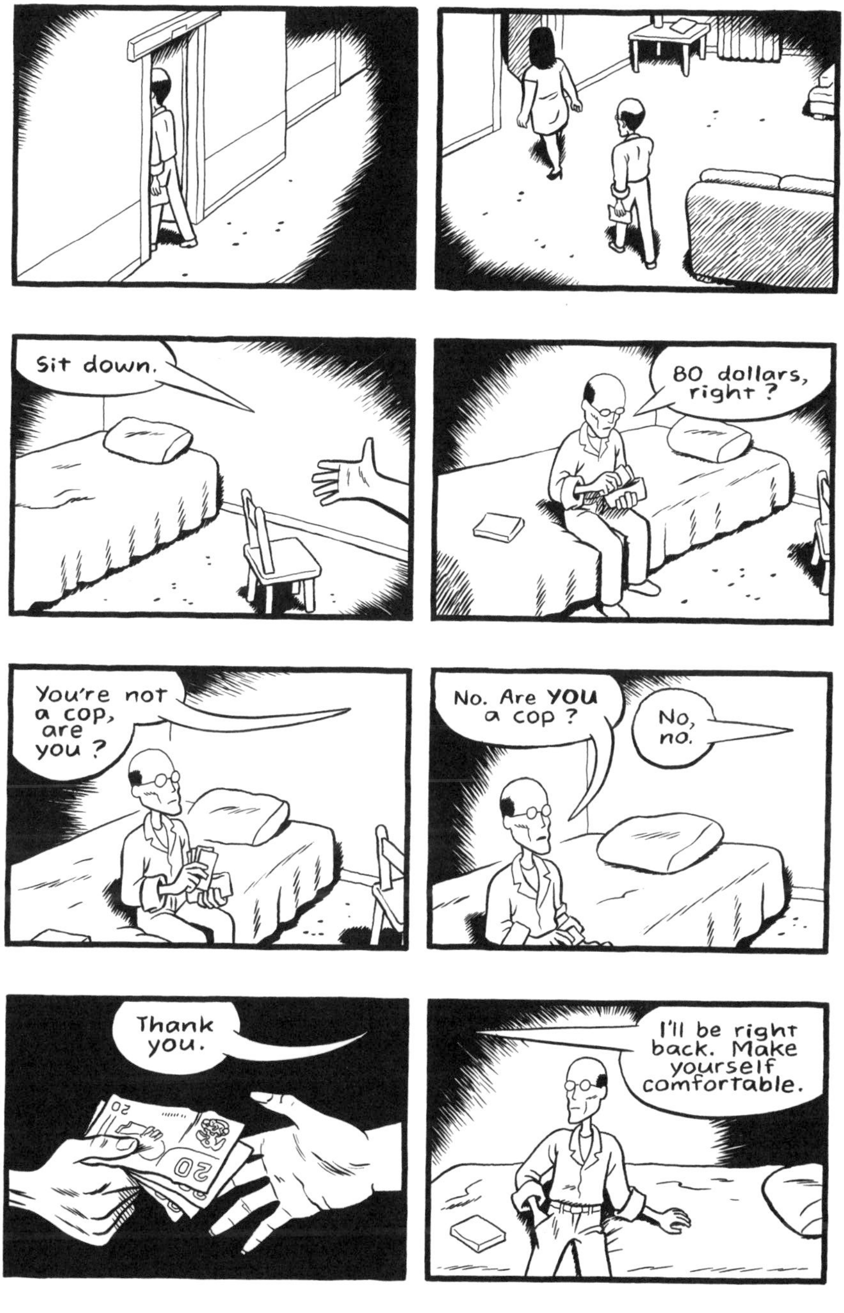
Sit down.
80 dollars, right?
You're not a cop, are you?
No. Are YOU a cop?
No, no.
Thank you.
I'll be right back. Make yourself comfortable.

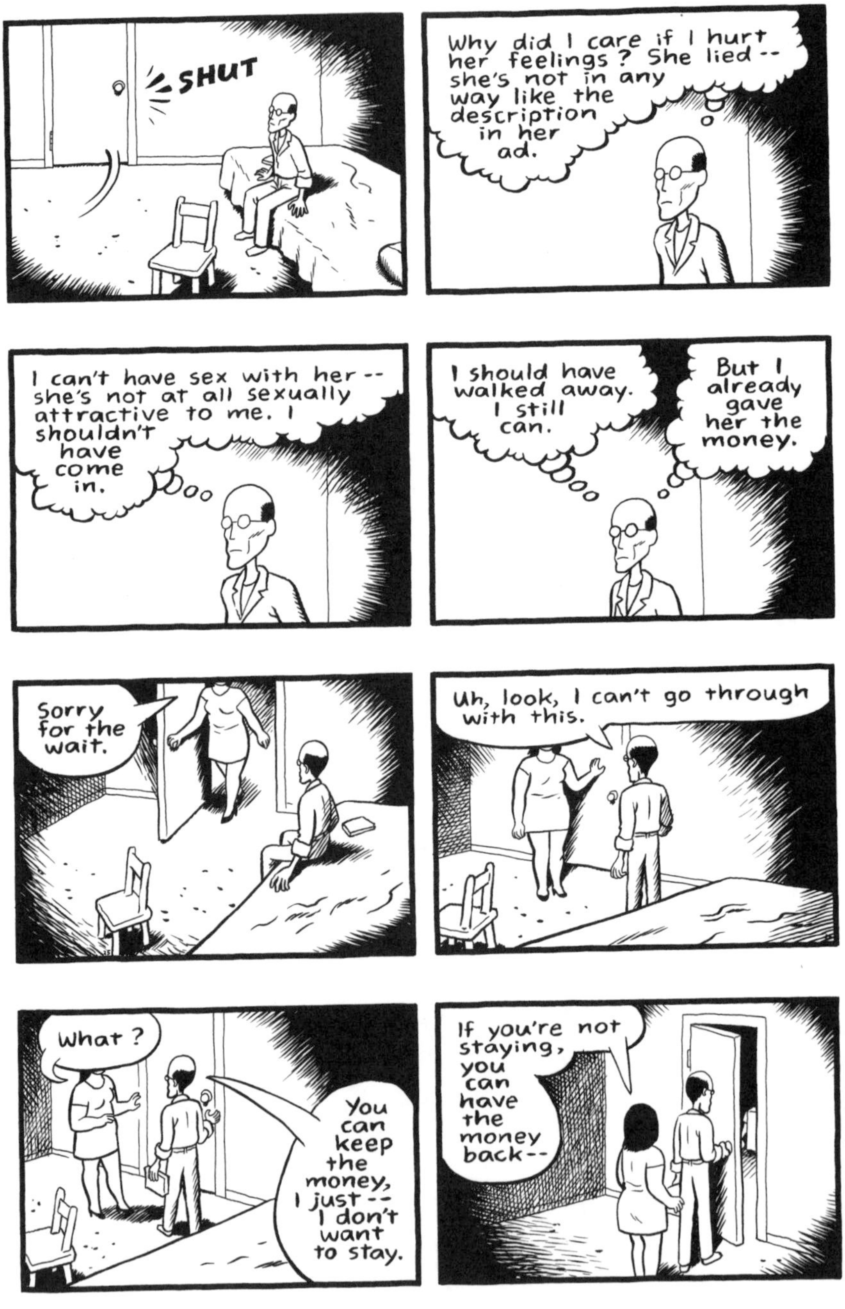
SHUT
Why did I care if I hurt her feelings? She lied -- she's not in any way like the description in her ad.
I can't have sex with her -- she's not at all sexually attractive to me. I shouldn't have come in.
I should have walked away. I still can.
But I already gave her the money.
Sorry for the wait.
Uh, look, I can't go through with this.
What?
You can keep the money, I just -- I don't want to stay.
If you're not staying, you can have the money back --

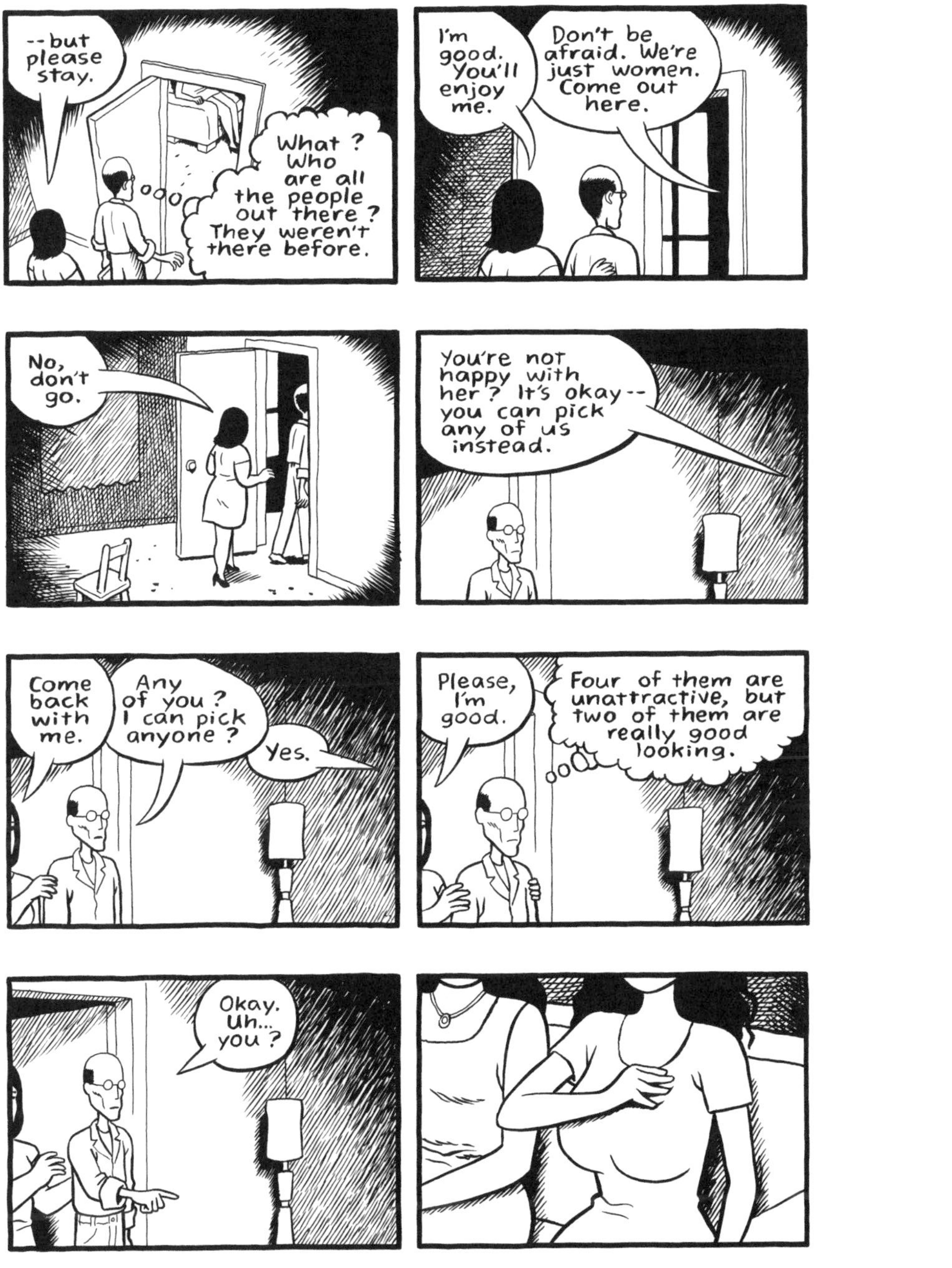
--but please stay.
What? Who are all the people out there? They weren't there before.
I'm good. You'll enjoy me.
Don't be afraid. We're just women. Come out here.
No, don't go.
You're not happy with her? It's okay--you can pick any of us instead.
Come back with me.
Any of you? I can pick anyone?
Yes.
Please, I'm good.
Four of them are unattractive, but two of them are really good looking.
Okay. Uh... you?

THE WOMAN I POINTED TO PUT HER HAND TO HER CHEST, SILENTLY ASKING, "ME?"

She looks... uncomfortable.

I'm getting the impression that she didn't want to be chosen.

Yeah, but if you don't want to...

SHE THEN LOOKED AT THE WOMAN WHO SEEMED TO BE THE MADAM.

THE MADAM GAVE A GESTURE WHICH SAID, "GO WITH HIM!"

Uh, if you'd rather not, I can pick one of the other girls.

It's okay.

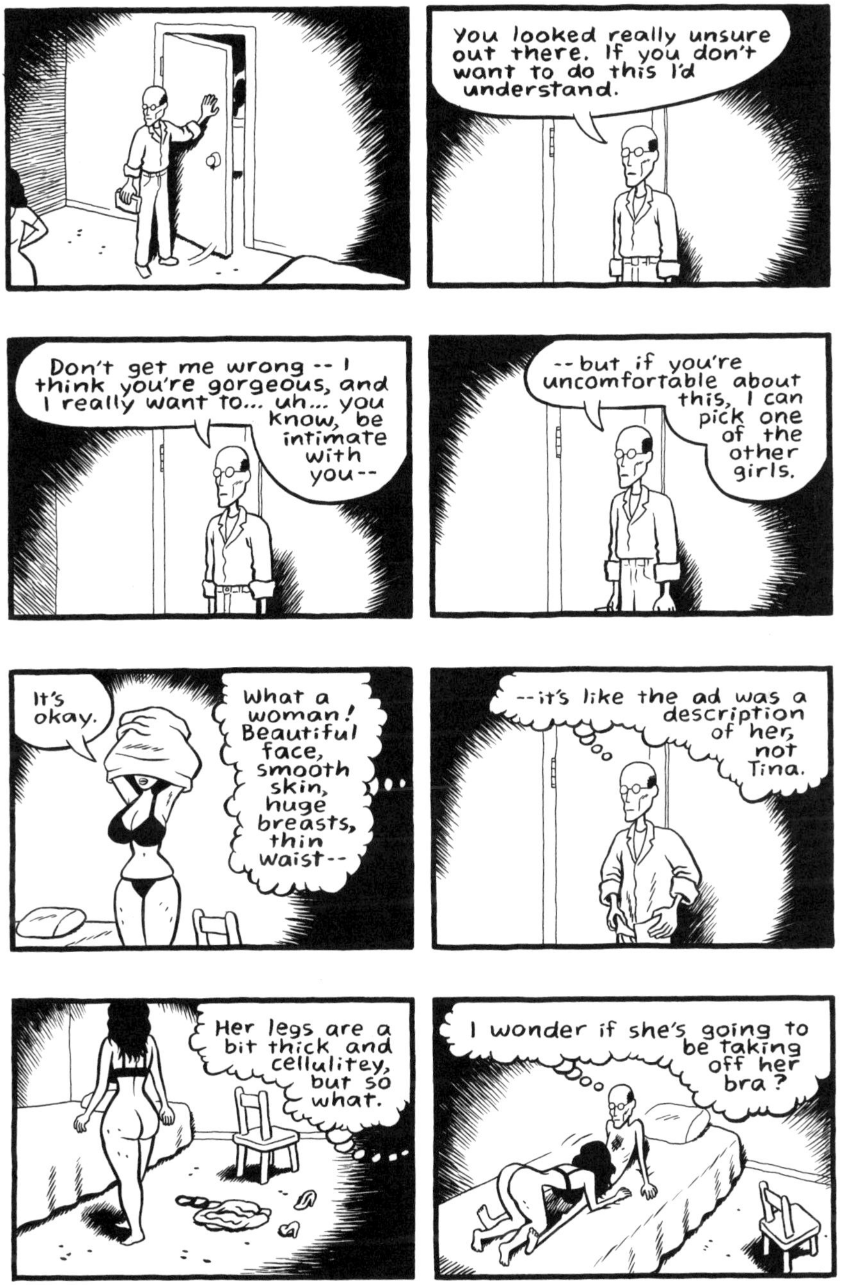

You looked really unsure out there. If you don't want to do this I'd understand.
Don't get me wrong -- I think you're gorgeous, and I really want to... uh... you know, be intimate with you--
--but if you're uncomfortable about this, I can pick one of the other girls.
It's okay.
What a woman! Beautiful face, smooth skin, huge breasts, thin waist--
--it's like the ad was a description of her, not Tina.
Her legs are a bit thick and cellulitey, but so what.
I wonder if she's going to be taking off her bra?

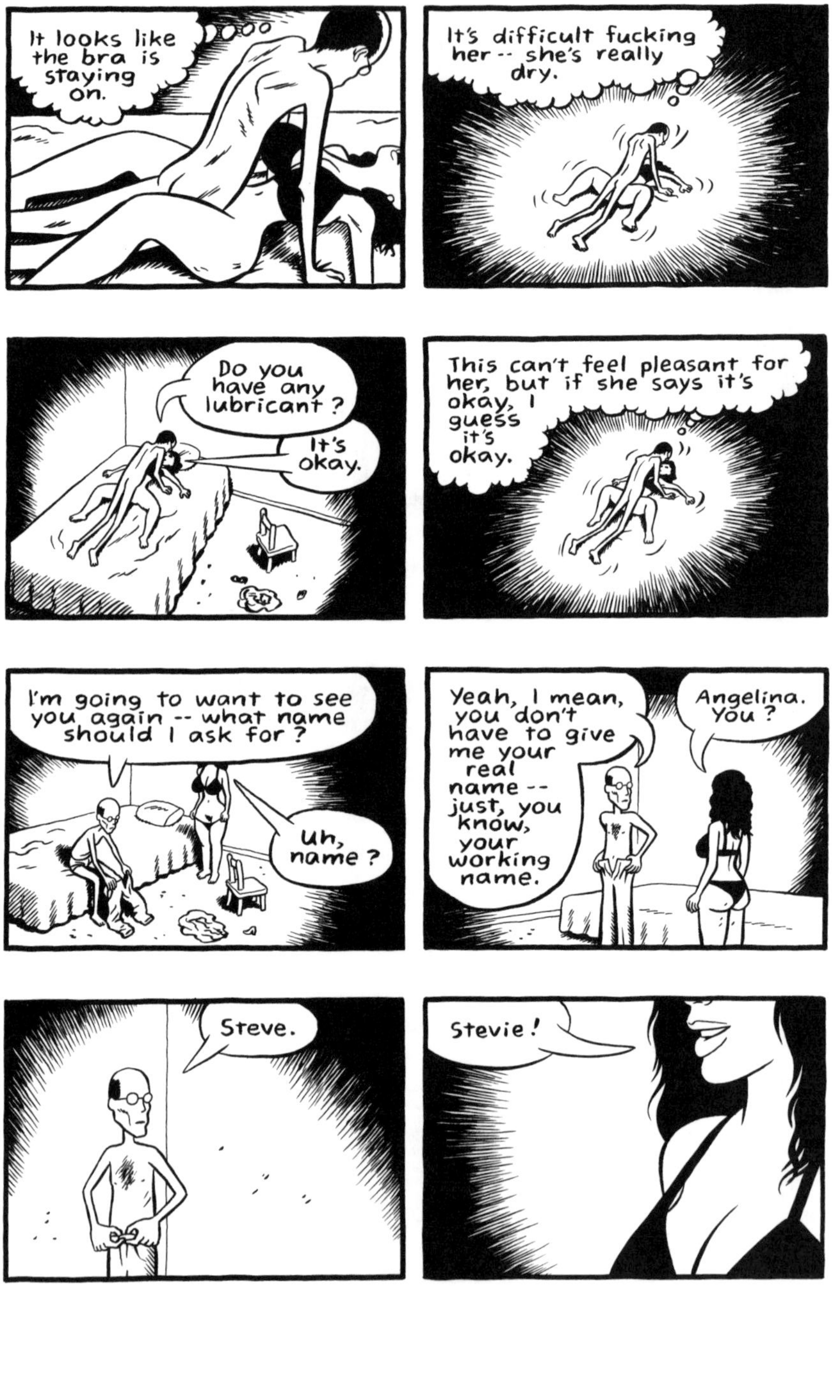
It looks like the bra is staying on.
It's difficult fucking her -- she's really dry.
Do you have any lubricant?
It's okay.
This can't feel pleasant for her, but if she says it's okay, I guess it's okay.
I'm going to want to see you again -- what name should I ask for?
Uh, name?
Yeah, I mean, you don't have to give me your real name -- just, you know, your working name.
Angelina. You?
Steve.
Stevie!

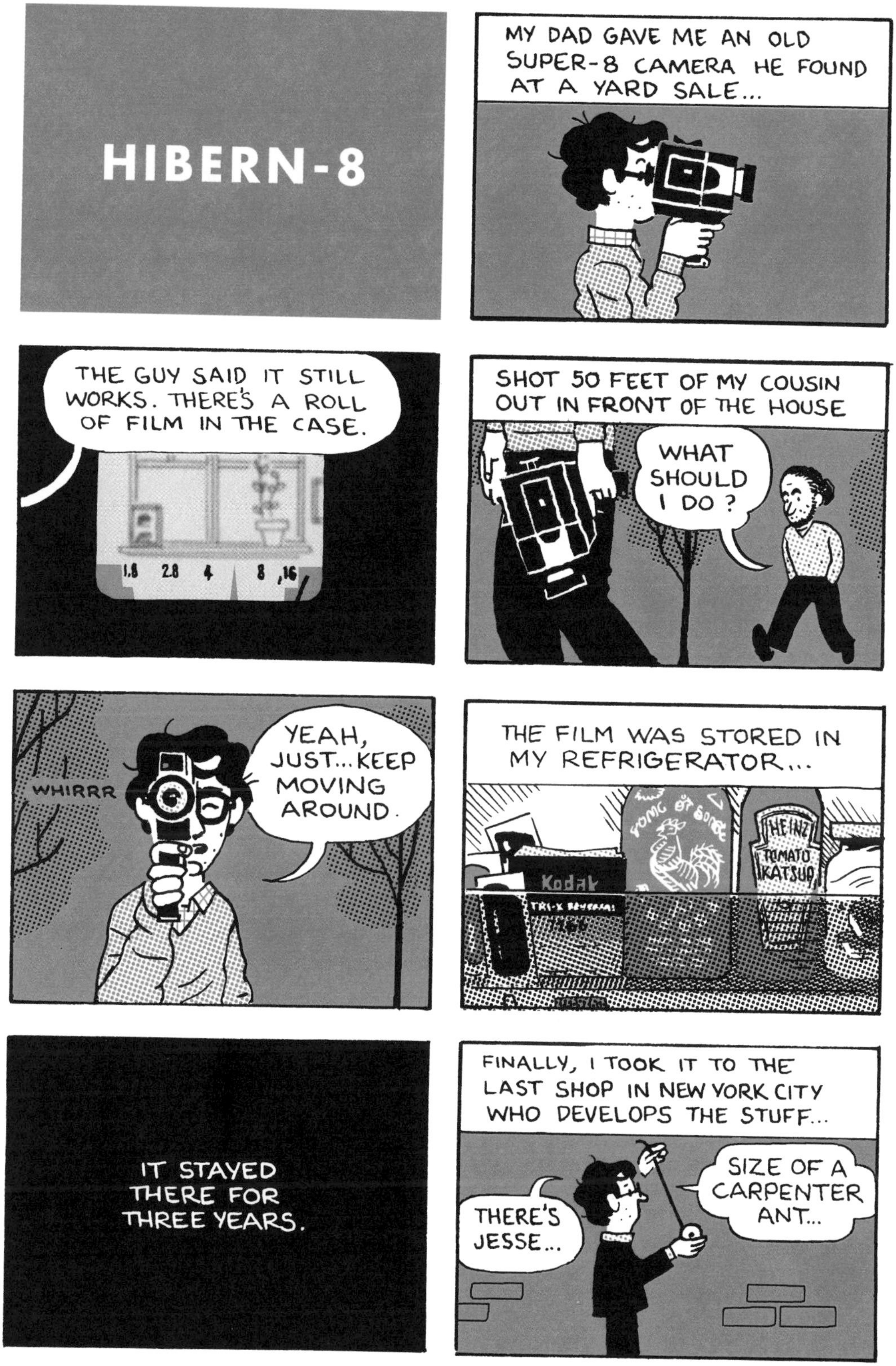
HIBERN-8
MY DAD GAVE ME AN OLD SUPER-8 CAMERA HE FOUND AT A YARD SALE...
THE GUY SAID IT STILL WORKS. THERE'S A ROLL OF FILM IN THE CASE.
1.8 2.8 4 8 16
SHOT 50 FEET OF MY COUSIN OUT IN FRONT OF THE HOUSE
WHAT SHOULD I DO?
WHIRRR
YEAH, JUST...KEEP MOVING AROUND.
THE FILM WAS STORED IN MY REFRIGERATOR...
Kodak
HEINZ
TOMATO KATSUP
IT STAYED THERE FOR THREE YEARS.
FINALLY, I TOOK IT TO THE LAST SHOP IN NEW YORK CITY WHO DEVELOPS THE STUFF...
THERE'S JESSE...
SIZE OF A CARPENTER ANT...

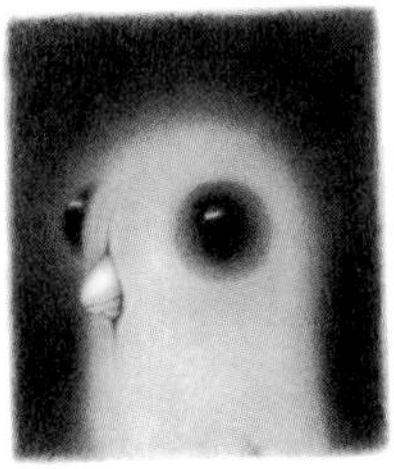

RENÉE FRENCH

Stage 6

from *H Day*

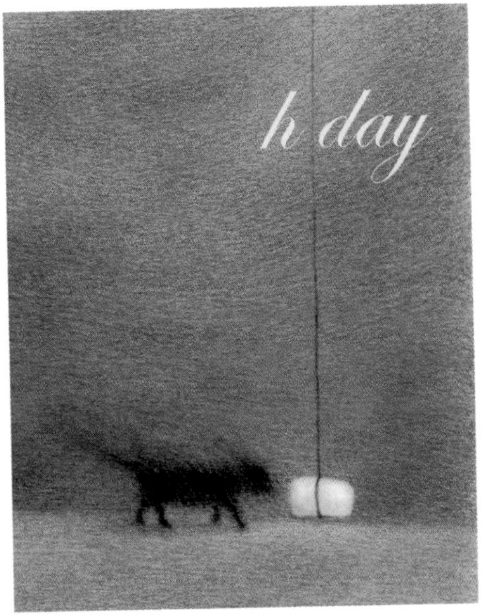
h day

FOR ME, DRAWING COMICS IS

Something I can't not do.

THE SELECTION

The last chapter of my book, *H Day*. A giant ship comes to rescue a black dog and the headache character's restraints finally let go, allowing him to leave the bed.

PUBLICATIONS MY WORK HAS APPEARED IN

The *New York Times*, *The Village Voice*, *Interview Magazine*, the *Paris Review*, *Salon/MOME*, *Kramer's Ergot*, the *Ganzfeld*, *Zero Zero*, *Lapin*, *Last Gasp*, *Comix 2000*.

AWARDS

Inkpot Award; nominated for multiple Harvey, Eisner, and Ignatz awards.

WHAT I'M KNOWN FOR

Marbles in My Underpants (Oni Press), *The Soap Lady* (Top Shelf), *Tinka* (Atheneum), *My Best Sweet Potato* (Atheneum), *The Ticking* (Top Shelf), *Micrographica* (Top Shelf), *edison steelhead's lost portfolio* (Sparkplug), *H Day* (Picturebox).

WHERE I LIVE

Northern California and Sydney, Australia.

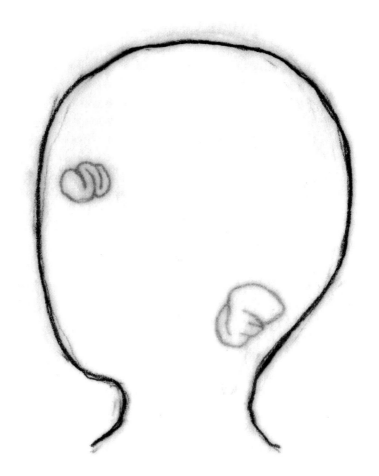

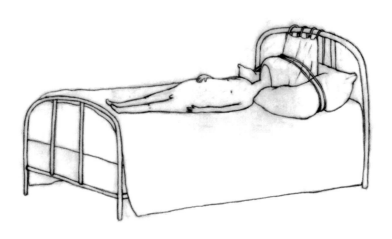

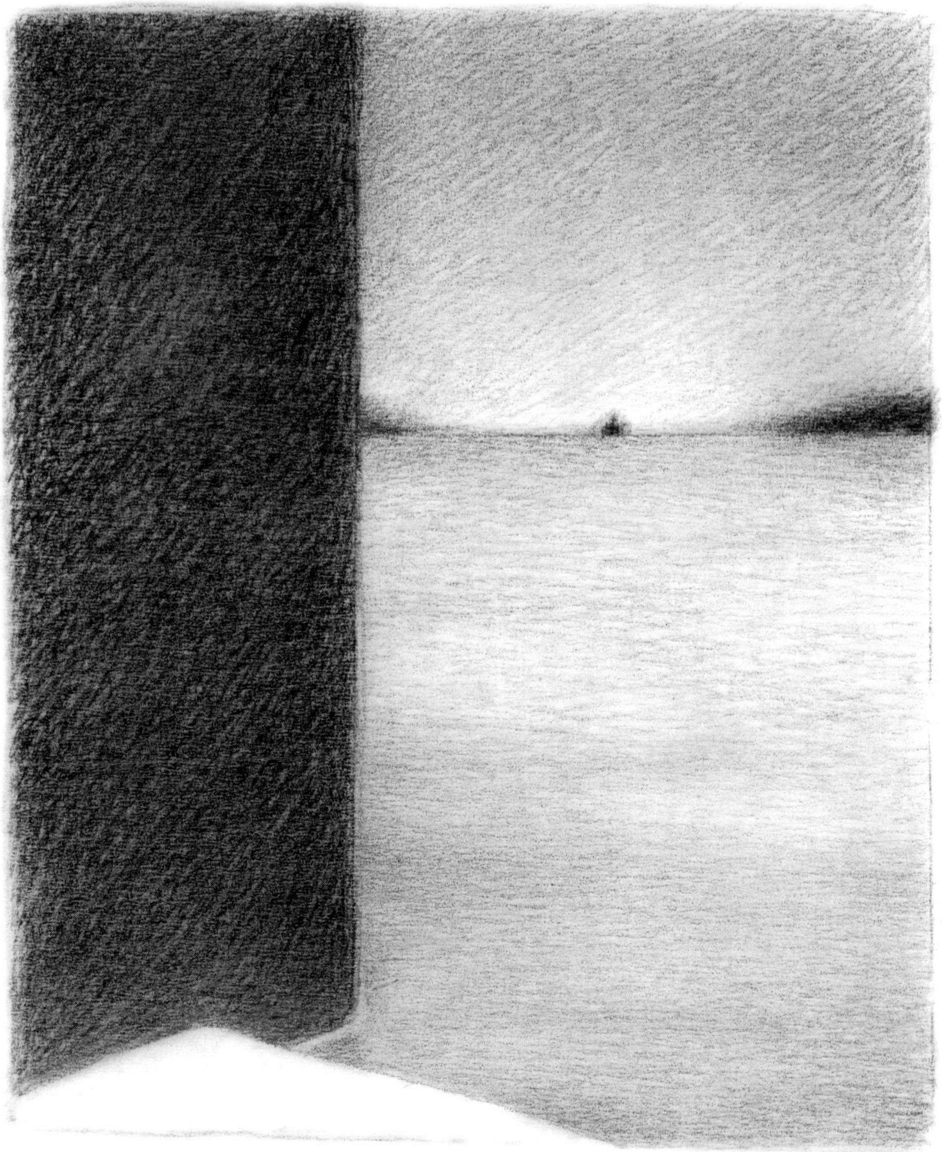

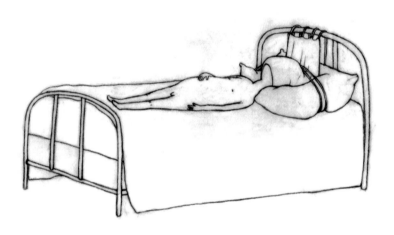

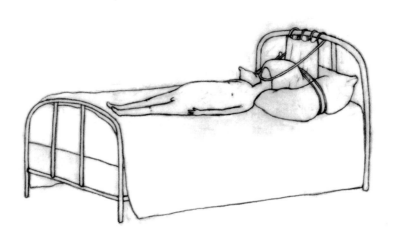

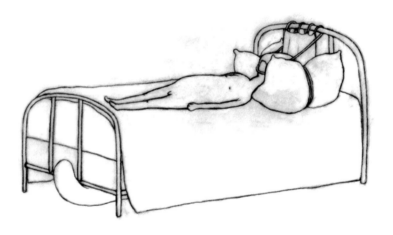

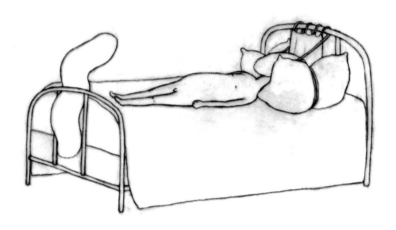

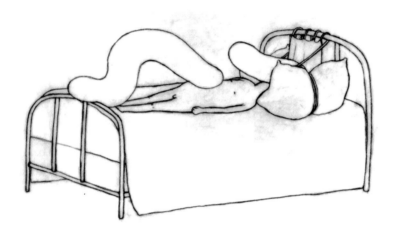

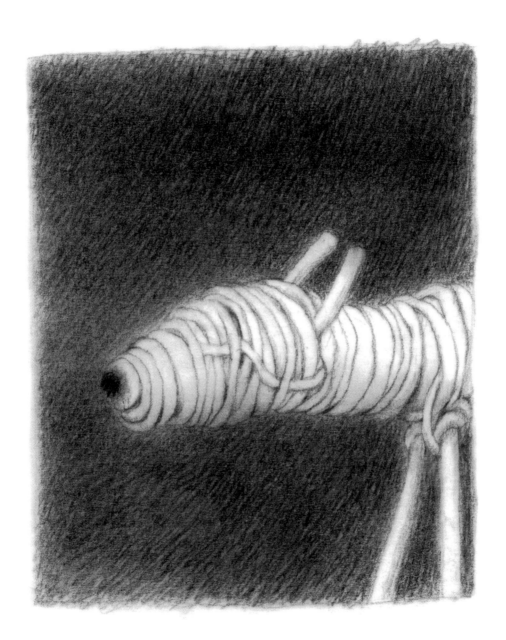

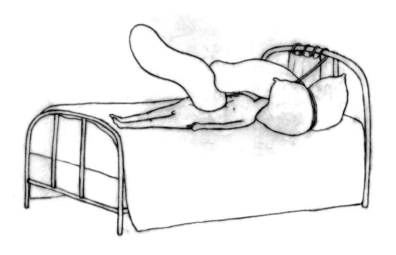

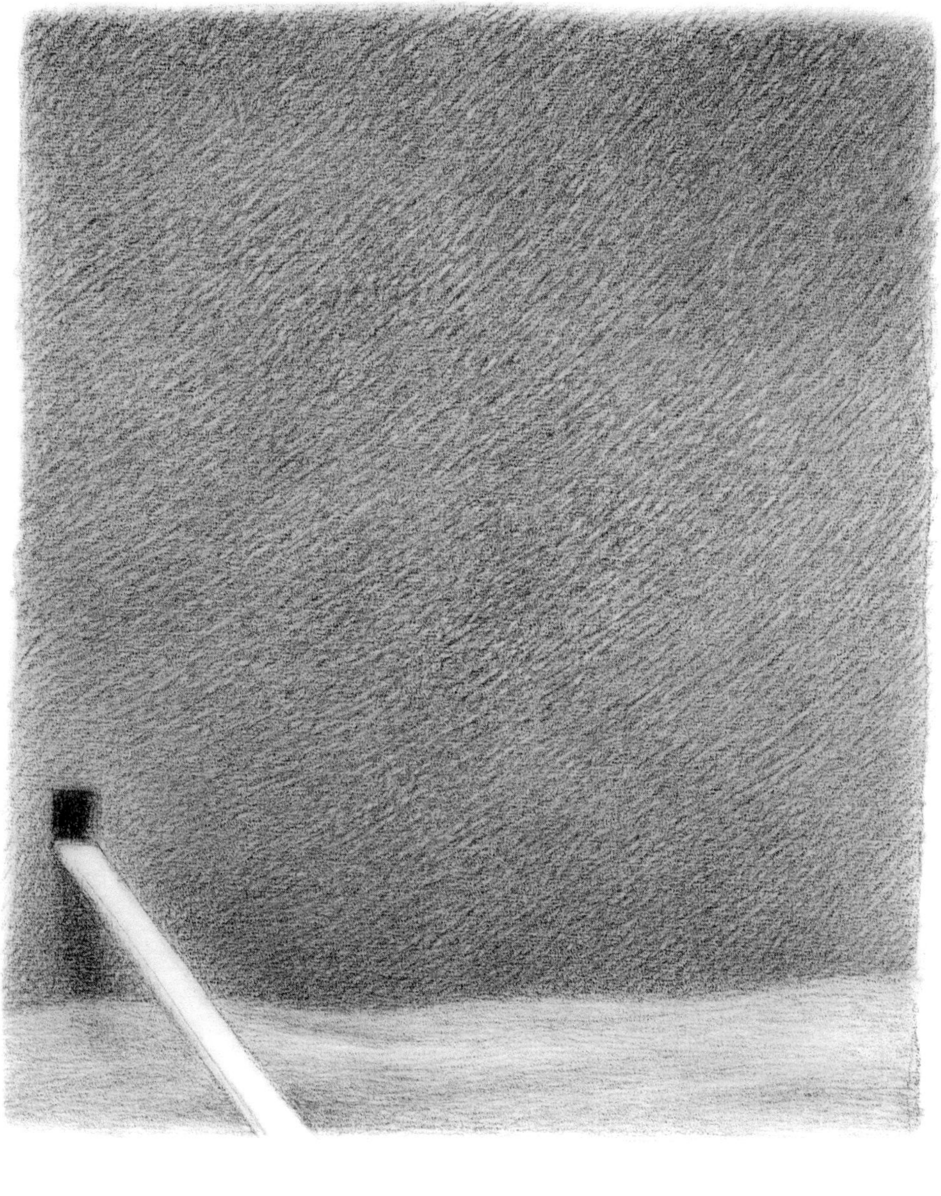

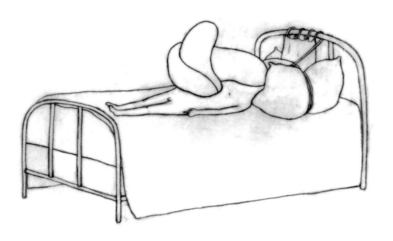

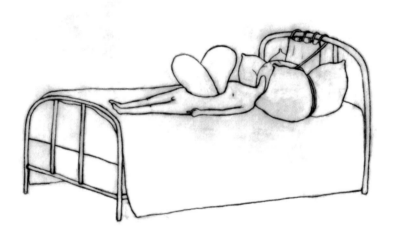

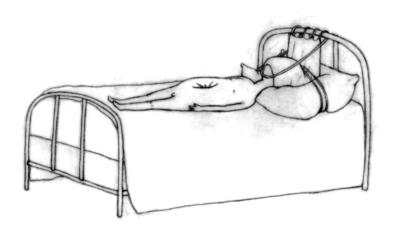

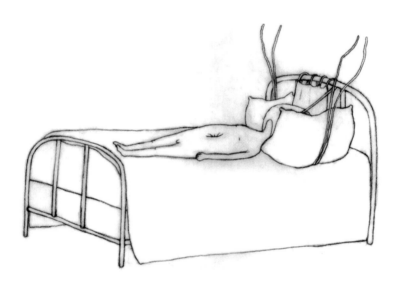

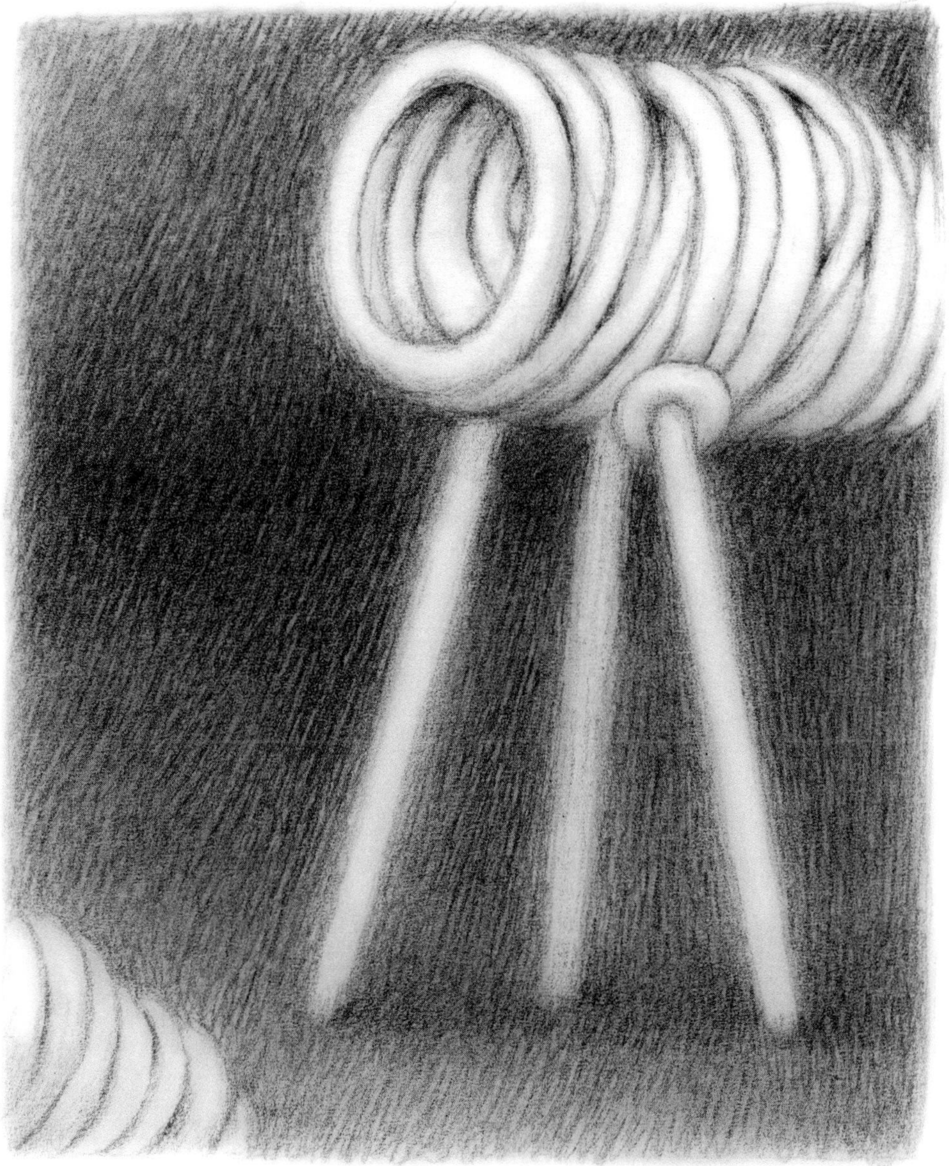

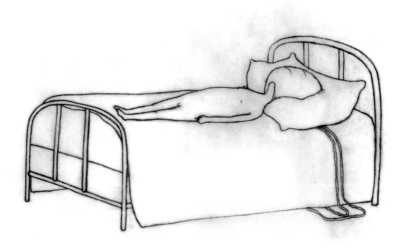

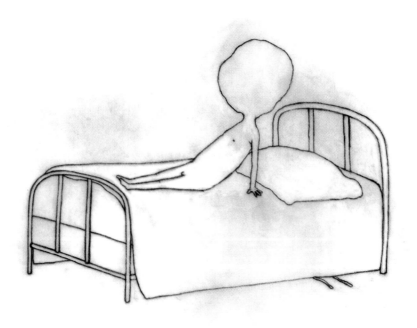

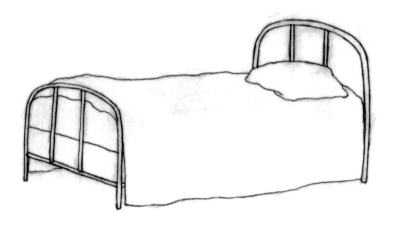

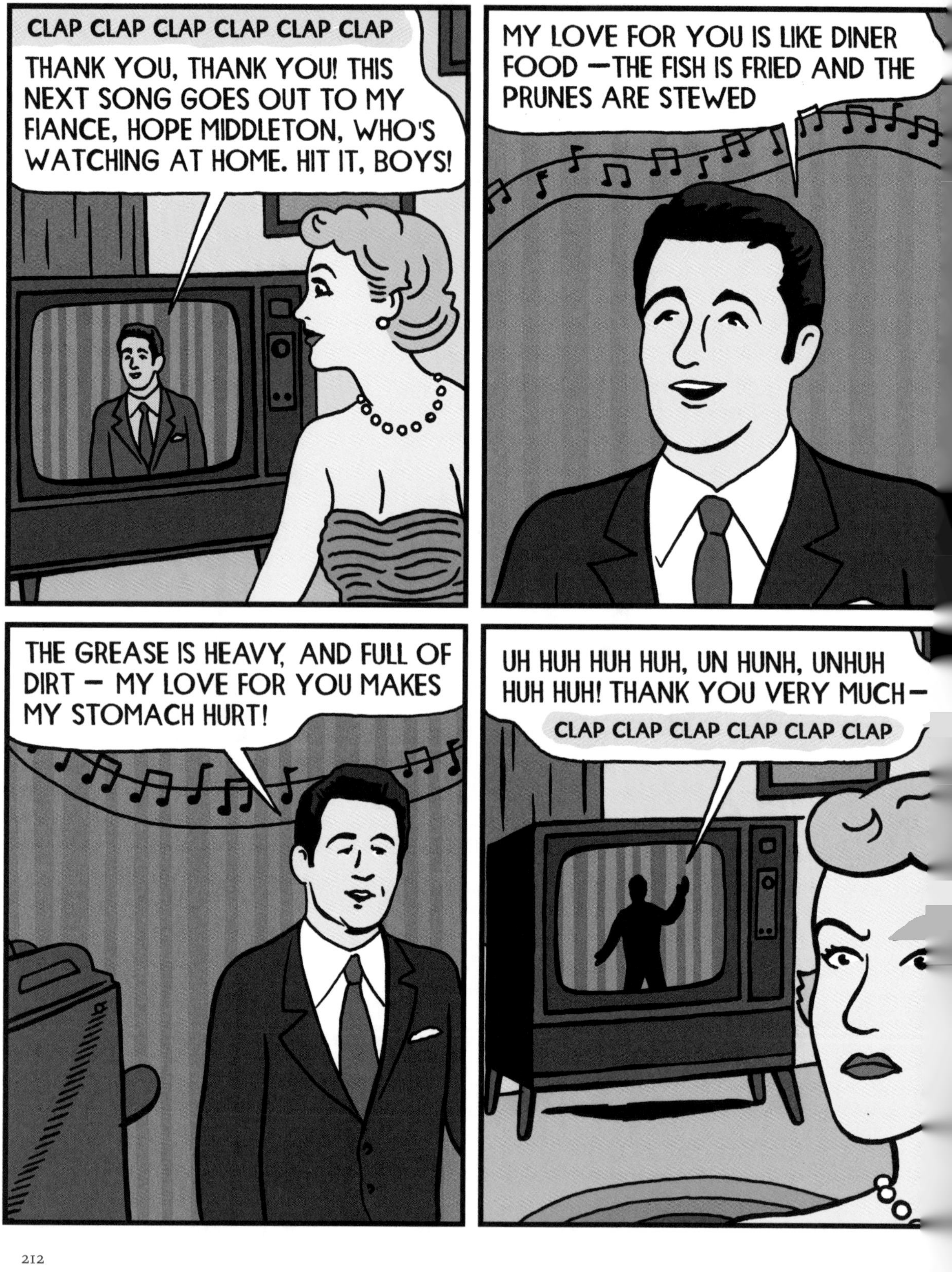
CLAP CLAP CLAP CLAP CLAP CLAP
THANK YOU, THANK YOU! THIS NEXT SONG GOES OUT TO MY FIANCE, HOPE MIDDLETON, WHO'S WATCHING AT HOME. HIT IT, BOYS!
MY LOVE FOR YOU IS LIKE DINER FOOD —THE FISH IS FRIED AND THE PRUNES ARE STEWED
THE GREASE IS HEAVY, AND FULL OF DIRT — MY LOVE FOR YOU MAKES MY STOMACH HURT!
UH HUH HUH HUH, UN HUNH, UNHUH HUH HUH! THANK YOU VERY MUCH—
CLAP CLAP CLAP CLAP CLAP CLAP

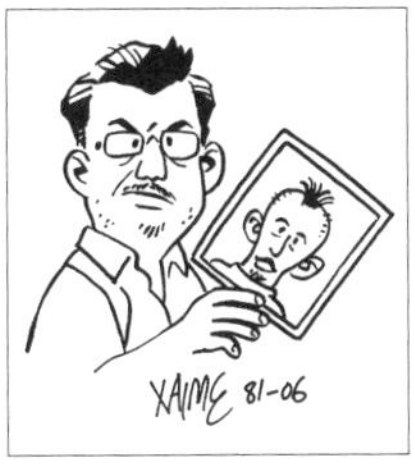
XAIME 81-06

JAIME HERNANDEZ

The Love Bunglers: Part Four *(Excerpt)*

from *Love and Rockets*

FOR ME, DRAWING COMICS IS

All I want to do for the rest of my life.

THE SELECTION

An excerpt from "The Love Bunglers: Part Four," which appeared in *Love and Rockets*, vol. 3, issue #4.

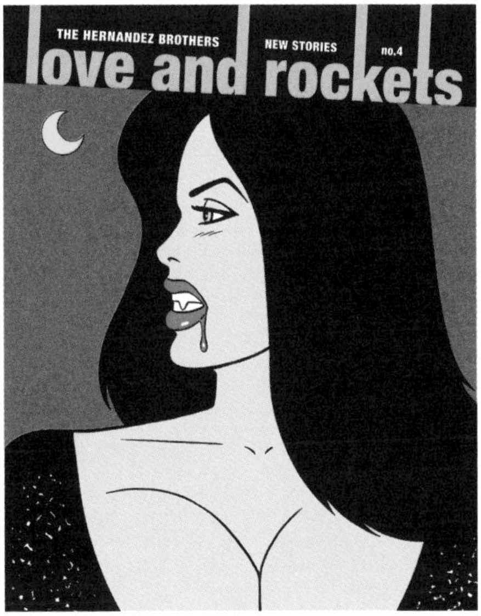
THE HERNANDEZ BROTHERS
NEW STORIES
no.4
love and rockets

THE CONTEXT

Maggie is trying to rent a space to start an auto repair business, and Ray has offered to help financially—but only because he is in love with Maggie and doesn't want her out of his life.

PUBLICATIONS MY WORK HAS APPEARED IN

The New Yorker, the *New York Times*, *Spin*.

AWARDS

Several Harvey Awards.

WHERE I LIVE

Altadena, California.

RENO! HI!

HEY, MAGGIE.

DOIN' SOME SHOPPIN'...?

YEAH, I WAS JUST GETTING SOMETHING TO TAKE TO A PARTY.

DO YOU KNOW MIKE VARAN?

YEAH, I USED TO WORK WIT' HIM. NICE ENOUGH DUDE.

WELL, GREAT. DO YOU WANNA COME? I'VE ALWAYS HATED GOING TO PARTIES ALL BY MY LONESOME.

SURE, I'M MEETIN' FRIENDS LATER BUT I COULD GO FOR AWHILE.

THANKS SO MUCH FOR DOING THIS. IF THERE'S ANYTHING I CAN DO FOR YOU, RENO...

YOU CAN KISS AGAI

MAGGIE!

ANGEL, HI. WHAT'S UP?

I CAN'T GO BACK IN THERE.

I DON'T KNOW HOW MANY TIMES I CAN WALK BY HIM AND SAY HI.

I MUST HAVE DONE IT A HUNDRED TIMES. MIKEY MUST THINK I'M A TOTAL DITZ.

THEN IT'S TIME TO CHANGE STRATEGY. COME ON...

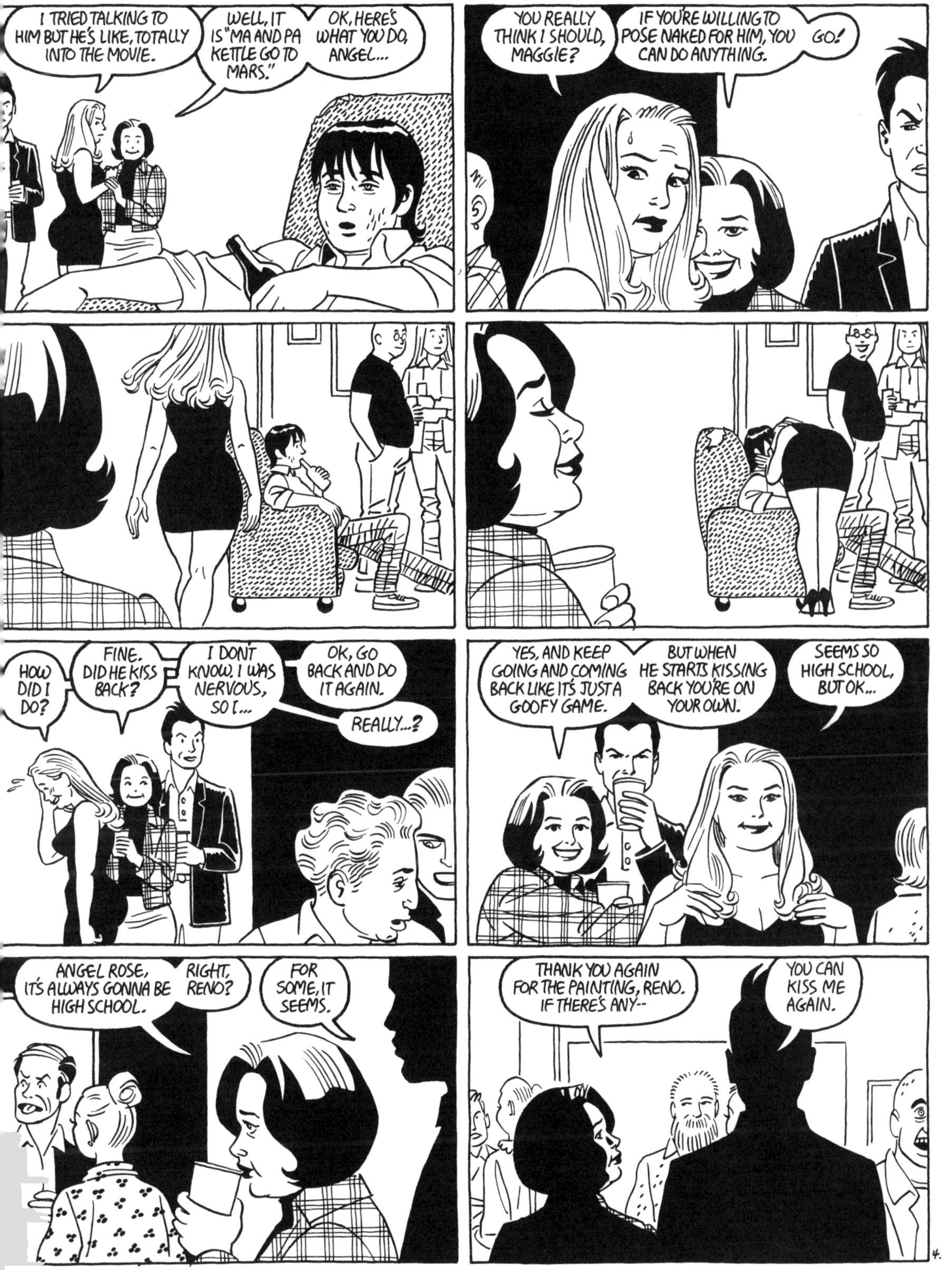

I TRIED TALKING TO HIM BUT HE'S LIKE, TOTALLY INTO THE MOVIE.
WELL, IT IS "MA AND PA KETTLE GO TO MARS."
OK, HERE'S WHAT YOU DO, ANGEL...
YOU REALLY THINK I SHOULD, MAGGIE?
IF YOU'RE WILLING TO POSE NAKED FOR HIM, YOU CAN DO ANYTHING.
GO!
HOW DID I DO?
FINE. DID HE KISS BACK?
I DON'T KNOW. I WAS NERVOUS, SO I...
OK, GO BACK AND DO IT AGAIN.
REALLY...?
YES, AND KEEP GOING AND COMING BACK LIKE IT'S JUST A GOOFY GAME.
BUT WHEN HE STARTS KISSING BACK YOU'RE ON YOUR OWN.
SEEMS SO HIGH SCHOOL, BUT OK...
ANGEL ROSE, IT'S ALWAYS GONNA BE HIGH SCHOOL.
RIGHT, RENO?
FOR SOME, IT SEEMS.
THANK YOU AGAIN FOR THE PAINTING, RENO. IF THERE'S ANY--
YOU CAN KISS ME AGAIN.
4.

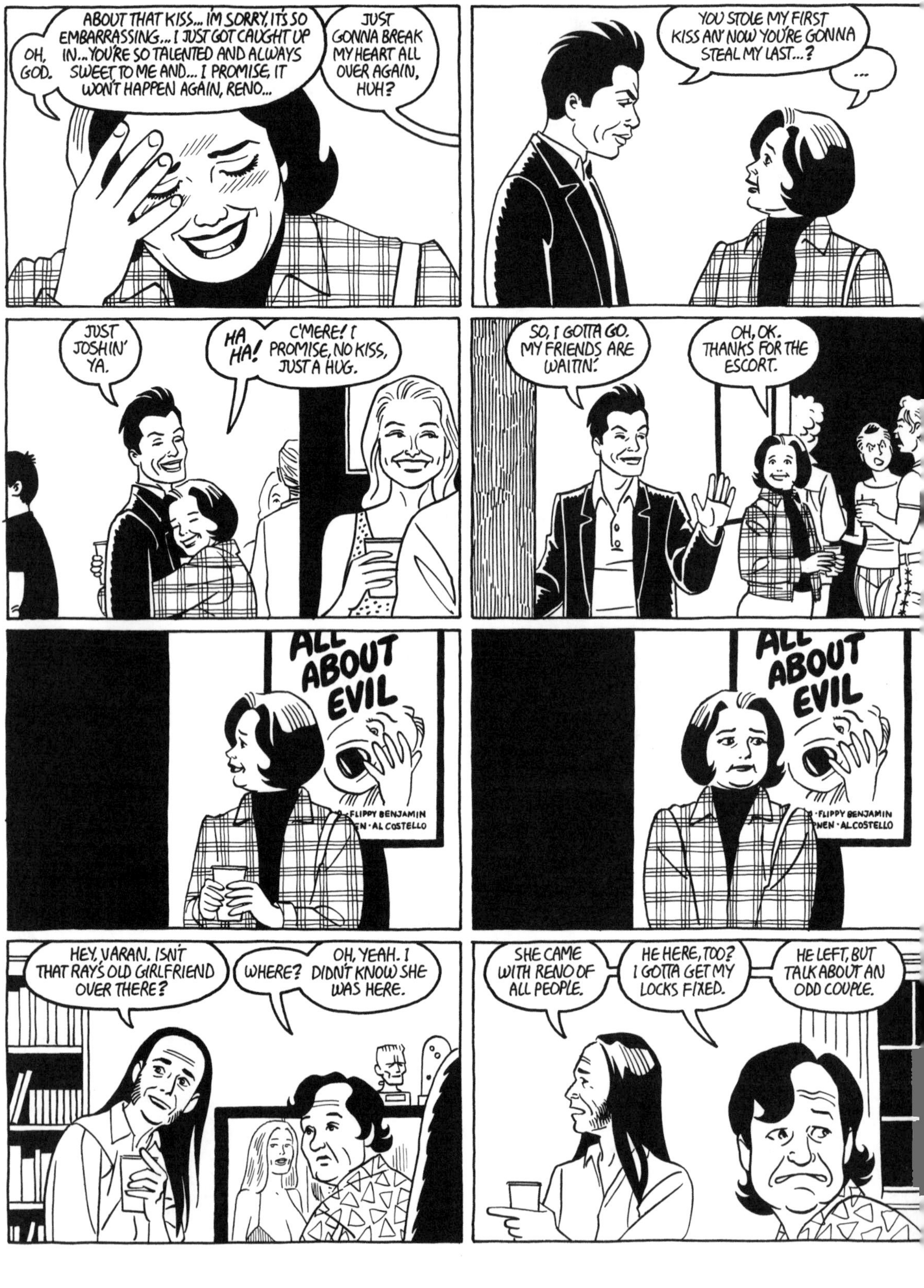
OH, GOD.
ABOUT THAT KISS... I'M SORRY, IT'S SO EMBARRASSING... I JUST GOT CAUGHT UP IN... YOU'RE SO TALENTED AND ALWAYS SWEET TO ME AND... I PROMISE, IT WON'T HAPPEN AGAIN, RENO...
JUST GONNA BREAK MY HEART ALL OVER AGAIN, HUH?
YOU STOLE MY FIRST KISS AN' NOW YOU'RE GONNA STEAL MY LAST...?
...
JUST JOSHIN' YA.
HA HA!
C'MERE! I PROMISE, NO KISS, JUST A HUG.
SO, I GOTTA GO. MY FRIENDS ARE WAITIN'.
OH, OK. THANKS FOR THE ESCORT.
ALL ABOUT EVIL
FLIPPY BENJAMIN
AL COSTELLO
ALL ABOUT EVIL
FLIPPY BENJAMIN
AL COSTELLO
HEY, VARAN. ISN'T THAT RAY'S OLD GIRLFRIEND OVER THERE?
WHERE?
OH, YEAH. I DIDN'T KNOW SHE WAS HERE.
SHE CAME WITH RENO OF ALL PEOPLE.
HE HERE, TOO? I GOTTA GET MY LOCKS FIXED.
HE LEFT, BUT TALK ABOUT AN ODD COUPLE.

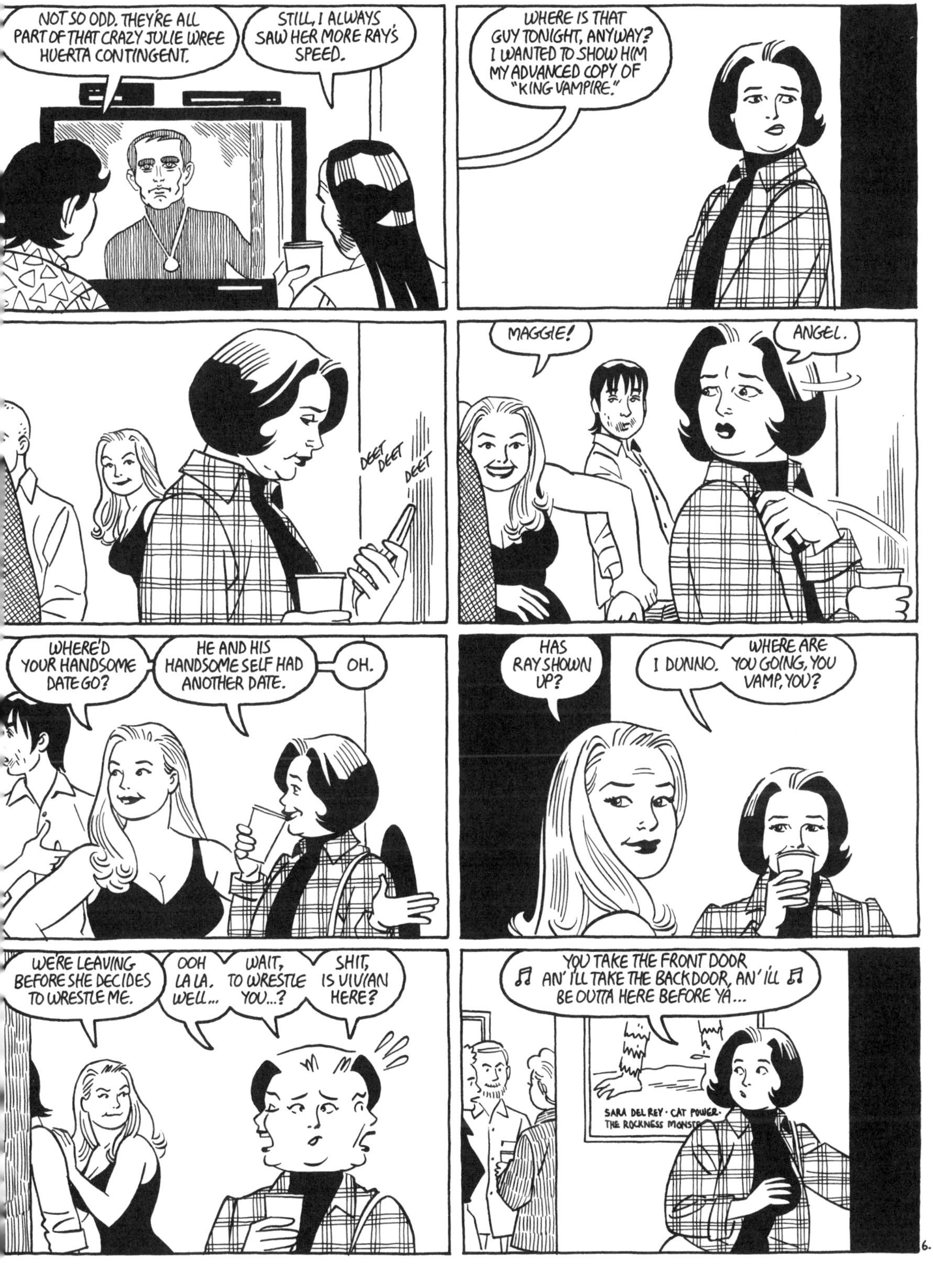
NOT SO ODD. THEY'RE ALL PART OF THAT CRAZY JULIE WREE HUERTA CONTINGENT.
STILL, I ALWAYS SAW HER MORE RAY'S SPEED.
WHERE IS THAT GUY TONIGHT, ANYWAY? I WANTED TO SHOW HIM MY ADVANCED COPY OF "KING VAMPIRE."
DEET DEET DEET
MAGGIE!
ANGEL.
WHERE'D YOUR HANDSOME DATE GO?
HE AND HIS HANDSOME SELF HAD ANOTHER DATE.
OH.
HAS RAY SHOWN UP?
I DUNNO.
WHERE ARE YOU GOING, YOU VAMP, YOU?
WE'RE LEAVING BEFORE SHE DECIDES TO WRESTLE ME.
OOH LA LA. WELL...
WAIT, TO WRESTLE YOU...?
SHIT, IS VIVIAN HERE?
♫ YOU TAKE THE FRONT DOOR AN' I'LL TAKE THE BACKDOOR, AN' I'LL BE OUTTA HERE BEFORE YA... ♫
SARA DEL REY · CAT POWER · THE ROCKNESS MONST
6.

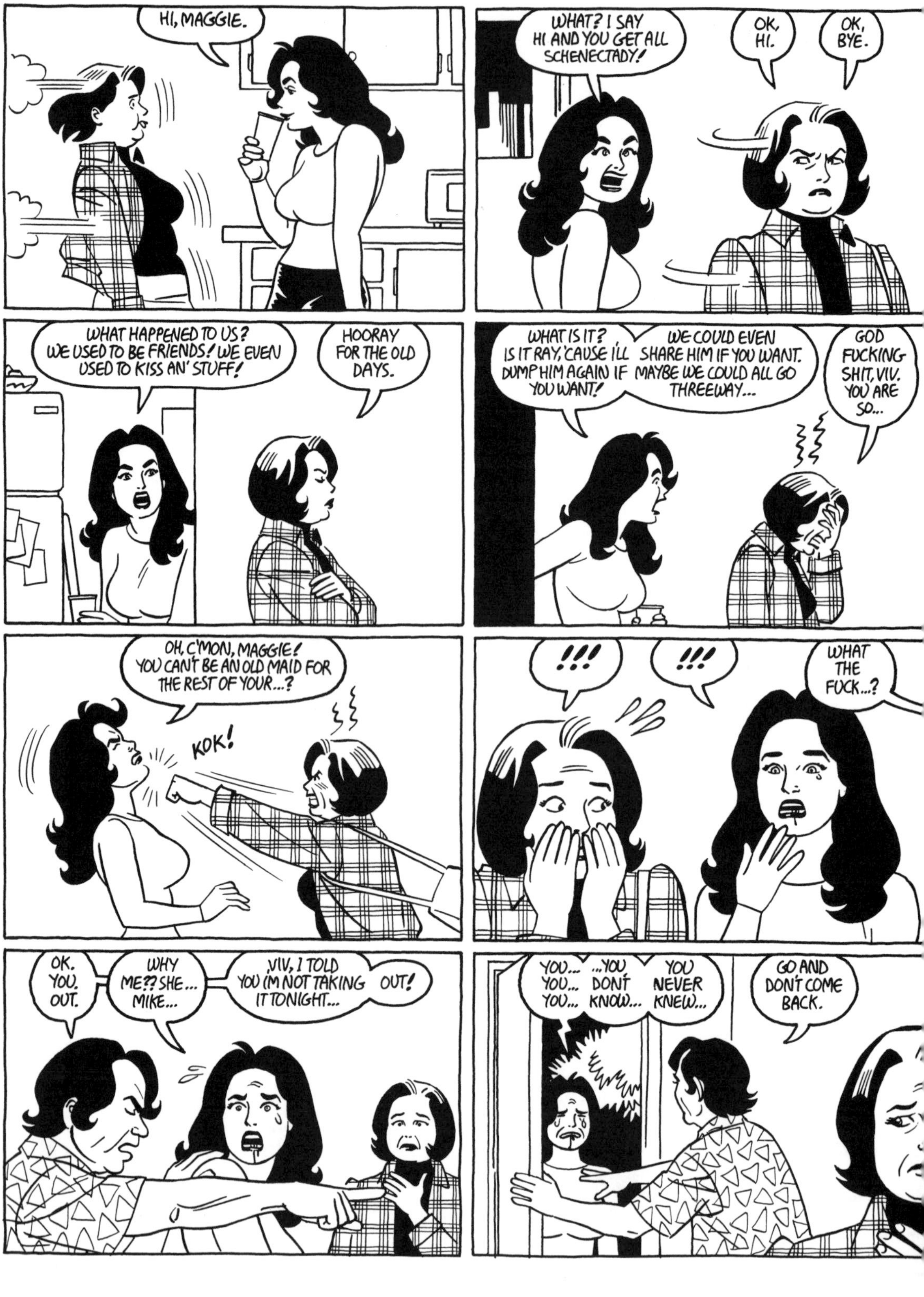
HI, MAGGIE.
WHAT? I SAY HI AND YOU GET ALL SCHENECTADY!
OK, HI.
OK, BYE.
WHAT HAPPENED TO US? WE USED TO BE FRIENDS! WE EVEN USED TO KISS AN' STUFF!
HOORAY FOR THE OLD DAYS.
WHAT IS IT? IS IT RAY, 'CAUSE I'LL DUMP HIM AGAIN IF YOU WANT!
WE COULD EVEN SHARE HIM IF YOU WANT. MAYBE WE COULD ALL GO THREEWAY...
GOD FUCKING SHIT, VIV. YOU ARE SO...
OH, C'MON, MAGGIE! YOU CAN'T BE AN OLD MAID FOR THE REST OF YOUR...?
KOK!
!!!
!!!
WHAT THE FUCK...?
OK. YOU. OUT.
WHY ME?? SHE... MIKE...
VIV, I TOLD YOU I'M NOT TAKING IT TONIGHT...
OUT!
YOU... YOU... YOU...
...YOU DON'T KNOW...
YOU NEVER KNEW...
GO AND DON'T COME BACK.

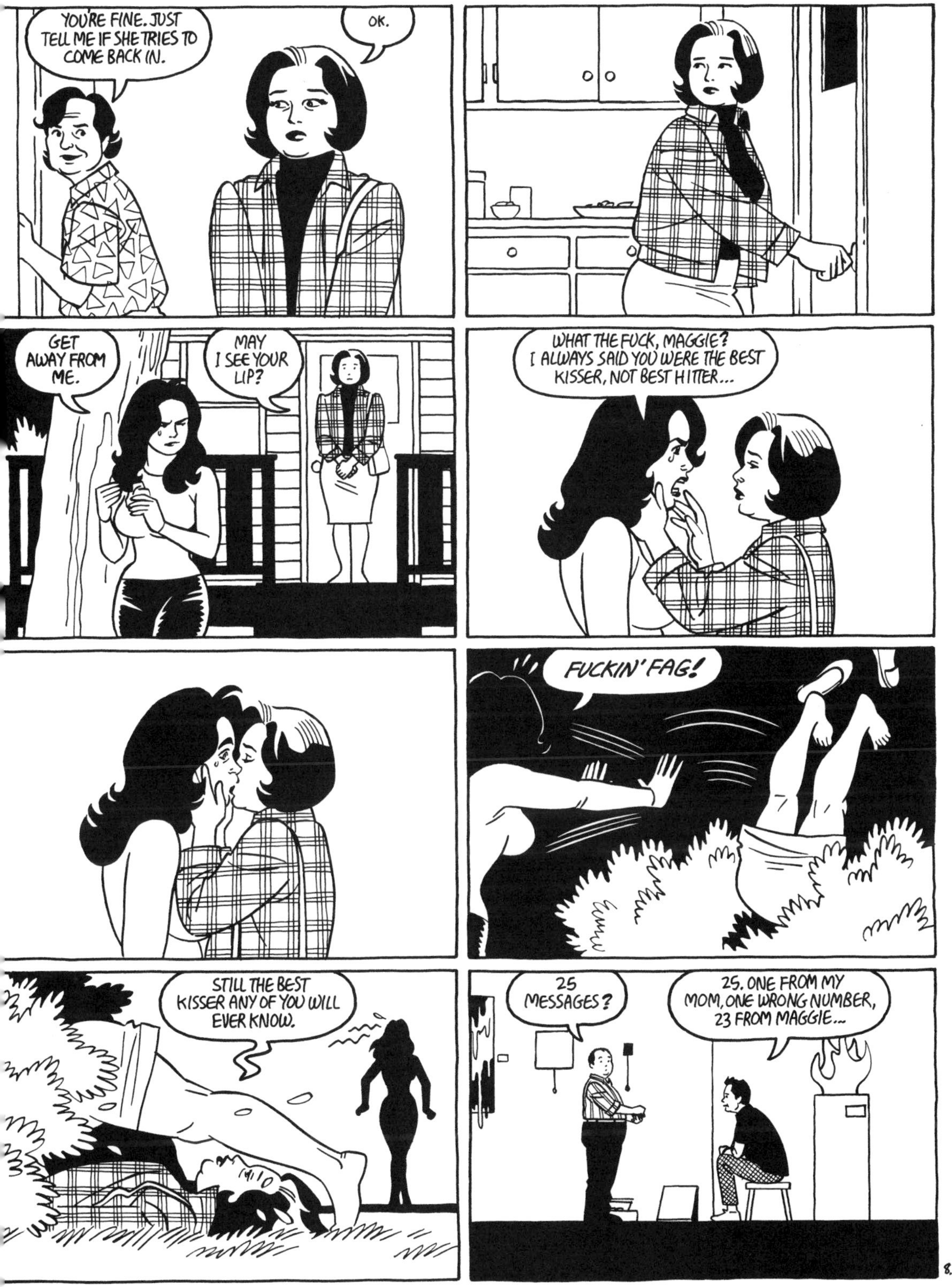
YOU'RE FINE. JUST TELL ME IF SHE TRIES TO COME BACK IN.
OK.
GET AWAY FROM ME.
MAY I SEE YOUR LIP?
WHAT THE FUCK, MAGGIE? I ALWAYS SAID YOU WERE THE BEST KISSER, NOT BEST HITTER...
FUCKIN' FAG!
STILL THE BEST KISSER ANY OF YOU WILL EVER KNOW.
25 MESSAGES?
25. ONE FROM MY MOM, ONE WRONG NUMBER, 23 FROM MAGGIE...
8.

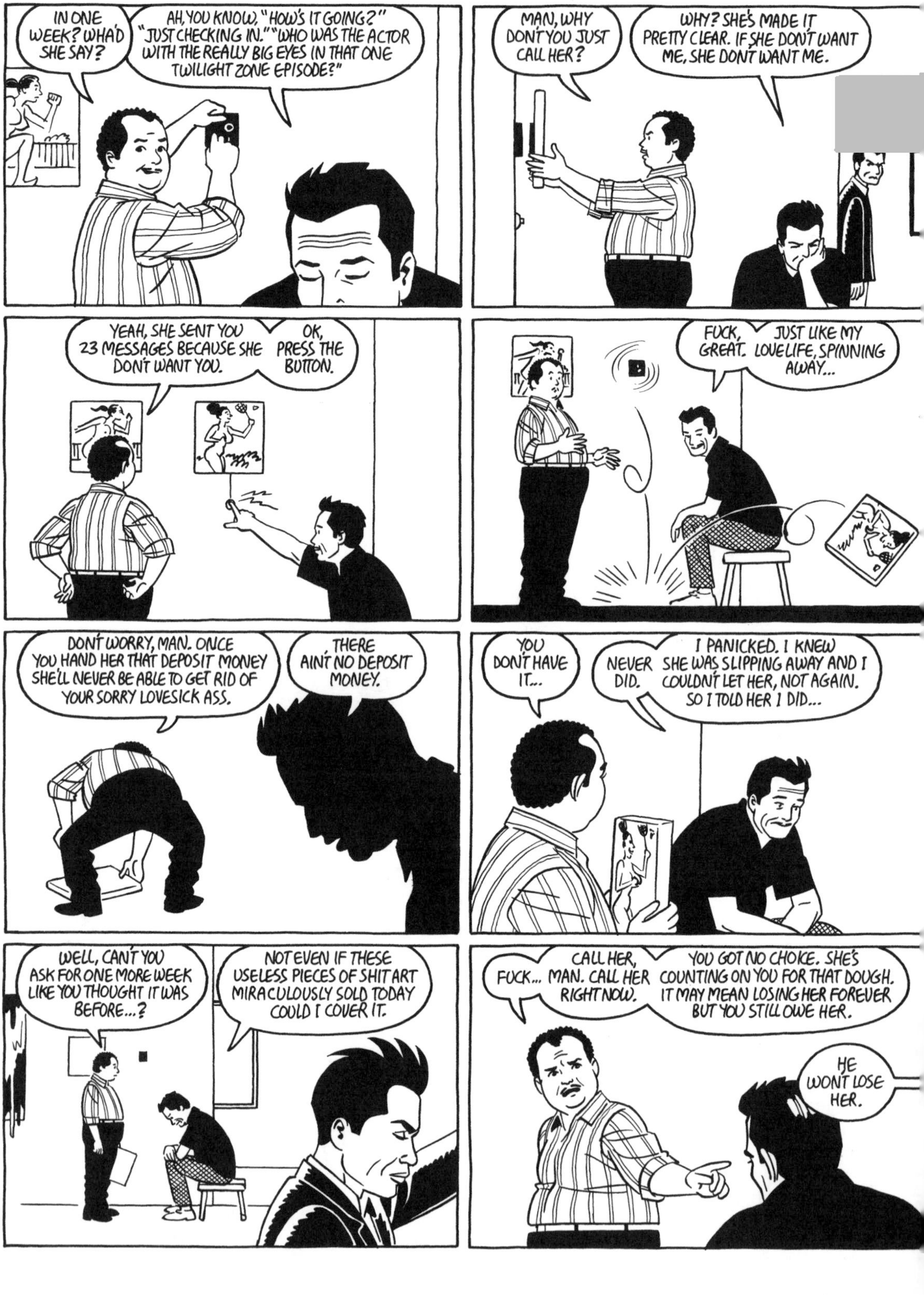

IN ONE WEEK? WHA'D SHE SAY?
AH, YOU KNOW, "HOW'S IT GOING?" "JUST CHECKING IN." "WHO WAS THE ACTOR WITH THE REALLY BIG EYES IN THAT ONE TWILIGHT ZONE EPISODE?"
MAN, WHY DON'T YOU JUST CALL HER?
WHY? SHE'S MADE IT PRETTY CLEAR. IF SHE DON'T WANT ME, SHE DON'T WANT ME.
YEAH, SHE SENT YOU 23 MESSAGES BECAUSE SHE DON'T WANT YOU.
OK, PRESS THE BUTTON.
FUCK, GREAT.
JUST LIKE MY LOVELIFE, SPINNING AWAY...
DON'T WORRY, MAN. ONCE YOU HAND HER THAT DEPOSIT MONEY SHE'LL NEVER BE ABLE TO GET RID OF YOUR SORRY LOVESICK ASS.
THERE AIN'T NO DEPOSIT MONEY.
YOU DON'T HAVE IT...
NEVER DID.
I PANICKED. I KNEW SHE WAS SLIPPING AWAY AND I COULDN'T LET HER, NOT AGAIN. SO I TOLD HER I DID...
WELL, CAN'T YOU ASK FOR ONE MORE WEEK LIKE YOU THOUGHT IT WAS BEFORE...?
NOT EVEN IF THESE USELESS PIECES OF SHIT ART MIRACULOUSLY SOLD TODAY COULD I COVER IT.
FUCK...
CALL HER, MAN. CALL HER RIGHT NOW.
YOU GOT NO CHOICE. SHE'S COUNTING ON YOU FOR THAT DOUGH. IT MAY MEAN LOSING HER FOREVER BUT YOU STILL OWE HER.
HE WON'T LOSE HER.

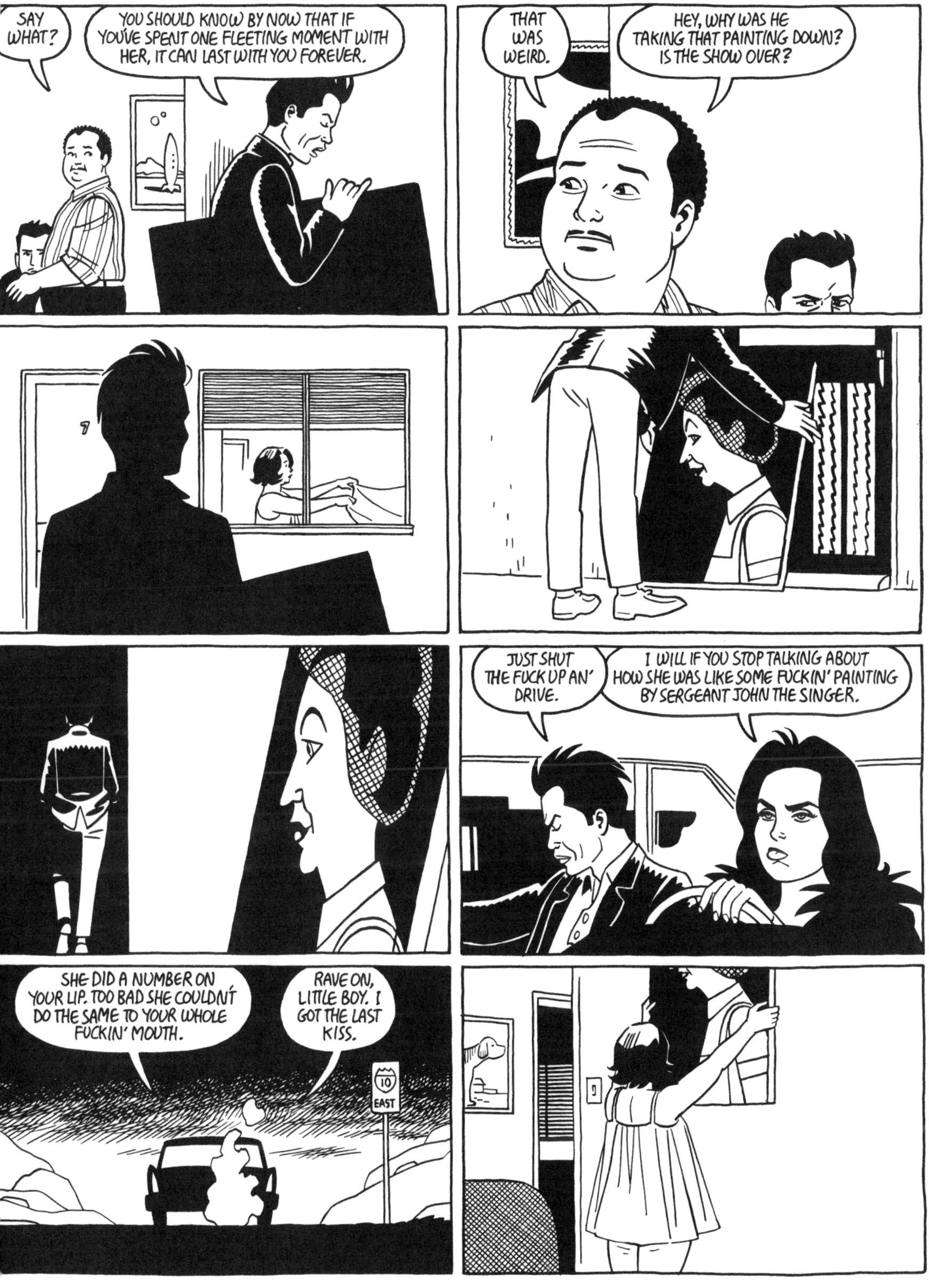
SAY WHAT?
YOU SHOULD KNOW BY NOW THAT IF YOU'VE SPENT ONE FLEETING MOMENT WITH HER, IT CAN LAST WITH YOU FOREVER.
THAT WAS WEIRD.
HEY, WHY WAS HE TAKING THAT PAINTING DOWN? IS THE SHOW OVER?
JUST SHUT THE FUCK UP AN' DRIVE.
I WILL IF YOU STOP TALKING ABOUT HOW SHE WAS LIKE SOME FUCKIN' PAINTING BY SERGEANT JOHN THE SINGER.
SHE DID A NUMBER ON YOUR LIP. TOO BAD SHE COULDN'T DO THE SAME TO YOUR WHOLE FUCKIN' MOUTH.
RAVE ON, LITTLE BOY. I GOT THE LAST KISS.
10
EAST
10.

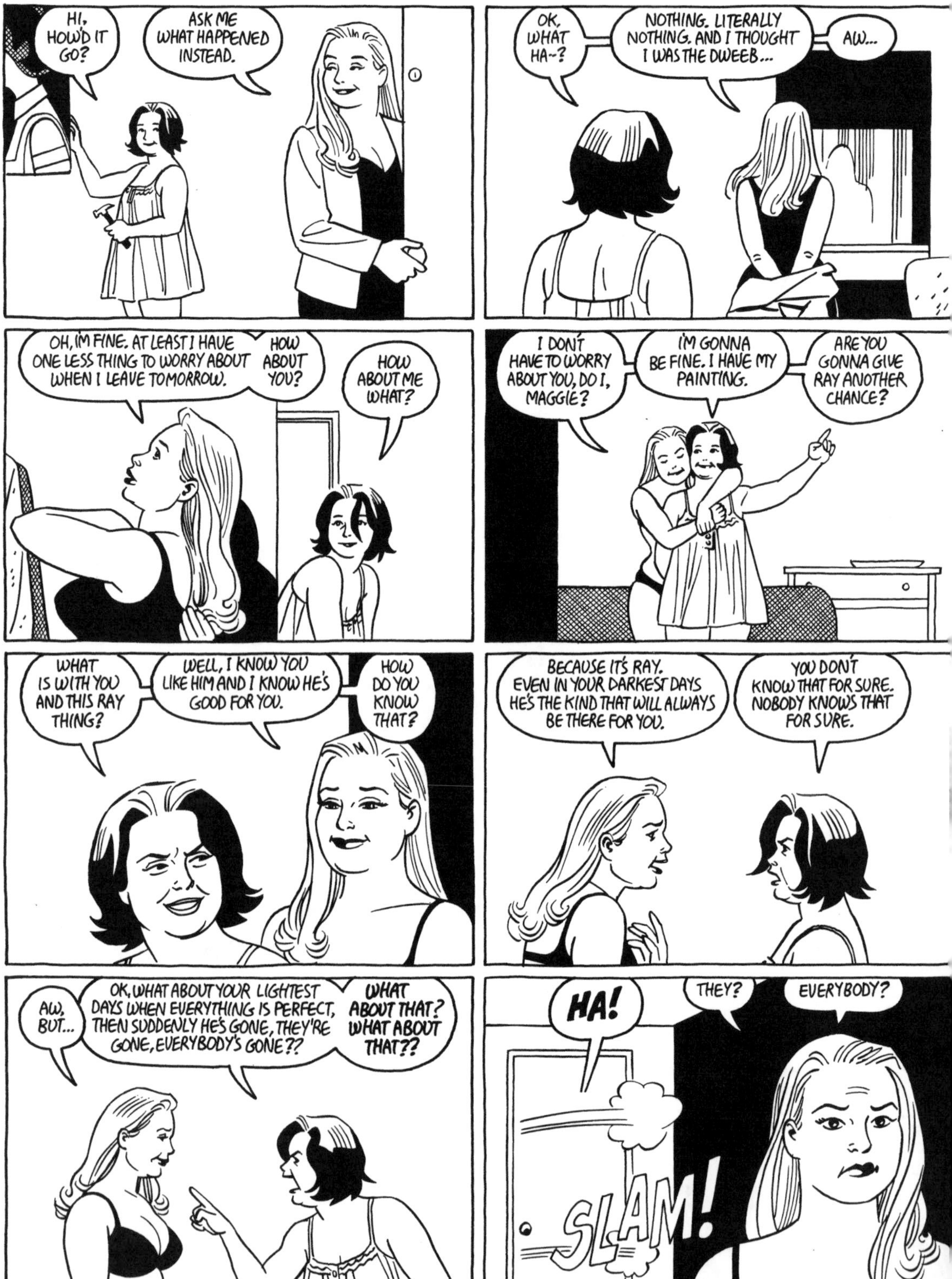
HI, HOW'D IT GO?
ASK ME WHAT HAPPENED INSTEAD.
OK, WHAT HA--?
NOTHING. LITERALLY NOTHING. AND I THOUGHT I WAS THE DWEEB...
AW...
OH, I'M FINE. AT LEAST I HAVE ONE LESS THING TO WORRY ABOUT WHEN I LEAVE TOMORROW.
HOW ABOUT YOU?
HOW ABOUT ME WHAT?
I DON'T HAVE TO WORRY ABOUT YOU, DO I, MAGGIE?
I'M GONNA BE FINE. I HAVE MY PAINTING.
ARE YOU GONNA GIVE RAY ANOTHER CHANCE?
WHAT IS WITH YOU AND THIS RAY THING?
WELL, I KNOW YOU LIKE HIM AND I KNOW HE'S GOOD FOR YOU.
HOW DO YOU KNOW THAT?
BECAUSE IT'S RAY. EVEN IN YOUR DARKEST DAYS HE'S THE KIND THAT WILL ALWAYS BE THERE FOR YOU.
YOU DON'T KNOW THAT FOR SURE. NOBODY KNOWS THAT FOR SURE.
AW, BUT...
OK, WHAT ABOUT YOUR LIGHTEST DAYS WHEN EVERYTHING IS PERFECT, THEN SUDDENLY HE'S GONE, THEY'RE GONE, EVERYBODY'S GONE??
WHAT ABOUT THAT? WHAT ABOUT THAT??
HA!
THEY?
EVERYBODY?
SLAM!

PROPHETS

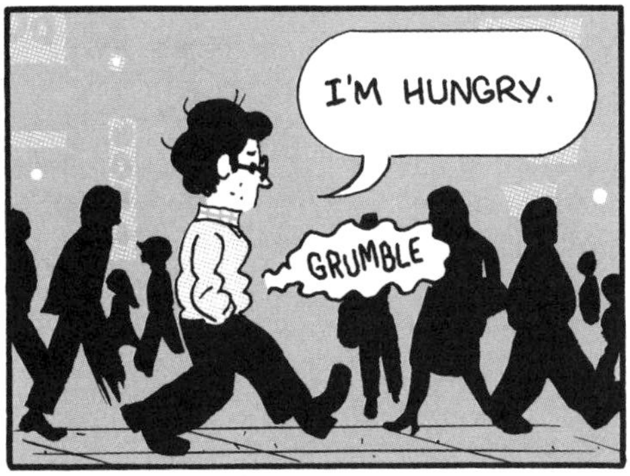
I'M HUNGRY.
GRUMBLE

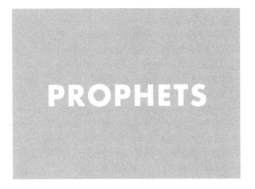

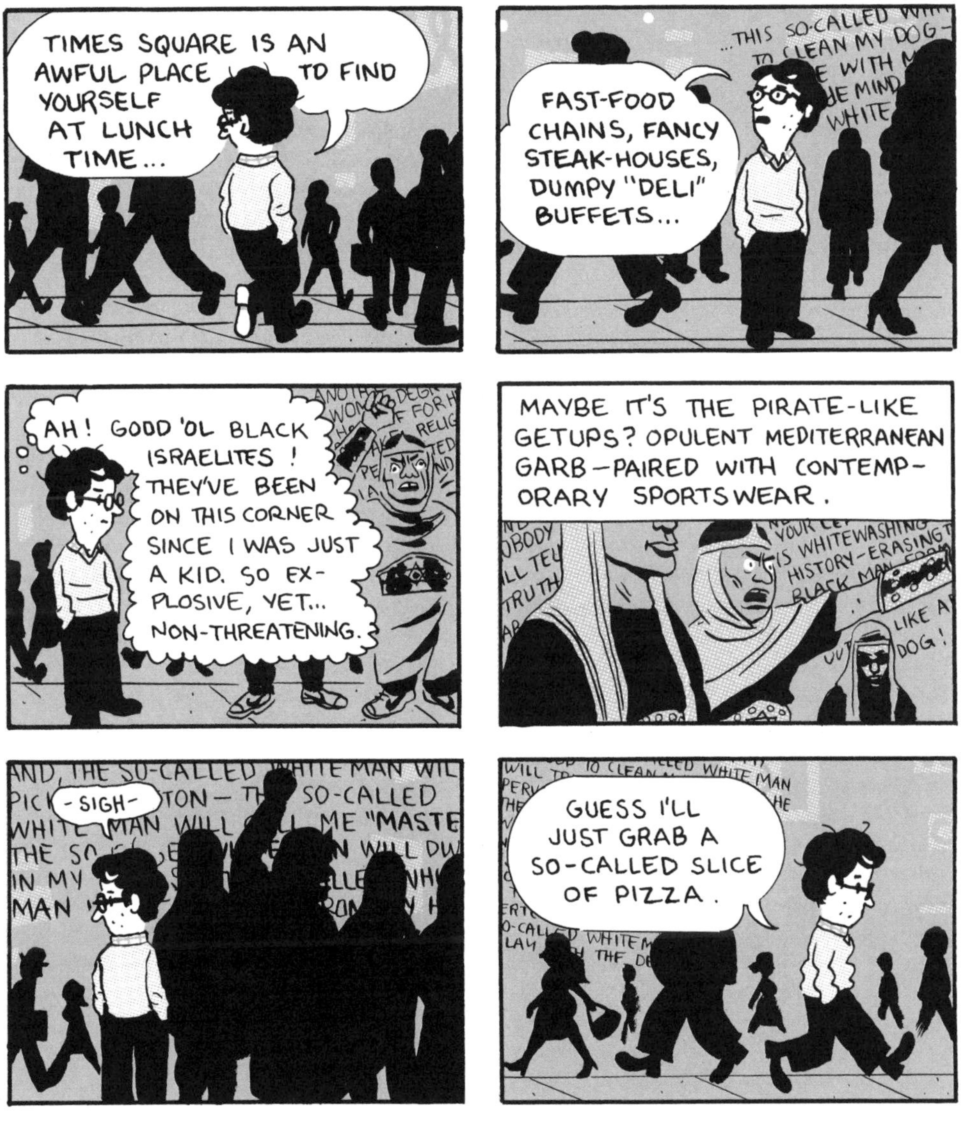
TIMES SQUARE IS AN AWFUL PLACE TO FIND YOURSELF AT LUNCH TIME...
FAST-FOOD CHAINS, FANCY STEAK-HOUSES, DUMPY "DELI" BUFFETS...
AH! GOOD 'OL BLACK ISRAELITES! THEY'VE BEEN ON THIS CORNER SINCE I WAS JUST A KID. SO EX-PLOSIVE, YET... NON-THREATENING.
MAYBE IT'S THE PIRATE-LIKE GETUPS? OPULENT MEDITERRANEAN GARB—PAIRED WITH CONTEMP-ORARY SPORTSWEAR.
-SIGH-
GUESS I'LL JUST GRAB A SO-CALLED SLICE OF PIZZA.

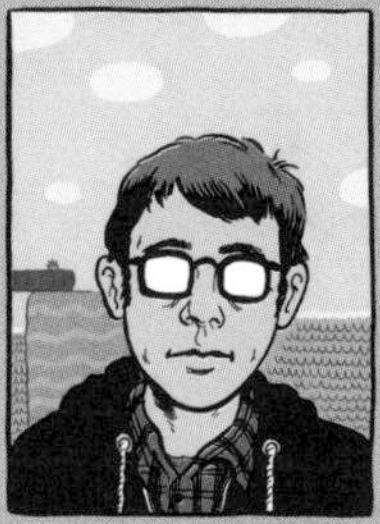

DAKOTA McFADZEAN

Leave Luck to Heaven

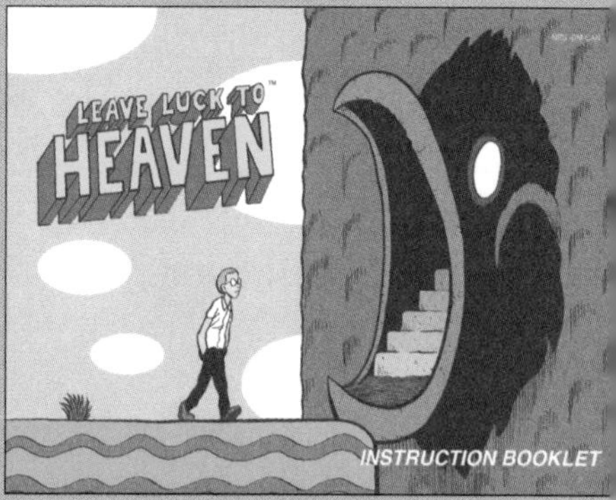
LEAVE LUCK TO™
HEAVEN
INSTRUCTION BOOKLET

FOR ME, DRAWING COMICS IS

Something that has somehow been at the center of everything I've ever done or wanted to do. Not just a reason to get up in the morning, but a reason to go to bed at night.

THE SELECTION

Leave Luck to Heaven is about an unnamed master teaching his apprentice how to play and appreciate old video games in a basement. It also serves as a useful instruction manual for the enjoyment of other media, experiences, textures, shapes . . .

AWARDS

A finalist for the Joe Shuster Awards: Gene Day Award for Self Publishers (2009); shortlisted for Expozine: Best English Comic (2008 and 2009); Independent Artist Grant, Saskatchewan Arts Board (2007).

WHAT I'M KNOWN FOR

The Dailies, a daily comic strip I've been doing since January 2010, available as a webcomic at dakotamcfadzean.com, and *Ghost Rabbit*, a minicomic about a little girl, a cartoon rabbit, memories, ghosts, dot screens, and photographs.

WHERE I LIVE

Montreal, Quebec.

*L*ook for this seal on all *Leave Luck to Heaven* products, accessories, software, and related ephemera. It represents our company's commitment to bringing you only the highest quality products. Items not carrying this seal are likely to be of an inferior quality and will serve as entertainment products only. This will limit the depth of the experience and will render it as a joke that has been told too many times.

THIS SEAL IS YOUR ASSURANCE THAT

Leave Luck to Heaven®

HAS APPROVED AND GUARANTEES THE QUALITY OF THIS PRODUCT

Thank you for purchasing the Leave Luck to Heaven® Instruction Manual®, which will assist you with the sublime enjoyment of a wide variety of Game Paks.

Please read this instruction booklet to ensure proper aesthetic appreciation of most games, and then save the booklet for future reference.

CONTENTS

PRECAUTIONS

1) This is a high precision activity. Proper care should be taken to avoid injury to the body, eyes and other vulnerable areas.
2) Should you find yourself returning to the same games over and over, determine whether this is a ritualized routine of nostalgia, a deeper exploration, or a bad habit.
3) Do not clean with benzene, paint thinner, alcohol, or other such solvents.

Note: In the interest of product improvement, the specifications of this experience are subject to change without prior notice.

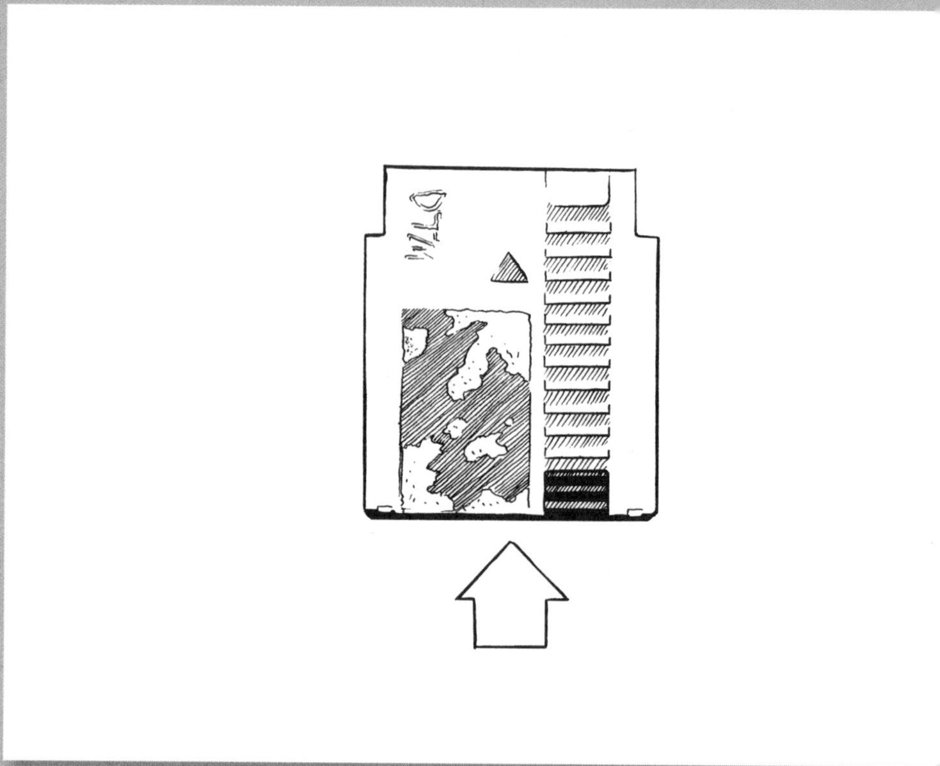

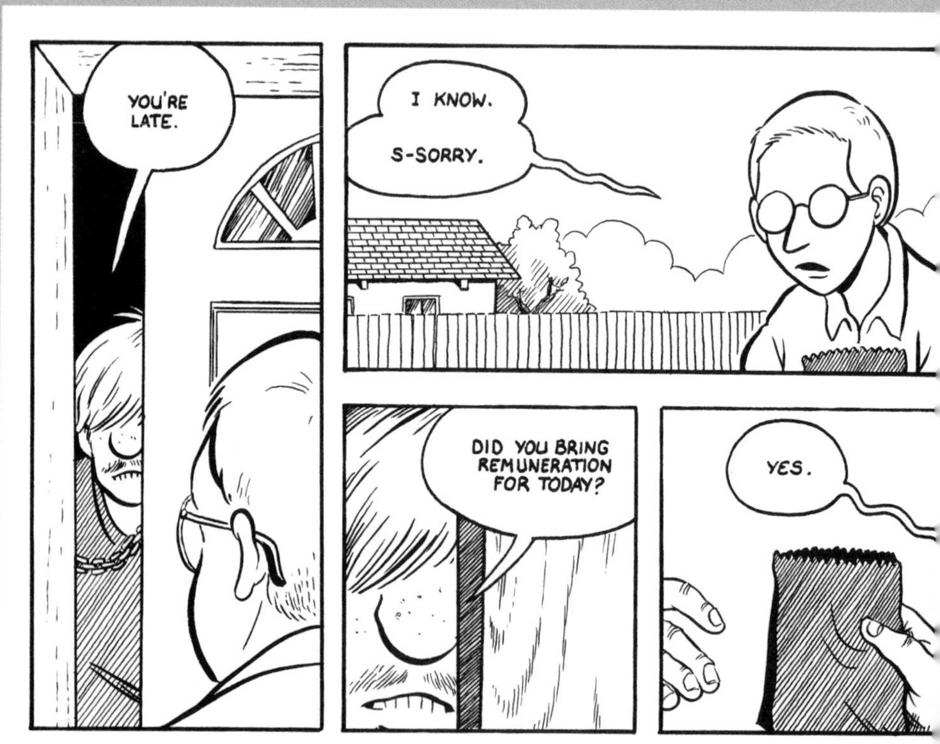
YOU'RE LATE.
I KNOW.
S-SORRY.
DID YOU BRING REMUNERATION FOR TODAY?
YES.

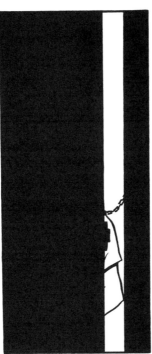

NINETY-NINE
SECONDS LEFT.

FAST MUSIC.

MM-HM

S-SORRY?
IT'S A PLAIN QUESTION.
SALVATION ARMY? VALUE VILLAGE? A GARAGE SALE?
WHERE DID YOU ACQUIRE THE GAME PAK?
OH, UH, I'VE HAD AN EXTRA COPY FOR A WHILE
I MEAN, IT'S PRETTY COMMON.
BUT THAT'S JUST IT. ALMOST EVERYONE HAS A COPY OF THIS GAME. MAYBE EVEN TWO OR THREE. NOT REALLY SURPRISING. IT CAME AS A PACK-IN WITH THE CONSOLE.

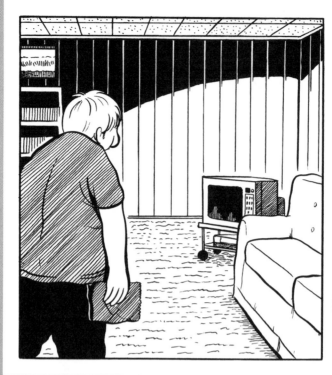

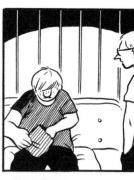

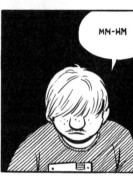

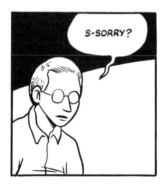

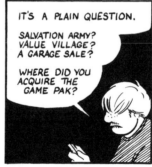

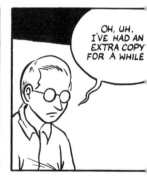

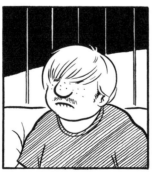

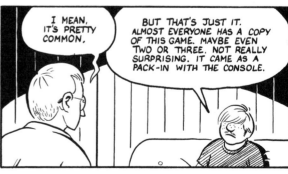

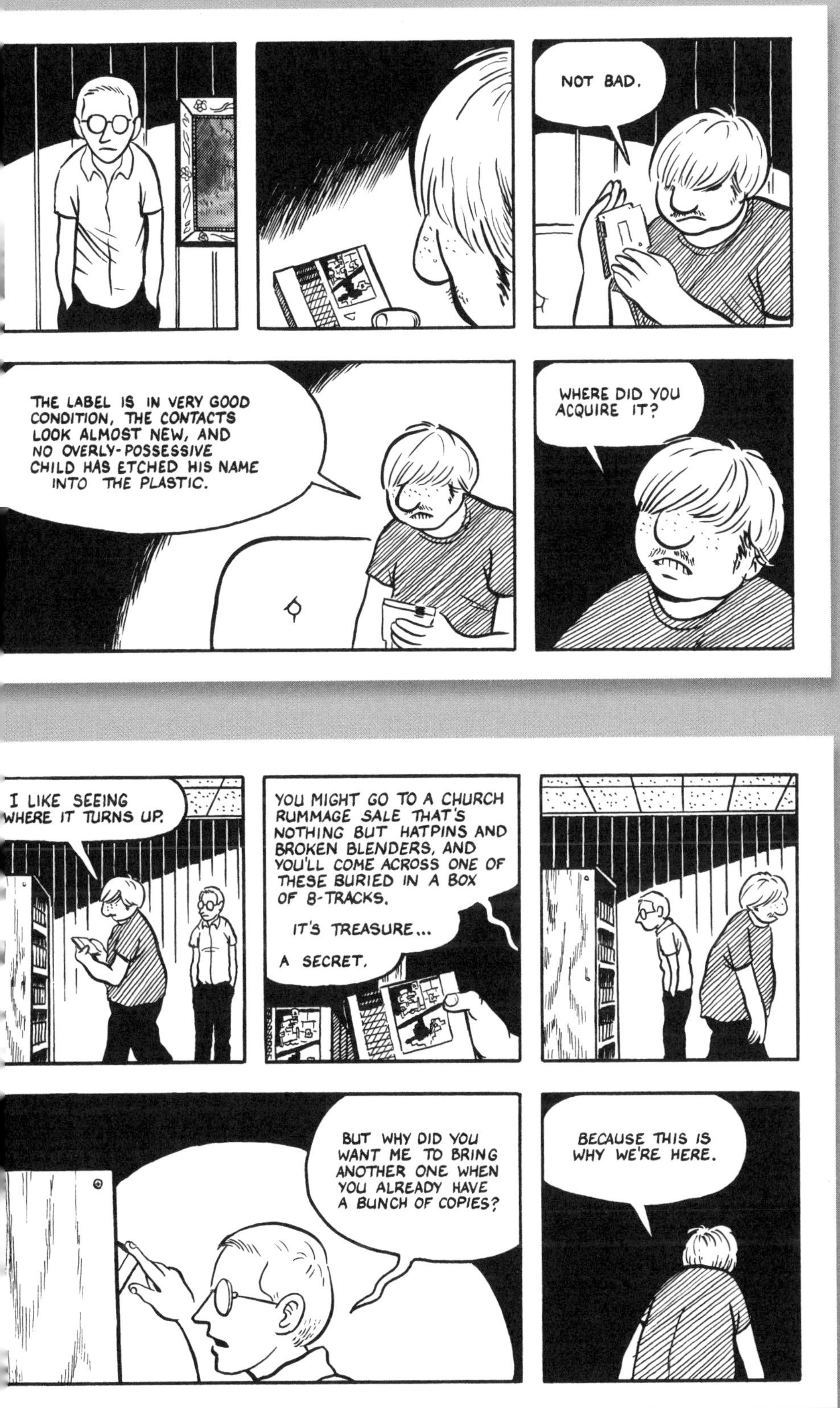
NOT BAD.
THE LABEL IS IN VERY GOOD CONDITION, THE CONTACTS LOOK ALMOST NEW, AND NO OVERLY-POSSESSIVE CHILD HAS ETCHED HIS NAME INTO THE PLASTIC.
WHERE DID YOU ACQUIRE IT?
I LIKE SEEING WHERE IT TURNS UP.
YOU MIGHT GO TO A CHURCH RUMMAGE SALE THAT'S NOTHING BUT HATPINS AND BROKEN BLENDERS, AND YOU'LL COME ACROSS ONE OF THESE BURIED IN A BOX OF 8-TRACKS.
IT'S TREASURE...
A SECRET.
BUT WHY DID YOU WANT ME TO BRING ANOTHER ONE WHEN YOU ALREADY HAVE A BUNCH OF COPIES?
BECAUSE THIS IS WHY WE'RE HERE.

NOW, LET'S BEGIN YOUR SESSION, SHALL WE?

POWER

INTERESTING! YOU DIDN'T EVEN LOOK IN THE CONTROL DECK TO SEE WHAT GAME WE'RE PLAYING TODAY.

SH-SHOULD I HAVE?

IT'S A PERSONAL DECISION. CHANCE VERSUS CHOICE.

ANYHOW, YOU DON'T GET A SAY THIS TIME. I CHOSE TODAY'S GAME FOR A REASON.

WHAT? W-WHY?

I'M SORRY!

YOU DON'T EVEN KNOW WHY YOU'RE APOLOGIZING.

THE PAINT-BY-NUMBER COMMENTS OF THE DIGITAL STATUS QUO HAVE NO PLACE HERE!

THIS ISN'T ABOUT LORDING TRIVIAL FACTOIDS AND CANON THEORIES OVER THE UNINITIATED.

AND IT'S NOT ABOUT WAXING NOSTALGIC OVER SOME IDEALIZED MEMORY OF BOYHOOD AFTERNOONS SPENT COMATOSE IN FRONT OF A TELEVISION SCREEN.

GO BACK TO YOUR PHILISTINE MASH-UPS AND FAN-FICS, AND LEAVE ME IN PEACE.

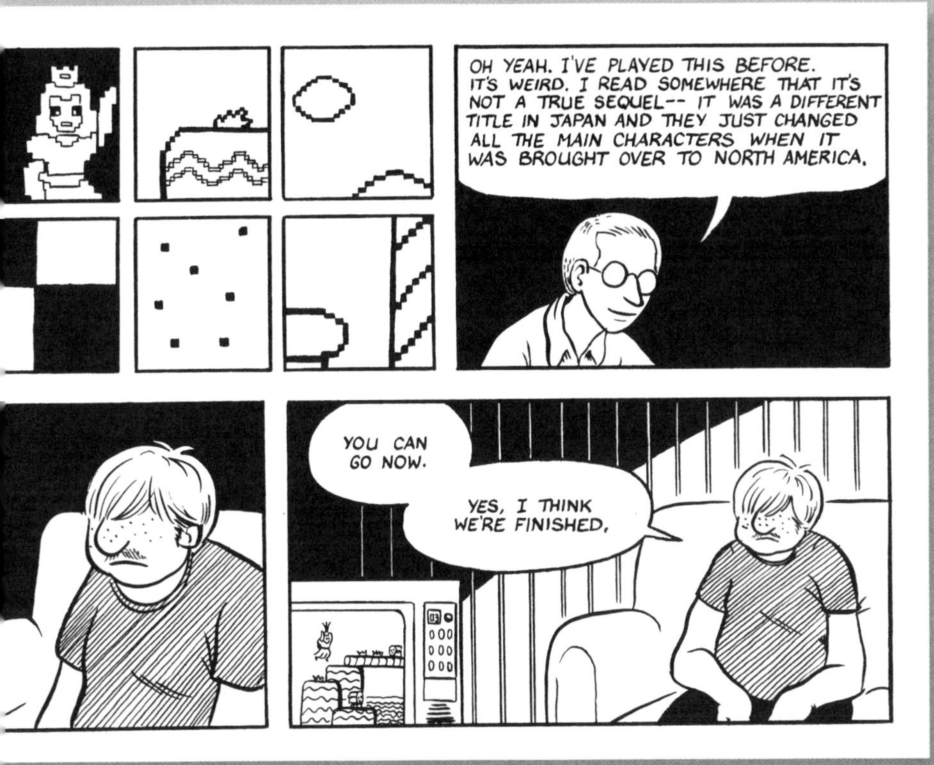

OH YEAH. I'VE PLAYED THIS BEFORE. IT'S WEIRD. I READ SOMEWHERE THAT IT'S NOT A TRUE SEQUEL-- IT WAS A DIFFERENT TITLE IN JAPAN AND THEY JUST CHANGED ALL THE MAIN CHARACTERS WHEN IT WAS BROUGHT OVER TO NORTH AMERICA.
YOU CAN GO NOW.
YES, I THINK WE'RE FINISHED.

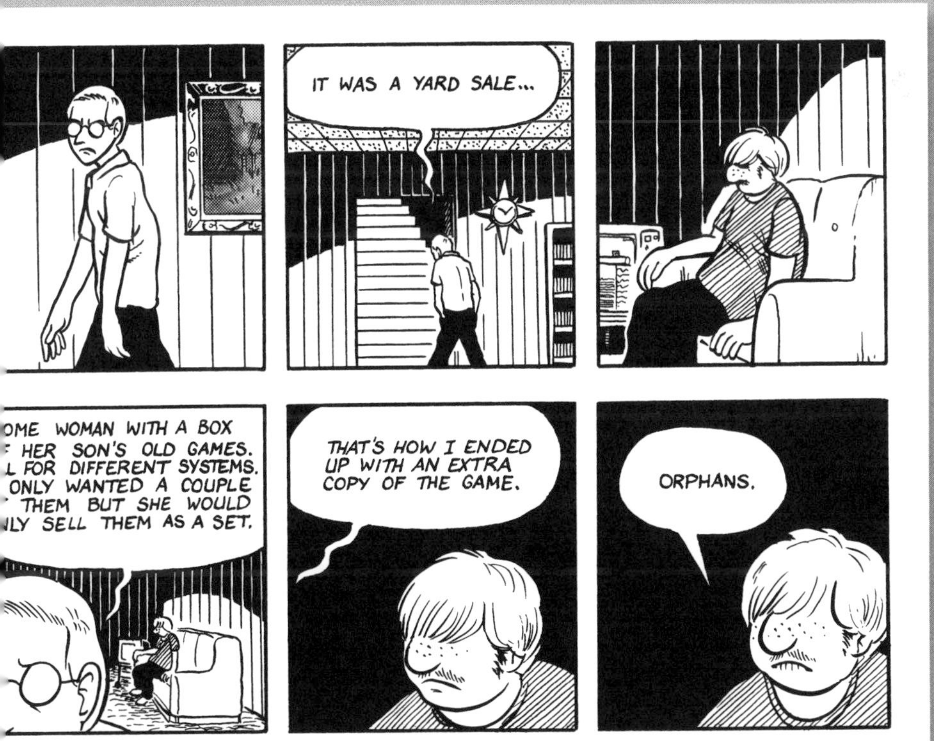

IT WAS A YARD SALE...
OME WOMAN WITH A BOX F HER SON'S OLD GAMES. L FOR DIFFERENT SYSTEMS. ONLY WANTED A COUPLE THEM BUT SHE WOULD NLY SELL THEM AS A SET.
THAT'S HOW I ENDED UP WITH AN EXTRA COPY OF THE GAME.
ORPHANS.

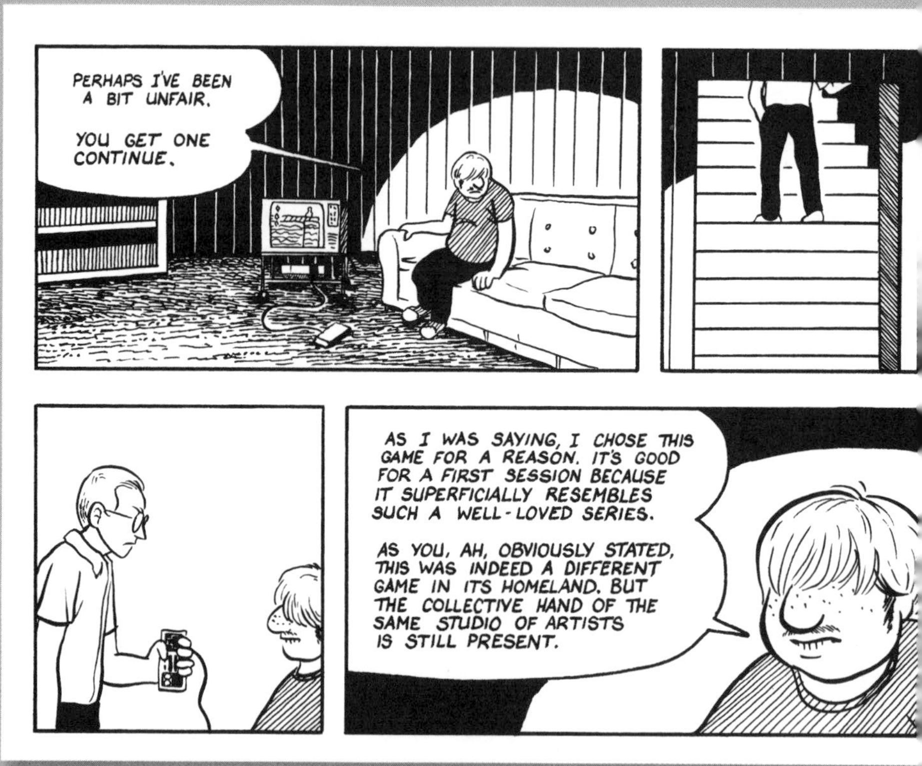
PERHAPS I'VE BEEN A BIT UNFAIR.
YOU GET ONE CONTINUE.
AS I WAS SAYING, I CHOSE THIS GAME FOR A REASON. IT'S GOOD FOR A FIRST SESSION BECAUSE IT SUPERFICIALLY RESEMBLES SUCH A WELL-LOVED SERIES.
AS YOU, AH, OBVIOUSLY STATED, THIS WAS INDEED A DIFFERENT GAME IN ITS HOMELAND. BUT THE COLLECTIVE HAND OF THE SAME STUDIO OF ARTISTS IS STILL PRESENT.

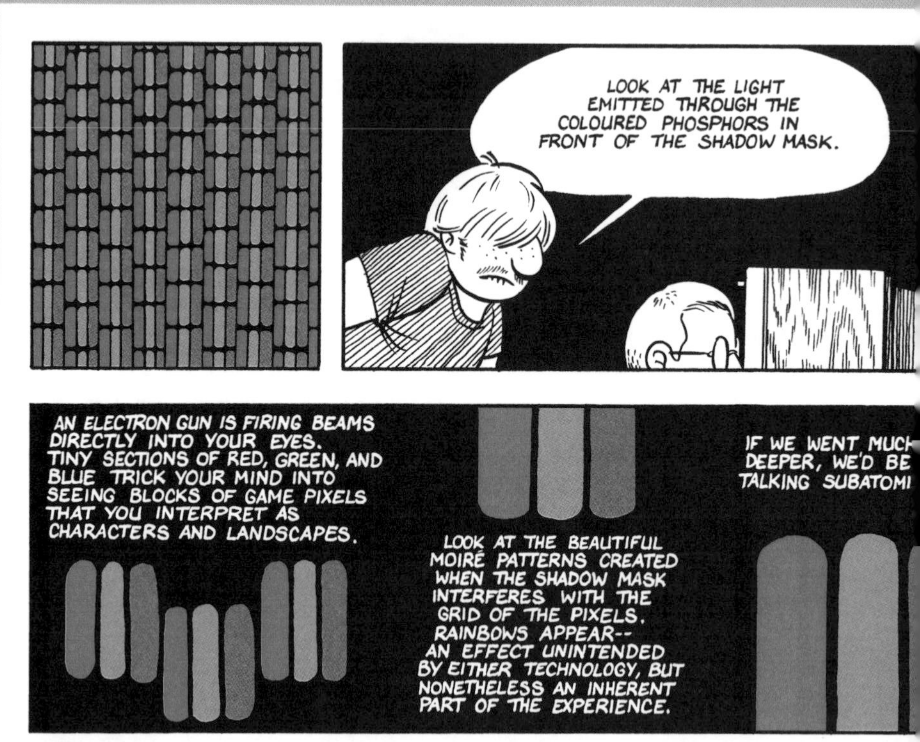
LOOK AT THE LIGHT EMITTED THROUGH THE COLOURED PHOSPHORS IN FRONT OF THE SHADOW MASK.
AN ELECTRON GUN IS FIRING BEAMS DIRECTLY INTO YOUR EYES. TINY SECTIONS OF RED, GREEN, AND BLUE TRICK YOUR MIND INTO SEEING BLOCKS OF GAME PIXELS THAT YOU INTERPRET AS CHARACTERS AND LANDSCAPES.
LOOK AT THE BEAUTIFUL MOIRÉ PATTERNS CREATED WHEN THE SHADOW MASK INTERFERES WITH THE GRID OF THE PIXELS. RAINBOWS APPEAR-- AN EFFECT UNINTENDED BY EITHER TECHNOLOGY, BUT NONETHELESS AN INHERENT PART OF THE EXPERIENCE.
IF WE WENT MUC DEEPER, WE'D BE TALKING SUBATOMI

U SEE, THIS IS SOMETHING AT TRANSCENDS THE WORLD CORPORATE MASCOTS AND E BRAND-RECOGNITION OF NOTORIOUS FRANCHISES.

GARDLESS OF YOUR IN-GAME ATAR, IT'S THE GAMEPLAY MECHANICS AND THE PLICATIONS OF THE WORLD WHICH YOU'RE PLAYING HAT TRULY MATTER.

THIS BASTARD GAME IS TELLING US THE SAME THING ITS BETTER-LOVED SIBLINGS TELL US.

SO WHAT IS IT TELLING YOU?

UH... J-JUMP?

AN OSTENSIBLE ACTION-- WHAT ELSE?

TH-THAT THERE'S MORE THAN MEETS THE EYE?

A CANNED SLOGAN FROM A MEDIOCRE TOY LINE, BUT YES. THIS GAME, LIKE SO MANY OTHERS, IS TELLING US THAT WHAT WE SEE MIGHT BE MORE THAN WHAT WE SEE. IT IS BEGGING US TO LOOK CLOSER...

SO LOOK CLOSER.

BUT HOW AM I SUPPOSED TO PLAY THE GAME WHEN I'M THIS CLOSE TO THE TV?

ARE YOU SURE YOU REALLY JUST WANT TO PLAY A GAME? ANYONE CAN DO THAT. IT IS A TRIVIAL MATTER.

HOPSCOTCH IS A GAME. TAG IS A GAME.

THIS IS MORE.

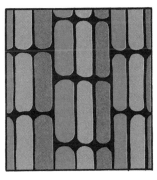

M NOT SURE IF I NDERSTAND. AREN'T I RYING TO FINISH THE AME? TO BEAT IT?

TO WIN?

IF YOU LIKE.

OR YOU CAN REALIZE THAT YOU ARE GIVEN EXTRA LIVES IN THIS GAME.

AND LIVES ARE MEANT TO BE LIVED.

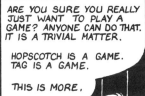

CONSIDER THE GAME'S STORYLINE: YOU HAD A DREAM IN WHICH A VOICE AT THE END OF A LONG STAIRCASE CALLED FOR HELP. WHEN YOU AWOKE, YOU WENT TO A NEARBY CAVE AND SAW EXACTLY WHAT YOU SAW IN YOUR DREAM, *THE WORLD OF SUBCON.*

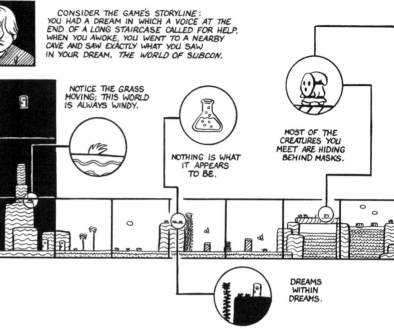

NOTICE THE GRASS MOVING; THIS WORLD IS ALWAYS WINDY.

NOTHING IS WHAT IT APPEARS TO BE.

MOST OF THE CREATURES YOU MEET ARE HIDING BEHIND MASKS.

DREAMS WITHIN DREAMS.

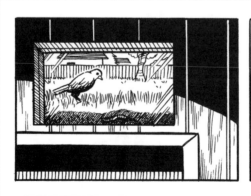

NO, NO, YOU'RE STILL PLAYING LIKE A PRE-PROGRAMMED ALGORITHM, WALKING ACROSS THE SCREEN JUST LIKE THE GAME PROGRAMMER INTENDED.

HIT RESET AGAIN.

HOW AM I SUPPOSED TO GET ANYWHERE IF YOU KEEP MAKING ME START OVER?

WHEN YOU FINISH THE GAME, THE END SCREEN IS DISPLAYED... IT LOOPS ENDLESSLY UNTIL YOU HIT THE RESET BUTTON.

HOW IS THIS ANY DIFFERENT?

WHEN YOU GET TO THE END, ANY SENSE OF ACCOMPLISHMENT YOU FEEL IS IMAGINARY.

CURSED KEYS TO LOCKED DOORS.
SWIMMING THROUGH QUICKSAND.
POW
AND BIRDS.
BIRDS ARE EVERYWHERE.
HOPPING
NIGHTMARISH
PROTANDROUS
BIRDS
SWALLOWING YOU WHOLE.

WELL THEN WHAT'S THE POINT OF PLAYING AT ALL?! IF THE WHOLE THING IS JUST A FUTILE LOOP OF CODE, THEN WHY ARE WE WASTING ALL DAY DOING THIS?!
I THOUGHT THIS WAS GOING TO BE INTERESTING, BUT YOU'RE JUST A PRETENTIOUS SNOB WHO READS WAY TOO MUCH INTO YOUR STUPID CHILDHOOD TOYS!
F YOU WISH TO LEAVE, THERE IS NOTHING EEPING YOU HERE.
GO HOME.
EAT A MEAL.
SLEEP.
ND CONTINUE YOUR NIMAL REPETITION NTIL YOUR ELDERLY ODY ONE DAY STOPS.
POWER
RESET
OR WE CAN TAKE A SHORT BREAK.

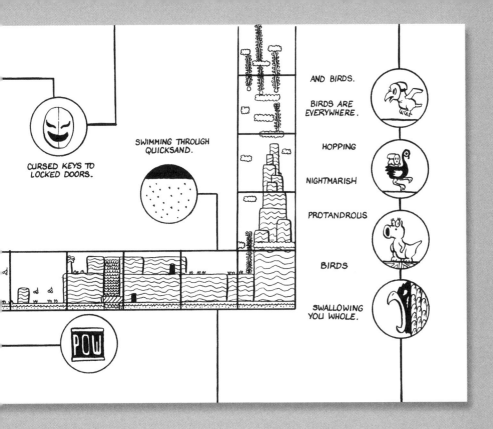

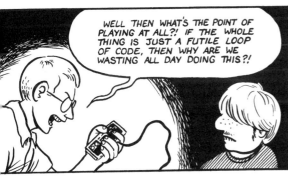

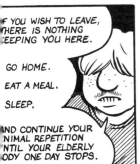

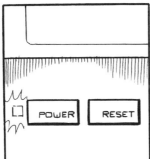

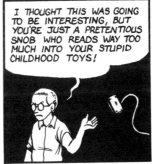

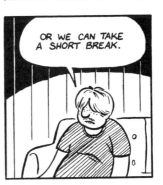

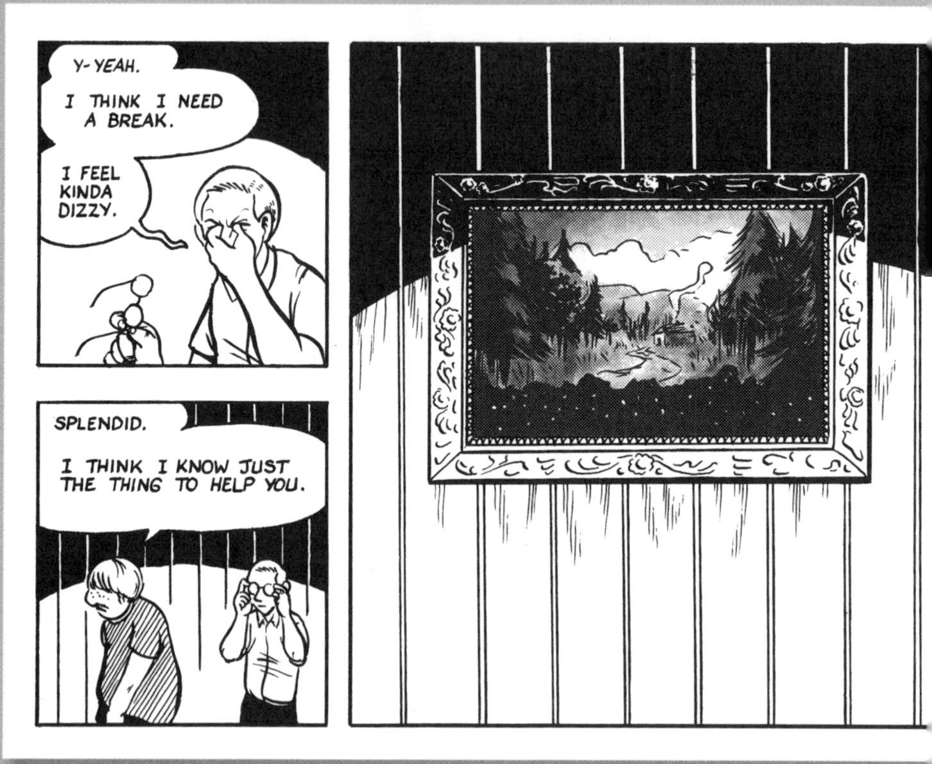
Y-YEAH.
I THINK I NEED A BREAK.
I FEEL KINDA DIZZY.
SPLENDID.
I THINK I KNOW JUST THE THING TO HELP YOU.

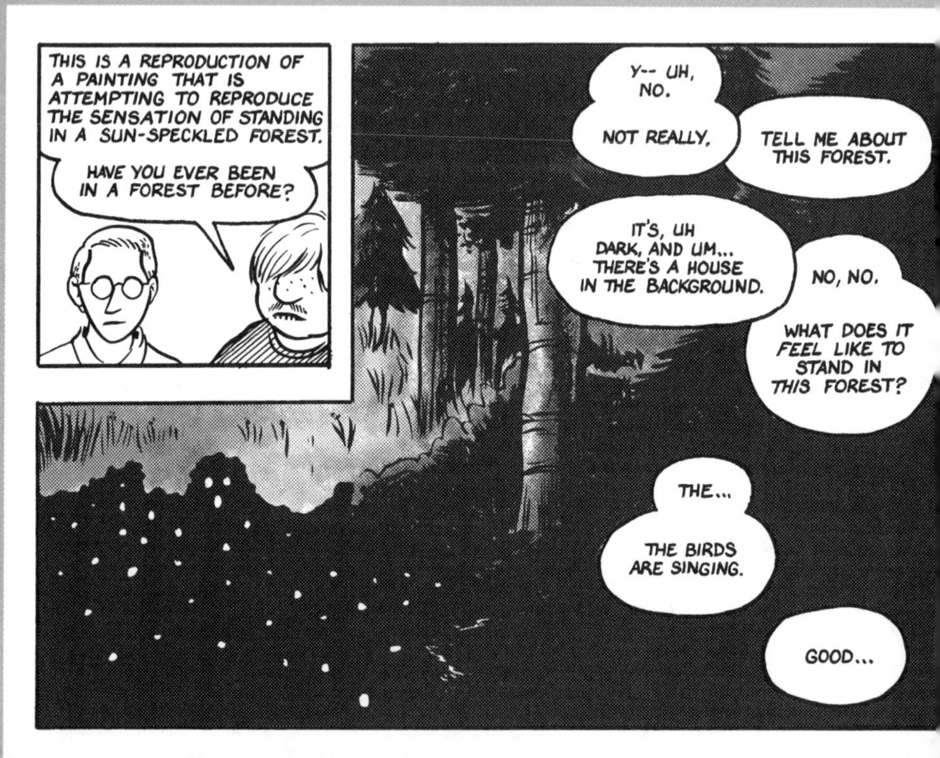
THIS IS A REPRODUCTION OF A PAINTING THAT IS ATTEMPTING TO REPRODUCE THE SENSATION OF STANDING IN A SUN-SPECKLED FOREST.
HAVE YOU EVER BEEN IN A FOREST BEFORE?
Y-- UH, NO.
NOT REALLY.
TELL ME ABOUT THIS FOREST.
IT'S, UH DARK, AND UM... THERE'S A HOUSE IN THE BACKGROUND.
NO, NO.
WHAT DOES IT FEEL LIKE TO STAND IN THIS FOREST?
THE...
THE BIRDS ARE SINGING.
GOOD...

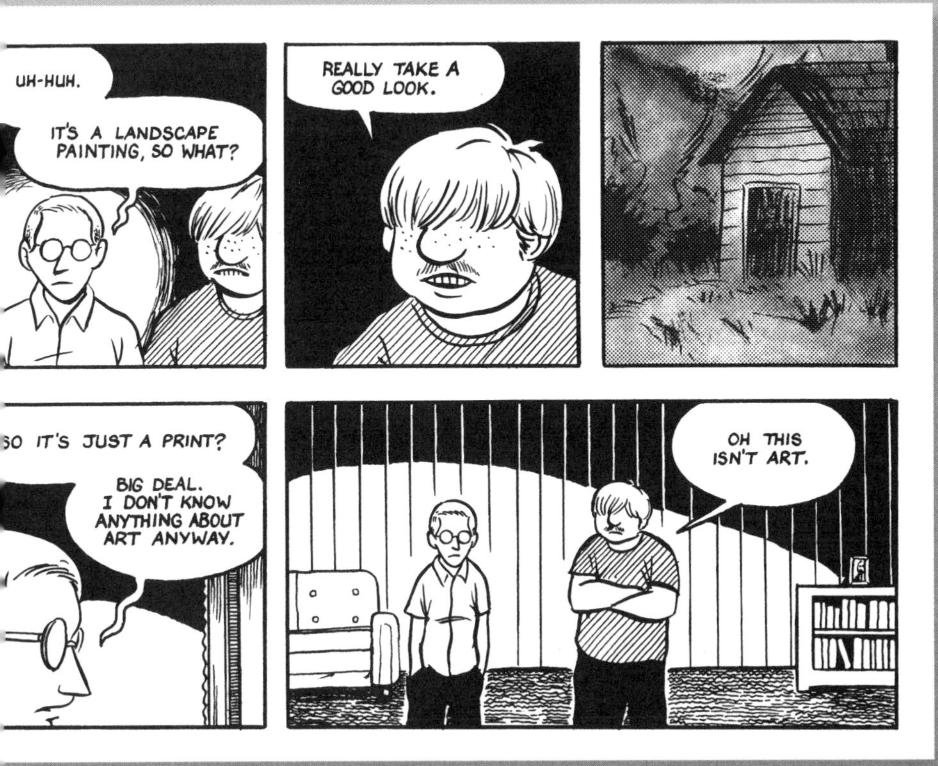
UH-HUH.
IT'S A LANDSCAPE PAINTING, SO WHAT?
REALLY TAKE A GOOD LOOK.
SO IT'S JUST A PRINT?
BIG DEAL. I DON'T KNOW ANYTHING ABOUT ART ANYWAY.
OH THIS ISN'T ART.

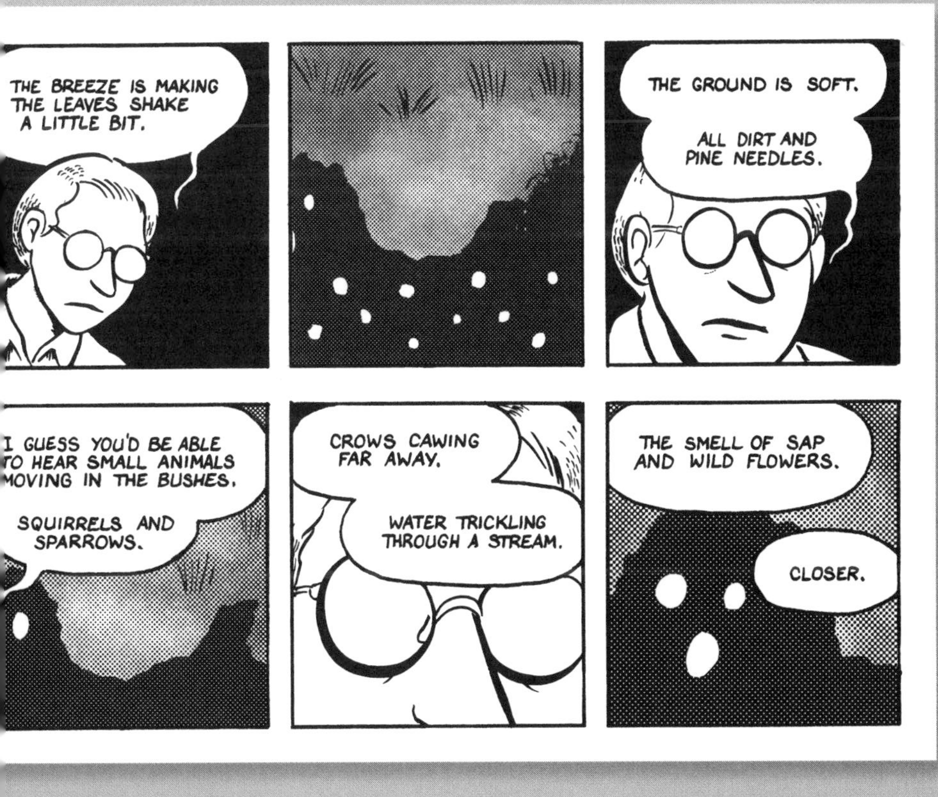
THE BREEZE IS MAKING THE LEAVES SHAKE A LITTLE BIT.
THE GROUND IS SOFT.
ALL DIRT AND PINE NEEDLES.
I GUESS YOU'D BE ABLE TO HEAR SMALL ANIMALS MOVING IN THE BUSHES.
SQUIRRELS AND SPARROWS.
CROWS CAWING FAR AWAY.
WATER TRICKLING THROUGH A STREAM.
THE SMELL OF SAP AND WILD FLOWERS.
CLOSER.

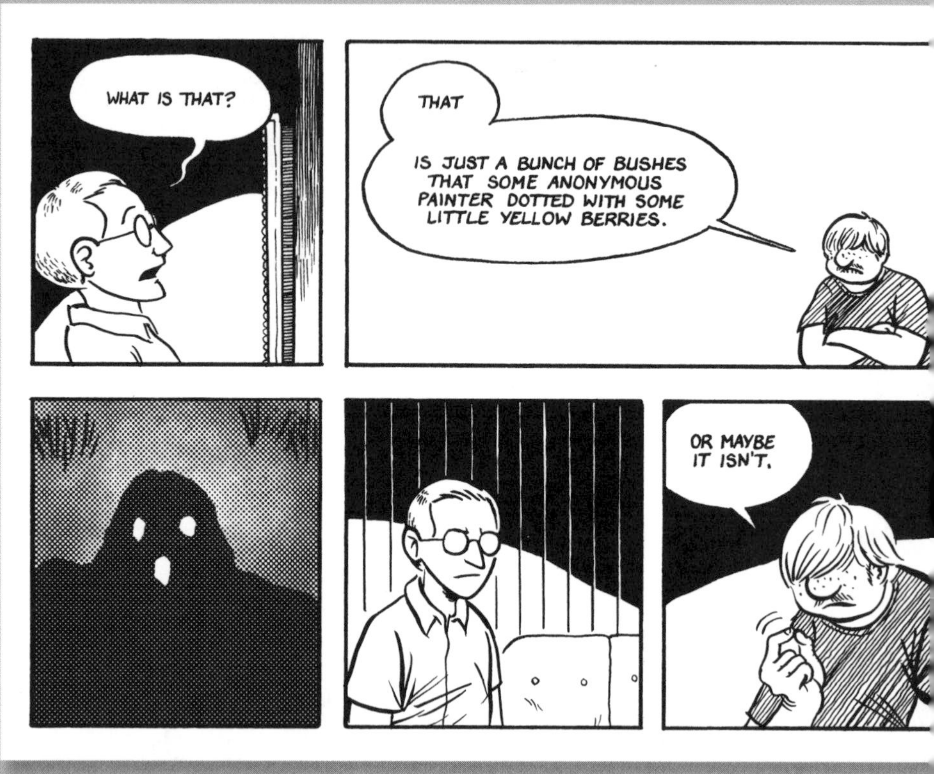
WHAT IS THAT?
THAT
IS JUST A BUNCH OF BUSHES THAT SOME ANONYMOUS PAINTER DOTTED WITH SOME LITTLE YELLOW BERRIES.
OR MAYBE IT ISN'T.

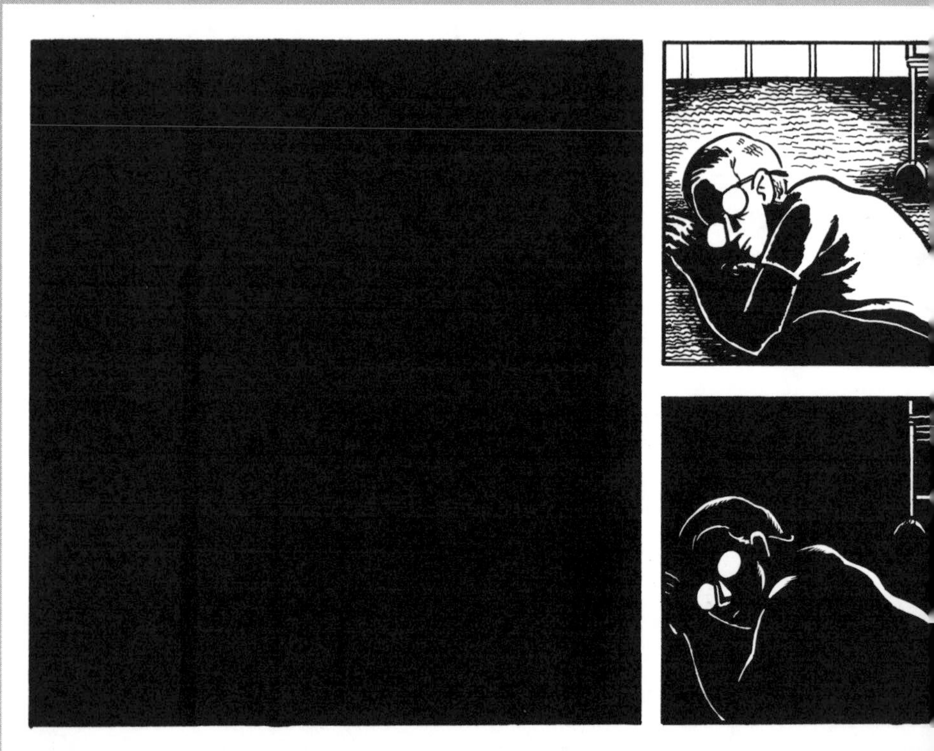

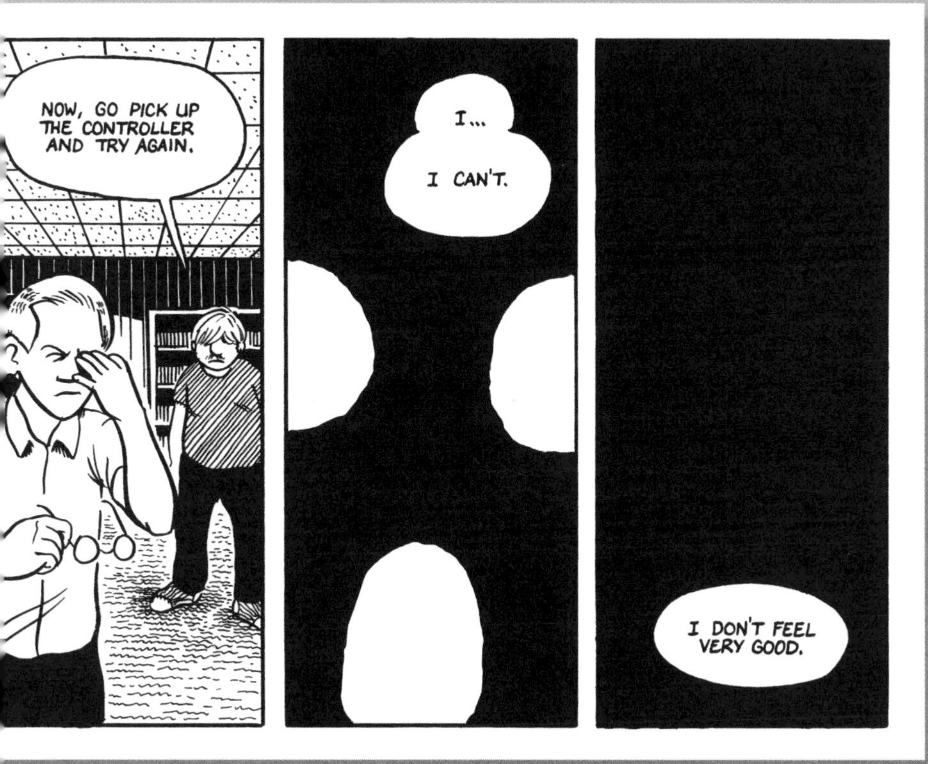
NOW, GO PICK UP THE CONTROLLER AND TRY AGAIN.
I...
I CAN'T.
I DON'T FEEL VERY GOOD.

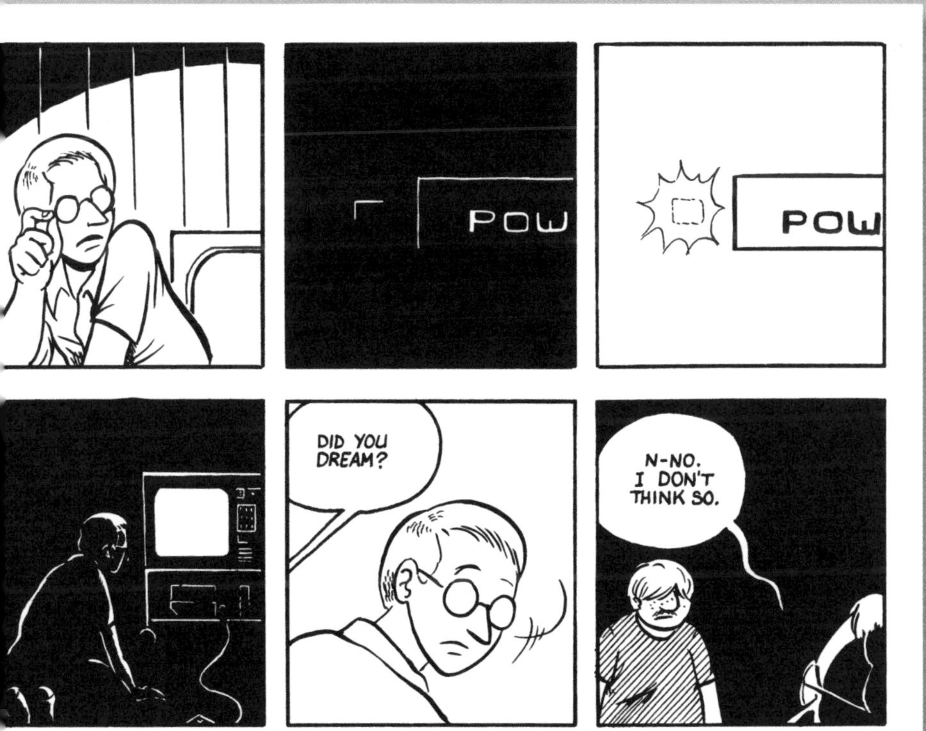
POW
POW
DID YOU DREAM?
N-NO. I DON'T THINK SO.

DID YOU MAKE IT TO THE END OF THE GAME?
N-NO.
AH. IT'S JUST AS WELL, I SUPPOSE. THE ENDING REVEALS THAT THE WHOLE THING WAS A DREAM.
SOME PEOPLE ARE DISAPPOINTED.
BUT YOU WON'T REMEMBER IT THAT WAY, WILL YOU?
IF YOU RETURN NEXT WEEK, MAKE SURE TO BRING FURTHER PAYMENT.

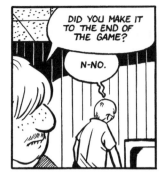

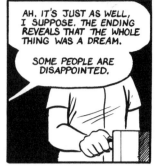

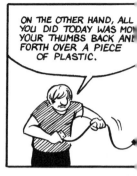

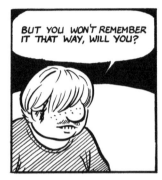

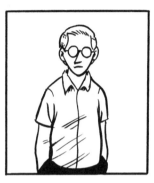

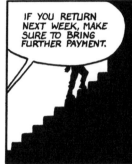

NOTES

90-MINUTE LIMITED WARRANTY LEAVE LUCK TO HEAVEN GAME EXPERIENCES

-MINUTE LIMITED WARRANTY:

ave Luck to Heaven Entertainment Concern ("Leave Luck to aven") warrants to the original consumer purchaser that this Game k Manual ("Manual") shall be free from defects in content, world- w, and resulting gameplay experiences for a period of 90 minutes m the time of purchasing. If a defect covered by this warranty occurs ring this 90-minute period, Leave Luck to Heaven will offer an ernative perspective free of charge.

receive this warranty service:

1. DO NOT return the Manual to the retailer.

2. Notify the Leave Luck to Heaven Consumer Service Department of the problem requiring warranty service by calling:
   dakota@dakotamcfadzean.com
   or by visiting our offices:
   http://www.dakotamcfadzean.com
   Our Consumer Service Department is in operation from 9:00 A.M. to 12:00 A.M. Central Standard Time Monday through Saturday. Please Do Not return unwanted Manuals to Leave Luck to Heaven. Instead, give it to a friend or relative.

3. If the Leave Luck to Heaven Service Representative is unable to provide a satisfactory discussion, try applying the ideas to a different Game Pak. Is it possible that cynicism or ennui have compromised the ability to view the experience with earnest eyes? If the problem persists, try limiting contact with the online game community and try again.

is warranty shall not apply if the contents of the Manual have been tentionally misinterpreted or misunderstood, or if the contents of the anual have been applied to an irredeemable game.

REPAIR/SERVICE AFTER EXPIRATION OF WARRANTY:

If successive readings of the manual results in defective content after the 90-minute warranty period, you may consider other techniques that may elicit a similar experience. Listen to a favourite album on headphones in a darkened room. Watch a familiar movie as though you have no idea what will happen next. Go for a long walk through a neighbourhood you've never visited before.

Incidentally, it is worth noting that it is possible to prevent the Phanto mask from chasing you by repeatedly throwing blocks at its key. If you do this enough times, the key will cry out in pain, and Phanto will no longer follow you when you are holding the key. Try it in World 1-3.

WARRANTY LIMITATIONS:

ANY APPLICABLE IMPLIED WARRANTIES INCLUDING WARRANTIES OF MERCHANTABILITY AND FITNESS ARE FOR A PARTICULAR PURPOSE, ARE HEREBY LIMITED TO NINETY MINUTES FROM THE DATE OF PURCHASE AND ARE SUBJECT TO THE CONDITIONS SET FORTH HEREIN. IN NO EVENT SHALL LEAVE LUCK TO HEAVEN BE LIABLE FOR CONSEQUENTIAL OR INCIDENTAL DAMAGES RESULTING FROM UNDERWHELMING EFFECTS DUE TO ANY OF THE TECHNIQUES IN THIS MANUAL.

The provisions of this warranty are valid in the United States and Canada only. The legal rights described above may vary from state to state and province to province. If nothing else, it should be relatively simple to find others who are unable to stop thinking about a digital memory that often seems more emotionally vivid than most real ones. The only problem is getting them to remember what it felt like before a basic understanding of computer programming developed. If such a thought seems impossible, the above limitations and exclusion may not apply to you.

33

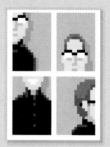

CHRISTOPH NIEMANN

Red Eye

from *NewYorkTimes.com*

Magazine
Abstract Sunday
CHRISTOPH NIEMANN
RED EYE

FOR ME, DRAWING COMICS IS

Exhausting.

THE SELECTION

A visual diary of a flight from New York to Berlin, with a stopover in London.

THE CONTEXT

Abstract City blog for the *New York Times*.

PUBLICATIONS MY WORK HAS APPEARED IN

The *New York Times, The New Yorker, Wired.*

AWARDS

Art Directors Club Hall of Fame (2010).

WHAT I'M KNOWN FOR

I Lego New York.

WHERE I LIVE

Germany.

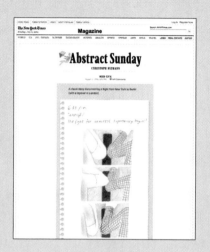

6:53 p.m.
Takeoff!
The fight for armrest supremacy begins!

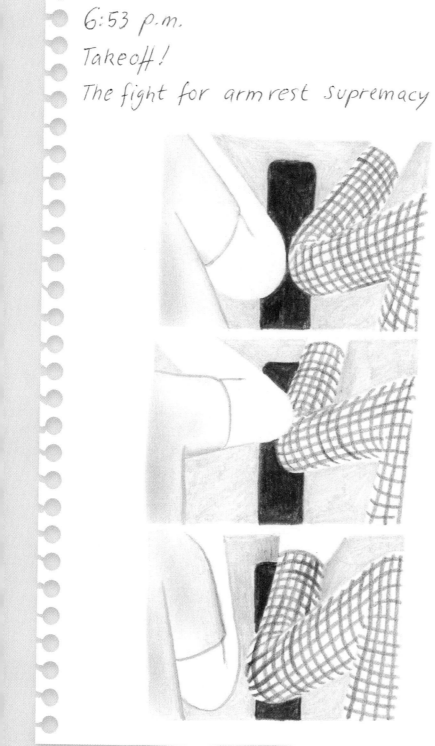

8:15 p.m. Maine

Peanuts.

8:16 p.m.
Trying not to devour them right away.
What if I stack them to pass more time?

8:17 p.m.

Could have sworn there was one left.

9:05 p.m.
Dinner !

THE
CHICKEN

THE
PASTA

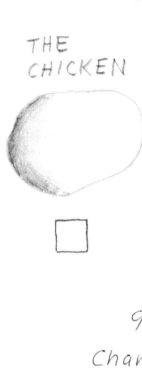

☐

☑

9:06 p.m.
Change of heart.

THE
CHICKEN

THE
PASTA

☑

10:00 p.m.

Wish my seat would recline further.

20°, MAYBE 25°

BANANA

LIKE 5°?

L.T. OF PISA

2° TOPS!

MY SEAT

10:43 p.m., 10:47 p.m., 10:50 p.m. Halifax

I ♥ my seat back monitor.

HALIFAX
HALIFAX
HALIFAX

10.08 p.m. St. John, New Brunswick

Cool! Seems that my remote has a button to delete neighbor.

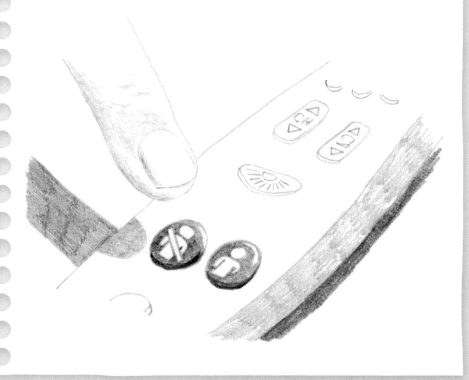

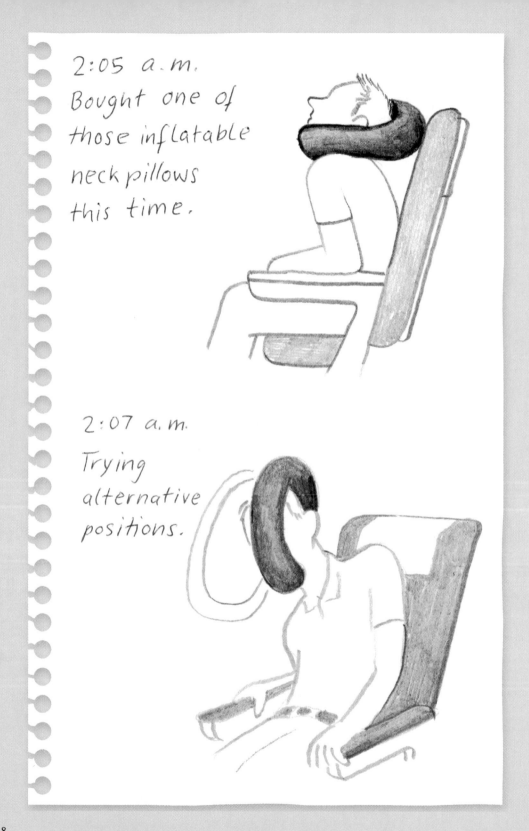

2:05 a.m.
Bought one of
those inflatable
neck pillows
this time.

2:07 a.m.
Trying
alternative
positions.

2:15 a.m.

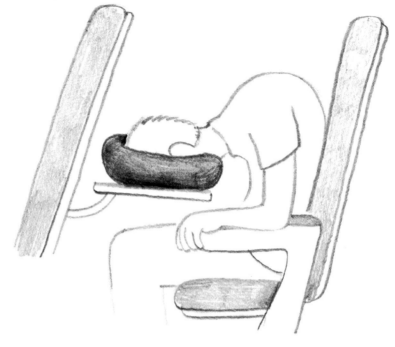

4:12 a.m.   North Atlantic

Not sure if I slept or just entered brief coma.
Not sure how to describe taste in my mouth either.

5:10 a.m.

Giving baby girl in front row the evil eye.

I don't mind that the poor thing is crying.
I'm just envious of her bassinet.

7:50 a.m.   Cork, Ireland

"Put your seat in the upright position!"
You mean, as opposed to where it is now?

8:05 a.m.
Cleanup.

CRUMPLED NEWSPAPER

NOVEL

ALL SORTS OF GARBAGE. AND GLASSES.

BROKEN PLASTIC CUP

8:07 a.m.
By the way:

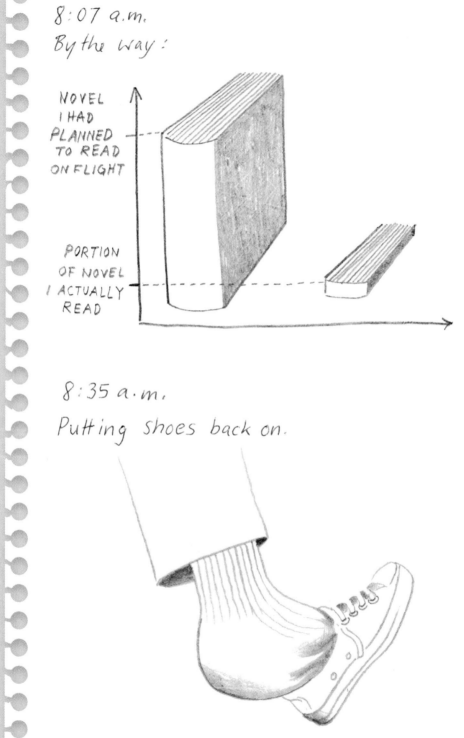

NOVEL I HAD PLANNED TO READ ON FLIGHT

PORTION OF NOVEL I ACTUALLY READ

8:35 a.m.

Putting shoes back on.

9:30 a.m. London Heathrow
Layover.
Heathrow bathrooms equipped with
nuclear-powered hand dryers.

9:50 a.m. Heathrow food court
They have awesome poppy seed pretzels here!

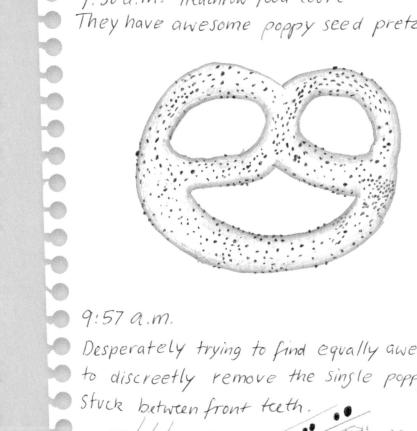

9:57 a.m.

Desperately trying to find equally awesome spot
to discreetly remove the single poppy seed
stuck between front teeth.

11:30 a.m. Groningen Netherlands
Back in the air.
Wow! Cloud outside looks just like
Henry Moore's "Reclining Figure" (1939).

11:35 a.m.
So does the "croissant."

11:52 a.m.

Unable to sleep, read, or even think.
Spending the remaining 45 minutes contemplating
the little hole in airplane window.

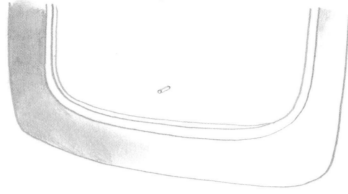

12:46 p.m. Berlin, Tegel airport (baggage claim)

A glimpse of happiness at last.
Looks like it wasn't <u>my</u> suitcase that
broke open during the flight.

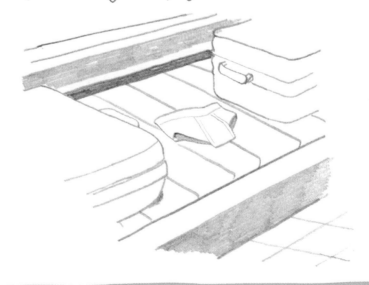

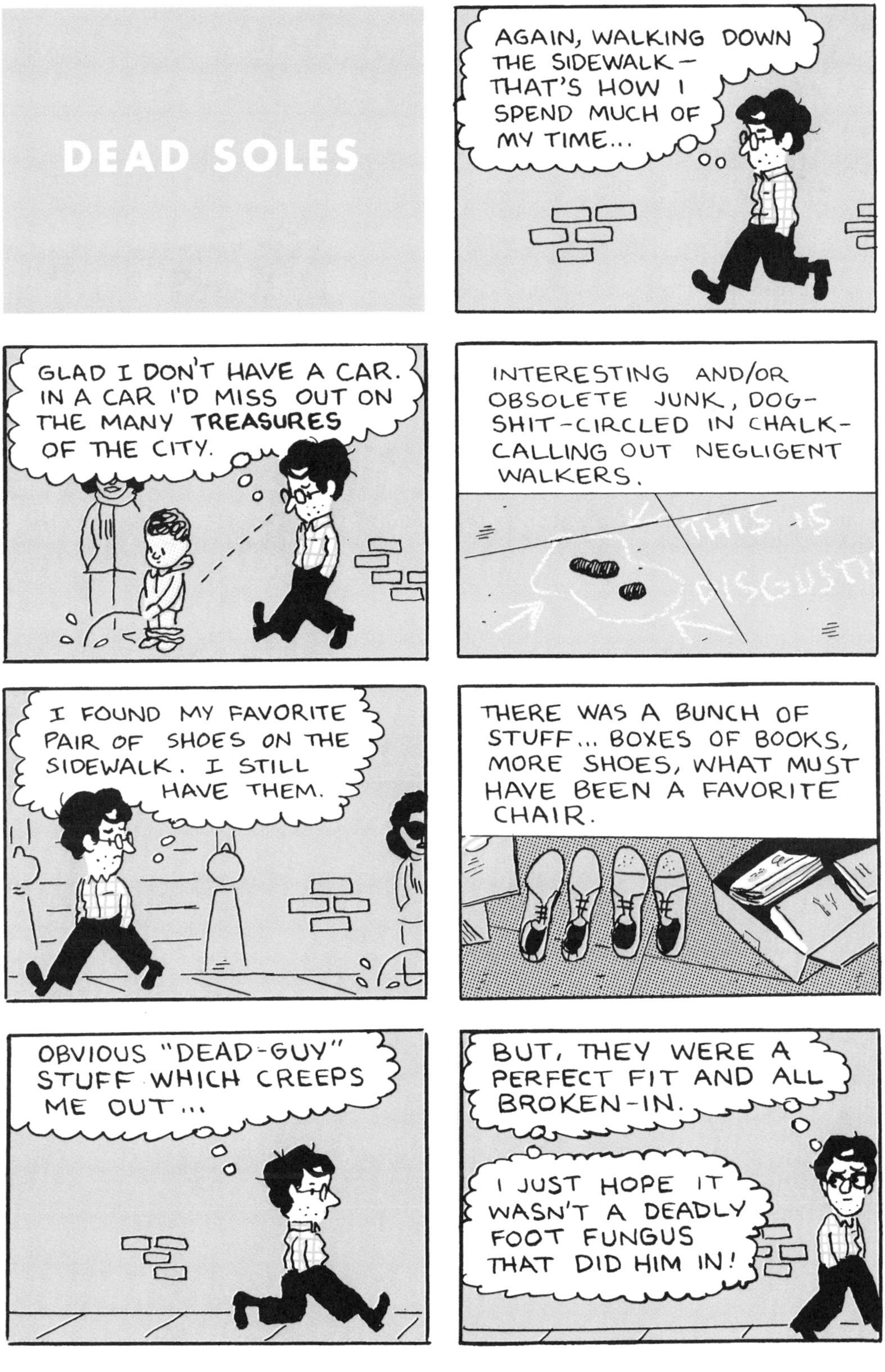
DEAD SOLES
AGAIN, WALKING DOWN THE SIDEWALK— THAT'S HOW I SPEND MUCH OF MY TIME...
GLAD I DON'T HAVE A CAR. IN A CAR I'D MISS OUT ON THE MANY **TREASURES** OF THE CITY.
INTERESTING AND/OR OBSOLETE JUNK, DOG-SHIT-CIRCLED IN CHALK-CALLING OUT NEGLIGENT WALKERS.
THIS IS
I FOUND MY FAVORITE PAIR OF SHOES ON THE SIDEWALK. I STILL HAVE THEM.
THERE WAS A BUNCH OF STUFF... BOXES OF BOOKS, MORE SHOES, WHAT MUST HAVE BEEN A FAVORITE CHAIR.
OBVIOUS "DEAD-GUY" STUFF WHICH CREEPS ME OUT...
BUT, THEY WERE A PERFECT FIT AND ALL BROKEN-IN.
I JUST HOPE IT WASN'T A DEADLY FOOT FUNGUS THAT DID HIM IN!

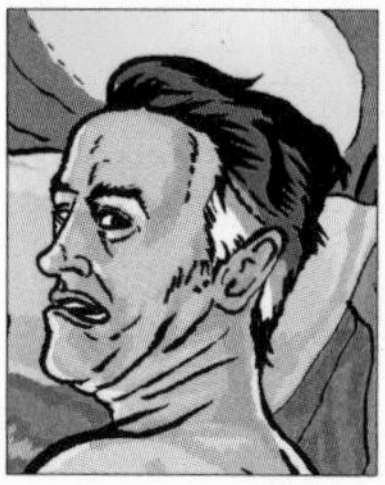

DAVID SANDLIN

House of Debt

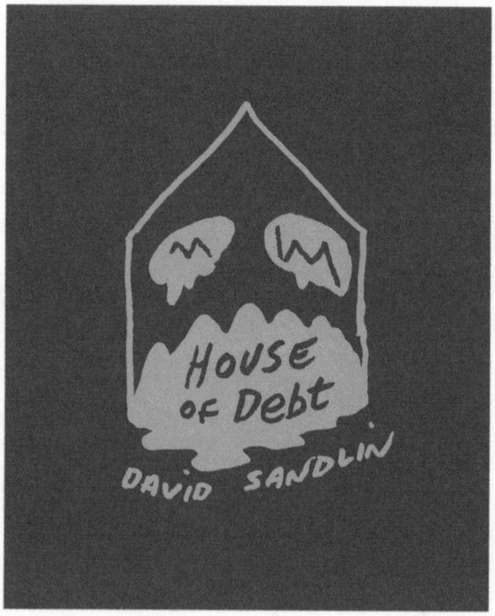
HOUSE
OF Debt
DAVID SANDLIN

FOR ME, DRAWING COMICS IS

An outgrowth of my silkscreen artist's books, which in turn were inspired by comics I read as a kid in Ireland.

THE SELECTION

When I was invited to participate in a *Strapazin* issue devoted to John Divola's iconic photographs, I used his images of abandoned houses as a starting point for a meditation on the housing and financial collapse of 2008 and beyond.

THE CONTEXT

I expanded the original idea into a larger book called *Mort-Gage,* published by Dernier Cri, France.

PUBLICATIONS MY WORK HAS APPEARED IN

The New Yorker, the *New York Times, RAW, Hotwire, Strapazin.*

AWARDS

Fellow at the Cullman Center for Scholars and Writers, New York Public Library (2010 to 2011); Swann Award; New York Foundation for the Arts Awards (four times).

WHAT I'M KNOWN FOR

A Sinner's Progress (1995 to 2009: an eight-volume series of artist's books, with associated paintings, installations, and printed multiples); *Land of 1,000 Beers* (1983).

WHERE I LIVE

New York, New York.

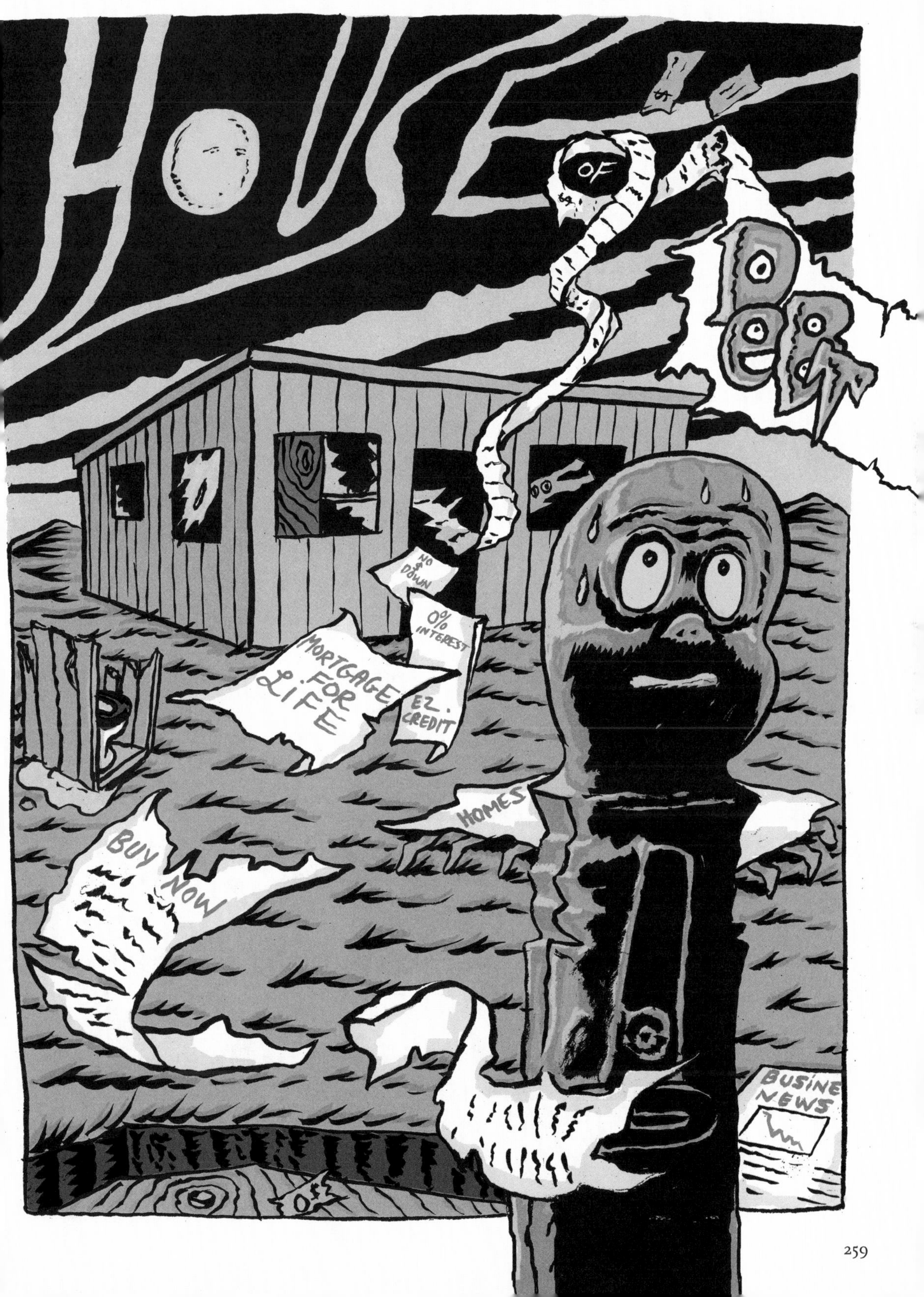
HOUSE
OF
DEBT
NO $ DOWN
0% INTEREST
MORTGAGE FOR LIFE
EZ. CREDIT
HOMES
BUY NOW
BUSINE NEWS

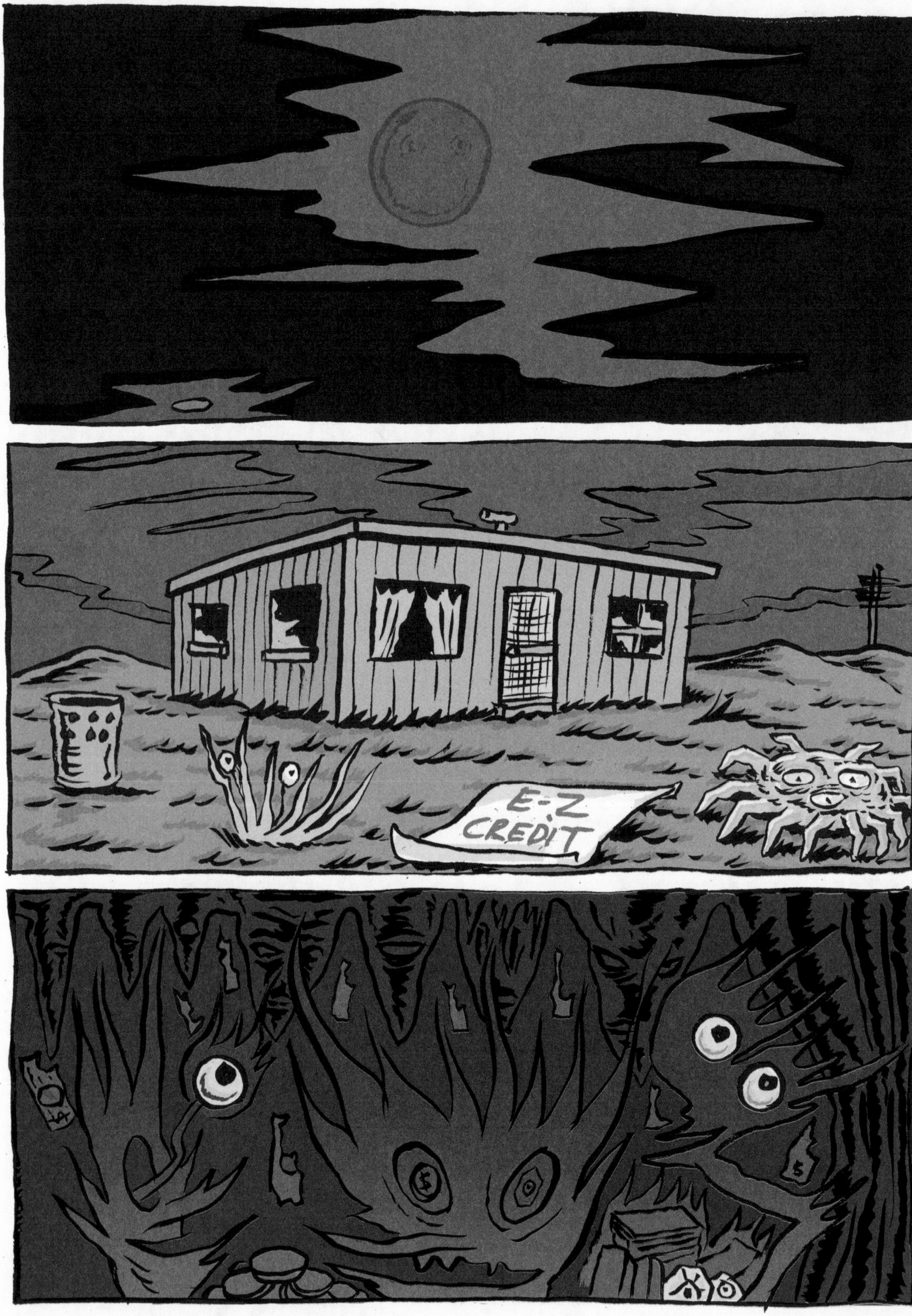
E-Z
CREDIT

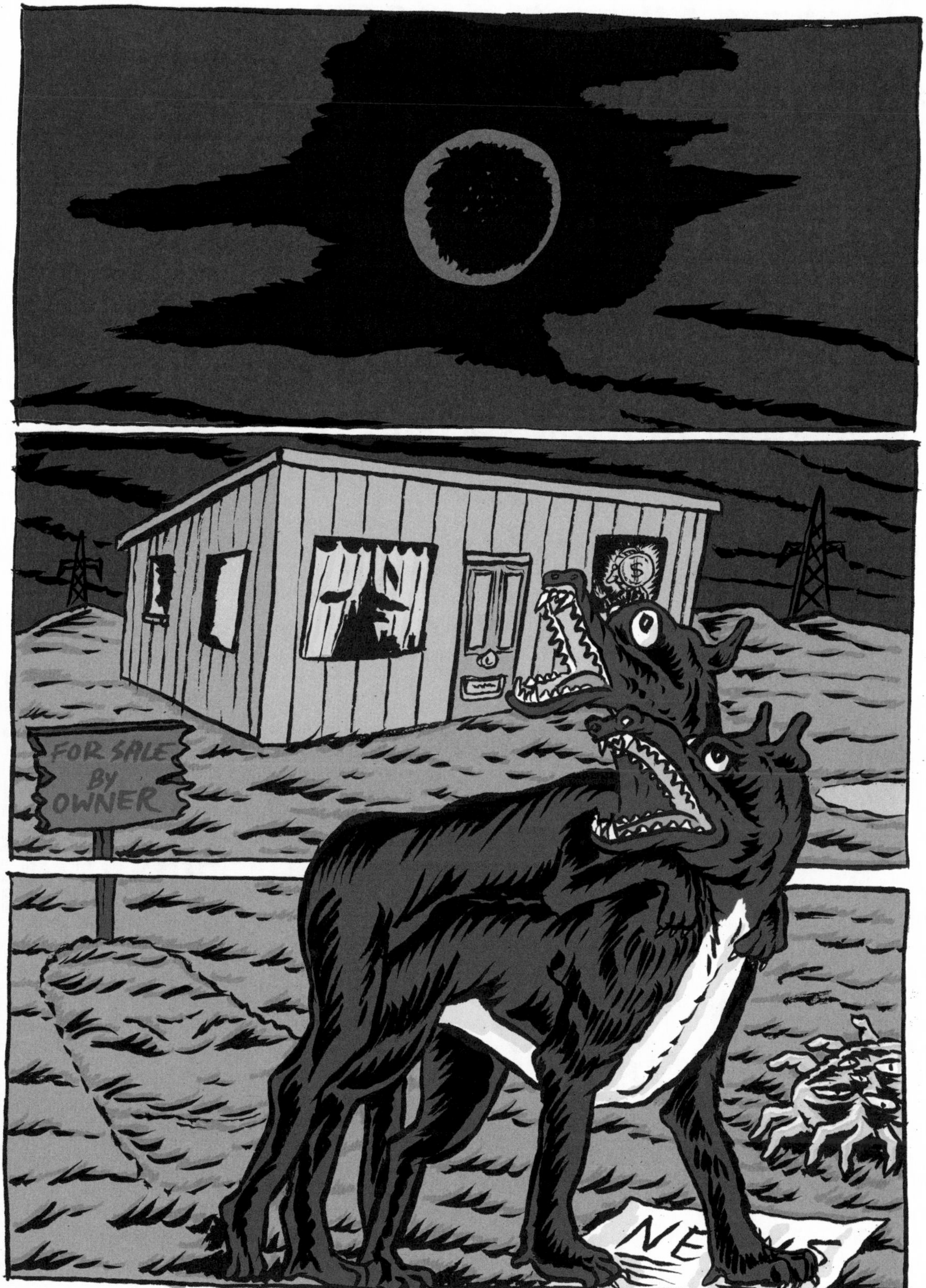
FOR SALE
BY
OWNER
NE S

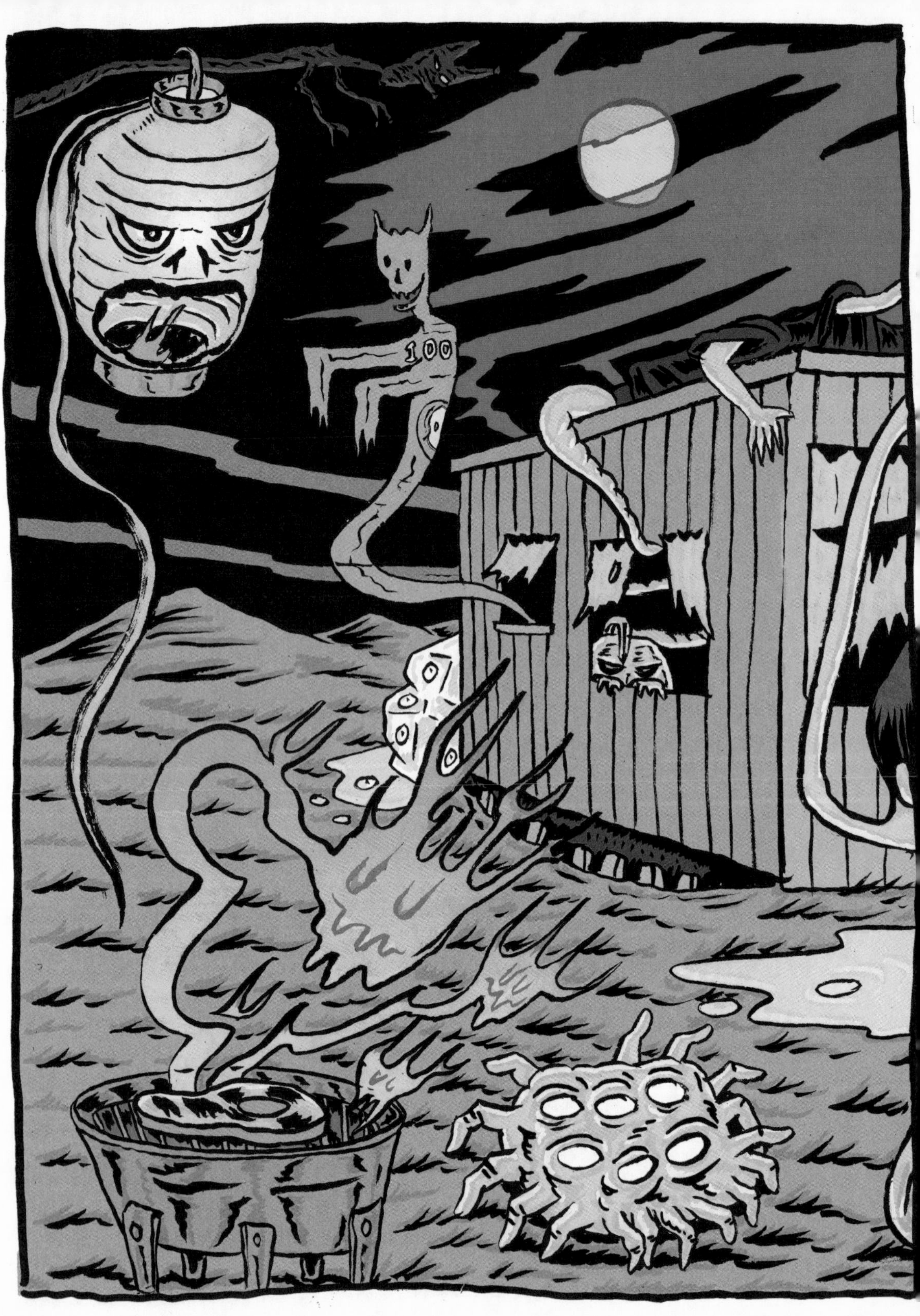
100

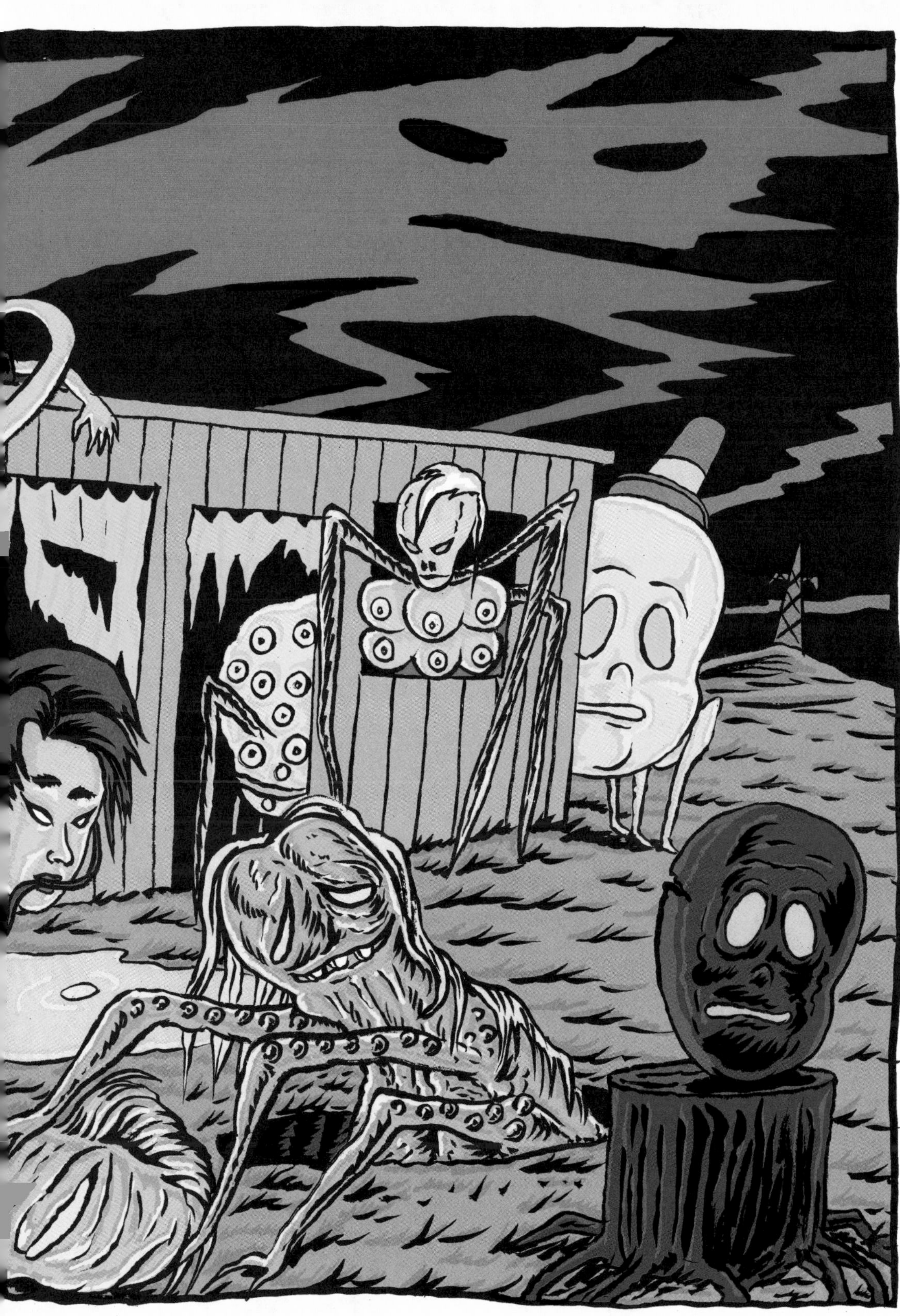

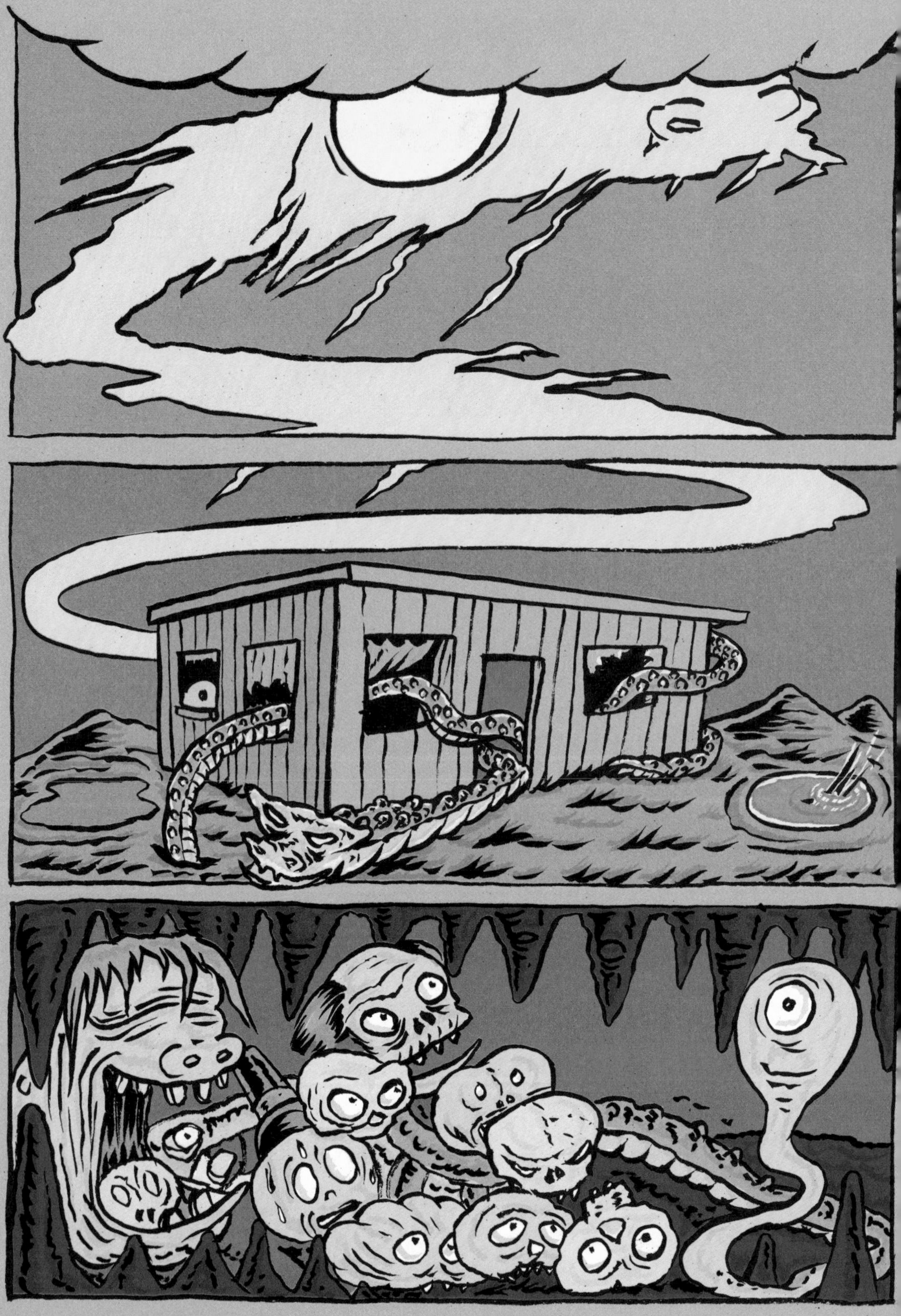

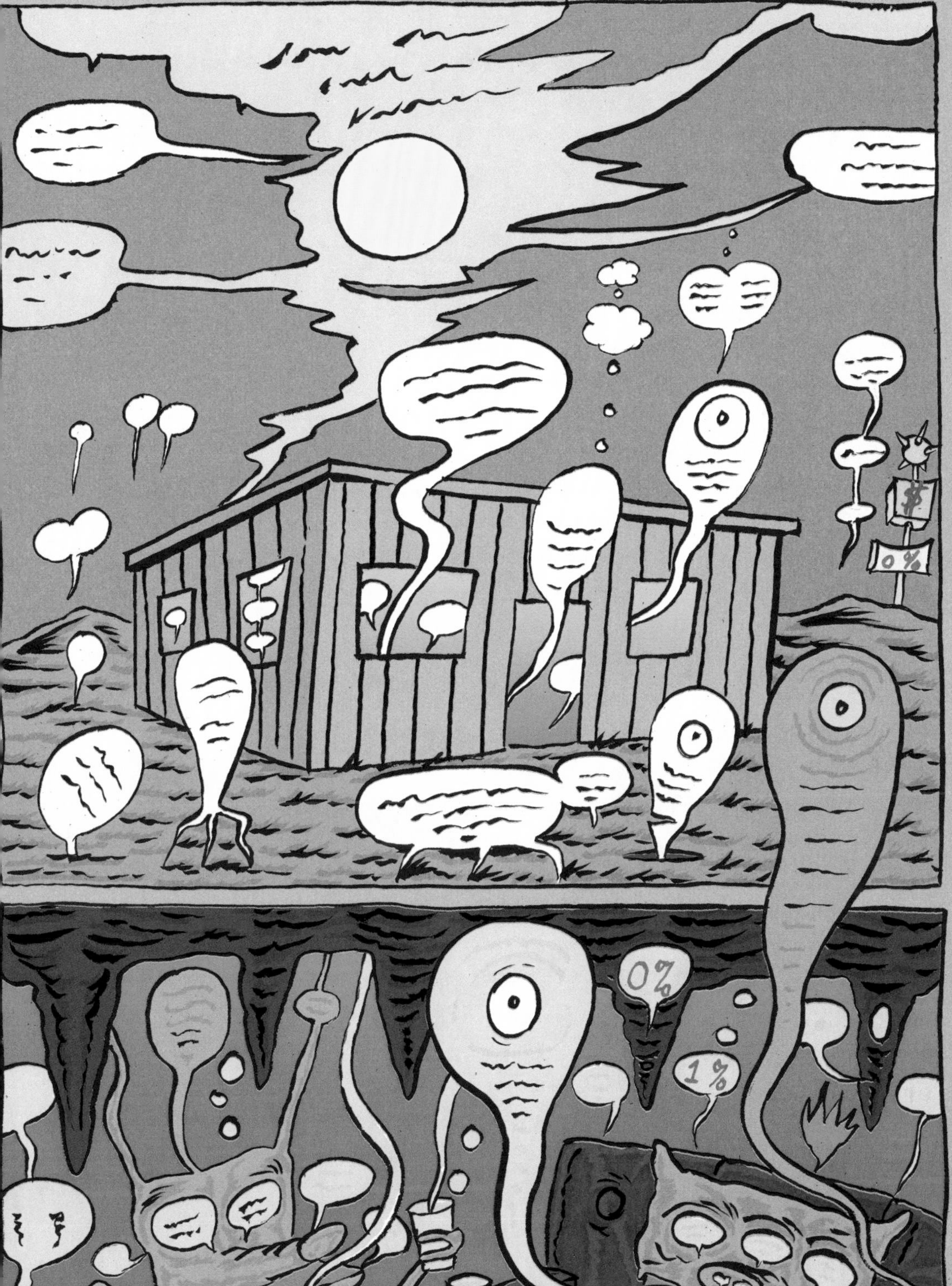
0%
0%
1%

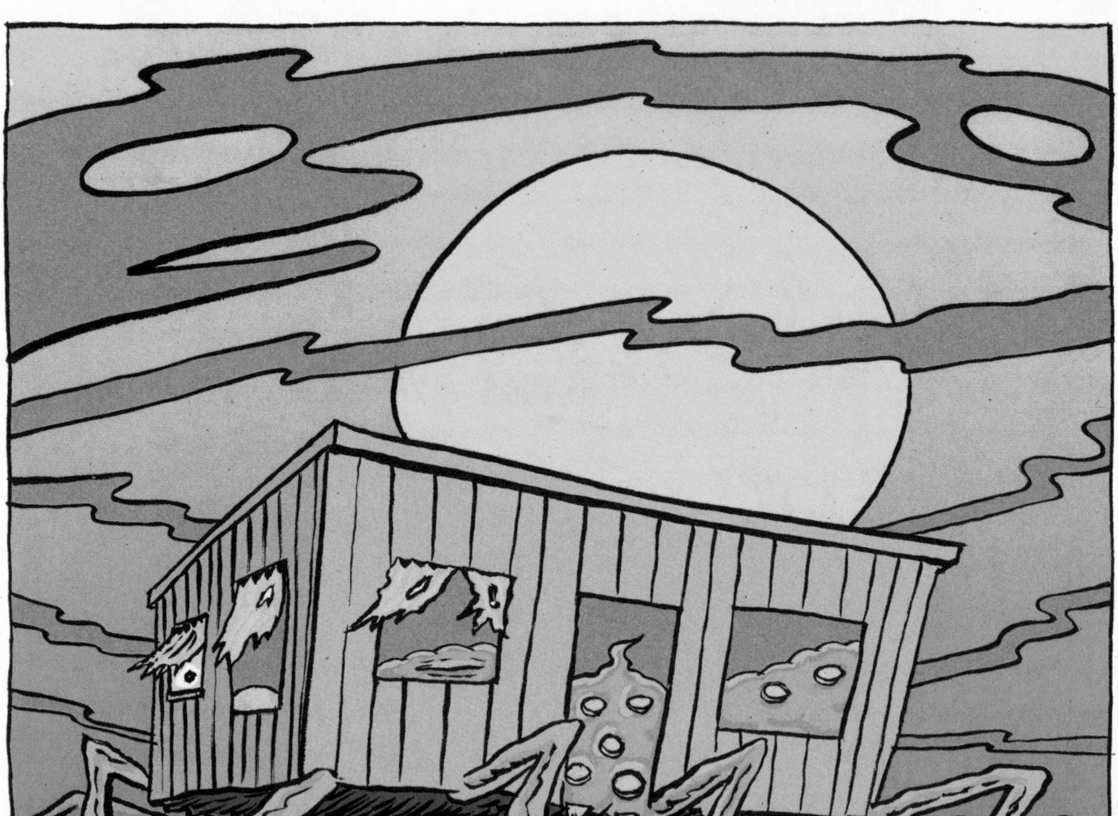

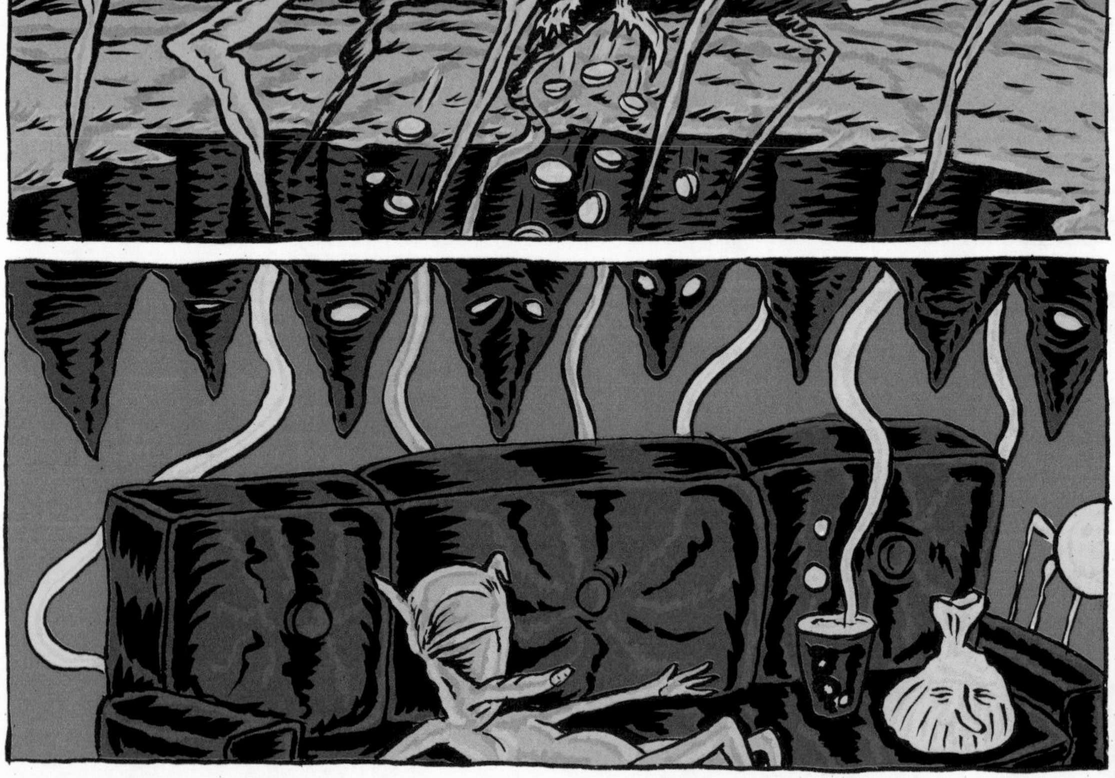

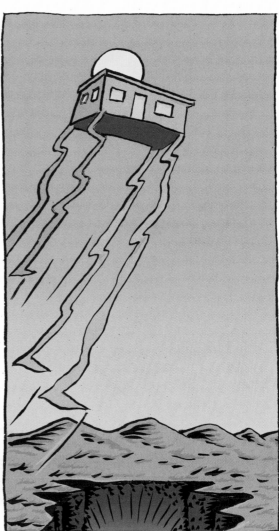

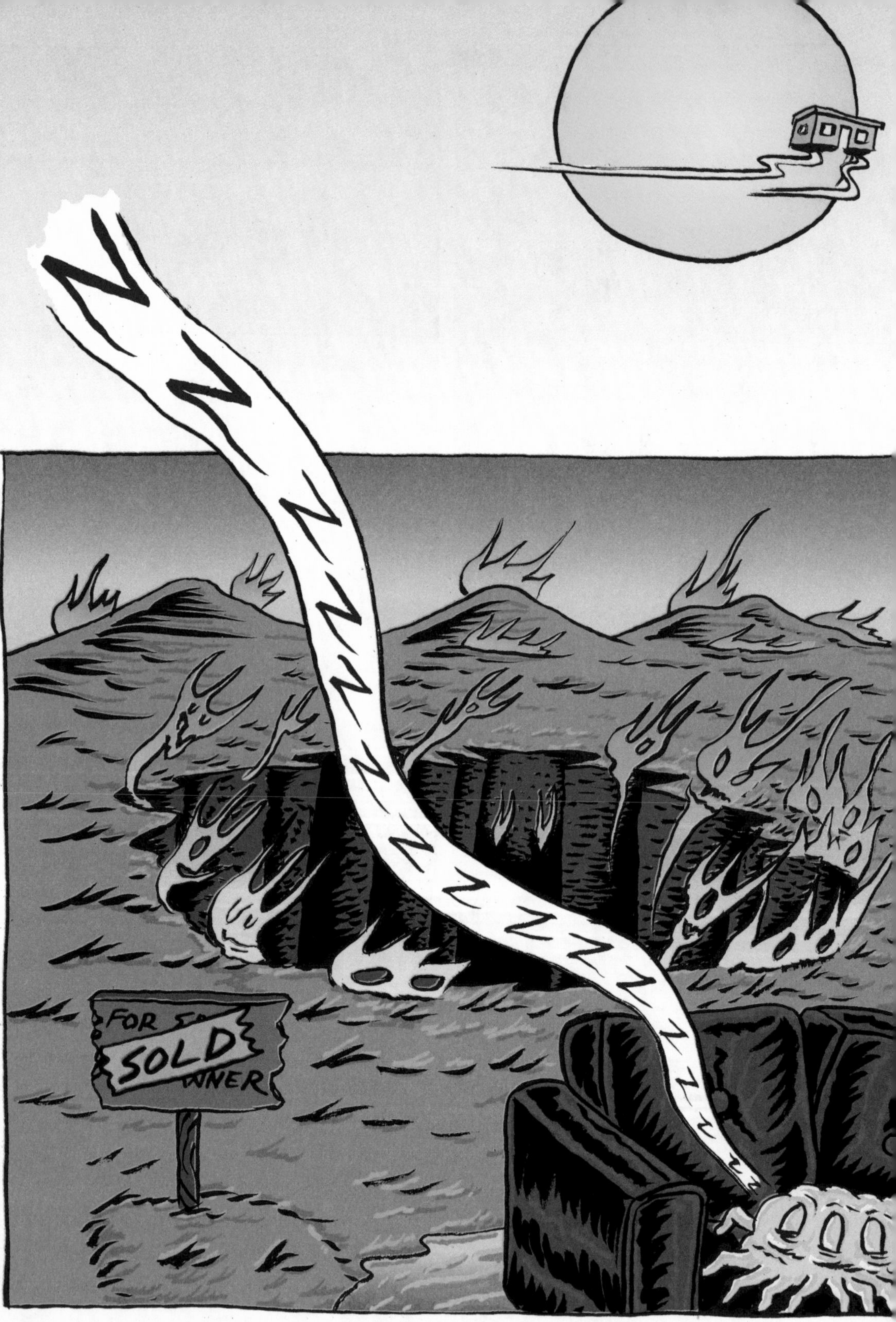
FOR
SOLD

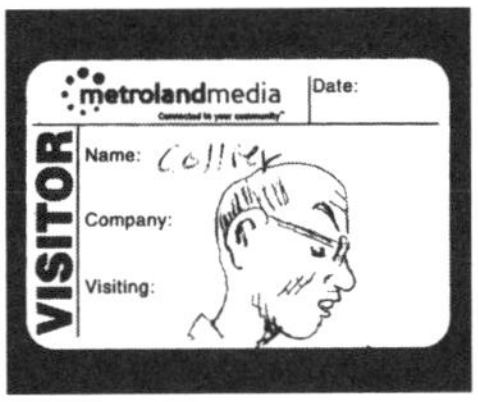
metrolandmedia
Date:
VISITOR
Name: Collier
Company:
Visiting:

DAVID COLLIER

The Irish Table

from *Chimo*

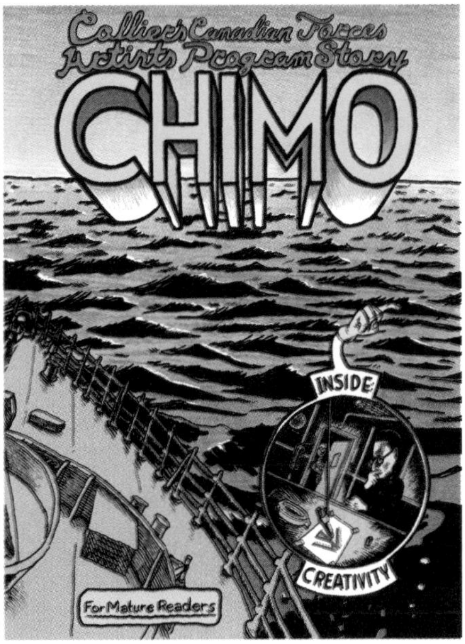
Collier's Canadian Forces Artists Program Story
CHIMO
INSIDE
CREATIVITY
For Mature Readers

FOR ME, DRAWING COMICS IS

A constant source of revelation.

THE SELECTION

When you leave the army and live as an artist for fifteen years, all your military qualifications expire. Rejoining at age forty-two, I had to do basic training over again.

THE CONTEXT

Using a Harvey Pekar book I illustrated as support material (*American Splendor: Unsung Hero*), I was accepted into the civilian Canadian Forces Artists Program. But in order to build on the legacy of the original "war artists" who inspired the program, I came to the conclusion that I had to get back into uniform.

PUBLICATIONS MY WORK HAS APPEARED IN

Weirdo, *Mineshaft*, the *Globe and Mail*, the *National Post*.

AWARDS

2010 Hamilton Music Award for Album Art, for a comic book created for Luke Doucet and the White Falcon's *Steel City Trawler*.

WHAT I'M KNOWN FOR

Collier's *Popular Press*, a book collecting thirty years on the newsstand, which is in wide release this year.

WHERE I LIVE

Hamilton, Ontario.

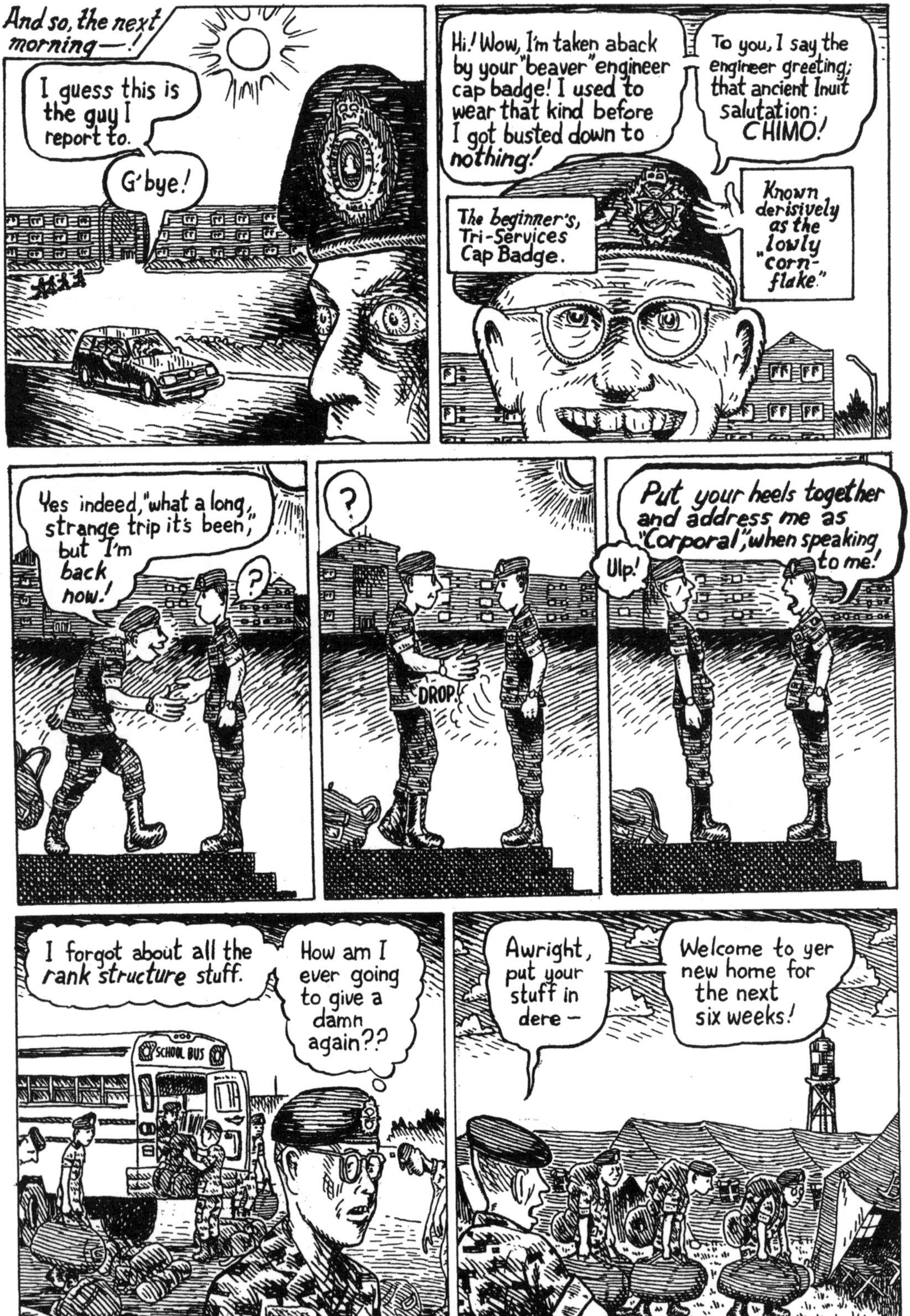

And so, the next morning—!
I guess this is the guy I report to.
G'bye!
Hi! Wow, I'm taken aback by your "beaver" engineer cap badge! I used to wear that kind before I got busted down to *nothing*!
To you, I say the engineer greeting; that ancient Inuit salutation: CHIMO!
The beginner's, Tri-Services Cap Badge.
Known derisively as the lowly "corn-flake."
Yes indeed, "what a long, strange trip it's been," but I'm *back* now!
?
?
DROP.
Ulp!
Put your heels together and address me as "Corporal", when speaking to me!
I forgot about all the *rank structure* stuff.
How am I ever going to give a damn again??
SCHOOL BUS
Awright, put your stuff in dere—
Welcome to yer new home for the next six weeks!

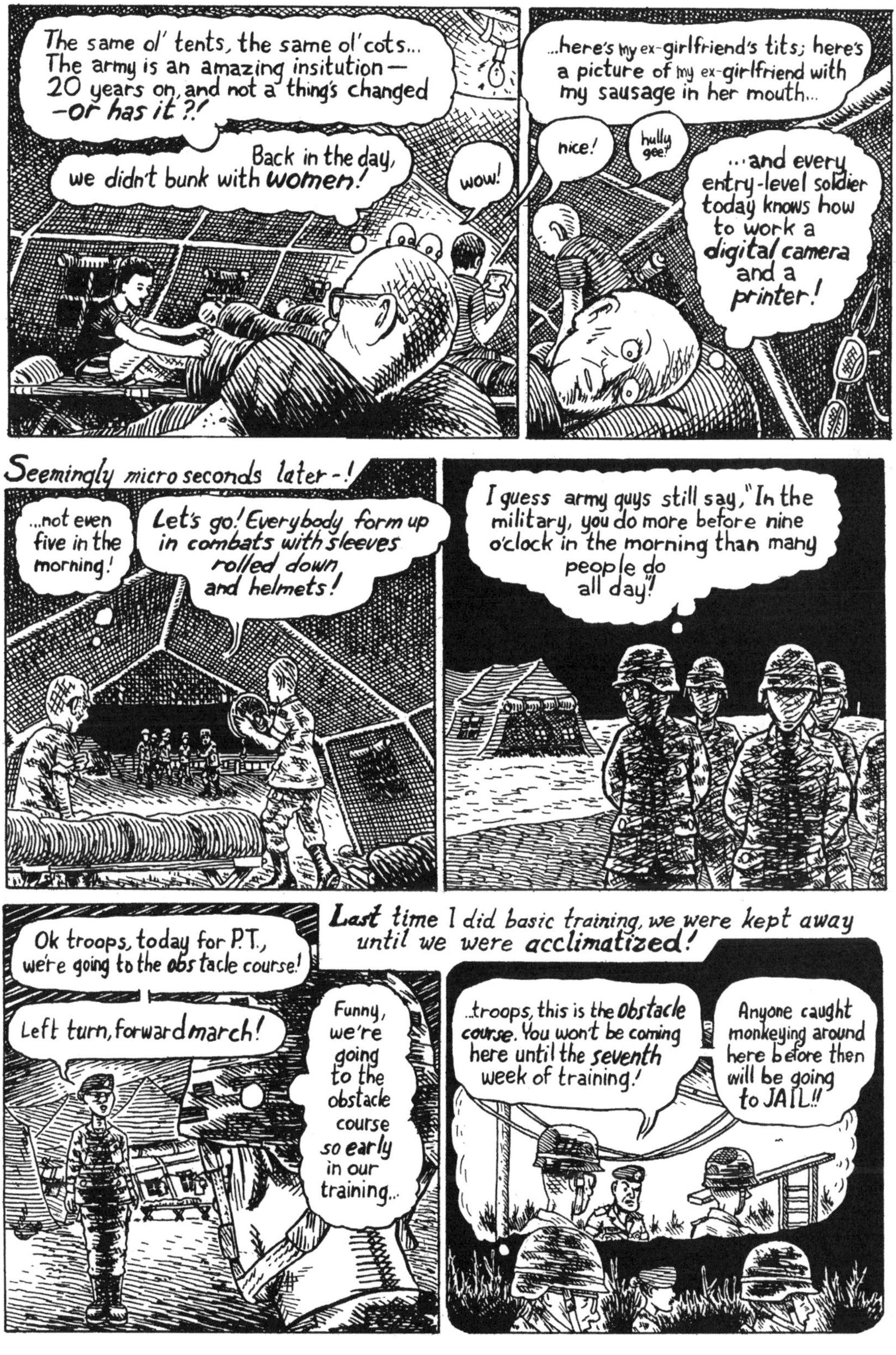
The same ol' tents, the same ol' cots... The army is an amazing insitution— 20 years on, and not a thing's changed —or has it?!
Back in the day, we didn't bunk with women!
wow!
...here's my ex-girlfriend's tits; here's a picture of my ex-girlfriend with my sausage in her mouth...
nice!
hully gee!
...and every entry-level soldier today knows how to work a digital camera and a printer!
Seemingly micro seconds later-!
...not even five in the morning!
Let's go! Everybody form up in combats with sleeves rolled down, and helmets!
I guess army guys still say, "In the military, you do more before nine o'clock in the morning than many people do all day!"
Ok troops, today for P.T., we're going to the obstacle course!
Left turn, forward march!
Funny, we're going to the obstacle course so early in our training...
Last time I did basic training, we were kept away until we were acclimatized!
...troops, this is the obstacle course. You won't be coming here until the seventh week of training!
Anyone caught monkeying around here before then will be going to JAIL!!

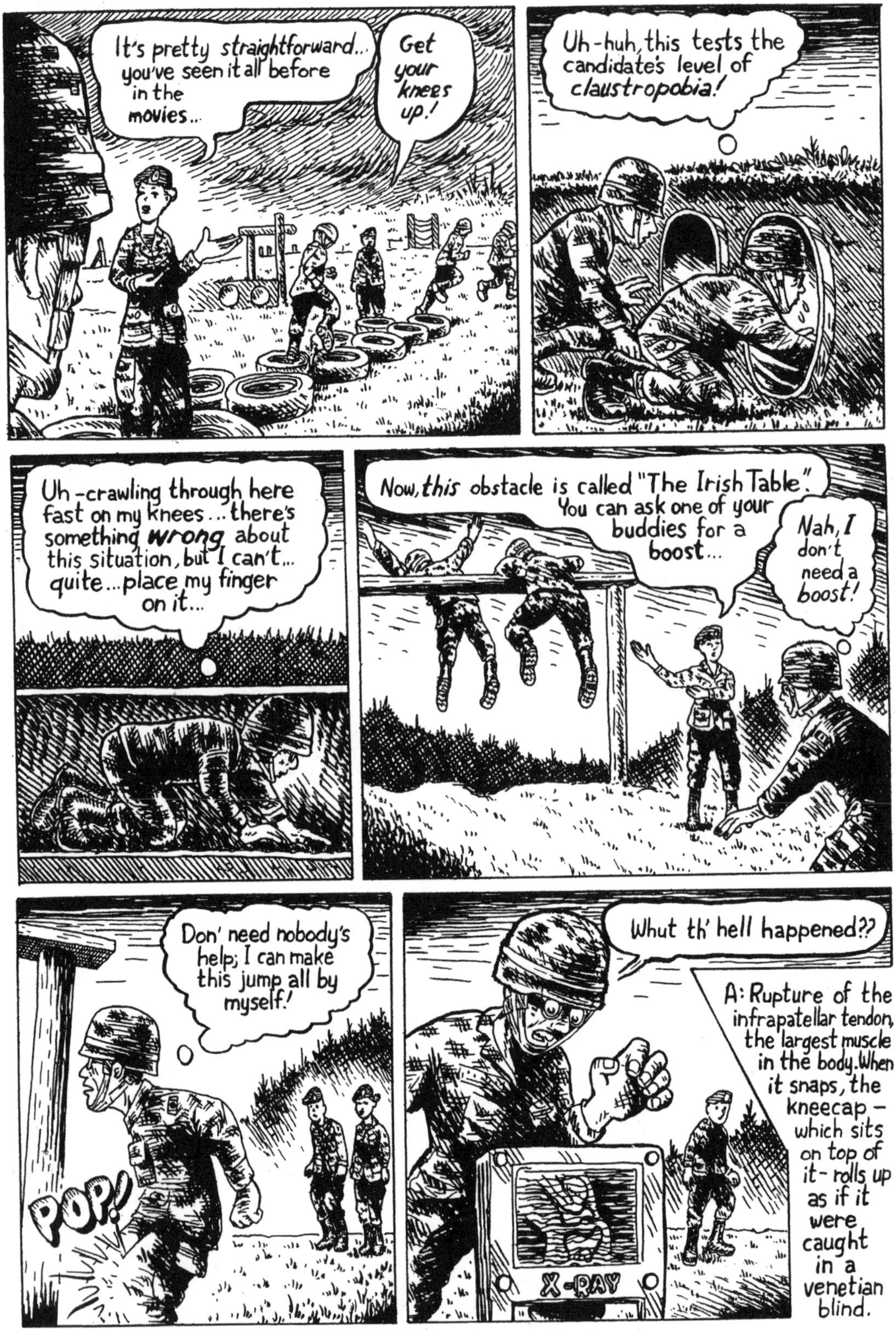
It's pretty straightforward... you've seen it all before in the movies...
Get your knees up!
Uh-huh, this tests the candidate's level of claustropobia!
Uh-crawling through here fast on my knees... there's something wrong about this situation, but I can't... quite... place my finger on it...
Now, this obstacle is called "The Irish Table". You can ask one of your buddies for a boost...
Nah, I don't need a boost!
Don' need nobody's help; I can make this jump all by myself!
POP!
Whut th' hell happened??
A: Rupture of the infrapatellar tendon, the largest muscle in the body. When it snaps, the kneecap – which sits on top of it – rolls up as if it were caught in a venetian blind.
X-RAY

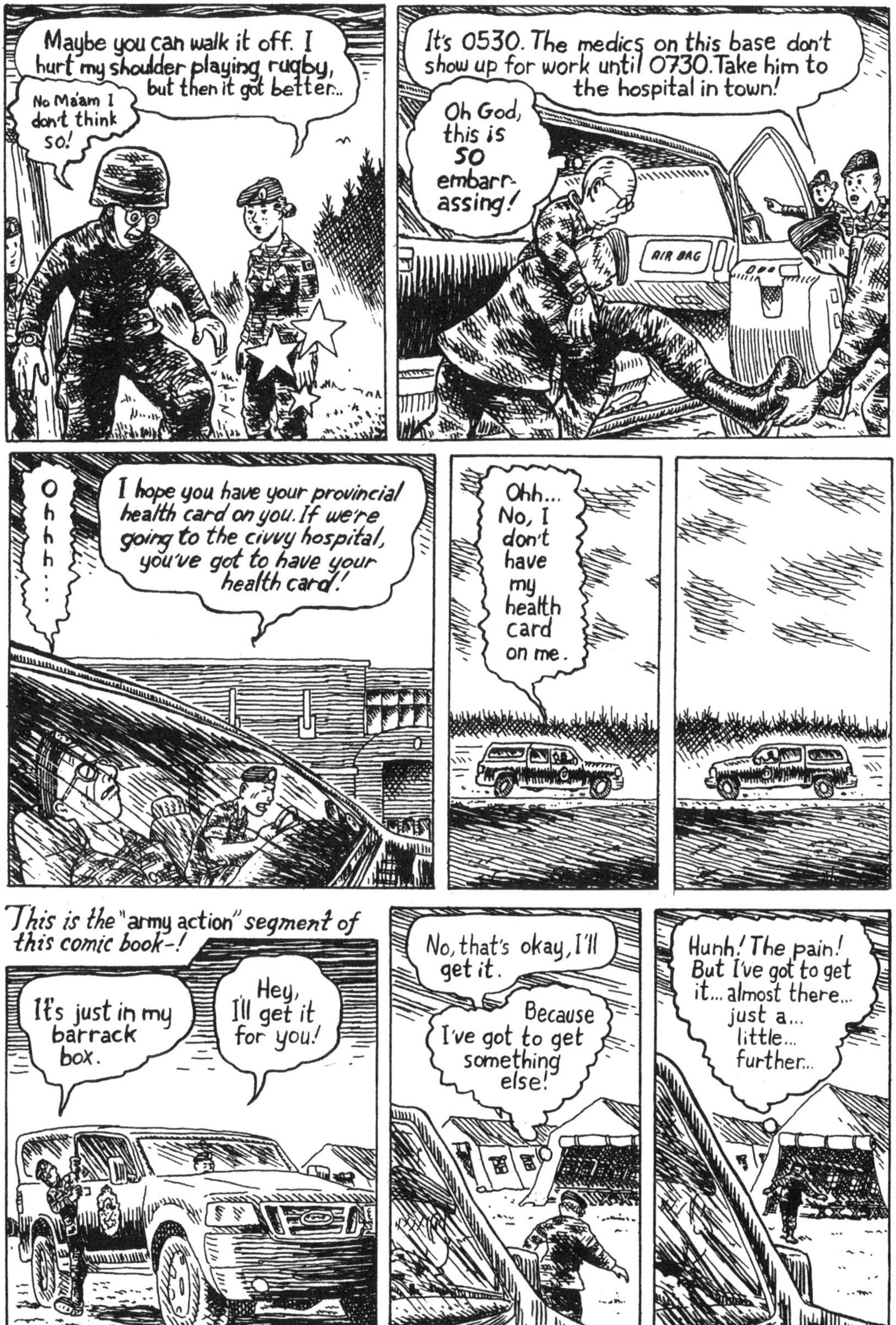

Maybe you can walk it off. I hurt my shoulder playing rugby, but then it got better...
No Ma'am I don't think so!
It's 0530. The medics on this base don't show up for work until 0730. Take him to the hospital in town!
Oh God, this is SO embarrassing!
AIR BAG
Ohhh...
I hope you have your provincial health card on you. If we're going to the civvy hospital, you've got to have your health card!
Ohh... No, I don't have my health card on me.
This is the "army action" segment of this comic book-!
It's just in my barrack box.
Hey, I'll get it for you!
No, that's okay, I'll get it.
Because I've got to get something else!
Hunh! The pain! But I've got to get it... almost there... just a... little... further...

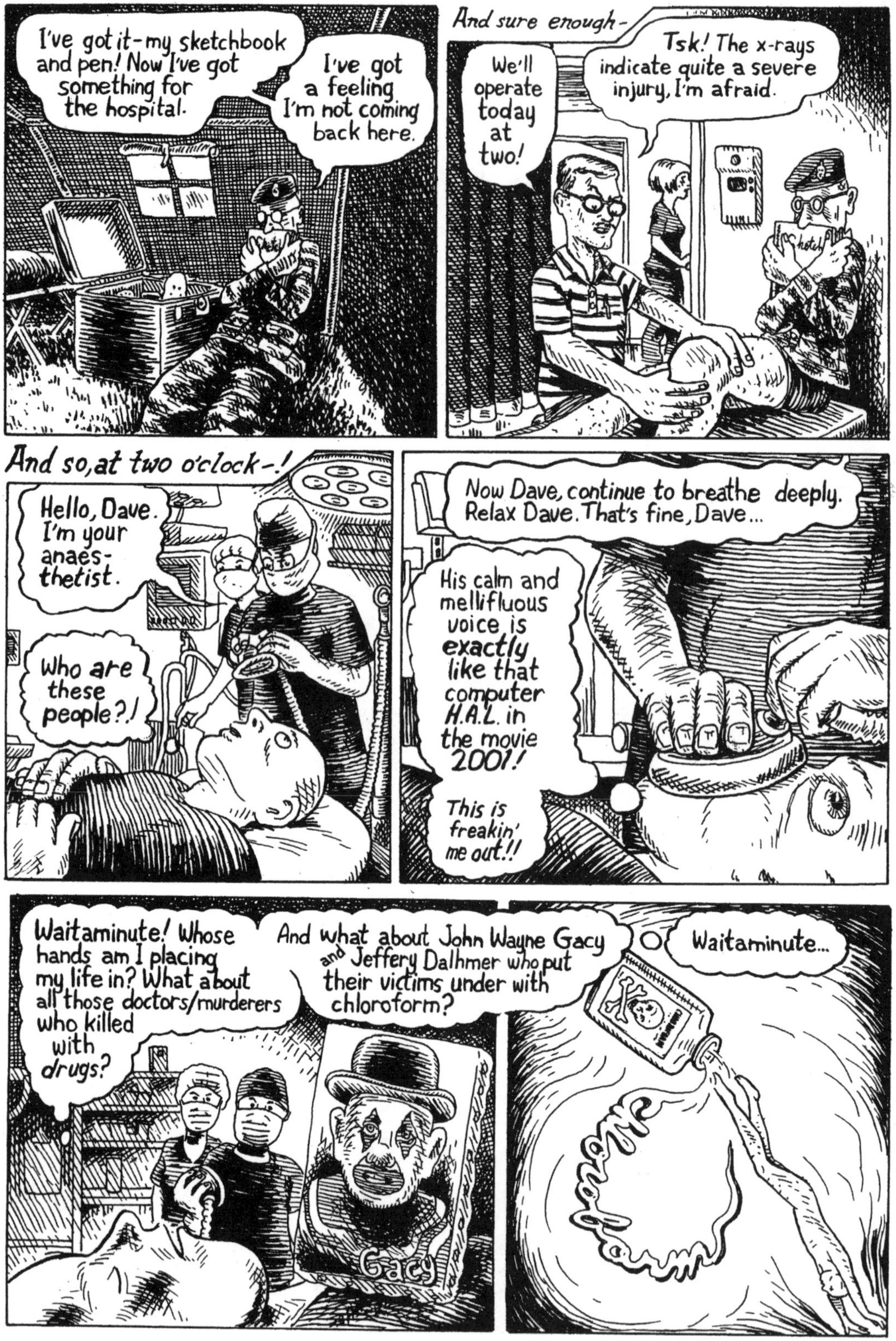
I've got it-my sketchbook and pen! Now I've got something for the hospital.
I've got a feeling I'm not coming back here.
And sure enough-
We'll operate today at two!
Tsk! The x-rays indicate quite a severe injury, I'm afraid.
And so, at two o'clock-!
Hello, Dave. I'm your anaes-thetist.
Who are these people?!
Now Dave, continue to breathe deeply. Relax Dave. That's fine, Dave...
His calm and mellifluous voice is exactly like that computer H.A.L. in the movie 2001!
This is freakin' me out!!
Waitaminute! Whose hands am I placing my life in? What about all those doctors/murderers who killed with drugs?
And what about John Wayne Gacy and Jeffery Dalhmer who put their victims under with chloroform?
Gacy
Waitaminute...
chloroform

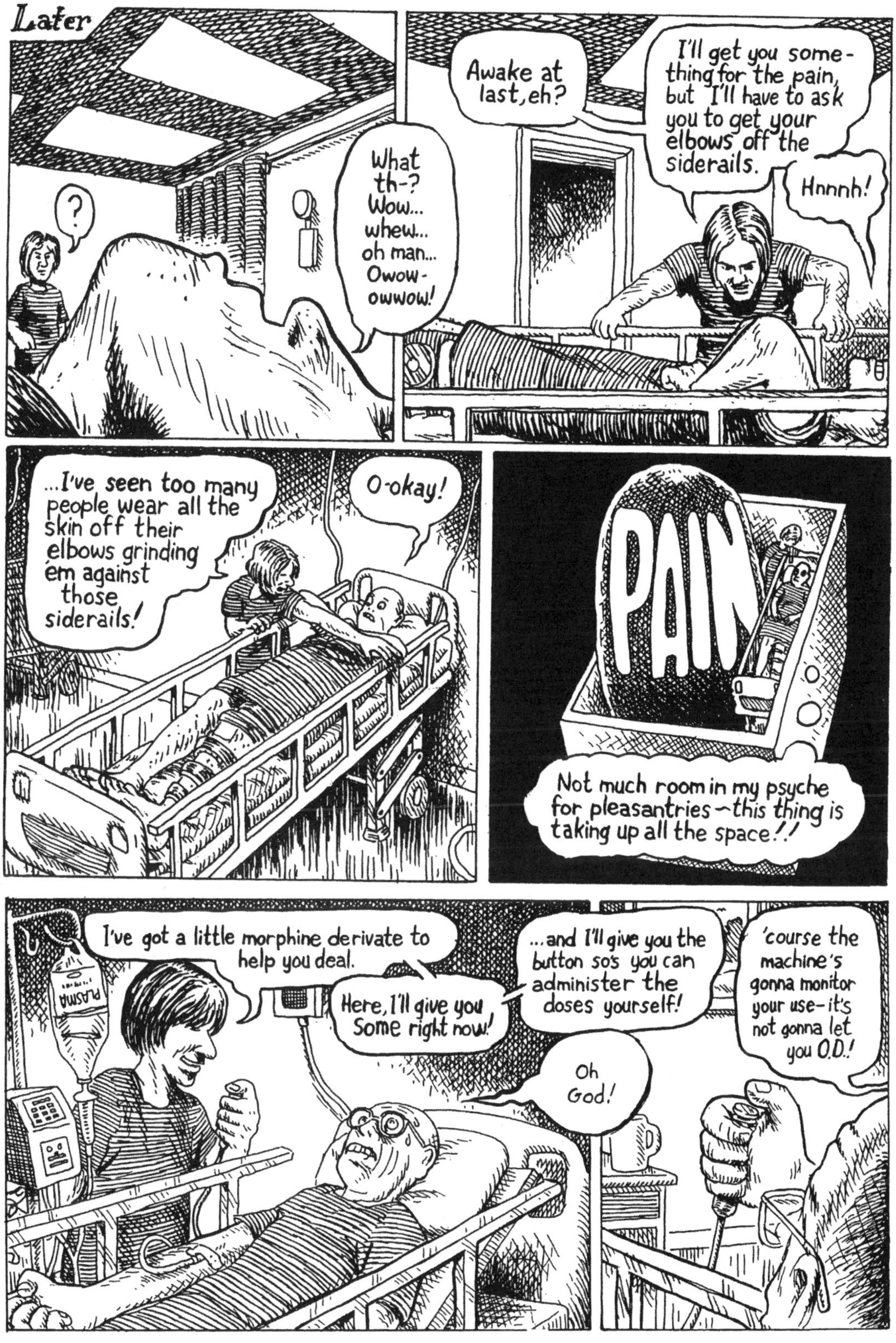
Later
?
What th-? Wow... whew... oh man... Owow-owwow!
Awake at last, eh?
I'll get you something for the pain, but I'll have to ask you to get your elbows off the siderails.
Hnnnh!
...I've seen too many people wear all the skin off their elbows grinding 'em against those siderails!
O-okay!
PAIN
Not much room in my psyche for pleasantries—this thing is taking up all the space!!
I've got a little morphine derivate to help you deal.
PLASMA
Here, I'll give you Some right now!
...and I'll give you the button so's you can administer the doses yourself!
Oh God!
'course the machine's gonna monitor your use—it's not gonna let you O.D.!

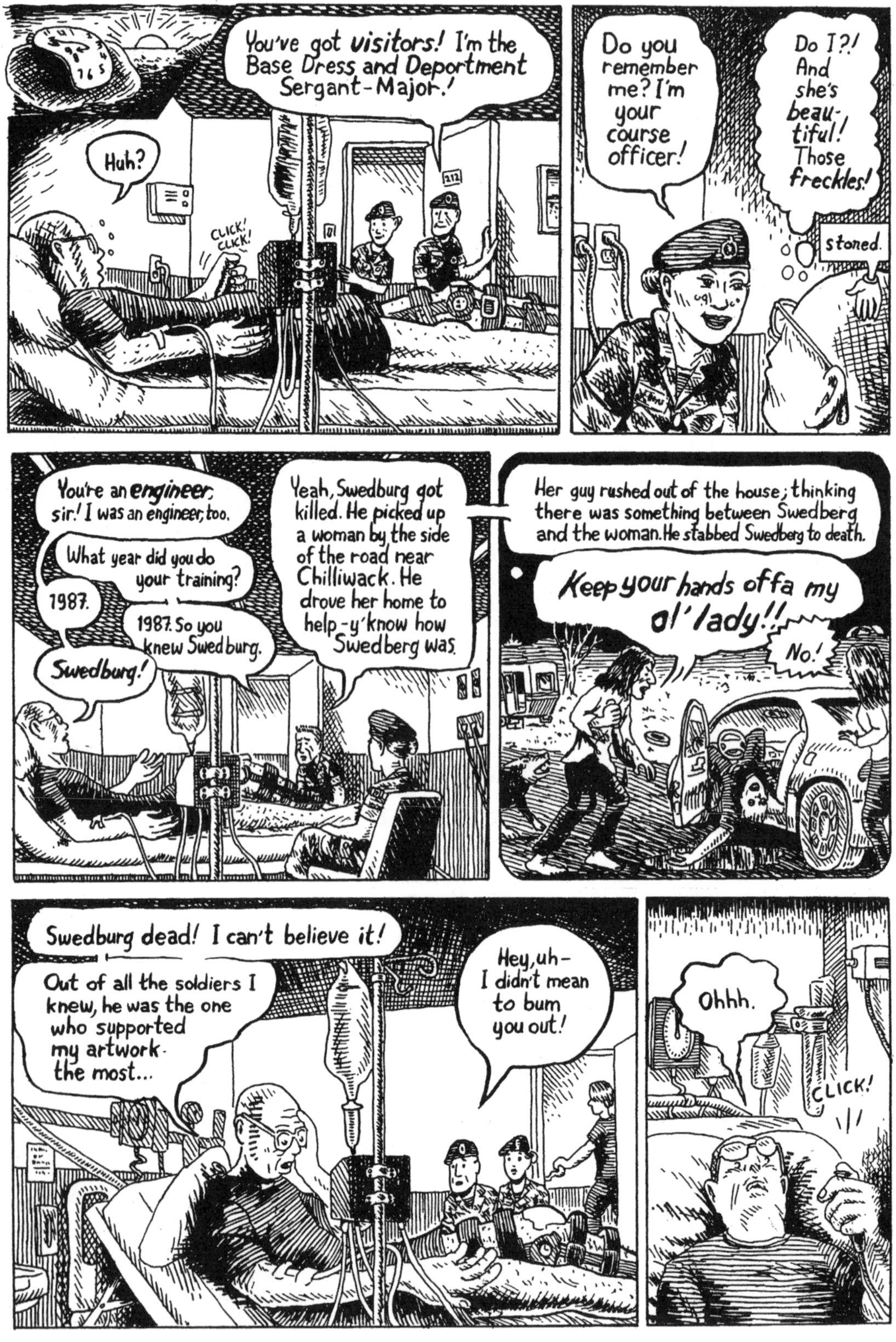
You've got visitors! I'm the Base Dress and Deportment Sergant-Major!
Huh?
CLICK! CLICK!
Do you remember me? I'm your course officer!
Do I?! And she's beau-tiful! Those freckles!
stoned.
You're an engineer, sir! I was an engineer, too.
What year did you do your training?
1987.
1987. So you knew Swedburg.
Swedburg!
Yeah, Swedburg got killed. He picked up a woman by the side of the road near Chilliwack. He drove her home to help-y'know how Swedberg was.
Her guy rushed out of the house; thinking there was something between Swedberg and the woman. He stabbed Swedberg to death.
Keep your hands offa my ol' lady!!
No!
Swedburg dead! I can't believe it!
Out of all the soldiers I knew, he was the one who supported my artwork the most...
Hey, uh- I didn't mean to bum you out!
Ohhh.
CLICK!

This whole army thing is almost too much. It's all about **people** —often **good, kind** people— putting themselves in **harm's** way.

CLICK!

But these days, one feels that one has to do **something**.

I couldn't stand it; living like a poet at the time of the fall of Rome - off at a country villa. A quiet, removed existence doesn't work when the barbarians are getting closer, ever closer.

In my lifetime, the world has changed so much. When I was a kid in the 1970's hippies were backpacking in to Kabul—then a cosmopolitian city!

It seemed all peace and love then, as if the world had this chance to get together.

The Beatles!

Beatles, yes!

RUBBER SOUL

Now, dem days of universal harmony are gone and we're left with **our** times!

CLICK!

Like, according to this magazine I've been reading, the Pentagon says we'll soon face even **greater** threats to our way o'life. "Forget the Middle East," they say, "In the future, the greatest source of danger will be China"!

HOW WE WOULD FIGHT CHINA

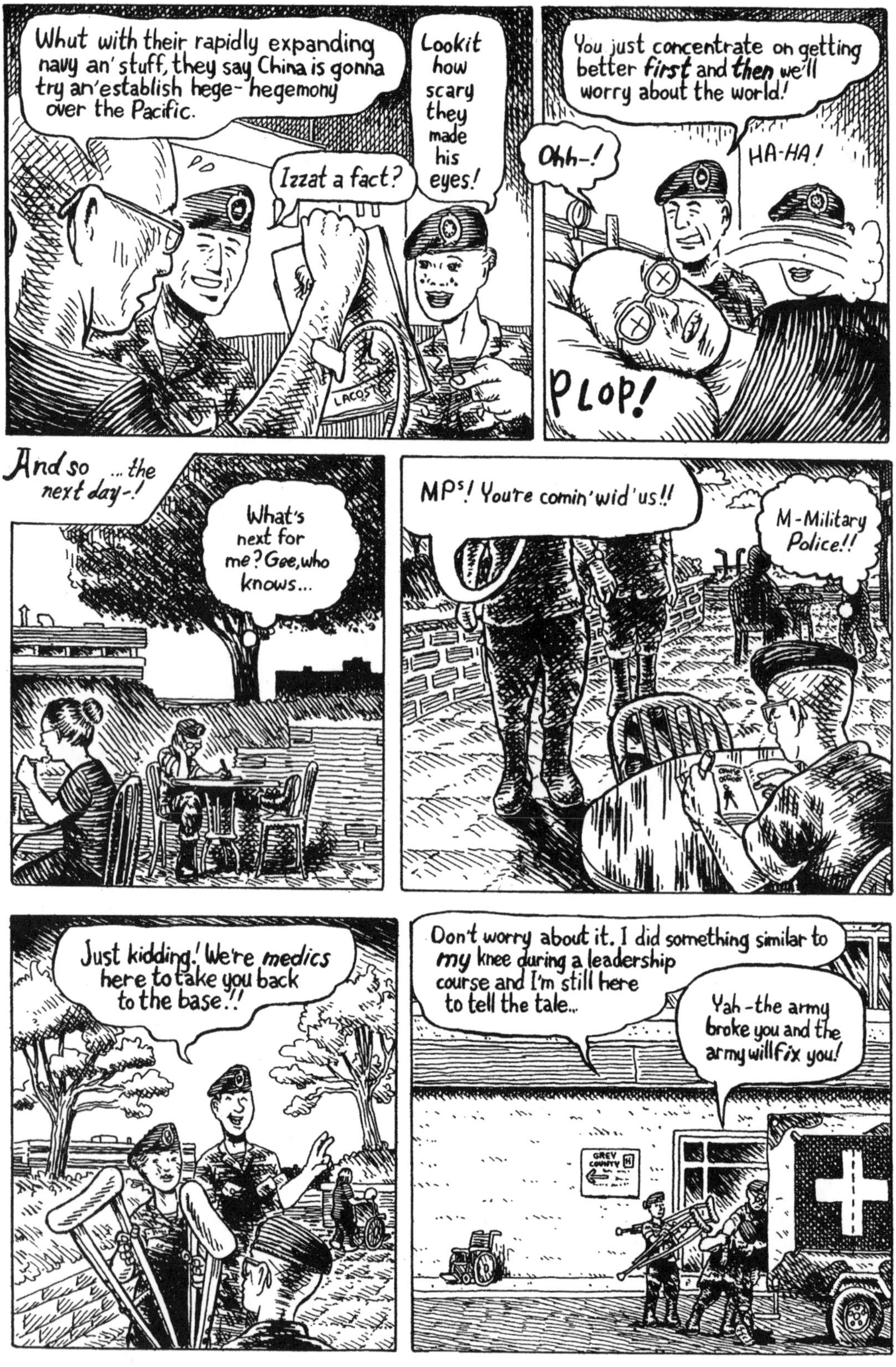

Whut with their rapidly expanding navy an' stuff, they say China is gonna try an' establish hege- hegemony over the Pacific.
Izzat a fact?
Lookit how scary they made his eyes!
LACOST
You just concentrate on getting better *first* and *then* we'll worry about the world!
Ohh-!
HA-HA!
PLOP!
And so ... the next day-!
What's next for me? Gee, who knows...
MPs! You're comin' wid 'us!!
M-Military Police!!
Just kidding! We're *medics* here to take you back to the base.!!
Don't worry about it. I did something similar to *my* knee during a leadership course and I'm still here to tell the tale...
Yah-the army broke you and the army will *fix* you!
GREY COUNTY

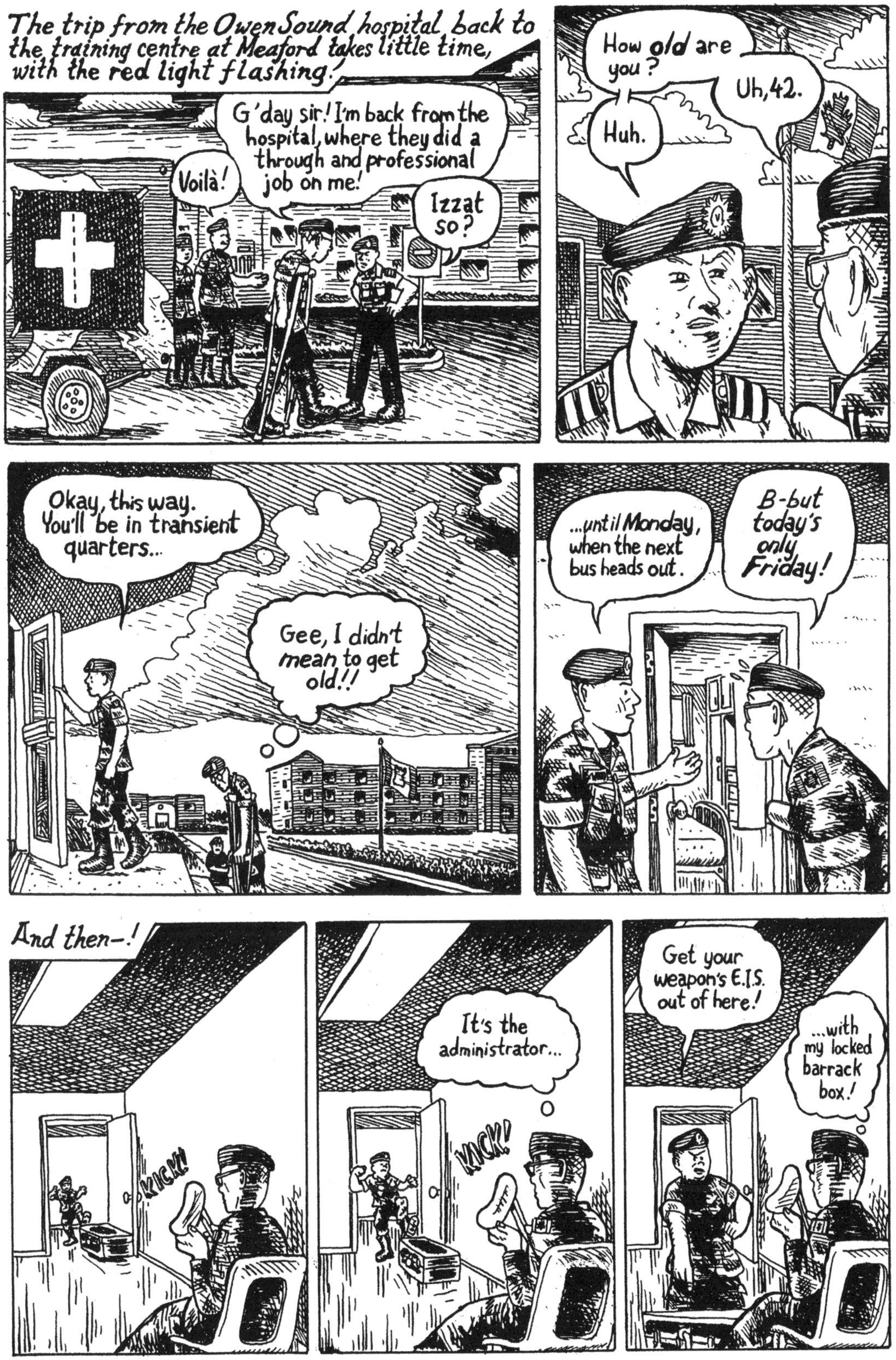

The trip from the Owen Sound hospital back to the training centre at Meaford takes little time, with the red light flashing!
Voilà!
G'day sir! I'm back from the hospital, where they did a through and professional job on me!
Izzat so?
How old are you?
Uh, 42.
Huh.
Okay, this way. You'll be in transient quarters...
Gee, I didn't mean to get old!!
...until Monday, when the next bus heads out.
B-but today's only Friday!
And then-!
KICK!
KICK!
It's the administrator...
Get your weapon's E.I.S. out of here!
...with my locked barrack box!

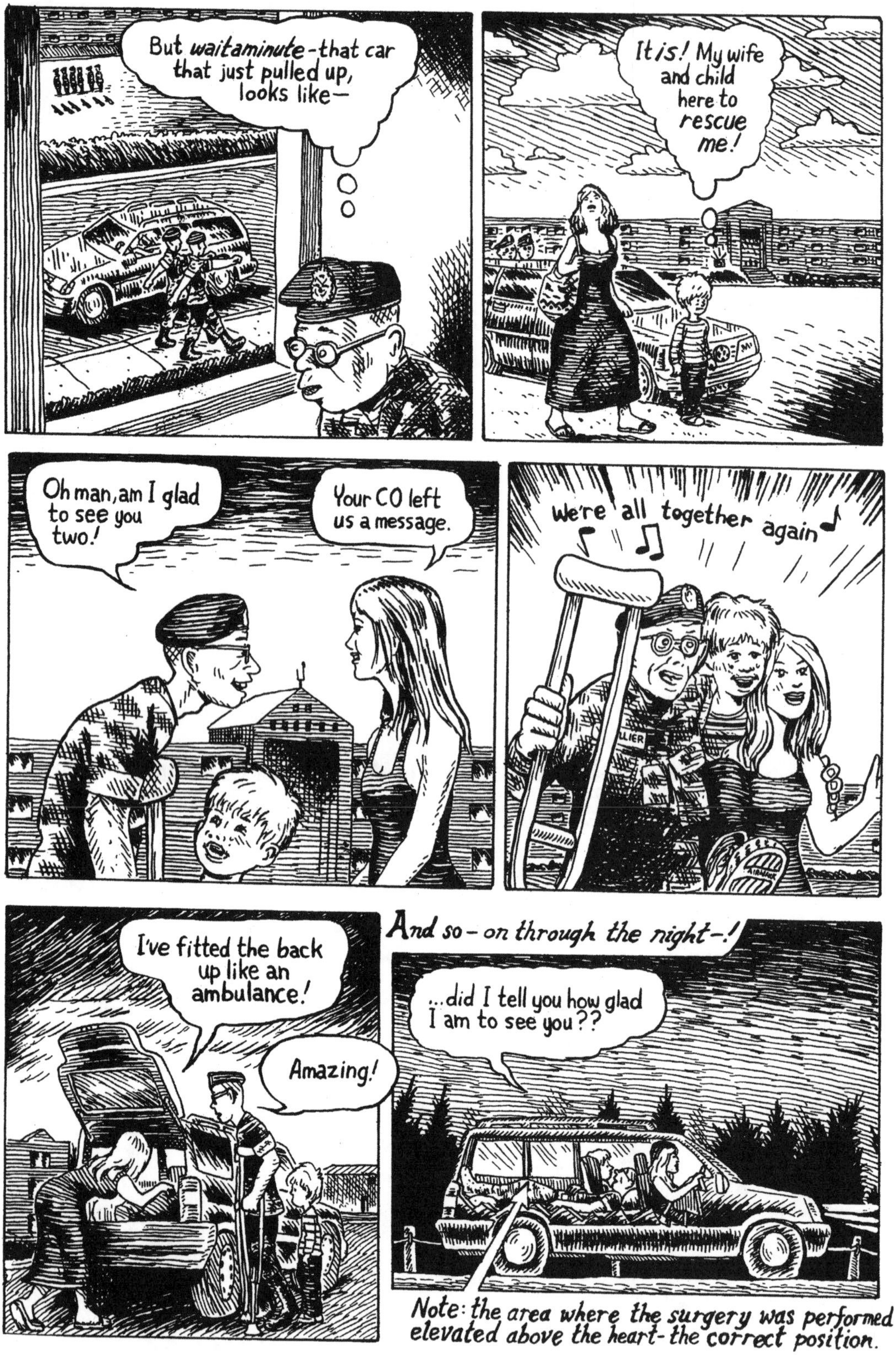
But waitaminute-that car that just pulled up, looks like—
It is! My wife and child here to rescue me!
Oh man, am I glad to see you two!
Your CO left us a message.
We're all together again
I've fitted the back up like an ambulance!
Amazing!
And so-on through the night-!
...did I tell you how glad I am to see you??
Note: the area where the surgery was performed elevated above the heart-the correct position.

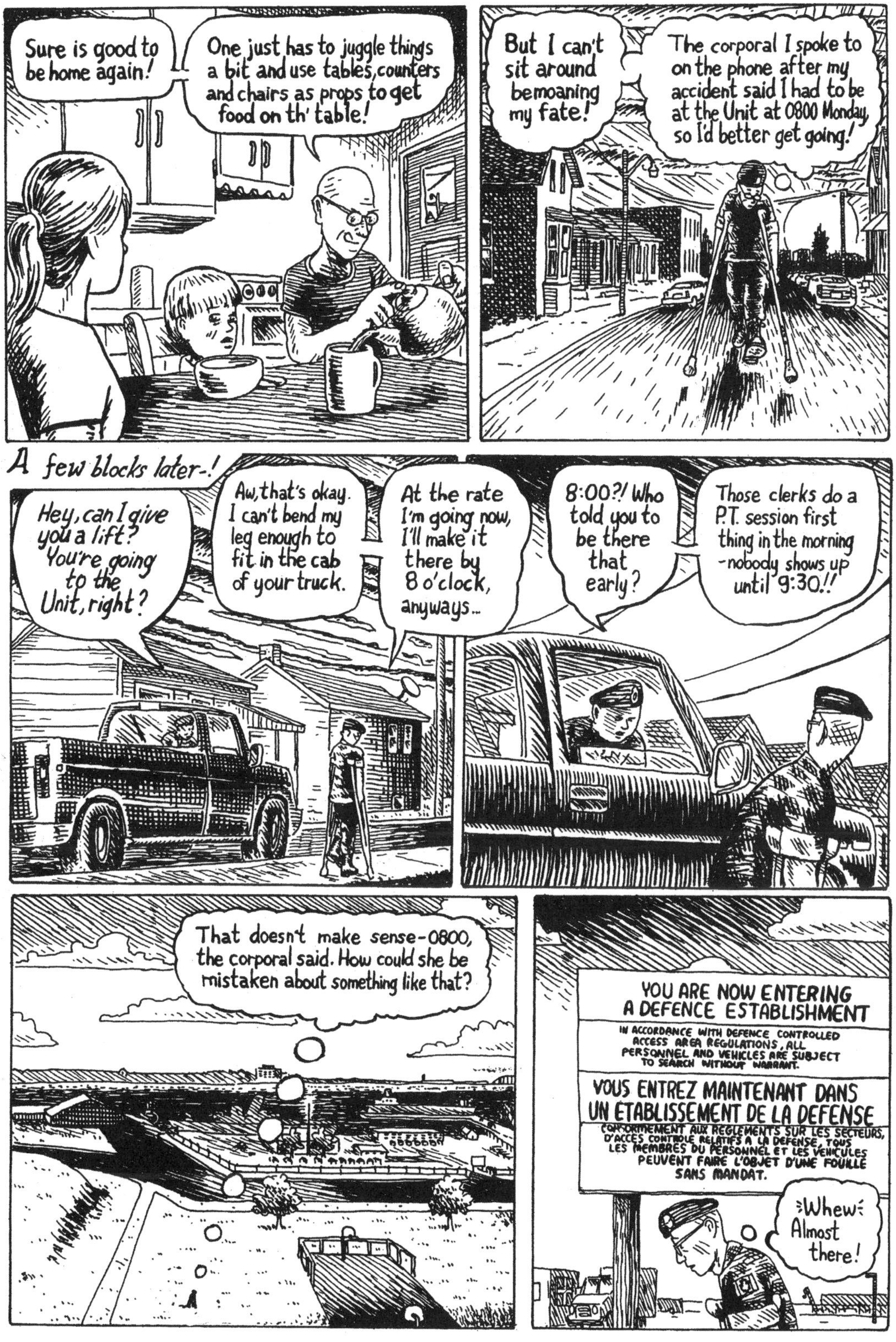
Sure is good to be home again!
One just has to juggle things a bit and use tables, counters and chairs as props to get food on th' table!
But I can't sit around bemoaning my fate!
The corporal I spoke to on the phone after my accident said I had to be at the Unit at 0800 Monday, so I'd better get going!
A few blocks later-!
Hey, can I give you a lift? You're going to the Unit, right?
Aw, that's okay. I can't bend my leg enough to fit in the cab of your truck.
At the rate I'm going now, I'll make it there by 8 o'clock, anyways...
8:00?! Who told you to be there that early?
Those clerks do a P.T. session first thing in the morning -nobody shows up until 9:30!!
That doesn't make sense-0800, the corporal said. How could she be mistaken about something like that?
YOU ARE NOW ENTERING A DEFENCE ESTABLISHMENT
IN ACCORDANCE WITH DEFENCE CONTROLLED ACCESS AREA REGULATIONS, ALL PERSONNEL AND VEHICLES ARE SUBJECT TO SEARCH WITHOUT WARRANT.
VOUS ENTREZ MAINTENANT DANS UN ETABLISSEMENT DE LA DEFENSE
CONFORMEMENT AUX REGLEMENTS SUR LES SECTEURS, D'ACCES CONTROLE RELATIFS A LA DEFENSE, TOUS LES MEMBRES DU PERSONNEL ET LES VEHICULES PEUVENT FAIRE L'OBJET D'UNE FOUILLE SANS MANDAT.
Whew Almost there!

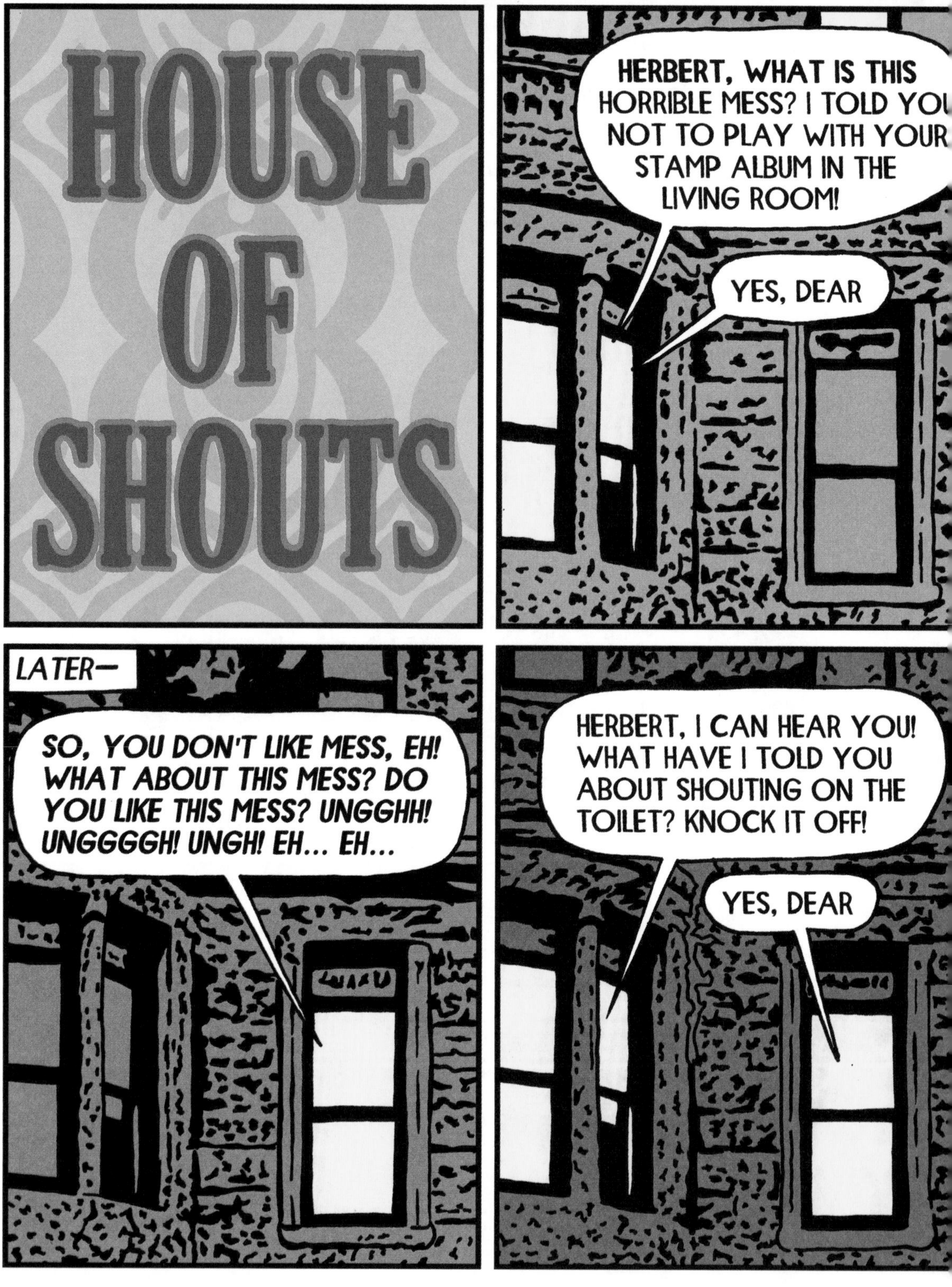
HOUSE OF SHOUTS
HERBERT, WHAT IS THIS HORRIBLE MESS? I TOLD YOU NOT TO PLAY WITH YOUR STAMP ALBUM IN THE LIVING ROOM!
YES, DEAR
LATER—
SO, YOU DON'T LIKE MESS, EH! WHAT ABOUT THIS MESS? DO YOU LIKE THIS MESS? UNGGHH! UNGGGGH! UNGH! EH... EH...
HERBERT, I CAN HEAR YOU! WHAT HAVE I TOLD YOU ABOUT SHOUTING ON THE TOILET? KNOCK IT OFF!
YES, DEAR

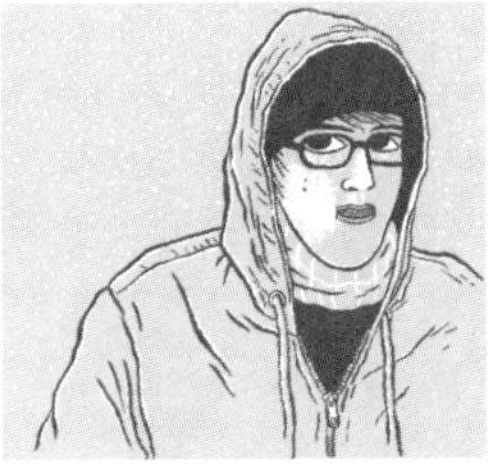

JESSE JACOBS

Even the Giants Get the Blues *(Excerpt)*

from *Even the Giants*

(see also endpapers)

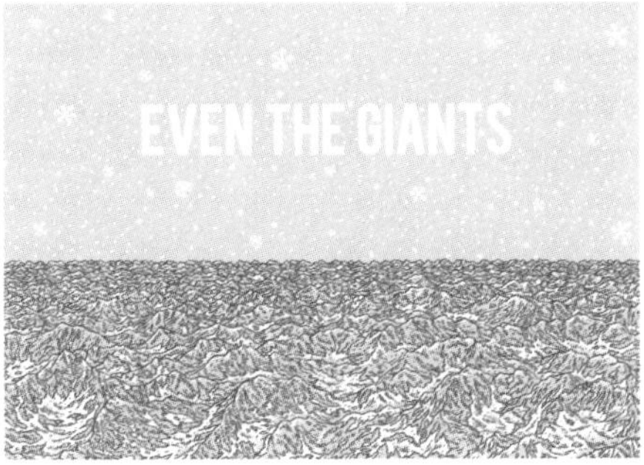
EVEN THE GIANTS

FOR ME, DRAWING COMICS IS

The best way I've found to amalgamate my scattered ideas. I enjoy the way in which the drawing and the writing inform one another.

THE SELECTION

Even the Giants includes a number of interwoven stories interspersed with short strips. The central narrative follows a pair of giants in an arctic alien landscape.

THE CONTEXT

This excerpt is indicative of the work as a whole, wobbling from story to story, framed within the larger narrative of arctic isolation.

PUBLICATIONS MY WORK HAS APPEARED IN

Le Monde Diplomatique, *Root Rot* (Koyama), *NoBrow 6* (NoBrow).

AWARDS

Nominated for a 2011 Ignatz Award for Promising New Talent; winner of the Gene Day Award for a Canadian Comic Book Self-Publisher of 2008; nominated for the 2009 Doug Wright Awards, Best Emerging Talent, and Pigskin Peters Award for Avant-Garde Canadian Comics.

WHAT I'M KNOWN FOR

Even the Giants is the first book I haven't published myself. *Blue Winter Shapes in the Snow* and *Small Victories* were my best minicomic efforts. Koyama Press released my graphic novel, *By This Shall You Know Him*, in May 2012.

WHERE I LIVE

London, Ontario.

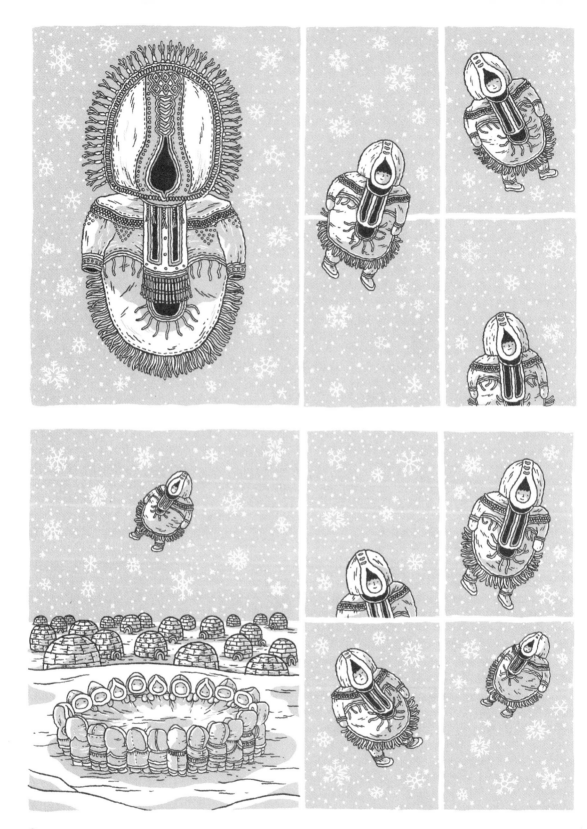

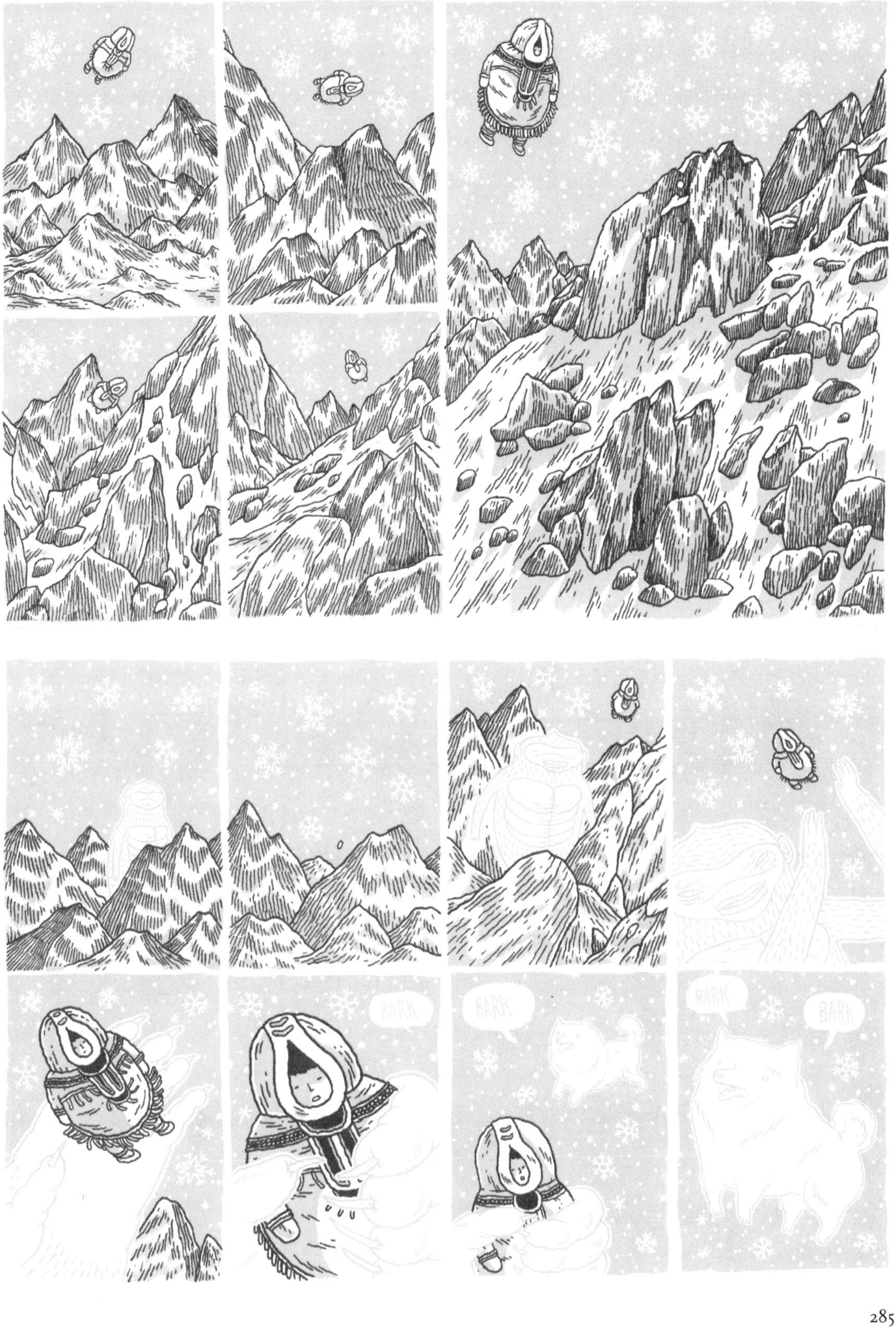
BARK
BARK
BARK
BARK

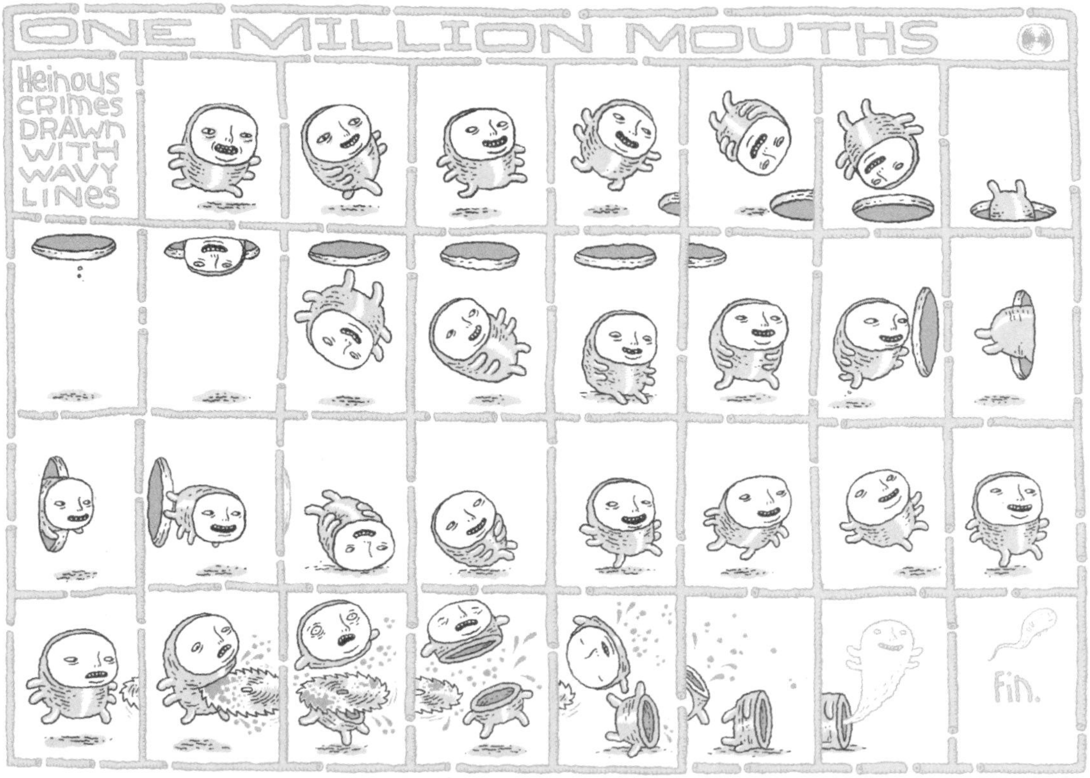
ONE MILLION MOUTHS
Heinous crimes drawn with wavy lines
Fin.

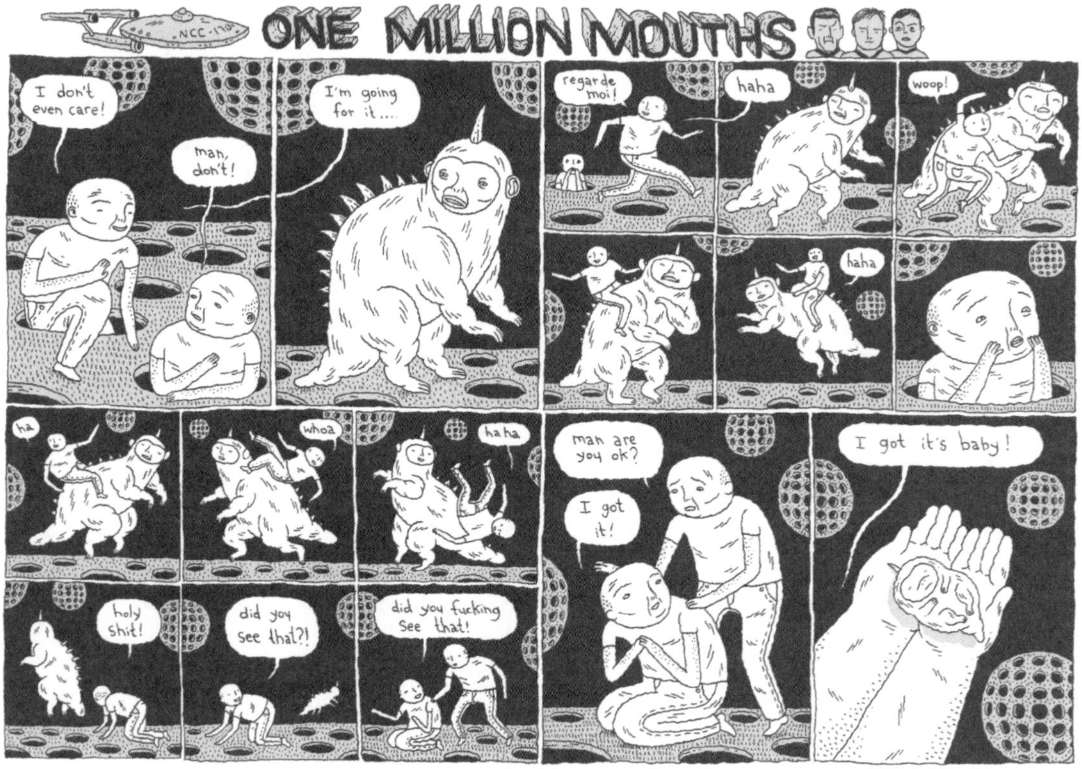
NCC-1701
ONE MILLION MOUTHS
I don't even care!
man, don't!
I'm going for it....
regarde moi!
haha
woop!
haha
ha
whoa
haha
man are you ok?
I got it!
I got it's baby!
holy shit!
did you see that?!
did you fucking see that!

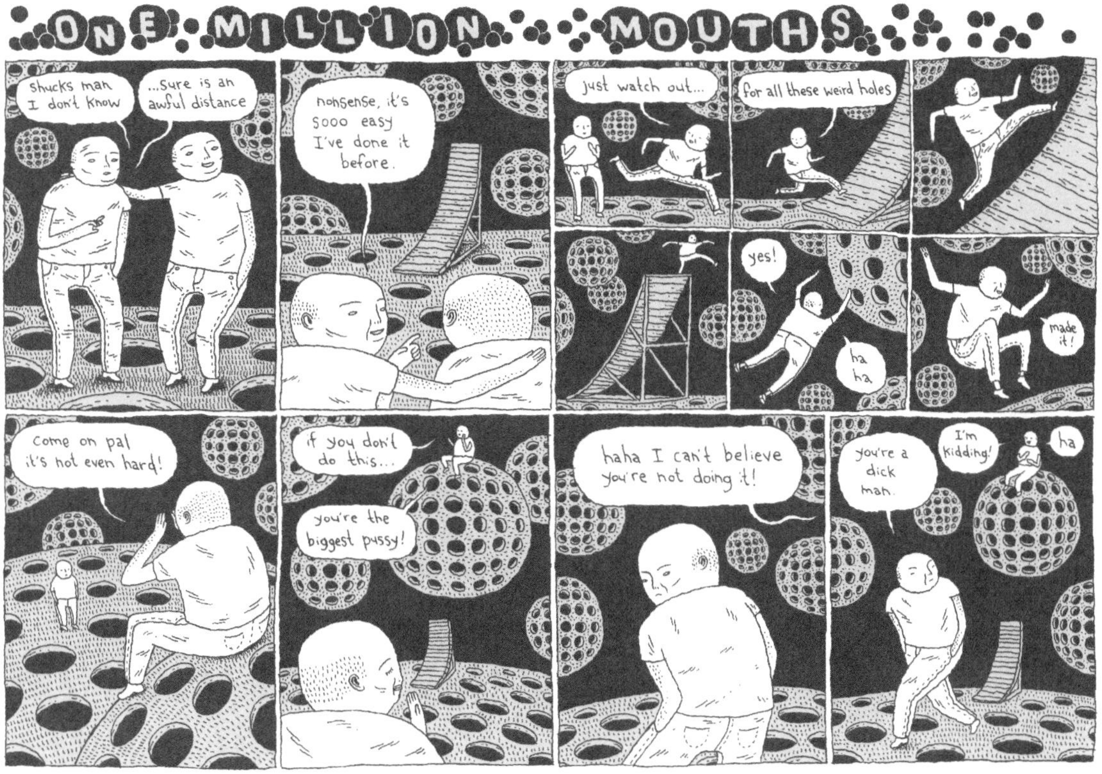
ONE MILLION MOUTHS
shucks man I don't know
...sure is an awful distance
nonsense, it's sooo easy I've done it before.
just watch out...
for all these weird holes
yes!
ha ha
made it!
come on pal it's not even hard!
if you don't do this...
you're the biggest pussy!
haha I can't believe you're not doing it!
you're a dick man.
I'm kidding!
ha

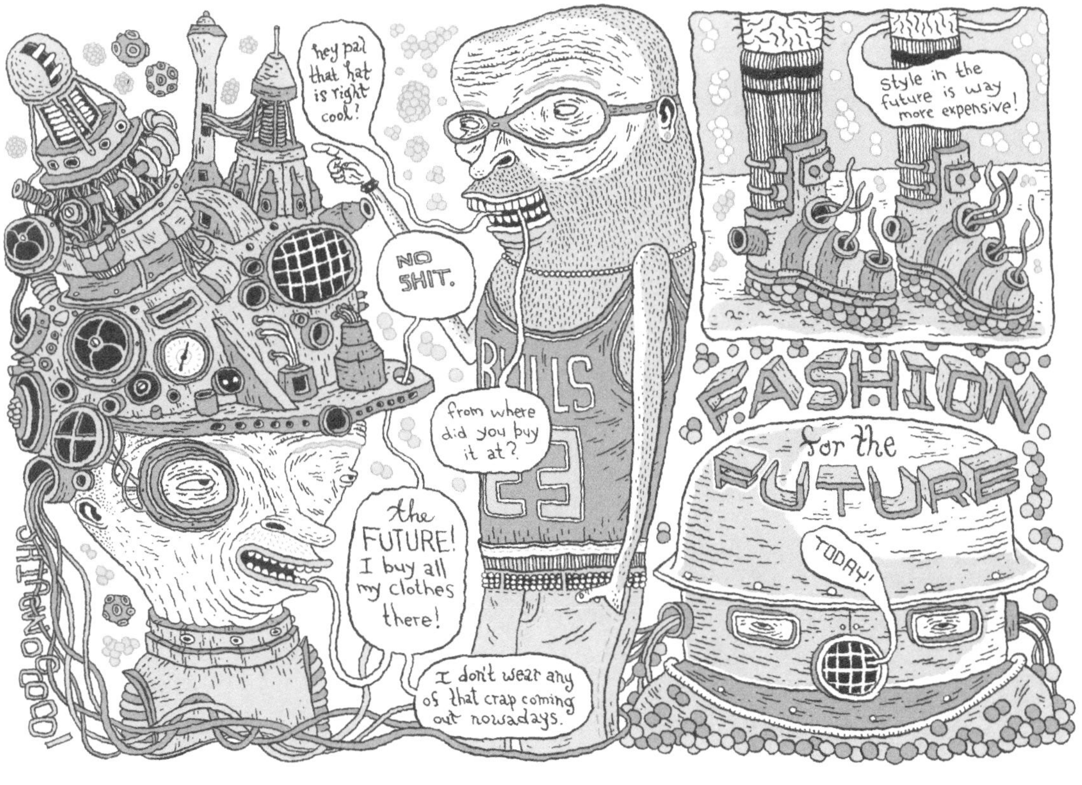
hey pal that hat is right cool!
NO SHIT.
from where did you buy it at?
the FUTURE! I buy all my clothes there!
I don't wear any of that crap coming out nowadays.
style in the future is way more expensive!
FASHION for the FUTURE
TODAY!

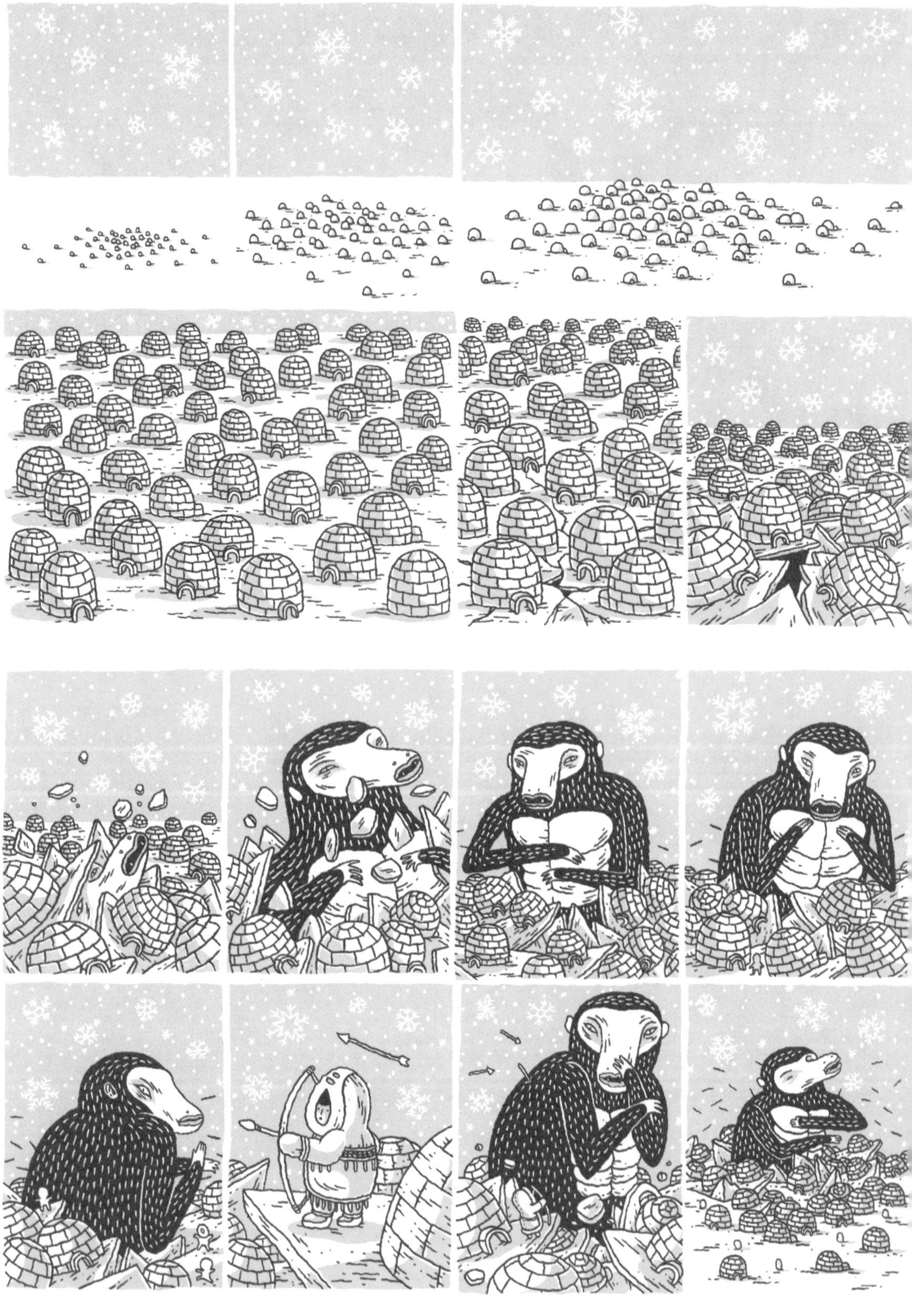

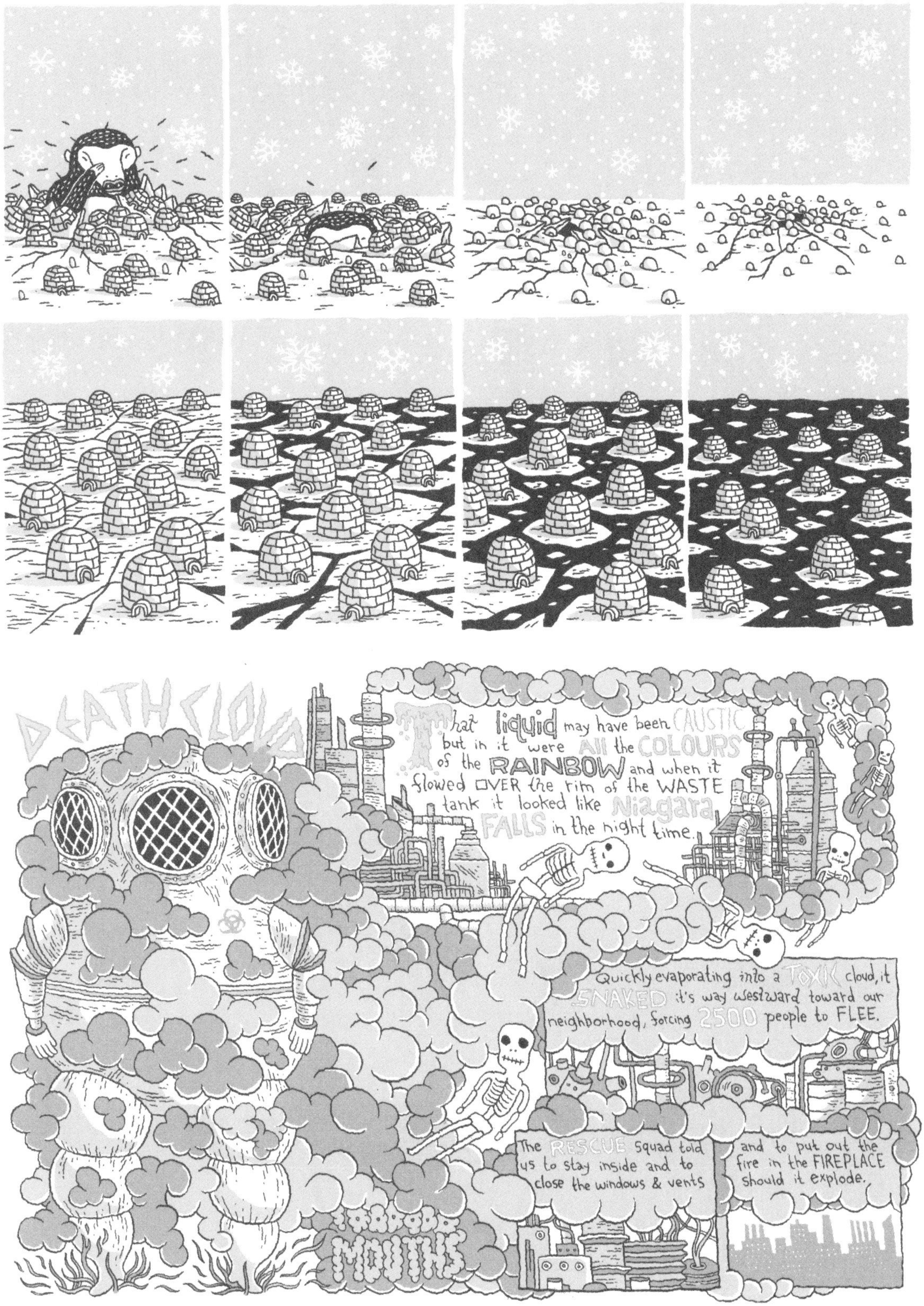
DEATH CLOUD
That liquid may have been CAUSTIC but in it were All the COLOURS of the RAINBOW and when it flowed OVER the rim of the WASTE tank it looked like Niagara FALLS in the night time.
Quickly evaporating into a TOXIC cloud, it SNAKED it's way westward toward our neighborhood, forcing 2500 people to FLEE.
The RESCUE squad told us to stay inside and to close the windows & vents
and to put out the fire in the FIREPLACE should it explode.
MOUTHS

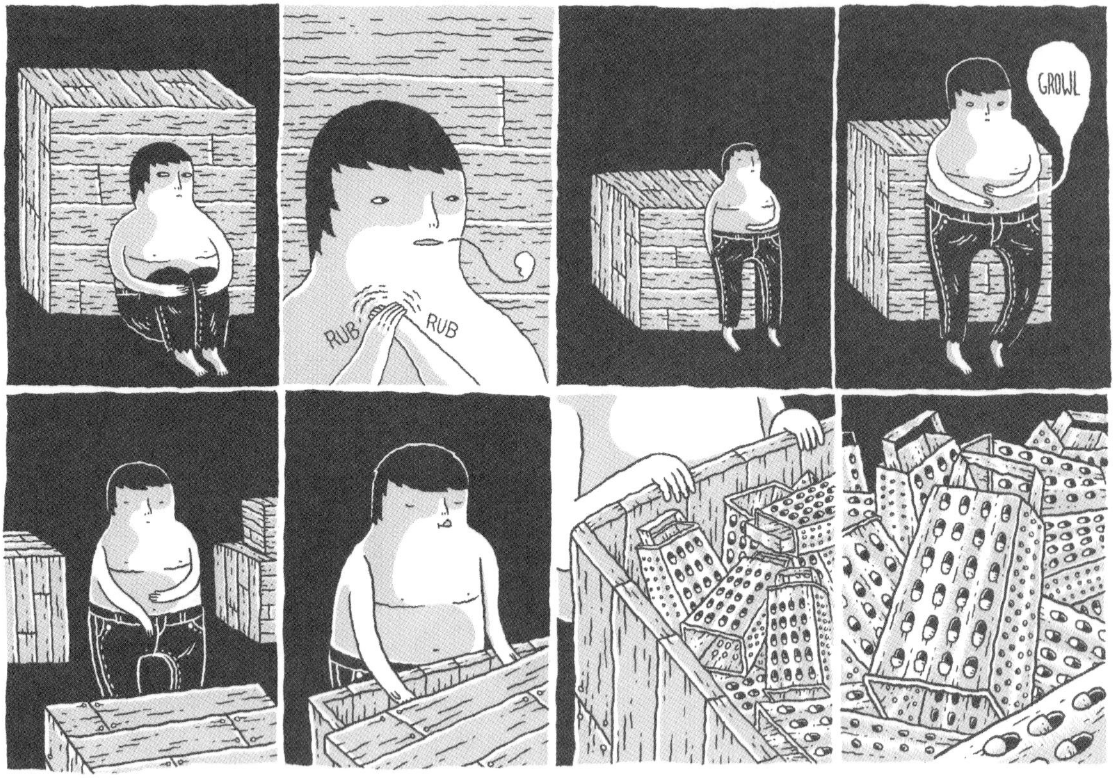
RUB RUB
GROWL

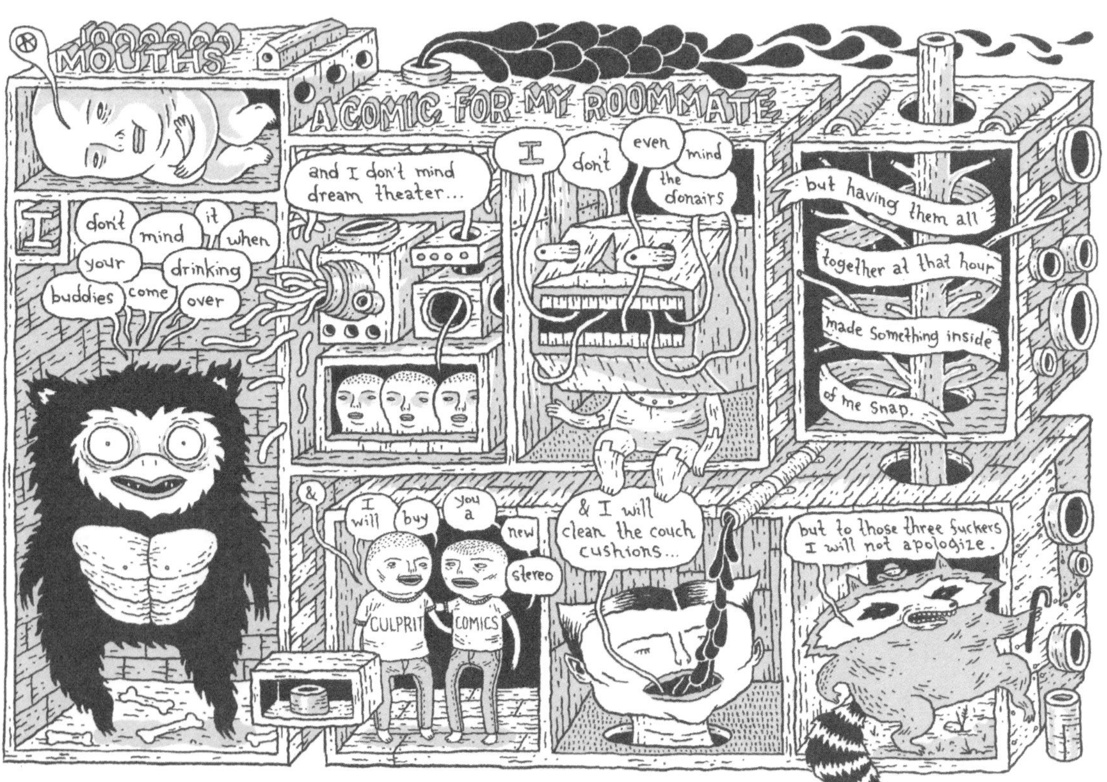
1000000 MOUTHS
A COMIC FOR MY ROOMMATE
I don't mind it when your drinking buddies come over
and I don't mind dream theater...
I don't even mind the donairs
but having them all together at that hour made something inside of me snap.
& I will buy you a new stereo
CULPRIT
COMICS
& I will clean the couch cushions...
but to those three fuckers I will not apologize.

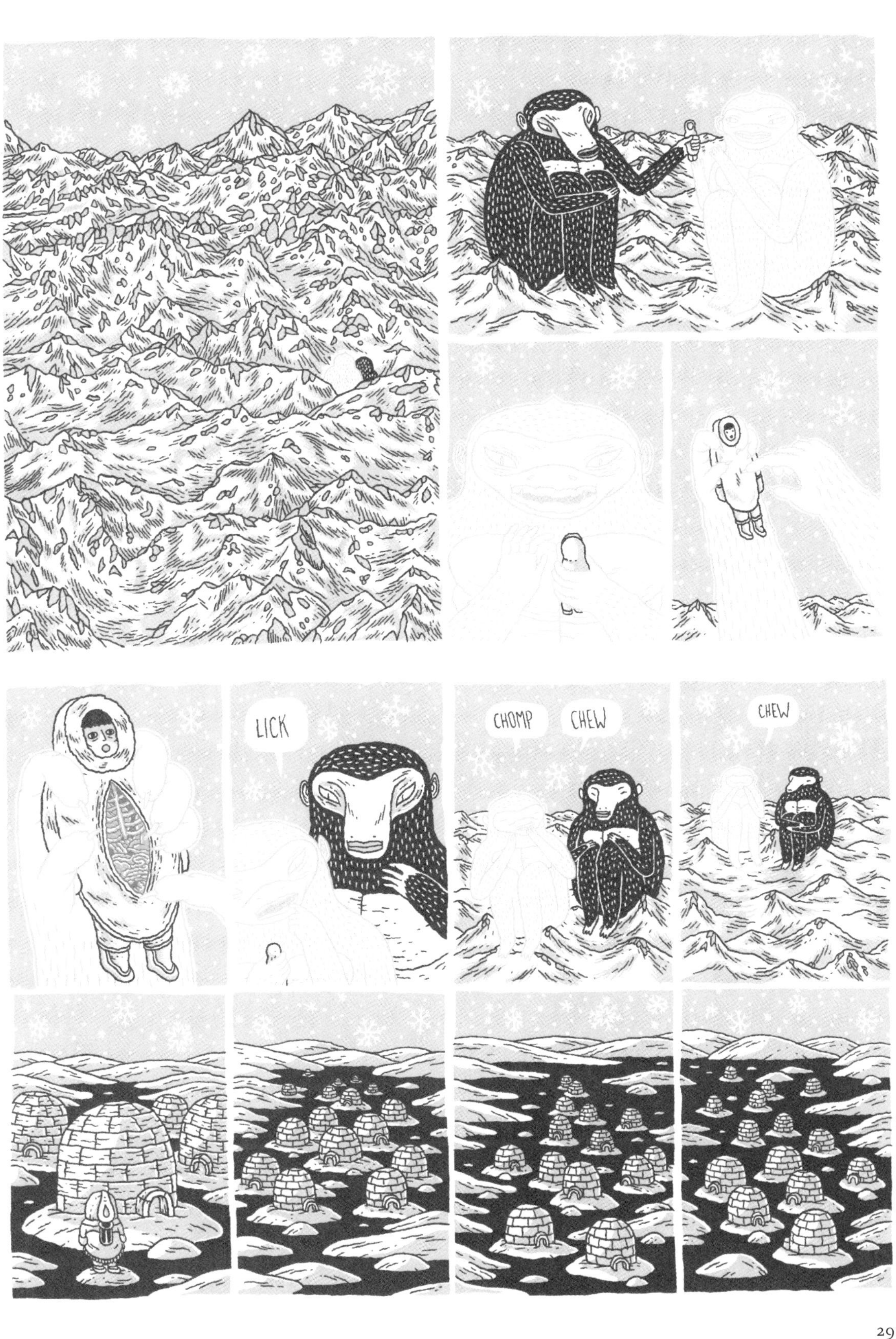
LICK
CHOMP
CHEW
CHEW

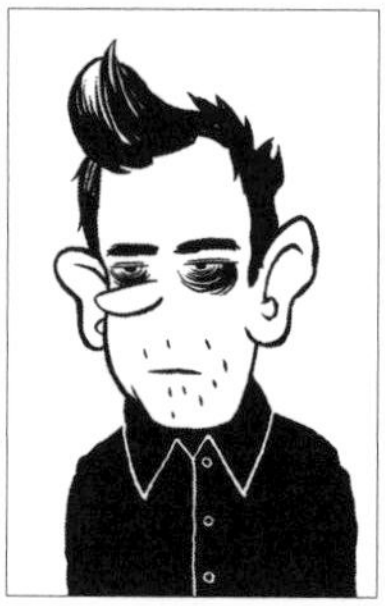

JORDAN CRANE

Elsewheres

from *Keeping Two*

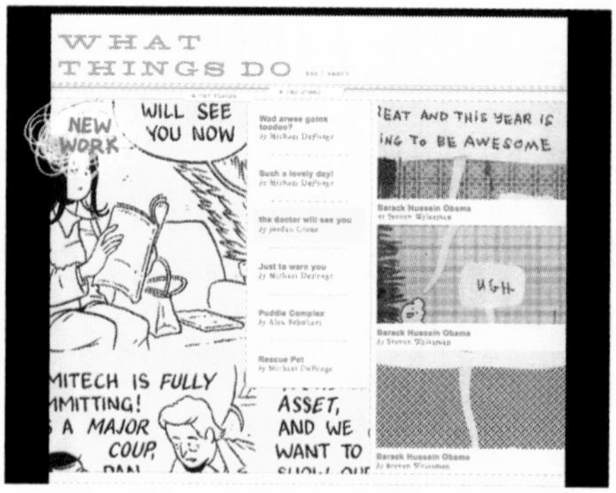
WHAT THINGS DO
NEW WORK
WILL SEE YOU NOW
UGH
ASSET, AND WE WANT TO

FOR ME, DRAWING COMICS IS

What I prefer to be doing.

THE SELECTION

William examines a large swath of ruin left in the wake of his girlfriend's disappearance. It's a soup-to-nuts tour of loss.

THE CONTEXT

This is an excerpt from *Keeping Two*. We arrive at this point in the story after William's girlfriend has been missing quite some time.

PUBLICATIONS MY WORK HAS APPEARED IN

Atlantic Monthly (cover), *Nickelodeon, GOOD, What Things Do.*

AWARDS

American Institute of Graphic Arts Award 2002 for Book Design; Ignatz awards for Outstanding Series and Outstanding Comic in 2010.

WHAT I'M KNOWN FOR

Uptight, my semiregular comic book; the kids' books *The Clouds Above* and *Keep Our Secrets; NON,* an anthology published in the late 1990s, with five issues through 2001.

WHERE I LIVE

Los Angeles, California.

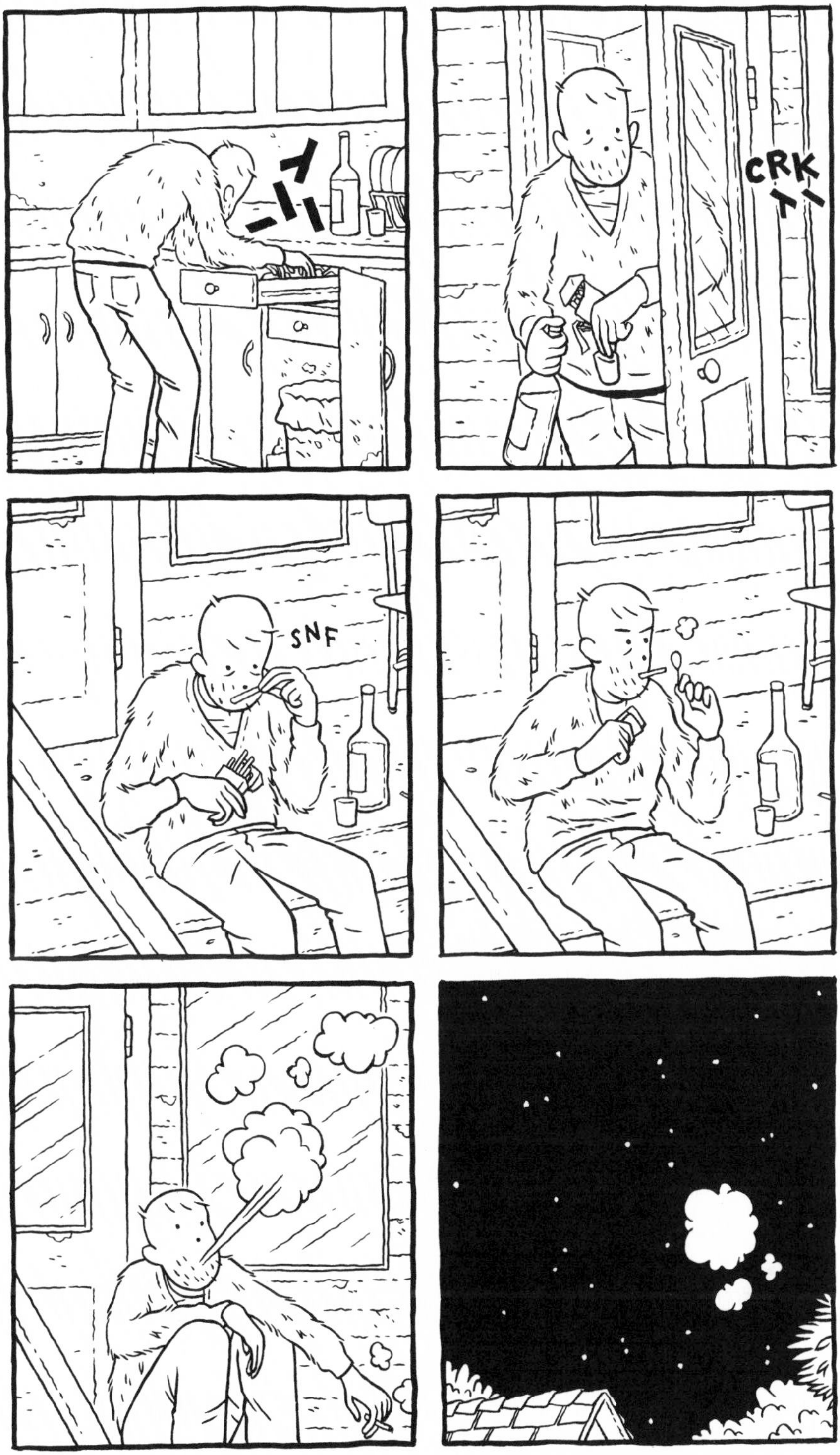
CRK
SNF

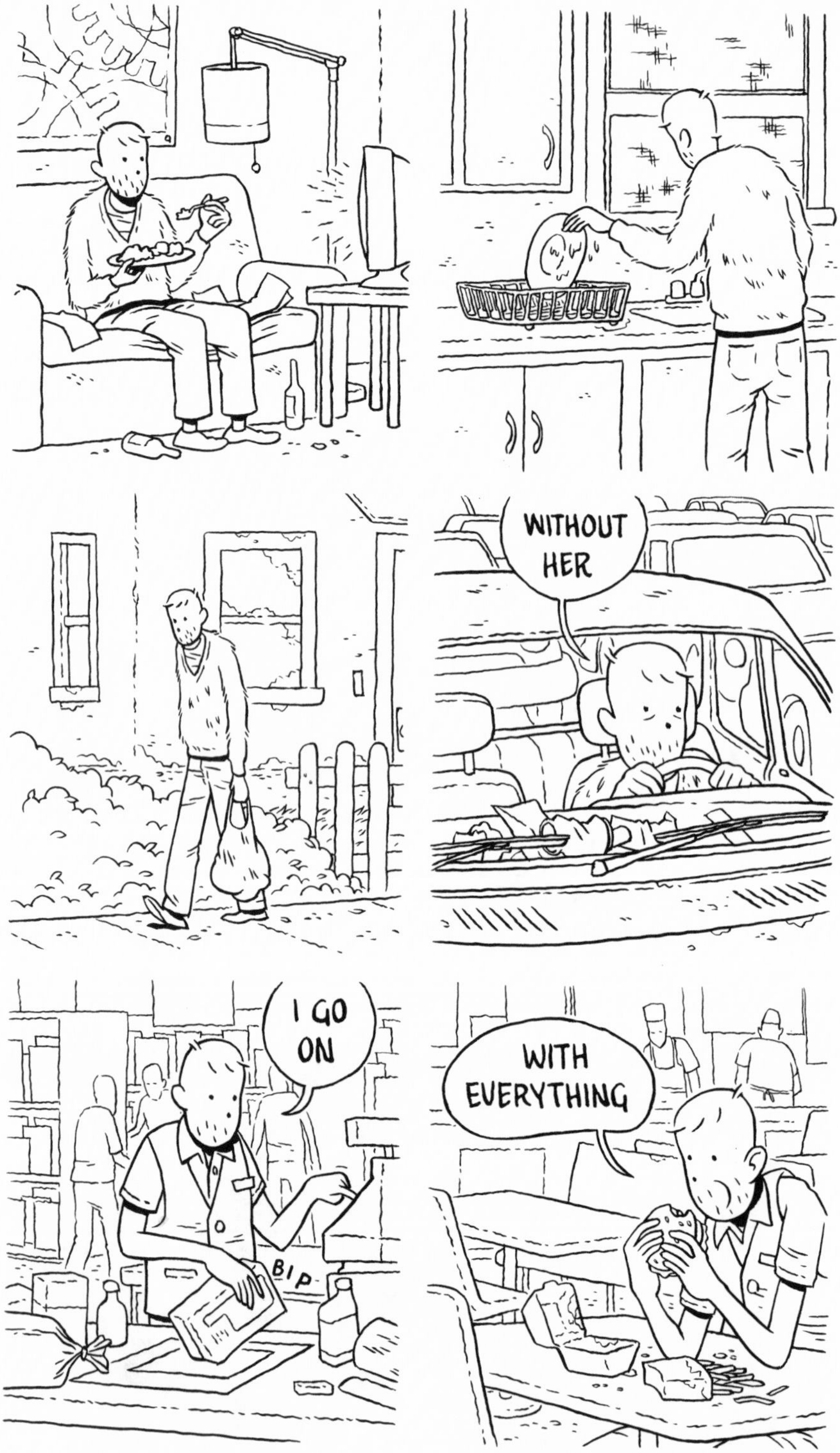
WITHOUT HER
I GO ON
BIP
WITH EVERYTHING

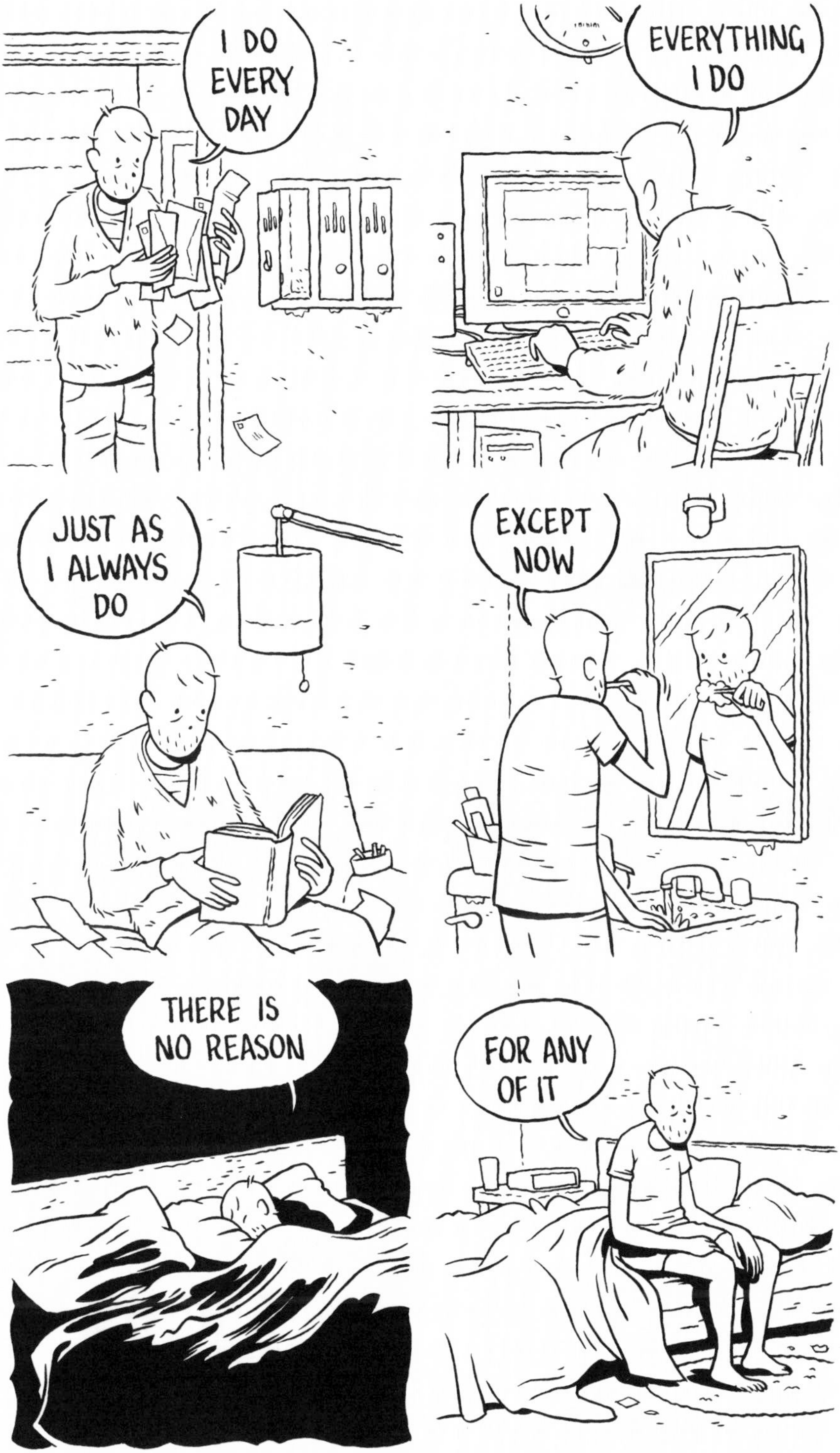
I DO EVERY DAY
EVERYTHING I DO
JUST AS I ALWAYS DO
EXCEPT NOW
THERE IS NO REASON
FOR ANY OF IT

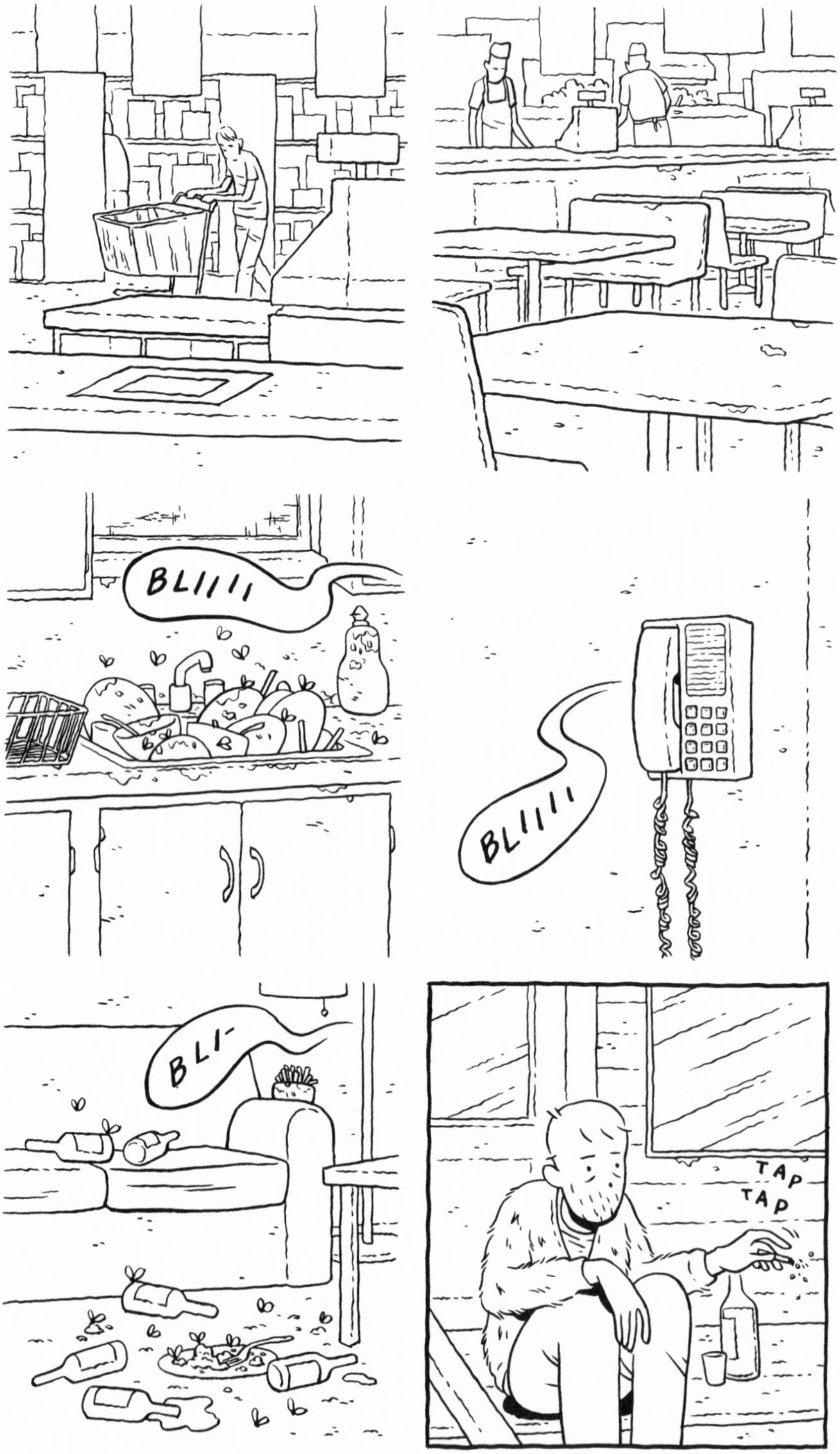
BLIIII
BLIIII
BLI-
TAP
TAP

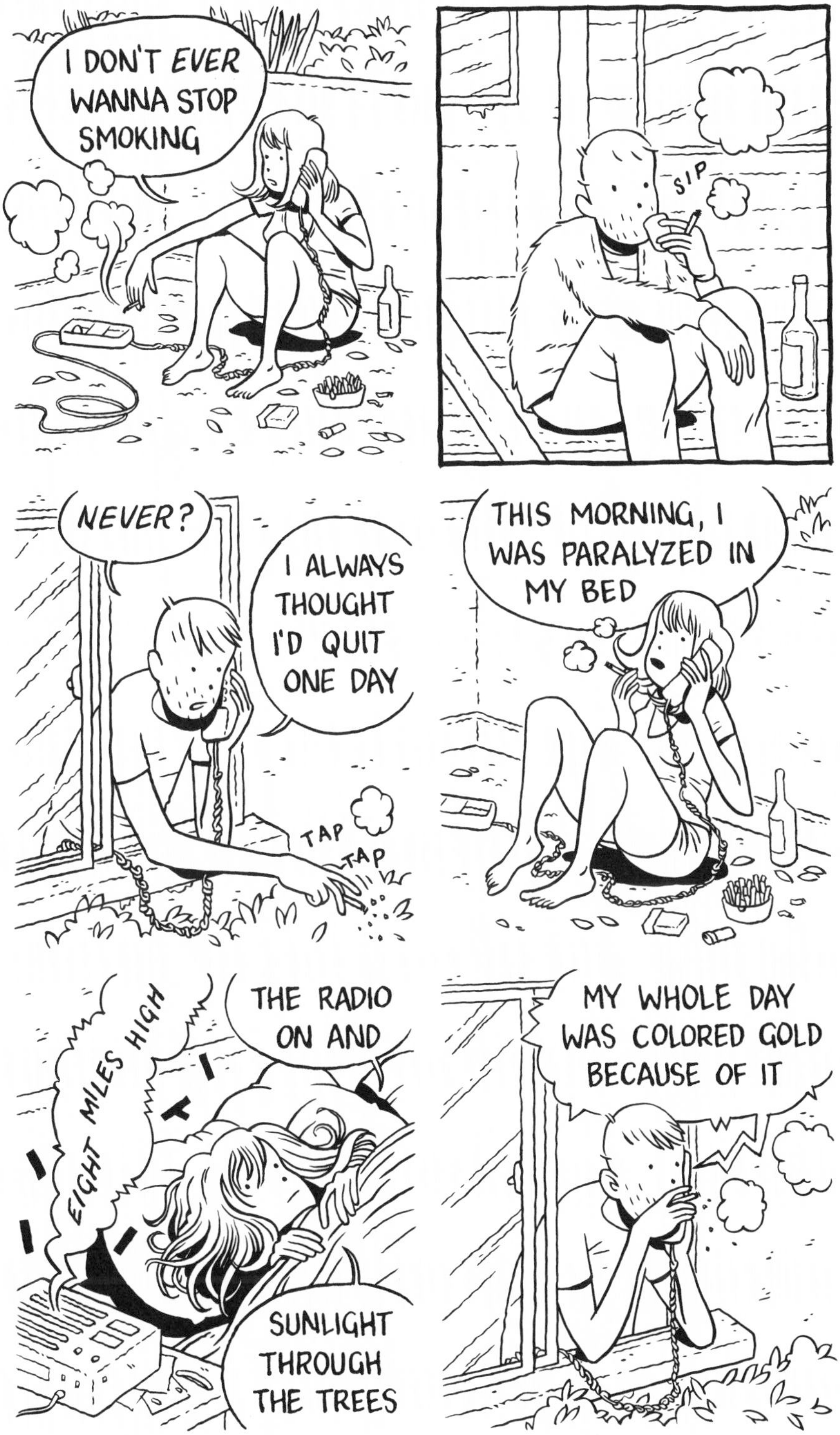

I DON'T EVER WANNA STOP SMOKING
SIP
NEVER?
I ALWAYS THOUGHT I'D QUIT ONE DAY
TAP TAP
THIS MORNING, I WAS PARALYZED IN MY BED
EIGHT MILES HIGH
THE RADIO ON AND
SUNLIGHT THROUGH THE TREES
MY WHOLE DAY WAS COLORED GOLD BECAUSE OF IT

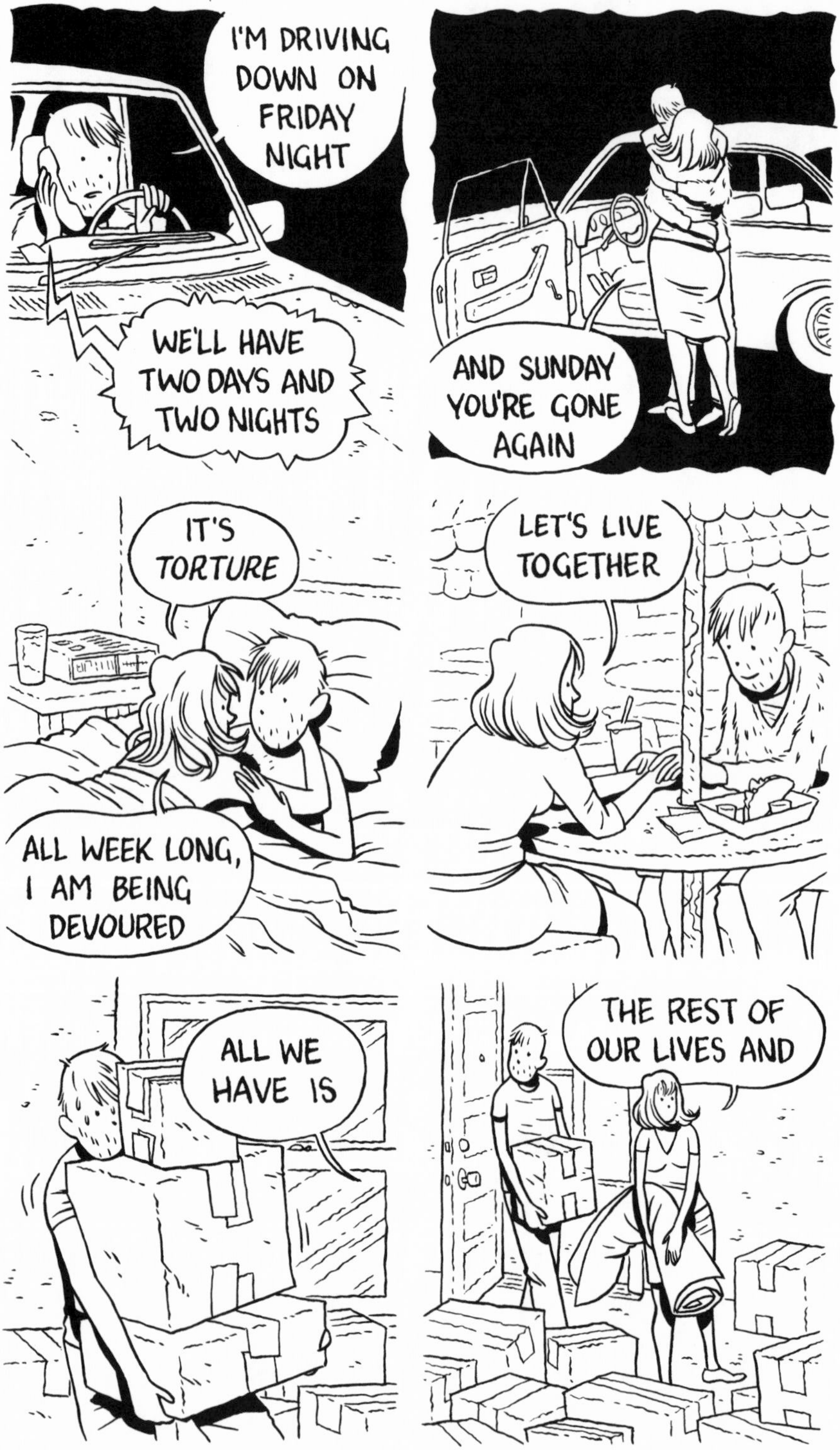
I'M DRIVING DOWN ON FRIDAY NIGHT
WE'LL HAVE TWO DAYS AND TWO NIGHTS
AND SUNDAY YOU'RE GONE AGAIN
IT'S TORTURE
ALL WEEK LONG, I AM BEING DEVOURED
LET'S LIVE TOGETHER
ALL WE HAVE IS
THE REST OF OUR LIVES AND

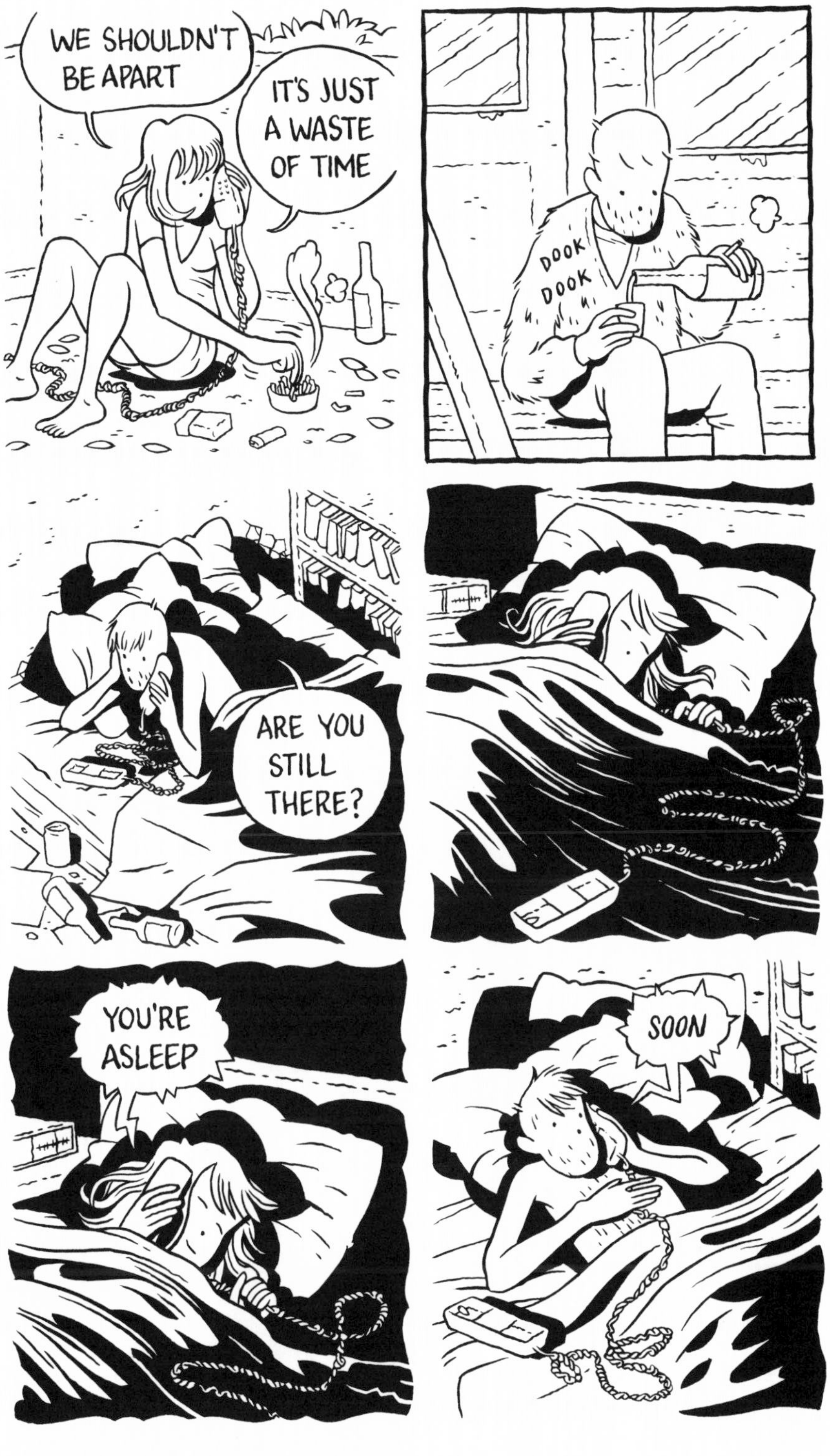
WE SHOULDN'T BE APART
IT'S JUST A WASTE OF TIME
DOOK DOOK
ARE YOU STILL THERE?
YOU'RE ASLEEP
SOON

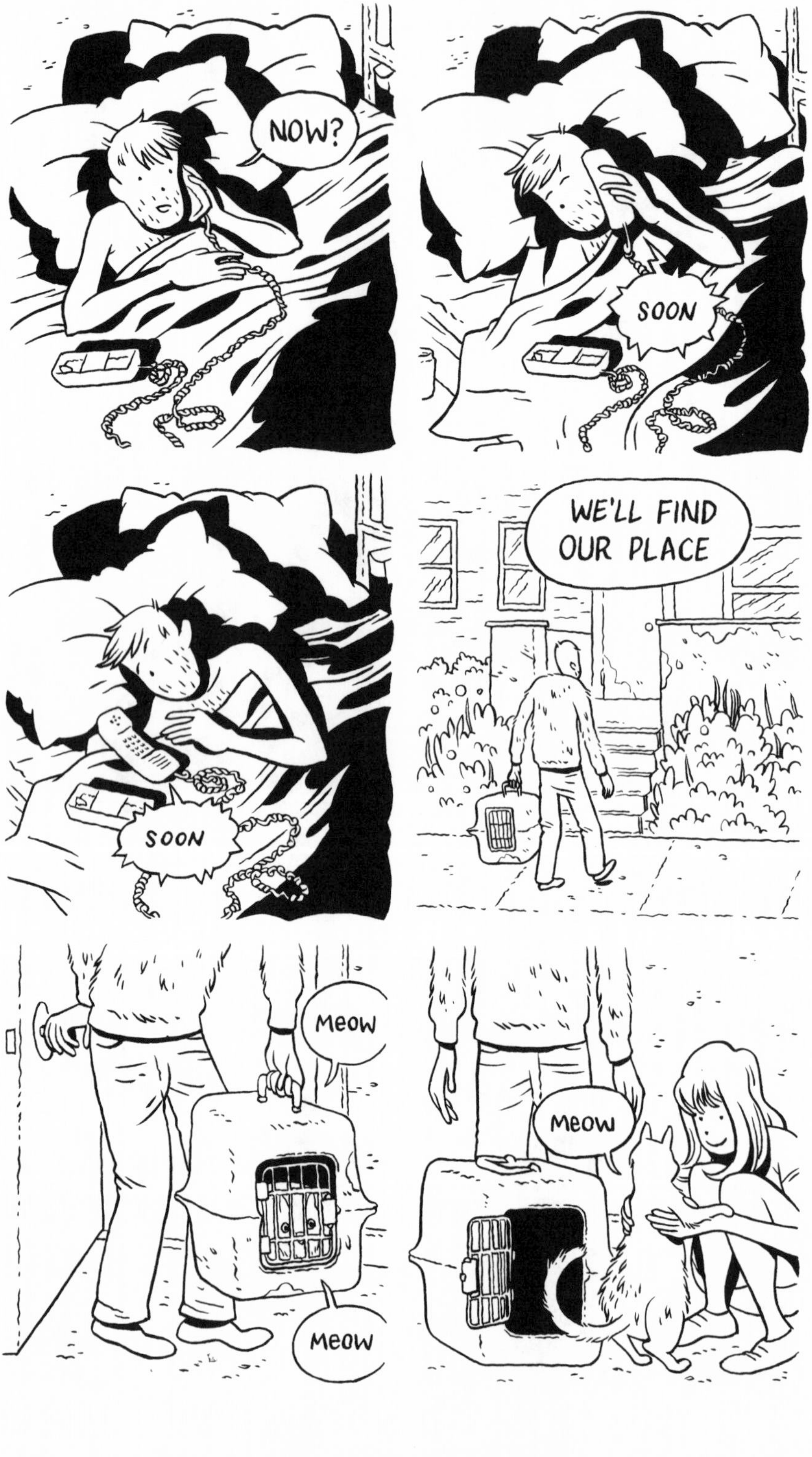
NOW?
SOON
SOON
WE'LL FIND OUR PLACE
MEOW
MEOW
MEOW

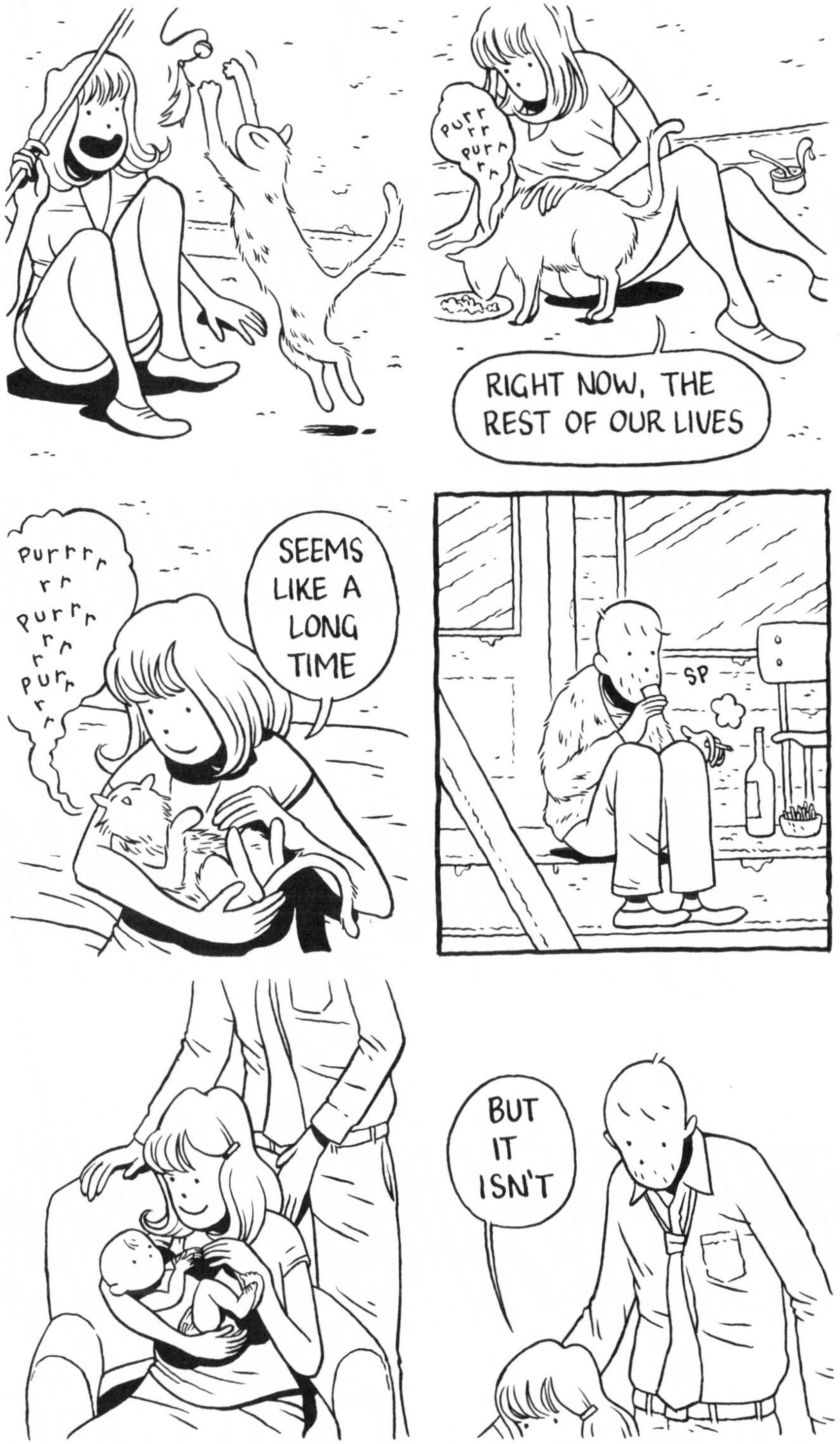
purr rr purr rr
RIGHT NOW, THE REST OF OUR LIVES
purrrr rr purrrr rr purr rr
SEEMS LIKE A LONG TIME
SP
BUT IT ISN'T

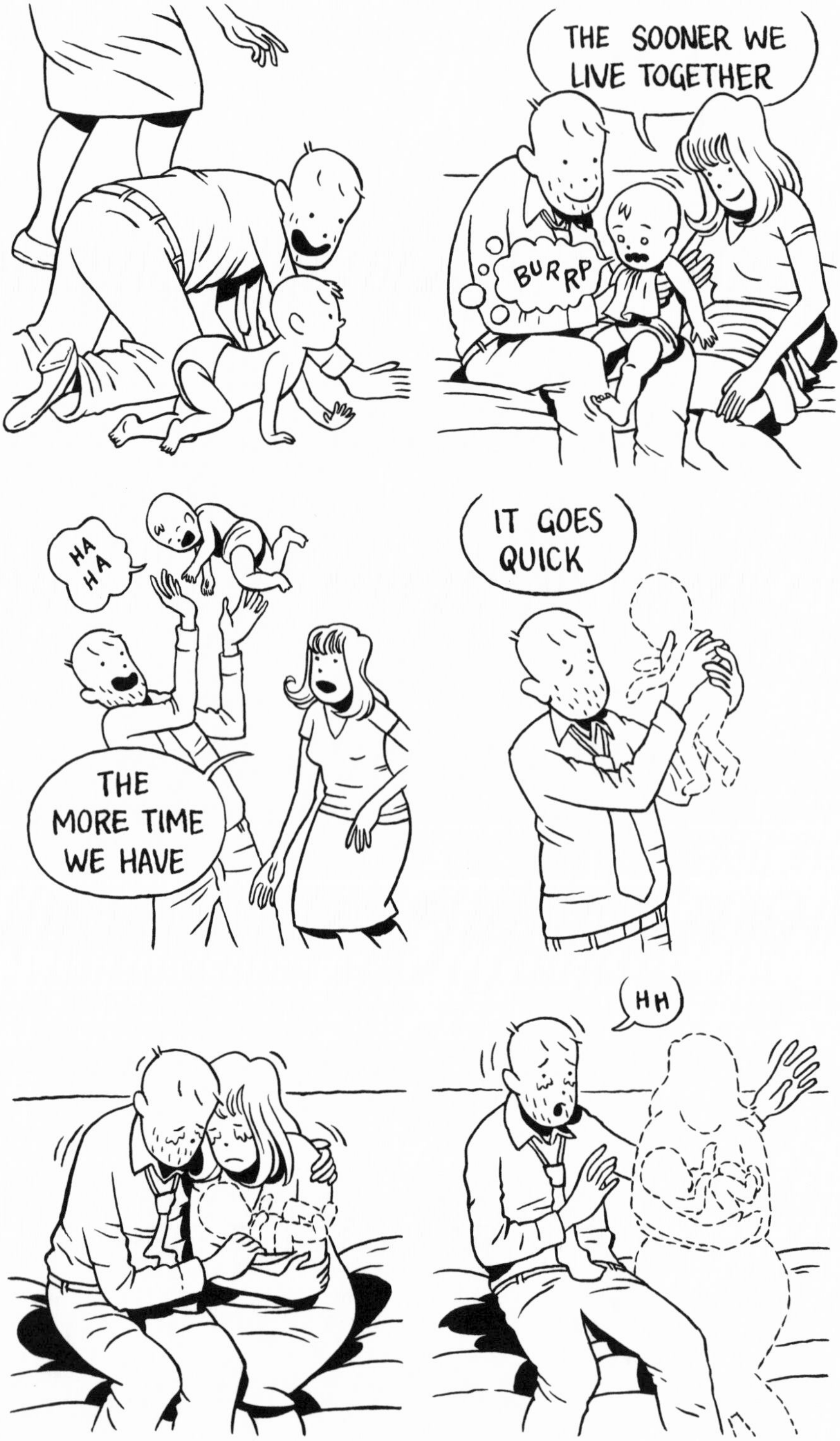
THE SOONER WE LIVE TOGETHER
BURRP
HA HA
THE MORE TIME WE HAVE
IT GOES QUICK
HH

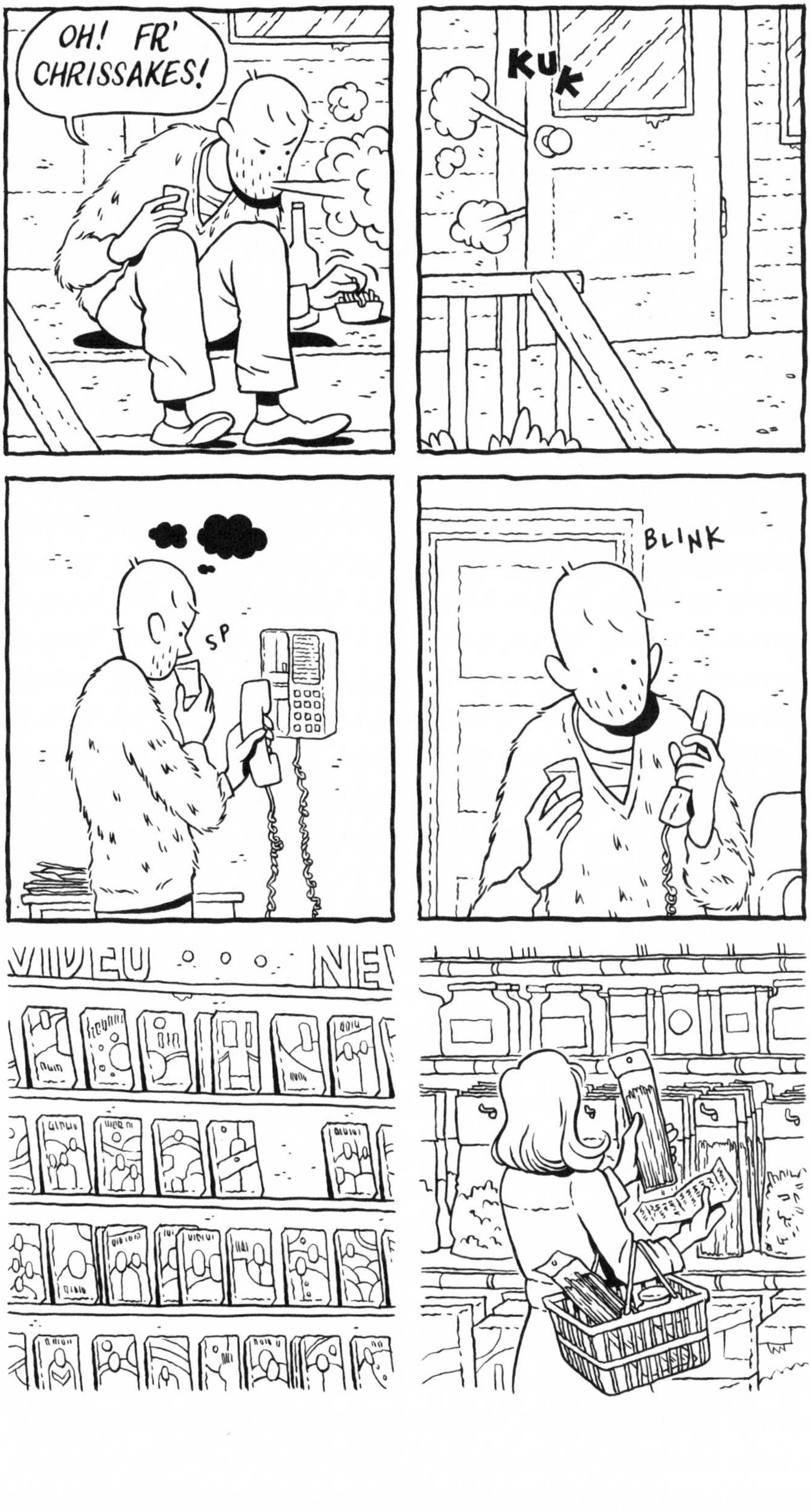
OH! FR' CHRISSAKES!
KUK
SP
BLINK
VIDEO
NEW

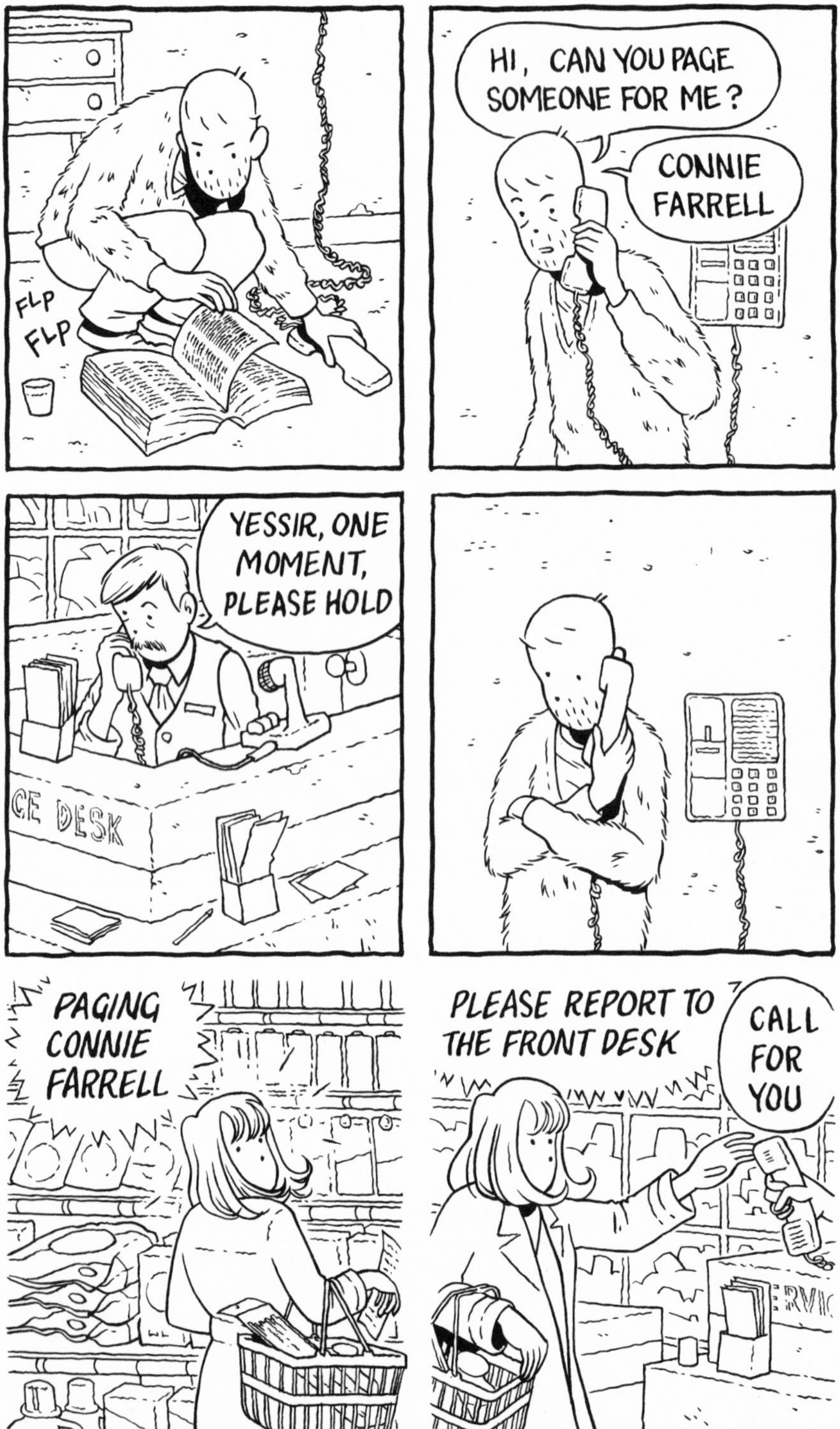
FLP
FLP
HI, CAN YOU PAGE SOMEONE FOR ME?
CONNIE FARRELL
YESSIR, ONE MOMENT, PLEASE HOLD
CE DESK
PAGING CONNIE FARRELL
PLEASE REPORT TO THE FRONT DESK
CALL FOR YOU

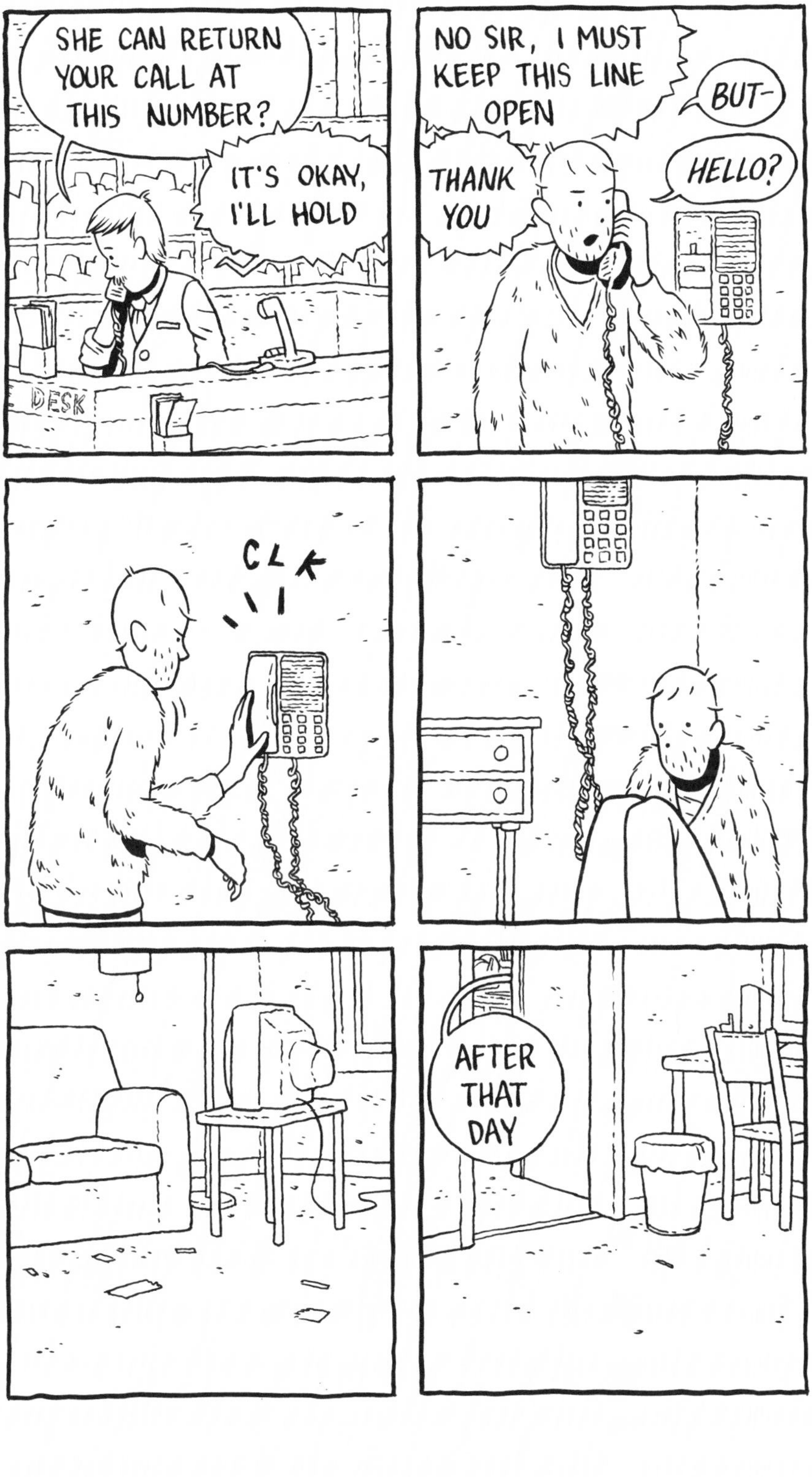
SHE CAN RETURN YOUR CALL AT THIS NUMBER?
IT'S OKAY, I'LL HOLD
DESK
NO SIR, I MUST KEEP THIS LINE OPEN
BUT-
THANK YOU
HELLO?
CLK
AFTER THAT DAY

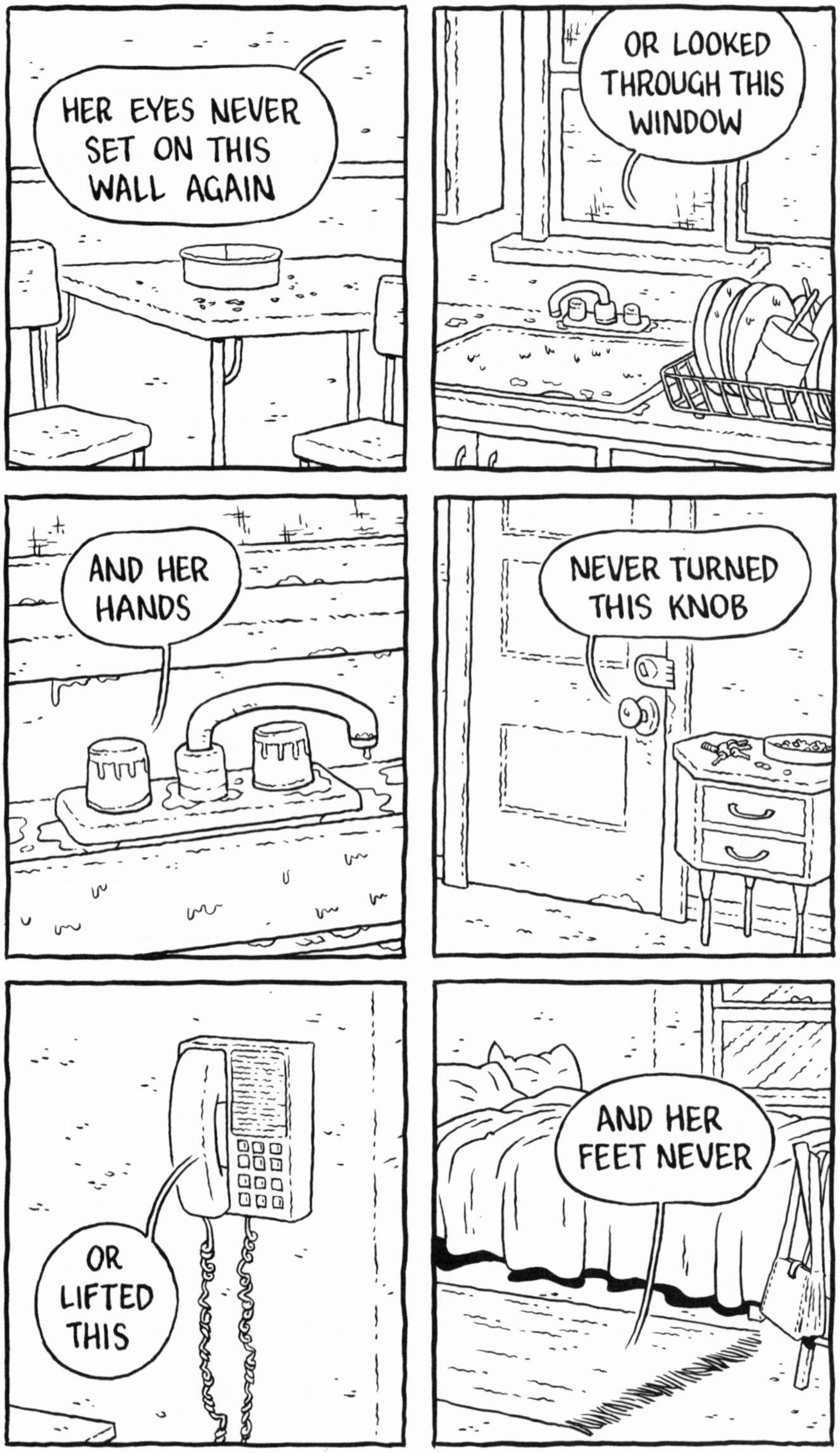
HER EYES NEVER SET ON THIS WALL AGAIN
OR LOOKED THROUGH THIS WINDOW
AND HER HANDS
NEVER TURNED THIS KNOB
OR LIFTED THIS
AND HER FEET NEVER

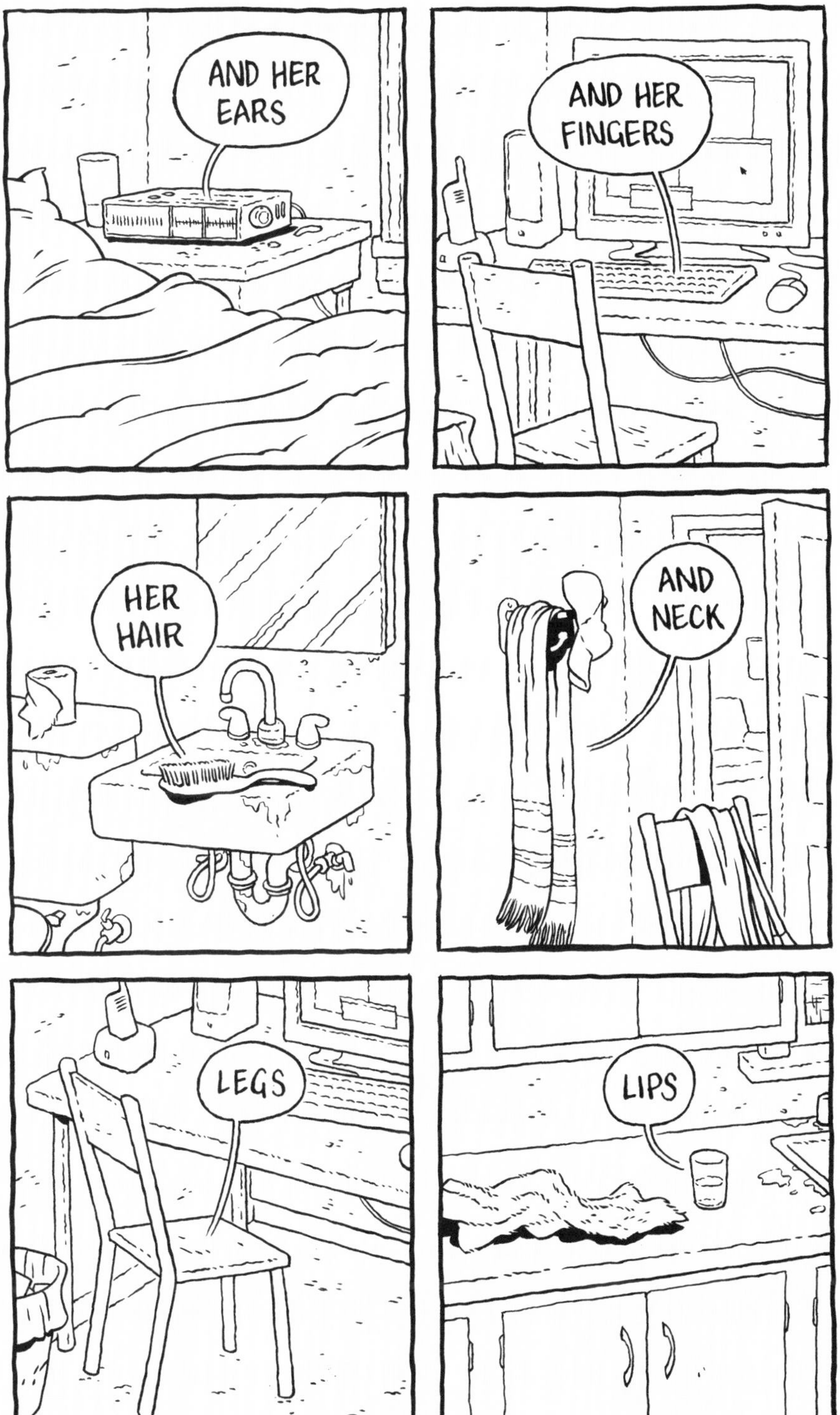
AND HER EARS
AND HER FINGERS
HER HAIR
AND NECK
LEGS
LIPS

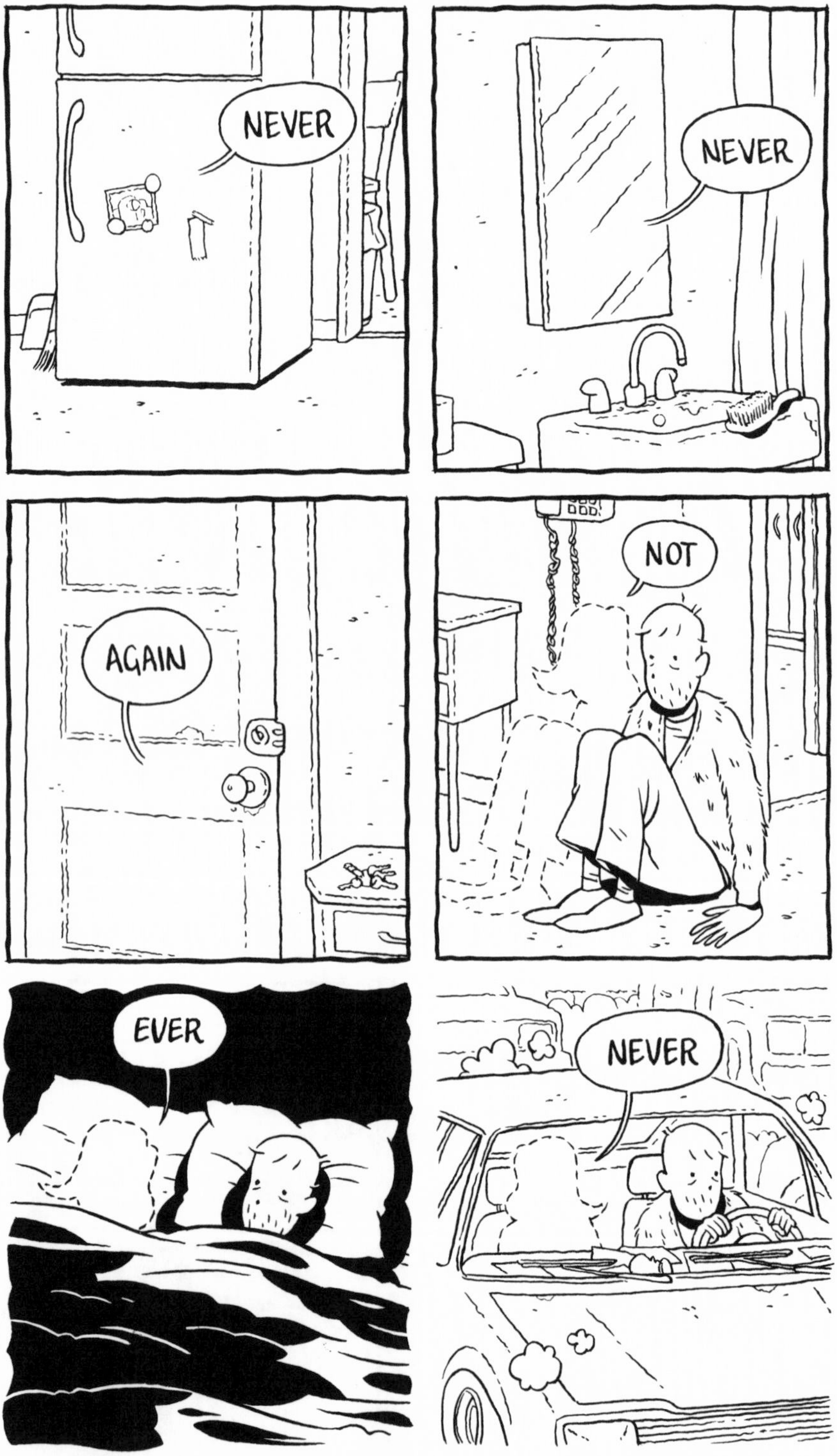
NEVER
NEVER
AGAIN
NOT
EVER
NEVER

HAGGLING

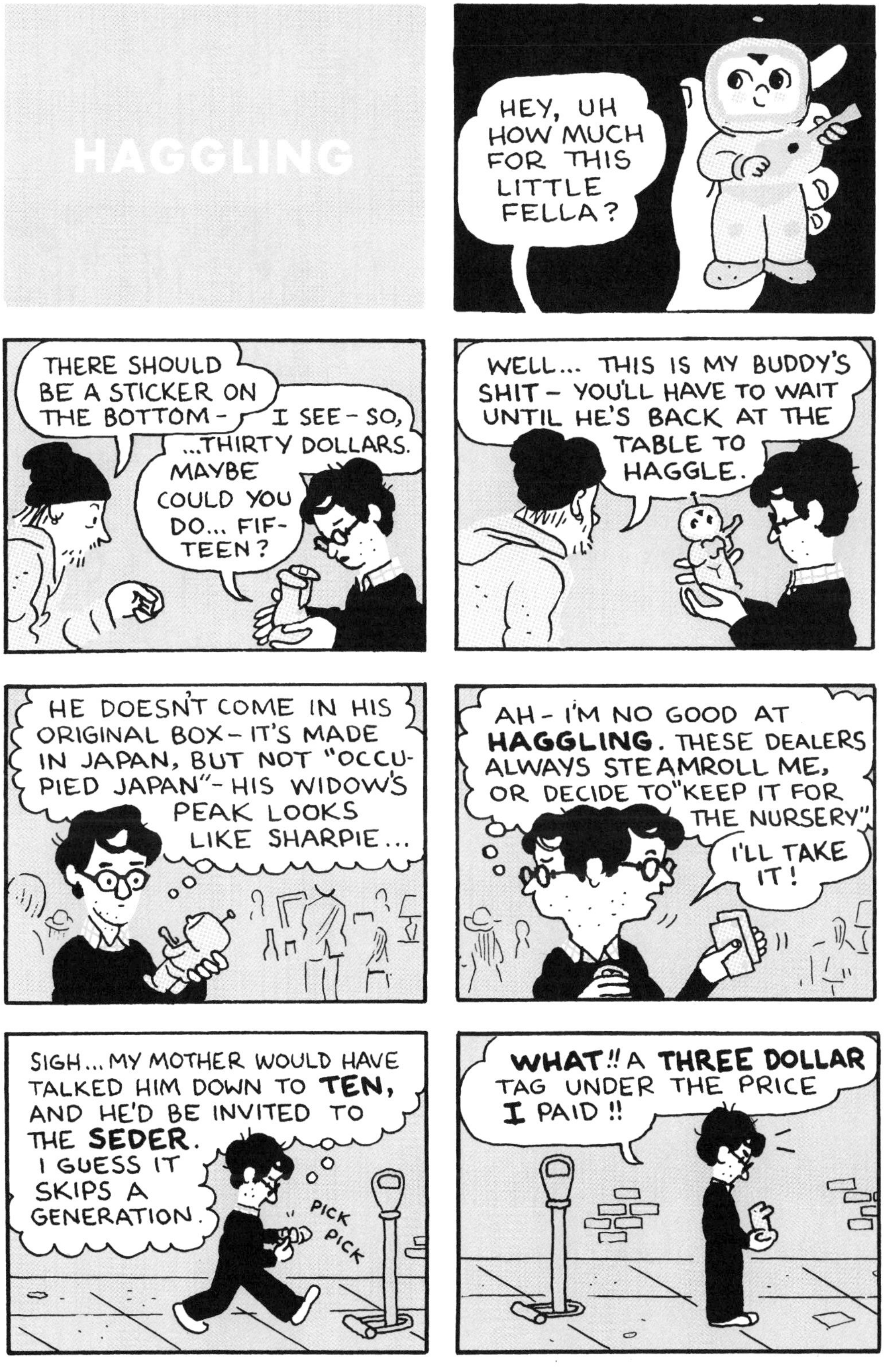
HEY, UH HOW MUCH FOR THIS LITTLE FELLA?
THERE SHOULD BE A STICKER ON THE BOTTOM -
I SEE - SO, ...THIRTY DOLLARS. MAYBE COULD YOU DO... FIF-TEEN?
WELL... THIS IS MY BUDDY'S SHIT - YOU'LL HAVE TO WAIT UNTIL HE'S BACK AT THE TABLE TO HAGGLE.
HE DOESN'T COME IN HIS ORIGINAL BOX - IT'S MADE IN JAPAN, BUT NOT "OCCU-PIED JAPAN" - HIS WIDOW'S PEAK LOOKS LIKE SHARPIE...
AH - I'M NO GOOD AT **HAGGLING**. THESE DEALERS ALWAYS STEAMROLL ME, OR DECIDE TO "KEEP IT FOR THE NURSERY"
I'LL TAKE IT!
SIGH... MY MOTHER WOULD HAVE TALKED HIM DOWN TO **TEN**, AND HE'D BE INVITED TO THE **SEDER**. I GUESS IT SKIPS A GENERATION.
PICK PICK
WHAT!! A **THREE DOLLAR** TAG UNDER THE PRICE **I** PAID!!

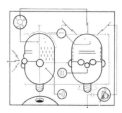

CHRIS WARE

Money

from *The New Yorker*

FOR ME, DRAWING COMICS IS

A labor-intensive, isolating, monomaniacal way of avoiding the painful minefields of actual human interaction.

THE SELECTION

This is a short strip for the "Money" issue of *The New Yorker*, created to accommodate a gatefold cover to which the strip was compositionally linked, granting the usual single-panel gag function of the cover the double duty of also being the first panel in a connected comic strip. It ran on the week of Columbus Day and was printed so that the dollar bill was life-size.

THE CONTEXT

The strip is also a part of *Building Stories* (Pantheon, 2012).

PUBLICATIONS MY WORK HAS APPEARED IN

The New Yorker.

AWARDS

Guardian First Book Award, 2002; United States Artists Hoi Fellowship, 2006.

WHAT I'M KNOWN FOR

Jimmy Corrigan, the Smartest Kid on Earth; *The ACME Novelty Library*; various collaborations with Ira Glass for *This American Life*.

WHERE I LIVE

Oak Park, Illinois.

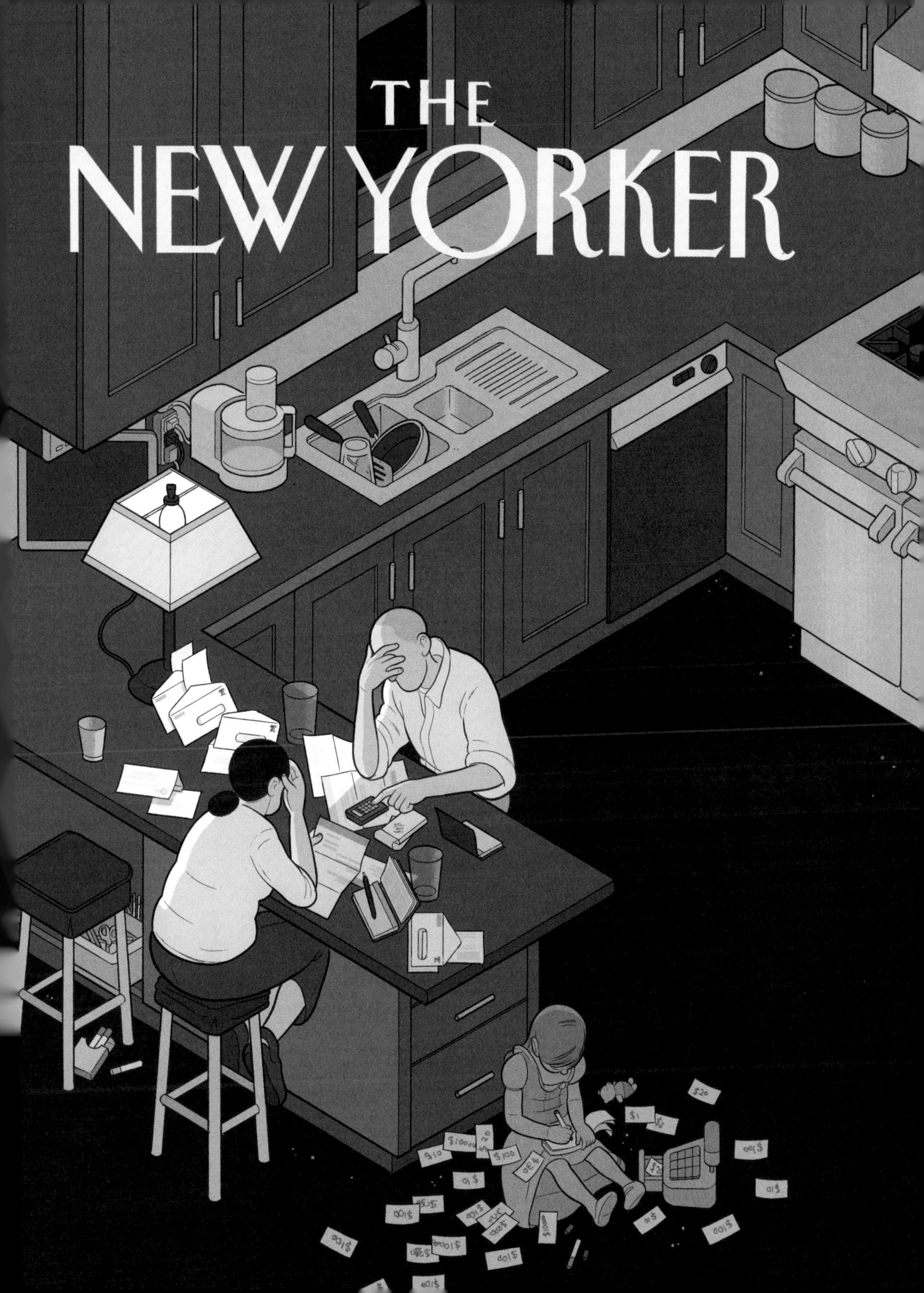
THE
NEW YORKER

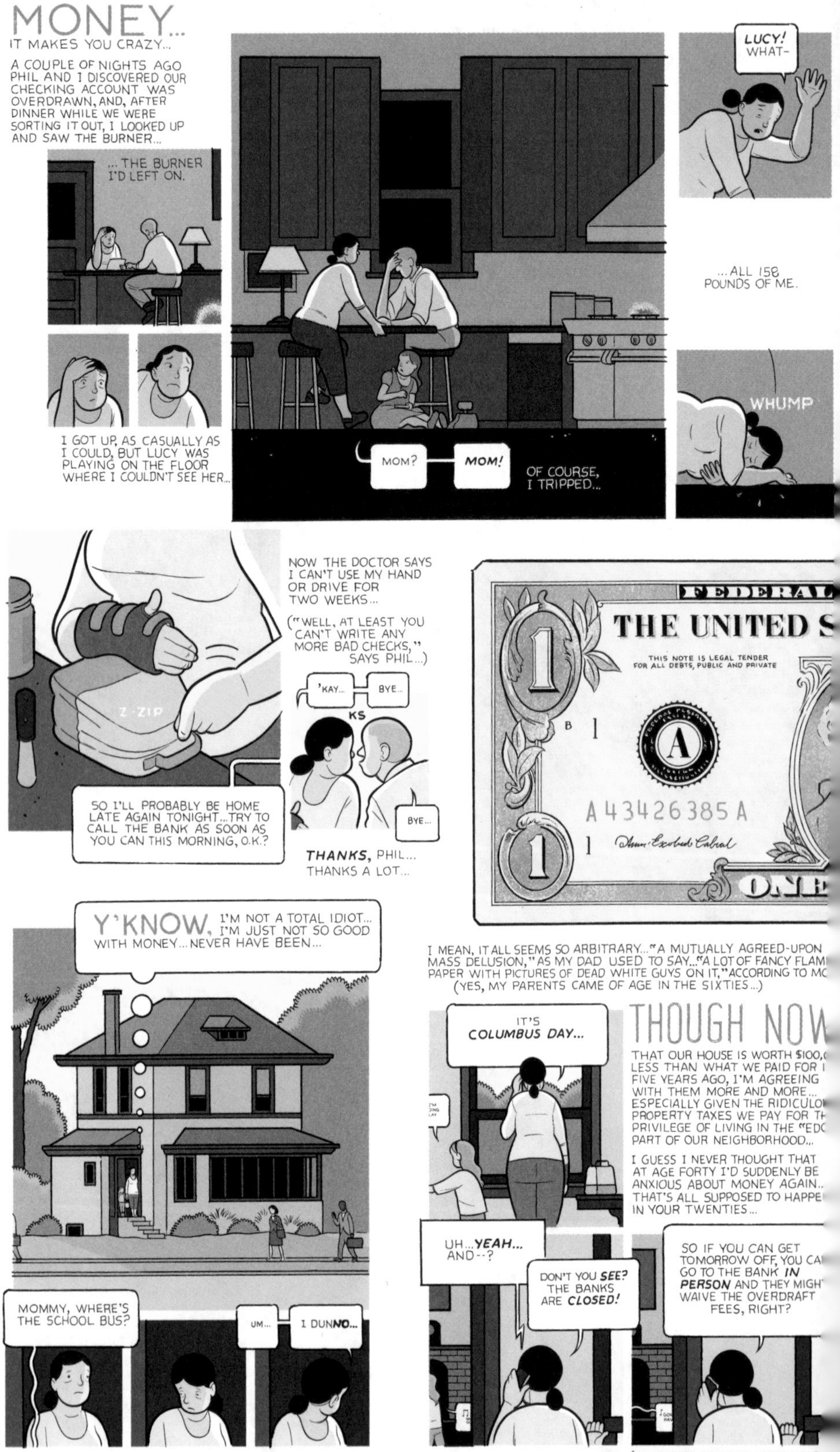
MONEY...
IT MAKES YOU CRAZY...
A COUPLE OF NIGHTS AGO PHIL AND I DISCOVERED OUR CHECKING ACCOUNT WAS OVERDRAWN, AND, AFTER DINNER WHILE WE WERE SORTING IT OUT, I LOOKED UP AND SAW THE BURNER...
...THE BURNER I'D LEFT ON.
I GOT UP, AS CASUALLY AS I COULD, BUT LUCY WAS PLAYING ON THE FLOOR WHERE I COULDN'T SEE HER...
MOM?
MOM!
OF COURSE, I TRIPPED...
LUCY! WHAT-
...ALL 158 POUNDS OF ME.
WHUMP
Z-ZIP
SO I'LL PROBABLY BE HOME LATE AGAIN TONIGHT...TRY TO CALL THE BANK AS SOON AS YOU CAN THIS MORNING, O.K.?
NOW THE DOCTOR SAYS I CAN'T USE MY HAND OR DRIVE FOR TWO WEEKS...
("WELL, AT LEAST YOU CAN'T WRITE ANY MORE BAD CHECKS," SAYS PHIL...)
'KAY...
BYE...
KS
BYE...
THANKS, PHIL... THANKS A LOT...
FEDERAL
THE UNITED S
THIS NOTE IS LEGAL TENDER FOR ALL DEBTS, PUBLIC AND PRIVATE
A
A 43426385 A
ONE
Y'KNOW, I'M NOT A TOTAL IDIOT... I'M JUST NOT SO GOOD WITH MONEY... NEVER HAVE BEEN...
I MEAN, IT ALL SEEMS SO ARBITRARY..."A MUTUALLY AGREED-UPON MASS DELUSION," AS MY DAD USED TO SAY..."A LOT OF FANCY FLAM PAPER WITH PICTURES OF DEAD WHITE GUYS ON IT," ACCORDING TO MO
(YES, MY PARENTS CAME OF AGE IN THE SIXTIES...)
THOUGH NOW
THAT OUR HOUSE IS WORTH $100, LESS THAN WHAT WE PAID FOR I FIVE YEARS AGO, I'M AGREEING WITH THEM MORE AND MORE... ESPECIALLY GIVEN THE RIDICULO PROPERTY TAXES WE PAY FOR TH PRIVILEGE OF LIVING IN THE "ED PART OF OUR NEIGHBORHOOD...
I GUESS I NEVER THOUGHT THAT AT AGE FORTY I'D SUDDENLY BE ANXIOUS ABOUT MONEY AGAIN... THAT'S ALL SUPPOSED TO HAPPE IN YOUR TWENTIES...
IT'S COLUMBUS DAY...
MOMMY, WHERE'S THE SCHOOL BUS?
UM...
I DUNNO...
UH...YEAH... AND--?
DON'T YOU SEE? THE BANKS ARE CLOSED!
SO IF YOU CAN GET TOMORROW OFF, YOU CA GO TO THE BANK IN PERSON AND THEY MIGH WAIVE THE OVERDRAFT FEES, RIGHT?
(ISN'T FACE TO FACE BETTER FOR THESE THINGS, ANYWAY

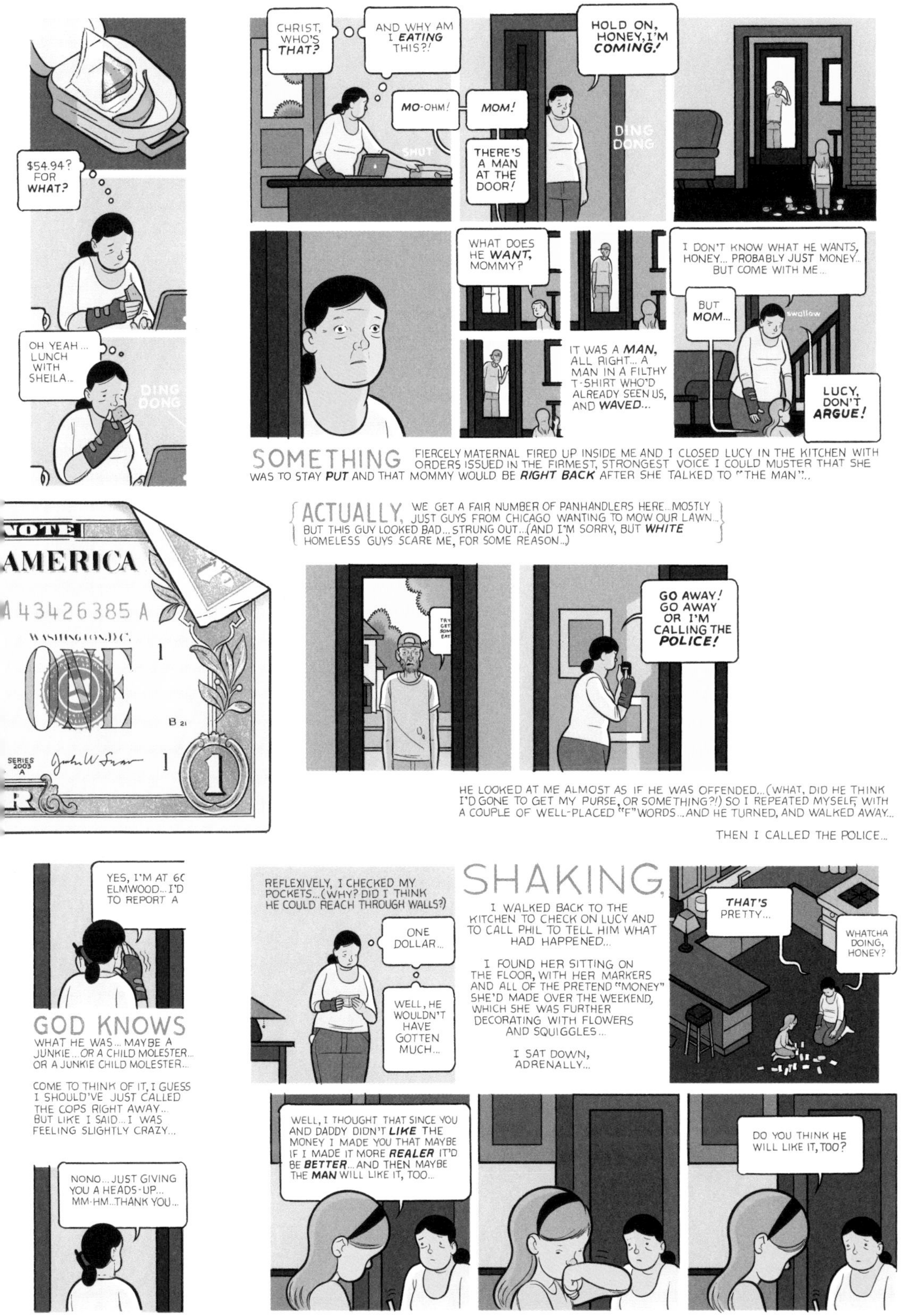
$54.94? FOR WHAT?
OH YEAH... LUNCH WITH SHEILA...
DING DONG
CHRIST, WHO'S THAT?
AND WHY AM I EATING THIS?!
SHUT
MO-OHM!
MOM!
THERE'S A MAN AT THE DOOR!
HOLD ON, HONEY, I'M COMING!
DING DONG
WHAT DOES HE WANT, MOMMY?
IT WAS A MAN, ALL RIGHT... A MAN IN A FILTHY T-SHIRT WHO'D ALREADY SEEN US, AND WAVED...
I DON'T KNOW WHAT HE WANTS, HONEY... PROBABLY JUST MONEY... BUT COME WITH ME...
BUT MOM...
swallow
LUCY, DON'T ARGUE!
SOMETHING FIERCELY MATERNAL FIRED UP INSIDE ME AND I CLOSED LUCY IN THE KITCHEN WITH ORDERS ISSUED IN THE FIRMEST, STRONGEST VOICE I COULD MUSTER THAT SHE WAS TO STAY PUT AND THAT MOMMY WOULD BE RIGHT BACK AFTER SHE TALKED TO "THE MAN"...
NOTE
AMERICA
A 43426385 A
WASHINGTON, D.C.
ONE
B 21
SERIES 2003 A
1
(ACTUALLY, WE GET A FAIR NUMBER OF PANHANDLERS HERE... MOSTLY JUST GUYS FROM CHICAGO WANTING TO MOW OUR LAWN... BUT THIS GUY LOOKED BAD... STRUNG OUT... (AND I'M SORRY, BUT WHITE HOMELESS GUYS SCARE ME, FOR SOME REASON...)
GO AWAY! GO AWAY OR I'M CALLING THE POLICE!
HE LOOKED AT ME ALMOST AS IF HE WAS OFFENDED... (WHAT, DID HE THINK I'D GONE TO GET MY PURSE, OR SOMETHING?!) SO I REPEATED MYSELF, WITH A COUPLE OF WELL-PLACED "F" WORDS... AND HE TURNED, AND WALKED AWAY...
THEN I CALLED THE POLICE...
YES, I'M AT 6C ELMWOOD... I'D TO REPORT A
GOD KNOWS WHAT HE WAS... MAYBE A JUNKIE... OR A CHILD MOLESTER... OR A JUNKIE CHILD MOLESTER...
COME TO THINK OF IT, I GUESS I SHOULD'VE JUST CALLED THE COPS RIGHT AWAY... BUT LIKE I SAID... I WAS FEELING SLIGHTLY CRAZY...
NONO... JUST GIVING YOU A HEADS-UP... MM-HM... THANK YOU...
REFLEXIVELY, I CHECKED MY POCKETS... (WHY? DID I THINK HE COULD REACH THROUGH WALLS?)
ONE DOLLAR...
WELL, HE WOULDN'T HAVE GOTTEN MUCH...
SHAKING, I WALKED BACK TO THE KITCHEN TO CHECK ON LUCY AND TO CALL PHIL TO TELL HIM WHAT HAD HAPPENED...
I FOUND HER SITTING ON THE FLOOR, WITH HER MARKERS AND ALL OF THE PRETEND "MONEY" SHE'D MADE OVER THE WEEKEND, WHICH SHE WAS FURTHER DECORATING WITH FLOWERS AND SQUIGGLES...
I SAT DOWN, ADRENALLY...
THAT'S PRETTY...
WHATCHA DOING, HONEY?
WELL, I THOUGHT THAT SINCE YOU AND DADDY DIDN'T LIKE THE MONEY I MADE YOU THAT MAYBE IF I MADE IT MORE REALER IT'D BE BETTER... AND THEN MAYBE THE MAN WILL LIKE IT, TOO...
DO YOU THINK HE WILL LIKE IT, TOO?

Comics for Kids

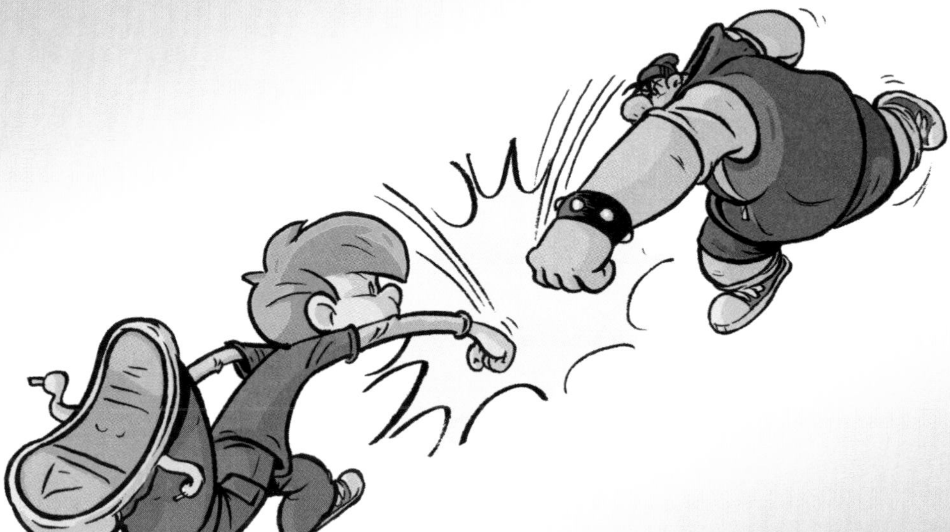

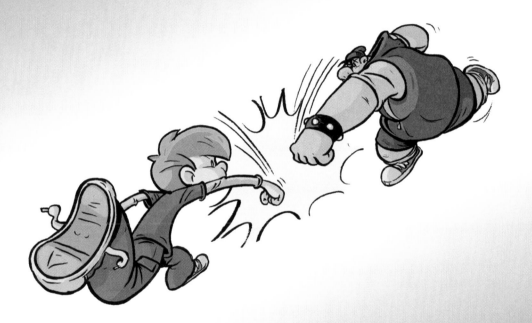

Sergio Aragonés Funnies

SERGIO ARGONÉS

Vacation / Doctor Costume

from *Sergio Aragonés Funnies*

#2
$3.50
Sergio Aragonés
Funnies
bongocomics.com

FOR ME, DRAWING COMICS IS

My life . . . besides my wife and daughter.

THE SELECTION

The selected pages are two one-page gag strips of the type that I include in every issue of *Sergio Aragonés Funnies* alongside longer stories. Normally the gags appear in black-and-white, but these strips appeared in color on the books' back covers.

WHAT I'M KNOWN FOR

Laugh-In bloopers and practical jokes animation; *Mad* pocket books; "A *Mad* look at . . ." marginals (the little cartoons that appear in the margins of the pages of *Mad* magazine).

WHERE I LIVE

Ojai, California.

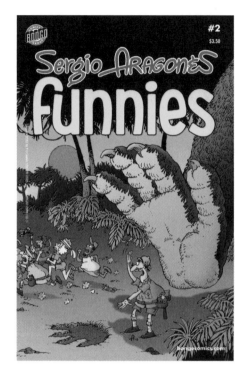

VACATION
HOTEL
$ $ $ $ $ $ $ $
PUZASKIS
SODAS
JARRITOS
AGUAS
TACOS .. BIRRIA
TORTAS .. LENGUA
ANTOJOS . TRIPA
SODAS
HOT
HOTEL

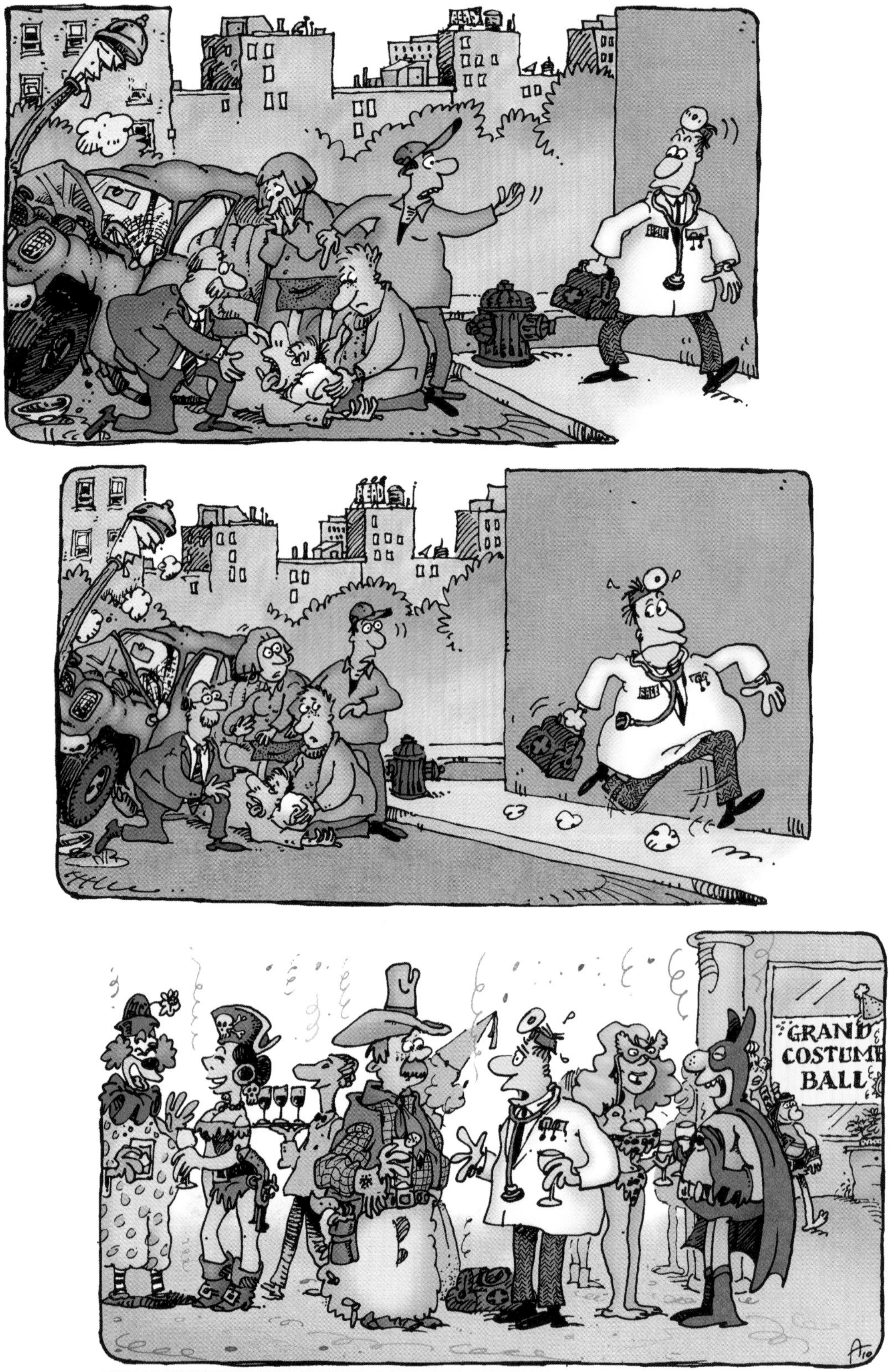
GRAND COSTUME BALL

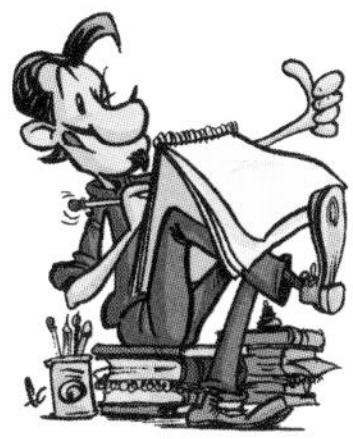

FRANK CAMMUSO

Rock, Scissors, Paper

from *Knights of the Lunch Table*

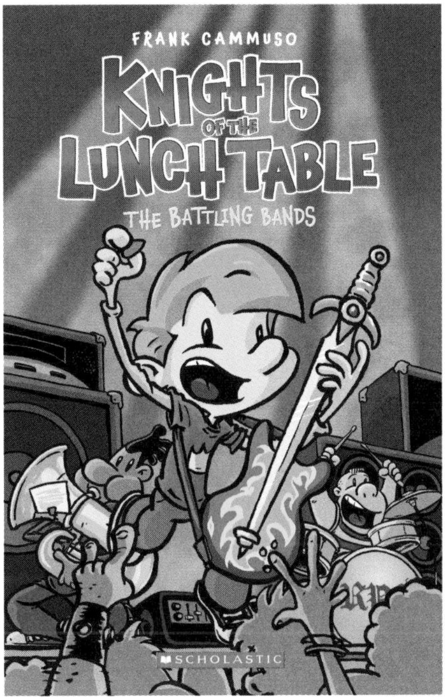
FRANK CAMMUSO
KNIGHTS OF THE LUNCH TABLE
THE BATTLING BANDS
SCHOLASTIC

FOR ME, DRAWING COMICS IS

The only thing I know how to do.

THE SELECTION

A short scene from the kids' graphic novel *Knights of the Lunch Table #3: The Battling Bands.*

THE CONTEXT

Class geek Artie King is desperately trying to avoid school bully Joe Roman—who is on the rampage because Artie accidentally broke his guitar.

WHAT I'M KNOWN FOR

Max Hamm Fairy Tale Detective; *Otto's Orange Day*; Knights of the Lunch Table series; and twenty years of political cartooning for the *Post-Standard.*

WHERE I LIVE

Syracuse, New York.

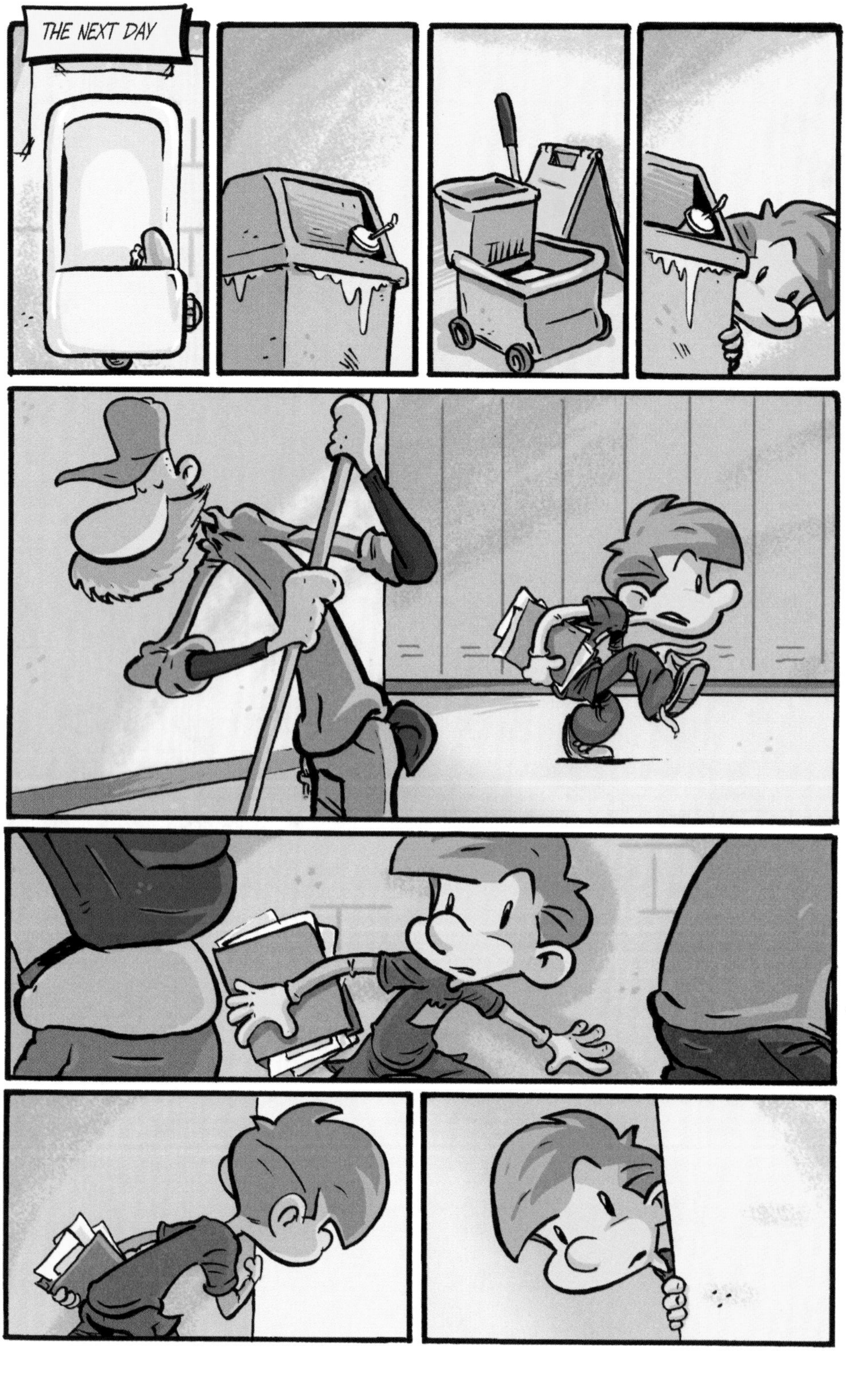
THE NEXT DAY

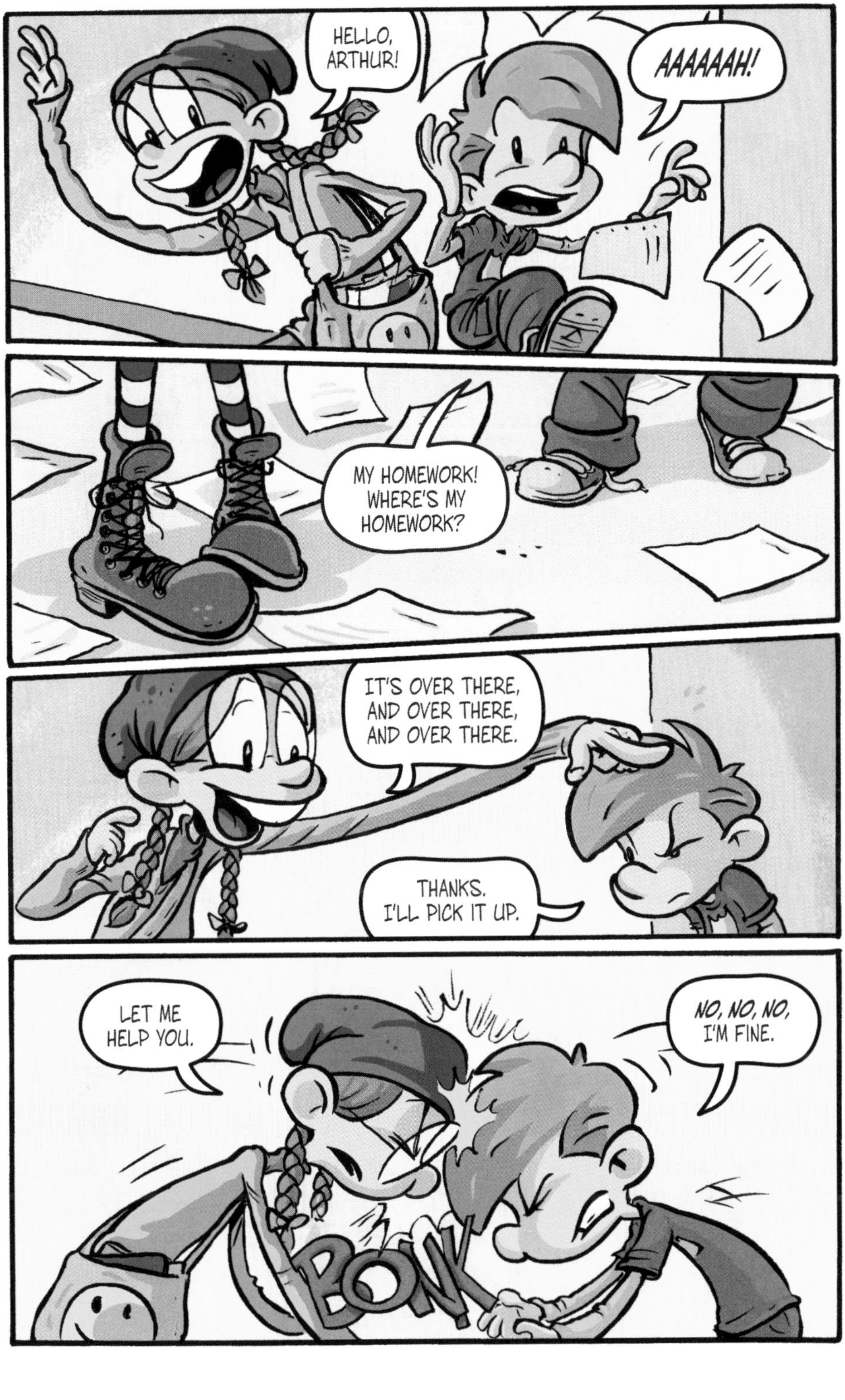

HELLO, ARTHUR!
AAAAAAH!
MY HOMEWORK! WHERE'S MY HOMEWORK?
IT'S OVER THERE, AND OVER THERE, AND OVER THERE.
THANKS. I'LL PICK IT UP.
LET ME HELP YOU.
NO, NO, NO, I'M FINE.
BONK

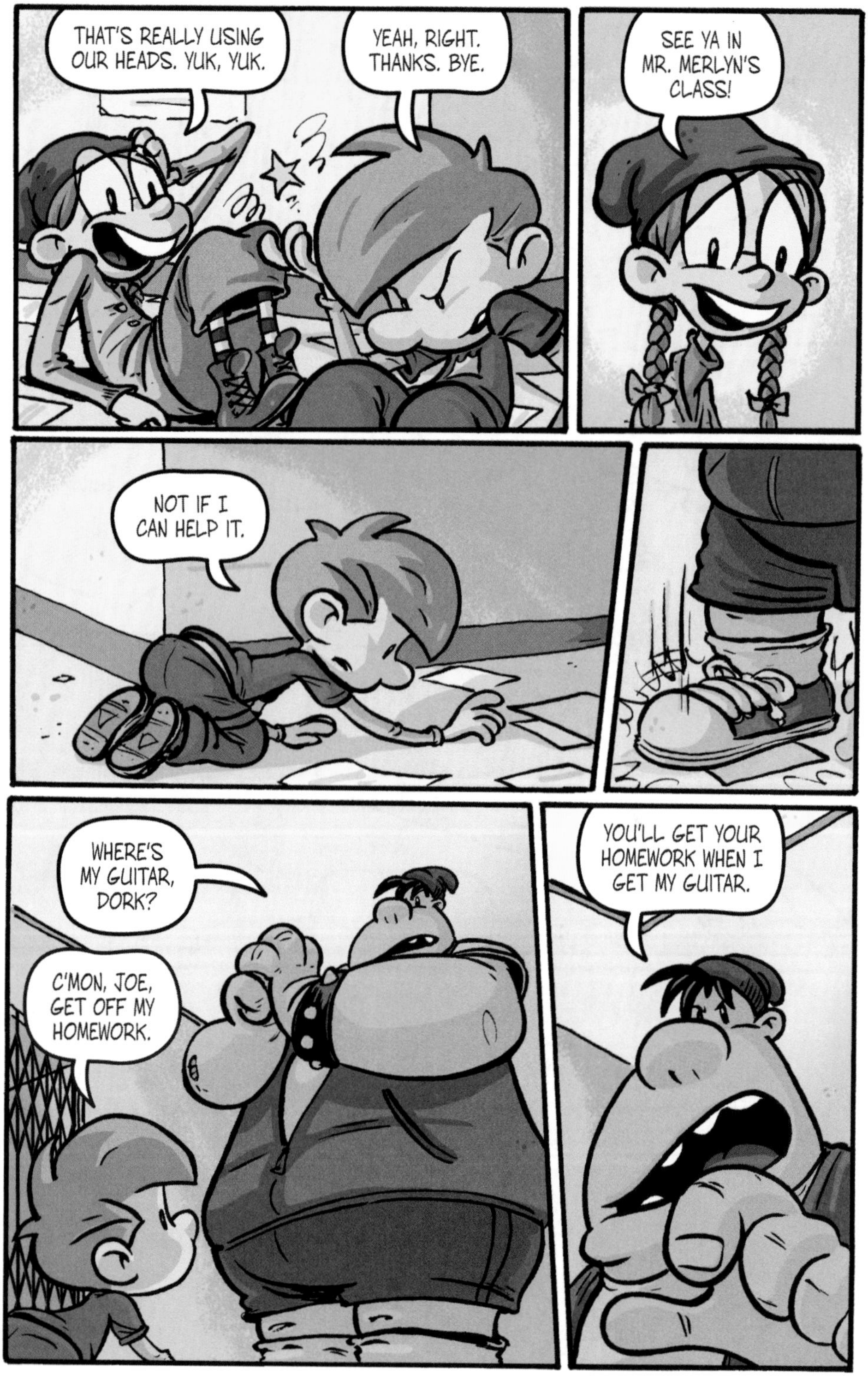
THAT'S REALLY USING OUR HEADS. YUK, YUK.
YEAH, RIGHT. THANKS. BYE.
SEE YA IN MR. MERLYN'S CLASS!
NOT IF I CAN HELP IT.
WHERE'S MY GUITAR, DORK?
C'MON, JOE, GET OFF MY HOMEWORK.
YOU'LL GET YOUR HOMEWORK WHEN I GET MY GUITAR.

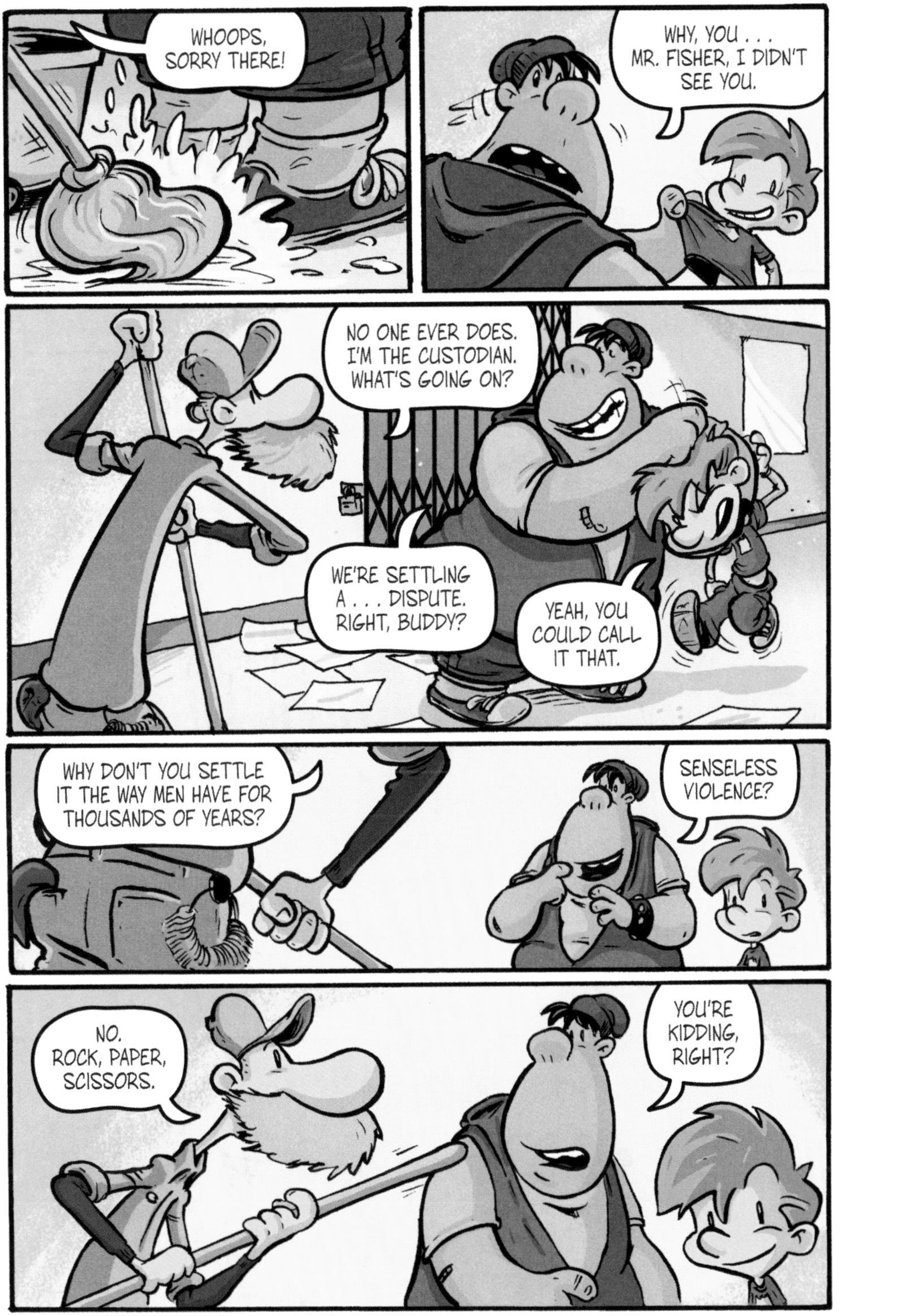
WHOOPS, SORRY THERE!
WHY, YOU . . . MR. FISHER, I DIDN'T SEE YOU.
NO ONE EVER DOES. I'M THE CUSTODIAN. WHAT'S GOING ON?
WE'RE SETTLING A . . . DISPUTE. RIGHT, BUDDY?
YEAH, YOU COULD CALL IT THAT.
WHY DON'T YOU SETTLE IT THE WAY MEN HAVE FOR THOUSANDS OF YEARS?
SENSELESS VIOLENCE?
NO. ROCK, PAPER, SCISSORS.
YOU'RE KIDDING, RIGHT?

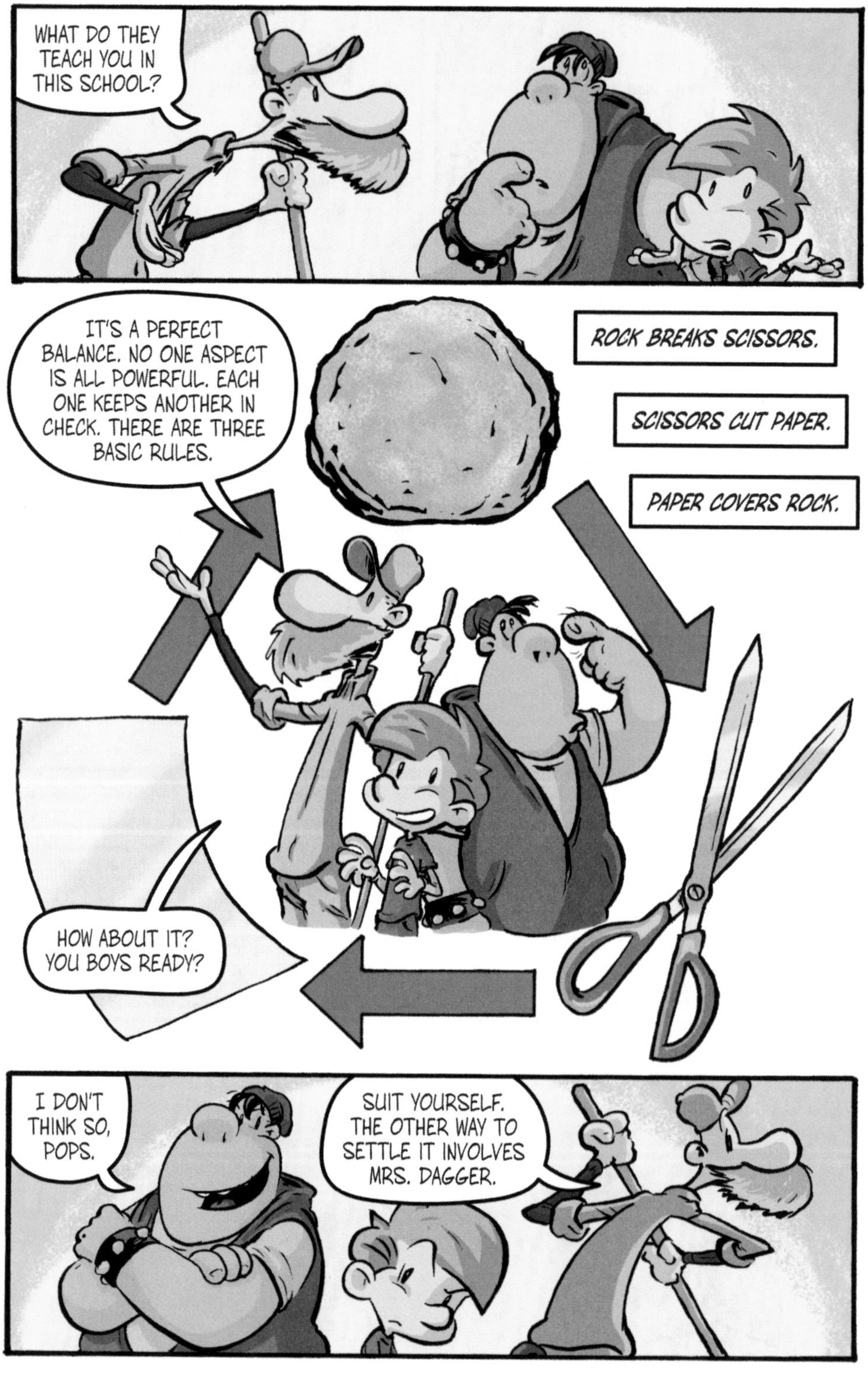
WHAT DO THEY TEACH YOU IN THIS SCHOOL?
IT'S A PERFECT BALANCE. NO ONE ASPECT IS ALL POWERFUL. EACH ONE KEEPS ANOTHER IN CHECK. THERE ARE THREE BASIC RULES.
ROCK BREAKS SCISSORS.
SCISSORS CUT PAPER.
PAPER COVERS ROCK.
HOW ABOUT IT? YOU BOYS READY?
I DON'T THINK SO, POPS.
SUIT YOURSELF. THE OTHER WAY TO SETTLE IT INVOLVES MRS. DAGGER.

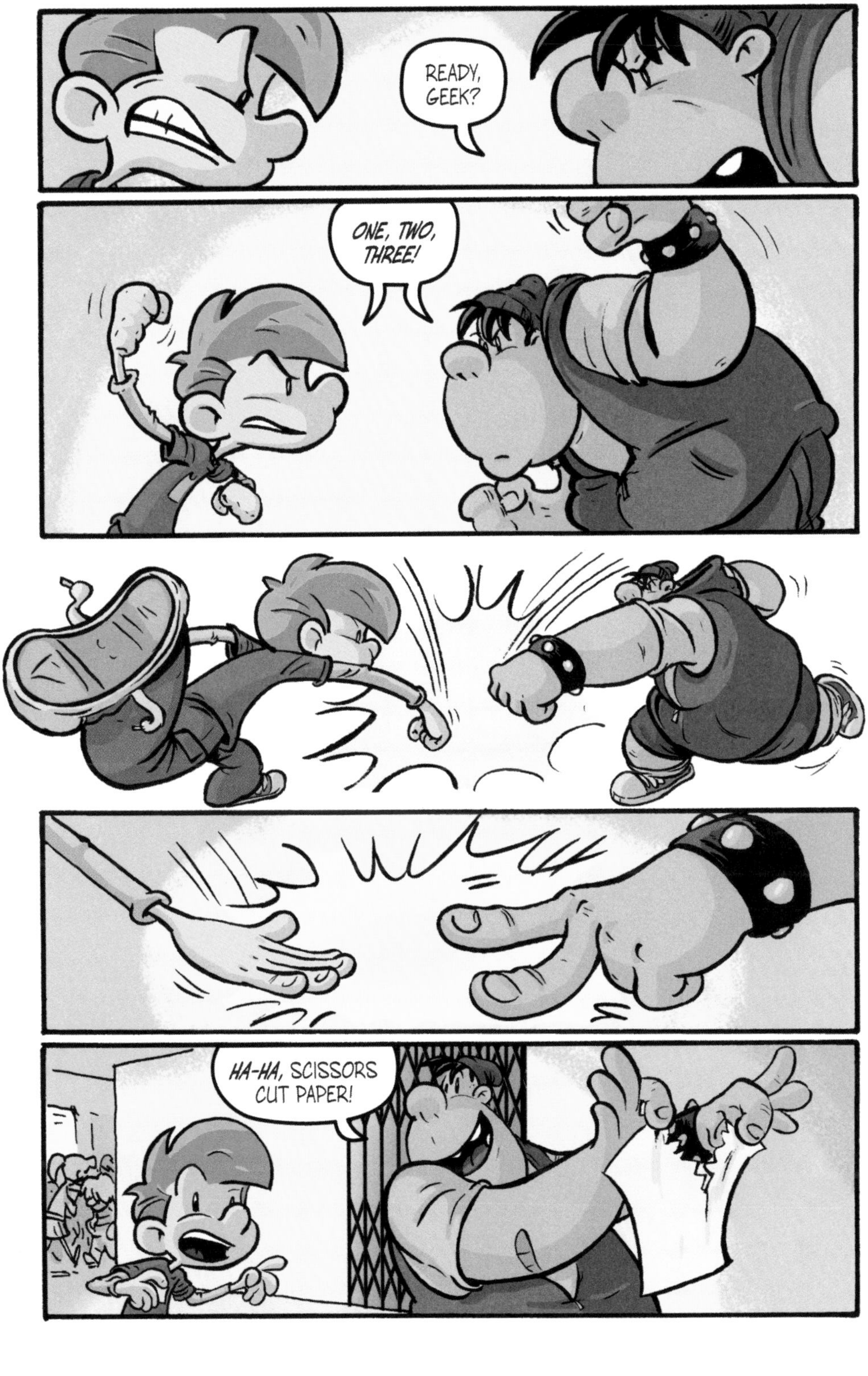
READY, GEEK?
ONE, TWO, THREE!
HA-HA, SCISSORS CUT PAPER!

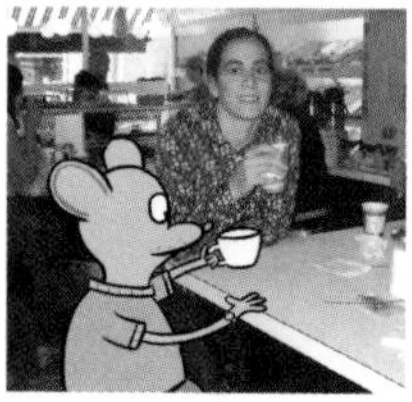

SARA VARON

Baking Failure #1

from *Bake Sale*

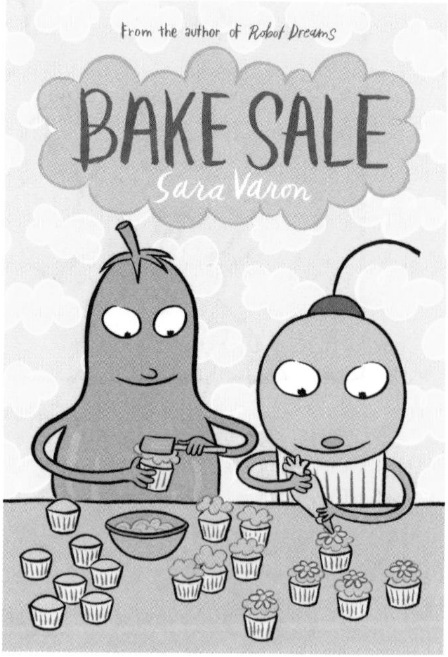
From the author of Robot Dreams
BAKE SALE
Sara Varon

FOR ME, DRAWING COMICS IS

1. A way for the characters in my head to come alive.
2. A really great job.

THE SELECTION

Bake Sale is the story of a cupcake who longs to travel abroad to meet the pastry of his dreams. He is convinced that this celebrity pastry will reveal the answers he is seeking, but he ultimately finds that the solution to his problems is hiding close to home.

THE CONTEXT

The main character is in the midst of trying unsuccessfully to diversify his baking skills.

WHAT I'M KNOWN FOR

The children's books *Chicken and Cat* and *Chicken and Cat Clean Up*; and the graphic novels *Sweaterweather, Robot Dreams,* and *Bake Sale.*

WHERE I LIVE

Brooklyn, New York.

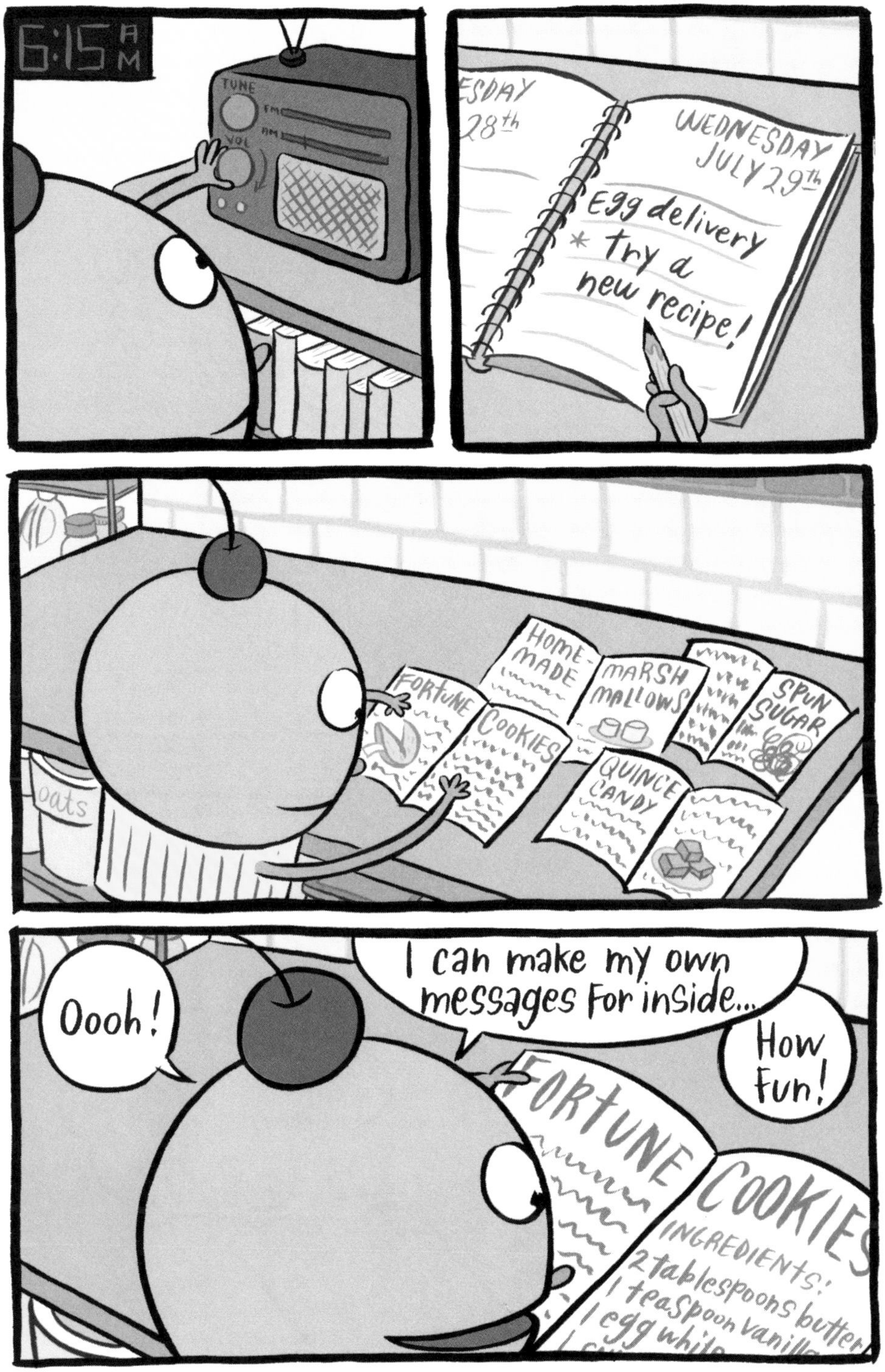
6:15 AM
TUNE
FM
AM
VOL
ESDAY
28th
WEDNESDAY
JULY 29th
Egg delivery
* try a new recipe!
HOME-MADE
MARSHMALLOWS
SPUN SUGAR
FORTUNE COOKIES
QUINCE CANDY
oats
Oooh!
I can make my own messages for inside...
How Fun!
FORTUNE COOKIES
INGREDIENTS:
2 tablespoons butter
1 teaspoon vanill
1 egg whit

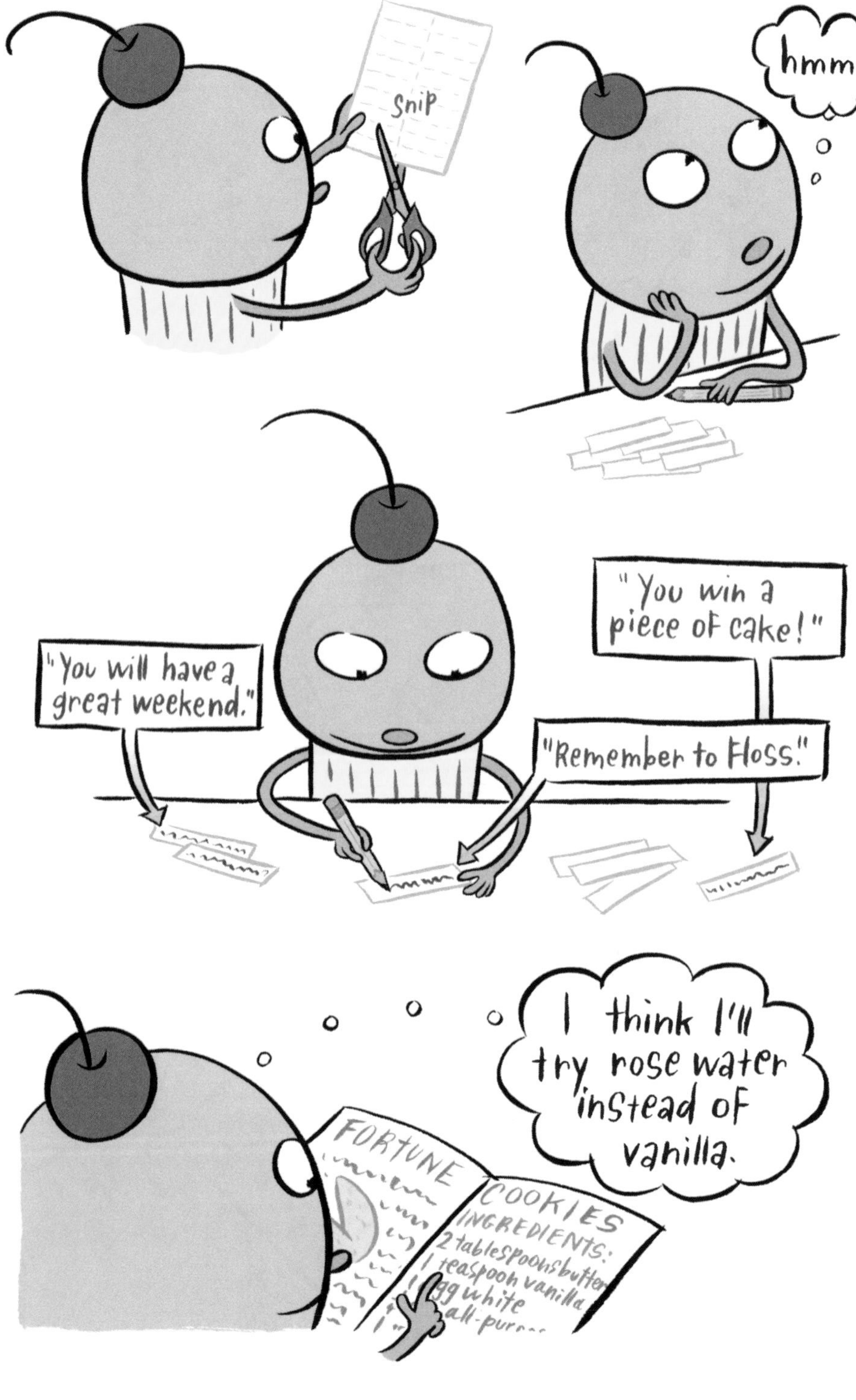
snip
hmm...
"You will have a great weekend."
"You win a piece of cake!"
"Remember to Floss."
I think I'll try rose water instead of vanilla.
FORTUNE COOKIES
INGREDIENTS:
2 tablespoons butter
1 teaspoon vanilla

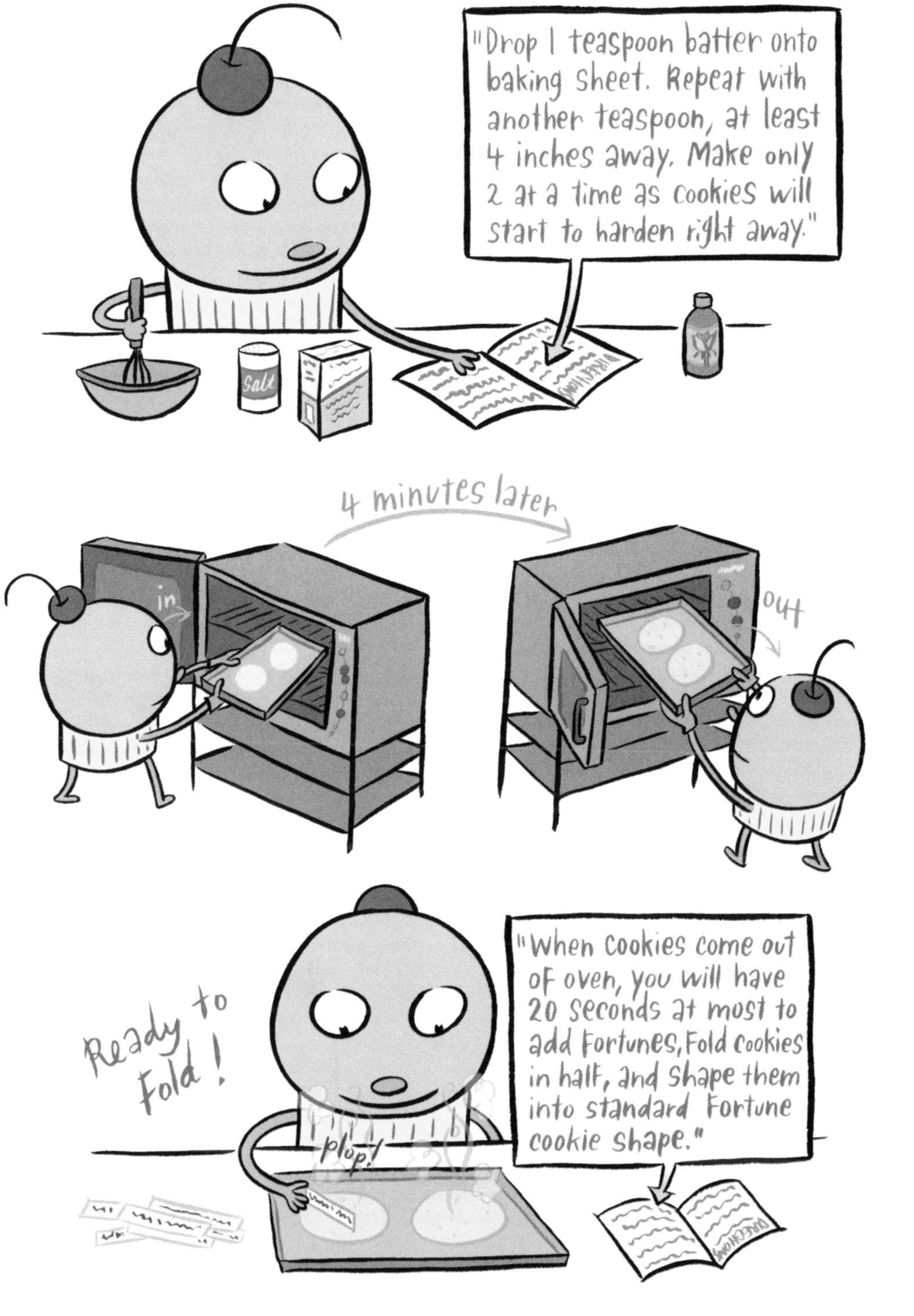

"Drop 1 teaspoon batter onto baking sheet. Repeat with another teaspoon, at least 4 inches away. Make only 2 at a time as cookies will start to harden right away."
Salt
4 minutes later
in
out
Ready to Fold!
"When cookies come out of oven, you will have 20 seconds at most to add fortunes, fold cookies in half, and shape them into standard fortune cookie shape."
plop!

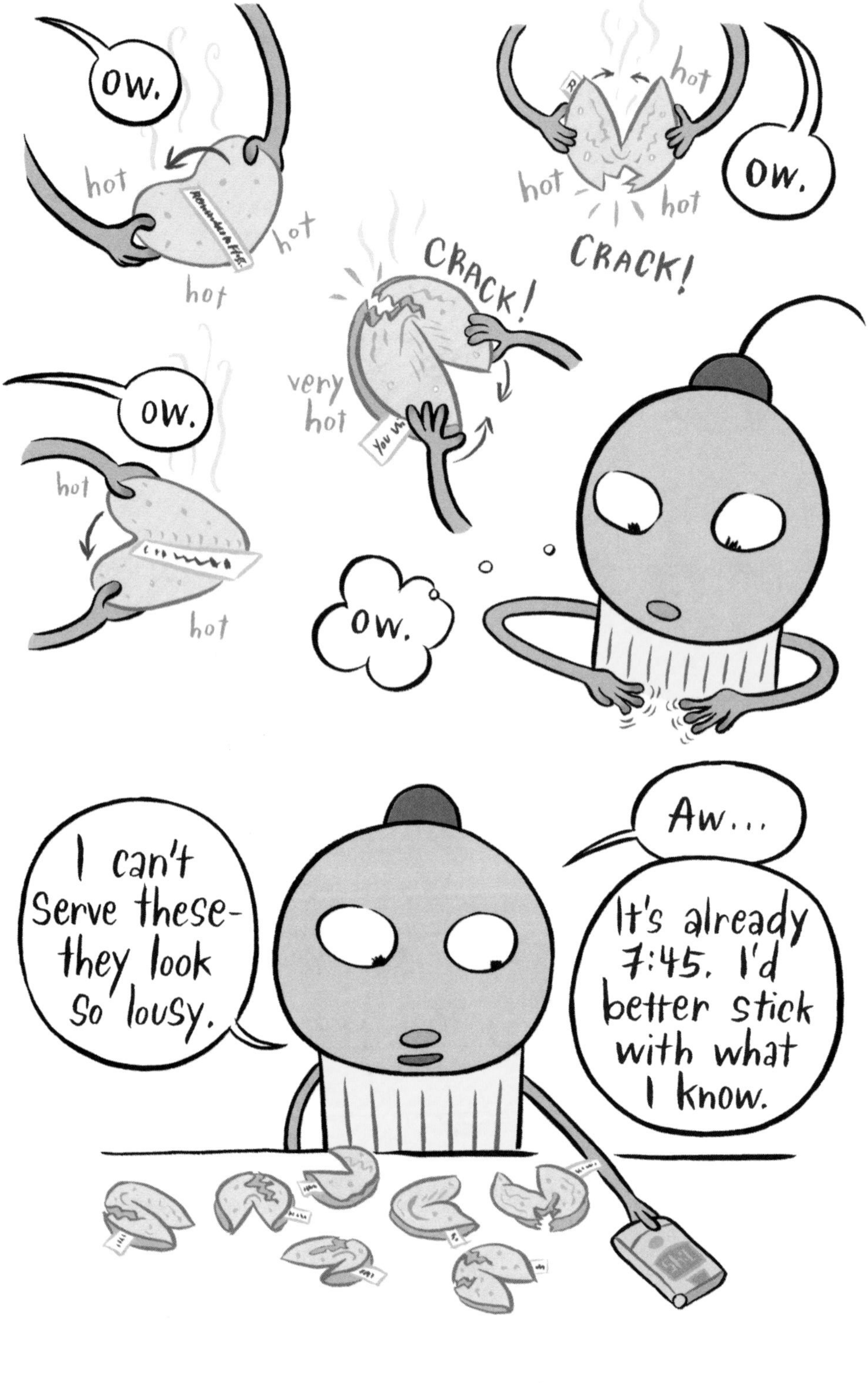
OW.
hot
hot
hot
hot
OW.
hot
hot
hot
CRACK!
OW.
CRACK!
very hot
OW.
hot
hot
OW.
I can't serve these- they look so lousy.
Aw...
It's already 7:45. I'd better stick with what I know.

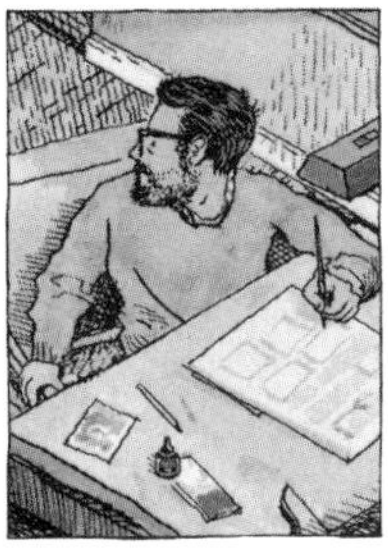

MICHAEL J. BUCKLEY

Read a Book / Draw Your Sister a Picture

from *60 Ways to Leave Your Mother (Alone)*

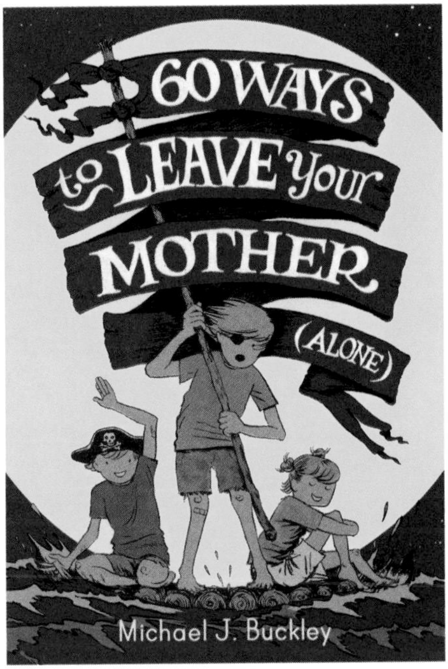
60 WAYS to LEAVE your MOTHER (ALONE)
Michael J. Buckley

FOR ME, DRAWING COMICS IS

Comics are many small tasks that must be done. Maybe comics are the many things that must be done before you can load a brush with ink? Sometimes it seems that way. The act of loading a brush with ink, the act of drawing, doesn't cause carpal tunnel like a keyboard. A puzzle without the box top. If I don't draw or work on the tasks, I am unhappy. You are unhappy.

THE SELECTION

I find it exasperating when my kids bicker over the plainest of activities—like reading a book. But I do enjoy drawing these imaginary slapstick fights!

THE CONTEXT

60 Ways was originally a list of things to do, literally, a list of things to do so as not to bother your mother, written by my wife for our kids. It's a tongue-in-cheek take on a theme familiar to any parent.

WHERE I LIVE

Kansas City, Missouri.

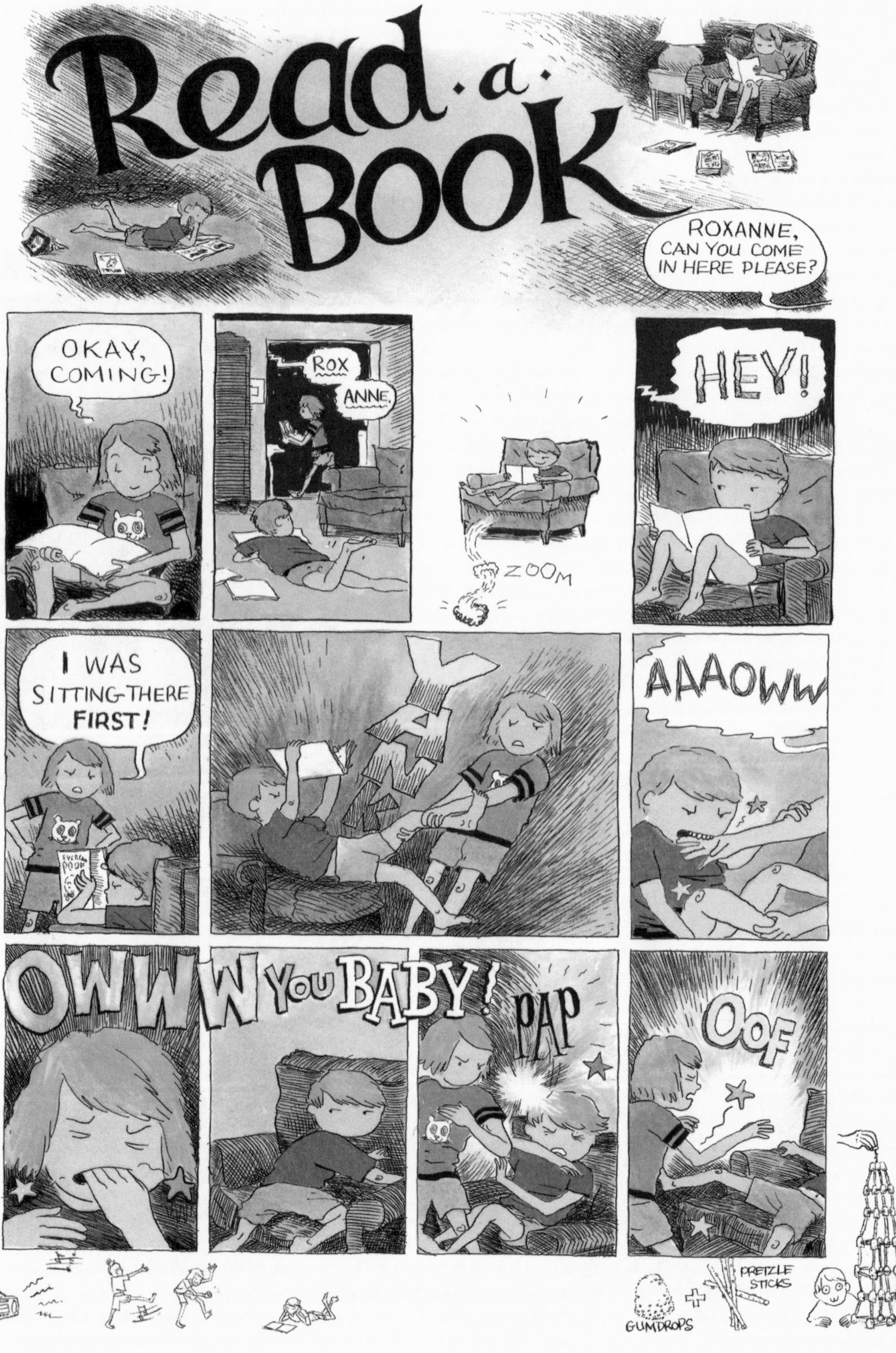
Read a Book
ROXANNE, CAN YOU COME IN HERE PLEASE?
OKAY, COMING!
ROX
ANNE,
ZOOM
HEY!
I WAS SITTING THERE FIRST!
AAAOWW
OWWW
YOU BABY!
PAP
OOF
PRETZLE STICKS
GUMDROPS

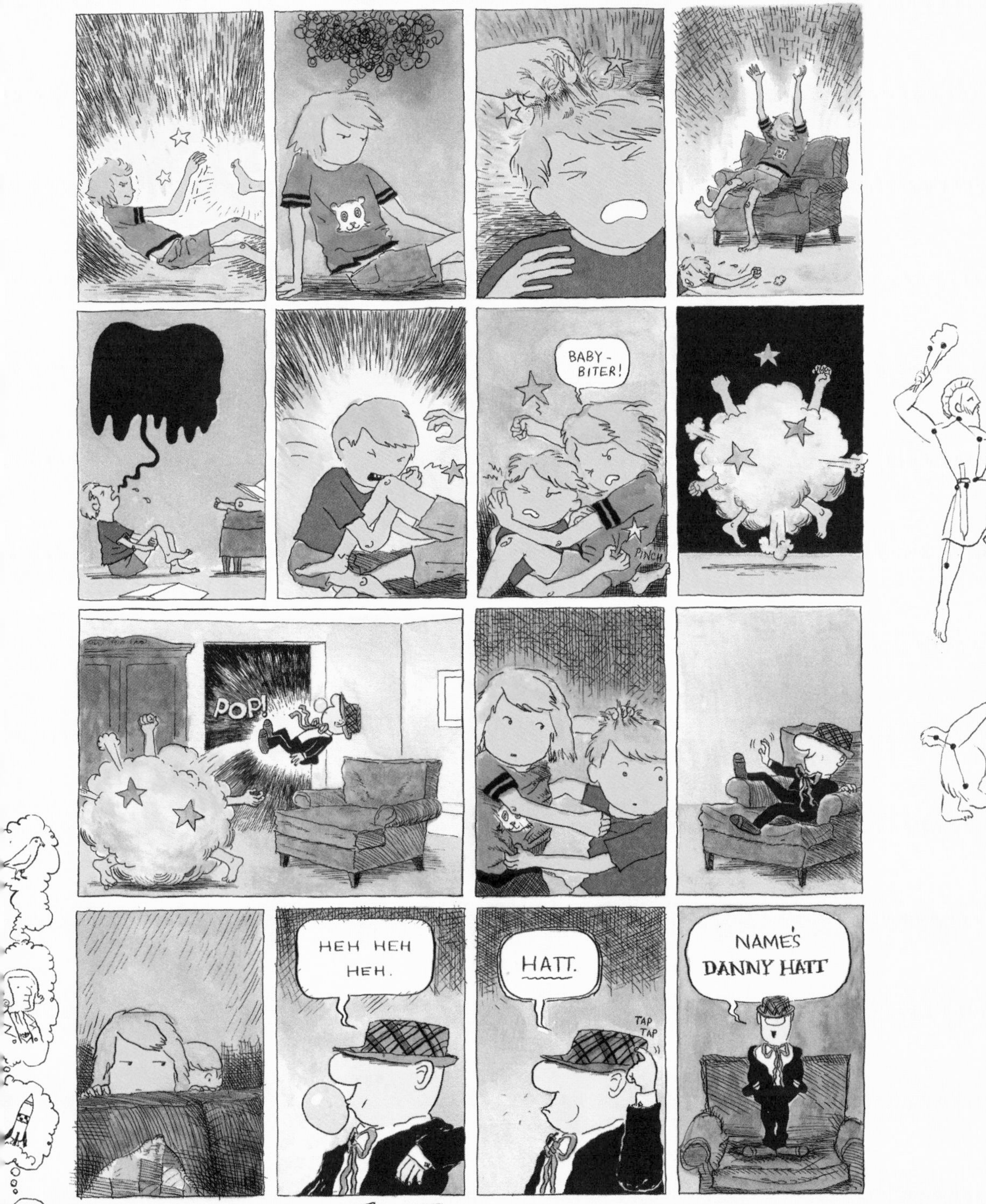
BABY-BITER!
PINCH
POP!
HEH HEH HEH.
HATT.
TAP TAP
NAME'S DANNY HATT
LIBRARY
Birds
GREAT INVENTORS
SPACE

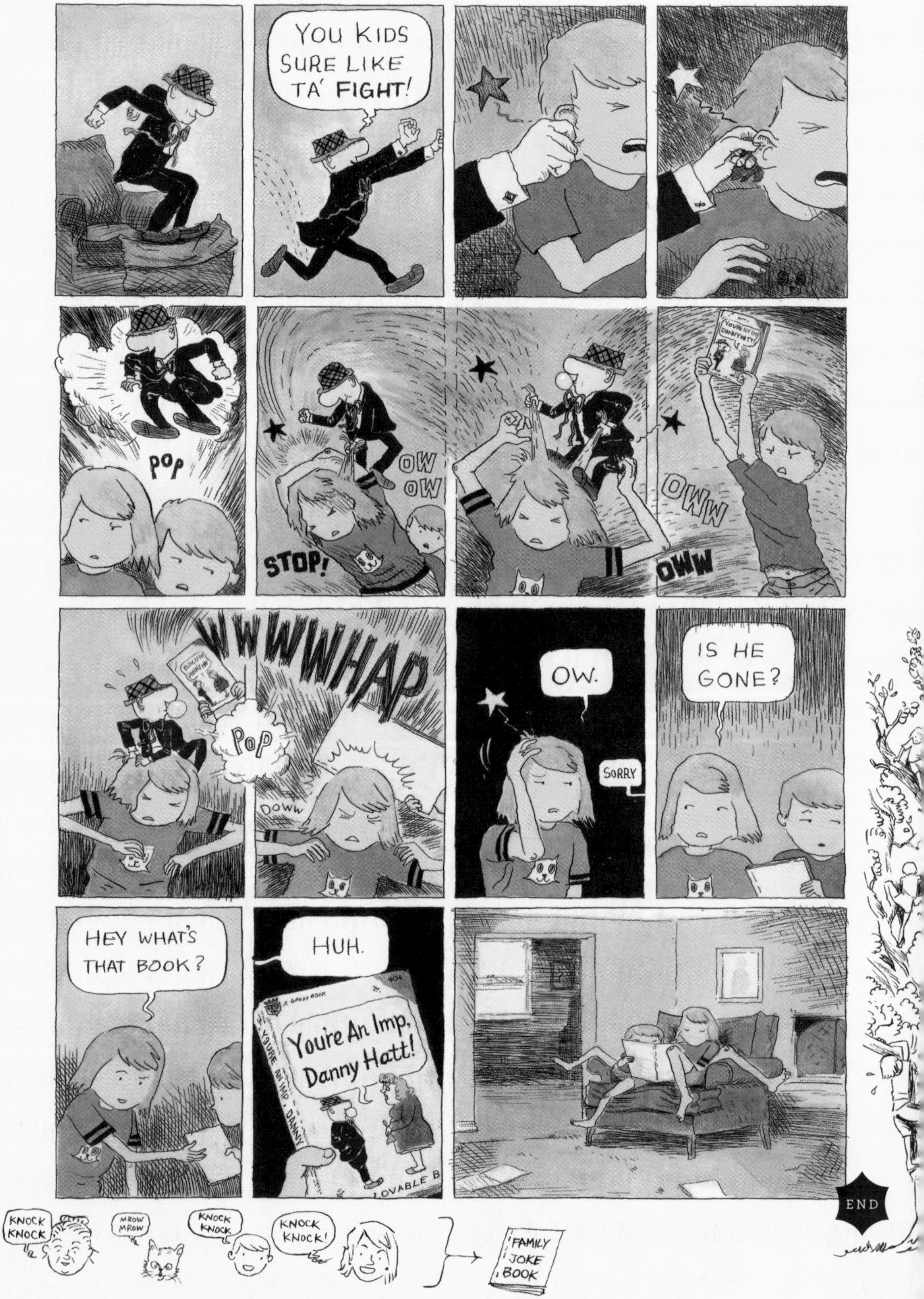

YOU KIDS SURE LIKE TA' FIGHT!
POP
OW OW
STOP!
OWW
OWW
WWWWHAP
POP
OW.
SORRY
IS HE GONE?
HEY WHAT'S THAT BOOK?
HUH.
A GREAT BOOK
You're An Imp, Danny Hatt!
LOVABLE B
END
KNOCK KNOCK
MROW MROW
KNOCK KNOCK
KNOCK KNOCK!
FAMILY JOKE BOOK

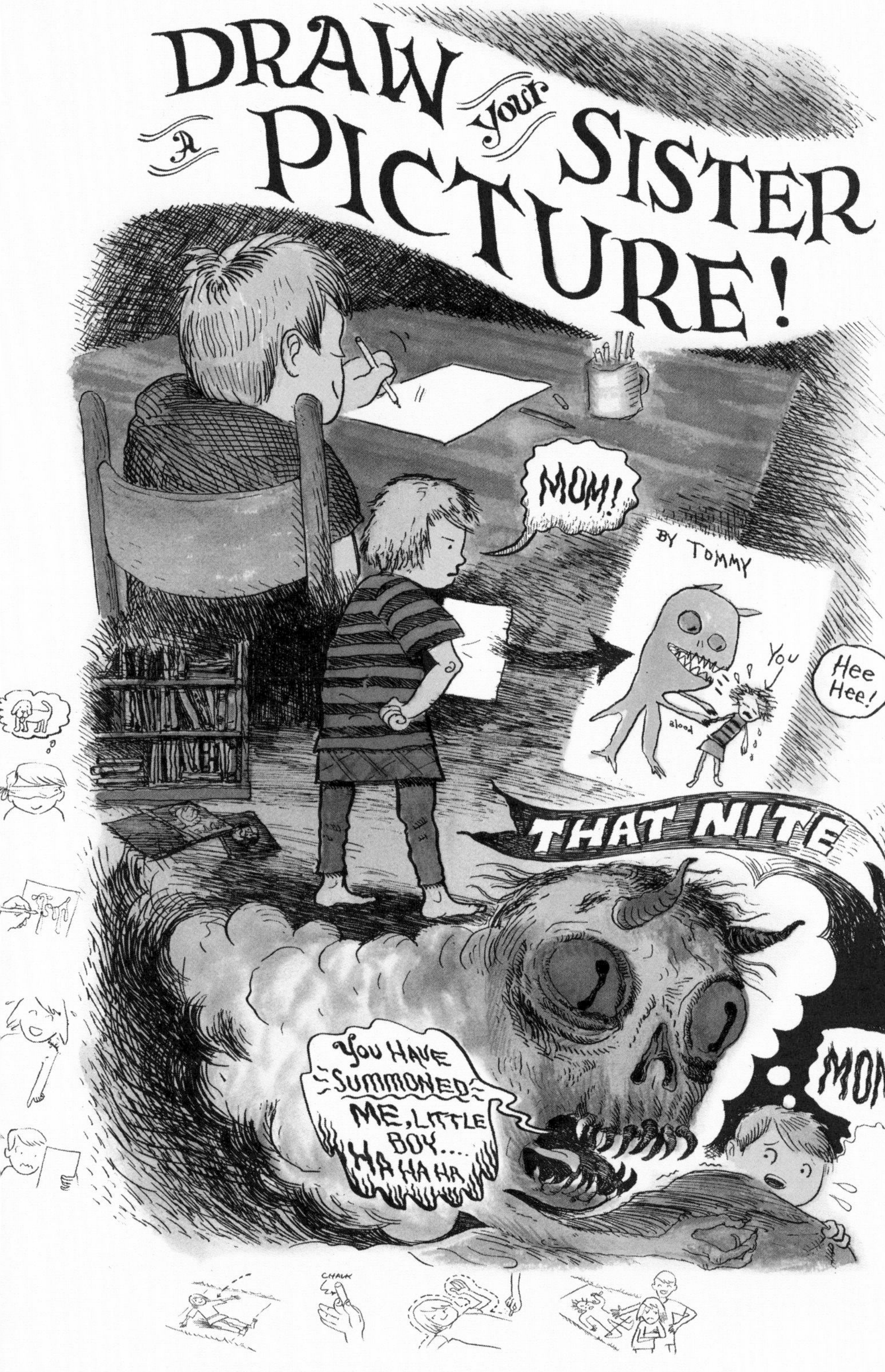
DRAW your SISTER A PICTURE!
MOM!
BY TOMMY
You
blood
Hee Hee!
THAT NITE
YOU HAVE SUMMONED ME, LITTLE BOY.... HA HA HA
MOM
CHALK

GEOFFREY HAYES

Patrick and Big Bear

from *Patrick in a Teddy Bear's Picnic and Other Stories*

PATRICK
IN
A TEDDY BEAR'S PICNIC
and other stories
Ma, today the park is all *ours*!
A TOON BOOK BY
GEOFFREY HAYES

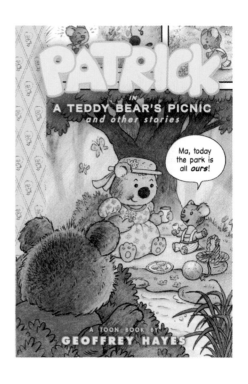

FOR ME, DRAWING COMICS IS

As natural as breathing and more satisfying than any other type of storytelling.

THE SELECTION

When Patrick's mother sends him to the store to buy cookies, he encounters Big Bear, the neighborhood bully. Patrick finds a way to escape Big Bear and express his inner dragon.

THE CONTEXT

Earlier, Big Bear popped Patrick's red balloon, and Patrick is intimidated by him.

WHAT I'M KNOWN FOR

Otto and Uncle Tooth Step Into Reading series; *Bear by Himself*; *Patrick Eats His Dinner*; *Thump and Plunk*.

WHERE I LIVE

Brooklyn, New York.

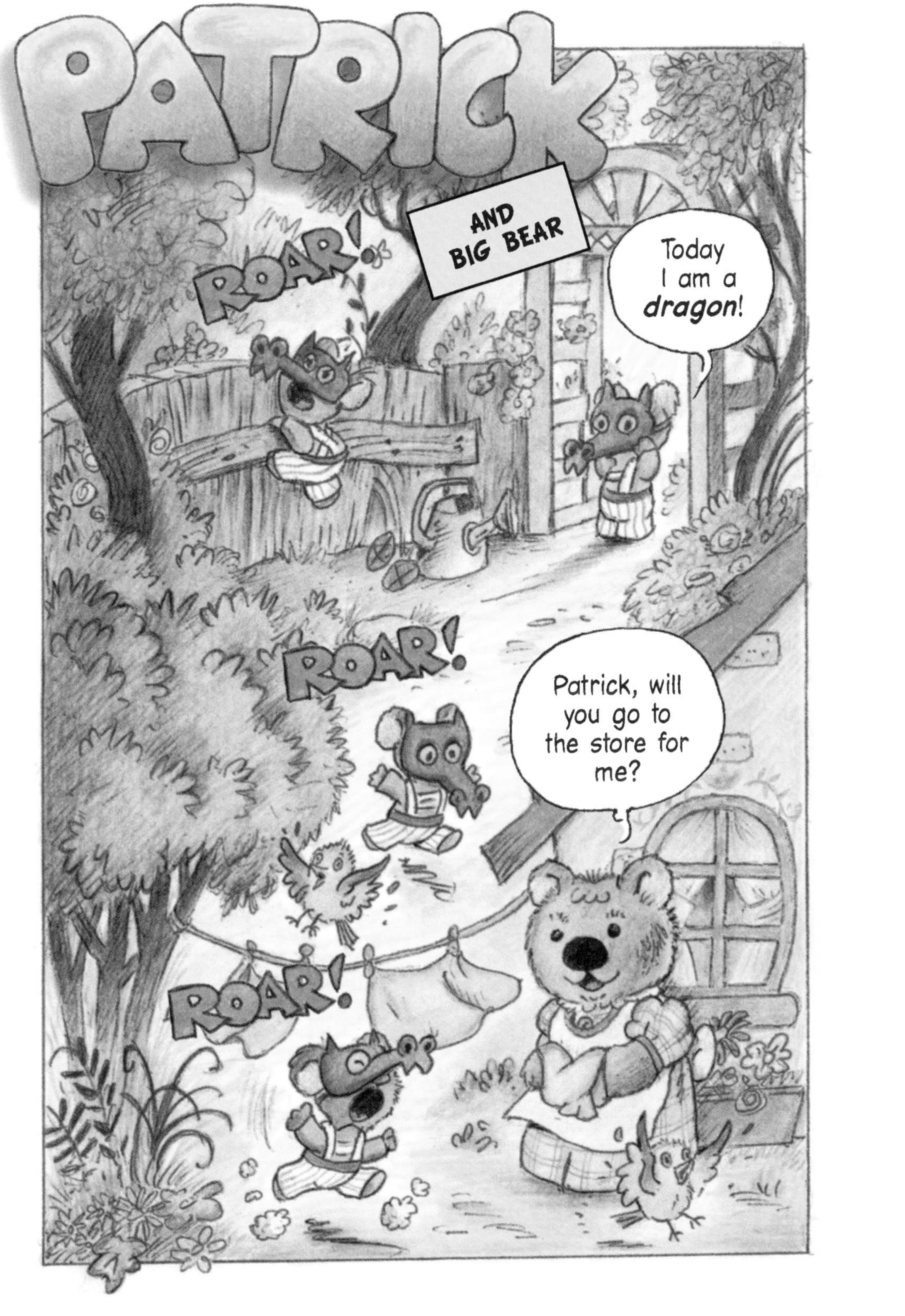
PATRICK
AND BIG BEAR
ROAR!
Today I am a *dragon*!
ROAR!
Patrick, will you go to the store for me?
ROAR!

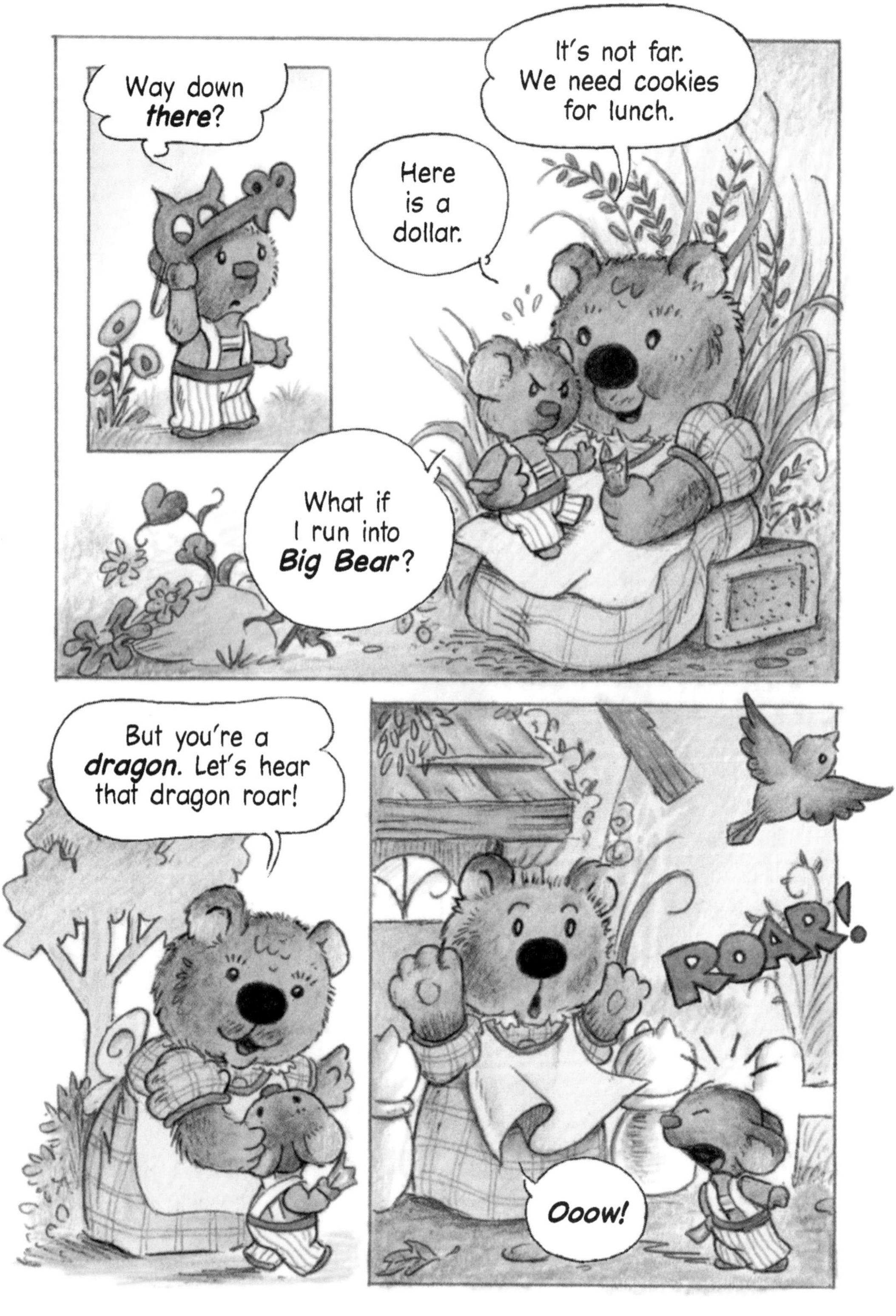
Way down ***there***?
It's not far. We need cookies for lunch.
Here is a dollar.
What if I run into ***Big Bear***?
But you're a ***dragon***. Let's hear that dragon roar!
ROAR!
Ooow!

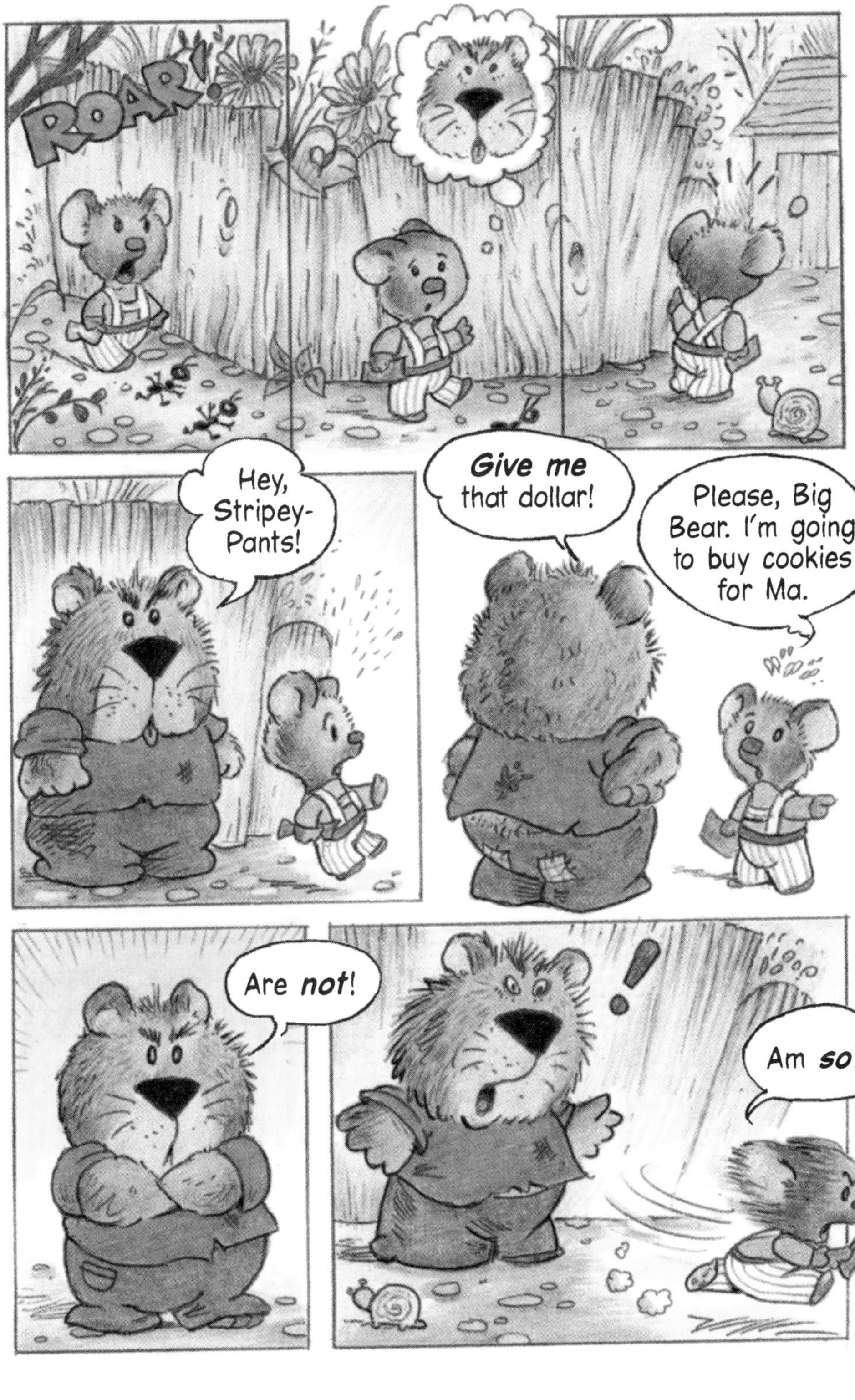
ROAR!
Hey, Stripey-Pants!
Give me that dollar!
Please, Big Bear. I'm going to buy cookies for Ma.
Are not!
Am so!

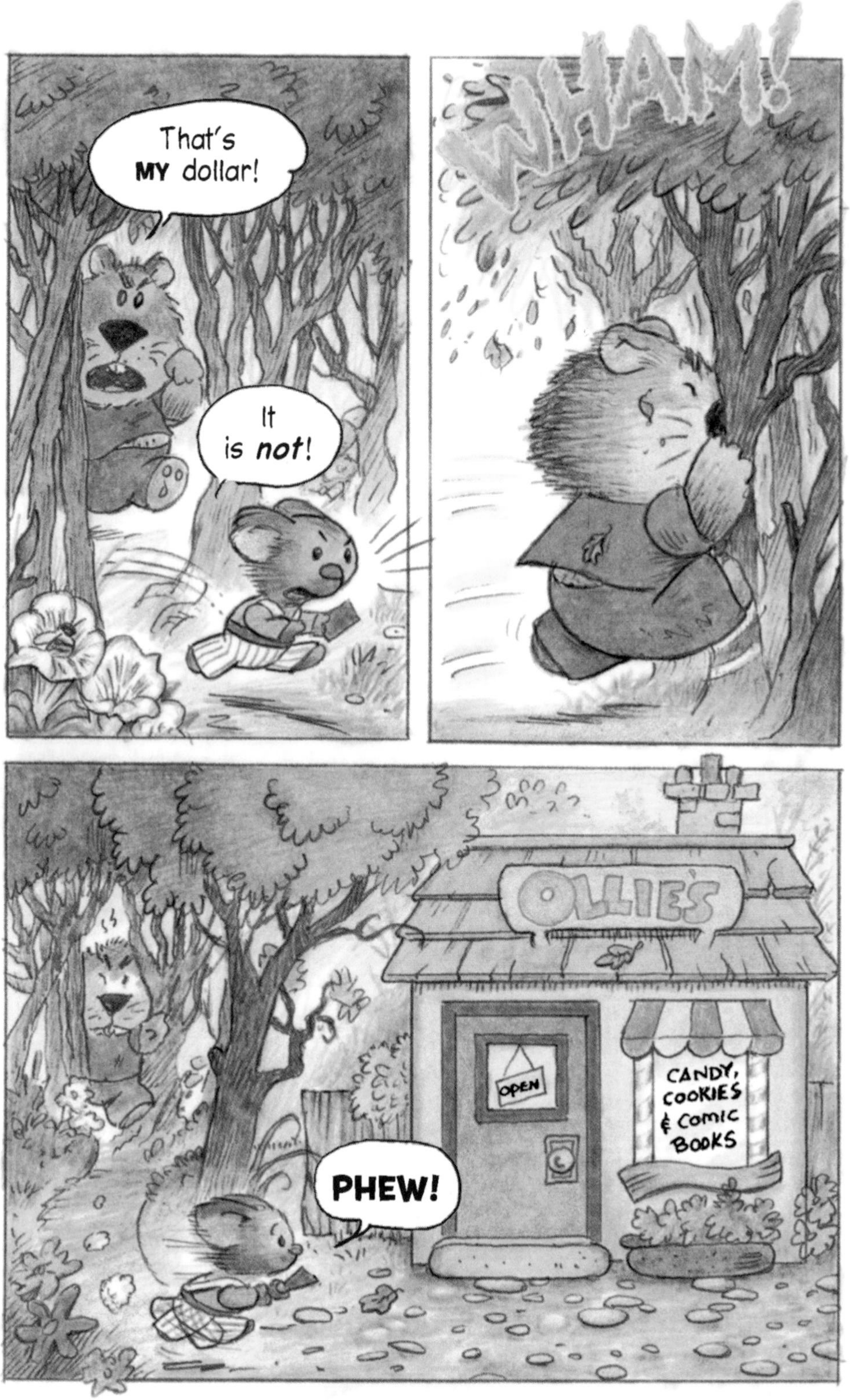
That's **MY** dollar!
It is *not*!
WHAM!
OLLIE'S
OPEN
CANDY, COOKIES & COMIC BOOKS
PHEW!

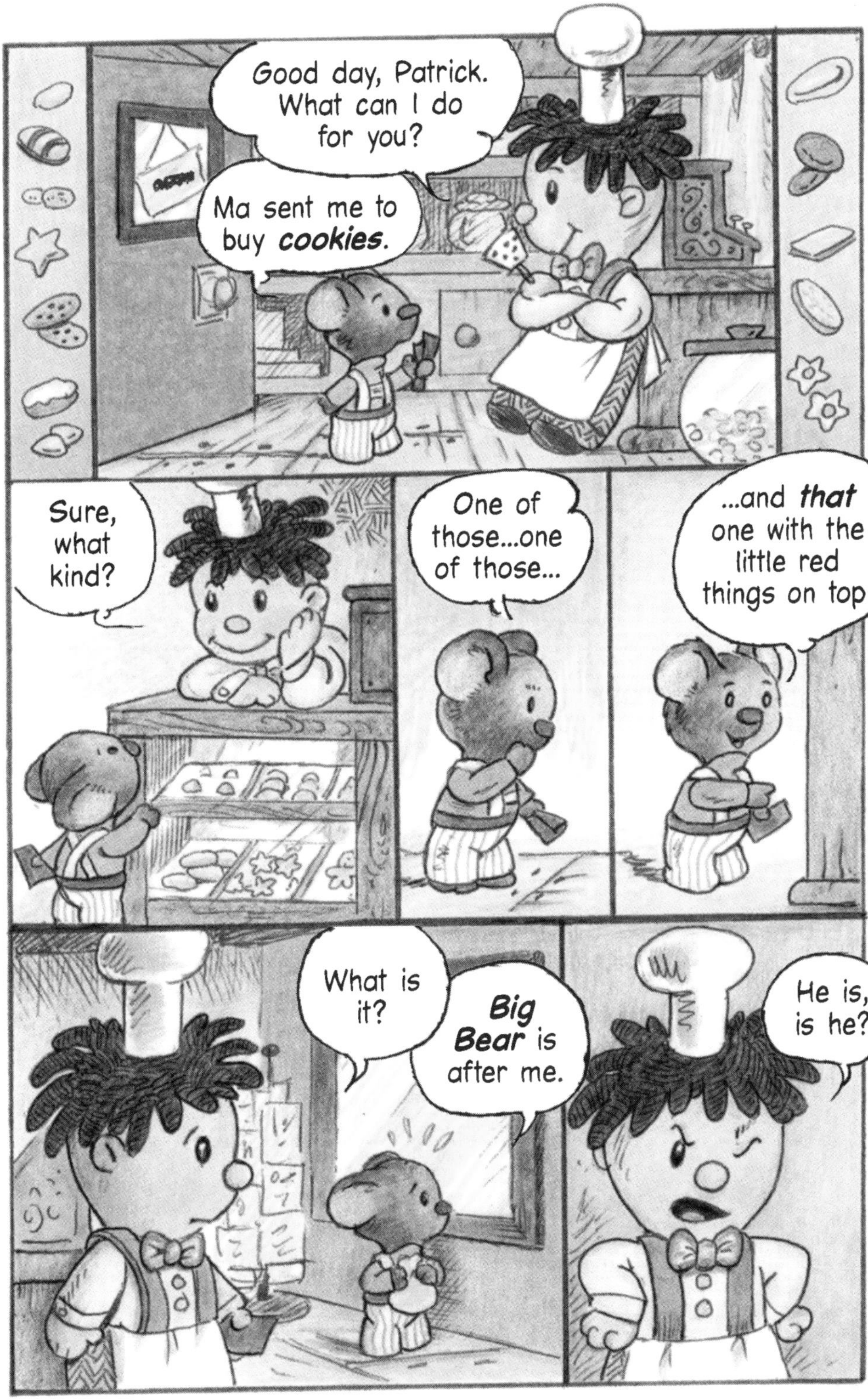
Good day, Patrick. What can I do for you?
Ma sent me to buy ***cookies***.
Sure, what kind?
One of those...one of those...
...and ***that*** one with the little red things on top.
What is it?
Big Bear is after me.
He is, is he?

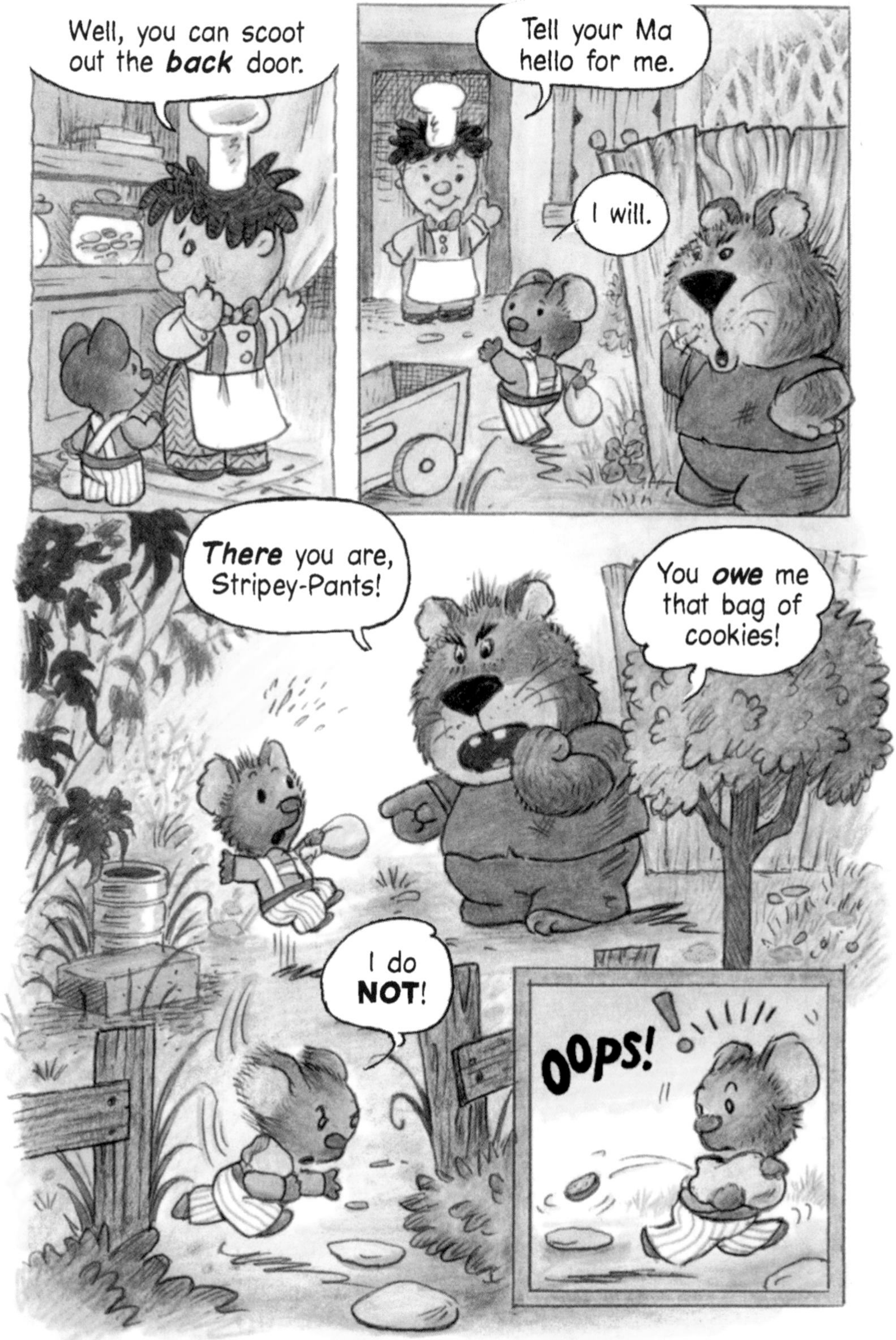
Well, you can scoot out the ***back*** door.
Tell your Ma hello for me.
I will.
There you are, Stripey-Pants!
You ***owe*** me that bag of cookies!
I do **NOT**!
OOPS!

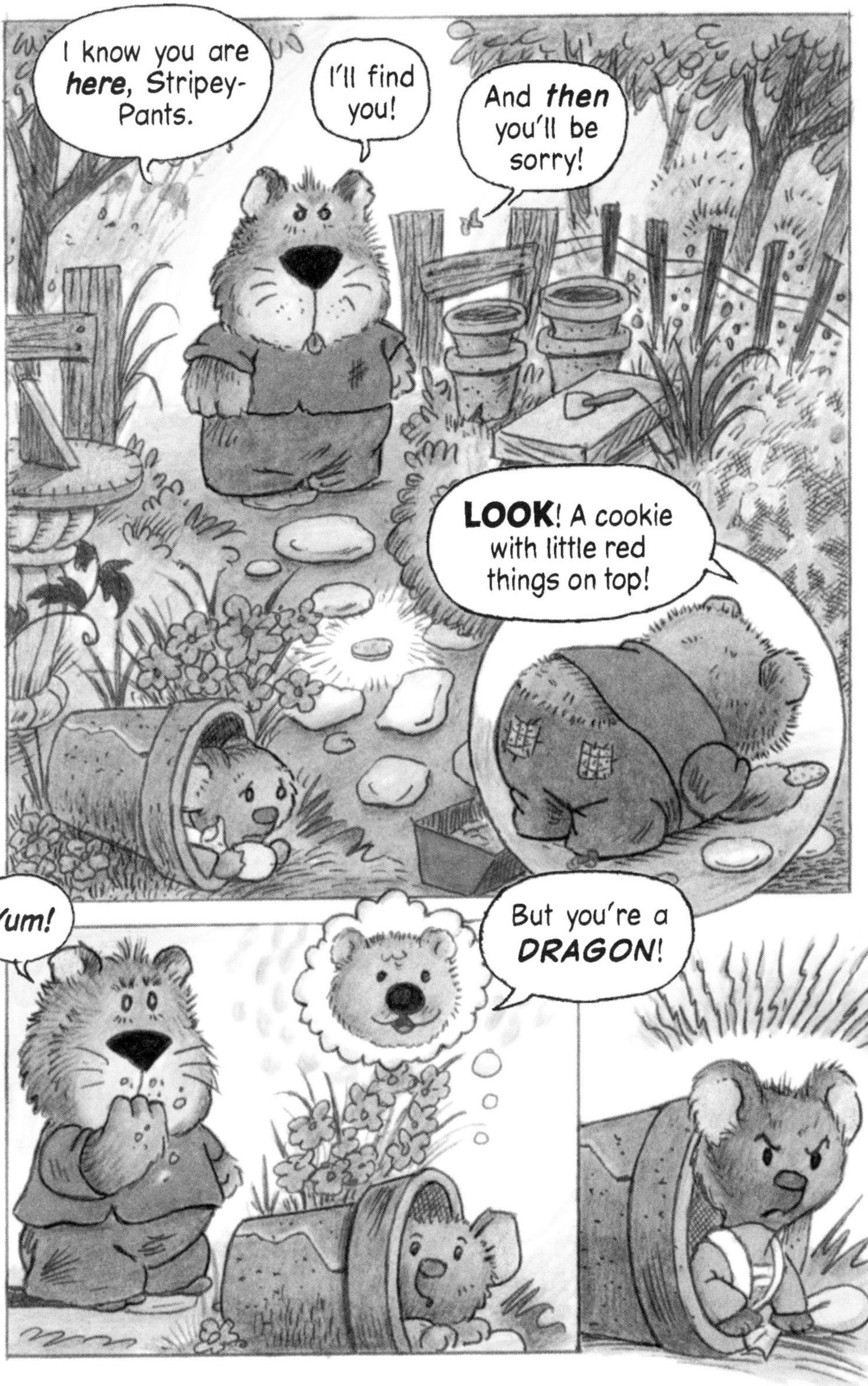
I know you are here, Stripey-Pants.
I'll find you!
And then you'll be sorry!
LOOK! A cookie with little red things on top!
Yum!
But you're a DRAGON!

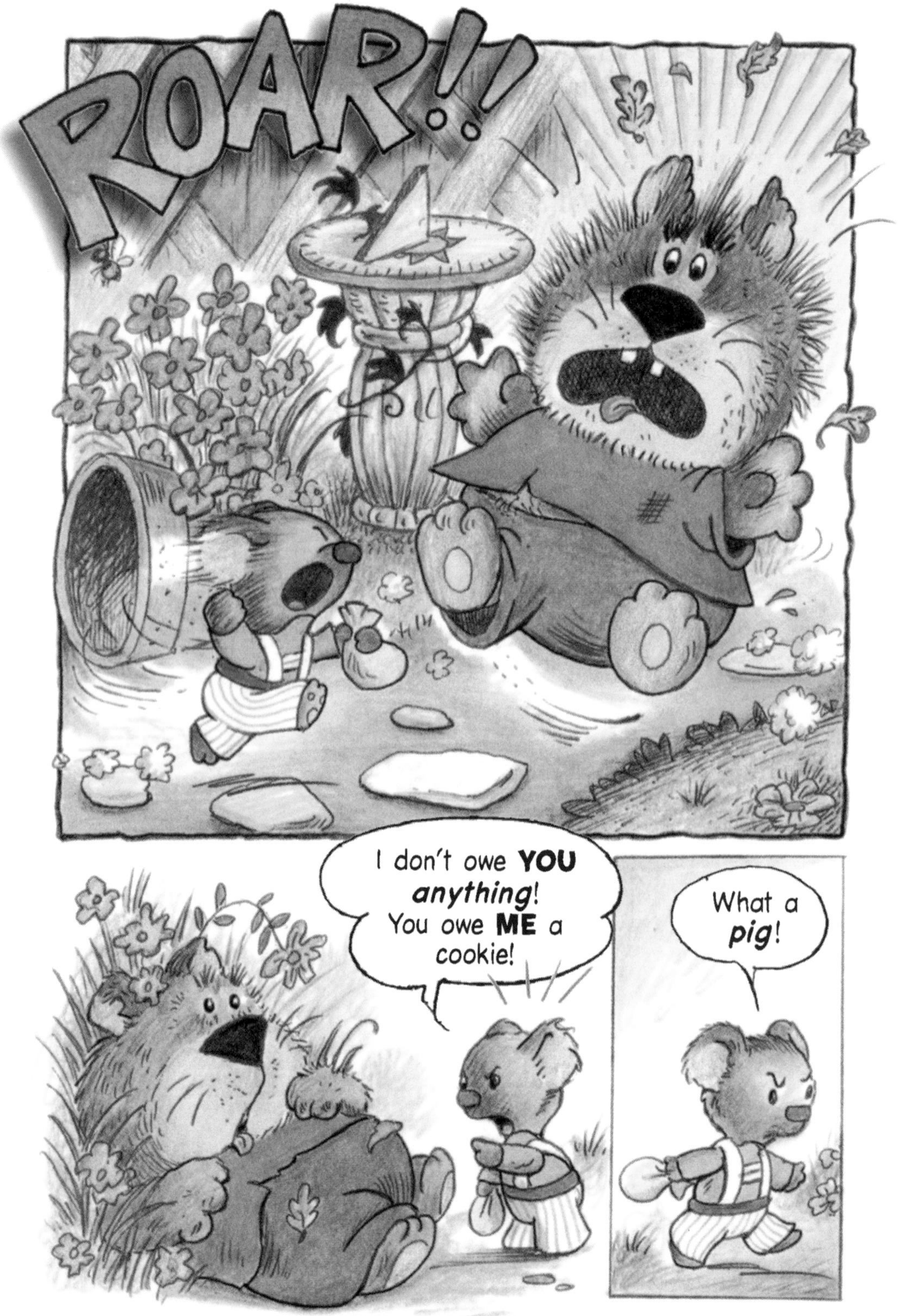
ROAR!!
I don't owe **YOU** ***anything***! You owe **ME** a cookie!
What a ***pig***!

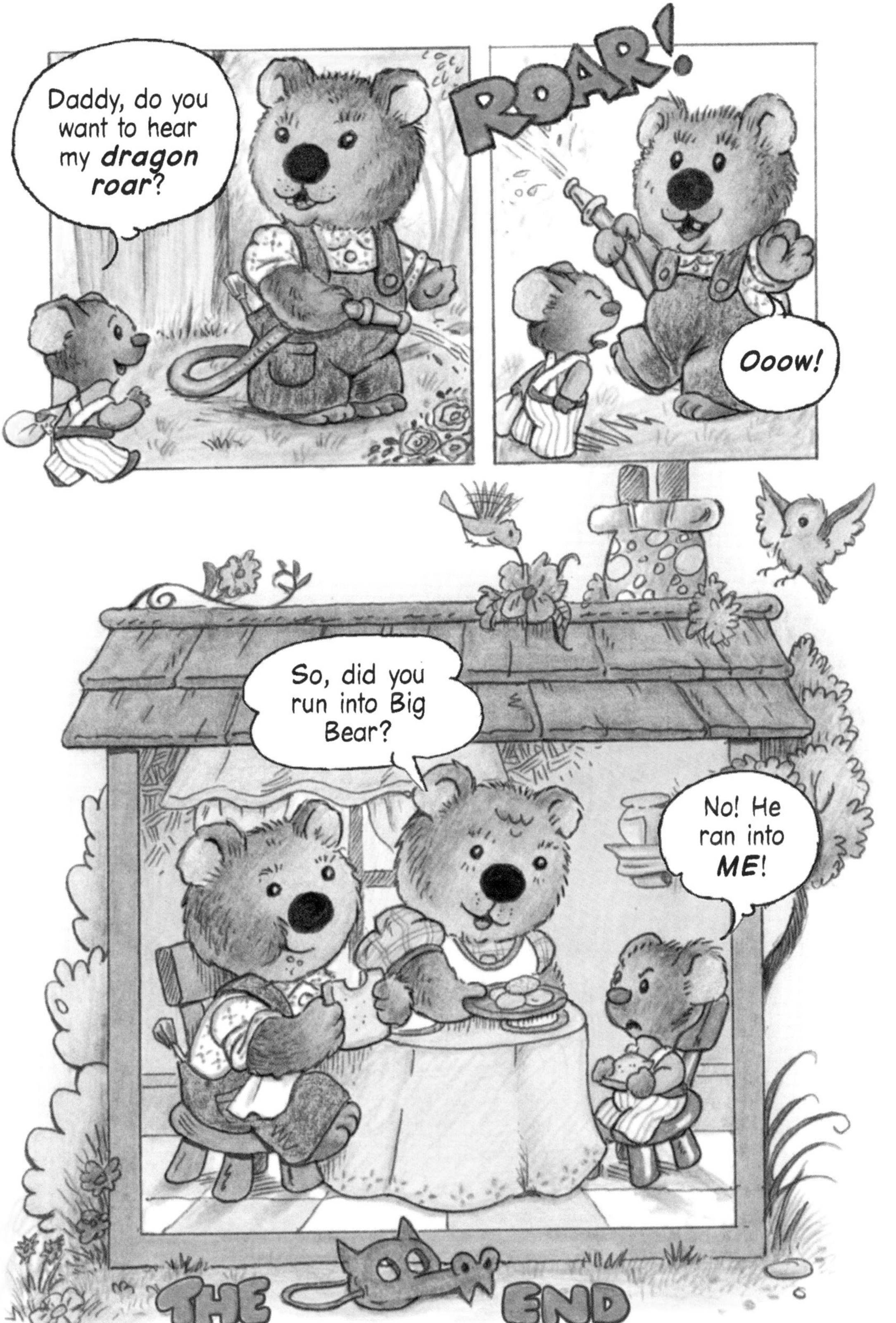
Daddy, do you want to hear my *dragon roar*?
ROAR!
Ooow!
So, did you run into Big Bear?
No! He ran into *ME*!
THE END

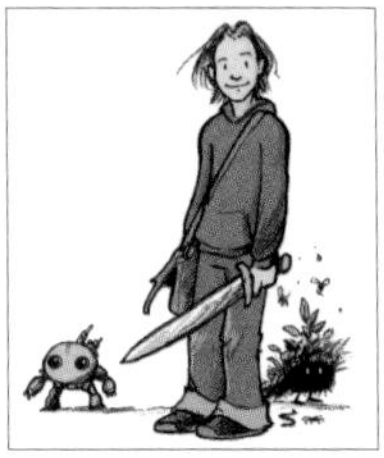

BEN HATKE

A Button in the Woods

from *Zita the Spacegirl*

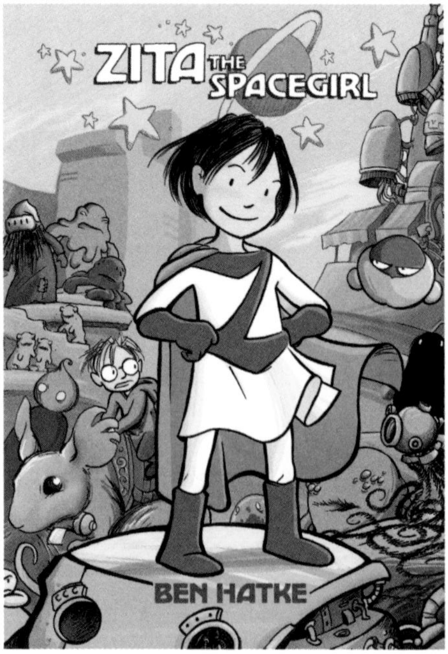
ZITA THE SPACEGIRL
BEN HATKE

FOR ME, DRAWING COMICS IS

An amazing dance of pictures and words and a form of art that I return to time and time again. Also, it's a great way to tell stories!

THE SELECTION

An excerpt from *Zita the Spacegirl* in which young Zita presses a mysterious red button and watches her friend get pulled into another world.

THE CONTEXT

While walking home from school, Zita and Joseph have happened upon a meteorite in a crater. Joseph urges Zita to leave it alone, but Zita slides down into the pit and finds a device with a tempting red button.

WHERE I LIVE

Strasburg, Virginia.

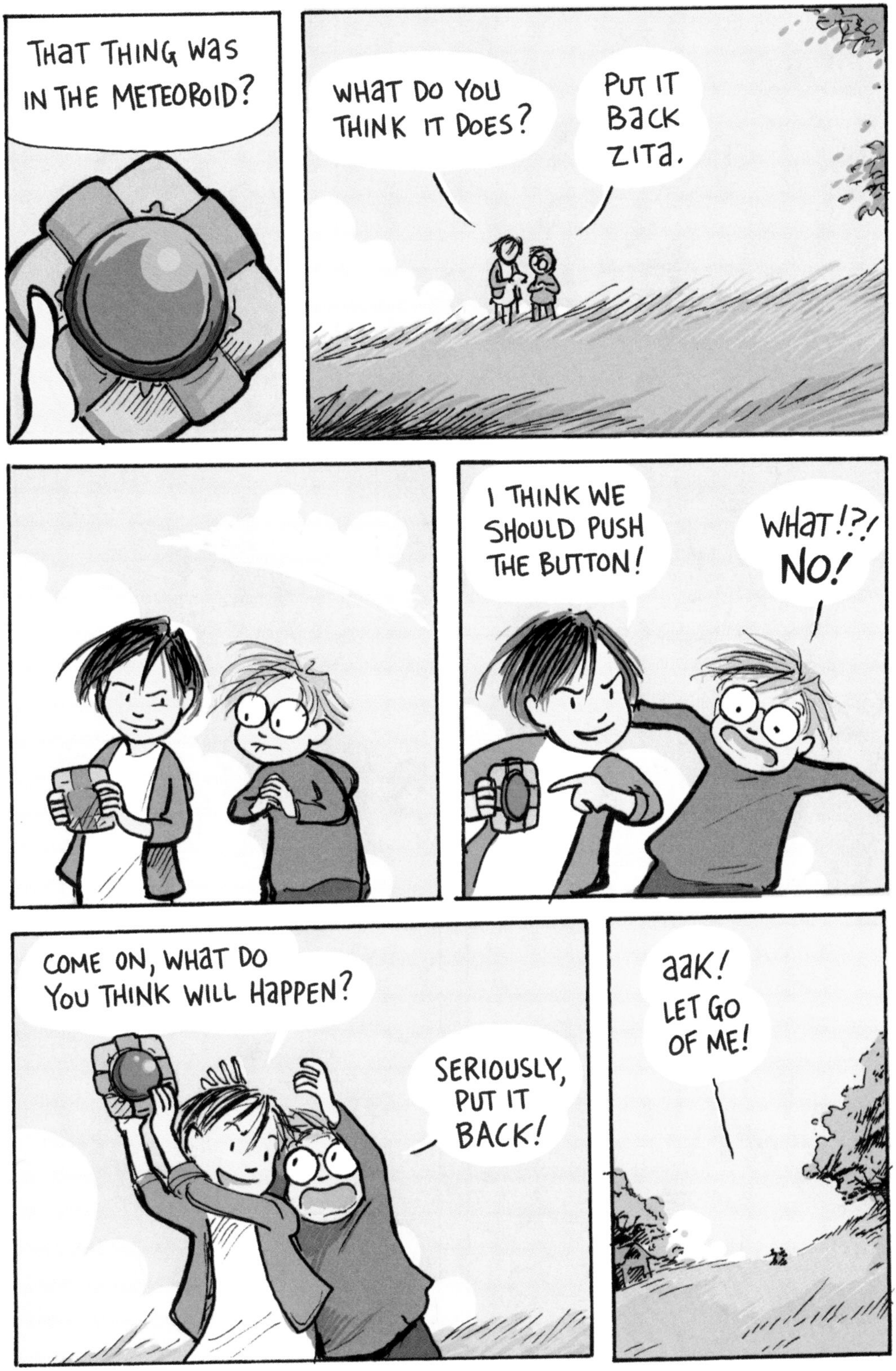
THAT THING WAS IN THE METEOROID?
WHAT DO YOU THINK IT DOES?
PUT IT BACK ZITA.
I THINK WE SHOULD PUSH THE BUTTON!
WHAT!?! NO!
COME ON, WHAT DO YOU THINK WILL HAPPEN?
SERIOUSLY, PUT IT BACK!
AAK! LET GO OF ME!

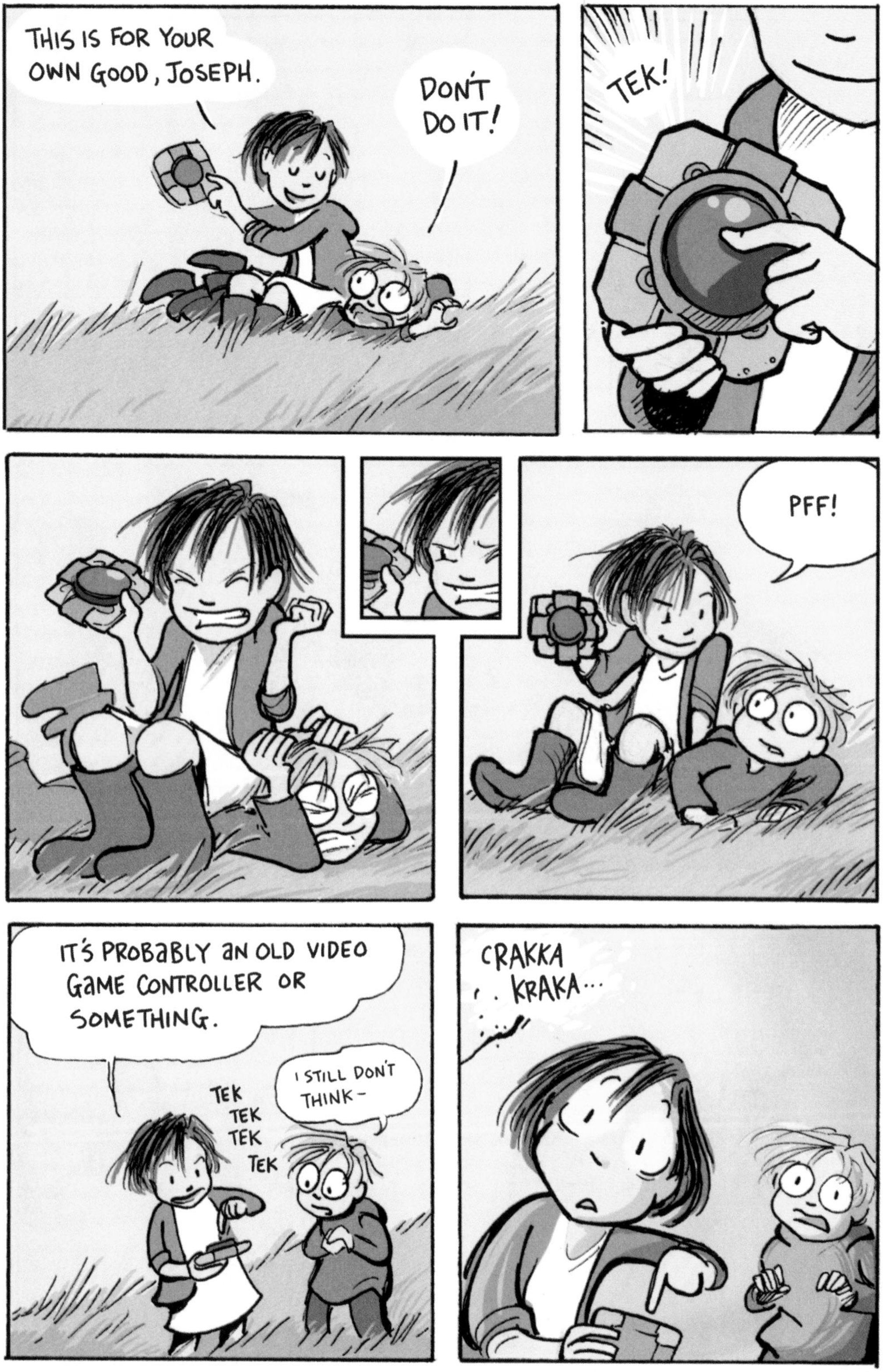
THIS IS FOR YOUR OWN GOOD, JOSEPH.
DON'T DO IT!
TEK!
PFF!
IT'S PROBABLY AN OLD VIDEO GAME CONTROLLER OR SOMETHING.
TEK TEK TEK TEK
I STILL DON'T THINK-
CRAKKA . . KRAKA...

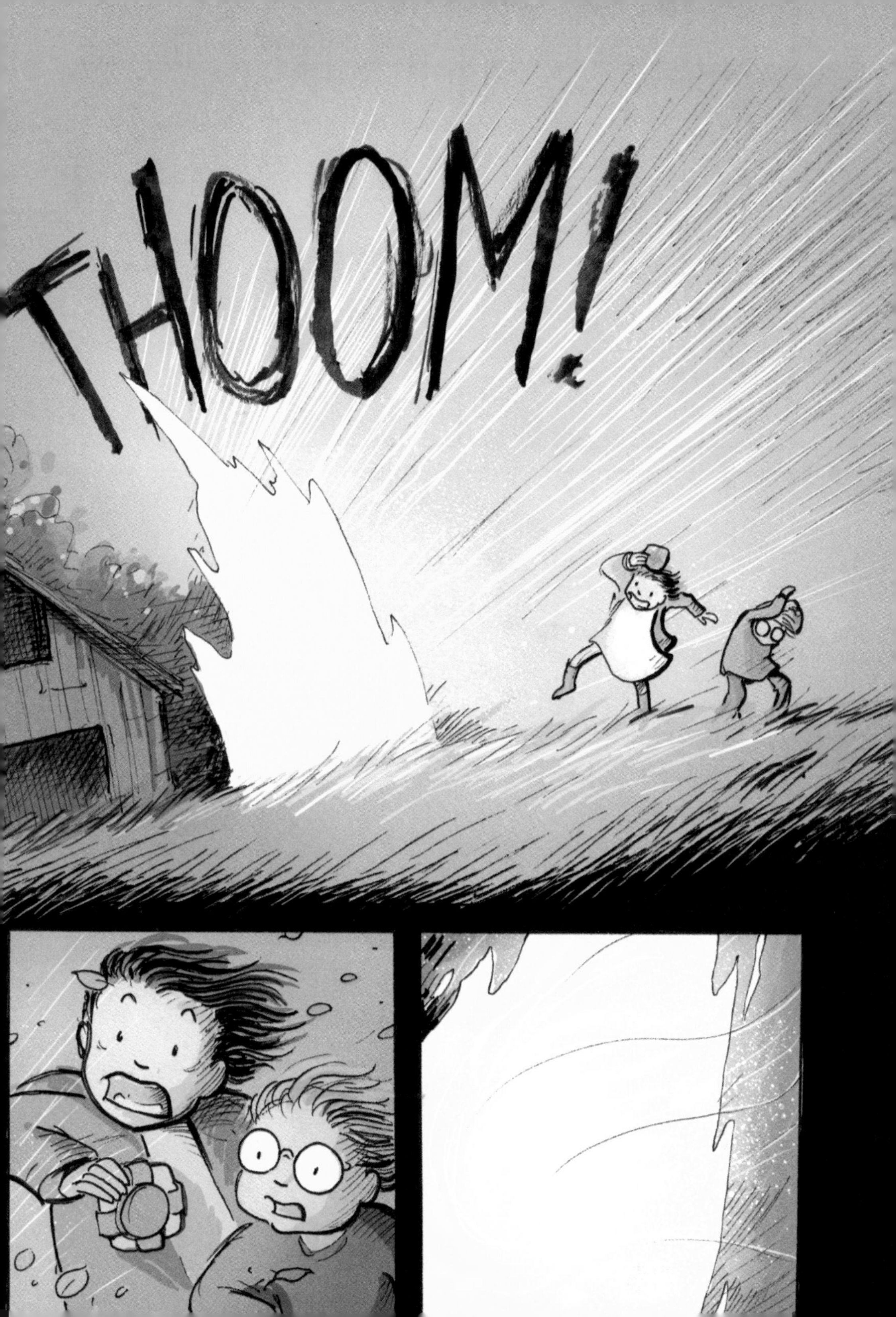
THOOM!

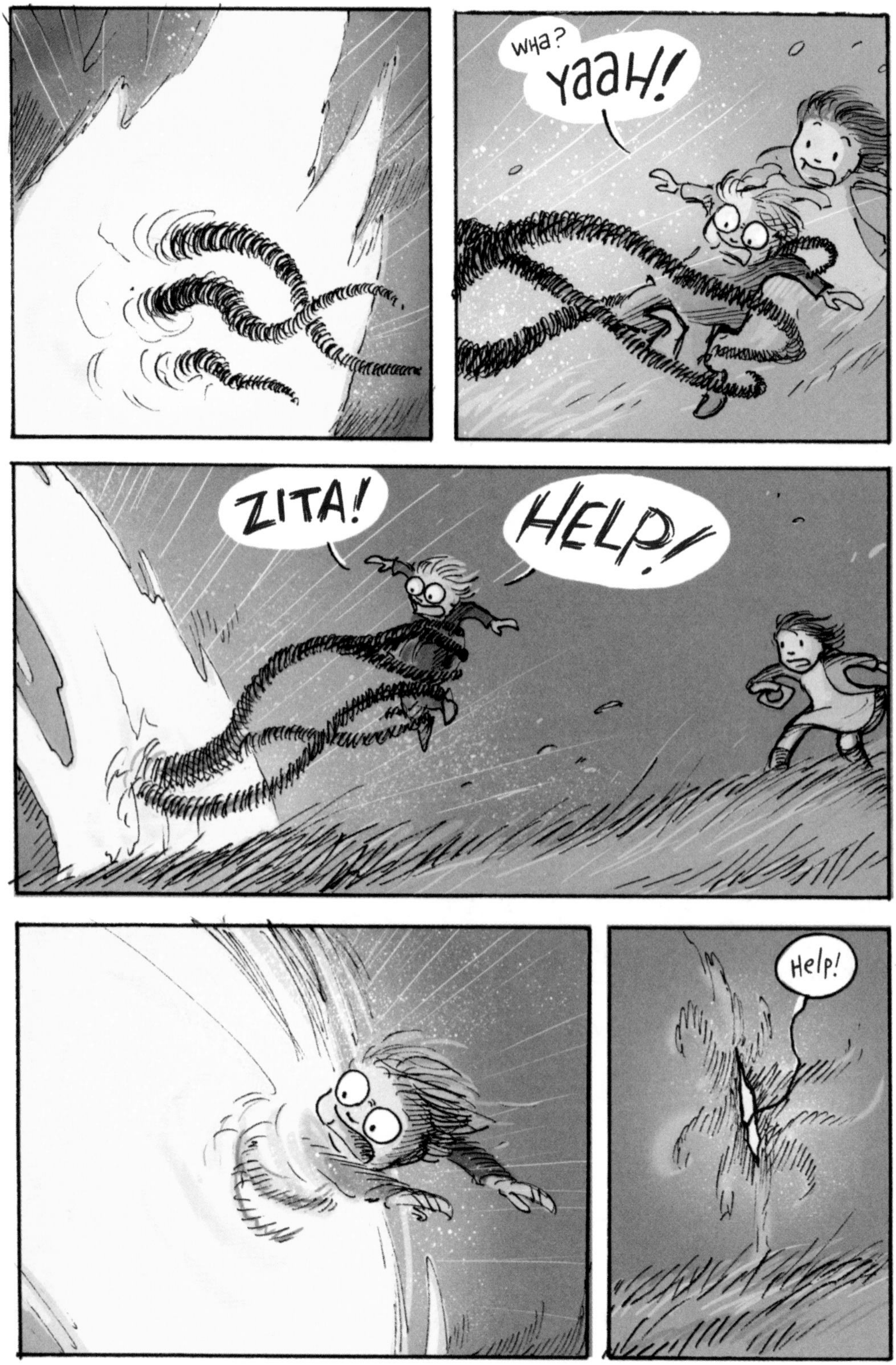
WHA?
YAAH!
ZITA!
HELP!
Help!

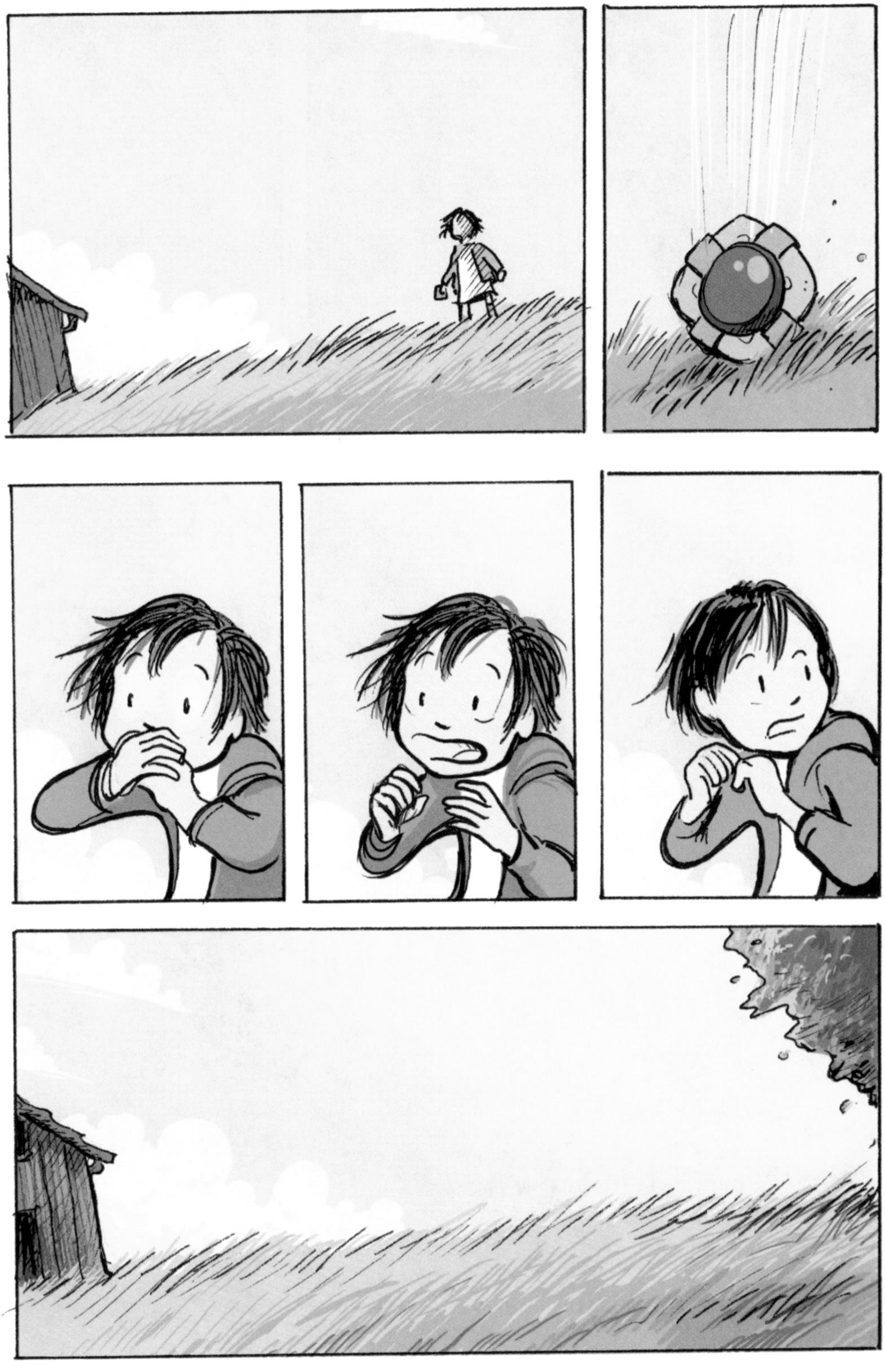

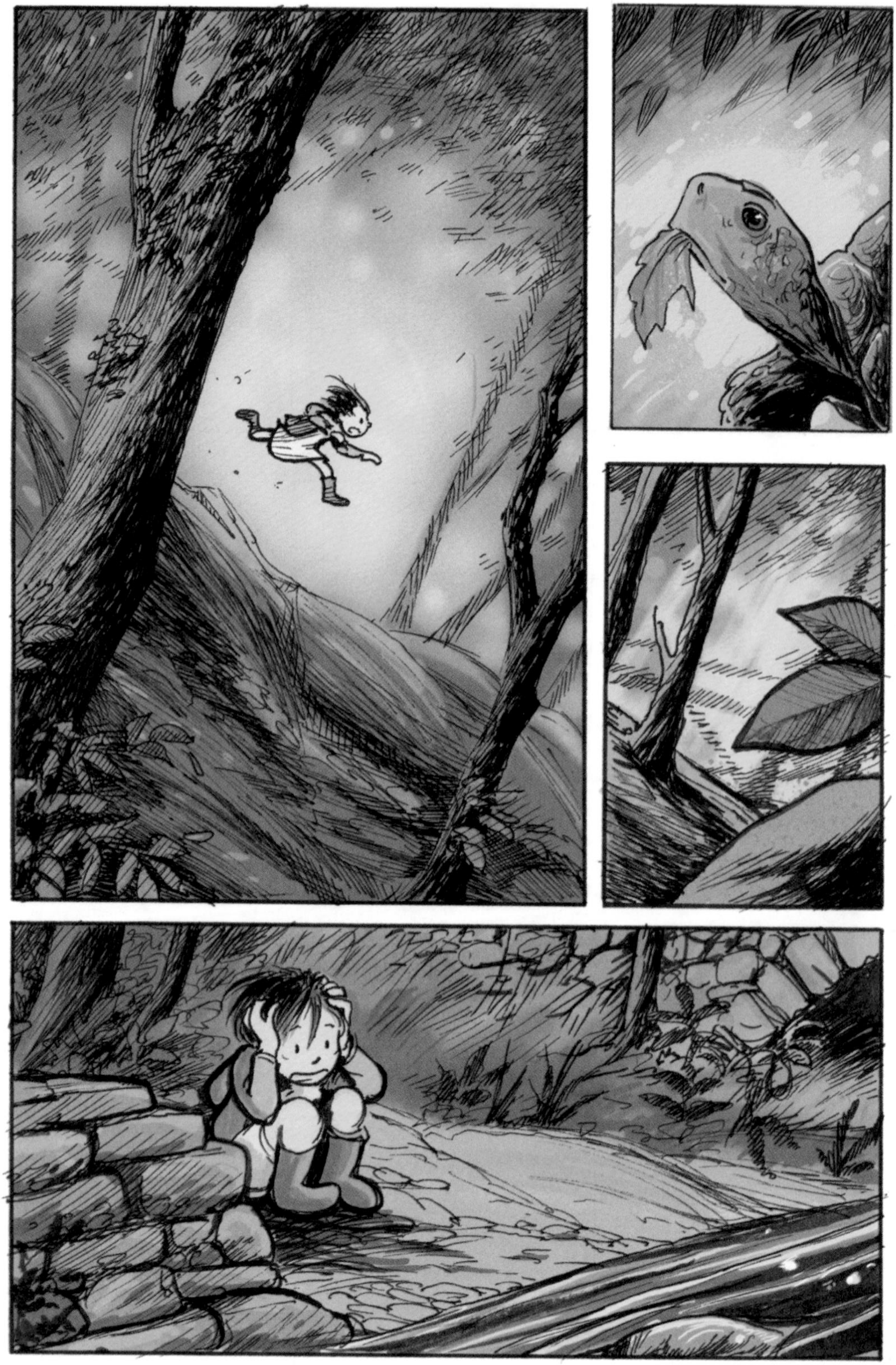

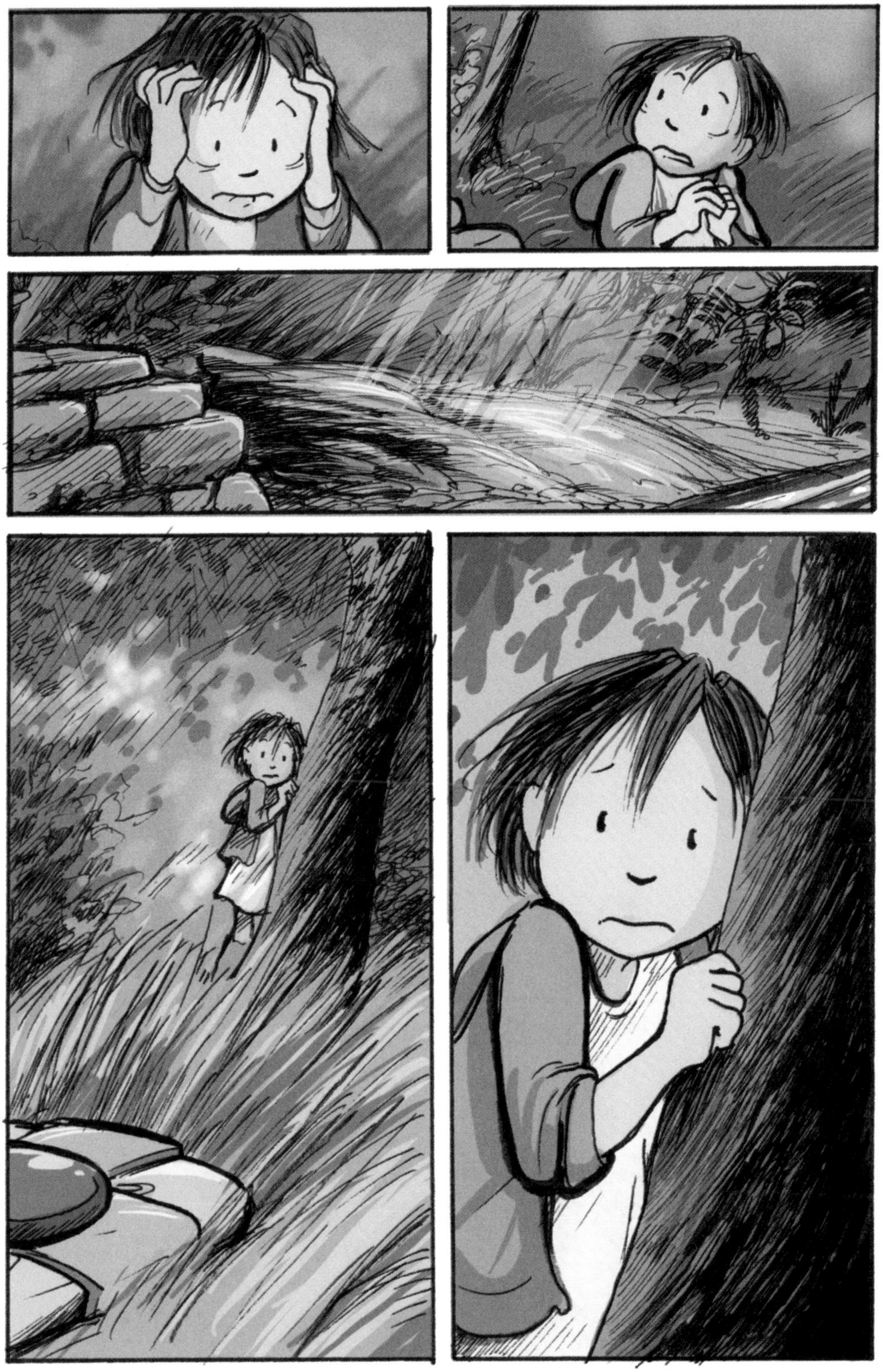

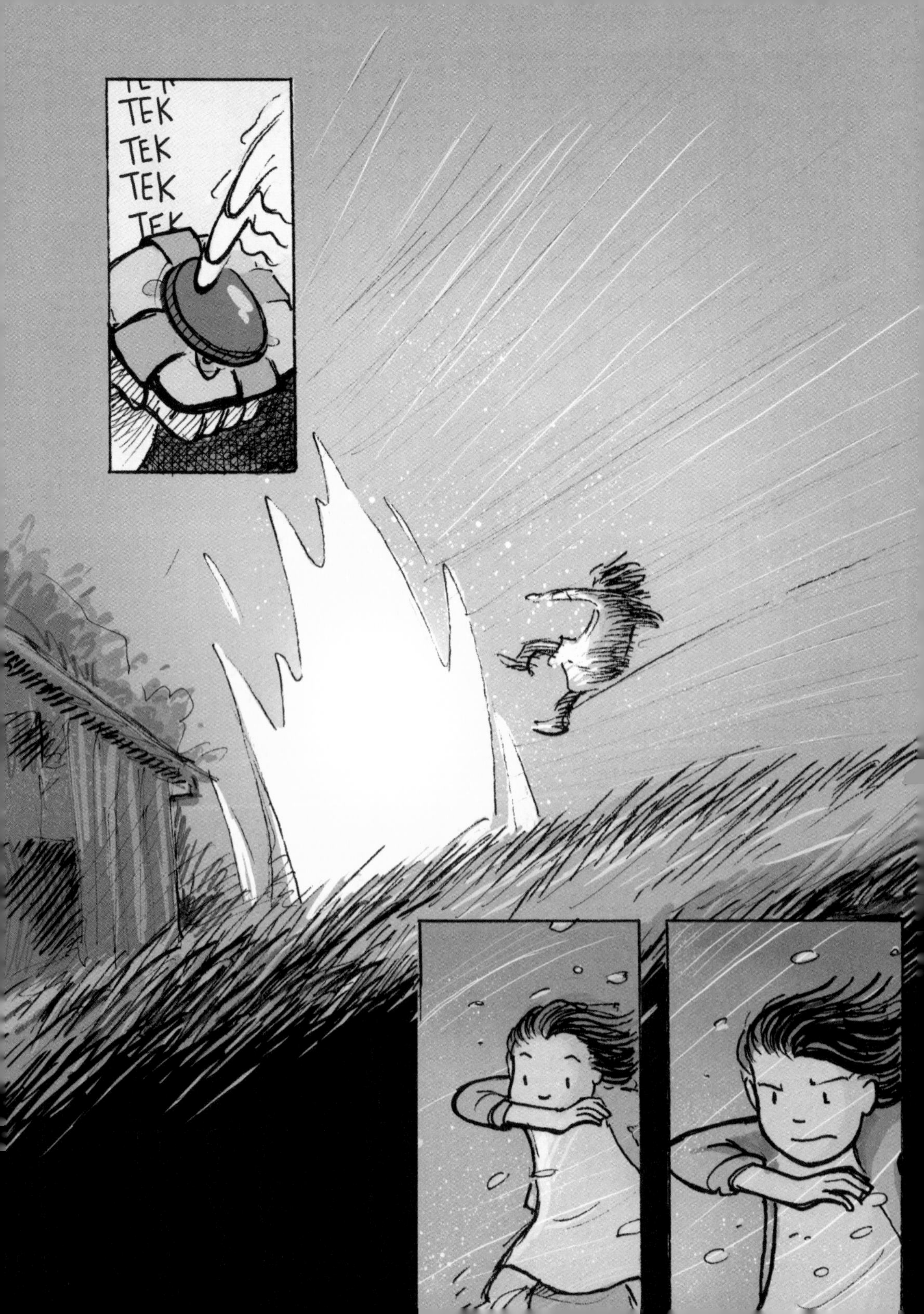
TEK
TEK
TEK

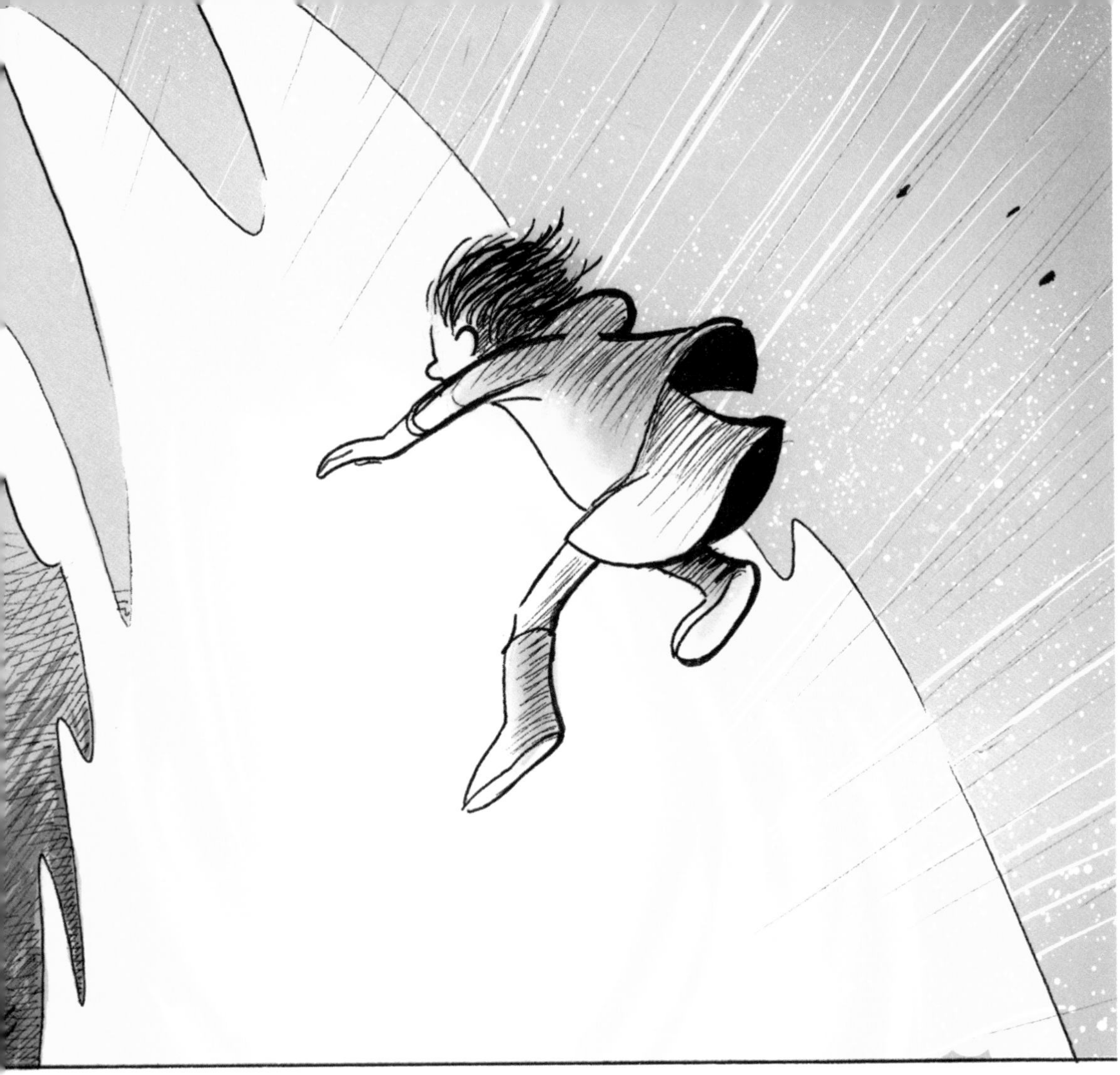

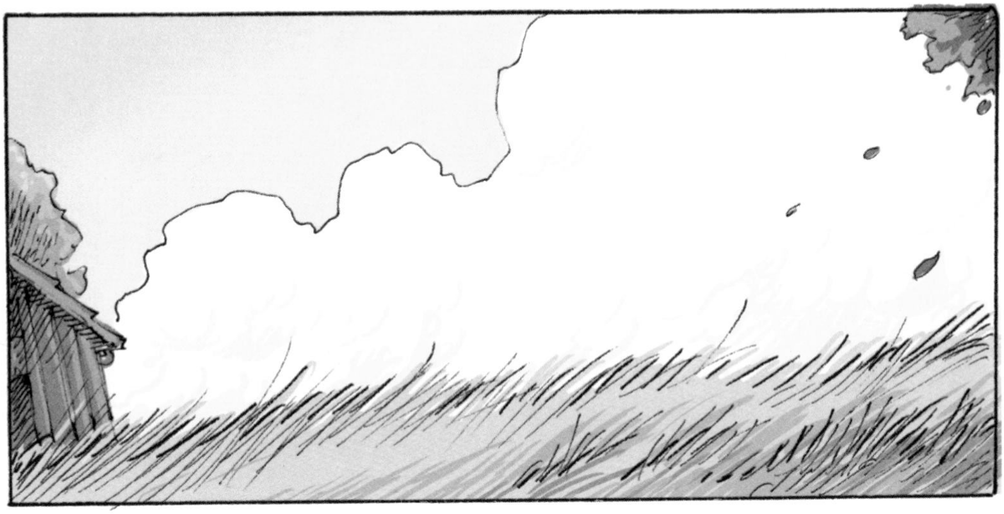

Notable Comics

from September 1, 2010, to August 31, 2011

Selected by Jessica Abel and Matt Madden

DERIK A. BADMAN
  Badman's Cave.
LYNDA BARRY
  Picture This: The Near-sighted Monkey Book.
JOSH BAYER
  ROM.
KATE BEATON
  1980's Businesswoman Comics. *Hark! A Vagrant.*
  Dracula. *Hark! A Vagrant.*
GABRIELLE BELL
  Sa Vie. *Lucky.*
NICK BERTOZZI
  Lewis & Clark.
PATRICIO BETTEO
  Mundo Invisible.
VERA BROSGOL
  Anya's Ghost.
BOX BROWN
  Ben Died of a Train.
ED BRUBAKER AND SEAN PHILLIPS
  Incognito, Vol. 2: Bad Influences.
JAN BURGER
  Earth and Sky.
MIKE CAREY AND PETER GROSS
  The Unwritten Vol. 3: Dead Man's Knock.
EMILY CARROLL
  His Face All Red.
STEPHEN DESTEFANO AND GEORGE CHIEFFET
  Lucky in Love: A Poor Man's History, vol. 1.
BRIAN CHIPPENDALE
  If 'n Oof.
DANIEL CLOWES
  Mister Wonderful: A Love Story.
PHILIPPE R. GIRARD
  Killing Velazquez.

MAREK COLEK
  Baba Yaga and the Wolf.
STEPHANIE CRAGG
  Midcentury Modern.
WARREN CRAGHEAD
  A Sound of the World. A Thing. *www.craghead.com.*
TRAVIS EDWARD DANDRO
  Journal, no. 3.
MIKE DAWSON
  Troop 142.
MICHAEL DEFORGE
  Spotting Deer.
  S M.
MICKEY DUZYJ
  Miss Chris.
JOSHUA DYSART, ALBERTO PONTICELLI, AND RICK VEITCH
  Unknown Soldier, Vol. 4: Beautiful World, "Kalashnikov."
CF
  Powr Mastrs, NO. 3.
EDIE FAKE
  Gaylord Phoenix.
GLYNNIS FAWKES
  The Terrible Story of Kinyras and Myrrha.
RAY FAWKES
  One Soul.
MICHEL FIFFE
  Zegas, no. 1.
MARIA FORDE
  Marlon Brando, vol. 2.
BERNARDO FERNÁNDEZ (BEF)
  Espiral.
RICK GEARY
  The Lives of Sacco & Vanzetti (A Treasury of Victorian Murder).

JULIA GFRÖRER
Too Dark to See.
PASCAL GIRARD
Bigfoot.
BROOKE GLADSTONE AND JOSH NEUFELD
The Influencing Machine: Brooke Gladstone on the Media.
CHARLES GLAUBITZ
Crystal Sigil. *Panel to Panel,* no. 1.
LISA HANAWALT
Worst Sandwiches. *I Want You,* no. 2.
How to get a Haircut. *I Want You,* no. 2.
TOM HART
The Dodgers. *Suspect Device,* no. 1.
JENNIFER HAYDEN
S'crapbook.
ADAM HINES
Duncan the Wonder Dog.
JAY HOSLER, ZANDER CANNON, AND KEVIN CANNON
Evolution: The Story of Life on Earth.
ARI HUFF
The Magnificent Osterman Brothers.
KEVIN HUIZENGA
Rumbling. *What Things Do.*
DAVID ISERI AND DAVID LAU
Summer Oddity.
SAM ITA
Frankenstein: A Pop-Up Book.
DUNJA JANKOVIC
Habitat, NO. 2.
TOM KACZYNSKI
Trans Utopia.
The Cozy Apocalypse. *Mome,* no. 21.
BEN KATCHOR
The Cardboard Valise.
KAZU KIBUISHI
Amulet #4: The Last Council.
ALEX KIM
Night Machine.
DAVID KING
Lemon Styles.
AIDAN KOCH
The Whale.
BLAISE LARMEE
2001.
SHARON LINTZ AND NICHOLAS BREUTZMAN
Photo Meetings. *Porn Hounds 2.*
SHARON LINTZ AND NATHAN SCHREIBER
Cancer. *Porn Hounds 2.*
JASON LITTLE
Motel Art Improvement Service.
JONAS MADDEN-CONNOR
The Most Gripping Mind-Exploding Triumphantly Electric of Our Time. *Papercutter,* no. 15.
BENJAMIN MARRA
The Incredibly Fantastic Adventures of Maureen Dowd.
JED McGOWAN
Lone Pine.
KAGAN McLEOD
Infinite Kung Fu.
CARLA SPEED McNEIL
Finder: Voice.
MAX MOSE
All Aboard.
ANNIE MURPHY
Truth: Stranger than Fiction. *Gay Genius.*
NATE NEAL
The Sanctuary.
TOM NEELY
The Wolf.
AUDREY NIFFINEGGER
The Night Bookmobile.
DAVID ORTEGA
Abuela y los Dead Mexicans.
JIM OTTAVIANI AND LELAND MYRICK
Feynman.
JASON OVERBY
2101.
PAT PALERMO
Live / Work, no. 1.
NATE POWELL
Any Empire.
LAUREN REDNISS
Radioactive.
JESSE REKLAW
N.Y.D.I., no. 1.
JAMES ROMBERGER AND WALLACE STEVENS
Madame La Fleurie. *Hooded Utilitarian.*
SIMON ROY
Shipwrecked with Dan the Gorilla.
GREG RUCKA AND J.H. WILLIAMS III
Batwoman: Elegy.

YUMI SAKUGAWA
Mundane Fortunes for the Next Ten Billion Years.

SETH
Palookaville, NO. 20.

MATT SHEEAN AND MALACHI WARD
Expansion, nos. 1 and 2.

MAHENDRA SINGH AND LEWIS CARROLL
The Hunting of the Snark.

JEFF SMITH
RASL, no. 11.

GRANT SNIDER
Incidental Comics.

BISHAKH SOM
Untitled. *Pood,* no. 2.

LESLIE STEIN
Eye of the Majestic Creature, no. 6.

KARL STEVENS
The Lodger.

MATT SUNDSTROM
Second Chances.

MATTHEW THURBER
1-800-Mice, no. 5.

MARK TODD AND ESTHER WATSON
Nubbin & Nutz.

GB TRAN
Vietnamerica: A Family's Journey.

NOAH VAN SCIVER
Blammo, no. 7.

CONNOR WILUMSEN
Rich Richmond. *Pood,* no. 2.

BRIAN WOOD AND BECKY CLOONAN
The Waking Life of Angels. *Demo,* no. 2.
Volume One Love Story. *Demo,* no. 2.

ZACH WORTON
The Klondike.

J. T. YOST
Losers Weepers, no. 3.

DAN ZETTWOCH
Motor Lodge. *Root Rot.*

Key to the Introduction

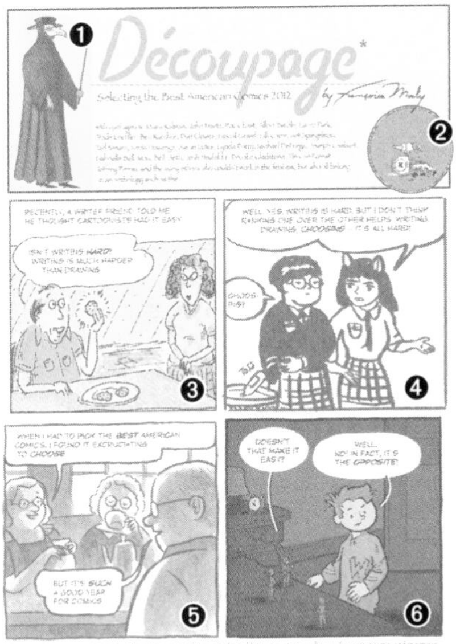
Découpage*
Selecting the Best American Comics 2012
by Françoise Mouly
RECENTLY, A WRITER FRIEND TOLD ME HE THOUGHT CARTOONISTS HAD IT EASY
ISN'T WRITING HARD? WRITING IS MUCH HARDER THAN DRAWING
WELL, YES, WRITING IS HARD, BUT I DON'T THINK RANKING ONE OVER THE OTHER HELPS. WRITING, DRAWING, CHOOSING — IT IS ALL HARD!
CHOOS-ING?
WHEN I HAD TO PICK THE BEST AMERICAN COMICS, I FOUND IT EXCRUCIATING TO CHOOSE
BUT IT'S SUCH A GOOD YEAR FOR COMICS
DOESN'T THAT MAKE IT EASY?
WELL, NO! IN FACT, IT'S THE OPPOSITE!

❶ MAIRA KALMAN
I Can't Go On, I'll Go On. *The New Yorker.*

❷ JOHN MARTZ
Heaven All Day.

❸ ROZ CHAST
Holiday Visit: Day No. 53, 267, 598. *The New Yorker.*

❹ JILLIAN TAMAKI
SuperMutant Magic Academy. *mutantmagic.com.*

❺ LAURA PARK
George. *Mome,* no. 22.

❻ TRADE LOEFFLER
Zip and Li'l Bit in The Captain's Quest. *zipandbit.com.*

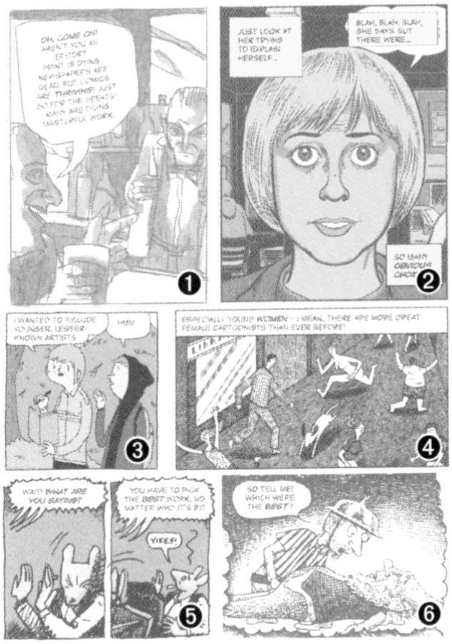
OH, COME ON! AREN'T YOU AN EDITOR? PRINT IS DYING, NEWSPAPERS ARE DEAD, BUT COMICS ARE THRIVING! JUST SO FOR THE GREATS! MANY ARE DOING MASTERFUL WORK.
JUST LOOK AT HER TRYING TO EXPLAIN HERSELF...
BLAH, BLAH, BLAH, SHE SAYS. BUT THERE WERE...
SO MANY OBVIOUS CHOI
I WANTED TO INCLUDE YOUNGER, LESSER-KNOWN ARTISTS
HMM
ESPECIALLY YOUNG WOMEN — I MEAN, THERE ARE MORE GREAT FEMALE CARTOONISTS THAN EVER BEFORE!
WAIT! WHAT ARE YOU SAYING?
YOU HAVE TO PICK THE BEST WORK, NO MATTER WHO IT'S BY!
YIKES!
SO TELL ME! WHICH WERE THE BEST?

❶ BEN KATCHOR
The Cardboard Valise.

❷ DANIEL CLOWES
Mister Wonderful: A Love Story.

❸ PASCAL GIRARD
Bigfoot.

❹ LILLI CARRÉ
Into the Night. *Mome,* no. 22.

❺ ART SPIEGELMAN
MetaMaus.

❻ TED STEARN
The Moolah Tree, Part 5. *Mome,* no. 22.

WAIT! LET ME EXPLAIN. WHEN I STARTED RAW MAGAZINE, IN THE 80'S...
THERE WERE MOSTLY SUPERHEROES, A FEW CHILDREN'S COMICS...
AND THE DIRTY, INTENTIONALLY LOWBROW, UNDERGROUND COMIX.
AND NOW...
YES?
...COMICS CAN TACKLE ANY TOPIC.
I SEE A FEW STRONG TENDENCIES: ONE IS AUTOBIOGRAPHY, WHICH TAKES ADVANTAGE OF THE FACT THAT COMICS ARE A HANDWRITTEN MEDIUM.
WHATCHA DOIN'?
NOTHIN'.
THEN WHY YA DOIN' IT?
WATCH TV WITH
ANOTHER IS DOCUMENTARY OR HISTORICAL FICTION, AND THERE'S ALSO THE YIN TO THAT YANG—PURELY VISUAL DREAM COMICS.
ANOTHER EXCITING TREND IS THE GREAT NEW KIDS COMICS.
HA! YOU SAID THERE USED TO BE SOME. DID THEY DISAPPEAR?...
...AND AREN'T ALL COMICS FOR KIDS ANYWAY?
NO! MOST COMICS ARE NOT FOR KIDS!

❶ KEVIN HUIZENGA
Rumbling. *What Things Do.*

❷ JASON LUTES
Berlin.

❸ LYNDA BARRY
Picture This: The Near-sighted Monkey Book.

❹ MICHAEL DeFORGE
Spotting Deer.

❺ JOSEPH LAMBERT
Root Rot.

❻ GABRIELLE BELL
Smoke Signal, no. 8.

BUT THIS IS THE FIRST TIME THERE'S A KIDS COMICS SECTION IN BEST AMERICAN. GOOD COMICS ARE GREAT FOR KIDS!
ROCK!
I ALSO WANTED TO BROADEN THE DEFINITION OF "COMICS" TO INCLUDE NARRATIVE SERIES OF IMAGES, WHICH ARE OFTEN FOUND ON BLOGS. THAT'S A NEW AND THRIVING VENUE FOR CARTOONISTS.
BACK IN THE RAW DAYS, MANY CARTOONISTS CAME TO COMICS THROUGH DRAWING—AND LEARNED TO WRITE.
NOW IT SEEMS MORE YOUNG WRITERS ARE LEARNING TO DRAW.
THERE'RE SOME WONDERFUL STRIPS IN HERE, BUT IT'S ONLY A TINY TASTE OF WHAT'S HAPPENING IN COMICS. YOU JUST HAVE TO ENTER INTO IT WITH AN OPEN MIND...
YOU SAID YOU HAVE STUFF FOR KIDS, SO YOU PUT IN WIMPY KID, RIGHT?
WELL, ACTUALLY, NO, THAT'S NOT IN.
THE END

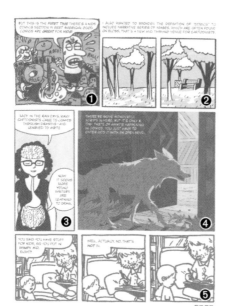

❶ MARC BELL
Smoke Signal, no. 8.

❷ SETH
Palookaville 20.

❸ BROOKE GLADSTONE AND JOSH NEUFELD
The Influencing Machine: Brooke Gladstone on the Media.

❹ TIN CAN FOREST
Baba Yaga and the Wolf.

❺ JEFFREY BROWN
Good at Playing. *nycgraphicnovelists.com.*

CREDITS

"Doctor Costume" by Sergio Aragonés. Reprinted from *Sergio Aragonés Funnies*, Issue #1 © 2011 by Bongo Entertainment, Inc. *Sergio Aragonés Funnies*™ and © Sergio Aragonés. All Rights Reserved. Reprinted by permission of Bongo Entertainment, Inc. "Vacation" by Sergio Aragonés. Reprinted from *Sergio Aragonés Funnies*, Issue #2 © 2011 by Bongo Entertainment, Inc. *Sergio Aragonés Funnies*™ and © Sergio Aragonés. All Rights Reserved. Reprinted by permission of Bongo Entertainment, Inc. "Haggling"; "Hot Stuff"; "Skyline"; "Hibern-8"; "Dead Soles"; "Prophets" by Jonathan Bennett. First published in *The Believer*. Copyright © 2012 by Jonathan Bennett. Reprinted by permission of Jonathan Bennett. "Angelina" by Chester Brown. First published in *Paying for It*. "The Pilot Learns to Fly" by Anders Brekhus Nilsen. First published in *Big Questions*. "Untitled" by Adrian Tomine. First published in *Scenes from an Impending Marriage*. Copyright © 2011 by Chester Brown, Anders Brekhus Nilsen, Adrian Tomine. Reprinted by permission of *Drawn & Quarterly*. "Draw Your Sister a Picture" and "Read a Book" by Michael J. Buckley. First published in *60 Ways to Leave Your Mother (Alone)*. Copyright © 2011 by Toil and Toil Books. Reprinted by permission of the Author. "X-Ed Out" by Charles Burns. First published in *X-Ed Out*, Pantheon Books. Copyright © 2012 by Charles Burns. Reprinted by permission of Charles Burns. "Rock, Scissors, Paper" by Frank Cammuso. First published in *Knights of the Lunch Table* #3. Copyright © 2011 by Frank Cammuso. Reprinted by permission of Frank Cammuso. "The Battle of Buron" by Scott Chantler is excerpted from *Two Generals* by Scott Chantler. Copyright © 2010. Reprinted by permission of McClelland & Stewart. "The Irish Table" by David Collier. First published in *Chimo*. Copyright © 2011 by David Collier. Reprinted by permission of Conundrum Press. "Elsewheres" by Jordan Crane. First published on whatthingsdo.com. Copyright © 2001 by Jordan Crane. Reprinted by permission of Jordan Crane. Untitled excerpt by Joyce Farmer. First published in *Special Exits*. Copyright © 2010 by Joyce Farmer. Reprinted by permission of Joyce Farmer. "Stage 6" by Renée French. First published in *H Day*. Copyright © 2010 by Picturebox. Reprinted by permission of Renée French. "The Golan Heights" by Sarah Glidden. First published in *How to Understand Israel in 60 Days or Less* © 2010 by Sarah Glidden. Used with permission of DC Comics. An excerpt from "Blood of the Virgin" by Sammy Harkham. First published in *Crickets* #3. Copyright © 2012 by Sammy Harkham. Reprinted by permission of Sammy Harkham. "A Button in the Woods" from pages 17–25 in *Zita the Spacegirl* by Ben Hatke. Text and illustrations copyright © 2010 by Ben Hatke. Reprinted by permission of Henry Holt and Company, LLC. "Patrick and Big Bear" by Geoffrey Hayes. First published in *Patrick in a Teddy Bear's Picnic and Other Stories—A TOON Book*. Copyright © 2010 by Geoffrey Hayes and Raw Junior. Reprinted by permission of Geoffrey Hayes. Excerpt from "The Love Bunglers: Part Four" by Jaime Hernandez. First published in *Love and Rockets*, vol. 3, #4. Copyright © 2012 by Jaime Hernandez. Reprinted by permission of Jaime Hernandez. "Even the Giants Get the Blues" by Jesse Jacobs. First published in *Even the Giants*. Copyright © 2011 by Jesse Jacobs. Reprinted by permission of Jesse Jacobs. "Kamikaze" by Nora Krug. First published in *A Public Space*. Copyright © 2011 by Nora Krug. Reprinted by permission of Nora Krug. "Are Comics Moronic Dribble?," "Skull Groin," "Diner Food," and "House of Shouts" from *Up All Night* by Michael Kupperman. First published in *Washington City Paper*. Copyright © 2011 by Michael Kupperman. Reprinted by permission of Michael Kupperman. "Leave Luck to Heaven" by Dakota McFadzean. First published in *Leave Luck to Heaven*. Copyright © 2011 by Dakota McFadzean. Reprinted by permission of Dakota McFadzean. "Red Eye" by Christoph Niemann. First published in NewYorkTimes.com. Copyright © 2012 by Christoph Niemann. Reprinted by permission of Christoph Niemann. "Jimbo" by Gary Panter. First published in *Jimbo* minicomic. Copyright © 2012 by Gary Panter. Reprinted by permission of Gary Panter. "House of Debt" by David Sandlin. First published in *House of Debt: Mini-Comic*. Copyright © 2011 by David Sandlin. Reprinted by permission of David Sandlin. "A Month of . . . " by Leanne Shapton. First published in the *New York Times* Opinion section, January 2011 to November 2011. Copyright © 2011 by Leanne Shapton. Reprinted by permission of Leanne Shapton. "Baking Failure #1" from *Bake Sale* by Sara Varon. Copyright © 2011 by Sara Varon. Reprinted by permission of Henry Holt and Company, LLC. "Money" by Chris Ware. First published in *The New Yorker*. Copyright © 2010 Chris Ware and *The New Yorker*/Condé Nast Archive. Reprinted by permission of Chris Ware and *The New Yorker*/Condé Nast. "Frank Among the Gut-Worshippers" by Jim Woodring. First published in *Congress of the Animals*. Copyright © 2011 by Jim Woodring. Reprinted by permission of Jim Woodring.

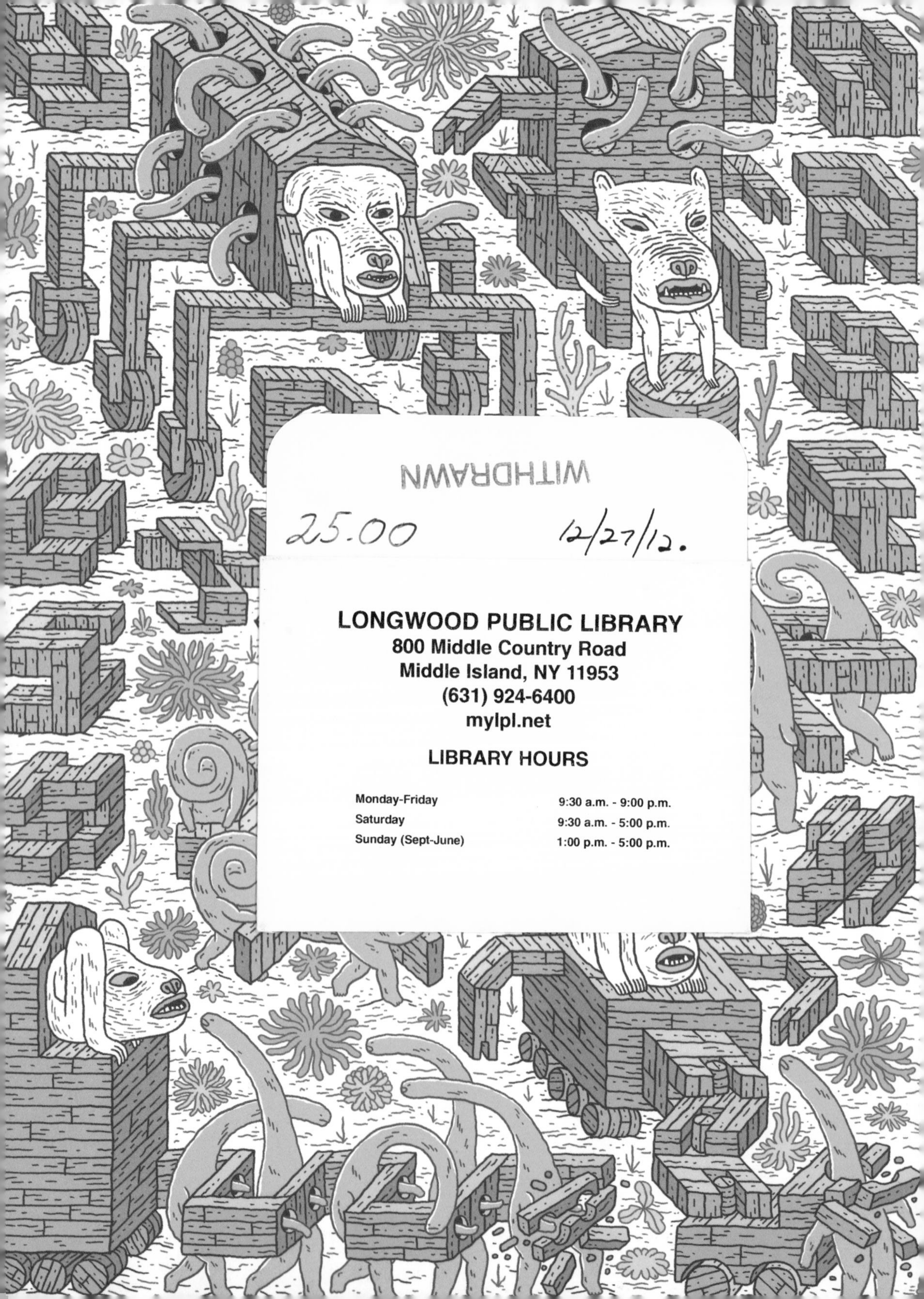